The Complete Works of
WASHINGTON
IRVING

Henry A. Pochmann
General Editor

MAHOMET AND
HIS SUCCESSORS

WASHINGTON IRVING

MAHOMET AND HIS SUCCESSORS

Edited by

Henry A. Pochmann and

E. N. Feltskog

The University of Wisconsin Press

Madison, Milwaukee, London

1970

Published by the University of Wisconsin Press
Box 1379, Madison, Wisconsin 53701
The University of Wisconsin Press, Ltd.
27–29 Whitfield Street, London W. 1
Copyright © 1970 by the
Regents of the University of Wisconsin
Printed in the United States of America by
George Banta Company, Inc., Menasha, Wisconsin
ISBN 0–299–05740–2
Library of Congress Catalog
Card Number 69–16115

CONTENTS

VOLUME I

VOLUME II

EDITORIAL APPENDIX

CONTENTS

MAHOMET AND HIS SUCCESSORS

Volume I

PREFACE

Some apology may seem necessary for presenting a life of Mahomet at the present day, when no new fact can be added to those already known concerning him. Many years since, during a residence in Madrid, the author projected a series of writings illustrative of the domination of the Arabs in Spain. These were to be introduced by a sketch of the life of the founder of the Islam Faith, and the first mover of Arabian conquest. Most of the particulars for this were drawn from Spanish sources, and from Gagnier's translation of the Arabian historian Abulfeda, a copy of which the author found in the Jesuits' Library of the Convent of St. Isidro, at Madrid.

Not having followed out, in its extent, the literary plan devised, the manuscript life lay neglected among the author's papers until the year 1831, when he revised and enlarged it for the Family Library of Mr. John Murray. Circumstances prevented its publication at the time, and it again was thrown aside for years.

During his last residence in Spain, the author beguiled the tediousness of a lingering indisposition, by again revising the manuscript, profiting in so doing by recent lights thrown on the subject by different writers, and particularly by Dr. Gustav Weil, the very intelligent and learned librarian of the University of Heidelberg, to whose industrious researches and able disquisitions, he acknowledges himself greatly indebted.[*]

Such is the origin of the work now given to the public; on which the author lays no claim to novelty of fact, nor profundity of research. It still bears the type of a work intended for a Family Library; in constructing which the whole aim of the writer has been to digest into an easy, perspicuous and flowing narrative, the admitted facts concerning Mahomet, together with such legends and traditions as have been wrought into the whole system of oriental literature; and at the same time to give such a summary of his faith as might be sufficient for the

[*] Mohammed der Prophet, sein Leben und seine Lehre. Stuttgart. 1843.

3

more general reader. Under such circumstances, he has not thought it worth while to encumber his pages with a scaffolding of references and citations, nor depart from the old English nomenclature of oriental names.

W. I.

SUNNYSIDE, 1849.

CHAPTER I

Preliminary notice of Arabia and the Arabs

During a long succession of ages, extending from the earliest period of recorded history down to the seventh century of the Christian era, that great chersonese or peninsula formed by the Red Sea, the Euphrates, the Gulf of Persia, and the Indian Ocean, and known by the name of Arabia, remained unchanged and almost unaffected by the events which convulsed the rest of Asia, and shook Europe and Africa to their centre. While kingdoms and empires rose and fell; while ancient dynasties passed away; while the boundaries and names of countries were changed, and their inhabitants were exterminated or carried into captivity, Arabia, though its frontier provinces experienced some vicissitudes, preserved in the depths of its deserts its primitive character and independence, nor had its nomadic tribes ever bent their haughty necks to servitude.

The Arabs carry back the traditions of their country to the highest antiquity. It was peopled, they say, soon after the deluge, by the progeny of Shem the son of Noah, who gradually formed themselves into several tribes, the most noted of which are the Adites and Thamudites. All these primitive tribes are said to have been either swept from the earth in punishment of their iniquities, or obliterated in subsequent modifications of the races, so that little remains concerning them but shadowy traditions and a few passages in the Koran. They are occasionally mentioned in oriental history as the "old primitive Arabians," – the "lost tribes."

The permanent population of the peninsula is ascribed, by the same authorities, to Kahtan or Joctan, a descendant in the fourth generation from Shem. His posterity spread over the southern part of the peninsula and along the Red Sea. Yarab, one of his sons, founded the kingdom of Yemen, where the territory of Araba was called after him; whence the Arabs derive the names of themselves and their country. Jurham, another son, founded the kingdom of Hedjaz, over which his descendants bore sway for many generations. Among these people Hagar and her son Ishmael were kindly received, when exiled from their home by the patriarch Abraham. In the process of time Ishmael married the daughter of Modâd, a reigning prince of the line of Jurham; and thus a stranger and a Hebrew became grafted on the original Arabian stock. It proved a vigorous graft. Ishmael's wife bore him

5

twelve sons, who acquired dominion over the country, and whose prolific race, divided into twelve tribes, expelled or overran and obliterated the primitive stock of Joctan.

Such is the account given by the peninsular Arabs of their origin;*
and Christian writers cite it as containing the fulfilment of the covenant of God with Abraham, as recorded in Holy Writ. "And Abraham
said unto God, O that Ishmael might live before thee! And God said, As
for Ishamael, I have heard thee. Behold, I have blessed him, and will
make him fruitful, and will multiply him exceedingly: *twelve princes*
shall he beget, and I will make him a great nation." (Genesis xvii.18,
20.)

These twelve princes with their tribes are further spoken of in the
Scriptures (Genesis xxv.18) as occupying the country "from Havilah
unto Shur, that is before Egypt, as thou goest towards Assyria;" a region identified by sacred geographers with part of Arabia. The description of them agrees with that of the Arabs of the present day. Some are
mentioned as holding towns and castles, others as dwelling in tents, or
having villages in the wilderness. Nebaioth and Kedar, the two first-
born of Ishmael, are most noted among the princes for their wealth in
flocks and herds, and for the fine wool of their sheep. From Nebaioth
came the Nabathai who inhabited Stony Arabia; while the name of
Kedar is occasionally given in Holy Writ to designate the whole Arabian nation. "Woe is me," says the Psalmist, "that I sojourn in Mesech,
that I dwell in the tents of Kedar." Both appear to have been the progenitors of the wandering or pastoral Arabs; the free rovers of the desert. "The wealthy nation," says the prophet Jeremiah, "that dwelleth
without care; which have neither gates nor bars, which dwell alone."

A strong distinction grew up in the earliest times between the Arabs
who "held towns and castles," and those who "dwelt in tents." Some of
the former occupied the fertile wadies, or valleys, scattered here and
there among the mountains, where these towns and castles were sur-

---

* Beside the Arabs of the peninsula, who were all of the Shemitic race, there
were others called Cushites, being descended from Cush the son of Ham. They inhabited the banks of the Euphrates and the Persian Gulf. The name of Cush is
often given in Scripture to the Arabs generally as well as to their country. It must
be the Arabs of this race who at present roam the deserted regions of ancient Assyria, and have been employed recently in disinterring the long-buried ruins of
Nineveh. They are sometimes distinguished as the Syro-Arabians. The present work
relates only to the Arabs of the peninsula, or Arabia Proper.

rounded by vineyards and orchards, groves of palm-trees, fields of grain, and well-stocked pastures. They were settled in their habits, devoting themselves to the cultivation of the soil and the breeding of cattle.

Others of this class gave themselves up to commerce, having ports and cities along the Red Sea; the southern shores of the peninsula and the Gulf of Persia, and carrying on foreign trade by means of ships and caravans. Such especially were the people of Yemen, or Arabia the Happy, that land of spices, perfumes and frankincense; the Sabæa of the poets; the Sheba of the sacred Scriptures. They were among the most active mercantile navigators of the eastern seas. Their ships brought to their shores the myrrh and balsams of the opposite coast of Berbera, with the gold, the spices, and other rich commodities of India and tropical Africa. These, with the products of their own country, were transported by caravans across the deserts to the semi-Arabian states of Ammon, Moab, and Edom or Idumea, to the Phœnician ports of the Mediterranean, and thence distributed to the western world.

The camel has been termed the ship of the desert, the caravan may be termed its fleet. The caravans of Yemen were generally fitted out, manned, conducted and guarded by the nomadic Arabs, the dwellers in tents, who, in this respect, might be called the navigators of the desert. They furnished the innumerable camels required, and also contributed to the freight by the fine fleeces of their countless flocks. The writings of the prophets show the importance, in scriptural times, of this inland chain of commerce by which the rich countries of the south, India, Ethiopia, and Arabia the Happy, were linked with ancient Syria.

Ezekiel, in his lamentations for Tyre, exclaims, "Arabia, and all the princes of Kedar, they occupied with thee in lambs, and rams, and goats; in these were they thy merchants. The merchants of Sheba and Raamah occupied in thy fairs with chief of all spices, and with all precious stones and gold. Haran, and Canneh, and Eden,* the merchants of Sheba, Asshur, and Chelmad, were thy merchants." And Isaiah, speaking to Jerusalem, says – "The multitude of camels shall cover thee; the dromedaries of Midian and Ephah; all they from Sheba shall come; they shall bring gold and incense. * * * * All the flocks of Kedar shall be gathered together unto thee; the rams of Nebaioth shall minister unto thee." (Isaiah lx. 6, 7.)

* Haran, Canna, and Aden, ports on the Indian Sea.

The agricultural and trading Arabs, however, the dwellers in towns and cities, have never been considered the true type of the race. They became softened by settled and peaceful occupations, and lost much of their original stamp by an intercourse with strangers. Yemen, too, being more accessible than the other parts of Arabia, and offering greater temptation to the spoiler, had been repeatedly invaded and subdued.

It was among the other class of Arabs, the rovers of the desert, the "dwellers in tents," by far the most numerous of the two, that the national character was preserved in all its primitive force and freshness. Nomadic in their habits, pastoral in their occupations, and acquainted by experience and tradition with all the hidden resources of the desert, they led a wandering life, roaming from place to place in quest of those wells and springs which had been the resort of their forefathers since the days of the patriarchs; encamping wherever they could find date-trees for shade, and sustenance and pasturage for their flocks, and herds, and camels; and shifting their abode whenever the temporary supply was exhausted.

These nomadic Arabs were divided and subdivided into innumerable petty tribes or families, each with its Sheikh or Emir, the representative of the patriarch of yore, whose spear, planted beside his tent, was the ensign of command. His office, however, though continued for many generations in the same family, was not strictly hereditary; but depended upon the good-will of the tribe. He might be deposed, and another of a different line elected in his place. His power, too, was limited, and depended upon his personal merit and the confidence reposed in him. His prerogative consisted in conducting negotiations of peace and war; in leading his tribe against the enemy; in choosing the place of encampment, and in receiving and entertaining strangers of note. Yet, even in these and similar privileges, he was controlled by the opinions and inclinations of his people.*

---

* In summer the wandering Arabs, says Burckhardt, seldom remain above three or four days on the same spot; as soon as their cattle have consumed the herbage near a watering place, the tribe removes in search of pasture, and the grass again springing up, serves for a succeeding camp. The encampments vary in the number of tents, from six to eight hundred; when the tents are but few, they are pitched in a circle; but more considerable numbers in a straight line, or a row of single tents, especially along a rivulet, sometimes three or four behind as many others. In winter, when water and pasture never fail, the whole tribe spreads itself over the plain in parties of three or four tents each, with an interval of half an hour's dis-

However numerous and minute might be the divisions of a tribe, the links of affinity were carefully kept in mind by the several sections. All the Sheikhs of the same tribe acknowledge a common chief called the Sheikh of Sheikhs, who, whether ensconced in a rock-built castle, or encamped amid his flocks and herds in the desert, might assemble under his standard all the scattered branches on any emergency affecting the common weal.

The multiplicity of these wandering tribes, each with its petty prince and petty territory, but without a national head, produced frequent collisions. Revenge, too, was almost a religious principle among them. To avenge a relative slain was the duty of his family, and often involved the honor of his tribe; and these debts of blood sometimes remained unsettled for generations, producing deadly feuds.

The necessity of being always on the alert to defend his flocks and herds, made the Arab of the desert familiar from his infancy with the exercise of arms. None could excel him in the use of the bow, the lance and the scimetar, and the adroit and graceful management of the horse. He was a predatory warrior also; for though at times he was engaged in the service of the merchant, furnishing him with camels and guides and drivers for the transportation of his merchandise, he was more apt to lay contributions on the caravan or plunder it outright in

---

tance between each party. The Sheikh's tent is always on the side on which enemies or guests may be expected. To oppose the former, and to honor the latter, is the Sheikh's principal business. Every father of a family sticks his lance into the ground by the side of his tent, and ties his horse in front. There also his camels repose at night. – Burckhardt, Notes on Bedouins, vol. i. p. 33.

The following is descriptive of the Arabs of Assyria, though it is applicable, in a great degree, to the whole race.

"It would be difficult to describe the appearance of a large tribe when migrating to new pastures. We soon found ourselves in the midst of wide-spreading flocks of sheep and camels. As far as the eye could reach, to the right, to the left, and in front, still the same moving crowd. Long lines of asses and bullocks, laden with black tents, huge caldrons, and variegated carpets; aged women and men, no longer able to walk, tied on the heap of domestic furniture; infants crammed into saddle-bags, their tiny heads thrust through the narrow opening, balanced on the animal's back by kids or lambs tied on the opposite side; young girls clothed only in the close-fitting Arab shirt, which displayed rather than concealed their graceful forms; mothers with their children on their shoulders; boys driving flocks of lambs; horsemen armed with their long tufted spears, scouring the plain on their fleet mares; riders urging their dromedaries with their short-hooked sticks, and leading their high-bred steeds by the halter; colts galloping among the throng; such was the motley crowd through which we had to wend our way." – Layard's Nineveh, i. ch. 4.

its toilful progress through the desert. All this he regarded as a legitimate exercise of arms; looking down upon the gainful sons of traffic as
an inferior race, debased by sordid habits and pursuits.

Such was the Arab of the desert, the dweller in tents, in whom was
fulfilled the prophetic destiny of his ancestor Ishmael. "He will be a
wild man; his hand will be against every man, and every man's hand
against him."* Nature had fitted him for his destiny. His form was light
and meagre, but sinewy and active, and capable of sustaining great
fatigue and hardship. He was temperate and even abstemious, requiring but little food, and that of the simplest kind. His mind like his
body was light and agile. He eminently possessed the intellectual attributes of the Shemitic race, penetrating sagacity, subtle wit, a ready
conception, and a brilliant imagination. His sensibilities were quick
and acute, though not lasting; a proud and daring spirit was stamped
on his sallow visage and flashed from his dark and kindling eye. He
was easily aroused by the appeals of eloquence, and charmed by the
graces of poetry. Speaking a language copious in the extreme, the
words of which have been compared to gems and flowers, he was naturally an orator; but he delighted in proverbs and apothegms, rather
than in sustained flights of declamation, and was prone to convey his
ideas in the oriental style by apologue and parable.

Though a restless and predatory warrior, he was generous and hospitable. He delighted in giving gifts; his door was always open to the
wayfarer, with whom he was ready to share his last morsel; and his
deadliest foe, having once broken bread with him, might repose securely beneath the inviolable sanctity of his tent.

In religion the Arabs, in what they term the Days of Ignorance, partook largely of the two faiths, the Sabean and the Magian, which at
that time prevailed over the eastern world. The Sabean, however, was
the one to which they most adhered. They pretended to derive it from
Sabi the son of Seth, whom, with his father and his brother Enoch, they
suppose to be buried in the pyramids. Others derive the name from the
Hebrew word, Saba, or the Stars, and trace the origin of the faith to
the Assyrian shepherds, who as they watched their flocks by night on
their level plains, and beneath their cloudless skies, noted the aspects
and movements of the heavenly bodies, and formed theories of their
good and evil influences on human affairs; vague notions which the

* Genesis xvi. 12.

Chaldean philosophers and priests reduced to a system, supposed to be more ancient even than that of the Egyptians.

By others it is derived from still higher authority, and claimed to be the religion of the antediluvian world. It survived, say they, the deluge, and was continued among the patriarchs. It was taught by Abraham, adopted by his descendants, the children of Israel, and sanctified and confirmed in the tablets of the law delivered unto Moses, amid the thunder and lightning of Mount Sinai.

In its original state the Sabean faith was pure and spiritual; inculcating a belief in the unity of God, the doctrine of a future state of rewards and punishments, and the necessity of a virtuous and holy life to obtain a happy immortality. So profound was the reverence of the Sabeans for the Supreme Being, that they never mentioned his name, nor did they venture to approach him, but through intermediate intelligences or angels. These were supposed to inhabit and animate the heavenly bodies, in the same way as the human body is inhabited and animated by a soul. They were placed in their respective spheres to supervise and govern the universe in subserviency to the Most High. In addressing themselves to the stars and other celestial luminaries, therefore, the Sabeans did not worship them as deities, but sought only to propitiate their angelic occupants as intercessors with the Supreme Being; looking up through these created things to God the great creator.

By degrees this religion lost its original simplicity and purity, and became obscured by mysteries, and degraded by idolatries. The Sabeans, instead of regarding the heavenly bodies as the habitations of intermediate agents, worshipped them as deities; set up graven images in honor of them, in sacred groves and in the gloom of forests; and at length enshrined these idols in temples, and worshipped them as if instinct with divinity. The Sabean faith too underwent changes and modifications in the various countries through which it was diffused. Egypt has long been accused of reducing it to the most abject state of degradation; the statues, hieroglyphics, and painted sepulchres of that mysterious country, being considered records of the worship, not merely of celestial intelligences, but of the lowest order of created beings, and even of inanimate objects. Modern investigation and research, however, are gradually rescuing the most intellectual nation of antiquity from this aspersion, and as they slowly lift the veil of mystery which hangs over the tombs of Egypt, are discovering that all these apparent

objects of adoration were but symbols of the varied attributes of the
one Supreme Being, whose name was too sacred to be pronounced by
mortals. Among the Arabs the Sabean faith became mingled with wild
superstitions, and degraded by gross idolatry. Each tribe worshipped
its particular star or planet, or set up its particular idol. Infanticide
mingled its horrors with their religious rites. Among the nomadic tribes
the birth of a daughter was considered a misfortune, her sex rendering
her of little service in a wandering and predatory life, while she might
bring disgrace upon her family by misconduct or captivity. Motives of
unnatural policy, therefore, may have mingled with their religious feelings, in offering up female infants as sacrifices to their idols, or in burying them alive.

The rival sect of Magians or Guebres (fire-worshippers), which, as
we have said, divided the religious empire of the East, took its rise in
Persia, where, after a while, its oral doctrines were reduced to writing
by its great prophet and teacher Zoroaster, in his volume of the Zen-
davesta. The creed, like that of the Sabeans, was originally simple and
spiritual, inculcating a belief in one supreme and eternal God, in whom
and by whom the universe exists: that he produced, through his creat-
ing word, two active principles, Ormusd, the principle or angel of light
or good, and Ahriman, the principle or angel of darkness or evil: that
these formed the world out of a mixture of their opposite elements, and
were engaged in a perpetual contest in the regulation of its affairs.
Hence the vicissitudes of good and evil, accordingly as the angel of
light or darkness has the upper hand: this contest would continue until
the end of the world, when there would be a general resurrection and
a day of judgment; the angel of darkness and his disciples would then
be banished to an abode of woful gloom, and their opponents would
enter the blissful realms of ever during light.

The primitive rites of this religion were extremely simple. The Magians had neither temples, altars, nor religious symbols of any kind, but
addressed their prayers and hymns directly to the Deity, in what they
conceived to be his residence, the sun. They reverenced this luminary
as being his abode, and as the source of the light and heat of which all
the other heavenly bodies were composed; and they kindled fires upon
the mountain tops to supply light during its absence. Zoroaster first introduced the use of temples, wherein sacred fire, pretended to be derived from heaven, was kept perpetually alive through the guardianship of priests, who maintained a watch over it night and day.

In process of time this sect, like that of the Sabeans, lost sight of the divine principle in the symbol, and came to worship light or fire, as the real Deity, and to abhor darkness as Satan or the devil. In their fanatic zeal the Magians would seize upon unbelievers and offer them up in the flames to propitiate their fiery deity.

To the tenets of these two sects reference is made in that beautiful text of the Wisdom of Solomon: "Surely vain are all men by nature who are ignorant of God, and could not, by considering the work, acknowledge the work master; but deemed either fire, or wind, or the swift air, or the circle of the stars, or the violent water, or the lights of heaven, to be gods, which govern the world."

Of these two faiths the Sabean, as we have before observed, was much the most prevalent among the Arabs; but in an extremely degraded form, mingled with all kinds of abuses, and varying among the various tribes. The Magian faith prevailed among those tribes which, from their frontier position, had frequent intercourse with Persia; while other tribes partook of the superstitions and idolatries of the nations on which they bordered.

Judaism had made its way into Arabia at an early period, but very vaguely and imperfectly. Still many of its rites and ceremonies, and fanciful traditions, became implanted in the country. At a later day, however, when Palestine was ravaged by the Romans, and the city of Jerusalem taken and sacked, many of the Jews took refuge among the Arabs; became incorporated with the native tribes; formed themselves into communities; acquired possession of fertile tracts; built castles and strongholds, and rose to considerable power and influence.

The Christian religion had likewise its adherents among the Arabs. St. Paul himself declares in his epistle to the Galatians, that soon after he had been called to preach Christianity among the heathens, he "went into Arabia." The dissensions, also, which rose in the Eastern church, in the early part of the third century, breaking it up into sects, each persecuting the others as it gained the ascendency, drove many into exile into remote parts of the East; filled the deserts of Arabia with anchorites, and planted the Christian faith among some of the principal tribes.

The foregoing circumstances, physical and moral, may give an idea of the causes which maintained the Arabs for ages in an unchanged condition. While their isolated position and their vast deserts protected them from conquest, their internal feuds, and their want of a common tie, political or religious, kept them from being formidable as conquerors. They were a vast aggregation of distinct parts; full of individual vigor, but wanting coherent strength. Although their nomadic life rendered them hardy and active; although the greater part of them were warriors from infancy, yet their arms were only wielded against each other, excepting some of the frontier tribes, which occasionally engaged as mercenaries in external wars. While, therefore, the other nomadic races of Central Asia, possessing no greater aptness for warfare, had, during a course of ages, successively overrun and conquered the civilized world, this warrior race, unconscious of its power, remained disjointed and harmless in the depths of its native deserts.

The time at length arrived when its discordant tribes were to be united in one creed, and animated by one common cause; when a mighty genius was to arise, who should bring together these scattered limbs, animate them with his own enthusiastic and daring spirit, and lead them forth, a giant of the desert, to shake and overturn the empires of the earth.

CHAPTER II

Birth and parentage of Mahomet – His infancy and childhood

Mahomet, the great founder of the faith of Islam, was born in Mecca, in April, in the year 569 of the Christian era. He was of the valiant and illustrious tribe of Koreish, of which there were two branches, descended from two brothers, Haschem and Abd Schems. Haschem, the progenitor of Mahomet, was a great benefactor of Mecca. This city is situated in the midst of a barren and stony country, and in former times was often subject to scarcity of provisions. At the beginning of the sixth century Haschem established two yearly caravans, one in the winter to South Arabia or Yemen; the other in the summer to Syria. By these means abundant supplies were brought to Mecca, as well as a great variety of merchandise. The city became a commercial mart, and the tribe of Koreish, which engaged largely in these expeditions, became wealthy and powerful. Haschem, at this time, was the guardian of the Caaba, the great shrine of Arabian pilgrimage and worship, the custody of which was confided to none but the most honorable tribes and families, in the same manner, as in old times, the temple of Jerusalem was intrusted only to the care of the Levites. In fact the guardianship of the Caaba was connected with civil dignities and privileges, and gave the holder of it the control of the sacred city.

On the death of Haschem, his son, Abd al Motâlleb, succeeded to his honors, and inherited his patriotism. He delivered the holy city from an invading army of troops and elephants, sent by the Christian princes of Abyssinia, who at that time held Yemen in subjection. These signal services rendered by father and son, confirmed the guardianship of the Caaba in the line of Haschem; to the great discontent and envy of the line of Abd Schems.

Abd al Motâlleb had several sons and daughters. Those of his sons who figure in history were, Abu Taleb, Abu Lahab, Abbas, Hamza, and Abdallah. The last named was the youngest and best beloved. He married Amina, a maiden of a distant branch of the same illustrious stock of Koreish. So remarkable was Abdallah for personal beauty and those qualities which win the affections of women, that, if Moslem traditions are to be credited, on the night of his marriage with Amina, two hundred virgins of the tribe of Koreish died of broken hearts.

Mahomet was the first and only fruit of the marriage thus sadly celebrated. His birth, according to similar traditions with the one just

15

cited, was accompanied by signs and portents announcing a child of wonder. His mother suffered none of the pangs of travail. At the moment of his coming into the world, a celestial light illumined the surrounding country, and the new-born child, raising his eyes to heaven, exclaimed: "God is great! There is no God but God, and I am his prophet."

Heaven and earth, we are assured, were agitated at his advent. The Lake Sawa shrank back to its secret springs, leaving its borders dry; while the Tigris, bursting its bounds, overflowed the neighboring lands. The palace of Khosru the king of Persia shook to its foundations, and several of its towers were toppled to the earth. In that troubled night the Kadhi, or Judge of Persia, beheld, in a dream, a ferocious camel conquered by an Arabian courser. He related his dream in the morning to the Persian monarch, and interpreted it to portend danger from the quarter of Arabia.

In the same eventful night the sacred fire of Zoroaster, which, guarded by the Magi, had burned without interruption for upwards of a thousand years, was suddenly extinguished, and all the idols in the world fell down. The demons, or evil genii, which lurk in the stars and the signs of the zodiac, and exert a malignant influence over the children of men, were cast forth by the pure angels, and hurled, with their arch leader, Eblis, or Lucifer, into the depths of the sea.

The relatives of the new-born child, say the like authorities, were filled with awe and wonder. His mother's brother, an astrologer, cast his nativity, and predicted that he would rise to vast power, found an empire, and establish a new faith among men. His grandfather, Abd al Motâlleb, gave a feast to the principal Koreishites, the seventh day after his birth, at which he presented this child, as the dawning glory of their race, and gave him the name of Mahomet (or Muhamed), indicative of his future renown.

Such are the marvellous accounts given by Moslem writers of the infancy of Mahomet, and we have little else than similar fables about his early years. He was scarce two months old when his father died, leaving him no other inheritance than five camels, a few sheep, and a female slave of Ethiopia, named Barakat. His mother, Amina, had hitherto nurtured him, but care and sorrow dried the fountains of her breast, and the air of Mecca being unhealthy for children, she sought a nurse for him among the females of the neighboring Bedouin tribes. These were accustomed to come to Mecca twice a year, in spring and autumn, to foster the children of its inhabitants; but they looked for the offspring of the rich, where they were sure of ample recompense, and turned with contempt from this heir of poverty. At length Halêma, the wife of a Saadite shepherd, was moved to compassion, and took the helpless infant to her home. It was in one of the pastoral valleys of the mountains.*

Many were the wonders related by Halêma of her infant charge. On the journey from Mecca, the mule which bore him became miraculously endowed with speech, and proclaimed aloud that he bore on his back the greatest of prophets, the chief of ambassadors, the favorite of the Almighty. The sheep bowed to him as he passed; as he lay in his cradle and gazed at the moon, it stooped to him in reverence.

The blessing of heaven, say the Arabian writers, rewarded the charity of Halêma. While the child remained under her roof, every thing around her prospered. The wells and springs were never dried up; the pastures were always green; her flocks and herds increased tenfold; a marvellous abundance reigned over her fields, and peace prevailed in her dwelling.

The Arabian legends go on to extol the almost supernatural powers, bodily and mental, manifested by this wonderful child at a very early age. He could stand alone when three months old; run abroad when he was seven, and at ten could join other children in their sports with bows and arrows. At eight months he could speak so as to be understood; and in the course of another month could converse with fluency, displaying a wisdom astonishing to all who heard him.

At the age of three years, while playing in the fields with his foster brother, Masroud, two angels in shining apparel appeared before them. They laid Mahomet gently upon the ground, and Gabriel, one of the angels, opened his breast, but without inflicting any pain. Then taking forth his heart, he cleansed it from all impurity, wringing from it those black and bitter drops of original sin, inherited from our forefather Adam, and which lurk in the hearts of the best of his descendants, inciting them to crime. When he had thoroughly purified it, he filled it with faith and knowledge and prophetic light, and replaced it in the bosom of the child. Now, we are assured by the same authorities,

---

* The Beni Sad (or children of Sad) date from the most remote antiquity, and, with the Kahtan Arabs, are the only remnants of the primitive tribes of Arabia. Their valley is among the mountains which range southwardly from the Tayef. — *Burckhardt on the Bedouins*, vol. ii. p. 47.

began to emanate from his countenance that mysterious light which had continued down from Adam, through the sacred line of prophets, until the time of Isaac and Ishmael; but which had lain dormant in the descendants of the latter, until it thus shone forth with renewed radiance from the features of Mahomet.

At this supernatural visitation, it is added, was impressed between the shoulders of the child the seal of prophecy, which continued throughout life the symbol and credential of his divine mission; though unbelievers saw nothing in it but a large mole, the size of a pigeon's egg.

When the marvellous visitation of the angel was related to Halêma and her husband, they were alarmed lest some misfortune should be impending over the child, or that his supernatural visitors might be of the race of evil spirits or genii, which haunt the solitudes of the desert, wreaking mischief on the children of men. His Saadite nurse, therefore, carried him back to Mecca, and delivered him to his mother Amina.

He remained with his parent until his sixth year, when she took him with her to Medina, on a visit to her relatives of the tribe of Adij, but on her journey homeward she died, and was buried at Abwa, a village between Medina and Mecca. Her grave it will be found, was a place of pious resort and tender recollection to her son, at the latest period of his life.

The faithful Abyssinian slave Barakat, now acted as a mother to the orphan child, and conducted him to his grandfather Abd al Motâlleb, in whose household he remained for two years, treated with care and tenderness. Abd al Motâlleb was now well stricken in years; having outlived the ordinary term of human existence. Finding his end approaching, he called to him his eldest son Abu Taleb, and bequeathed Mahomet to his especial protection. The good Abu Taleb took his nephew to his bosom, and ever afterwards was to him as a parent. As the former succeeded to the guardianship of the Caaba at the death of his father, Mahomet continued for several years in a kind of sacerdotal household, where the rites and ceremonies of the sacred house were rigidly observed. And here we deem it necessary to give a more especial notice of the alleged origin of the Caaba, and of the rites and traditions and superstitions connected with it, closely interwoven as they are with the faith of Islam and the story of its founder.

CHAPTER III

Traditions concerning Mecca and the Caaba

When Adam and Eve were cast forth from Paradise, say Arabian traditions, they fell in different parts of the earth; Adam on a mountain of the island of Serendib, or Ceylon; Eve in Arabia on the borders of the Red Sea, where the port of Jidda is now situated. For two hundred years they wandered separate and lonely about the earth, until, in consideration of their penitence and wretchedness, they were permitted to come together again on Mount Arafat, not far from the present city of Mecca. In the depth of his sorrow and repentance, Adam, it is said, raised his hands and eyes to heaven, and implored the clemency of God; entreating that a shrine might be vouchsafed to him similar to that at which he had worshipped when in Paradise, and round which the angels used to move in adoring processions.

The supplication of Adam was effectual. A tabernacle or temple formed of radiant clouds was lowered down by the hands of angels, and placed immediately below its prototype in the celestial paradise. Towards his heaven-descended shrine, Adam thenceforth turned when in prayer, and round it he daily made seven circuits in imitation of the rites of the adoring angels.

At the death of Adam, say the same traditions, the tabernacle of clouds passed away, or was again drawn up to heaven; but another, of the same form and in the same place, was built of stone and clay by Seth, the son of Adam. This was swept away by the deluge. Many generations afterwards, in the time of the patriarchs, when Hagar and her child Ishmael were near perishing with thirst in the desert, an angel revealed to them a spring or well of water, near to the ancient site of the tabernacle. This was the well of Zem Zem, held sacred by the progeny of Ishmael to the present day. Shortly afterwards two individuals of the gigantic race of the Amalekites, in quest of a camel which had strayed from their camp, discovered this well, and, having slaked their thirst, brought their companions to the place. Here they founded the city of Mecca, taking Ishmael and his mother under their protection. They were soon expelled by the proper inhabitants of the country, among whom Ishmael remained. When grown to man's estate, he married the daughter of the ruling prince, by whom he had a numerous progeny, the ancestors of the Arabian people. In process of time, by God's command he undertook to rebuild the Caaba, on the precise site

19

of the original tabernacle of clouds. In this pious work he was assisted
by his father Abraham. A miraculous stone served Abraham as a scaf-
fold, rising and sinking with him as he built the walls of the sacred
edifice. It still remains there an inestimable relic, and the print of the
patriarch's foot is clearly to be perceived on it by all true believers.

While Abraham and Ishmael were thus occupied, the angel Gabriel
brought them a stone, about which traditional accounts are a little at
variance; by some it is said to have been one of the precious stones of
Paradise, which fell to the earth with Adam, and was afterwards lost in
the slime of the deluge, until retrieved by the angel Gabriel. The more
received tradition is, that it was originally the guardian angel appointed to watch over Adam in Paradise, but changed into a stone and
ejected thence with him at his fall, as a punishment for not having
been more vigilant. This stone Abraham and Ishmael received with
proper reverence, and inserted it in a corner of the exterior wall of the
Caaba, where it remains to the present day, devoutly kissed by worshippers each time they make a circuit of the temple. When first inserted in the wall it was, we are told, a single jacinth of dazzling
whiteness, but became gradually blackened by the kisses of sinful mortals. At the resurrection it will recover its angelic form, and stand forth
a testimony before God in favor of those who have faithfully performed the rites of pilgrimage.

Such are the Arabian traditions, which rendered the Caaba and the
well of Zem Zem, objects of extraordinary veneration from the remotest
antiquity among the people of the East, and especially the descendants
of Ishmael. Mecca, which incloses these sacred objects within its walls,
was a holy city many ages before the rise of Mahometanism, and was
the resort of pilgrims from all parts of Arabia. So universal and profound was the religious feeling respecting this observance, that four
months in every year were devoted to the rites of pilgrimage, and held
sacred from all violence and warfare. Hostile tribes then laid aside
their arms; took the heads from their spears; traversed the late dangerous deserts in security; thronged the gates of Mecca clad in the pilgrim's garb; made their seven circuits round the Caaba in imitation of
the angelic host; touched and kissed the mysterious black stone; drank
and made ablutions at the well Zem Zem in memory of their ancestor
Ishmael; and having performed all the other primitive rites of pilgrimage returned home in safety, again to resume their weapons and their
wars.

Among the religious observances of the Arabs in these their "days of ignorance;" that is to say, before the promulgation of the Moslem doctrines, fasting and prayer had a foremost place. They had three principal fasts within the year; one of seven, one of nine, and one of thirty days. They prayed three times each day; about sunrise, at noon, and about sunset; turning their faces in the direction of the Caaba, which was their Kebla, or point of adoration. They had many religious traditions, some of them acquired in early times from the Jews, and they are said to have nurtured their devotional feelings with the book of Psalms, and with a book said to be by Seth, and filled with moral discourses.

Brought up, as Mahomet was, in the house of the guardian of the Caaba, the ceremonies and devotions connected with the sacred edifice may have given an early bias to his mind, and inclined it to those speculations in matters of religion by which it eventually became engrossed. Though his Moslem biographers would fain persuade us his high destiny was clearly foretold in his childhood by signs and prodigies, yet his education appears to have been as much neglected as that of ordinary Arab children; for we find that he was not taught either to read or write. He was a thoughtful child, however; quick to observe, prone to meditate on all that he observed, and possessed of an imagination fertile, daring, and expansive. The yearly influx of pilgrims from distant parts made Mecca a receptacle for all kinds of floating knowledge, which he appears to have imbibed with eagerness and retained in a tenacious memory; and as he increased in years, a more extended sphere of observation was gradually opened to him.

CHAPTER IV

First journey of Mahomet with the caravan to Syria

Mahomet was now twelve years of age, but, as we have shown, he had an intelligence far beyond his years. The spirit of inquiry was awake within him, quickened by intercourse with pilgrims from all parts of Arabia. His uncle Abu Taleb, too, beside his sacerdotal character as guardian of the Caaba, was one of the most enterprising merchants of the tribe of Koreish, and had much to do with those caravans set on foot by his ancestor Haschem, which traded to Syria and Yemen. The arrival and departure of those caravans, which thronged the gates of Mecca and filled its streets with pleasing tumult, were exciting events to a youth like Mahomet, and carried his imagination to foreign parts. He could no longer repress the ardent curiosity thus aroused; but once, when his uncle was about to mount his camel to depart with the caravan for Syria, clung to him, and entreated to be permitted to accompany him: "For who, oh my uncle," said he, "will take care of me when thou art away?"

The appeal was not lost upon the kind-hearted Abu Taleb. He bethought him, too, that the youth was of an age to enter upon the active scenes of Arab life, and of a capacity to render essential service in the duties of the caravan; he readily, therefore, granted his prayer, and took him with him on the journey to Syria.

The route lay through regions fertile in fables and traditions, which it is the delight of the Arabs to recount in the evening halts of the caravan. The vast solitudes of the desert, in which that wandering people pass so much of their lives, are prone to engender superstitious fancies; they have accordingly peopled them with good and evil genii, and clothed them with tales of enchantment, mingled up with wonderful events which happened in days of old. In these evening halts of the caravan, the youthful mind of Mahomet doubtless imbibed many of those superstitions of the desert which ever afterwards dwelt in his memory, and had a powerful influence over his imagination. We may especially note two traditions which he must have heard at this time, and which we find recorded by him in after years in the Koran. One related to the mountainous district of Hedjar. Here, as the caravan wound its way through silent and deserted valleys, caves were pointed out in the sides of the mountains once inhabited by the Beni Thamud, or children of Thamud, one of the "lost tribes" of Arabia; and this was the tradition concerning them.

They were a proud and gigantic race, existing before the time of the patriarch Abraham. Having fallen into blind idolatry, God sent a prophet of the name of Saleh, to restore them to the right way. They refused, however, to listen to him, unless he should prove the divinity of his mission by causing a camel, big with young, to issue from the entrails of a mountain. Saleh accordingly prayed, and lo! a rock opened, and a female camel came forth, which soon produced a foal. Some of the Thamudites were convinced by the miracle, and were converted by the prophet from their idolatry; the greater part, however, remained in unbelief. Saleh left the camel among them as a sign, warning them that a judgment from heaven would fall on them, should they do her any harm. For a time the camel was suffered to feed quietly in their pastures, going forth in the morning, and returning in the evening. It is true, that when she bowed her head to drink from a brook or well, she never raised it until she had drained the last drop of water; but then in return she yielded milk enough to supply the whole tribe. As, however, she frightened the other camels from the pasture, she became an object of offence to the Thamudites, who hamstrung and slew her. Upon this there was a fearful cry from heaven, and great claps of thunder, and in the morning all the offenders were found lying on their faces, dead. Thus the whole race was swept from the earth, and their country was laid for ever afterward under the ban of heaven.

This story made a powerful impression on the mind of Mahomet, insomuch that, in after years, he refused to let his people encamp in the neighborhood, but hurried them away from it as an accursed region.

Another tradition, gathered on this journey, related to the city of Eyla, situated near the Red Sea. This place, he was told, had been inhabited in old times by a tribe of Jews, who lapsed into idolatry and profaned the Sabbath, by fishing on that sacred day; whereupon the old men were transformed into swine, and the young men into monkeys.

We have noted these two traditions especially because they are both cited by Mahomet as instances of divine judgment on the crime of idolatry, and evince the bias his youthful mind was already taking on that important subject.

Moslem writers tell us, as usual, of wonderful circumstances which attended the youth throughout this journey, giving evidence of the

continual guardianship of heaven. At one time, as he traversed the
burning sands of the desert, an angel hovered over him unseen, sheltering him with his wings; a miracle, however, which evidently does not
rest on the evidence of an eye-witness; at another time he was protected by a cloud which hung over his head during the noontide heat;
and on another occasion, as he sought the scanty shade of a withered
tree, it suddenly put forth leaves and blossoms.

After skirting the ancient domains of the Moabites and the Ammon-
ites, often mentioned in the sacred Scriptures, the caravan arrived at
Bosra, or Bostra, on the confines of Syria, in the country of the tribe of
Manasseh, beyond the Jordan. In Scripture days it had been a city of
the Levites, but now was inhabited by Nestorian Christians. It was a
great mart, annually visited by the caravans; and here our wayfarers
came to a halt, and encamped near a convent of Nestorian monks.

By this fraternity Abu Taleb and his nephew were entertained with
great hospitality. One of the monks, by some called Sergius, by others
Bahira,* on conversing with Mahomet, was surprised at the precocity
of his intellect, and interested by his eager desire for information,
which appears to have had reference, principally, to matters of religion. They had frequent conversations together on such subjects, in the
course of which the efforts of the monk must have been mainly directed against that idolatry in which the youthful Mahomet had hitherto been educated; for the Nestorian Christians were strenuous in condemning not merely the worship of images, but even the casual exhibi-
tion of them; indeed, so far did they carry their scruples on this point,
that even the cross, that general emblem of Christianity, was in a great
degree included in this prohibition.

Many have ascribed that knowledge of the principles and traditions
of the Christian faith displayed by Mahomet in after life, to those early
conversations with this monk; it is probable, however, that he had further intercourse with the latter in the course of subsequent visits which
he made to Syria.

Moslem writers pretend that the interest taken by the monk in the
youthful stranger, arose from his having accidentally perceived between his shoulders the seal of prophecy. He warned Abu Taleb, say
they, when about to set out on his return to Mecca, to take care that

---

* Some assert that these two names indicate two monks, who held conversations
with Mahomet.

his nephew did not fall into the hands of the Jews; foreseeing with the eye of prophecy the trouble and opposition he was to encounter from that people.

It required no miraculous sign, however, to interest a sectarian monk, anxious to make proselytes, in an intelligent and inquiring youth, nephew of the guardian of the Caaba, who might carry back with him to Mecca the seeds of Christianity sown in his tender mind; and it was natural that the monk should be eager to prevent his hoped-for convert, in the present unsettled state of his religious opinions, from being beguiled into the Jewish faith.

Mahomet returned to Mecca, his imagination teeming with the wild tales and traditions picked up in the desert, and his mind deeply impressed with the doctrines imparted to him in the Nestorian convent. He seems ever afterwards to have entertained a mysterious reverence for Syria, probably from the religious impressions received there. It was the land whither Abraham the patriarch had repaired from Chaldea, taking with him the primitive worship of the one true God. "Verily," he used to say in after years, "God has ever maintained guardians of his word in Syria; forty in number; when one dies another is sent in his room; and through them the land is blessed." And again – "Joy be to the people of Syria, for the angels of the kind God spread their wings over them."*

NOTE — The conversion of Abraham from the idolatry into which the world had fallen after the deluge, is related in the Sixth Chapter of the Koran. Abraham's father, Azer, or Zerah, as his name is given in the Scriptures, was a statuary and an idolater.

"And Abraham said unto his father Azer, 'Why dost thou take graven images for gods? Verily, thou and thy people are in error.'

"Then was the firmament of heaven displayed unto Abraham, that he might see how the world was governed.

"When night came, and darkness overshadowed the earth, he beheld a bright star shining in the firmament, and cried out to his people who were astrologers: 'This, according to your assertions, is the Lord.'

"But the star set, and Abraham said, 'I have no faith in gods that set.'

"He beheld the moon rising, and exclaimed, 'Assuredly, this is the Lord.' But the moon likewise set, and he was confounded, and prayed unto God, saying, 'Direct me, lest I become as one of these people, who go astray.'

"When he saw the sun rising, he cried out, 'This is the most glorious of all; this of a certainty is the Lord.' But the sun also set. Then said Abraham, 'I believe not, oh my people, in those things which ye call gods. Verily, I turn my face unto Him, the Creator, who hath formed both the heavens and the earth.' "

* Mishcât-ul-Masâbih, vol. ii. p. 812.

CHAPTER V

Commercial occupations of Mahomet – His marriage with Cadijah

Mahomet was now completely launched in active life, accompanying his uncles in various expeditions. At one time, when about sixteen years of age, we find him with his uncle Zobeir, journeying with the caravan to Yemen; at another time acting as armor-bearer to the same uncle, who led a warlike expedition of Koreishites in aid of the Kenanites against the tribe of Hawazan. This is cited as Mahomet's first essay in arms, though he did little else than supply his uncle with arrows in the heat of the action, and shield him from the darts of the enemy. It is stigmatized among Arabian writers as al Fadjar, or the impious war, having been carried on during the sacred months of pilgrimage.

As Mahomet advanced in years, he was employed by different persons as commercial agent or factor in caravan journeys to Syria, Yemen, and elsewhere; all which tended to enlarge the sphere of his observation, and to give him a quick insight into character and a knowledge of human affairs.

He was a frequent attender of fairs also, which, in Arabia, were not always mere resorts of traffic, but occasionally scenes of poetical contests between different tribes, where prizes were adjudged to the victors, and their prize poems treasured up in the archives of princes. Such, especially, was the case with the fair of Ocadh; and seven of the prize poems adjudged there, were hung up as trophies in the Caaba. At these fairs, also, were recited the popular traditions of the Arabs, and inculcated the various religious faiths which were afloat in Arabia. From oral sources of this kind, Mahomet gradually accumulated much of that varied information as to creeds and doctrines which he afterwards displayed.

There was at this time residing in Mecca a widow, named Cadijah (or Khadijah), of the tribe of Koreish. She had been twice married. Her last husband, a wealthy merchant, had recently died, and the extensive concerns of the house were in need of a conductor. A nephew of the widow, named Chuzima, had become acquainted with Mahomet in the course of his commercial expeditions, and had noticed the ability and integrity with which he acquitted himself on all occasions. He pointed him out to his aunt as a person well qualified to be her factor. The personal appearance of Mahomet may have strongly seconded this recommendation; for he was now about twenty-five years of age, and

extolled by Arabian writers for his manly beauty and engaging manners. So desirous was Cadijah of securing his services, that she offered
him double wages to conduct a caravan which she was on the point of
sending off to Syria. Mahomet consulted his uncle Abu Taleb, and by
his advice, accepted the offer. He was accompanied and aided in the
expedition by the nephew of the widow, and by her slave Maïsara, and
so highly satisfied was Cadijah with the way in which he discharged
his duties, that, on his return, she paid him double the amount of his
stipulated wages. She afterwards sent him to the southern parts of Arabia on similar expeditions, in all which he gave like satisfaction.

Cadijah was now in her fortieth year, a woman of judgment and experience. The mental qualities of Mahomet rose more and more in her
estimation, and her heart began to yearn toward the fresh and comely
youth. According to Arabian legends, a miracle occurred most opportunely to confirm and sanctify the bias of her inclinations. She was one
day with her handmaids, at the hour of noon, on the terraced roof of
her dwelling, watching the arrival of a caravan conducted by Mahomet. As it approached, she beheld, with astonishment, two angels
overshadowing him with their wings to protect him from the sun. Turning, with emotion, to her handmaids, "Behold!" said she, "the beloved
of Allah, who sends two angels to watch over him!"

Whether or not the handmaidens looked forth with the same eyes of
devotion as their mistress, and likewise discerned the angels, the legend does not mention. Suffice it to say, the widow was filled with a
lively faith in the superhuman merits of her youthful steward, and
forthwith commissioned her trusty slave, Maïsara, to offer him her
hand. The negotiation is recorded with simple brevity. "Mahomet," demanded Maïsara, "why dost thou not marry?" "I have not the means,"
replied Mahomet. "Well, but if a wealthy dame should offer thee her
hand: one also who is handsome and of high birth?" "And who is she?"
"Cadijah!" "How is that possible?" "Let me manage it." Maïsara returned to his mistress and reported what had passed. An hour was appointed for an interview, and the affair was brought to a satisfactory
arrangement with that promptness and sagacity which had distinguished Mahomet in all his dealings with the widow. The father of
Cadijah made some opposition to the match, on account of the poverty
of Mahomet, following the common notion that wealth should be
added to wealth: but the widow wisely considered her riches only as
the means of enabling her to follow the dictates of her heart. She gave

a great feast, to which were invited her father and the rest of her relatives, and Mahomet's uncles Abu Taleb and Hamza, together with several other of the Koreishites. At this banquet wine was served in abundance, and soon diffused good humor round the board. The objections to Mahomet's poverty were forgotten; speeches were made by Abu Taleb on the one side, and by Waraka, a kinsman of Cadijah, on the other, in praise of the proposed nuptials; the dowry was arranged, and the marriage formally concluded.

Mahomet then caused a camel to be killed before his door, and the flesh distributed among the poor. The house was thrown open to all comers; the female slaves of Cadijah danced to the sound of timbrels, and all was revelry and rejoicing. Abu Taleb, forgetting his age and his habitual melancholy, made merry on the occasion. He had paid down from his purse a dower of twelve-and-a-half okks of gold, equivalent to twenty young camels. Halêma, who had nursed Mahomet in his infancy, was summoned to rejoice at his nuptials, and was presented with a flock of forty sheep, with which she returned, enriched and contented, to her native valley, in the desert of the Saadites.

CHAPTER VI

Conduct of Mahomet after his marriage – Becomes anxious for re-
ligious reform – His habits of solitary abstraction – The vision of the
cave – His annunciation as a prophet

The marriage with Cadijah placed Mahomet among the most wealthy of his native city. His moral worth also gave him great influence in the community. Allah, says the historian Abulfeda, had endowed him with every gift necessary to accomplish and adorn an honest man; he was so pure and sincere; so free from every evil thought, that he was commonly known by the name of Al Amin, or The Faithful.

The great confidence reposed in his judgment and probity, caused him to be frequently referred to as arbiter in disputes between his townsmen. An anecdote is given as illustrative of his sagacity on such occasions. The Caaba having been injured by fire, was undergoing repairs, in the course of which the sacred black stone was to be replaced. A dispute arose among the chiefs of the various tribes, as to which was entitled to perform so august an office, and they agreed to abide by the decision of the first person who should enter by the gate al Harâm. That person happened to be Mahomet. Upon hearing their different claims, he directed that a great cloth should be spread upon the ground, and the stone laid thereon; and that a man from each tribe should take hold of the border of the cloth. In this way the sacred stone was raised equally and at the same time by them all to a level with its allotted place, in which Mahomet fixed it with his own hands.

Four daughters and one son, were the fruit of the marriage with Cadijah. The son was named Kasim, whence Mahomet was occasionally called Abu Kasim, or the father of Kasim, according to Arabian nomenclature. This son, however, died in his infancy.

For several years after his marriage he continued in commerce, visiting the great Arabian fairs, and making distant journeys with the caravans. His expeditions were not as profitable as in the days of his stewardship, and the wealth acquired with his wife diminished, rather than increased in the course of his operations. That wealth, in fact, had raised him above the necessity of toiling for subsistence, and given him leisure to indulge the original bias of his mind; a turn for reverie and religious speculation, which he had evinced from his earliest years. This had been fostered in the course of his journeyings, by his intercourse with Jews and Christians, originally fugitives from persecution, but now gathered into tribes, or forming part of the population of cities. The Arabian deserts too, rife as we have shown them with fanciful superstitions, had furnished aliment for his enthusiastic reveries. Since his marriage with Cadijah, also, he had a household oracle to influence him in his religious opinions. This was his wife's cousin Waraka, a man of speculative mind and flexible faith; originally a Jew; subsequently a Christian; and withal a pretender to astrology. He is worthy of note as being the first on record to translate parts of the Old and New Testament into Arabic. From him Mahomet is supposed to have derived much of his information respecting those writings, and many of the traditions of the Mishnu and the Talmud, on which he draws so copiously in his Koran.

The knowledge thus variously acquired and treasured up in an uncommonly retentive memory, was in direct hostility to the gross idolatry prevalent in Arabia, and practised at the Caaba. That sacred edifice had gradually become filled and surrounded by idols, to the number of three hundred and sixty, being one for every day of the Arab year. Hither had been brought idols from various parts, the deities of other nations, the chief of which, Hobal, was from Syria, and supposed to have the power of giving rain. Among these idols too, were Abraham and Ishmael, once revered as prophets and progenitors, now represented with divining arrows in their hands, symbols of magic.

Mahomet became more and more sensible of the grossness and absurdity of this idolatry, in proportion as his intelligent mind contrasted it with the spiritual religions, which had been the subjects of his inquiries. Various passages in the Koran show the ruling idea which gradually sprang up in his mind, until it engrossed his thoughts and influenced all his actions. That idea was a religious reform. It had become his fixed belief, deduced from all that he had learnt and meditated, that the only true religion had been revealed to Adam at his creation, and been promulgated and practised in the days of innocence. That religion inculcated the direct and spiritual worship of one true and only God, the creator of the universe.

It was his belief, furthermore, that this religion, so elevated and simple, had repeatedly been corrupted and debased by man, and especially outraged by idolatry; wherefore a succession of prophets, each inspired by a revelation from the Most High, had been sent from time to time, and at distant periods, to restore it to its original purity. Such was Noah, such was Abraham, such was Moses, and such was Jesus

Christ. By each of these, the true religion had been reinstated upon earth, but had again been vitiated by their followers. The faith as taught and practised by Abraham when he came out of the land of Chaldea, seems especially to have formed a religious standard in his mind, from his veneration for the patriarch as the father of Ishmael, the progenitor of his race.

It appeared to Mahomet that the time for another reform was again arrived. The world had once more lapsed into blind idolatry. It needed the advent of another prophet, authorized by a mandate from on high, to restore the erring children of men to the right path, and to bring back the worship of the Caaba to what it had been in the days of Abraham and the patriarchs. The probability of such an advent, with its attendant reforms, seems to have taken possession of his mind, and produced habits of reverie and meditation, incompatible with the ordinary concerns of life and the bustle of the world. We are told that he gradually absented himself from society, and sought the solitude of a cavern on Mount Hara, about three leagues north of Mecca, where, in emulation of the Christian anchorites of the desert, he would remain days and nights together, engaged in prayer and meditation. In this way he always passed the month of Ramadhan, the holy month of the Arabs. Such intense occupation of the mind on one subject, accompanied by fervent enthusiasm of spirit, could not but have a powerful effect upon his frame. He became subject to dreams, to ecstasies and trances. For six months successively, according to one of his historians, he had constant dreams bearing on the subject of his waking thoughts. Often he would lose all consciousness of surrounding objects, and lie upon the ground as if insensible. Cadijah, who was sometimes the faithful companion of his solitude, beheld these paroxysms with anxious solicitude, and entreated to know the cause; but he evaded her inquiries, or answered them mysteriously. Some of his adversaries have attributed them to epilepsy, but devout Moslems declare them to have been the workings of prophecy; for already, say they, the intimations of the Most High began to dawn, though vaguely, on his spirit; and his mind labored with conceptions too great for mortal thought. At length, say they, what had hitherto been shadowed out in dreams, was made apparent and distinct by an angelic apparition and a divine annunciation.

It was in the fortieth year of his age, when this famous revelation took place. Accounts are given of it by Moslem writers as if received from his own lips, and it is alluded to in certain passages of the Koran. He was passing, as was his wont, the month of Ramadhan in the cavern of Mount Hara, endeavoring by fasting, prayer, and solitary meditation, to elevate his thoughts to the contemplation of divine truth. It was on the night called by Arabs Al Kader, or the Divine Decree; a night in which, according to the Koran, angels descend to earth, and Gabriel brings down the decrees of God. During that night there is peace on earth, and a holy quiet reigns over all nature until the rising of the morn.

As Mahomet, in the silent watches of the night, lay wrapped in his mantle, he heard a voice calling upon him; uncovering his head, a flood of light broke upon him of such intolerable splendor that he swooned away. On regaining his senses, he beheld an angel in a human form, which, approaching from a distance, displayed a silken cloth covered with written characters. "Read!" said the angel.

"I know not how to read!" replied Mahomet.

"Read!" repeated the angel, "in the name of the Lord, who has created all things; who created man from a clot of blood. Read in the name of the Most High, who taught man the use of the pen; who sheds on his soul the ray of knowledge, and teaches him what before he knew not."

Upon this Mahomet instantly felt his understanding illumined with celestial light, and read what was written on the cloth, which contained the decrees of God, as afterwards promulgated in the Koran. When he had finished the perusal, the heavenly messenger announced, "Oh Mahomet, of a verity, thou art the prophet of God! and I am his angel Gabriel."

Mahomet, we are told, came trembling and agitated to Cadijah in the morning, not knowing whether what he had heard and seen was indeed true, and that he was a prophet decreed to effect that reform so long the object of his meditations; or whether it might not be a mere vision, a delusion of the senses, or worse than all, the apparition of an evil spirit.

Cadijah, however, saw every thing with the eye of faith, and the credulity of an affectionate woman. She saw in it the fruition of her husband's wishes, and the end of his paroxysms and privations. "Joyful tidings dost thou bring!" exclaimed she. "By him, in whose hand is the soul of Cadijah, I will henceforth regard thee as the prophet of our nation. Rejoice," added she, seeing him still cast down; "Allah will not suffer thee to fall to shame. Hast thou not been loving to thy kinsfolk, kind to thy neighbors, charitable to the poor, hospitable to the stranger, faithful to thy word, and ever a defender of the truth?"

Cadijah hastened to communicate what she had heard to her cousin Waraka, the translator of the Scriptures; who, as we have shown, had been a household oracle of Mahomet in matters of religion. He caught at once, and with eagerness, at this miraculous annunciation. "By him in whose hand is the soul of Waraka," exclaimed he; "thou speakest true, oh Cadijah! The angel who has appeared to thy husband is the same who, in days of old, was sent to Moses the son of Amram. His annunciation is true. Thy husband is indeed a prophet!"

The zealous concurrence of the learned Waraka, is said to have had a powerful effect in fortifying the dubious mind of Mahomet.

NOTE – Dr. Gustav Weil, in a note to *Mohammed der Prophet,* discusses the question of Mahomet's being subject to attacks of epilepsy; which has generally been represented as a slander of his enemies and of Christian writers. It appears, however, to have been asserted by some of the oldest Moslem biographers, and given on the authority of persons about him. He would be seized, they said, with violent trembling, followed by a kind of swoon, or rather convulsion, during which perspiration would stream from his forehead in the coldest weather; he would lie with his eyes closed, foaming at the mouth and bellowing like a young camel. Ayesha one of his wives, and Zeid one of his disciples, are among the persons cited as testifying to that effect. They considered him at such times as under the influence of a revelation. He had such attacks, however, in Mecca, before the Koran was revealed to him. Cadijah feared that he was possessed by evil spirits, and would have called in the aid of a conjurer to exorcise them, but he forbade her. He did not like that any one should see him during these paroxysms. His visions, however, were not always preceded by such attacks. Hareth Ibn Haschem, it is said, once asked him in what manner the revelations were made. "Often," replied he, "the angel appears to me in a human form, and speaks to me. Sometimes I hear sounds like the tinkling of a bell, but see nothing. [A ringing in the ears is a symptom of epilepsy.] When the invisible angel has departed, I am possessed of what he has revealed." Some of his revelations he professed to receive direct from God, others in dreams; for the dreams of prophets, he used to say, are revelations.

The reader will find this note of service in throwing some degree of light upon the enigmatical career of this extraordinary man.

Mahomet inculcates his doctrines secretly and slowly — Receives further revelations and commands — Announces it to his kindred — Manner in which it was received — Enthusiastic devotion of Ali — Christian portents

For a time Mahomet confided his revelations merely to his own household. One of the first to avow himself a believer, was his servant Zeid, an Arab of the tribe of Kalb. This youth had been captured in childhood by a freebooting party of Koreishites, and had come by purchase or lot into the possession of Mahomet. Several years afterwards his father, hearing of his being in Mecca, repaired thither and offered a considerable sum for his ransom. "If he chooses to go with thee," said Mahomet, "he shall go without ransom: but if he chooses to remain with me, why should I not keep him?" Zeid preferred to remain, having ever, he said, been treated more as a son than as a slave. Upon this, Mahomet publicly adopted him, and he had ever since remained with him in affectionate servitude. Now, on embracing the new faith he was set entirely free, but it will be found that he continued through life that devoted attachment which Mahomet seems to have had the gift of inspiring in his followers and dependents.

The early steps of Mahomet in his prophetic career, were perilous and doubtful, and taken in secrecy. He had hostility to apprehend on every side; from his immediate kindred, the Koreishites of the line of Haschem, whose power and prosperity were identified with idolatry; and still more from the rival line of Abd Schems, who had long looked with envy and jealousy on the Haschemites, and would eagerly raise the cry of heresy and impiety to dispossess them of the guardianship of the Caaba. At the head of this rival branch of Koreish was Abu Sofian, the son of Harb, grandson of Omeya, and great-grandson of Abd Schems. He was an able and ambitious man, of great wealth and influence, and will be found one of the most persevering and powerful opponents of Mahomet.*

---

* Niebuhr (Travels, vol. ii.) speaks of the tribe of Harb, which possessed several cities and a number of villages in the highlands of Hedjas, a mountainous range between Mecca and Medina. They have castles on precipitous rocks, and harass and lay under contribution the caravans. It is presumed that this tribe takes its name from the father of Abu Sofian; as did the great line of the Omeyades from his grandfather.

Under these adverse circumstances the new faith was propagated secretly and slowly, insomuch that for the first three years the number of
converts did not exceed forty; these, too, for the most part, were young
persons, strangers, and slaves. Their meetings for prayer were held in
private, either at the house of one of the initiated, or in a cave near
Mecca. Their secrecy, however, did not protect them from outrage.
Their meetings were discovered; a rabble broke into their cavern and a
scuffle ensued. One of the assailants was wounded in the head by Saad,
an armorer, thenceforth renowned among the faithful, as the first of
their number who shed blood in the cause of Islam.

One of the bitterest opponents of Mahomet, was his uncle Abu
Lahab, a wealthy man, of proud spirit and irritable temper. His son
Otha had married Mahomet's third daughter, Rokaia, so that they were
doubly allied. Abu Lahab, however, was also allied to the rival line of
Koreish, having married Omm Jemil, sister of Abu Sofian, and he was
greatly under the control of his wife and his brother-in-law. He reprobated what he termed the heresies of his nephew, as calculated to
bring disgrace upon their immediate line, and to draw upon it the hostilities of the rest of the tribe of Koreish. Mahomet was keenly sensible
of the rancorous opposition of this uncle, which he attributed to the
instigations of his wife, Omm Jemil. He especially deplored it, as he
saw that it affected the happiness of his daughter Rokaia, whose inclination to his doctrines brought on her the reproaches of her husband
and his family.

These and other causes of solicitude preyed upon his spirits, and increased the perturbation of his mind. He became worn and haggard,
and subject more and more to fits of abstraction. Those of his relatives
who were attached to him, noticed his altered mien, and dreaded an
attack of illness; others scoffingly accused him of mental hallucination;
and the foremost among these scoffers was his uncle's wife, Omm
Jemil, the sister of Abu Sofian.

The result of this disordered state of mind and body was another vision, or revelation, commanding him to "arise, preach, and magnify the
Lord." He was now to announce, publicly and boldly, his doctrines, beginning with his kindred and tribe. Accordingly, in the fourth year of
what is called his mission, he summoned all the Koreishites of the line
of Haschem to meet him on the hill of Safa, in the vicinity of Mecca,
when he would unfold matters important to their welfare. They assembled there, accordingly, and among them came Mahomet's hostile

uncle Abu Lahab, and with him his scoffing wife, Omm Jemil. Scarce had the prophet begun to discourse of his mission, and to impart his revelations, when Abu Lahab started up in a rage, reviled him for calling them together on so idle an errand, and catching up a stone, would have hurled it at him. Mahomet turned upon him a withering look; cursed the hand thus raised in menace, and predicted his doom to the fire of Jehennam; with the assurance that his wife, Omm Jemil, would bear the bundle of thorns with which the fire would be kindled.

The assembly broke up in confusion. Abu Lahab and his wife, exasperated at the curse dealt out to them, compelled their son, Otha, to repudiate his wife, Rokaia, and sent her back weeping to Mahomet. She was soon indemnified, however, by having a husband of the true faith, being eagerly taken to wife by Mahomet's zealous disciple, Othman Ibn Affan.

Nothing discouraged by the failure of his first attempt, Mahomet called a second meeting of the Haschemites at his own house, where, having regaled them with the flesh of a lamb, and given them milk to drink, he stood forth and announced, at full length, his revelations received from heaven, and the divine command to impart them to those of his immediate line.

"Oh children of Abd al Motâlleb," cried he, with enthusiasm, "to you, of all men, has Allah vouchsafed these most precious gifts. In his name I offer you the blessings of this world, and endless joys hereafter. Who among you will share the burden of my offer? Who will be my brother, my lieutenant, my vizier?"

All remained silent; some wondering; others smiling with incredulity and derision. At length Ali, starting up with youthful zeal, offered himself to the service of the prophet, though modestly acknowledging his youth and physical weakness.* Mahomet threw his arms round the generous youth, and pressed him to his bosom. "Behold my brother, my vizier, my vicegerent," exclaimed he; "let all listen to his words, and obey him."

The outbreak of such a stripling as Ali, however, was answered by a scornful burst of laughter of the Koreishites; who taunted Abu Taleb, the father of the youthful proselyte, with having to bow down before his son, and yield him obedience.

---

* By an error of translators, Ali is made to accompany his offer of adhesion by an extravagant threat against all who should oppose Mahomet.

But though the doctrines of Mahomet was thus ungraciously re-ceived by his kindred and friends, they found favor among the people at large, especially among the women, who are ever prone to befriend a persecuted cause. Many of the Jews, also, followed him for a time, but when they found that he permitted his disciples to eat the flesh of the camel, and of other animals forbidden by their law, they drew back and rejected his religion as unclean.

Mahomet now threw off all reserve, or rather was inspired with in-creasing enthusiasm, and went about openly and earnestly proclaiming his doctrines, and giving himself out as a prophet, sent by God to put an end to idolatry, and to mitigate the rigor of the Jewish and the Christian law. The hills of Safa and Kubeis, sanctified by traditions concerning Hagar and Ishmael, were his favorite places of preaching, and Mount Hara was his Sinai, whither he retired occasionally, in fits of excitement and enthusiasm, to return from its solitary cave with fresh revelations of the Koran.

The good old Christian writers, on treating of the advent of one whom they denounce as the Arab enemy of the church, make supersti-tious record of divers prodigies which occurred, about this time, awful forerunners of the troubles about to agitate the world. In Constantino-ple, at that time the seat of Christian empire, were several monstrous births and prodigious apparitions, which struck dismay into the hearts of all beholders. In certain religious processions in that neighborhood, the crosses on a sudden moved of themselves, and were violently agi-tated, causing astonishment and terror. The Nile, too, that ancient mother of wonders, gave birth to two hideous forms, seemingly man and woman, which rose out of its waters, gazed about them for a time with terrific aspect, and sank again beneath the waves. For a whole day the sun appeared to be diminished to one-third of its usual size, shedding pale and baleful rays. During a moonless night a furnace light glowed throughout the heavens, and bloody lances glittered in the sky.

All these, and sundry other like marvels, were interpreted into signs of coming troubles. The ancient servants of God shook their heads mournfully, predicting the reign of Antichrist at hand; with vehement persecution of the Christian faith, and great desolation of the churches; and to such holy men who have passed through the trials and troubles of the faith, adds the venerable Padre Jayme Bleda, it is given to un-derstand and explain these mysterious portents, which forerun disasters of the church; even as it is given to ancient mariners to read in the signs of the air, the heavens and the deep, the coming tempest which is to overwhelm their bark.

Many of these sainted men were gathered to glory before the completion of their prophecies. There, seated securely in the empyreal heavens, they may have looked down with compassion upon the troubles of the Christian world; as men on the serene heights of mountains look down upon the tempests which sweep the earth and sea, wrecking tall ships, and rending lofty towers.

CHAPTER VIII

Outlines of the Mahometan Faith

Though it is not intended in this place to go fully into the doctrines promulgated by Mahomet, yet it is important to the right appreciation of his character and conduct, and of the events and circumstances set forth in the following narrative, to give their main features.

It must be particularly borne in mind, that Mahomet did not profess to set up a new religion; but to restore that derived in the earliest times, from God himself. "We follow," says the Koran, "the religion of Abraham the orthodox, who was no idolater. We believe in God and that which hath been sent down to us, and that which hath been sent down unto Abraham and Ishmael, and Isaac and Jacob and the tribes, and that which was delivered unto Moses and Jesus, and that which was delivered unto the prophets from the Lord: we make no distinction between any of them, and to God we are resigned."*

The Koran,† which was the great book of faith, was delivered in portions from time to time, according to the excitement of his feelings, or the exigency of circumstances. It was not given as his own work, but as a divine revelation; as the very words of God. The Deity is supposed to speak in every instance. "We have sent thee down the book of truth, confirming the scripture which was revealed before it, and preserving the same in its purity."‡

The law of Moses, it was said, had for a time been the guide and rule of human conduct. At the coming of Jesus Christ it was superseded by the Gospel; both were now to give place to the Koran, which was more full and explicit than the preceding codes, and intended to reform the abuses which had crept into them through the negligence or the corruptions of their professors. It was the completion of the law; after it there would be no more divine revelations. Mahomet was the last, as he was the greatest, of the line of prophets sent to make known the will of God.

The unity of God was the corner stone of this reformed religion. "There is no God but God," was its leading dogma. Hence, it received

---

* Koran, chap. ii
† Derived from the Arabic word Kora, to read or teach.
‡ Koran, ch. v.

the name of the religion of Islam,* an Arabian word, implying submission to God. To this leading dogma, was added, "Mahomet is the prophet of God;" an addition authorized, as it was maintained, by the divine annunciation, and important to procure a ready acceptation of his revelations.

Beside the unity of God, a belief was inculcated in his angels or ministering spirits; in his prophets; in the resurrection of the body; in the last judgment and a future state of rewards and punishments, and in predestination. Much of the Koran may be traced to the Bible, the Mishnu and the Talmud of the Jews,† especially its wild though often beautiful traditions concerning the angels, the prophets, the patriarchs, and the good and evil genii. He had at an early age imbibed a reverence for the Jewish faith, his mother, it is suggested, having been of that religion.

The system laid down in the Koran, however, was essentially founded on the Christian doctrines inculcated in the New Testament; as they had been expounded to him by the Christian sectarians of Arabia. Our Saviour was to be held in the highest reverence as an inspired prophet, the greatest that had been sent before the time of Mahomet, to reform the law; but all idea of his divinity was rejected as impious, and the doctrine of the Trinity was denounced as an outrage on the unity of God. Both were pronounced errors and interpolations of the

---

* Some Etymologists derive Islam from Salem or Aslama, which signifies salvation. The Christians form from it the term Islamism, and the Jews have varied it into Ismailism, which they intend as a reproach, and an allusion to the origin of the Arabs as descendants of Ishmael.

From Islam the Arabians drew the terms Moslem or Muslem, and Musulman, a professor of the faith of Islam. These terms are in the singular number and make Musliman in the dual, and Muslimen in the plural. The French and some other nations follow the idioms of their own languages in adopting or translating the Arabic terms, and form the plural by the addition of the letter s; writing Musulman and Musulmans. A few English writers, of whom Gibbon is the chief, have imitated them, imagining that they were following the Arabian usage. Most English authors, however, follow the idiom of their own language, writing Moslem and Moslems, Musulman and Musulmen; this usage is also the more harmonious.

† *The Mishnu* of the Jews like the Sonna of the Mahometans, is a collection of traditions forming the Oral law. It was compiled in the second century by Judah Hakkodish, a learned Jewish Rabbi, during the reign of Antoninus Pius, the Roman Emperor.

The Jerusalem Talmud and the Babylonish Talmud, are both commentaries on the Mishnu. The former was compiled at Jerusalem, about three hundred years after Christ, and the latter in Babylonia, about two centuries later. The Mishnu is the most ancient record possessed by the Jews except the Bible.

expounders; and this, it will be observed, was the opinion of some of the Arabian sects of Christians.

The worship of saints and the introduction of images and paintings representing them, were condemned as idolatrous lapses from the pure faith of Christ, and such, we have already observed, were the tenets of the Nestorians with whom Mahomet is known to have had much communication.

All pictures representing living things were prohibited. Mahomet used to say, that the angels would not enter a house in which there were such pictures, and that those who made them would be sentenced in the next world, to find souls for them, or be punished.

Most of the benignant precepts of our Saviour were incorporated in the Koran. Frequent alms-giving was enjoined as an imperative duty, and the immutable law of right and wrong, "Do unto another, as thou wouldst he should do unto thee," was given for the moral conduct of the faithful.

"Deal not unjustly with others," says the Koran, "and ye shall not be dealt with unjustly. If there be any debtor under a difficulty of paying his debt, let his creditor wait until it be easy for him to do it; but if he remit it in alms, it will be better for him."

Mahomet inculcated a noble fairness and sincerity in dealing. "Oh merchants!" would he say, "falsehood and deception are apt to prevail in traffic, purify it therefore with alms; give something in charity as an atonement; for God is incensed by deceit in dealing, but charity appeases his anger. He who sells a defective thing, concealing its defect, will provoke the anger of God and the curses of the angels.

"Take not advantage of the necessities of another to buy things at a sacrifice; rather relieve his indigence.

"Feed the hungry; visit the sick, and free the captive if confined unjustly.

"Look not scornfully upon thy fellow-man; neither walk the earth with insolence; for God loveth not the arrogant and vainglorious. Be moderate in thy pace, and speak with a moderate tone; for the most ungrateful of all voices, is the voice of asses."*

Idolatry of all kinds was strictly forbidden; indeed it was what Ma-

---

* The following words of Mahomet, treasured up by one of his disciples, appear to have been suggested by a passage in Matthew xxv. 35–45:

"Verily, God will say at the day of resurrection, 'Oh sons of Adam! I was sick, and ye did not visit me.' Then they will say, 'How could we visit thee? for thou art the Lord of the universe, and art free from sickness.' And God will reply, 'Knew ye

homet held in most abhorrence. Many of the religious usages, however, prevalent since time immemorial among the Arabs, to which he had been accustomed from infancy, and which were not incompatible with the doctrine of the unity of God, were still retained. Such was the pilgrimage to Mecca, including all the rites connected with the Caaba, the well of Zem Zem, and other sacred places in the vicinity; apart from any worship of the idols by which they had been profaned.

The old Arabian rite of prayer, accompanied or rather preceded by ablution, was still continued. Prayers indeed were enjoined at certain hours of the day and night; they were simple in form and phrase, addressed directly to the Deity with certain inflexions, or at times a total prostration of the body, and with the face turned towards the Kebla, or point of adoration.

At the end of each prayer, the following verse from the second chapter of the Koran was recited. It is said to have great beauty in the original Arabic, and is engraved on gold and silver ornaments, and on precious stones worn as amulets. "God! There is no God but He, the living, the ever living; he sleepeth not, neither doth he slumber. To him belongeth the heavens, and the earth, and all that they contain. Who shall intercede with him unless by his permission? He knoweth the past and the future, but no one can comprehend any thing of his knowledge but that which he revealeth. His sway extendeth over the heavens and the earth, and to sustain them both is no burthen to him. He is the High, the Mighty!"

Mahomet was strenuous in enforcing the importance and efficacy of prayer. "Angels," said he, "come among you both by night and day; after which those of the night ascend to heaven, and God asks them how they left his creatures. We found them, say they, at their prayers, and we left them at their prayers."

The doctrines in the Koran respecting the resurrection and final

---

not that such a one of my servants was sick, and ye did not visit him? Had you visited that servant, it would have been counted to you as righteousness.' And God will say, 'Oh sons of Adam! I asked you for food, and ye gave it me not.' And the sons of Adam will say, 'How could we give thee food, seeing thou art the sustainer of the universe, and art free from hunger?' And God will say, 'Such a one of my servants asked you for bread, and ye refused it. Had you given him to eat, ye would have received your reward from me.' And God will say, 'Oh sons of Adam, I asked you for water, and ye gave it me not.' They will reply, 'Oh, our supporter! How could we give thee water, seeing thou art the sustainer of the universe, and not subject to thirst?' And God will say, 'Such a one of my servants asked you for water, and ye did not give it to him. Had ye done so, ye would have received your reward from me.' "

judgment, were in some respects similar to those of the Christian religion, but were mixed up with wild notions derived from other sources; while the joys of the Moslem heaven, though partly spiritual, were clogged and debased by the sensualities of earth, and infinitely below the ineffable purity and spiritual blessedness of the heaven promised by our Saviour.

Nevertheless, the description of the last day, as contained in the eighty-first chapter of the Koran, and which must have been given by Mahomet at the outset of his mission at Mecca, as one of the first of his revelations, partakes of sublimity.

"In the name of the all merciful God! a day shall come when the sun will be shrouded, and the stars will fall from the heavens.

"When the camels about to foal will be neglected, and wild beasts will herd together through fear.

"When the waves of the ocean will boil, and the souls of the dead again be united to the bodies.

"When the female infant that has been buried alive will demand, for what crime was I sacrificed? and the eternal books will be laid open.

"When the heavens will pass away like a scroll, and hell will burn fiercely; and the joys of paradise will be made manifest.

"On that day shall every soul make known that which it hath performed.

"Verily, I swear to you by the stars which move swiftly and are lost in the brightness of the sun, and by the darkness of the night, and by the dawning of the day, these are not the words of an evil spirit, but of an angel of dignity and power, who possesses the confidence of Allah, and is revered by the angels under his command. Neither is your companion, Mahomet, distracted. He beheld the celestial messenger in the light of the clear horizon, and the words revealed to him are intended as an admonition unto all creatures."

NOTE – To exhibit the perplexed maze of controversial doctrines from which Mahomet had to acquire his notions of the Christian faith, we subjoin the leading points of the jarring sects of oriental Christians alluded to in the foregoing article; all of which have been pronounced heretical or schismatic.

The Sabellians, so called from Sabellius, a Libyan priest of the third century, believed in the unity of God, and that the Trinty expressed but three different states or relations, Father, Son, and Holy Ghost, all forming but one substance, as a man consists of body and soul.

The Arians, from Arius, an ecclesiastic of Alexandria in the fourth century, affirmed Christ to be the Son of God, but distinct from him and inferior to him, and denied the Holy Ghost to be God.

The Nestorians, from Nestorius, Bishop of Constantinople in the fifth century, maintained that Christ had two distinct natures, divine and human; that Mary was only his mother, and Jesus a man, and that it was an abomination to style her, as was the custom of the church, the Mother of God.

The Monophysites maintained the single nature of Christ, as their name betokens. They affirmed that he was combined of God and man, so mingled and united as to form but one nature.

The Eutychians, from Eutyches, abbot of a convent in Constantinople in the fifth century, were a branch of the Monophysites, expressly opposed to the Nestorians. They denied the double nature of Christ, declaring that he was entirely God previous to the incarnation, and entirely man during the incarnation.

The Jacobites, from Jacobus, bishop of Edessa, in Syria, in the sixth century, were a very numerous branch of the Monophysites, varying but little from the Eutychians. Most of the Christian tribes of Arabs were Jacobites.

The Mariamites, or worshippers of Mary, regarded the Trinity as consisting of God the Father, God the Son, and God the Virgin Mary.

The Collyridians were a sect of Arabian Christians, composed chiefly of females. They worshiped the Virgin Mary as possessed of divinity, and made offerings to her of a twisted cake, called collyris, whence they derived their name.

The Nazaræans, or Nazarenes, were a sect of Jewish Christians, who considered Christ as the Messiah, as born of a Virgin by the Holy Ghost, and as possessing something of a divine nature; but they conformed in all other respects to the rites and ceremonies of the Mosaic law.

The Ebionites, from Ebion, a converted Jew, who lived in the first century, were also a sect of judaizing Christians, little differing from the Nazaræans. They believed Christ to be a pure man, the greatest of the prophets, but denied that he had any existence previous to being born of the Virgin Mary. This sect, as well as that of the Nazaræans, had many adherents in Arabia.

Many other sects might be enumerated, such as the Corinthians, Maronites, and Marcionites, who took their names from learned and zealous leaders; and the Docetes and Gnostics, who were subdivided into various sects of subtle enthuiasts. Some of these asserted the immaculate purity of the Virgin Mary, affirming that her conception and delivery were effected like the transmission of the rays of light through a pane of glass, without impairing her virginity; an opinion still maintained strenuously in substance by Spanish Catholics.

Most of the Docetes asserted that Jesus Christ was of a nature entirely divine; that a phantom, a mere form without substance, was crucified by the deluded Jews, and that the crucifixion and resurrection were deceptive mystical exhibitions at Jerusalem for the benefit of the human race.

The Carpocratians, Basilidians, and Valentinians, named after three Egyptian controversialists, contended that Jesus Christ was merely a wise and virtuous mortal, the son of Joseph and Mary, selected by God to reform and instruct mankind; but that a divine nature was imparted to him at the maturity of his age, and period of his baptism, by St. John. The former part of this creed, which is that of the Ebionites, has been revived, and is professed by some of the Unitarian Christians, a numerous and increasing sect of Protestants of the present day.

It is sufficient to glance at these dissensions, which we have not arranged in chronological order, but which convulsed the early Christian church, and continued to prevail at the era of Mahomet, to acquit him of any charge of conscious blasphemy in the opinions he inculcated concerning the nature and mission of our Saviour.

CHAPTER IX

Ridicule cast on Mahomet and his doctrines – Demand for miracles – Conduct of Abu Taleb – Violence of the Koreishites – Mahomet's daughter Rokaia, with her husband Othman, and a number of disciples take refuge in Abyssinia – Mahomet in the house of Orkham – Hostility of Abu Jahl; his punishment

The greatest difficulty with which Mahomet had to contend at the outset of his prophetic career, was the ridicule of his opponents. Those who had known him from his infancy – who had seen him a boy about the streets of Mecca; and afterwards occupied in all the ordinary concerns of life, scoffed at his assumption of the apostolic character. They pointed with a sneer at him as he passed, exclaiming, "Behold the grandson of Abd al Motâlleb, who pretends to know what is going on in heaven!" Some who had witnessed his fits of mental excitement and ecstasy, considered him insane; others declared that he was possessed with a devil, and some charged him with sorcery and magic.

When he walked the streets he was subject to those jeers, and taunts, and insults which the vulgar are apt to vent upon men of eccentric conduct and unsettled mind. If he attempted to preach, his voice was drowned by discordant noises and ribald songs: nay, dirt was thrown upon him when he was praying in the Caaba.

Nor was it the vulgar and ignorant alone who thus insulted him. One of his most redoubtable assailants was a youth named Amru; and as he subsequently made a distinguished figure in Mahometan history, we would impress the circumstances of this, his first appearance, upon the mind of the reader. He was the son of a courtezan of Mecca; who seems to have rivalled in fascination the Phrynes and Aspasias of Greece, and to have numbered some of the noblest of the land among her lovers. When she gave birth to this child, she mentioned several of the tribe of Koreish who had equal claims to the paternity. The infant was declared to have most resemblance to Aass, the oldest of her admirers, whence, in addition to his name of Amru, he received the designation of Ibn al Aass, the son of Aass.

Nature had lavished her choicest gifts upon this natural child, as if to atone for the blemish of his birth. Though young, he was already one of the most popular poets of Arabia, and equally distinguished for the pungency of his satirical effusions and the captivating sweetness of his serious lays.

When Mahomet first announced his mission, this youth assailed him

45

with lampoons and humorous madrigals; which, falling in with the poetic taste of the Arabs, were widely circulated, and proved greater impediments to the growth of Islamism than the bitterest persecution.

Those who were more serious in their opposition demanded of Mahomet supernatural proofs of what he asserted. "Moses and Jesus, and the rest of the prophets," said they, "wrought miracles to prove the divinity of their missions. If thou art indeed a prophet, greater than they, work the like miracles."

The reply of Mahomet may be gathered from his own words in the Koran. "What greater miracle could they have than the Koran itself: a book revealed by means of an unlettered man; so elevated in language, so incontrovertible in argument, that the united skill of men and devils could compose nothing comparable? What greater proof could there be that it came from none but God himself? The Koran itself is a miracle."

They demanded, however, more palpable evidence; miracles addressed to the senses; that he should cause the dumb to speak, the deaf to hear, the blind to see, the dead to rise; or that he should work changes in the face of nature; cause fountains to gush forth; change a sterile place into a garden, with palm-trees, and vines, and running streams; cause a palace of gold to rise, decked with jewels and precious stones; or ascend by a ladder into heaven in their presence. Or, if the Koran did indeed, as he affirmed, come down from heaven; that they might see it as it descended, or behold the angel who brought it; and then they would believe.

Mahomet replied sometimes by arguments, sometimes by denunciations. He claimed to be nothing more than a man sent by God as an apostle. Had angels, said he, walked familiarly on earth, an angel had assuredly been sent on this mission; but woful had been the case of those who, as in the present instance, doubted his word. They would not have been able, as with him, to argue, and dispute, and take time to be convinced; their perdition would have been instantaneous. "God," added he, "needs no angel to enforce my mission. He is a sufficient witness between you and me. Those whom he shall dispose to be convinced, will truly believe; those whom he shall permit to remain in error, will find none to help their unbelief. On the day of resurrection they will appear blind, and deaf, and dumb, and grovelling on their faces. Their abode will be in the eternal flames of Jehennam. Such will be the reward of their unbelief.

"You insist on miracles. God gave to Moses the power of working miracles. What was the consequence? Pharaoh disregarded his mira-

cles, accused him of sorcery, and sought to drive him and his people
from the land; but Pharaoh was drowned, and with him all his host.
Would ye tempt God to miracles, and risk the punishment of Pharaoh?"

It is recorded by Al Maalem, an Arabian writer, that some of Mahomet's disciples at one time joined with the multitude in this cry for
miracles, and besought him to prove, at once, the divinity of his mission, by turning the hill of Safa into gold. Being thus closely urged, he
betook himself to prayer; and having finished, assured his followers
that the angel Gabriel had appeared to him, and informed him that,
should God grant his prayer, and work the desired miracle, all who dis-
believed it would be exterminated. In pity to the multitude, therefore,
who appeared to be a stiff-necked generation, he would not expose
them to destruction: so the hill of Safa was permitted to remain in its
pristine state.

Other Moslem writers assert that Mahomet departed from his self-
prescribed rule, and wrought occasional miracles, when he found his
hearers unusually slow of belief. Thus we are told that, at one time, in
presence of a multitude, he called to him a bull, and took from his
horns a scroll containing a chapter of the Koran, just sent down from
heaven. At another time, while discoursing in public, a white dove hovered over him, and, alighting on his shoulder, appeared to whisper in
his ear; being, as he said, a messenger from the Deity. On another occasion he ordered the earth before him to be opened, when two jars
were found, one filled with honey, the other with milk, which he pronounced emblems of the abundance promised by heaven to all who
should obey his law.

Christian writers have scoffed at these miracles; suggesting that the
dove had been tutored to its task, and sought grains of wheat which it
had been accustomed to find in the ear of Mahomet; that the scroll had
previously been tied to the horns of the bull, and the vessels of milk
and honey deposited in the ground. The truer course would be to dis-
card these miraculous stories altogether, as fables devised by mistaken
zealots; and such they have been pronounced by the ablest of the Moslem commentators.

There is no proof that Mahomet descended to any artifices of the
kind to enforce his doctrines or establish his apostolic claims. He appears to have relied entirely on reason and eloquence, and to have
been supported by religious enthusiasm in this early and dubious stage
of his career. His earnest attacks upon the idolatry which had vitiated

and superseded the primitive worship of the Caaba, began to have a sensible effect, and alarmed the Koreishites. They urged Abu Taleb to silence his nephew or to send him away; but finding their entreaties unavailing, they informed the old man that if this pretended prophet and his followers persisted in their heresies, they should pay for them with their lives.

Abu Taleb hastened to inform Mahomet of these menaces, imploring him not to provoke against himself and family such numerous and powerful foes.

The enthusiastic spirit of Mahomet kindled at the words. "Oh my uncle!" exclaimed he, "though they should array the sun against me on my right hand, and the moon on my left, yet, until God should command me, or should take me hence, would I not depart from my purpose."

He was retiring with dejected countenance, when Abu Taleb called him back. The old man was as yet unconverted, but he was struck with admiration of the undaunted firmness of his nephew, and declared that, preach what he might, he would never abandon him to his enemies. Feeling that of himself he could not yield sufficient protection, he called upon the other descendants of Haschem and Abd al Motâlleb to aid in shielding their kinsman from the persecution of the rest of the tribe of Koreish; and so strong is the family tie among the Arabs, that though it was protecting him in what they considered a dangerous heresy, they all consented excepting his uncle Abu Lahab.

The animosity of the Koreishites became more and more virulent, and proceeded to personal violence. Mahomet was assailed and nearly strangled in the Caaba, and was rescued with difficulty by Abu Beker, who himself suffered personal injury in the affray. His immediate family became objects of hatred, especially his daughter Rokaia and her husband Othman Ibn Affan. Such of his disciples as had no powerful friends to protect them were in peril of their lives. Full of anxiety for their safety, Mahomet advised them to leave his dangerous companionship for the present, and take refuge in Abyssinia. The narrowness of the Red Sea made it easy to reach the African shore. The Abyssinians were Nestorian Christians, elevated by their religion above their barbarous neighbors. Their najashee or king was reputed to be tolerant and just. With him Mahomet trusted his daughter and his fugitive disciples would find refuge.

Othman Ibn Affan was the leader of this little band of Moslems, consisting of eleven men and four women. They took the way by the sea-coast to Jidda, a port about two days' journey to the west of Mecca, where they found two Abyssinian vessels at anchor, in which they embarked, and sailed for the land of refuge.

This event, which happened in the fifth year of the mission of Mahomet, is called the first Hegira or Flight, to distinguish it from the second Hegira, the flight of the prophet himself from Mecca to Medina. The kind treatment experienced by the fugutives induced others of the same faith to follow their example, until the number of Moslem refugees in Abyssinia amounted to eighty-three men and eighteen women, besides children.

The Koreishites finding that Mahomet was not to be silenced, and was daily making converts, passed a law banishing all who should embrace his faith. Mahomet retired before the storm, and took refuge in the house of a disciple named Orkham, situated on the hill of Safa. This hill, as has already been mentioned, was renowned in Arabian tradition as the one on which Adam and Eve were permitted to come once more together, after the long solitary wandering about the earth which followed their expulsion from paradise. It was likewise connected in tradition with the fortunes of Hagar and Ishmael.

Mahomet remained for a month in the house of Orkham, continuing his revelations and drawing to him sectaries from various parts of Arabia. The hostility of the Koreishites followed him to his retreat. Abu Jahl, an Arab of that tribe, sought him out, insulted him with opprobrious language, and even personally maltreated him. The outrage was reported to Hamza an uncle of Mahomet, as he returned to Mecca from hunting. Hamza was no proselyte to Islamism, but he was pledged to protect his nephew. Marching with his bow unstrung in his hand to an assemblage of the Koreishites, where Abu Jahl was vaunting his recent triumph, he dealt the boaster a blow over the head, that inflicted a grievous wound. The kinsfolk of Abu Jahl rushed to his assistance, but the brawler stood in awe of the vigorous arm and fiery spirit of Hamza, and sought to pacify him. "Let him alone," said he to his kinsfolk; "in truth I have treated his nephew very roughly." He alleged in palliation of his outrage the apostasy of Mahomet; but Hamza was not to be appeased. "Well!" cried he, fiercely and scornfully, "I also do not believe in your gods of stone; can you compel me?" Anger produced in his bosom what reasoning might have attempted in vain. He forthwith declared himself a convert; took the oath of adhesion to the prophet, and became one of the most zealous and valiant champions of the new faith.

CHAPTER X

Omar Ibn al Khattâb, nephew of Abu Jahl, undertakes to revenge his uncle by slaying Mahomet – His wonderful conversion to the faith – Mahomet takes refuge in a castle of Abu Taleb – Abu Sofian, at the head of the rival branch of Koreishites, persecutes Mahomet and his followers – Obtains a decree of non-intercourse with them – Mahomet leaves his retreat and makes converts during the month of pilgrimage – Legend of the conversion of Habib the Wise

The hatred of Abu Jahl to the prophet was increased by the severe punishment received at the hands of Hamza. He had a nephew named Omar Ibn al Khattâb; twenty-six years of age; of gigantic stature, prodigious strength, and great courage. His savage aspect appalled the bold, and his very walking-staff struck more terror into beholders than another man's sword. Such are the words of the Arabian historian, Abu Abdallah Mohamed Ibn Omal Alwakedi, and the subsequent feats of this warrior prove that they were scarce chargeable with exaggeration.

Instigated by his uncle Abu Jahl, this fierce Arab undertook to penetrate to the retreat of Mahomet, who was still in the house of Orkham, and to strike a poniard to his heart. The Koreishites are accused of having promised him one hundred camels and one thousand ounces of gold for this deed of blood; but this is improbable, nor did the vengeful nephew of Abu Jahl need a bribe.

As he was on his way to the house of Orkham he met a Koreishite, to whom he imparted his design. The Koreishite was a secret convert to Islamism, and sought to turn him from his bloody errand. "Before you slay Mahomet," said he, "and draw upon yourself the vengeance of his relatives, see that your own are free from heresy." "Are any of mine guilty of backsliding?" demanded Omar with astonishment. "Even so," was the reply; "thy sister Amina and her husband Seid."

Omar hastened to the dwelling of his sister, and, entering it abruptly, found her and her husband reading the Koran. Seid attempted to conceal it, but his confusion convinced Omar of the truth of the accusation, and heightened his fury. In his rage he struck Seid to the earth; placed his foot upon his breast, and would have plunged his sword into it, had not his sister interposed. A blow on the face bathed her visage in blood. "Enemy of Allah!" sobbed Amina, "dost thou strike me thus for believing in the only true God? In despite of thee and thy violence, I will persevere in the true faith. Yes," added she with fervor, "'There is no God but God, and Mahomet is his prophet: – And now, Omar, finish thy work!"

Omar paused; repented of his violence, and took his foot from the bosom of Seid.

"Show me the writing," said he. Amina, however, refused to let him touch the sacred scroll until he had washed his hands. The passage which he read, is said to have been the twentieth chapter of the Koran, which thus begins:

"In the name of the most merciful God! We have not sent down the Koran to inflict misery on mankind, but as a monitor, to teach him to believe in the true God, the creator of the earth and the lofty heavens.

"The all merciful is enthroned on high, to him belongeth whatsoever is in the heavens above, and in the earth beneath, and in the regions under the earth.

"Dost thou utter thy prayers with a loud voice? know that there is no need. God knoweth the secrets of thy heart; yea, that which is most hidden.

"Verily, I am God; there is none beside me. Serve me, serve none other. Offer up thy prayer to none but me."

The words of the Koran sank deep into the heart of Omar. He read farther, and was more and more moved; but when he came to the parts treating of the resurrection and of judgment, his conversion was complete.

He pursued his way to the house of Orkham, but with an altered heart. Knocking humbly at the door, he craved admission. "Come in, son of al Khattâb," exclaimed Mahomet. "What brings thee hither?"

"I come to enroll my name among the believers of God and his prophet." So saying, he made the Moslem profession of faith.

He was not content until his conversion was publicly known. At his request, Mahomet accompanied him instantly to the Caaba, to perform openly the rites of Islamism. Omar walked on the left hand of the prophet, and Hamza on the right, to protect him from injury and insult, and they were followed by upwards of forty disciples. They passed in open day through the streets of Mecca, to the astonishment of its inhabitants. Seven times did they make the circuit of the Caaba, touching each time the sacred black stone, and complying with all the other ceremonials. The Koreishites regarded this procession with dismay, but dared not approach nor molest the prophet, being deterred by the looks of those terrible men of battle Hamza and Omar; who, it is said, glared upon them like two lions that had been robbed of their young.

Fearless and resolute in every thing, Omar went by himself the next day to pray as a Moslem in the Caaba, in open defiance of the Koreishites. Another Moslem, who entered the temple, was interrupted in his worship, and rudely treated; but no one molested Omar, because he was the nephew of Abu Jahl. Omar repaired to his uncle. "I renounce thy protection," said he. "I will not be better off than my fellow-believers." From that time he cast his lot with the followers of Mahomet, and was one of his most strenuous defenders.

Such was the wonderful conversion of Omar, afterwards the most famous champion of the Islam faith. So exasperated were the Koreishites by this new triumph of Mahomet, that his uncle Abu Taleb feared they might attempt the life of his nephew, either by treachery, or open violence. At his earnest entreaties, therefore, the latter, accompanied by some of his principal disciples, withdrew to a kind of castle, or stronghold, belonging to Abu Taleb, in the neighborhood of the city.

The protection thus given by Abu Taleb, the head of the Haschemites, and by others of his line, to Mahomet and his followers, although differing from them in faith, drew on them the wrath of the rival branch of the Koreishites, and produced a schism in the tribe. Abu Sofian, the head of that branch, availed himself of the heresies of the prophet to throw discredit, not merely upon such of his kindred as had embraced his faith, but upon the whole line of Haschem, which, though dissenting from his doctrines, had, through mere clannish feelings, protected him. It is evident the hostility of Abu Sofian arose, not merely from personal hatred or religious scruples, but from family feud. He was ambitious of transferring to his own line the honors of the city so long engrossed by the Haschemites. The last measure of the kind-hearted Abu Taleb, in placing Mahomet beyond the reach of persecution, and giving him a castle as a refuge, was seized upon by Abu Sofian and his adherents, as a pretext for a general ban of the rival line. They accordingly issued a decree, forbidding the rest of the tribe of Koreish from intermarrying, or holding any intercourse, even of bargain or sale, with the Haschemites, until they should deliver up their kinsman, Mahomet, for punishment. This decree, which took place in the seventh year of what is called the mission of the prophet, was written on parchment, and hung up in the Caaba. It reduced Mahomet and his disciples to great straits, being almost famished at times in the stronghold in which they had taken refuge. The fortress was also beleaguered occasionally by the Koreishites, to enforce the ban in all its rigor, and to prevent the possibility of supplies.

The annual season of pilgrimage, however, when hosts of pilgrims repair from all parts of Arabia to Mecca, brought transient relief to the persecuted Moslems. During that sacred season, according to immemorial law and usage among the Arabs, all hostilities were suspended, and warring tribes met in temporary peace to worship at the Caaba. At such times Mahomet and his disciples would venture from their stronghold and return to Mecca. Protected also by the immunity of the holy month, Mahomet would mingle among the pilgrims and preach and pray; propound his doctrines, and proclaim his revelations. In this way he made many converts, who, on their return to their several homes, carried with them the seeds of the new faith to distant regions. Among these converts were occasionally the princes or heads of tribes, whose examples had an influence on their adherents. Arabian legends give a pompous and extravagant account of the conversion of one of these princes; which, as it was attended by some of the most noted miracles recorded of Mahomet, may not be unworthy of an abbreviated insertion.

The prince in question was Habib Ibn Malec, surnamed the Wise on account of his vast knowledge and erudition; for he is represented as deeply versed in magic and the sciences, and acquainted with all religions, to their very foundations, having read all that had been written concerning them, and also acquired practical information, for he had belonged to them all by turns, having been Jew, Christian, and one of the Magi. It is true, he had had more than usual time for his studies and experience, having, according to Arabian legend, attained to the age of one hundred and forty years. He now came to Mecca at the head of a powerful host of twenty thousand men, bringing with him a youthful daughter, Satiha, whom he must have begotten in a ripe old age; and for whom he was putting up prayers at the Caaba, she having been struck dumb, and deaf, and blind, and deprived of the use of her limbs.

Abu Sofian and Abu Jahl, according to the legend, thought the presence of this very powerful, very idolatrous, and very wise old prince, at the head of so formidable a host, a favorable opportunity to effect the ruin of Mahomet. They accordingly informed Habib the Wise of the heresies of the pretended prophet; and prevailed upon the venerable prince to summon him into his presence, at his encampment in the Valley of Flints, there to defend his doctrines; in the hope that his obstinacy in error would draw upon him banishment or death.

The legend gives a magnificent account of the issuing forth of the

idolatrous Koreishites, in proud array, on horseback and on foot, led by
Abu Sofian and Abu Jahl, to attend the grand inquisition in the Valley
of Flints; and of the oriental state in which they were received by
Habib the Wise, seated under a tent of crimson, on a throne of ebony,
inlaid with ivory and sandal-wood, and covered with plates of gold.

Mahomet was in the dwelling of Cadijah when he received a summons to this formidable tribunal. Cadijah was loud in her expressions
of alarm; and his daughters hung about his neck, weeping and lamenting, for they thought him going to certain death; but he gently rebuked
their fears, and bade them trust in Allah.

Unlike the ostentatious state of his enemies, Abu Sofian and Abu
Jahl, he approached the scene of trial in simple guise, clad in a white
garment, with a black turban, and a mantle which had belonged to his
grandfather Abd al Motálleb, and was made of the stuff of Aden. His
hair floated below his shoulders, the mysterious light of prophecy
beamed from his countenance; and though he had not anointed his
beard, nor used any perfumes, excepting a little musk and camphor for
the hair of his upper lip, yet wherever he passed a bland odor diffused
itself around, being, say the Arabian writers, the fragrant emanations
from his person.

He was preceded by the zealous Abu Beker, clad in a scarlet vest
and a white turban; with his mantle gathered up under his arms, so as
to display his scarlet slippers.

A silent awe, continues the legend, fell upon the vast assemblage as
the prophet approached. Not a murmur, not a whisper was to be
heard. The very brute animals were charmed to silence; and the neighing of the steed, the bellowing of the camel, and the braying of the ass
were mute.

The venerable Habib received him graciously: his first question was
to the point. "They tell thou dost pretend to be a prophet sent from
God? Is it so?"

"Even so," replied Mahomet. "Allah has sent me to proclaim the veritable faith."

"Good," rejoined the wary sage, "but every prophet has given proof
of his mission by signs and miracles. Noah had his rainbow: Solomon
his mysterious ring: Abraham the fire of the furnace, which became
cool at his command: Isaac the ram, which was sacrificed in his stead:
Moses his wonder-working rod, and Jesus brought the dead to life, and

appeased tempests with a word. If, then, thou art really a prophet, give us a miracle in proof."

The adherents of Mahomet trembled for him when they heard this request, and Abu Jahl clapped his hands and extolled the sagacity of Habib the Wise. But the prophet rebuked him with scorn. "Peace! dog of thy race!" exclaimed he; "disgrace of thy kindred, and of thy tribe." He then calmly proceeded to execute the wishes of Habib.

The first miracle demanded of Mahomet was to reveal what Habib had within his tent, and why he had brought it to Mecca.

Upon this, says the legend, Mahomet bent toward the earth and traced figures upon the sand. Then raising his head, he replied, "Oh Habib! thou hast brought hither thy daughter, Satiha, deaf and dumb, and lame and blind, in the hope of obtaining relief of Heaven. Go to thy tent; speak to her, and hear her reply, and know that God is all powerful."

The aged prince hastened to his tent. His daughter met him with light step and extended arms, perfect in all her faculties, her eyes beaming with joy, her face clothed with smiles, and more beauteous than the moon in an unclouded night.

The second miracle demanded by Habib was still more difficult. It was that Mahomet should cover the noontide heaven with supernatural darkness, and cause the moon to descend and rest upon the top of the Caaba.

The prophet performed this miracle as easily as the first. At his summons, a darkness blotted out the whole light of day. The moon was then seen straying from her course and wandering about the firmament. By the irresistible power of the prophet, she was drawn from the heavens and rested on the top of the Caaba. She then performed seven circuits about it, after the manner of the pilgrims, and having made a profound reverence to Mahomet, stood before him with lambent wavering motion, like a flaming sword; giving him the salutation of peace, and hailing him as a prophet.

Not content with this miracle, pursues the legend, Mahomet compelled the obedient luminary to enter by the right sleeve of his mantle, and go out by the left; then to divide into two parts, one of which went towards the east, and the other towards the west, and meeting in the centre of the firmament reunited themselves into a round and glorious orb.

It is needless to say that Habib the Wise was convinced and converted by these miracles, as were also four hundred and seventy of the
inhabitants of Mecca. Abu Jahl, however, was hardened in unbelief, exclaiming that all was illusion and enchantment produced by the magic
of Mahomet.

NOTE – The miracles here recorded are not to be found in the pages of the
accurate Abulfeda, nor are they maintained by any of the graver of the Moslem
writers; but they exist in tradition, and are set forth with great prolixity by
apocryphal authors, who insist that they are alluded to in the fifty-fourth chapter
of the Koran. They are probably as true as many other of the wonders related of
the prophet. It will be remembered that he himself claimed but one miracle, "the
Koran."

CHAPTER XI

The ban of non-intercourse mysteriously destroyed – Mahomet en-
abled to return to Mecca – Death of Abu Taleb; of Cadijah –
Mahomet betroths himself to Ayesha – Marries Sawda – The Koreish-
ites renew their persecution – Mahomet seeks an asylum in Tayef
– His expulsion thence – Visited by genii in the desert of Naklah

Three years had elapsed since Mahomet and his disciples took refuge in the castle of Abu Taleb. The ban or decree still existed in the Caaba, cutting them off from all intercourse with the rest of their tribe. The sect, as usual, increased under persecution. Many joined it in Mecca; murmurs arose against the unnatural feud engendered among the Koreishites, and Abu Sofian was made to blush for the lengths to which he had carried his hostility against some of his kindred.

All at once it was discovered that the parchment in the Caaba, on which the decree had been written, was so substantially destroyed, that nothing of the writing remained but the initial words, "In thy name, Oh Almighty God!" The decree was, therefore, declared to be annulled, and Mahomet and his followers were permitted to return to Mecca unmolested. The mysterious removal of this legal obstacle has been considered by pious Moslems, another miracle wrought by supernatural agency in favor of the prophet; though unbelievers have surmised that the document, which was becoming embarrassing in its effects to Abu Sofian himself, was secretly destroyed by mortal hands.

The return of Mahomet and his disciples to Mecca, was followed by important conversions, both of inhabitants of the city and of pilgrims from afar. The chagrin experienced by the Koreishites from the growth of this new sect, was soothed by tidings of victories of the Persians over the Greeks, by which they conquered Syria and a part of Egypt. The idolatrous Koreishites exulted in the defeat of the Christian Greeks, whose faith, being opposed to the worship of idols, they assimilated to that preached by Mahomet. The latter replied to their taunts and exultations, by producing the thirtieth chapter of the Koran, opening with these words: "The Greeks have been overcome by the Persians, but they shall overcome the latter in the course of a few years."

The zealous and believing Abu Beker, made a wager of ten camels, that this prediction would be accomplished within three years. "Increase the wager, but lengthen the time," whispered Mahomet. Abu Beker staked one hundred camels, but made the time nine years. The prediction was verified and the wager won. This anecdote is confidently cited by Moslem doctors, as a proof that the Koran came down from heaven, and that Mahomet possessed the gift of prophecy. The whole, if true, was no doubt a shrewd guess into futurity, suggested by a knowledge of the actual state of the warring powers.

Not long after his return to Mecca, Mahomet was summoned to close the eyes of his uncle Abu Taleb, then upwards of fourscore years of age, and venerable in character as in person. As the hour of death drew nigh, Mahomet exhorted his uncle to make the profession of faith necessary, according to the Islam creed, to secure a blissful resurrection.

A spark of earthly pride lingered in the breast of the dying patriarch. "Oh son of my brother!" replied he, "should I repeat those words, the Koreishites would say, I did so through fear of death."

Abulfeda, the historian, insists that Abu Taleb actually died in the faith. Al Abbas, he says, hung over the bed of his expiring brother, and perceiving his lips to move, approached his ear to catch his dying words. They were the wished-for confession. Others affirm that his last words were, "I die in the faith of Abd al Motålleb." Commentators have sought to reconcile the two accounts, by asserting that Abd al Motålleb, in his latter days renounced the worship of idols, and believed in the unity of God.

Scarce three days had elapsed from the death of the venerable Abu Taleb, when Cadijah, the faithful and devoted wife of Mahomet, likewise sank into the grave. She was sixty-five years of age. Mahomet wept bitterly at her tomb, and clothed himself in mourning for her, and for Abu Taleb, so that this year was called the year of mourning. He was comforted in his affliction, says the Arabian author, Abu Horaira, by an assurance from the angel Gabriel, that a silver palace was allotted to Cadijah in Paradise, as a reward for her great faith and her early services to the cause.

Though Cadijah had been much older than Mahomet at the time of their marriage, and past the bloom of years when women are desirable in the East, and though the prophet was noted for an amorous temperament, yet he is said to have remained true to her to the last; nor ever availed himself of the Arabian law, permitting a plurality of wives, to give her a rival in his house. When, however, she was laid in the grave, and the first transport of his grief had subsided, he sought to console himself for her loss, by entering anew into wedlock; and henceforth indulged in a plurality of wives. He permitted, by his law, four wives to each of his followers; but did not limit himself to that number; for he observed that a prophet, being peculiarly gifted and privileged, was not bound to restrict himself to the same laws as ordinary mortals.

His first choice was made within a month after the death of Cadijah, and fell upon a beautiful child named Ayesha, the daughter of his faithful adherent, Abu Beker. Perhaps he sought, by this alliance, to grapple Abu Beker still more strongly to his side; he being one of the bravest and most popular of his tribe. Ayesha, however, was but seven years of age, and, though females soon bloom and ripen in those eastern climes, she was yet too young to enter into the married state. He was merely betrothed to her, therefore, and postponed their nuptials for two years, during which time he caused her to be carefully instructed in the accomplishments proper to an Arabian maiden of distinguished rank.

Upon this wife, thus chosen in the very blossom of her years, the prophet doted more passionately than upon any of those whom he subsequently married. All these had been previously experienced in wedlock; Ayesha, he said, was the only one who came a pure unspotted virgin to his arms.

Still, that he might not be without due solace while Ayesha was attaining the marriageable age, he took, as a wife, Sawda, the widow of Sokran, one of his followers. She had been nurse to his daughter Fatima, and was one of the faithful who fled into Abyssinia from the early persecutions of the people of Mecca. It is pretended that, while in exile, she had a mysterious intimation of the future honor which awaited her; for she dreamt that Mahomet laid his head upon her bosom. She recounted the dream to her husband Sokran, who interpreted it as a prediction of his speedy death, and of her marriage with the prophet.

The marriage, whether predicted or not, was one of mere expediency. Mahomet never loved Sawda with the affection he manifested for his other wives. He would even have put her away in after years, but she implored to be allowed the honor of still calling herself his wife; proffering that, whenever it should come to her turn to share the marriage bed, she would relinquish her right to Ayesha. Mahomet consented to an arrangement which favored his love for the latter, and Sawda continued, as long as she lived, to be nominally his wife.

Mahomet soon became sensible of the loss he had sustained in the death of Abu Taleb; who had been not merely an affectionate relative, but a steadfast and powerful protector, from his great influence in

Mecca. At his death there was no one to check and counteract the hostilities of Abu Sofian and Abu Jahl; who soon raised up such a spirit of persecution among the Koreishites, that Mahomet found it unsafe to continue in his native place. He set out, therefore, accompanied by his freedman Zeid, to seek a refuge at Tayef, a small walled town, about seventy miles from Mecca, inhabited by the Thakifites, or Arabs of the tribe of Thakeef. It was one of the favored places of Arabia, situated among vineyards and gardens. Here grew peaches and plums, melons and pomegranates; figs, blue and green, the nebeck-tree producing the lotus, and palm-trees with their clusters of green and golden fruit. So fresh were its pastures and fruitful its fields, contrasted with the sterility of the neighboring deserts, that the Arabs fabled it to have originally been a part of Syria, broken off and floated hither at the time of the deluge.

Mahomet entered the gates of Tayef with some degree of confidence, trusting for protection to the influence of his uncle Al Abbas, who had possessions there. He could not have chosen a worse place of refuge. Tayef was one of the strongholds of idolatry. Here was maintained in all its force the worship of Al Lat, one of the female idols already mentioned. Her image of stone was covered with jewels and precious stones, the offerings of her votaries; it was believed to be inspired with life, and the intercession of Al Lat was implored as one of the daughters of God.

Mahomet remained about a month in Tayef, seeking in vain to make proselytes among its inhabitants. When he attempted to preach his doctrines, his voice was drowned by clamors. More than once he was wounded by stones thrown at him, and which the faithful Zeid endeavored in vain to ward off. So violent did the popular fury become at last, that he was driven from the city, and even pursued for some distance beyond the walls by an insulting rabble of slaves and children.

Thus driven ignominiously from his hoped-for place of refuge, and not daring to return openly to his native city, he remained in the desert until Zeid should procure a secret asylum for him among his friends in Mecca. In this extremity, he had one of those visions or supernatural visitations which appear always to have occurred in lonely or agitated moments, when we may suppose him to have been in a state of mental excitement. It was after the evening prayer, he says, in a solitary place in the valley of Naklah, between Mecca and Tayef. He was reading the

Koran, when he was overheard by a passing company of Gins or Genii. These are spiritual beings, some good, others bad, and liable like man to future rewards and punishments. "Hark! give ear!" said the Genii one to the other. They paused and listened as Mahomet continued to read. "Verily," said they at the end, "we have heard an admirable discourse, which directeth unto the right institution; wherefore we believe therein."

This spiritual visitation consoled Mahomet for his expulsion from Tayef, showing that though he and his doctrines might be rejected by men, they were held in reverence by spiritual intelligences. At least so we may infer from the mention he makes of it in the forty-sixth and seventy-second chapters of the Koran. Thenceforward, he declared himself sent for the conversion of these genii as well as of the human race.

NOTE – The belief in genii was prevalent throughout the East, long before the time of Mahomet. They were supposed to haunt solitary places, particularly toward nightfall; a superstition congenial to the habits and notions of the inhabitants of lonely and desert countries. The Arabs supposed every valley and barren waste to have its tribe of genii, who were subject to a dominant spirit, and roamed forth at night to beset the pilgrim and the traveller. Whenever, therefore, they entered a lonely valley toward the close of evening, they used to supplicate the presiding spirit or lord of the place, to protect them from the evil genii under his command.

Those columns of dust raised by whirling eddies of wind, and which sweep across the desert, are supposed to be caused by some evil genius or sprite of gigantic size.

The serpents which occasionally infest houses were thought to be often genii, some infidels and some believers. Mahomet cautioned his followers to be slow to kill a house serpent. "Warn him to depart; if he do not obey, then kill him, for it is a sign that he is a mere reptile or an infidel genius."

It is fabled that in earlier times, the genii had admission to heaven, but were expelled on account of their meddling propensities. They have ever since been of a curious and prying nature, often attempting to clamber up to the constellations; thence to peep into heaven, and see and overhear what is going on there. They are, however, driven thence by angels with flaming swords; and those meteors called shooting stars are supposed by Mahometans to be darted by the guardian angels at these intrusive genii.

Other legends pretend that the earth was originally peopled by these genii, but they rebelled against the Most High, and usurped terrestrial dominion, which they maintained for two thousand years. At length, Azazil, or Lucifer, was sent against them and defeated them, overthrowing their mighty king Gian ben Gian, the founder of the pyramids; whose magic buckler of talismanic virtue fell subsequently into the hands of king Solomon the Wise, giving him power over the spells and charms of magicians and evil genii. The rebel spirits, defeated and humiliated, were driven into an obscure corner of the earth. Then it was that God created man, with less dangerous faculties and powers, and gave him the world for a habitation.

The angels according to Moslem notions were created from bright gems; the genii from fire without smoke, and Adam from clay.

Mahomet, when in the seventy-second chapter of the Koran, he alludes to the visitation of the genii in the valley of Naklah, makes them give the following frank account of themselves:

"We formerly attempted to pry into what was transacting in heaven, but we found the same guarded by angels with flaming darts; and we sat on some of the seats thereof to hear the discourse of its inhabitants; but whoso listeneth now finds a flame prepared to guard the celestial confines. There are some among us who are Moslems, and there are others who swerve from righteousness. Whoso embraceth Islamism seeketh the true direction; but those who swerve from righteousness shall be fuel for the fire of Jehennam."

CHAPTER XII

*Night journey of the prophet from Mecca to Jerusalem; and thence to
the seventh heaven*

An asylum being provided for Mahomet in the house of Mutem Ibn
Adi, one of his disciples, he ventured to return to Mecca. The supernatural visitation of genii in the valley of Naklah, was soon followed by a
vision or revelation far more extraordinary, and which has ever since
remained a theme of comment and conjecture among devout Mahometans. We allude to the famous night journey to Jerusalem, and thence
to the seventh heaven. The particulars of it, though given as if in the
very words of Mahomet, rest merely on tradition; some, however, cite
texts corroborative of it, scattered here and there in the Koran.

We do not pretend to give this vision or revelation in its amplitude
and wild extravagance, but will endeavor to seize upon its most essential features.

The night on which it occurred, is described as one of the darkest
and most awfully silent that had ever been known. There was no crowing of cocks nor barking of dogs; no howling of wild beasts nor hooting
of owls. The very waters ceased to murmur, and the winds to whistle;
all nature seemed motionless and dead. In the mid watches of the
night, Mahomet was roused by a voice crying, "Awake, thou sleeper!"
The angel Gabriel stood before him. His forehead was clear and serene, his complexion white as snow, his hair floated on his shoulders;
he had wings of many dazzling hues, and his robes were sewn with
pearls and embroidered with gold.

He brought Mahomet a white steed of wonderful form and qualities,
unlike any animal he had ever seen; and in truth, it differs from any
animal ever before described. It had a human face, but the cheeks of
a horse: its eyes were as jacinths and radiant as stars. It had eagle's
wings all glittering with rays of light; and its whole form was resplendent with gems and precious stones. It was a female, and from its dazzling splendor and incredible velocity was called Al Borak, or Lightning.

Mahomet prepared to mount this supernatural steed, but as he extended his hand, it drew back and reared.

"Be still, Oh Borak!" said Gabriel; "respect the prophet of God.
Never wert thou mounted by mortal man more honored of Allah."

"Oh Gabriel!" replied Al Borak, who at this time was miraculously endowed with speech; "did not Abraham of old, the friend of God, bestride me when he visited his son Ishmael? Oh Gabriel! is not this the mediator, the intercessor, the author of the profession of faith?"

"Even so, Oh Borak, this is Mahomet Ibn Abdallah, of one of the tribes of Arabia the Happy, and of the true faith. He is chief of the sons of Adam, the greatest of the divine legates, the seal of the prophets. All creatures must have his intercession before they can enter paradise. Heaven is on his right hand, to be the reward of those who believe in him; the fire of Jehennam is on his left hand, into which all shall be thrust who oppose his doctrines."

"Oh Gabriel!" entreated Al Borak; "by the faith existing between thee and him, prevail on him to intercede for me at the day of the resurrection."

"Be assured, Oh Borak!" exclaimed Mahomet, "that through my intercession thou shalt enter paradise."

No sooner had he uttered these words, than the animal approached and submitted to be mounted, then rising with Mahomet on its back, it soared aloft far above the mountains of Mecca.

As they passed like lightning between heaven and earth, Gabriel cried aloud, "Stop, Oh Mahomet! descend to the earth, and make the prayer with two inflections of the body."

They alighted on the earth, and having made the prayer –

"Oh friend and well beloved of my soul!" said Mahomet; "why dost thou command me to pray in this place?"

"Because it is Mount Sinai, on which God communed with Moses."

Mounting aloft, they again passed rapidly between heaven and earth, until Gabriel called out a second time, "Stop, Oh Mahomet! descend, and make the prayer with two inflections."

They descended, Mahomet prayed, and again demanded, "Why didst thou command me to pray in this place?"

"Because it is Bethlehem, where Jesus the Son of Mary was born."

They resumed their course through the air, until a voice was heard on the right, exclaiming, "Oh Mahomet, tarry a moment, that I may speak to thee; of all created beings I am most devoted to thee."

But Borak pressed forward, and Mahomet forbore to tarry, for he felt that it was not with him to stay his course, but with God the all-powerful and glorious.

Another voice was now heard on the left, calling on Mahomet in like words to tarry; but Borak still pressed forward, and Mahomet tarried not. He now beheld before him a damsel of ravishing beauty, adorned with all the luxury and riches of the earth. She beckoned him with alluring smiles: "Tarry a moment, Oh Mahomet, that I may talk with thee, I, who, of all beings, am the most devoted to thee." But still Borak pressed on, and Mahomet tarried not; considering that it was not with him to stay his course, but with God the all-powerful and glorious.

Addressing himself, however, to Gabriel, "What voices are those I have heard?" said he; "and what damsel is this who has beckoned to me?"

"The first, Oh Mahomet, was the voice of a Jew; hadst thou listened to him, all thy nation would have been won to Judaism.

"The second was the voice of a Christian: hadst thou listened to him, thy people would have inclined to Christianity.

"The damsel was the world, with all its riches, its vanities, and allurements; hadst thou listened to her, thy nation would have chosen the pleasures of this life, rather than the bliss of eternity, and all would have been doomed to perdition."

Continuing their aerial course, they arrived at the gate of the holy temple at Jerusalem, where, alighting from Al Borak, Mahomet fastened her to the rings where the prophets before him had fastened her. Then entering the temple, he found there Abraham, and Moses, and Isa (Jesus), and many more of the prophets. After he had prayed in company with them for a time, a ladder of light was let down from heaven, until the lower end rested on the Shakra, or foundation-stone of the sacred house, being the stone of Jacob. Aided by the angel Gabriel, Mahomet ascended this ladder with the rapidity of lightning.

Being arrived at the first heaven, Gabriel knocked at the gate. Who is there? was demanded from within. Gabriel. Who is with thee? Mahomet. Has he received his mission? He has. Then he is welcome! and the gate was opened.

This first heaven was of pure silver, and in its resplendent vault the stars are suspended by chains of gold. In each star an angel is placed sentinel, to prevent the demons from scaling the sacred abodes. As Mahomet entered, an ancient man approached him, and Gabriel said, "Here is thy father Adam, pay him reverence." Mahomet did so, and Adam embraced him, calling him the greatest among his children, and the first among the prophets.

In this heaven were innumerable animals of all kinds, which Gabriel said were angels, who, under these forms, interceded with Allah for the various races of animals upon earth. Among these was a cock of dazzling whiteness, and of such marvellous height, that his crest touched the second heaven, though five hundred years' journey above the first. This wonderful bird saluted the ear of Allah each morning with his melodious chant. All creatures on earth, save man, are awakened by his voice, and all the fowls of his kind chant hallelujahs in emulation of his note. *

They now ascended to the second heaven. Gabriel, as before, knocked at the gate; the same questions and replies were exchanged; the door opened and they entered.

This heaven was all of polished steel, and dazzling splendor. Here they found Noah; who, embracing Mahomet, hailed him as the greatest among the prophets.

Arrived at the third heaven, they entered with the same ceremonies. It was all studded with precious stones, and too brilliant for mortal eyes. Here was seated an angel of immeasurable height, whose eyes were seventy thousand days' journey apart. He had at his command a hundred thousand battalions of armed men. Before him was spread a vast book, in which he was continually writing and blotting out.

"This, Oh Mahomet," said Gabriel, "is Asrael, the angel of death, who is in the confidence of Allah. In the book before him he is continually writing the names of those who are to be born, and blotting out the names of those who have lived their allotted time, and who, therefore, instantly die."

They now mounted to the fourth heaven, formed of the finest silver. Among the angels who inhabited it was one five hundred days' journey

* There are three to which, say the Moslem doctors, God always lends a willing ear: the voice of him who reads the Koran; of him who prays for pardon; and of this cock who crows to the glory of the Most High. When the last day is near, they add, Allah will bid this bird to close his wings and chant no more. Then all the cocks on earth will cease to crow, and their silence will be a sign that the great day of judgment is impending.

The Reverend Doctor Humphrey Prideaux, Dean of Norwich, in his life of Mahomet, accuses him of having stolen this wonderful cock from the tract Bava Bathra of the Babylonish Talmud, "wherein," says he, "we have a story of such a prodigious bird, called Ziz, which, standing with his feet on the earth, reacheth up to the heavens with his head, and with the spreading of his wings, darkeneth the whole orb of the sun, and causeth a total eclipse thereof. This bird the Chaldee paraphrast on the Psalms says is a cock, and that he crows before the Lord; and the Chaldee paraphrast on Job tells us of his crowing every morning before the Lord, and that God giveth him wisdom for that purpose."

in height. His countenance was troubled, and rivers of tears ran from his eyes. "This," said Gabriel, "is the angel of tears, appointed to weep over the sins of the children of men, and to predict the evils which await them."

The fifth heaven was of the finest gold. Here Mahomet was received by Aaron with embraces and congratulations. The avenging angel dwells in this heaven, and presides over the element of fire. Of all the angels seen by Mahomet, he was the most hideous and terrific. His visage seemed of copper, and was covered with wens and warts. His eyes flashed lightning, and he grasped a flaming lance. He sat on a throne surrounded by flames, and before him was a heap of red-hot chains. Were he to alight upon earth in his true form, the mountains would be consumed, the seas dried up, and all the inhabitants would die with terror. To him, and the angels his ministers, is intrusted the execution of divine vengeance on infidels and sinners.

Leaving this awful abode, they mounted to the sixth heaven, composed of a transparent stone, called Hasala, which may be rendered carbuncle. Here was a great angel, composed half of snow and half of fire; yet the snow melted not, nor was the fire extinguished. Around him a choir of lesser angels continually exclaimed, "Oh Allah! who hast united snow and fire, unite all thy faithful servants in obedience to thy law."

"This," said Gabriel, "is the guardian angel of heaven and earth. It is he who dispatches angels unto individuals of thy nation, to incline them in favor of thy mission, and call them to the service of God; and he will continue to do so until the day of resurrection."

Here was the prophet Musa (Moses), who, however, instead of welcoming Mahomet with joy, as the other prophets had done, shed tears at sight of him.

"Wherefore does thou weep?" inquired Mahomet.

"Because I behold a successor, who is destined to conduct more of his nation into paradise than ever I could of the backsliding children of Israel."

Mounting hence to the seventh heaven, Mahomet was received by the patriarch Abraham. This blissful abode is formed of divine light, and of such transcendent glory that the tongue of man cannot describe it. One of its celestial inhabitants will suffice to give an idea of the rest. He surpassed the whole earth in magnitude, and had seventy thousand heads; each head seventy thousand mouths; each mouth seventy thousand tongues; each tongue spoke seventy thousand different languages, and all these were incessantly employed in chanting the praises of the Most High.

While contemplating this wonderful being, Mahomet was suddenly transported aloft to the lotus-tree, called Sedrat, which flourishes on the right hand of the invisible throne of Allah. The branches of this tree extend wider than the distance between the sun and the earth. Angels more numerous than the sands of the sea-shore, or of the beds of all the streams and rivers, rejoice beneath its shade. The leaves resemble the ears of an elephant; thousands of immortal birds sport among its branches, repeating the sublime verses of the Koran. Its fruits are milder than milk and sweeter than honey. If all the creatures of God were assembled, one of these fruits would be sufficient for their sustenance. Each seed incloses a houri, or celestial virgin, provided for the felicity of true believers. From this tree issue four rivers; two flow into the interior of paradise, two issue beyond it, and become the Nile and Euphrates.

Mahomet and his celestial guide now proceeded to Al Mamour, or the House of Adoration; formed of red jacinths or rubies, and surrounded by innumerable lamps, perpetually burning. As Mahomet entered the portal, three vases were offered him, one containing wine, another milk, and the third, honey. He took and drank of the vase containing milk.

"Well hast thou done; auspicious is thy choice," exclaimed Gabriel. "Hadst thou drunk of the wine, thy people had all gone astray."

The sacred house resembles in form the Caaba at Mecca, and is perpendicularly above it in the seventh heaven. It is visited every day by seventy thousand angels of the highest order. They were at this very time making their holy circuit, and Mahomet, joining with them, walked round it seven times.

Gabriel could go no further. Mahomet now traversed, quicker than thought, an immense space; passing through two regions of dazzling light, and one of profound darkness. Emerging from this utter gloom, he was filled with awe and terror at finding himself in the presence of Allah, and but two bow-shots from his throne. The face of the Deity was covered with twenty thousand veils, for it would have annihilated man to look upon its glory. He put forth his hands, and placed one upon the breast and the other upon the shoulder of Mahomet, who felt a freezing chill penetrate to his heart and to the very marrow of his bones. It was followed by a feeling of ecstatic bliss, while a sweetness and fragrance prevailed around, which none can understand, but those who have been in the divine presence.

Mahomet now received from the Deity himself, many of the doctrines contained in the Koran; and fifty prayers were prescribed as the daily duty of all true believers.

When he descended from the divine presence and again met with Moses, the latter demanded what Allah had required. "That I should make fifty prayers every day."

"And thinkest thou to accomplish such a task? I have made the experiment before thee. I tried it with the children of Israel, but in vain; return, then, and beg a diminution of the task."

Mahomet returned accordingly, and obtained a diminution of ten prayers; but when he related his success to Moses, the latter made the same objection to the daily amount of forty. By his advice Mahomet returned repeatedly, until the number was reduced to five.

Moses still objected. "Thinkest thou to exact five prayers daily from they people? By Allah! I have had experience with the children of Israel, and such a demand is vain; return, therefore, and entreat still further mitigation of the task."

"No," replied Mahomet, "I have already asked indulgence until I am ashamed." With these words he saluted Moses and departed.

By the ladder of light he descended to the temple of Jerusalem, where he found Borak fastened as he had left her, and mounting, was borne back in an instant to the place whence he had first been taken.

This account of the vision, or nocturnal journey, is chiefly according to the words of the historians Abulfeda, Al Bokhari, and Abu Horaira, and is given more at large in the Life of Mahomet, by Gagnier. The journey itself has given rise to endless commentaries and disputes among the doctors. Some affirm that it was no more than a dream or vision of the night; and support their assertion by a tradition derived from Ayesha, the wife of Mahomet, who declared that, on the night in question, his body remained perfectly still, and it was only in spirit that he made his nocturnal journey. In giving this tradition, however, they did not consider that at the time the journey was said to have taken place, Ayesha was still a child, and, though espoused, had not become the wife of Mahomet.

Others insist that he made the celestial journey bodily, and that the whole was miraculously effected in so short a space of time, that, on his return, he was able to prevent the complete overturn of a vase of water, which the angel Gabriel had struck with his wing on his departure.

Others say that Mahomet only pretended to have made the nocturnal journey to the temple of Jerusalem, and that the subsequent ascent to heaven was a vision. According to Ahmed ben Joseph, the nocturnal visit to the temple was testified by the patriarch of Jerusalem himself. "At the time," says he, "that Mahomet sent an envoy to the emperor Heraclius, at Constantinople, inviting him to embrace Islamism, the patriarch was in the presence of the emperor. The envoy having related the nocturnal journey of the prophet, the patriach was seized with astonishment, and informed the emperor of a circumstance coinciding with the narrative of the envoy. 'It is my custom,' said he, 'never to retire to rest at night until I have fastened every door of the temple. On the night here mentioned, I closed them according to my custom, but there was one which it was impossible to move. Upon this, I sent for the carpenters, who, having inspected the door, declared that the lintel over the portal, and the edifice itself, had settled to such a degree, that it was out of their power to close the door. I was obliged, therefore, to leave it open. Early in the morning, at the break of day, I repaired thither, and behold, the stone placed at the corner of the temple was perforated, and there were vestiges of the place where Al Borak had been fastened. Then, said I, to those present, this portal would not have remained fixed unless some prophet had been here to pray.'"

Traditions go on to say, that when Mahomet narrated his nocturnal journey to a large assembly in Mecca, many marvelled yet believed, some were perplexed with doubt, but the Koreishites laughed it to scorn. "Thou sayest that thou hast been to the temple of Jerusalem," said Abu Jahl; "prove the truth of thy words, by giving a description of it."

For a moment Mahomet was embarrassed by the demand, for he had visited the temple in the night, when its form was not discernible; suddenly, however, the angel Gabriel stood by his side, and placed before his eyes an exact type of the sacred edifice, so that he was enabled instantly to answer the most minute questions.

The story still transcended the belief even of some of his disciples, until Abu Beker, seeing them wavering in their faith, and in danger of backsliding, roundly vouched for the truth of it; in reward for which support, Mahomet gave him the title of Al Seddek, or the Testifier to the Truth, by which he was thenceforth distinguished.

As we have already observed, this nocturnal journey rests almost entirely upon tradition, though some of its circumstances are vaguely alluded to in the Koran. The whole may be a fanciful superstructure of Moslem fanatics on one of these visions or ecstasies to which Mahomet was prone, and the relation of which caused him to be stigmatized by the Koreishites as a madman.

CHAPTER XIII

Mahomet makes converts of pilgrims from Medina – Determines to fly to that city – A plot to slay him – His miraculous escape – His Hegira, or flight – His reception at Medina

The fortunes of Mahomet were becoming darker and darker in his native place. Cadijah, his original benefactress, the devoted companion of his solitude and seclusion, the zealous believer in his doctrines, was in her grave: so also was Abu Taleb, once his faithful and efficient protector. Deprived of the sheltering influence of the latter, Mahomet had become, in a manner, an outlaw in Mecca; obliged to conceal himself, and remain a burthen on the hospitality of those whom his own doctrines had involved in persecution. If worldly advantage had been his object, how had it been attained? Upwards of ten years had elapsed since first he announced his prophetic mission; ten long years of enmity, trouble, and misfortune. Still he persevered, and now, at a period of life when men seek to enjoy in repose the fruition of the past, rather than risk all in new schemes for the future, we find him, after having sacrificed ease, fortune, and friends, prepared to give up home and country also, rather than his religious creed.

As soon as the privileged time of pilgrimage arrived, he emerged once more from his concealment, and mingled with the multitude assembled from all parts of Arabia. His earnest desire was to find some powerful tribe, or the inhabitants of some important city, capable and willing to receive him as a guest, and protect him in the enjoyment and propagation of his faith.

His quest was for a time unsuccessful. Those who had come to worship at the Caaba, drew back from a man stigmatized as an apostate; and the worldly-minded were unwilling to befriend one proscribed by the powerful of his native place.

At length, as he was one day preaching on the hill Al Akaba, a little to the north of Mecca, he drew the attention of certain pilgrims from the city of Yathreb. This city, since called Medina, was about two hundred and seventy miles north of Mecca. Many of its inhabitants were Jews and heretical Christians. The pilgrims in question were pure Arabs of the ancient and powerful tribe of Khazradites, and in habits of friendly intercourse with the Keneedites and Naderites, two Jewish tribes inhabiting Mecca, who claimed to be of the sacerdotal line of

Aaron. The pilgrims had often heard their Jewish friends explain the mysteries of their faith, and talk of an expected Messiah. They were moved by the eloquence of Mahomet, and struck with the resemblance of his doctrines to those of the Jewish law; insomuch that when they heard him proclaim himself a prophet, sent by heaven to restore the ancient faith, they said, one to another, "Surely this must be the promised Messiah of which we have been told." The more they listened, the stronger became their persuasion of the fact, until in the end they avowed their conviction, and made a final profession of the faith.

As the Khazradites belonged to one of the most powerful tribes of Yathreb, Mahomet sought to secure their protection, and proposed to accompany them on their return; but they informed him that they were at deadly feud with the Awsites, another powerful tribe of that city, and advised him to defer his coming until they should be at peace. He consented; but on the return home of the pilgrims, he sent with them Musab Ibn Omeir, one of the most learned and able of his disciples, with instructions to strengthen them in the faith, and to preach it to their townsmen. Thus were the seeds of Islamism first sown in the city of Medina. For a time they thrived but slowly. Musab was opposed by the idolaters, and his life threatened; but he persisted in his exertions, and gradually made converts among the principal inhabitants. Among these were Saad Ibn Maadi, a prince or chief of the Awsites; and Osaid Ibn Hodheir, a man of great authority in the city. Numbers of the Moslems of Mecca also, driven away by persecution, took refuge in Medina, and aided in propagating the new faith among its inhabitants, until it found its way into almost every household.

Feeling now assured of being able to give Mahomet an asylum in the city, upwards of seventy of the converts of Medina, led by Musab Ibn Omeir, repaired to Mecca with the pilgrims in the holy month of the thirteenth year of "the mission," to invite him to take up his abode in their city. Mahomet gave them a midnight meeting on the hill Al Akaba. His uncle Al Abbas, who, like the deceased Abu Taleb, took an affectionate interest in his welfare, though no convert to his doctrines, accompanied him to this secret conference, which he feared might lead him into danger. He entreated the pilgrims from Medina not to entice his nephew to their city until more able to protect him: warning them that their open adoption of the new faith would bring all Arabia in arms against them. His warnings and entreaties were in vain: a solemn compact was made between the parties. Mahomet demanded that they should abjure idolatry, and worship the one true God openly and fearlessly. For himself he exacted obedience in weal and woe; and for the disciples who might accompany him, protection; even such as they would render to their own wives and children. On these terms he offered to bind himself to remain among them, to be the friend of their friends, the enemy of their enemies. "But, should we perish in your cause," asked they, "what will be our reward?" "Paradise!" replied the prophet.

The terms were accepted; the emissaries from Medina placed their hands in the hands of Mahomet, and swore to abide by the compact. The latter then singled out twelve from among them, whom he designated as his apostles; in imitation, it is supposed, of the example of our Saviour. Just then a voice was heard from the summit of the hill, denouncing them as apostates, and menacing them with punishment. The sound of this voice, heard in the darkness of the night, inspired temporary dismay. "It is the voice of the fiend Eblis," said Mahomet, scornfully; "he is the foe of God: fear him not." It was probably the voice of some spy or evesdropper of the Koreishites; for the very next morning they manifested a knowledge of what had taken place in the night; and treated the new confederates with great harshness as they were departing from the city.

It was this early accession to the faith, and this timely aid proffered and subsequently afforded to Mahomet and his disciples, which procured for the Moslems of Medina the appellation of Ansarians, or auxiliaries, by which they were afterwards distinguished.

After the departure of the Ansarians, and the expiration of the holy month, the persecutions of the Moslems were resumed with increased virulence, insomuch that Mahomet, seeing a crisis was at hand, and being resolved to leave the city, advised his adherents generally to provide for their safety. For himself, he still lingered in Mecca with a few devoted followers.

Abu Sofian, his implacable foe, was at this time governor of the city. He was both incensed and alarmed at the spreading growth of the new faith, and held a meeting of the chief of the Koreishites to devise some means of effectually putting a stop to it. Some advised that Mahomet should be banished the city; but it was objected that he might gain other tribes to his interest, or perhaps the people of Medina, and return at their head to take his revenge. Others proposed to wall him up in a dungeon, and supply him with food until he died; but it was surmised that his friends might effect his escape. All these objections were raised by a violent and pragmatical old man, a stranger from the province of Nedja, who, say the Moslem writers, was no other than the devil in disguise, breathing his malignant spirit into those present. At length it was declared by Abu Jahl, that the only effectual check on the growing evil was to put Mahomet to death. To this all agreed, and as a means of sharing the odium of the deed, and withstanding the vengeance it might awaken among the relatives of the victim, it was arranged that a member of each family should plunge his sword into the body of Mahomet.

It is to this conspiracy that allusion is made in the eighth chapter of the Koran. "And call to mind how the unbelievers plotted against thee, that they might either detain thee in bonds, or put thee to death, or expel thee the city; but God laid a plot against them; and God is the best layer of plots."

In fact, by the time the murderers arrived before the dwelling of Mahomet, he was apprised of the impending danger. As usual, the warning is attributed to the angel Gabriel, but it is probable it was given by some Koreishite, less bloody-minded than his confederates. It came just in time to save Mahomet from the hands of his enemies. They paused at his door, but hesitated to enter. Looking through a crevice they beheld, as they thought, Mahomet wrapped in his green mantle, and lying asleep on his couch. They waited for a while, consulting whether to fall on him while sleeping, or wait until he should go forth. At length they burst open the door and rushed toward the couch. The sleeper started up; but, instead of Mahomet, Ali stood before them. Amazed and confounded, they demanded, "Where is Mahomet?" "I know not," replied Ali, sternly, and walked forth; nor did any one venture to molest him. Enraged at the escape of their victim, however, the Koreishites proclaimed a reward of a hundred camels to any one who should bring them Mahomet alive or dead.

Divers accounts are given of the mode in which Mahomet made his escape from the house after the faithful Ali had wrapped himself in his mantle and taken his place upon the couch. The most miraculous account is, that he opened the door silently, as the Koreishites stood before it, and, scattering a handful of dust in the air, cast such blindness upon them, that he walked through the midst of them without being perceived. This, it is added, is confirmed by the verse of the 30th chapter of the Koran: "We have thrown blindness upon them, that they shall not see."

The most probable account is, that he clambered over the wall in the rear of the house, by the help of a servant, who bent his back for him to step upon it.

He repaired immediately to the house of Abu Beker, and they arranged for instant flight. It was agreed that they should take refuge in a cave in Mount Thor, about an hour's distance from Mecca, and wait there until they could proceed safely to Medina: and in the meantime the children of Abu Beker should secretly bring them food. They left Mecca while it was yet dark, making their way on foot by the light of the stars, and the day dawned as they found themselves at the foot of Mount Thor. Scarce were they within the cave, when they heard the sound of pursuit. Abu Beker, though a brave man, quaked with fear. "Our pursuers," said he, "are many, and we are but two." "Nay," replied Mahomet, "there is a third; God is with us!" And here the Moslem writers relate a miracle, dear to the minds of all true believers. By the time, say they, that the Koreishites reached the mouth of the cavern, an acacia tree had sprung up before it, in the spreading branches of which a pigeon had made its nest, and laid its eggs, and over the whole a spider had woven its web. When the Koreishites beheld these signs of undisturbed quiet, they concluded that no one could recently have entered the cavern; so they turned away, and pursued their search in another direction.

Whether protected by miracle or not, the fugitives remained for three days undiscovered in the cave, and Asama, the daughter of Abu Beker, brought them food in the dusk of the evenings.

On the fourth day, when they presumed the ardor of pursuit had abated, the fugitives ventured forth, and set out for Medina, on camels which a servant of Abu Beker had brought in the night for them. Avoiding the main road usually taken by the caravans, they bent their course nearer to the coast of the Red Sea. They had not proceeded far, however, before they were overtaken by a troop of horse, headed by Soraka Ibn Malec. Abu Beker was again dismayed by the number of their pursuers; but Mahomet repeated the assurance, "Be not troubled; Allah is with us." Soraka was a grim warrior, with shagged iron-gray locks, and naked sinewy arms rough with hair. As he overtook Mahomet, his horse reared and fell with him. His superstitious mind was struck with it as an evil sign. Mahomet perceived the stage of his feelings, and by an eloquent appeal wrought upon him to such degree, that Soraka, filled with awe, entreated his forgiveness; and turning back with his troop, suffered him to proceed on his way unmolested.

The fugitives continued their journey without further interruption, until they arrived at Koba, a hill about two miles from Medina. It was a favorite resort of the inhabitants of the city, and a place to which they sent their sick and infirm, for the air was pure and salubrious. Hence, too, the city was supplied with fruit; the hill and its environs being covered with vineyards, and with groves of the date and lotus; with gardens producing citrons, oranges, pomegranates, figs, peaches, and apricots; and being irrigated with limpid streams.

On arriving at this fruitful spot, Al Kaswa, the camel of Mahomet, crouched on her knees, and would go no further. The prophet interpreted it as a favorable sign, and determined to remain at Koba, and prepare for entering the city. The place where his camel knelt is still pointed out by pious Moslems, a mosque named Al Takwa having been built there to commemorate the circumstance. Some affirm that it was actually founded by the prophet. A deep well is also shown in the vicinity, beside which Mahomet reposed under the shade of the trees, and into which he dropped his seal ring. It is believed still to remain there, and has given sanctity to the well; the waters of which are conducted by subterraneous conduits to Medina. At Koba he remained four days, residing in the house of an Awsite named Colthum Ibn Hadem. While at this village he was joined by a distinguished chief, Boreida Ibn Hoseib, with seventy followers, all of the tribe of Saham. These made profession of faith between the hands of Mahomet.

Another renowned proselyte who repaired to the prophet at this village, was Salman al Parsi (or the Persian). He is said to have been a native of a small place near Ispahan, and that, on passing one day by a Christian church, he was so much struck by the devotion of the people, and the solemnity of the worship, that he became disgusted with the idolatrous faith in which he had been brought up. He afterwards wandered about the east, from city to city, and convent to convent, in quest of a religion, until an ancient monk, full of years and infirmities, told him of a prophet who had arisen in Arabia to restore the pure faith of Abraham.

This Salman rose to power in after years, and was reputed by the unbelievers of Mecca to have assisted Mahomet in compiling his doctrine. This is alluded to in the sixteenth chapter of the Koran. "Verily, the idolaters say, that a certain man assisted to compose the Koran; but the language of this man is Ajami (or Persian), and the Koran is indited in the pure Arabian tongue."*

The Moslems of Mecca, who had taken refuge some time before in Medina, hearing that Mahomet was at hand, came forth to meet him at Koba; among these was the early convert Talha, and Zobeir, the nephew of Cadijah. These, seeing the travel-stained garments of Mahomet and Abu Beker, gave them white mantles, with which to make their entrance into Medina. Numbers of the Ansarians, or auxiliaries, of Medina, who had made their compact with Mahomet in the preceding year, now hastened to renew their vow of fidelity.

Learning from them that the number of proselytes in the city was rapidly augmenting, and that there was a general disposition to receive him favorably, he appointed Friday, the Moslem sabbath, the sixteenth day of the month Rabi, for his public entrance.

Accordingly, on the morning of that day he assembled all his followers to prayer; and after a sermon, in which he expounded the main principles of his faith, he mounted his camel Al Kaswa, and set forth for that city which was to become renowned in after ages as his city of refuge.

Boreida Ibn al Hoseib, with his seventy horsemen of the tribe of Saham, accompanied him as a guard. Some of the disciples took turns to hold a canopy of palm-leaves over his head, and by his side rode Abu Beker. "Oh apostle of God!" cried Boreida, "thou shalt not enter Medina without a standard;" so saying, he unfolded his turban, and tying one end of it to the point of his lance, bore it aloft before the prophet.

The city of Medina was fair to approach, being extolled for beauty of situation, salubrity of climate, and fertility of soil; for the luxuriance of its palm-trees, and the fragrance of its shrubs and flowers. At a short distance from the city a crowd of new proselytes to the faith, came forth in sun and dust to meet the cavalcade. Most of them had never seen Mahomet, and paid reverence to Abu Beker through mistake; but the latter put aside the screen of palm-leaves, and pointed out the real

* The renowned and learned Humphrey Prideaux, Doctor of Divinity and Dean of Norwich, in his Life of Mahomet, confounds this Salman the Persian with Abdallah Ibu Salem, a learned Jew; by some called Abdias Ben Salan in the Hebrew dialect, and by others Abdallah Salen; who is accused by Christian writers of assisting Mahomet in fabricating his revelations.

object of homage, who was greeted with loud acclamations.

In this way did Mahomet, so recently a fugitive from his native city, with a price upon his head, enter Medina, more as a conqueror in triumph than an exile seeking an asylum. He alighted at the house of a Khazradite, named Abu Ayub, a devout Moslem, to whom moreover he was distantly related; here he was hospitably received, and took up his abode in the basement story.

Shortly after his arrival he was joined by the faithful Ali, who had fled from Mecca, and journeyed on foot, hiding himself in the day and travelling only at night, lest he should fall into the hands of the Koreishites. He arrived weary and wayworn, his feet bleeding with the roughness of the journey.

Within a few days more came Ayesha, and the rest of Abu Beker's household, together with the family of Mahomet, conducted by his faithful freedman Zeid, and by Abu Beker's servant Abdallah.

Such is the story of the memorable Hegira, or "Flight of the prophet;" – the era of the Arabian calendar from which time is calculated by all true Moslems: it corresponds to the 622d year of the Christian era.

CHAPTER XIV

Moslems in Medina, Mohadjerins and Ansarians – The party of Abdallah Ibn Obba and the Hypocrites – Mahomet builds a mosque; preaches; makes converts among the Christians – The Jews slow to believe – Brotherhood established between fugitives and allies

Mahomet soon found himself at the head of a numerous and powerful sect in Medina; partly made up of those of his disciples who had fled from Mecca, and were thence called Mohadjerins or Fugitives, and partly of inhabitants of the place, who on joining the faith were called Ansarians or Auxiliaries. Most of these latter were of the powerful tribes of the Awsites and Khazradites, which, though descended from two brothers, Al Aws and Al Khazraj, had for a hundred and twenty years distracted Medina by their inveterate and mortal feuds, but had now become united in the bonds of faith. With such of these tribes as did not immediately adopt his doctrines he made a covenant.

The Khazradites were very much under the sway of a prince or chief, named Abdallah Ibn Obba; who, it is said, was on the point of being made king, when the arrival of Mahomet and the excitement caused by his doctrines gave the popular feeling a new direction. Abdallah was stately in person, of a graceful demeanor, and ready and eloquent tongue; he professed great friendship for Mahomet, and with several companions of his own type and character, used to attend the meetings of the Moslems. Mahomet was captivated at first by their personal appearance, their plausible conversation, and their apparent deference; but he found in the end that Abdallah was jealous of his popularity and cherished secret animosity against him, and that his companions were equally false in their pretended friendship; hence, he stamped them with the name of "The Hypocrites." Aballah Ibn Obba long continued his political rival in Medina.

Being now enabled publicly to exercise his faith and preach his doctrines, Mahomet proceeded to erect a mosque. The place chosen was a graveyard or burying-ground, shaded by date-trees. He is said to have been guided in his choice by what he considered a favorable omen; his camel having knelt opposite to this place on his public entry into the city. The dead were removed, and the trees cut down to make way for the intended edifice. It was simple in form and structure, suited to the unostentatious religion which he professed, and to the scanty and precarious means of its votaries. The walls were of earth and brick; the trunks of the palm-trees recently felled, served as pillars to support the roof, which was framed of their branches and thatched with their leaves. It was about a hundred ells square, and had three doors; one to the south, where the Kebla was afterwards established, another called the gate of Gabriel, and the third the gate of Mercy. A part of the edifice, called Soffat, was assigned as a habitation to such of the believers as were without a home.

Mahomet assisted with his own hands in the construction of this mosque. With all his foreknowledge, he little thought that he was building his own tomb and monument; for in that edifice his remains are deposited. It has in after times been repeatedly enlarged and beautified, but still bears the name Mesjed al Nebi (the Mosque of the Prophet), from having been founded by his hands. He was for some time at a loss in what manner his followers should be summoned to their devotions; whether with the sound of trumpets, as among the Jews, or by lighting fires on high places, or by the striking of timbrels. While in this perplexity, a form of words to be cried aloud, was suggested by Abdallah, the son of Zeid, who declared that it was revealed to him in a vision. It was instantly adopted by Mahomet, and such is given as the origin of the following summons, which is to this day heard from the lofty minarets throughout the East, calling the Moslems to the place of worship: "God is great! God is great! There is no God but God. Mahomet is the apostle of God. Come to prayers! come to prayers! God is great! God is great! There is no God but God." To which at dawn of day is added the exhortation, "Prayer is better than sleep! Prayer is better than sleep!"

Every thing in this humble mosque was at first conducted with great simplicity. At night it was lighted up by splinters of the date-tree; and it was some time before lamps and oil were introduced. The prophet stood on the ground and preached, leaning with his back against the trunk of one of the date-trees, which served as pillars. He afterwards had a pulpit or tribune erected, to which he ascended by three steps, so as to be elevated above the congregation. Tradition asserts, that when he first ascended this pulpit, the deserted date-tree uttered a groan; whereupon, as a consolation, he gave it the choice either to be transplanted to a garden again to flourish, or to be transferred to paradise, there to yield fruit, in after life, to true believers. The date-tree wisely chose the latter, and was subsequently buried beneath the pulpit, there to await its blissful resurrection.

Mahomet preached and prayed in the pulpit, sometimes sitting, sometimes standing and leaning on a staff. His precepts as yet were all peaceful and benignant, inculcating devotion to God and humanity to man. He seems to have emulated for a time the benignity of the Christian faith. "He who is not affectionate to God's creatures, and to his own children," would he say, "God will not be affectionate to him. Every Moslem who clothes the naked of his faith, will be clothed by Allah in the green robes of paradise."

In one of his traditional sermons transmitted by his disciples, is the following apologue on the subject of charity: "When God created the earth it shook and trembled, until he put mountains upon it, to make it firm. Then the angels asked, 'Oh God, is there any thing of thy creation stronger than these mountains?' And God replied, 'Iron is stronger than the mountains; for it breaks them.' 'And is there any thing of thy creation stronger than iron?' 'Yes; fire is stronger than iron, for it melts it.' 'Is there any thing of thy creation stronger than fire?' 'Yes; water, for it quenches fire.' 'Oh Lord, is there any thing of thy creation stronger than water?' 'Yes, wind; for it overcomes water and puts it in motion.' 'Oh, our Sustainer! is there any thing of thy creation stronger than wind?' 'Yes, a good man giving alms; if he give with his right hand and conceal it from his left, he overcomes all things.' "

His definition of charity embraced the wide circle of kindness. Every good act, he would say, is charity. Your smiling in your brother's face is charity; an exhortation of your fellow-man to virtuous deeds is equal to alms-giving; your putting a wanderer in the right road is charity; your assisting the blind is charity; your removing stones and thorns and other obstructions from the road is charity; your giving water to the thirsty is charity.

"A man's true wealth hereafter is the good he does in this world to his fellow-man. When he dies, people will say, 'What property has he left behind him?' But the angels, who examine him in the grave, will ask, 'What good deeds hast thou sent before thee?' "

"Oh prophet!" said one of his disciples, "my mother, Omm-Sad, is dead; what is the best alms I can send for the good of her soul?" "Water!" replied Mahomet, bethinking himself of the panting heats of the desert. "Dig a well for her, and give water to the thirsty." The man digged a well in his mother's name, and said, "This well is for my mother, that its rewards may reach her soul."

Charity of the tongue, also, that most important and least cultivated of charities, was likewise earnestly inculcated by Mahomet. Abu Jaraiya, an inhabitant of Basrah, coming to Medina, and being persuaded of the apostolical office of Mahomet, entreated him some great rule of conduct. "Speak evil of no one," answered the prophet. "From that time," says Abu Jaraiya, "I never did abuse any one, whether freeman or slave."

The rules of Islamism extended to the courtesies of life. Make a salam (or salutation) to a house on entering and leaving it. Return the salute of friends and acquaintances, and wayfarers on the road. He who rides must be the first to make the salute to him who walks; he who walks to him who is sitting; a small party to a large party, and the young to the old.

On the arrival of Mahomet at Medina, some of the Christians of the city promptly enrolled themselves among his followers; they were probably of those sectarians who held to the human nature of Christ, and found nothing repugnant in Islamism; which venerated Christ as the greatest among the prophets. The rest of the Christians resident there showed but little hostility to the new faith, considering it far better than the old idolatry. Indeed, the schisms and bitter dissensions among the Christians of the East had impaired their orthodoxy, weakened their zeal, and disposed them easily to be led away by new doctrines.

The Jews, of which there were rich and powerful families in Medina and its vicinity, showed a less favorable disposition. With some of them Mahomet made covenants of peace, and trusted to gain them in time to accept him as their promised Messiah or prophet. Biased, perhaps unconsciously, by such views, he had modelled many of his doctrines on the dogmas of their religion, and observed certain of their fasts and ordinances. He allowed such as embraced Islamism, to continue in the observance of their Sabbath, and of several of the Mosaic laws and ceremonies. It was the custom of the different religions of the East, to have each a Kebla or sacred point towards which they turned their faces in the act of adoration; the Sabeans toward the North Star; the Persian fire-worshipper towards the east, the place of the rising sun; the Jews toward their holy city of Jerusalem. Hitherto Mahomet had prescribed nothing of the kind; but now, out of deference to the Jews, he made Jerusalem the Kebla, toward which all Moslems were to turn their faces when in prayer.

While new converts were daily made among the inhabitants of Medina, sickness and discontent began to prevail among the fugitives from Mecca. They were not accustomed to the climate; many suffered from fevers, and in their sickness and debility languished after the home whence they were exiled.

To give them a new home, and link them closely with their new friends and allies, Mahomet established a brotherhood between fifty-four of them and as many of the inhabitants of Medina. Two persons thus linked together, were pledged to stand by each other in weal and woe; it was a tie which knit their interests more closely even than that of kindred, for they were to be heirs to each other in preference to blood relations.

This institution was one of expediency, and lasted only until the new comers had taken firm root in Medina; extended merely to those of the people of Mecca who had fled from persecution; and is alluded to in the following verse of the eighth chapter of the Koran: "They who have believed and have fled their country, and employed their substance and their persons in fighting for the faith, and they who have given the prophet a refuge among them, and have assisted him, these shall be deemed the one nearest of kin to the other."

In this shrewd, but simple way, were laid the foundations of that power which was soon to attain stupendous strength, and to shake the mightiest empires of the world.

CHAPTER XV

*Marriage of Mahomet with Ayesha – Of his daughter Fatima with
Ali – Their household arrangements*

The family relations of Mahomet had been much broken up by the
hostility brought upon him by his religious zeal. His daughter Rokaia
was still an exile with her husband, Othman Ibn Affan, in Abyssinia;
his daughter Zeinab had remained in Mecca with her husband, Abul
Aass, who was a stubborn opposer of the new faith. The family with
Mahomet in Medina consisted of his recently wedded wife Sawda, and
Fatima and Um Colthum, daughters of his late wife Cadijah. He had a
heart prone to affection, and subject to female influence, but he had
never entertained much love for Sawda; and though he always treated
her with kindness, he felt the want of some one to supply the place of
his deceased wife Cadijah.

"Oh Omar," said he one day, "the best of man's treasures is a virtuous woman, who acts by God's orders, and is obedient and pleasing
to her husband: he regards her personal and mental beauties with delight; when he orders her to do any thing she obeys him; and when he
is absent she guards his right in property and honor."

He now turned his eyes upon his betrothed spouse Ayesha, the beautiful daughter of Abu Beker. Two years had elapsed since they were
betrothed, and she had now attained her ninth year; an infantine age
it would seem, though the female form is wonderfully precocious in the
quickening climates of the East. Their nuptials took place a few months
after their arrival in Medina, and were celebrated with great simplicity;
the wedding supper was of milk, and the dowry of the bride was twelve
okks of silver.

The betrothing of Fatima, his youngest daughter, with his loyal disciple Ali, followed shortly after, and their marriage at a somewhat later
period. Fatima was between fifteen and sixteen years of age, of great
beauty, and extolled by Arabian writers as one of the four perfect
women with whom Allah has deigned to bless the earth. The age of Ali
was about twenty-two.

Heaven and earth, say the Moslem writers, joined in paying honor to
these happy espousals. Medina resounded with festivity, and blazed
with illuminations, and the atmosphere was laden with aromatic odors.
As Mahomet, on the nuptial night, conducted his daughter to her bridegroom, heaven sent down a celestial pomp to attend her: on her right

hand was the archangel Gabriel, on her left was Michael, and she was followed by a train of seventy thousand angels, who all night kept watch round the mansion of the youthful pair.

Such are the vaunting exaggerations with which Moslem writers are prone to overlay every event in the history of the prophet, and destroy the real grandeur of his career, which consists in its simplicity. A more reliable account states that the wedding feast was of dates and olives; that the nuptial couch was a sheep-skin; that the portion of the bride consisted of two skirts, one head-tire, two silver armlets, one leathern pillow stuffed with palm-leaves, one beaker or drinking cup, one hand-mill, two large jars for water, and one pitcher. All this was in unison with the simplicity of Arab housekeeping, and with the circumstances of the married couple; and to raise the dowry required of him, Ali, it is said, had to sell several camels and some shirts of mail.

The style of living of the prophet himself was not superior to that of his disciple. Ayesha, speaking of it in after years, observed: "For a whole month together we did not light a fire to dress victuals; our food was nothing but dates and water, unless any one sent us meat. The people of the prophet's household never got wheat-bread two successive days."

His food, in general, was dates and barley-bread, with milk and honey. He swept his chamber, lit his fire, mended his clothes, and was, in fact, his own servant. For each of his two wives he provided a separate house adjoining the mosque. He resided with them by turns, but Ayesha ever remained his favorite.

Mahomet has been extolled by Moslem writers for the chastity of his early life; and it is remarkable that, with all the plurality of wives indulged in by the Arabs, and which he permitted himself in subsequent years, and with all that constitutional fondness which he evinced for the sex, he remained single in his devotion to Cadijah to her dying day, never giving her a rival in his house, nor in his heart. Even the fresh and budding charms of Ayesha, which soon assumed such empire over him, could not obliterate the deep and mingled feeling of tenderness and gratitude for his early benefactress. Ayesha was piqued one day at hearing him indulge in these fond recollections: "Oh, apostle of God," demanded the youthful beauty, "was not Cadijah stricken in years? Has not Allah given thee a better wife in her stead?"

"Never!" exclaimed Mahomet, with an honest burst of feeling – "never did God give me a better! When I was poor, she enriched me; when I was pronounced a liar, she believed in me; when I was opposed by all the world, she remained true to me!"

CHAPTER XVI

The sword announced as the instrument of faith — First foray against
the Koreishites — Surprisal of a caravan

We come now to an important era in the career of Mahomet. Hitherto
he had relied on argument and persuasion to make proselytes; enjoin-
ing the same on his disciples. His exhortations to them to bear with patience and long-suffering the violence of their enemies, almost emulated the meek precept of our Saviour, "if they smite thee on the one
cheek, turn to them the other also." He now arrived at a point where
he completely diverged from the celestial spirit of the Christian doctrines, and stamped his religion with the alloy of fallible mortality. His
human nature was not capable of maintaining the sublime forbearance
he had hitherto inculcated. Thirteen years of meek endurance had
been rewarded by nothing but aggravated injury and insult. His greatest persecutors had been those of his own tribe, the Koreishites, especially those of the rival line of Abd Schems; whose vindictive chief,
Abu Sofian, had now the sway at Mecca. By their virulent hostility his
fortunes had been blasted; his family degraded, impoverished, and dispersed, and he himself driven into exile. All this he might have continued to bear with involuntary meekness, had not the means of retaliation unexpectedly sprung up within his reach. He had come to Medina a fugitive seeking an asylum, and craving merely a quiet home. In
a little while, and probably to his own surprise, he found an army at
his command: for among the many converts daily made in Medina, — the
fugitives flocking to him from Mecca, and proselytes from the tribes of
the desert, — were men of resolute spirit, skilled in the use of arms, and
fond of partisan warfare. Human passions and mortal resentments were
awakened by this sudden accession of power. They mingled with that
zeal for religious reform, which was still his predominant motive. In
the exaltations of his enthusiastic spirit he endeavored to persuade
himself, and perhaps did so effectually, that the power thus placed
within his reach was intended as a means of effecting his great purpose, and that he was called upon by divine command to use it. Such,
at least, is the purport of the memorable manifesto which he issued at
this epoch, and which changed the whole tone and fortunes of his
faith.

"Different prophets," said he, "have been sent by God to illustrate his
different attributes: Moses his clemency and providence; Solomon his

wisdom, majesty, and glory; Jesus Christ his righteousness, omni-
science, and power; – his righteousness by purity of conduct; his omni-
science by the knowledge he displayed of the secrets of all hearts; his
power by the miracles he wrought. None of these attributes, however,
have been sufficient to enforce conviction, and even the miracles of
Moses and Jesus have been treated with unbelief. I, therefore, the last
of the prophets, am sent with the sword! Let those who promulgate my
faith enter into no argument nor discussion; but slay all who refuse
obedience to the law. Whoever fights for the true faith, whether he fall
or conquer, will assuredly receive a glorious reward."

"The sword," added he, " is the key of heaven and hell; all who draw
it in the cause of the faith will be rewarded with temporal advantages;
every drop shed of their blood, every peril and hardship endured by
them, will be registered on high as more meritorious than even fasting
or praying. If they fall in battle, their sins will at once be blotted out,
and they will be transported to paradise, there to revel in eternal pleasures in the arms of black-eyed houris."

Predestination was brought to aid these belligerent doctrines. Every
event, according to the Koran, was predestined from eternity, and
could not be avoided. No man could die sooner or later than his allotted hour, and when it arrived, it would be the same, whether the angel
of death should find him in the quiet of his bed, or amid the storm of
battle.

Such were the doctrines and revelations which converted Islamism
of a sudden from a religion of meekness and philanthropy, to one of
violence and the sword. They were peculiarly acceptable to the Arabs,
harmonizing with their habits, and encouraging their predatory propensities. Virtually pirates of the desert, it is not to be wondered at
that, after this open promulgation of the Religion of the Sword, they
should flock in crowds to the standard of the prophet. Still no violence
was authorized by Mahomet against those who should persist in unbelief, provided they should readily submit to his temporal sway, and
agree to pay tribute; and here we see the first indication of worldly
ambition and a desire for temporal dominion dawning upon his mind.
Still it will be found, that the tribute thus exacted was subsidiary to his
ruling passion, and mainly expended by him in the extension of the
faith.

The first warlike enterprises of Mahomet betray the lurking resentment we have noted. They were directed against the caravans of

Mecca, belonging to his implacable enemies the Koreishites. The three first were headed by Mahomet in person, but without any material result. The fourth was confided to a Moslem, named Abdallah Ibn Jasch; who was sent out with eight or ten resolute followers on the road toward South Arabia. As it was now the holy month of Radjab, sacred from violence and rapine, Abdallah had sealed orders, not to be opened until the third day. These orders were vaguely yet significantly worded. Abdallah was to repair to the valley of Naklah, between Mecca and Tayef (the same in which Mahomet had the revelation of the Genii), where he was to watch for an expected caravan of the Koreishites. "Perhaps," added the letter of instructions shrewdly, – "perhaps thou mayest be able to bring us some tidings of it."

Abdallah understood the true meaning of the letter, and acted up to it. Arriving in the valley of Naklah, he descried the caravan, consisting of several camels laden with merchandise, and conducted by four men. Following it at a distance, he sent one of his men, disguised as a pilgrim, to overtake it. From the words of the latter the Koreishites supposed his companions to be like himself, pilgrims bound to Mecca. Beside, it was the month of Radjab, when the desert might be travelled in security. Scarce had they come to a halt, however, when Abdallah and his comrades fell on them; killed one and took two prisoners; the fourth escaped. The victors then returned to Medina with their prisoners and booty.

All Medina was scandalized at this breach of the holy month. Mahomet, finding that he had ventured too far, pretended to be angry with Abdallah, and refused to take the share of the booty offered to him. Confiding in the vagueness of his instructions, he insisted that he had not commanded Abdallah to shed blood, or commit any violence during the holy month.

The clamor still continuing, and being echoed by the Koreishites of Mecca, produced the following passage of the Koran:

"They will ask thee concerning the sacred month, whether they may make war therein. Answer: To war therein is grievous; but to deny God, to bar the path of God against his people, to drive true believers from his holy temple, and to worship idols, are sins far more grievous than to kill in the holy months."

Having thus proclaimed divine sanction for the deed, Mahomet no longer hesitated to take his share of the booty. He delivered one of the prisoners on ransom; the other embraced Islamism.

The above passage of the Koran, however satisfactory it may have been to devout Moslems, will scarcely serve to exculpate their prophet in the eyes of the profane. The expedition of Abdallah Ibn Jasch was a sad practical illustration of the new religion of the sword. It contemplated not merely an act of plunder and revenge, a venial act in the eyes of Arabs, and justified by the new doctrines by being exercised against the enemies of the faith, but an outrage also on the holy month, that period sacred from time immemorial against violence and bloodshed, and which Mahomet himself professed to hold in reverence. The craft and secrecy also with which the whole was devised and conducted, the sealed letter of instructions to Abdallah, to be opened only at the end of three days, at the scene of projected outrage, and couched in language vague, equivocal, yet sufficiently significant to the agent; all were in direct opposition to the conduct of Mahomet in the earlier part of his career, when he dared openly to pursue the path of duty, "though the sun should be arrayed against him on the right hand, and the moon on the left;" all showed that he was conscious of the turpitude of the act he was authorizing. His disavowal of the violence committed by Abdallah, yet his bringing the Koran to his aid to enable him to profit by it with impunity, give still darker shades to this transaction; which altogether shows how immediately and widely he went wrong the moment he departed from the benevolent spirit of Christianity, which he at first endeavored to emulate. Worldly passions and worldly interests were fast getting the ascendency over that religious enthusiasm which first inspired him. As has well been observed, "the first drop of blood shed in his name in the Holy Week, displayed him a man, in whom the slime of earth had quenched the holy flame of prophecy."

CHAPTER XVII

The Battle of Beder

In the second year of the Hegira Mahomet received intelligence that his arch foe, Abu Sofian, with a troop of thirty horsemen, was conducting back to Mecca a caravan of a thousand camels, laden with the merchandise of Syria. Their route lay through the country of Medina, between the range of mountains and the sea. Mahomet determined to intercept them. About the middle of the month Ramadhan, therefore, he sallied forth with three hundred and fourteen men, of whom eighty-three were Mohadjerins, or exiles from Mecca; sixty-one Awsites, and a hundred and seventy Khazradites. Each troop had its own banner. There were but two horses in this little army,* but there were seventy fleet camels, which the troop mounted by turns, so as to make a rapid march without much fatigue.

Othman Iban Affan, the son-in-law of Mahomet, was now returned with his wife Rokaia from their exile in Abyssinia, and would have joined the enterprise, but his wife was ill almost unto death, so that he was obliged reluctantly to remain in Medina.

Mahomet for a while took the main road to Mecca, then leaving it to the left, turned toward the Red Sea and entered a fertile valley, watered by the brook Beder. Here he lay in wait near a ford, over which the caravans were accustomed to pass. He caused his men to dig a deep trench, and to divert the water therein, so that they might resort thither to slake their thirst, out of reach of the enemy.

In the meantime, Abu Sofian having received early intelligence that Mahomet had sallied forth to waylay him with a superior force, dispatched a messenger named Omair, on a fleet dromedary, to summon instant relief from Mecca. The messenger arrived at the Caaba haggard and breathless. Abu Jahl mounted the roof and sounded the alarm. All Mecca was in confusion and consternation. Henda, the wife of Abu Sofian, a woman of a fierce and intrepid nature, called upon her

---

* "The Arabs of the desert," says Burckhardt, "are not rich in horses. Among the great tribes on the Red Sea, between Akaba and Mecca, and to the south and southeast of Mecca, as far as Yemen, horses are very scarce, especially among those of the mountainous districts. The settled inhabitants of Hedjaz and Yemen are not much in the habit of keeping horses. The tribes most rich in horses are those who dwell in the comparatively fertile plains of Mesopotamia, on the banks of the river Euphrates, and on the Syrian plains." – *Burckhardt*, II. 50.

father Otha, her brother Al Walid, her uncle Shaiba, and all the warriors of her kindred, to arm and hasten to the relief of her husband.
The brothers, too, of the Koreishite slain by Abdallah Ibn Jasch, in the
valley of Naklah, seized their weapons to avenge his death. Motives of
interest were mingled with eagerness for vengeance, for most of the
Koreishites had property embarked in the caravan. In a little while a
force of one hundred horse and seven hundred camels hurried forward
on the road toward Syria. It was led by Abu Jahl, now threescore and
ten years of age, a veteran warrior of the desert, who still retained the
fire, and almost the vigor and activity of youth, combined with the rancor of old age.

While Abu Jahl, with his forces, was hurrying on in one direction,
Abu Sofian was approaching in another. On arriving at the region of
danger, he preceded his caravan a considerable distance, carefully regarding every track and foot-print. At length he came upon the track of
the little army of Mahomet. He knew it from the size of the kernels of
the dates, which the troops had thrown by the wayside as they
marched, – those of Medina being remarkable for their smallness. On
such minute signs do the Arabs depend in tracking their foes through
the deserts.

Observing the course Mahomet had taken, Abu Sofian changed his
route, and passed along the coast of the Red Sea until he considered
himself out of danger. He then sent another messenger to meet any Koreishites that might have sallied forth, and to let them know that the
caravan was safe, and they might return to Mecca.

The messenger met the Koreishites when in full march. On hearing
that the caravan was safe, they came to a halt and held council. Some
were for pushing forward and inflicting a signal punishment on Mahomet and his followers; others were for turning back. In this dilemma,
they sent a scout to reconnoitre the enemy. He brought back word that
they were about three hundred strong; this increased the desire of
those who were for battle. Others remonstrated. "Consider," said they,
"these are men who have nothing to lose; they have nothing but their
swords; not one of them will fall without slaying his man. Beside, we
have relatives among them; if we conquer, we will not be able to look
each other in the face, having slain each other's relatives." These words
were producing their effect, but the brothers of the Koreishite who had
been slain in the valley of Naklah, were instigated by Abu Jahl to cry

for revenge. That fiery old Arab seconded their appeal. "Forward!" cried he; "let us get water from the brook Beder for the feast with which we shall make merry over the escape of our caravan." The main body of the troops, therefore, elevated their standards and resumed their march, though a considerable number turned back to Mecca.

The scouts of Mahomet brought him notice of the approach of this force. The hearts of some of his followers failed them; they had come forth in the expectation of little fighting and much plunder, and were dismayed at the thoughts of such an overwhelming host; but Mahomet bade them be of good cheer, for Allah had promised him an easy victory.

The Moslems posted themselves on a rising ground, with water at the foot of it. A hut, or shelter of the branches of trees, had been hastily erected on the summit for Mahomet, and a dromedary stood before it, on which he might fly to Medina in case of defeat.

The vanguard of the enemy entered the valley panting with thirst, and hastened to the stream to drink; but Hamza, the uncle of Mahomet, set upon them with a number of his men, and slew the leader with his own hand. Only one of the vanguard escaped, who was afterwards converted to the faith.

The main body of the enemy now approached with sound of trumpet. Three Koreishite warriors advancing in front, defied the bravest of the Moslems to equal combat. Two of these challengers were Otha, the father-in-law of Abu Sofian, and Al Walid, his brother-in-law. The third challenger was Shaiba, the brother of Otha. These it will be recollected had been instigated to sally forth from Mecca, by Henda, the wife of Abu Sofian. They were all men of rank in their tribe.

Three warriors of Medina stepped forward and accepted their challenge; but they cried, "No! Let the renegades of our own city of Mecca, advance, if they dare." Upon this Hamza and Ali, the uncle and cousin of Mahomet, and Obeidah Ibn al Hareth, undertook the fight. After a fierce and obstinate contest, Hamza and Ali each slew his antagonist. They then went to the aid of Obeidah, who was severely wounded and nearly overcome by Otha. They slew the Koreishite and bore away their associate, but he presently died of his wounds.

The battle now became general. The Moslems, aware of the inferiority of their number, at first merely stood on the defensive, maintaining their position on the rising ground, and galling the enemy with flights of arrows whenever they sought to slake their intolerable thirst at the stream below. Mahomet remained in his hut on the hill, accompanied by Abu Beker, and earnestly engaged in prayer. In the course of the battle he had a paroxysm, or fell into a kind of trance. Coming to himself, he declared that God in a vision had promised him the victory. Rushing out of the hut, he caught up a handful of dust and cast it into the air toward the Koreishites, exclaiming, "May confusion light upon their faces." Then ordering his followers to charge down upon the enemy: "Fight, and fear not," cried he; "the gates of paradise are under the shade of swords. He will assuredly find instant admission, who falls fighting for the faith."

In the shock of battle which ensued, Abu Jahl, who was urging his horse into the thickest of the conflict, received a blow of a scimetar in the thigh, which brought him to the ground. Abdallah Ibn Masoud put his foot upon his breast, and while the fiery veteran was still uttering imprecations and curses on Mahomet, severed his head from his body.

The Koreishites now gave way and fled. Seventy remained dead on the field, and nearly the same number were taken prisoners. Fourteen Moslems were slain, whose names remain on record as martyrs to the faith.

This signal victory was easily to be accounted for on natural principles; the Moslems being fresh and unwearied, and having the advantage of a rising ground, and a supply of water; while the Koreishites were fatigued by a hasty march, parched with thirst, and diminished in force, by the loss of numbers who had turned back to Mecca. Moslem writers, however, attribute this early triumph of the faith to supernatural agency. When Mahomet scattered dust in the air, say they, three thousand angelic warriors in white and yellow turbans, and long dazzling robes, and mounted on black and white steeds, came rushing like a blast, and swept the Koreishites before them. Nor is this affirmed on Moslem testimony alone, but given on the word of an idolater, a peasant who was attending sheep on an adjacent hill. "I was with a companion, my cousin," said the peasant, "upon the fold of the mountain watching the conflict, and waiting to join with the conquerors and share the spoil. Suddenly, we beheld a great cloud sailing toward us, and within it were the neighing of steeds and braying of trumpets. As it approached, squadrons of angels sallied forth, and we heard the terrific voice of the archangel as he urged his mare Haizum, 'Speed! speed! Oh Haizum!' At which awful sound the heart of my companion burst with terror, and he died on the spot; and I had well nigh shared his fate."*

When the conflict was over Abdallah Ibn Masoud brought the head of Abu Jahl to Mahomet, who eyed the grisly trophy with exultation, exclaiming, "This man was the Pharaoh of our nation." The true name of this veteran warrior was Amru Ibn Hasham. The Koreishites had given him the surname of Abu 'lhoem, or Father of Wisdom, on account of his sagacity. The Moslems had changed it to Abu Jahl, Father of Folly. The latter appellation has adhered to him in history, and he is never mentioned by true believers without the ejaculation, "May he be accursed of God."

The Moslems who had fallen in battle were honorably interred; as to the bodies of the Koreishites, they were contemptuously thrown into a pit which had been digged for them. The question was how to dispose of the prisoners. Omar was for striking off their heads; but Abu Beker advised that they should be given up on ransom. Mahomet observed that Omar was like Noah, who prayed for the destruction of the guilty by the deluge; but Abu Beker was like Abraham, who interceded for the guilty. He decided on the side of mercy. But two of the prisoners were put to death; one, named Nadhar, for having ridiculed the Koran as a collection of Persian tales and fables; the other, named Okba, for the attempt upon the life of Mahomet when he first preached in the Caaba, and when he was rescued by Abu Beker. Several of the prisoners who were poor, were liberated on merely making oath never again to take up arms against Mahomet or his followers. The rest were detained until ransoms should be sent by their friends.

Among the most important of the prisoners, was Al Abbas, the uncle of Mahomet. He had been captured by Abu Yaser, a man of small stature. As the bystanders scoffed at the disparity of size, Al Abbas pre-

---

* This miraculous aid is repeatedly mentioned in the Koran, e.g.:

"God had already given you the victory at Beder, when ye were inferior in number. When thou saidst unto the faithful, Is it not enough for you that your Lord should assist you with three thousand angels, sent down from heaven? Verily, if ye persevere, and fear God, and your enemies come upon you suddenly, your Lord will assist you with five thousand angels, distinguished by their horses and attire —

    *   *   *   *   *   *   *   *   *   *   *   *

"O true believers, ye slew not those who were slain at Beder yourselves, but God slew them. Neither didst thou, O Mahomet, cast the gravel into their eyes, when thou didst seem to cast it; but God cast it." — Sale's Koran, chap. iii.

tended that he really had surrendered to a horseman of gigantic size, mounted on a steed the like of which he had never seen before. Abu Yaser would have steadily maintained the truth of his capture, but Mahomet, willing to spare the humiliation of his uncle, intimated that the captor had been aided by the angel Gabriel.

Al Abbas would have excused himself from paying ransom, alleging that he was a Moslem in heart, and had only taken part in the battle on compulsion; but his excuse did not avail. It is thought by many that he really had a secret understanding with his nephew, and was employed by him as a spy in Mecca, both before and after the battle of Beder.

Another prisoner of great importance to Mahomet was Abul Aass, the husband of his daughter Zeinab. The prophet would fain have drawn his son-in-law to him and enrolled him among his disciples, but Abul Aass remained stubborn in unbelief. Mahomet then offered to set him at liberty on condition of his returning to him his daughter. To this the infidel agreed; and Zeid, the faithful freedman of the prophet, was sent with several companions to Mecca, to bring Zeinab to Medina; in the meantime, her husband Abul Aass, remained a hostage for the fulfilment of the compact.

Before the army returned to Medina there was a division of the spoil; for, though the caravan of Abu Sofian had escaped, yet considerable booty of weapons and camels had been taken in the battle, and a large sum of money would accrue from the ransom of the prisoners. On this occasion, Mahomet ordered that the whole should be equally divided among all the Moslems engaged in the enterprise; and though it was a long-established custom among the Arabs to give a fourth part of the booty to the chief, yet he contented himself with the same share as the rest. Among the spoil which fell to his lot was a famous sword of admirable temper, called Dhu'l Fakâr, or the Piercer. He ever afterwards bore it when in battle; and his son-in-law Ali inherited it at his death.

This equal distribution of the booty caused great murmurs among the troops. Those who had borne the brunt of the fight, and had been most active in taking the spoil, complained that they had to share alike with those who had stood aloof from the affray, and with the old men who had remained to guard the camp. The dispute, observes Sale, resembles that of the soldiers of David in relation to spoils taken from the Amalekites; those who had been in the action insisting that they who tarried by the stuff should have no share of the spoil. The decision was the same – that they should share alike. (1 Samuel, ch. xxx. 21–25.) Mahomet, from his knowledge of bible history, may have been guided by this decision. The division of the spoils was an important point to settle, for a leader about to enter on a career of predatory warfare. Fortunately, he had a timely revelation shortly after his return to Mecca, regulating for the future the division of all booty gained in fighting for the faith.

Such are the particulars of the famous battle of Beder, the first victory of the Saracens under the standard of Mahomet; inconsiderable, perhaps in itself, but stupendous in its results; being the commencement of a career of victories which changed the destinies of the world.

CHAPTER XVIII

Death of the prophet's daughter Rokaia — Restoration of his daughter Zeinab — Effect of the prophet's malediction on Abu Lahab and his family — Frantic rage of Henda, the wife of Abu Sofian — Mahomet narrowly escapes assassination — Embassy of the Koreishites — The King of Abyssinia

Mahomet returned in triumph to Medina with the spoils and prisoners 'aken in his first battle. His exultation, however, was checked by domestic grief. Rokaia, his beloved daughter, so recently restored from exile, was no more. The messenger who preceded Mahomet with tidings of his victory, met the funeral train at the gate of the city, bearing her body to the tomb.

The affliction of the prophet was soothed shortly afterward by the arrival from Mecca of his daughter Zeinab, conducted by the faithful Zeid. The mission of Zeid had been attended with difficulties. The people of Mecca were exasperated by the late defeat, and the necessity of ransoming the prisoners. Zeid remained, therefore, without the walls, and sent in a message to Kenanah, the brother of Abul Aass, informing him of the compact, and appointing a place where Zeinab should be delivered into his hands. Kenanah set out to conduct her thither in a litter. On the way he was beset by a throng of Koreishites, determined to prevent the daughter of Mahomet from being restored to him. In the confusion one Habbar Ibn Aswad made a thrust at the litter with a lance, which, had not Kenanah parried it with his bow, might have proved fatal to Zeinab. Abu Sofian was attracted to the place by the noise and tumult, and rebuked Kenanah for restoring Mahomet's daughter thus publicly, as it might be construed into a weak concession; Zeinab was taken back, therefore, to her home, and Kenanah delivered her up secretly to Zeid in the course of the following night.

Mahomet was so exasperated at hearing of the attack on his daughter, that he ordered whoever should take Habbar, to burn him alive. When his rage had subsided he modified this command. "It is for God alone," said he, "to punish man with fire. If taken, let Habbar be put to death with the sword."

The recent triumph of the Moslems at Beder struck the Koreishites of Mecca with astonishment and mortification. The man so recently driven a fugitive from their walls, had suddenly started up a powerful foe. Several of their bravest and most important men had fallen beneath his sword; others were his captives, and awaited a humiliating ransom. Abu Lahab, the uncle of Mahomet, and always his vehement opposer, had been unable, from illness, to take the field. He died a few days after hearing of the victory, his death being hastened by the exasperation of his spirits. Pious Moslems, however, attribute it to the curse pronounced by Mahomet aforetime on him and his family, when he raised his hand to hurl a stone at the prophet on the hill of Safa. That curse, say they, fell heavily also on his son Otha, who had repudiated the prophet's daughter Rokaia; he was torn to pieces by a lion, in the presence of a whole caravan, when on a journey to Syria.

By no one was the recent defeat at Beder felt so severely as by Abu Sofian. He reached Mecca in safety with his caravan, it is true; but it was to hear of the triumph of the man he detested, and to find his home desolate. His wife Henda met him with frantic lamentations for the death of her father, her uncle, and her brother. Rage mingled with her grief, and she cried night and day for vengeance on Hamza and Ali, by whose hands they had fallen.*

Abu Sofian summoned two hundred fleet horsemen, each with a sack of meal at his saddle-bow, the scanty provisions of an Arab for a foray; as he sallied forth he vowed neither to anoint his head, perfume his beard, nor approach a female, until he had met Mahomet face to face. Scouring the country to within three miles of the gates of Medina, he slew two of the prophet's followers, ravaged the fields, and burnt the date-trees.

Mahomet sallied forth to meet him at the head of a superior force. Abu Sofian, regardless of his vow, did not await his approach, but turned bridle and fled. His troop clattered after him, throwing off their sacks of meal in the hurry of their flight; whence this scampering affair was derisively called "The war of the meal sacks."

Moslem writers record an imminent risk of the prophet, while yet in

---

* It is a received law among all the Arabs, that whoever sheds the blood of a man, owes blood on that account to the family of the slain person. This ancient law is sanctioned by the Koran. "O true believers, the law of retaliation is ordained to you for the slain; the free shall die for the free." The Blood revenge, or Thar, as it is termed in Arabic, is claimed by the relatives of all who have been killed in open war, and not merely of the actual homicide, but of all his relations. For those killed in wars between two tribes, the price of blood is required from the persons who were known to have actually killed them.

The Arab regards this blood revenge as one of his most sacred rights, as well as duties; no earthly consideration could induce him to give it up. He has a proverbial saying, "Were hell-fire to be my lot, I would not relinquish the *Thar.*" – See *Burckhardt's Notes*, v. i. 314.

the field on this occasion. He was one day sleeping alone at the foot of a tree, at a distance from his camp, when he was awakened by a noise, and beheld Durthur, a hostile warrior, standing over him with a drawn sword. "Oh Mahomet," cried he, "who is there now to save thee?" "God!" replied the prophet. Struck with conviction, Durthur let fall his sword, which was instantly seized upon by Mahomet. Brandishing the weapon, he exclaimed in turn, "Who is there now to save thee, Oh Durthur?" "Alas, no one!" replied the soldier. "Then learn from me to be merciful." So saying, he returned the sword. The heart of the warrior was overcome; he acknowledged Mahomet as the prophet of God, and embraced the faith.

As if the anecdote were not sufficiently marvellous, other devout Moslems affirm that the deliverance of Mahomet was through the intervention of the angel Gabriel, who, at the moment Durthur was about to strike, gave him a blow on the breast with his invisible hand, which caused him to let fall his sword.

About this time the Koreishites of Mecca bethought themselves of the relatives and disciples of Mahomet who had taken refuge from their persecutions in Abyssinia; most of whom still remained there under the protection of the Najashee or Abyssinian king. To this potentate the Koreishites sent an embassy to obtain the persons of the fugitives. One of the ambassadors was Abdallah Ibn Rabia; another was Amru Ibn Al Aass, the distinguished poet who had assailed Mahomet at the outset of his mission with lampoons and madrigals. He was now more matured in years, and as remarkable for his acute sagacity as for his poetic talents. He was still a redoubtable opponent of the faith of Islam, of which in after years he was to prove one of the bravest and most distinguished champions.

Amru and Abdallah opened their embassy in the oriental style by the parade of rich presents, and then requested, in the name of the Koreish authorities of Mecca, that the fugitives might be delivered up to them. The king was a just man, and summoned the Moslems before him to explain this new and dangerous heresy of which they were accused. Among their number was Giafar, or Jaafar, the son of Abu Taleb, and brother of Ali, consequently the cousin of Mahomet. He was a man of persuasive eloquence and a most prepossessing appearance. He stood forth on this occasion, and expounded the doctrines of Islam with zeal and power. The king, who, as has been observed, was a Nestorian

Christian, found these doctrines so similar in many respects to those of his sect, and so opposed to the gross idolatry of the Koreishites, that, so far from giving up the fugitives, he took them more especially into favor and protection, and returning to Amru and Abdallah the presents they had brought, dismissed them from his court.

CHAPTER XIX

Growing power of Mahomet – His resentment against the Jews –
Insult to an Arab damsel by the Jewish tribe of Kainoka – A
tumult – The Beni Kainoka take refuge in their castle – Subdued
and punished by confiscation and banishment – Marriage of Othman
to the prophet's daughter Omm Kolthum, and of the prophet to
Hafza

The battle of Beder had completely changed the position of Mahomet; he was now a triumphant chief of a growing power. The idolatrous tribes of Arabia were easily converted to a faith which flattered their predatory inclinations with the hope of spoil, and which, after all, professed but to bring them back to the primitive religion of their ancestors; the first cavalcade, therefore, which entered the gates of Medina with the plunder of a camp, made converts of almost all its heathen inhabitants, and gave Mahomet the control of the city. His own tone now became altered, and he spoke as a lawgiver and a sovereign. The first evidence of this change of feeling was in his treatment of the Jews, of whom there were three principal and powerful families in Medina.

All the concessions made by him to that stiff-necked race had proved fruitless; they not only remained stubborn in unbelief, but treated him and his doctrines with ridicule. Assma, the daughter of Merwân, a Jewish poetess, wrote satires against him. She was put to death by one of his fanatic disciples. Abu Afak, an Israelite, one hundred and twenty years of age, was likewise slain for indulging in satire against the prophet. Kaab Ibn Aschraf, another Jewish poet, repaired to Mecca after the battle of Beder, and endeavored to stir up the Koreishites to vengeance, reciting verses in which he extolled the virtues and bewailed the death of those of their tribe who had fallen in the battle. Such was his infatuation, that he recited these verses in public, on his return to Medina, and in the presence of some of the prophet's adherents who were related to the slain. Stung by this invidious hostility, Mahomet one day exclaimed in his anger, "Who will rid me of this son of Aschraf?" Within a few days afterwards, Kaab paid for his poetry with his life; being slain by a zealous Ansarian of the Awsite tribe.

An event at length occurred, which caused the anger of Mahomet against the Jews to break out in open hostility. A damsel of one of the pastoral tribes of Arabs who brought milk to the city, was one day in the quarter inhabited by the Beni Kainoka, or children of Kainoka, one of the three principal Jewish families. Here she was accosted by a number of young Israelites, who having heard her beauty extolled, besought her to uncover her face. The damsel refused an act contrary to the laws of propriety among her people. A young goldsmith, whose shop was hard by, secretly fastened the end of her veil to the bench on which she was sitting, so that when she rose to depart, the garment remained, and her face was exposed to view. Upon this there was laughter and scoffing among the young Israelites, and the damsel stood in the midst confounded and abashed. A Moslem present, resenting the shame put upon her, drew his sword, and thrust it through the body of the goldsmith; he in his turn was instantly slain by the Israelites. The Moslems from a neighboring quarter flew to arms, the Beni Kainoka did the same, but being inferior in numbers, took refuge in a stronghold. Mahomet interfered to quell the tumult; but, being generally exasperated against the Israelites, insisted that the offending tribe should forthwith embrace the faith. They pleaded the treaty which he had made with them on his coming to Medina, by which they were allowed the enjoyment of their religion; but he was not to be moved. For some time the Beni Kainoka refused to yield, and remained obstinately shut up in their stronghold; but famine compelled them to surrender. Abdallah Ibn Obba Solul, the leader of the Khazradites, who was a protector of this Jewish tribe, interfered in their favor, and prevented their being put to the sword; but their wealth and effects were confiscated, and they were banished to Syria, to the number of seven hundred men.

The arms and riches accruing to the prophet and his followers from this confiscation, were of great avail in the ensuing wars of the faith. Among the weapons which fell to the share of Mahomet, are enumerated three swords; Medham, the Keen, al Battar, the Trenchant, and Hatef, the Deadly. Two lances, al Monthari, the Disperser, and al Monthawi, the Destroyer. A cuirass of silver, named al Fadha, and another named al Saadia, said to have been given by Saul to David, when about to encounter Goliath. There was a bow, too, called al Catûm, or the Strong, but it did not answer to its name, for in the first battle in which the prophet used it, he drew it with such force that he broke it in pieces. In general, he used the Arabian kind of bow, with appropriate arrows and lances, and forbade his followers to use those of Persia.

Mahomet now sought no longer to conciliate the Jews; on the contrary, they became objects of his religious hostility. He revoked the regulation by which he had made Jerusalem the Kebla or point of prayer, and established Mecca in its place; towards which, ever since, the Mahometans turn their faces when performing their devotions.

The death of the prophet's daughter Rokaia had been properly deplored by her husband Othman. To console the latter for his loss,
Omar, his brother in arms, offered him, in the course of the year, his
daughter Hafza for wife. She was the widow of Hobash, a Suhamite,
eighteen years of age, and of tempting beauty, yet Othman declined
the match. Omar was indignant at what he conceived a slight to his
daughter and to himself, and complained of it to Mahomet. "Be not
grieved, Omar," replied the prophet, "a better wife is destined for Othman, and a better husband for thy daughter." He in effect gave his
own daughter Omm Kolthum to Othman; and took the fair Hafza to
wife himself. By these politic alliances he grappled both Othman and
Omar more strongly to his side, while he gratified his own inclinations
for female beauty. Hafza, next to Ayesha, was the most favored of his
wives; and was intrusted with the coffer containing the chapters and
verses of the Koran as they were revealed.

CHAPTER XX

*Henda incites Abu Sofian and the Koreishites to revenge the death
of her relations slain in the battle of Beder – The Koreishites sally
forth, followed by Henda and her female companions – Battle of
Ohod – Ferocious triumph of Henda – Mahomet consoles himself by
marrying Hend, the daughter of Omeya*

As the power of Mahomet increased in Medina, the hostility of the Koreishites in Mecca augmented in virulence. Abu Sofian held command
in the sacred city, and was incessantly urged to warfare by his wife
Henda, whose fierce spirit could take no rest, until "blood revenge" had
been wreaked on those by whom her father and brother had been
slain. Akrema, also, a son of Abu Jahl, and who inherited his father's
hatred of the prophet, clamored for vengeance. In the third year of the
Hegira, therefore, the year after the battle of Beder, Abu Sofian took
the field at the head of three thousand men, most of them Koreishites,
though there were also Arabs of the tribes of Kanana and Tehama.
Seven hundred were armed with corselets, and two hundred were
horsemen. Akrema was one of the captains, as was also Khaled Ibn al
Waled, a warrior of indomitable valor, who afterwards rose to great renown. The banners were borne in front by the race of Abd al Dar, a
branch of the tribe of Koreish, who had a hereditary right to the foremost place in council, the foremost rank in battle, and to bear the standard in the advance of the army.

In the rear of the host followed the vindictive Henda, with fifteen
principal women of Mecca, relatives of those slain in the battle of
Beder; sometimes filling the air with wailings and lamentations for the
dead; at other times animating the troops with the sound of timbrels
and warlike chants. As they passed through the village of Abwa, where
Amina the mother of Mahomet was interred, Henda was with difficulty
prevented from tearing the mouldering bones out of the grave.

Al Abbas, the uncle of Mahomet, who still resided in Mecca, and was
considered hostile to the new faith, seeing that destruction threatened
his nephew should that army come upon him by surprise, sent secretly
a swift messenger to inform him of his danger. Mahomet was at the
village of Koba, when the message reached him. He immediately hastened back to Medina, and called a council of his principal adherents.
Representing the insufficiency of their force to take the field, he gave it
as his opinion that they should await an attack in Medina, where the
very women and children could aid them by hurling stones from the

house-tops. The elder among his followers joined in his opinion; but the young men, of heady valor at all times, and elated by the late victory at Beder, cried out for a fair fight in the open field.

Mahomet yielded to their clamors, but his forces, when mustered, were scarce a thousand men; one hundred only had curaisses, and but two were horsemen. The hearts of those recently so clamorous to sally forth, now misgave them, and they would fain await the encounter within the walls. "No," replied Mahomet, "it becomes not a prophet when once he has drawn the sword to sheathe it; nor when once he has advanced, to turn back, until God has decided between him and the foe." So saying, he led forth his army. Part of it was composed of Jews and Khazradites, led by Abdallah Ibn Obba Solul. Mahomet declined the assistance of the Jews, unless they embraced the faith of Islam, and as they refused, he ordered them back to Medina; upon which their protector, Abdallah, turned back also with his Khazradites; thus reducing the army to about seven hundred men.

With this small force Mahomet posted himself upon the hill of Ohod, about six miles from Medina. His position was partly defended by rocks and the asperities of the hill, and archers were stationed to protect him in flank and rear from the attacks of cavalry. He was armed with a helmet and two shirts of mail. On his sword was engraved, "Fear brings disgrace; forward lies honor. Cowardice saves no man from his fate." As he was not prone to take an active part in battle, he confided his sword to a brave warrior, Abu Dudjana, who swore to wield it as long as it had edge and temper. For himself, he, as usual, took a commanding stand whence he might overlook the field.

The Koreishites, confident in their numbers, came marching to the foot of the hill with banners flying. Abu Sofian led the centre; there were a hundred horsemen on each wing; the left commanded by Akrema, the son of Abu Jahl, the right by Khaled Ibn al Waled. As they advanced, Henda and her companions struck their timbrels and chanted their war song; shrieking out at intervals the names of those who had been slain in the battle of Beder. "Courage, sons of Abd al Dar!" cried they to the standard-bearers. "Forward to the fight! close with the foe! strike home and spare not. Sharp be your swords and pitiless your hearts!"

Mahomet restrained the impatience of his troops; ordering them not to commence the fight, but to stand firm and maintain their advantage of the rising ground. Above all, the archers were to keep to their post, let the battle go as it might, lest the cavalry should fall upon his rear.

The horsemen of the left wing, led by Akrema, now attempted to take the Moslems in flank, but were repulsed by the archers, and retreated in confusion. Upon this Hamza set up the Moslem war-cry, Amit! amit! (Death! death!) and rushed down with his forces upon the centre. Abu Dudjana was at his right hand, armed with the sword of Mahomet, and having a red band round his head, on which was written, "Help comes from God! victory is ours!"

The enemy were staggered by the shock. Abu Dudjana dashed into the midst of them, dealing deadly blows on every side, and exclaiming, "The sword of God and his prophet!" Seven standard-bearers, of the race of Abd el Dar, were, one after the other, struck down, and the centre began to yield. The Moslem archers, thinking the victory secure, forgot the commands of Mahomet, and leaving their post, dispersed in quest of spoil, crying "Booty! booty!" Upon this Khaled, rallying the horse, got possession of the ground abandoned by the archers, attacked the Moslems in rear, put some to flight, and threw the rest in confusion. In the midst of the confusion a horseman, Obbij Ibn Chalaf by name, pressed through the throng, crying, "Where is Mahomet? There is no safety while he lives." But Mahomet, seizing a lance from an attendant, thrust it through the throat of the idolater, who fell dead from his horse. "Thus," says the pious Al Jannabi, "died this enemy of God, who, some years before, had menaced the prophet, saying, 'I shall find a day to slay thee.' 'Have a care,' was the reply; 'if it please Allah, thou thyself shall fall beneath my hand.' "

In the midst of the melee a stone from a sling struck Mahomet on the mouth, cutting his lip and knocking out one of his front teeth; he was wounded in the face also by an arrow, the iron head of which remained in the wound. Hamza, too, while slaying a Koreishite, was transfixed by the lance of Wacksa, an Ethiopian slave, who had been promised his freedom if he should revenge the death of his master, slain by Hamza in the battle of Beder. Mosaab Ibn Omair, also, who bore the standard of Mahomet, was laid low, but Ali seized the sacred banner and bore it aloft amidst the storm of battle.

As Mosaab resembled the prophet in person, a shout was put up by the enemy that Mahomet was slain. The Koreishites were inspired with redoubled ardor at the sound; the Moslems fled in despair, bearing

with them Abu Beker and Omar, who were wounded. Raab, the son of
Malek, however, beheld Mahomet lying among the wounded in a
ditch, and knew him by his armor. "Oh believers!" cried he, "the
prophet of God yet lives. To the rescue! to the rescue!" Mahomet was
drawn forth and borne up the hill to the summit of a rock, where the
Moslems prepared for a desperate defence. The Koreishites, however,
thinking Mahomet slain, forbore to pursue them, contenting themselves
with plundering and mutilating the dead. Henda and her female companions were foremost in the savage work of vengeance; and the ferocious heroine sought to tear out and devour the heart of Hamza. Abu
Sofian bore a part of the mangled body upon his lance, and descending
the hill in triumph, exclaimed, exultingly, "War has its vicissitudes. The
battle of Ohod succeeds to the battle of Beder."

The Koreishites having withdrawn, Mahomet descended from the
rock and visited the field of battle. At sight of the body of his uncle
Hamza, so brutally mangled and mutilated, he vowed to inflict like
outrage on seventy of the enemy when in his power. His grief, we are
told, was soothed by the angel Gabriel, who assured him that Hamza
was enregistered an inhabitant of the seventh heaven, by the title of
"The lion of God and of his prophet."

The bodies of the slain were interred two and two, and three and
three, in the places where they had fallen. Mahomet forbade his followers to mourn for the dead by cutting off their hair, rending their
garments, and the other modes of lamentation usual among the Arabs;
but he consented that they should weep for the dead, as tears relieve
the overladen heart.

The night succeeding the battle was one of great disquietude, lest
the Koreishites should make another attack; or should surprise Medina.
On the following day he marched in the direction of that city, hovering
near the enemy, and on the return of night lighting numerous watch-
fires. Abu Sofian, however, had received intelligence that Mahomet was
still alive. He felt himself too weak to attack the city, therefore, while
Mahomet was in the field, and might come to its assistance; and he
feared that the latter might be reinforced by its inhabitants, and seek
him with superior numbers. Contenting himself, therefore, with the recent victory, he made a truce with the Moslems for a year, and returned in triumph to Mecca.

Mahomet sought consolation for this mortifying defeat by taking to
himself another wife, Hend, the daughter of Omeya, a man of great

influence. She was a widow, and had, with her husband, been among the number of the fugitives in Abyssinia. She was now twenty-eight years of age, and had a son named Salma, whence she was commonly called Omm Salma, or the Mother of Salma. Being distinguished for grace and beauty, she had been sought by Abu Beker and Omar, but without success. Even Mahomet at first met with difficulty. "Alas!" said she, "what happiness can the prophet of God expect with me? I am no longer young; I have a son, and I am of a jealous disposition." "As to thy age," replied Mahomet, "thou art much younger than I. As to thy son, I will be a father to him: as to thy jealous disposition, I will pray Allah to root it from thy heart."

A separate dwelling was prepared for the bride, adjacent to the mosque. The household goods, as stated by a Moslem writer, consisted of a sack of barley, a handmill, a pan, and a pot of lard or butter. Such were as yet the narrow means of the prophet; or rather, such the frugality of his habits and the simplicity of Arab life.

CHAPTER XXI

Treachery of certain Jewish tribes; their punishment – Devotion of the prophet's freedman Zeid; divorces his beautiful wife Zeinab, that she may become the wife of the prophet

The defeat of Mahomet at the battle of Ohod, acted for a time unfavorably to his cause among some of the Arab and Jewish tribes, as was evinced by certain acts of perfidy. The inhabitants of two towns, Adhal and Kara, sent a deputation to him, professing an inclination to embrace the faith, and requesting missionaries to teach them its doctrines. He accordingly sent six disciples to accompany the deputation; but on the journey, while reposing by the brook Radje within the boundaries of the Hodseitites, the deputies fell upon the unsuspecting Moslems, slew four of them, and carried the other two to Mecca, where they gave them up to the Koreishites, who put them to death.

A similar act of treachery was practised by the people of the province of Nadjed. Pretending to be Moslems, they sought succor from Mahomet against their enemies. He sent a number of his followers to their aid, who were attacked by the Beni Suleim or Suleimites, near the brook Manna, about four days' journey from Medina, and slain almost to a man. One of the Moslems, Amru Ibn Omeya, escaped the carnage and made for Medina. On the way he met two unarmed Jews of the Beni Amir; either mistaking these for enemies, or provoked to wanton rage by the death of his comrades, he fell upon them and slew them. The tribe, who were at peace with Mahomet, called upon him for redress. He referred the matter to the mediation of another Jewish tribe, the Beni Nadher, who had rich possessions and a castle, called Zohra, within three miles of Medina. This tribe had engaged by treaty, when he came a fugitive from Mecca, to maintain a neutrality between him and his opponents. The chief of this tribe being now applied to as a mediator, invited Mahomet to an interview. He went, accompanied by Abu Beker, Omar, Ali, and a few others. A repast was spread in the open air before the mansion of the chief. Mahomet, however, received private information that he had been treacherously decoyed hither, and was to be slain as he sat at the repast: it is said that he was to be crushed by a millstone, flung from the terraced roof of the house. Without intimating his knowledge of the treason, he left the company abruptly, and hastened back to Medina.

His rage was now kindled against the whole race of Nadher, and he ordered them to leave the country within ten days on pain of death. They would have departed, but Abdallah the Khazradite secretly persuaded them to stay by promising them aid. He failed in his promise. The Beni Nadher, thus disappointed by the "Chief of the Hypocrites," shut themselves up in their castle of Zohra, where they were besieged by Mahomet, who cut down and burnt the date-trees, on which they depended for supplies. At the end of six days they capitulated, and were permitted to depart, each with a camel load of effects, arms excepted. Some were banished to Syria, others to Khaïbar, a strong Jewish city and fortress, distant several days' journey from Medina. As the tribe was wealthy, there was great spoil, which Mahomet took entirely to himself. His followers demurred that this was contrary to the law of partition revealed in the Koran; but he let them know that according to another revelation, all booty gained, like the present, without striking a blow, was not won by man, but was a gift from God, and must be delivered over to the prophet to be expended by him in good works, and the relief of orphans, of the poor, and the traveller. Mahomet in effect did not appropriate it to his own benefit, but shared it among the Mohadjerins, or exiles from Mecca; two Nadherite Jews who had embraced Islamism, and two or three Ansarians or Auxiliaries of Medina, who had proved themselves worthy, and were poor.

We forbear to enter into details of various petty expeditions of Mahomet about this time, one of which extended to the neighborhood of Tabuc, on the Syrian frontier, to punish a horde which had plundered the caravans of Medina. These expeditions were checkered in their results, though mostly productive of booty; which now began to occupy the minds of the Moslems, almost as much as the propagation of the faith. The spoils thus suddenly gained may have led to riot and debauchery, as we find a revelation of the passage of the Koran, forbidding wine and games of hazard, those fruitful causes of strife and insubordination in predatory camps.

During this period of his career, Mahomet in more than one instance narrowly escaped falling by the hand of an assassin. He himself is charged with the use of insidious means to rid himself of an enemy; for it is said that he sent Amru Ibn Omeya on a secret errand to Mecca, to assassinate Abu Sofian, but that the plot was discovered, and the assassin only escaped by rapid flight. The charge, however, is not well substantiated, and is contrary to his general character and conduct.

If Mahomet had relentless enemies, he had devoted friends, an instance of which we have in the case of his freedman and adopted son Zeid Ibn Hareth. He had been one of the first converts to the faith, and one of its most valiant champions. Mahomet consulted him on all occasions, and employed him in his domestic concerns. One day he entered his house with the freedom with which a father enters the dwelling of a son. Zeid was absent, but Zeinab his wife, whom he had recently married, was at home. She was the daughter of Djasch, of the country of Kaiba, and considered the fairest of her tribe. In the privacy of home she had laid aside her veil and part of her attire, so that her beauty stood revealed to the gaze of Mahomet on his sudden entrance. He could not refrain from expressions of wonder and admiration, to which she made no reply, but repeated them all to her husband on his return. Zeid knew the amorous susceptibility of Mahomet, and saw that he had been captivated by the beauty of Zeinab. Hastening after him, he offered to repudiate his wife; but the prophet forbade it as contrary to the law. The zeal of Zeid was not to be checked; he loved his beautiful wife, but he venerated the prophet, and he divorced himself without delay. When the requisite term of separation had elapsed, Mahomet accepted, with gratitude, this pious sacrifice. His nuptials with Zeinab surpassed in splendor all his other marriages. His doors were thrown open to all comers; they were feasted with the flesh of sheep and lambs, with cakes of barley, with honey, and fruits, and favorite beverages; so they ate and drank their fill and then departed – railing against the divorce as shameful, and the marriage as incestuous.

At this critical juncture was revealed that part of the thirty-third chapter of the Koran, distinguishing relatives by adoption from relatives by blood, according to which there was no sin in marrying one who had been the wife of an adopted son. This timely revelation pacified the faithful; but, to destroy all shadow of a scruple, Mahomet revoked his adoption, and directed Zeid to resume his original appellation of Ibn Hareth, after his natural father. The beautiful Zeinab, however, boasted thenceforth a superiority over the other wives of the prophet on the score of the revelation, alleging that her marriage was ordained by heaven.*

* This was Mahomet's second wife of the name of Zeinab; the first, who had died some time previous, was the daughter of Chuzeima.

CHAPTER XXII

Expedition of Mahomet against the Beni Mostalek – He espouses Barra, a captive – Treachery of Abdallah Ibn Obba – Ayesha slandered – Her vindication – Her innocence proved by a revelation

Among the Arab tribes which ventured to take up arms against Mahomet after his defeat at Ohod, were the Beni Mostalek, a powerful race of Koreishite origin. Mahomet received intelligence of their being assembled in warlike guise under their prince Al Hareth, near the wells of Moraïsi, in the territory of Kedaid, and within five miles of the Red Sea. He immediately took the field at the head of a chosen band of the faithful, accompanied by numbers of the Khazradites, led by their chief Abdallah Ibn Obba. By a rapid movement he surprised the enemy; Al Hareth was killed at the onset by the flight shot of an arrow; his troops fled in confusion after a brief resistance, in which a few were slain. Two hundred prisoners, five thousand sheep, and one thousand camels, were the fruits of this easy victory. Among the captives was Barra, the daughter of Al Hareth, and wife to a young Arab of her kin. In the division of the spoil she fell to the lot of Thabet Ibn Reis, who demanded a high ransom. The captive appealed to Mahomet against this extortion, and prayed that the ransom might be mitigated. The prophet regarded her with eyes of desire, for she was fair to look upon. "I can serve thee better," said he, "than by abating thy ransom: be my wife." The beautiful Barra gave ready consent; her ransom was paid by the prophet to Thabet; her kindred were liberated by the Moslems, to whose lot they had fallen; most of them embraced the faith, and Barra became the wife of Mahomet after his return to Medina.

After the battle, the troops crowded round the wells of Moraïsi to assuage their thirst. In the press a quarrel rose between some of the Mohadjerins, or exiles of Mecca, and the Khazradites, in which one of the latter received a blow. His comrades rushed to revenge the insult, and blood would have been shed but for the interference of Mahomet. The Khazradites remained incensed, and other of the people of Medina made common cause with them. Abdallah Ibn Obba, eager to take advantage of every circumstance adverse to the rising power of Mahomet, drew his kindred and townsfolk apart. "Behold," said he, "the insults you have brought upon yourselves by harboring these fugitive Koreishites. You have taken them to your houses, and given them your goods, and now they turn upon and maltreat you. They would make

113

themselves your masters even in your own house; but by Allah, when we return to Medina, we will see which of us is strongest."

Secret word was brought to Mahomet of this seditious speech. Omar counselled him at once to make way with Abdallah; but the prophet feared to excite the vengeance of the kindred and adherents of the powerful Khazradite. To leave no time for mutiny, he set off immediately on the homeward march, although it was in the heat of the day, and continued on throughout the night, nor halted until the following noon, when the wearied soldiery cared for nothing but repose.

On arriving at Medina, he called Abdallah to account for his seditious expressions. He flatly denied them, pronouncing the one who had accused him a liar. A revelation from heaven, however, established the charge against him and his adherents. "These are the men," says the Koran, "who say to the inhabitants of Medina, do not bestow any thing on the refugees who are with the apostle of God, that they may be compelled to separate from him. They say, verily, if we return to Medina, the worthier will expel thence the meaner. God curse them! how are they turned aside from the truth."

Some of the friends of Abdallah, convinced by this revelation, advised him to ask pardon of the prophet; but he spurned their counsel. "You have already," said he, "persuaded me to give this man my countenance and friendship, and now you would have me put myself beneath his very feet."

Nothing could persuade him that Mahomet was not an idolater at heart, and his revelations all imposture and deceit. He considered him, however, a formidable rival, and sought in every way to injure and annoy him. To this implacable hostility is attributed a scandalous story which he propagated about Ayesha, the favorite wife of the prophet.

It was the custom with Mahomet always to have one of his wives with him, on his military expeditions, as companion and solace; she was taken by lot, and on the recent occasion the lot had fallen on Ayesha. She travelled in a litter, inclosed by curtains, and borne on the back of a camel, which was led by an attendant. On the return homeward the army, on one occasion, coming to a halt, the attendants of Ayesha were astonished to find the litter empty. Before they had recovered from their surprise, she arrived on a camel, led by a youthful Arab named Safwan Ibn al Moattel. This circumstance having come to the knowledge of Abdallah, he proclaimed it to the world after his return to Medina, affirming that Ayesha had been guilty of wantonness with the youthful Safwan.

The story was eagerly caught up and circulated by Hamna, the sister of the beautiful Zeinab, whom Mahomet had recently espoused, and who hoped to benefit her sister by the downfall of her deadly rival Ayesha; it was echoed also by Mistah, a kinsman of Abu Beker, and was celebrated in satirical verses by a poet named Hasan.

It was some time before Ayesha knew of the scandal thus circulating at her expense. Sickness had confined her to the house on her return to Medina, and no one ventured to tell her of what she was accused. She remarked, however, that the prophet was stern and silent, and no longer treated her with his usual tenderness. On her recovery, she heard with consternation the crime alleged against her, and protested her innocence. The following is her version of the story.

The army, on its homeward march, had encamped not far from Medina, when orders were given in the night to march. The attendants, as usual, brought a camel before the tent of Ayesha, and placing the litter on the ground, retired until she could take her seat within it. As she was about to enter, she missed her necklace, and returned into the tent to seek it. In the meantime the attendants lifted the litter upon the camel and strapped it fast, not perceiving that it was empty; she being slender and of little weight. When she returned from seeking the necklace, the camel was gone, and the army was on the march; whereupon she wrapped herself in her mantle and sat down, trusting that, when her absence should be discovered, some persons would be sent back in quest of her.

While thus seated, Safwan Ibn al Moattel, the young Arab, being one of the rear-guard, came up, and, recognizing her, accosted her with the usual Moslem salutation. "To God we belong, and to God we must return! Wife of the prophet, why dost thou remain behind?"

Ayesha made no reply, but drew her veil closer over her face. Safwan then alighted, aided her to mount the camel, and, taking the bridle, hastened to rejoin the army. The sun had risen, however, before he overtook it, just without the walls of Medina.

This account, given by Ayesha, and attested by Safwan Ibn al Moattel, was satisfactory to her parents and particular friends; but was scoffed at by Abdallah and his adherents, "the Hypocrites." Two parties thus arose on the subject, and great strife ensued. As to Ayesha, she shut herself up within her dwelling, refusing all food, and weeping day and night in the bitterness of her soul.

Mahomet was sorely troubled in mind, and asked counsel of Ali in his perplexity. The latter made light of the affair, observing that his

misfortune was the frequent lot of man. The prophet was but little consoled by his suggestion. He remained separated from Ayesha for a
month; but his heart yearned toward her; not merely on account of her
beauty, but because he loved her society. In a paroxysm of grief, he
fell into one of those trances, which unbelievers have attributed to epilepsy; in the course of which he received a seasonable revelation,
which will be found in a chapter of the Koran. It was to this effect.

They who accuse a reputable female of adultery, and produce not
four witnesses of the fact, shall be scourged with fourscore stripes, and
their testimony rejected. As to those who have made the charge against
Ayesha, have they produced four witnesses thereof? If they have not,
they are liars in the sight of God. Let them receive, therefore, the punishment of their crime.

The innocence of the beautiful Ayesha being thus miraculously made
manifest, the prophet took her to his bosom with augmented affection.
Nor was he slow in dealing the prescribed castigation. It is true, Abdallah Ibn Obba was too powerful a personage to be subjected to the
scourge, but it fell the heavier on the shoulders of his fellow calumnia-
tors. The poet Hasan was cured for some time of his propensity to
make satirical verses, nor could Hamna, though a female, and of great
personal charms, escape the infliction of stripes; for Mahomet observed
that such beauty should have been accompanied by a gentler nature.

The revelation at once convinced the pious Ali of the purity of Ayesha; but she never forgot nor forgave that he had doubted; and the
hatred thus implanted in her bosom, was manifested to his great detri-
ment in many of the most important concerns of his after life.

CHAPTER XXIII

The battle of the Moat – Bravery of Saad Ibn Moad – Defeat of the Koreishites – Capture of the Jewish castle of Koraida – Saad decides as to the punishment of the Jews – Mahomet espouses Rehana, a Jewish captive – His life endangered by sorcery; saved by a revelation of the angel Gabriel

During the year of truce which succeeded the battle of Ohod, Abu Sofian, the restless chief of the Koreishites, formed a confederacy with the Arab tribe of Ghatafan and other tribes of the desert, as well as with many of the Jews of the race of Nadher, whom Mahomet had driven from their homes. The truce being ended, he prepared to march upon Medina, with these confederates, their combined forces amounting to ten thousand men.

Mahomet had early intelligence of the meditated attack, but his late reverse at Ohod made him wary of taking the field against such numbers; especially as he feared the enemy might have secret allies in Medina; where he distrusted the Jewish inhabitants and the Hypocrites, the partisans of Abdallah Ibn Obba, who were numerous and powerful.

Great exertions were now made to put the city in a state of defence. Salmân the Persian, who had embraced the faith, advised that a deep moat should be digged at some distance beyond the wall, on the side on which the enemy would approach. This mode of defence, hitherto unused in Arabia, was eagerly adopted by Mahomet; who set a great number of men to dig the moat, and even assisted personally in the labor. Many miracles are recorded of him during the progress of this work. At one time, it is said, he fed a great multitude from a single basket of dates; which remained full after all were satisfied. At another time he feasted a thousand men upon a roasted lamb and a loaf of barley bread; yet enough remained for all his fellow-laborers in the moat. Nor must we omit to note the wonderful blows which he gave to a rock, with an iron mallet; striking off sparks which in one direction lighted up all Yemen, or Arabia the Happy; in another, revealed the imperial palace of Constantinople; and in a third, illumined the towers of the royal residence of Persia; all signs and portents of the future conquests of Islam.

Scarcely was the moat completed when the enemy appeared in great force on the neighboring hills. Leaving Ibn Omm Mactum, a trusty officer, to command in the city, and keep a vigilant eye on the disaffected, Mahomet sallied forth with three thousand men, whom he formed in battle array, having the deep moat in front. Abu Sofian advanced confidently with his combined force of Koreishites and Ghatafanites, but was unexpectedly checked by the moat, and by a galling fire from the Moslems drawn up beyond it. The enemy now encamped; the Koreishites in the lower part of the valley, and the Ghatafanites, in the upper; and for some days the armies remained on each side of the moat, keeping up a distant combat with slings and stones, and flights of arrows.

In the meantime, spies brought word to Mahomet that a Jewish tribe, the Beni Koraida, who had a strong castle near the city, and had made a covenant of peace with him, were in secret league with the enemy. He now saw the difficulty, with his scanty forces, to man the whole extent of the moat; to guard against a perfidious attack from the Koraidites; and to maintain quiet in the city where the Jews must have secret confederates. Summoning a council of war, he consulted with his captains on the policy of bribing the Ghatafanites to a separate peace, by offering them a third of the date-harvest of Medina. Upon this, Saad Ibn Moad, a stout leader of the Awsites of Medina, demanded: "Do you propose this by the command of Allah, or is it an idea of your own?" "If it had been a command of Allah," replied Mahomet, "I should never have asked your advice. I see you pressed by enemies on every side, and I seek to break their confederacy." "Oh prophet of God!" rejoined Saad, "when we were fellow-idolaters with these people of Ghatafan, they got none of our dates without paying for them; and shall we give them up gratuitously now that we are of the true faith, and led by thee? No, by Allah! if they want our dates they must win them with their swords."

The stout Saad had his courage soon put to the proof. A prowling party of Koreishite horsemen, among whom was Akrema the son of Abu Jahl, and Amru, uncle of Mahomet's first wife Cadijah, discovered a place where the moat was narrow, and putting spurs to their steeds succeeded in leaping over, followed by some of their comrades. They then challenged the bravest of the Moslems to equal combat. The challenge was accepted by Saad Ibn Moad, by Ali, and several of their companions. Ali had a close combat with Amru; they fought on horseback and on foot, until, grappling with each other, they rolled in the dust. In the end, Ali was victorious and slew his foe. The general conflict was maintained with great obstinacy; several were slain on both

sides, and Saad Ibn Moad was severely wounded. At length the Koreishites gave way, and spurred their horses to recross the moat. The
steed of one of them, Nawfal Ibn Abdallah, leaped short; his rider was
assailed with stones while in the moat, and defied the Moslems to attack him with nobler weapons. In an instant Ali sprang down into the
moat, and Nawfal soon fell beneath his sword. Ali then joined his companions in pursuit of the retreating foe, and wounded Akrema with a
javelin. This skirmish was dignified with the name of the Battle of the
Moat.

Mahomet, still unwilling to venture a pitched battle, sent Rueim, a
secretly converted Arab of the tribe of Ghatafan, to visit the camps of
the confederates and artfully to sow dissensions among them. Rueim
first repaired to the Koraidites, with whom he was in old habits of
friendship. "What folly is this," said he, "to suffer yourselves to be
drawn by the Koreishites of Mecca into their quarrel. Bethink you how
different is your situation from theirs. If defeated, they have only to
retreat to Mecca, and be secure. Their allies from the desert will also
retire to their distant homes, and you will be left to bear the whole
brunt of the vengeance of Mahomet and the people of Medina. Before
you make common cause with them, therefore, let them pledge themselves and give hostages, never to draw back until they have broken
the power of Mahomet."

He then went to the Koreishites and the tribe of Ghatafan, and
warned them against confiding in the Jews of Koraida, who intended to
get hostages from them, and deliver them up into the hands of Mahomet.

The distrust thus artfully sown among the confederates soon produced its effects. Abu Sofian sent word on Friday evening, to the Koraidites, to be ready to join next morning in a general assault. The Jews
replied, that the following day was their Sabbath, on which they could
not engage in battle; at the same time they declined to join in any hostile act, unless their allies should give hostages to stand by them to the
end.

The Koreishites and Ghatafanites were now convinced of the perfidy
of the Koraidites, and dared not venture upon the meditated attack,
lest these should fall upon them in the rear. While they lay idly in their
camp a cold storm came on, with drenching rain and sweeping blasts
from the desert. Their tents were blown down; their camp-fires were
extinguished; in the midst of the uproar, the alarm was given that Ma-

homet had raised the storm by enchantment, and was coming upon them with his forces. All now was panic and confusion. Abu Sofian, finding all efforts vain to produce order, mounted his camel in despair, and gave the word to retreat. The confederates hurried off from the scene of tumult and terror, the Koreishites towards Mecca, the others to their homes in the desert.

Abu Sofian, in rage and mortification, wrote a letter to Mahomet, upbraiding him with his cowardice in lurking behind a ditch, a thing unknown in Arabian warfare; and threatening to take his revenge on some future day, when they might meet in open fight, as in the field of Ohod. Mahomet hurled back a defiance, and predicted that the day was approaching when he would break in pieces the idols of the Koreishites.

The invaders having disappeared, Mahomet turned to take vengeance on the Beni Koraida; who shut themselves up in their castle, and withstood a siege of many days. At length, pinched by famine, they implored the intercession of their ancient friends and protectors, the Awsites. The latter entreated the prophet to grant these Hebrews the same terms he had formerly granted to the Beni Kainoka, at the prayer of Abdallah the Khazradite. Mahomet reflected a moment, and offered to leave their fate to the decision of Saad Ibn Moad, the Awsite chief. The Koraidites gladly agreed, knowing him to have been formerly their friend. They accordingly surrendered themselves, to the number of seven hundred, and were conducted in chains to Medina. Unfortunately for them, Saad considered their perfidious league with the enemy as one cause of the recent hostility. He was still smarting with the wound received in the battle of the Moat, and in his moments of pain and anger had repeatedly prayed that his life might be spared to see vengeance wreaked on the Koraidites. Such was the state of his feelings when summoned to decide upon their fate.

Being a gross, full-blooded man, he was with difficulty helped upon an ass, propped up by a leathern cushion, and supported in his seat until he arrived at the tribunal of justice. Before ascending it, he exacted an oath from all present to abide by his decision. The Jews readily took it, anticipating a favorable sentence. No sooner was he helped into the tribunal, than, extending his hand, he condemned the men to death, the women and children to slavery, and their effects to be shared among the victors.

The wretched Jews looked aghast, but there was no appeal. They were conducted to a public place since called the Market of the Koraidites, where great graves had been digged. Into these they were compelled to descend, one by one, their prince Hoya Ibn Ahktab among the number, and were successively put to death. Thus the prayer of Saad Ibn Moad for vengeance on the Koraidites was fully gratified. He witnessed the execution of the men he had condemned, but such was his excitement that his wound broke out afresh, and he died shortly afterwards.

In the Castle of Koraida was found a great quantity of pikes, lances, cuirasses, and other armor; and its lands were covered with flocks and herds and camels. In dividing the spoil each foot-soldier had one lot, each horseman three; two for his horse, and one for himself. A fifth part of the whole was set apart for the prophet.

The most precious prize in the eyes of Mahomet was Rihana, daughter of Simeon, a wealthy and powerful Jew; and the most beautiful female of her tribe. He took her to himself, and, having converted her to the faith, added her to the number of his wives.

But, though thus susceptible of the charms of the Israelitish women, Mahomet became more and more vindictive in his hatred of the men; no longer putting faith in their covenants, and suspecting them of the most insidious attempts upon his life. Moslem writers attribute to the spells of Jewish sorcerers a long and languishing illness, with which he was afflicted about this time, and which seemed to defy all remedy. They describe the very charm by which it was produced. It was prepared, say they, by a Jewish necromancer from the mountains, aided by his daughters, who were equally skilled in the diabolic art. They formed a small waxen effigy of Mahomet; wound round it some of his hair, and thrust through it eleven needles. They then made eleven knots in a bow-string, blowing with their breaths on each; and, winding the string round the effigy, threw the whole into a well.

Under the influence of this potent spell Mahomet wasted away, until his friend, the angel Gabriel, revealed the secret to him in a vision. On awaking, he sent Ali to the well, where the image was discovered. When it was brought to Mahomet, continues the legend, he repeated over it the two last chapters of the Koran, which had been communicated to him in the recent vision. They consist of eleven verses, and are to the following purport.

In the name of the all merciful God! I will fly for refuge to the Lord of the light of day.

That he may deliver me from the danger of beings and things created by himself.

From the dangers of the darksome night, and of the moon when in eclipse.

From the danger of sorcerers, who tie knots and blow on them with their breath.

From the danger of the envious, who devise deadly harm.

I will fly for refuge to Allah, the Lord of men.

To Allah, the King of men.

To Allah, the God of men.

That he may deliver me from the evil spirit who flies at the mention of his holy name.

Who suggests evil thoughts into the hearts of the children of men.

And from the evil Genii, and men who deal in magic.

At the repetition of each one of these verses, says the legend, a knot of the bow-string came loose, a needle fell from the effigy, and Mahomet gained strength. At the end of the eleventh verse he rose, renovated in health and vigor, as one restored to freedom after having been bound with cords.

The two final chapters of the Koran, which comprise these verses, are entitled the amulets, and considered by the superstitious Moslems effectual talismans against sorcery and magic charms.

The conduct of Mahomet in the affair narrated in this chapter, has been censured as weak and vacillating, and deficient in military decision, and his measures as wanting in true greatness of mind, and the following circumstances are adduced to support these charges. When threatened with violence from without, and perfidy from within, he is for bribing a part of his confederate foes to a separate peace; but suffers himself to be, in a manner, hectored out of this crafty policy by Saad Ibn Moad; yet, subsequently, he resorts to a scheme still more subtle and crafty, by which he sows dissension among his enemies. Above all, his conduct towards the Jews has been strongly reprobated. His referring the appeal of the Beni Koraida for mercy, to the decision of one whom he knew to be bent on their destruction, has been stigmatized as cruel mockery; and the massacre of those unfortunate men in the market-place of Medina, is pronounced one of the darkest pages of his history. In fact, his conduct towards this race from the time that he had power in his hands, forms an exception to the general tenor of his disposition, which was forgiving and humane. He may have been especially provoked against them by proofs of treachery and deadly rancor on their part; but we see in this, as in other parts of his policy in this part of his career, instances of that worldly alloy which at times was debasing his spirit, now that he had become the Apostle of the Sword.

CHAPTER XXIV

Mahomet undertakes a pilgrimage to Mecca – Evades Khaled and a troop of horse sent against him – Encamps near Mecca – Negotiates with the Koreishites for permission to enter and complete his pilgrimage – Treaty for ten years, by which he is permitted to make a yearly visit of three days – He returns to Medina

Six years had now elapsed since the flight of Mahomet from Mecca. As that city was sacred in the eyes of the Arabs and their great point of pilgrimage, his long exile from it, and his open warfare with the Koreishites, who had charge of the Caaba, prejudiced him in the opinion of many of the tribes, and retarded the spread of his doctrines. His followers, too, who had accompanied him in his flight, languished once more to see their native home, and there was danger of their faith becoming enfeebled under a protracted exile.

Mahomet felt more and more the importance of linking the sacred city with his religion, and maintaining the ancient usages of his race. Besides, he claimed but to be a reformer, anxious to restore the simplicity and purity of the patriarchal faith. The month Doul Kaada was at hand, the month of pilgrimage, when there was a truce to warfare, and enemies might meet in peace within the holy boundaries. A timely vision assured Mahomet that he and his followers might safely avail themselves of the protection of this venerable custom to revisit the ancient shrines of Arabian worship. The revelation was joyfully received by his followers, and in the holy month he set forth from Medina on his pilgrimage, at the head of fourteen hundred men; partly Mohadjerins or Fugitives, and partly Ansarians or Auxiliaries. They took with them seventy camels to be slain in sacrifice at the Caaba. To manifest publicly that they came in peace and not in war, they halted at Dsu Huleifa, a village about a day's journey from Medina, where they laid aside all their weapons, excepting their sheathed swords, and thence continued on in pilgrim garb.

In the meantime a confused rumor of this movement had reached Mecca. The Koreishites, suspecting hostilities, sent forth Khaled Ibn Waled with a powerful troop of horse, to take post in a valley about two days' journey from Mecca, and check the advance of the Moslems.

Mahomet, hearing that the main road was thus barred against him, took a rugged and difficult route through the defiles of the mountains, and, avoiding Khaled and his forces, descended into the plain near Mecca; where he encamped at Hodeïba, within the sacred boundaries.

Hence he sent assurances to the Koreishites of his peaccable intentions, and claimed the immunities and rights of pilgrimage.

Envoys from the Koreishites visited his camp to make observations. They were struck with the reverence with which he was regarded by his followers. The water with which he performed his ablutions became sanctified; a hair falling from his head, or the paring of a nail, was caught up as a precious relic. One of the envoys, in the course of conversation, unconsciously touched the flowing beard of the prophet; he was thrust back by the disciples, and warned of the impiety of the act. In making his report to the Koreishites on his return, "I have seen the king of Persia, and the emperor of Constantinople, surrounded by their courts," said he, "but never did I behold a sovereign so revered by his subjects, as is Mahomet by his followers."

The Koreishites were the more loth to admit into their city an adversary to their sect, so formidable in his influence over the minds and affections of his fellow-men. Mahomet sent repeated missions to treat for a safe access to the sacred shrines, but in vain. Othman Ibn Affan, his son-in-law, was his last envoy. Several days elapsed without his return, and it was rumored that he was slain. Mahomet determined to revenge his fall. Standing under a tree, and summoning his people around him, he exacted an oath to defend him even to the death, and never to desert the standard of the faith. This ceremony is known among Mahometans, by the name of the Spontaneous Inauguration.

The reappearance of Othman in the camp, restored tranquillity. He was accompanied by Solhail, an ambassador from the Koreishites, to arrange a treaty of peace. They perceived the impolicy of warring with a man whose power was incessantly increasing, and who was obeyed with such fanatic devotion. The treaty proposed was for ten years; during which time Mahomet and his adherents were to have free access to Mecca as pilgrims, there to remain, three days at a time, in the exercise of their religious rites. The terms were readily accepted, and Ali was employed to draw up the treaty. Mahomet dictated the words. "Write," said he, "these are the conditions of peace made by Mahomet the apostle of God." "Hold!" cried Solhail, the ambassador, "had I believed thee to be the apostle of God, I should never have taken up arms against thee. Write, therefore, simply thy name, and the name of thy father." Mahomet was fain to comply, for he felt he was not sufficiently in force at this moment to contend about forms; so he merely denominated himself in the treaty, Mahomet Ibn Abdallah (Mahomet the son of Abdallah), an abnegation which gave some little scandal to his followers. Their discontent was increased when he ordered them to shave their heads, and to sacrifice on the spot the camels brought to be offered up at the Caaba, as it showed he had not the intention of entering Mecca; these rites being properly done at the conclusion of the ceremonials of pilgrimage. They reminded him of his vision which promised a safe entrance of the sacred city; he replied, that the present treaty was an earnest of its fulfilment, which would assuredly take place on the following year. With this explanation they had to content themselves; and having performed the ceremony, and made the sacrifice prescribed, the camp was broken up, and the pilgrim host returned, somewhat disappointed and dejected, to Medina.

CHAPTER XXV

Expedition against the city of Khaïbar; siege – Exploits of Mahomet's captains – Battle of Ali and Marhab – Storming of the citadel – Ali makes a buckler of the gate – Capture of the place – Mahomet poisoned; he marries Safiya, a captive; also Omm Habiba, a widow

To console his followers for the check their religious devotion had experienced at Mecca, Mahomet now set on foot an expedition calculated to gratify that love of plunder, which began to rival fanaticism in attaching them to his standard.

About five days' journey to the northeast of Medina, was situated the city of Khaïbar, and its dependent territory. It was inhabited by Jews, who had grown wealthy by commerce, as well as agriculture. Their rich domain was partly cultivated with grain, and planted with groves of palm-trees; partly devoted to pasturage and covered with flocks and herds; and it was fortified by several castles. So venerable was its antiquity, that Abulfeda, the Arabian historian, assures us that Moses, after the passage of the Red Sea, sent an army against the Amalekites, inhabiting Yathreb (Medina), and the strong city of Khaïbar.

This region had become a place of refuge for the hostile Jews, driven by Mahomet from Medina and its environs, and for all those who had made themselves obnoxious to his vengeance. These circumstances, together with its teeming wealth, pointed it out as a fit and ripe object for that warfare which he had declared against all enemies of the faith.

In the beginning of the seventh year of the Hegira, he departed on an expedition against Khaïbar, at the head of twelve hundred foot and two hundred horse, accompanied by Abu Beker, by Ali, by Omar, and other of his principal officers. He had two standards; one represented the sun, the other a black eagle; which last became famous in after years as the standard of Khaled.

Entering the fertile territory of Khaïbar, he began his warfare by assailing the inferior castles with which it was studded. Some of these capitulated without making resistance; in which cases, being considered "gifts from God," the spoils went to the prophet, to be disposed of by him in the way before mentioned. Others of more strength, and garrisoned by stouter hearts, had to be taken by storm.

After the capture of these minor fortresses, Mahomet advanced against the city of Khaïbar. It was strongly defended by outworks, and its citadel, Al Kamus, built on a steep rock, was deemed impregnable, insomuch that Kenana Ibn al Rabi, the chief or king of the nation, had made it the depository of all his treasures.

The siege of this city was the most important enterprise the Moslems had yet undertaken. When Mahomet first came in sight of its strong and frowning walls, and its rock-built citadel, he is said to have put up the following prayer:

"Oh Allah! Lord of the seven heavens, and of all things which they cover! Lord of the seven earths, and all which they sustain! Lord of the evil spirits, and of all whom they lead astray! Lord of the winds, and of all whom they scatter and disperse! We supplicate thee to deliver into our hands this city, and all that it contains, and the riches of all its lands. To thee we look for aid against this people, and against all the perils by which we are environed."

To give more solemnity to his prayers, he chose as his place of worship a great rock, in a stony place called Mansela, and, during all the time that he remained encamped before Khaïbar, made daily seven circuits round it, as are made round the Caaba. A mosque was erected on this rock in after times in memorial of this devout ceremonial, and it became an object of veneration to all pious Moslems.

The siege of the citadel lasted for some time, and tasked the skill and patience of Mahomet and his troops; as yet but little practised in the attack of fortified places. They suffered too from want of provisions, for the Arabs in their hasty expeditions seldom burden themselves with supplies, and the Jews on their approach had laid waste the level country, and destroyed the palm-trees round their capital.

Mahomet directed the attacks in person: the besiegers protected themselves by trenches, and brought battering-rams to play upon the walls; a breach was at length effected, but for several days every attempt to enter was vigorously repelled. Abu Beker at one time led the assault, bearing the standard of the prophet; but, after fighting with great bravery, was compelled to retreat. The next attack was headed by Omar Ibn Khattâb, who fought until the close of day with no better success. A third attack was led by Ali, whom Mahomet armed with his own scimetar, called Dhu'l-Fakâr, or the Trenchant. On confiding to his hands the sacred banner, he pronounced him "a man who loved God and his prophet; and whom God and his prophet loved. A man who knew not fear, nor ever turned his back upon a foe."

And here it may be well to give a traditional account of the person and character of Ali. He was of the middle height, but robust and square, and of prodigious strength. He had a smiling countenance, exceedingly florid, with a bushy beard. He was distinguishcd for an amiable disposition, sagacious intellect, and religious zeal, and, from his undaunted courage, was surnamed the Lion of God.

Arabian writers dwell with fond exaggeration on the exploits, at Khaïbar, of this their favorite hero. He was clad, they say, in a scarlet vest, over which was buckled a cuirass of steel. Scrambling with his followers up the great heap of stones and rubbish in front of the breach, he planted his standard on the top, determined never to recede until the citadel was taken. The Jews sallied forth to drive down the assailants. In the conflict which ensued, Ali fought hand to hand with the Jewish commander, Al Hareth, whom he slew. The brother of the slain advanced to revenge his death. He was of gigantic stature; with a double cuirass, a double turban, wound round a helmet of proof, in front of which sparkled an immense diamond. He had a sword girt to each side, and brandished a three-pronged spear, like a trident. The warriors measured each other with the eye, and accosted each other in boasting oriental style.

"I," said the Jew, "am Marhab; armed at all points, and terrible in battle."

"And I am Ali, whom his mother, at his birth, surnamed Al Haïdara (the rugged lion)."

The Moslem writers make short work of the Jewish champion. He made a thrust at Ali with his three-pronged lance, but it was dexterously parried; and before he could recover himself, a blow from the scimetar Dhu'l-Fakâr divided his buckler, passed through the helm of proof, through doubled turban and stubborn skull, cleaving his head even to his teeth. His gigantic form fell lifeless to the earth.

The Jews now retreated into the citadel, and a general assault took place. In the heat of the action the shield of Ali was severed from his arm, leaving his body exposed: wrenching a gate, however, from its hinges, he used it as a buckler through the remainder of the fight. Abu Rafe, a servant of Mahomet, testifies to the fact. "I afterwards," says he, "examined this gate in company with seven men, and all eight of us attempted in vain to wield it."*

The citadel being captured, every vault and dungeon was ransacked for the wealth said to be deposited there by Kenana the Jewish prince.

---

* This stupendous feat is recorded by the historian Abulfeda, c. 24. "Abu Rafe," observes Gibbon, "was an eye-witness; but who will be witness for Abu Rafe?" We join with the distinguished historian in his doubt; yet if we scrupulously question the testimony of an eye-witness, what will become of history?

None being discovered, Mahomet demanded of him where he had concealed his treasure. He declared that it had all been expended in the
subsistence of his troops, and in preparations for defence. One of his
faithless subjects, however, revealed the place where a great amount
had been hidden. It did not equal the expectations of the victors, and
Kenana was put to the torture to reveal the rest of his supposed
wealth. He either could not or would not make further discoveries, so
he was delivered up to the vengeance of a Moslem, whose brother he
had crushed to death by a piece of a millstone hurled from the wall,
and who struck off his head with a single blow of his sabre.*

While in the citadel of Khaïbar, Mahomet came near falling a victim
to Jewish vengeance. Demanding something to eat, a shoulder of lamb
was set before him. At the first mouthful he perceived something unusual in the taste, and spat it forth, but instantly felt acute internal
pain. One of his followers, named Baschar, who had eaten more freely,
fell down and expired in convulsions. All now was confusion and consternation; on diligent inquiry, it was found that the lamb had been
cooked by Zaïnab, a female captive, niece to Marhab, the gigantic warrior slain by Ali. Being brought before Mahomet, and charged with
having infused poison into the viand, she boldly avowed it, vindicating
it as a justifiable revenge for the ills he had brought upon her tribe and
her family. "I thought," said she, "if thou wert indeed a prophet, thou
wouldst discover thy danger; if but a chieftain, thou wouldst fall, and
we should be delivered from a tyrant."

Arabian writers are divided as to the fate of this heroine. According
to some, she was delivered up to the vengeance of the relatives of Baschar, who had died of the poison. According to others, her beauty
pleaded in her behalf, and Mahomet restored her unharmed to her
family.

The same writers seldom permit any remarkable event of Mahomet's
life to pass without a miracle. In the present instance, they assure us
that the poisoned shoulder of lamb became miraculously gifted with
speech, and warned Mahomet of his danger. If so, it was rather slow of
speech, for he had imbibed sufficient poison to injure his constitution
throughout the remainder of his life; affecting him often with paroxysms of pain; and in his last moments he complained that the veins of

* The Jews inhabiting the tract of country called Khaïbar, are still known in
Arabia by the name of Beni Khiebar. They are divided into three tribes, under
independent Sheikhs, the Beni Missead, Beni Schahan, and Beni Anaesse. They
are accused of pillaging the caravans. – *Niebuhr*, v. ii. p. 43.

his heart throbbed with the poison of Khaïbar. He experienced kinder
treatment at the hands of Safiya (or Sophia), another female captive,
who had still greater motives for vengeance than Zaïnab; for she was
the recently espoused wife of Kenana, who had just been sacrificed for
his wealth, and she was the daughter of Hoya Ibn Ahktab, prince of
the Beni Koraida, who, with seven hundred of his people, had been
put to death in the square of Medina, as has been related.

This Safiya was of great beauty; it is not surprising, therefore, that
she should find instant favor in the eyes of Mahomet, and that he
should seek, as usual, to add her to his harem; but it may occasion surprise that she should contemplate such a lot with complacency. Moslem
writers, however, explain this by assuring us that she was supernatur-
ally prepared for the event.

While Mahomet was yet encamped before the city, and carrying on
the siege, she had a vision of the night, in which the sun descended
from the firmament and nestled in her bosom. On recounting her
dream to her husband Kenana in the morning, he smote her on the
face, exclaiming, "Woman, you speak in parables of this Arab chief
who has come against us."

The vision of Safiya was made true, for having converted her with all
decent haste to the faith of Islam, Mahomet took her to wife before he
left Khaïbar. Their nuptials took place on the homeward march, at Al
Sahba, where the army halted for three days. Abu Ayub, one of the
prophet's most ardent disciples and marshal of his household, patrolled
around the nuptial tent throughout the night, sword in hand. Safiya
was one of the most favored wives of Mahomet, whom she survived for
forty years of widowhood.

Besides the marriages of affection which we have recorded, the
prophet, about this time, made another of policy. Shortly after his return to Medina, he was gladdened by the arrival, from Abyssinia, of
the residue of the fugitives. Among these was a comely widow, thirty
years of age, whose husband, Abdallah, had died while in exile. She
was generally known by the name of Omm Habiba, the mother of Habiba, from a daughter to whom she had given birth. This widow was
the daughter of Mahomet's arch enemy, Abu Sofian; and the prophet
conceived that a marriage with the daughter might soften the hostility
of the father; a politic consideration, which is said to have been either
suggested or sanctioned by a revelation of a chapter of the Koran.

When Abu Sofian heard of the espousals, "By heaven," exclaimed he,
"this camel is so rampant, that no muzzle can restrain him."

CHAPTER XXVI

Missions to various Princes; to Heraclius; to Khosru II; to the Prefect of Egypt – Their result

During the residue of the year, Mahomet remained at Medina, sending forth his trusty disciples, by this time experienced captains, on various military expeditions; by which refractory tribes were rapidly brought into subjection. His views as a statesman widened as his territories increased. Though he professed, in cases of necessity, to propagate his religion by the sword, he was not neglectful of the peaceful measures of diplomacy, and sent envoys to various princes and potentates, whose dominions bordered on his political horizon, urging them to embrace the faith of Islam; which was, in effect, to acknowledge him, through his apostolic office, their superior.

Two of the most noted of these missions, were to Khosru II, king of Persia, and Heraclius, the Roman emperor, at Constantinople. The wars between the Romans and the Persians, for the dominion of the East, which had prevailed from time to time through several centuries, had been revived by these two potentates with varying fortunes, and for several years past had distracted the eastern world. Countries had been overrun by either power; states and kingdoms had changed hands under alternate invasions, and according to the conquests and defeats of the warring parties. At one time, Khosru with three armies, one vauntingly called the Fifty Thousand Golden Spears, had wrested Palestine, Cappadocia, Armenia, and several other great and wealthy provinces from the Roman emperor; had made himself master of Jerusalem, and carried off the Holy Cross to Persia; had invaded Africa, conquered Libya and Egypt, and extended his victories even to Carthage.

In the midst of his triumphant career, a Moslem envoy arrived bearing him a letter from Mahomet. Khosru sent for his secretary or interpreter, and ordered him to read it. The letter began as follows:

"In the name of the most merciful God! Mahomet, son of Abdallah, and apostle of God, to Khosru king of Persia."

"What!" cried Khosru, starting up in haughty indignation, "does one who is my slave, dare to put his name first in writing to me?" So saying, he seized the letter and tore it in pieces, without seeking to know its contents. He then wrote to his viceroy in Yemen, saying, "I am told there is in Medina a madman, of the tribe of Koreish, who pretends to be a prophet. Restore him to his senses; or if you cannot, send me his head."

When Mahomet was told how Khosru had torn his letter, "Even so," said he, "shall Allah rend his empire in pieces."

The letter from the prophet to Heraclius, was more favorably received, reaching him probably during his reverses. It was signed in characters of silver, Mahomet Azzarel, Mahomet the messenger of God, and invited the emperor to renounce Christianity, and embrace the faith of Islam. Heraclius, we are told, deposited the epistle respectfully upon his pillow, treated the envoy with distinction, and dismissed him with magnificent presents. Engrossed, however, by his Persian wars, he paid no further attention to this mission, from one whom he probably considered a mere Arab fanatic; nor attached sufficient importance to his military operations, which may have appeared mere predatory forays of the wild tribes of the desert.

Another mission of Mahomet was to the Mukowkis, or governor of Egypt, who had originally been sent there by Heraclius to collect tribute; but who, availing himself of the confusion produced by the wars between the Romans and Persians, had assumed sovereign power, and nearly thrown off all allegiance to the emperor. He received the envoy with signal honor, but evaded a direct reply to the invitation to embrace the faith, observing that it was a grave matter requiring much consideration. In the meantime, he sent presents to Mahomet of precious jewels; garments of Egyptian linen; exquisite honey and butter; a white she-ass, called Yafur; a white mule, called Daldal, and a fleet horse called Lazlos, or the Prancer. The most acceptable of his presents, however, were two Coptic damsels, sisters, called Mariyah (or Mary), and Shiren.

The beauty of Mariyah caused great perturbation in the mind of the prophet. He would fain have made her his concubine, but was impeded by his own law in the seventeenth chapter of the Koran, ordaining that fornication should be punished with stripes.

He was relieved from his dilemma, by another revelation revoking the law in regard to himself alone, allowing him intercourse with his handmaid. It remained in full force, however, against all other Moslems. Still, to avoid scandal, and above all, not to excite the jealousy of his wives, he carried on his intercourse with the beautiful Mariyah in secret; which may be one reason why she remained long a favorite.

CHAPTER XXVII

Mahomet's pilgrimage to Mecca; his marriage with Maimuna —
Khaled Ibn al Waled and Amru Ibn al Aass become proselytes

The time had now arrived when, by treaty with the Koreishites, Mahomet and his followers were permitted to make a pilgrimage to Mecca, and pass three days unmolested at the sacred shrines. He departed accordingly with a numerous and well-armed host, and seventy camels for sacrifices. His old adversaries would fain have impeded his progress, but they were overawed, and on his approach withdrew silently to the neighboring hills. On entering the bounds of Mecca, the pilgrims, according to compact and usage, laid aside all their warlike accoutrements excepting their swords, which they carried sheathed.

Great was their joy on beholding once more the walls and towers of the sacred city. They entered the gates in pilgrim garb, with devout and thankful hearts, and Mahomet performed all the ancient and customary rites, with a zeal and devotion which gratified beholders, and drew to him many converts. When he had complied with all the ceremonials he threw aside the Ihram or pilgrim's garb, and withdrew to Sarif, a hamlet two leagues distant, and without the sacred boundaries. Here he had a ceremonial of a different kind to perform, but one in which he was prone to act with unfeigned devotion. It was to complete his marriage with Maimuna, the daughter of Al Hareth, the Helalite. He had become betrothed to her on his arrival at Mecca, but had postponed the nuptials until after he had concluded the rites of pilgrimage. This was doubtless another marriage of policy, for Maimuna was fifty-one years of age, and a widow, but the connection gained him two powerful proselytes. One was Khaled Ibn al Waled, a nephew of the widow, an intrepid warrior who had come near destroying Mahomet at the battle of Ohod. He now became one of the most victorious champions of Islamism, and by his prowess obtained the appellation of "The Sword of God."

The other proselyte was Khaled's friend Amru Ibn al Aass; the same who assailed Mahomet with poetry and satire at the commencement of his prophetic career; who had been an ambassador from the Koreishites to the king of Abyssinia, to obtain the surrender of the fugitive Moslems, and who was henceforth destined with his sword to carry victoriously into foreign lands, the faith he had once so strenuously opposed.

NOTE – Maimuna was the last spouse of the prophet, and, old as she was at her marriage, survived all his other wives. She died many years after him, in a pavillion at Sarif, under the same tree in the shade of which her nuptial tent had been pitched, and was there interred. The pious historian, Al Jannabi, who styles himself "a poor servant of Allah, hoping for the pardon of his sins through the mercy of God," visited her tomb on returning from a pilgrimage to Mecca, in the year of the Hegira, 963, A.D. 1555. "I saw there," said he, "a dome of black marble erected in memory of Maimuna, on the very spot on which the apostle of God had reposed with her. God knows the truth! and also the reason of the black color of the stone. There is a place of ablution, and an oratory; but the building has fallen to decay."

CHAPTER XXVIII

A Moslem envoy slain in Syria – Expedition to avenge his death –
Battle of Muta – Its results

Among the different missions which had been sent by Mahomet beyond the bounds of Arabia to invite neighboring princes to embrace his religion, was one to the governor of Bosra, the great mart on the confines of Syria, to which he had made his first caravan journey in the days of his youth. Syria had been alternately under Roman and Persian domination, but was at that time subject to the emperor, though probably in a great state of confusion. The envoy of Mahomet was slain at Muta, a town about three days' journey eastward from Jerusalem. The one who slew him was an Arab of the Christian tribe of Gassan, and son to Shorhail, an emir, who governed Muta in the name of Heraclius.

To revenge the death of his legate, and to insure respect to his envoys in future, Mahomet prepared to send an army of three thousand men against the offending city. It was a momentous expedition, as it might, for the first time, bring the arms of Islam in collision with those of the Roman Empire; but Mahomet presumed upon his growing power, the energy of his troops, and the disordered state of Syrian affairs. The command was intrusted to his freedman Zeid, who had given such signal proof of devotion in surrendering to him his beautiful wife Zeinab. Several chosen officers were associated with him. One was Mahomet's cousin Jaafar, son of Abu Taleb, and brother of Ali; the same who, by his eloquence, had vindicated the doctrines of Islam before the king of Abyssinia, and defeated the Koreish embassy. He was now in the prime of life, and noted for great courage and manly beauty. Another of the associate officers was Abdallah Ibn Kawaha, the poet, but who had signalized himself in arms as well as poetry. A third was the new proselyte Khaled, who joined the expedition as a volunteer, being eager to prove by his sword the sincerity of his conversion.

The orders to Zeid were to march rapidly, so as to come upon Muta by surprise, to summon the inhabitants to embrace the faith, and to treat them with lenity. Women, children, monks, and the blind, were to be spared at all events; nor were any houses to be destroyed, nor trees cut down.

The little army sallied from Medina in the full confidence of coming upon the enemy unawares. On their march, however, they learned that a greatly superior force of Romans, or rather Greeks and Arabs, was advancing to meet them. A council of war was called. Some were for pausing, and awaiting further orders from Mahomet: but Abdallah, the poet, was for pushing fearlessly forward without regard to numbers. "We fight for the faith!" cried he; "if we fall, paradise is our reward. On, then, to victory or martyrdom!"

All caught a spark of the poet's fire, or rather, fanaticism. They met the enemy near Muta, and encountered them with fury rather than valor. In the heat of the conflict Zeid received a mortal wound. The sacred banner was falling from his grasp, but was seized and borne aloft by Jaafar. The battle thickened round him, for the banner was the object of fierce contention. He defended it with desperate valor. The hand by which he held it was struck off; he grasped it with the other. That, too, was severed; he embraced it with his bleeding arms. A blow from a scimetar cleft his skull; he sank dead upon the field, still clinging to the standard of the faith. Abdallah the poet next reared the banner; but he too fell beneath the sword. Khaled, the new convert, seeing the three Moslem leaders slain, now grasped the fatal standard, but in his hand it remained aloft. His voice rallied the wavering Moslems: his powerful arm cut its way through the thickest of the enemy. If his own account may be credited, and he was one whose deeds needed no exaggeration, nine scimetars were broken in his hand by the fury of the blows given by him in this deadly conflict.

Night separated the combatants. In the morning Khaled, whom the army acknowledged as their commander, proved himself as wary as he was valiant. By dint of marches and counter-marches, he presented his forces in so many points of view, that the enemy were deceived as to his number, and supposed he had received a strong reinforcement. At his first charge, therefore, they retreated: their retreat soon became a flight; in which they were pursued with great slaughter. Khaled then plundered their camp, in which was found great booty. Among the slain in the field of battle was found the body of Jaafar, covered with wounds, but all in front. Out of respect to his valor, and to his relationship with the prophet, Khaled ordered that his corpse should not be buried on the spot, but borne back for honorable interment at Medina.

The army, on its return, though laden with spoil, entered the city more like a funeral train than a triumphant pageant, and was received with mingled shouts and lamentations. While the people rejoiced in the success of their arms, they mourned the loss of three of their favorite generals. All bewailed the fate of Jaafar, brought home a ghastly corpse to that city whence they had so recently seen him sally forth in all the pride of valiant manhood, the admiration of every beholder. He had left behind him a beautiful wife and infant son. The heart of Mahomet was touched by her affliction. He took the orphan child in his arms and bathed it with his tears. But most he was affected when he beheld the young daughter of his faithful Zeid approaching him. He fell on her neck and wept in speechless emotion. A bystander expressed surprise that he should give way to tears for a death which, according to Moslem doctrine, was but a passport to paradise. "Alas!" replied the prophet, "these are the tears of friendship for the loss of a friend!"

The obsequies of Jaafar were performed on the third day after the arrival of the army. By that time Mahomet had recovered his self-possession, and was again the prophet. He gently rebuked the passionate lamentations of the multitude, taking occasion to inculcate one of the most politic and consolatory doctrines of his creed. "Weep no more," said he, "over the death of this my brother. In place of the two hands lost in defending the standard of the faith, two wings have been given him to bear him to paradise; there to enjoy the endless delights insured to all believers who fall in battle."

It was in consequence of the prowess and generalship displayed by Khaled in this perilous fight, that he was honored by Mahomet with the appellation of "The Sword of God," by which he was afterwards renowned.

CHAPTER XXIX

Designs upon Mecca – Mission of Abu Sofian – Its result

Mahomet, by force either of arms or eloquence, had now acquired dominion over a great number of the Arabian tribes. He had many thousand warriors under his command; sons of the desert inured to hunger, thirst, and the scorching rays of the sun, and to whom war was a sport rather than a toil. He had corrected their intemperance, disciplined their valor, and subjected them to rule. Repeated victories had given them confidence in themselves and in their leader; whose standard they followed with the implicit obedience of soldiers, and the blind fanaticism of disciples.

The views of Mahomet expanded with his means, and a grand enterprise now opened upon his mind. Mecca, his native city, the abode of his family for generations, the scene of his happiest years, was still in the hands of his implacable foes. The Caaba, the object of devotion and pilgrimage to all the children of Ishmael, the shrine of his earliest worship, was still profaned by the emblems and rites of idolatry. To plant the standard of the faith on the walls of his native city; to rescue the holy house from profanation; restore it to the spiritual worship of the one true God, and make it the rallying point of Islamism, formed now the leading object of his ambition.

The treaty of peace existing with the Koreishites was an impediment to any military enterprise; but some casual feuds and skirmishings soon gave a pretext for charging them with having violated the treaty stipulations. The Koreishites had by this time learned to appreciate and dread the rapidly increasing power of the Moslems, and were eager to explain away, or atone for, the quarrels and misdeeds of a few heedless individuals. They even prevailed on their leader, Abu Sofian, to repair to Medina as ambassador of peace, trusting that he might have some influence with the prophet through his daughter Omm Habiba.

It was a sore trial to this haughty chief to come almost a suppliant to the man whom he had scoffed at as an impostor, and treated with inveterate hostility; and his proud spirit was doomed to still further mortification, for Mahomet, judging from his errand of the weakness of his party, and being secretly bent on war, vouchsafed him no reply.

Repressing his rage, Abu Sofian sought the intermediation of Abu Beker, of Omar, and Ali; but they all rebuked and repulsed him; for they knew the secret wishes of Mahomet. He next endeavored to secure the favor of Fatima, the daughter of Mahomet and wife of Ali, by flattering a mother's pride, entreating her to let her son Hassan, a child but six years old, be his protector; but Fatima answered haughtily, "My son is too young to be a protector; and no protection can avail against the will of the prophet of God." Even his daughter, Omm Habiba, the wife of Mahomet, on whom Abu Sofian had calculated for influence, added to his mortification, for on his offering to seat himself on a mat in her dwelling, she hastily folded it up, exclaiming, "It is the bed of the prophet of God, and too sacred to be made the resting-place of an idolater."

The cup of humiliation was full to overflowing, and in the bitterness of his heart Abu Sofian cursed his daughter. He now turned again to Ali, beseeching his advice in the desperate state of his embassy.

"I can advise nothing better," replied Ali, "than for thee to promise, as the head of the Koreishites, a continuance of thy protection; and then to return to thy home."

"But thinkest thou, that promise will be of any avail?"

"I think not," replied Ali dryly; "but I know not to the contrary."

In pursuance of this advice, Abu Sofian repaired to the mosque, and made public declaration, in behalf of the Koreishites, that on their part the treaty of peace should be faithfully maintained; after which he returned to Mecca, deeply humiliated by the imperfect result of his mission. He was received with scoffs by the Koreishites, who observed that his declaration of peace availed nothing without the concurrence of Mahomet.

CHAPTER XXX

Surprise and capture of Mecca

Mahomet now prepared for a secret expedition to take Mecca by surprise. His allies were summoned from all quarters to Medina; but no intimation was given of the object he had in view. All the roads leading to Mecca were barred to prevent any intelligence of his movements being carried to the Koreishites. With all his precautions the secret came near being discovered. Among his followers, fugitives from Mecca, was one named Hateb, whose family had remained behind, and were without connections or friends to take an interest in their welfare. Hateb now thought to gain favor for them among the Koreishites, by betraying the plans of Mahomet. He accordingly wrote a letter revealing the intended enterprise, and gave it in charge to a singing woman, named Sara, a Haschemite slave, who undertook to carry it to Mecca.

She was already on the road when Mahomet was apprised of the treachery. Ali and five others, well mounted, were sent in pursuit of the messenger. They soon overtook her, but searched her person in vain. Most of them would have given up the search and turned back, but Ali was confident that the prophet of God could not be mistaken nor misinformed. Drawing his scimetar, he swore to strike off the head of the messenger, unless the letter were produced. The threat was effectual. She drew forth the letter from among her hair.

Hateb on being taxed with his perfidy, acknowledged it; but pleaded his anxiety to secure favor for his destitute family, and his certainty that the letter would be harmless, and of no avail against the purposes of the apostle of God. Omar spurned at his excuses and would have struck off his head; but Mahomet, calling to mind that Hateb had fought bravely in support of the faith in the battle of Beder, admitted his excuses and forgave him.

The prophet departed with ten thousand men on this momentous enterprise. Omar, who had charge of regulating the march, and appointing the encampments, led the army by lonely passes of the mountains; prohibiting the sound of attabal or trumpet, or any thing else that could betray their movements. While on the march, Mahomet was joined by his uncle Al Abbas, who had come forth with his family from Mecca, to rally under the standard of the faith. Mahomet received him graciously, yet with a hint at his tardiness. "Thou art the last of the emigrants," said he, "as I am the last of the prophets." Al Abbas sent his family forward to Medina, while he turned and accompanied the expedition. The army reached the valley of Marr Azzahran, near to the sacred city, without being discovered. It was nightfall when they silently pitched their tents, and now Omar for the first time permitted them to light their watch-fires.

In the meantime, though Al Abbas had joined the standard of the faith in all sincerity, yet he was sorely disquieted at seeing his nephew advancing against Mecca, with such a powerful force and such hostile intent; and feared the entire destruction of the Koreishites, unless they could be persuaded in time to capitulate. In the dead of the night, he mounted Mahomet's white mule Fadda, and rode forth to reconnoitre. In skirting the camp, he heard the tramp of men and sound of voices. A scouting party were bringing in two prisoners captured near the city. Al Abbas approached, and found the captives to be Abu Sofian, and one of his captains. They were conducted to the watch-fire of Omar, who recognized Abu Sofian by the light. "God be praised," cried he, "that I have such an enemy in my hands, and without conditions." His ready scimetar might have given fatal significance to his words, had not Al Abbas stepped forward and taken Abu Sofian under his protection, until the will of the prophet should be known. Omar rushed forth to ascertain that will, or rather to demand the life of the prisoner; but Al Abbas, taking the latter up behind him, put spurs to his mule, and was the first to reach the tent of the prophet, followed hard by Omar, clamoring for the head of Abu Sofian.

Mahomet thus beheld in his power his inveterate enemy, who had driven him from his home and country, and persecuted his family and friends; but he beheld in him the father of his wife Omm Habiba, and felt inclined to clemency. He postponed all decision in the matter until morning; giving Abu Sofian in charge of Al Abbas.

When the captain was brought before him on the following day: "Well, Abu Sofian," cried he, "is it not at length time to know that there is no other God but God?"

"That I already knew," replied Abu Sofian.

"Good! and is it not time for thee to acknowledge me as the apostle of God?"

"Dearer art thou to me than my father and my mother," replied Abu Sofian, using an oriental phrase of compliment; "but I am not yet prepared to acknowledge thee a prophet."

"Out upon thee!" cried Omar, "testify instantly to the truth, or thy head shall be severed from thy body."

To these threats were added the counsels and entreaties of Al Abbas, who showed himself a real friend in need. The rancor of Abu Sofian had already been partly subdued by the unexpected mildness of Mahomet; so, making a merit of necessity, he acknowledged the divinity of his mission; furnishing an illustration of the Mosleum maxim, "To convince stubborn unbelievers, there is no argument like the sword."

Having now embraced the faith, Abu Sofian obtained favorable terms for the people of Mecca, in case of their submission. None were to be harmed who should remain quietly in their houses; or should take refuge in the houses of Abu Sofian and Hakim; or under the banner of Abu Rawaiha.

That Abu Sofian might take back to the city a proper idea of the force brought against it, he was stationed with Al Abbas at a narrow defile where the whole army passed in review. As the various Arab tribes marched by with their different arms and ensigns, Al Abbas explained the name and country of each. Abu Sofian was surprised at the number, discipline, and equipment of the troops; for the Moslems had been rapidly improving in the means and art of war; but when Mahomet approached, in the midst of a chosen guard, armed at all points and glittering with steel, his astonishment passed all bounds. "There is no withstanding this!" cried he to Al Abbas, with an oath – "truly thy nephew wields a mighty power."

"Even so," replied the other; "return then to thy people; provide for their safety, and warn them not to oppose the apostle of God."

Abu Sofian hastened back to Mecca, and assembling the inhabitants, told them of the mighty host at hand, led on by Mahomet; of the favorable terms offered in case of their submission, and of the vanity of all resistance. As Abu Sofian had been the soul of the opposition to Mahomet and his doctrines, his words had instant effect in producing acquiescence in an event which seemed to leave no alternative. The greater part of the inhabitants, therefore, prepared to witness, without resistance, the entry of the prophet.

Mahomet, in the meantime, who knew not what resistance he might meet with, made a careful distribution of his forces as he approached the city. While the main body marched directly forward, strong detachments advanced over the hills on each side. To Ali, who commanded a large body of cavalry, was confided the sacred banner, which he was to plant on Mount Hadjun, and maintain it there until joined by the prophet. Express orders were given to all the generals to practise forbearance, and in no instance to make the first attack; for it was the earnest desire of Mahomet to win Mecca by moderation and clemency, rather than subdue it by violence. It is true, all who offered armed resistance were to be cut down, but none were to be harmed who submitted quietly. Overhearing one of his captains exclaim, in the heat of his zeal, that "no place was sacred on the day of battle," he instantly appointed a cooler-headed commander in his place.

The main body of the army advanced without molestation. Mahomet brought up the rear-guard, clad in a scarlet vest, and mounted on his favorite camel Al Kaswa. He proceeded but slowly, however; his movements being impeded by the immense multitude which thronged around him. Arrived on Mount Hadjun, where Ali had planted the standard of the faith, a tent was pitched for him. Here he alighted, put off his scarlet garment, and assumed the black turban and the pilgrim garb. Casting a look down into the plain, however, he beheld, with grief and indignation, the gleam of swords and lances, and Khaled, who commanded the left wing, in a full career of carnage. His troops, composed of Arab tribes converted to the faith, had been galled by a flight of arrows from a body of Koreishites; whereupon the fiery warrior charged into the thickest of them with sword and lance; his troops pressed after him; they put the enemy to flight, entered the gates of Mecca pell-mell with them, and nothing but the swift commands of Mahomet preserved the city from a general massacre.

The carnage being stopped, and no further opposition manifested, the prophet descended from the mount and approached the gates, seated on his camel, accompanied by Abu Beker on his right hand, and followed by Osama, the son of Zeid. The sun was just rising as he entered the gates of his native city, with the glory of a conqueror, but the garb and humility of a pilgrim. He entered, repeating verses of the Koran, which he said had been revealed to him at Medina, and were prophetic of the event. He triumphed in the spirit of a religious zealot, not of a warrior. "Unto God," said he, "belong the hosts of heaven and earth, and God is mighty and wise. Now hath God verified unto his apostle the vision, wherein he said, ye shall surely enter the holy temple of Mecca in full security."

Without dismounting, Mahomet repaired directly to the Caaba, the scene of his early devotions, the sacred shrine of worship since the days of the patriarchs, and which he regarded as the primitive temple of the one true God. Here he made the seven circuits round the sacred edifice, a reverential rite from the days of religious purity; with the same devout feeling he each time touched the black stone with his staff; regarding it as a holy relic. He would have entered the Caaba, but Othman Ibn Talha, the ancient custodian, locked the door. Ali snatched the keys, but Mahomet caused them to be returned to the venerable officer, and so won him by his kindness, that he not merely threw open the doors, but subsequently embraced the faith of Islam; whereupon he was continued in his office.

Mahomet now proceeded to execute the great object of his religious aspirations, the purifying of the sacred edifice from the symbols of idolatry, with which it was crowded. All the idols in and about it, to the number of three hundred and sixty, were thrown down and destroyed. Among these, the most renowned was Hobal, an idol brought from Balka, in Syria, and fabled to have the power of granting rain. It was, of course, a great object of worship among the inhabitants of the thirsty desert. There were statues of Abraham and Ishmael also, represented with divining arrows in their hands; "an outrage on their memories," said Mahomet, "being symbols of a diabolical art which they had never practised." In reverence of their memories, therefore, these statues were demolished. There were paintings, also, depicting angels in the guise of beautiful women. "The angels," said Mahomet, indignantly, "are no such beings. There are celestial houris provided in paradise for the solace of true believers; but angels are ministering spirits of the Most High, and of too pure a nature to admit of sex." The paintings were accordingly obliterated.

Even a dove, curiously carved of wood, he broke with his own hands, and cast upon the ground, as savoring of idolatry.

From the Caaba he proceeded to the well of Zem Zem. It was sacred in his eyes, from his belief that it was the identical well revealed by the angel to Hagar and Ishmael, in their extremity; he considered the rite connected with it as pure and holy, and continued it in his faith. As he approached the well, his uncle Al Abbas presented him a cruise of the water, that he might drink, and make the customary ablution. In commemoration of this pious act, he appointed his uncle guardian of the cup of the well; an office of sacred dignity, which his descendants retain to this day.

At noon one of his followers, at his command, summoned the people to prayer from the top of the Caaba, a custom continued ever since throughout Mahometan countries, from minarets or towers provided in every mosque. He also established the Kebla, toward which the faithful in every part of the world should turn their faces in prayer.

He afterwards addressed the people in a kind of sermon, setting forth his principal doctrines, and announcing the triumph of the faith as a fulfilment of prophetic promise. Shouts burst from the multitude in reply. "Allah Achbar! God is great!" cried they. "There is no God but God, and Mahomet is his prophet."

The religious ceremonials being ended, Mahomet took his station on the hill Al Safa, and the people of Mecca, male and female, passed before him, taking the oath of fidelity to him as the prophet of God, and renouncing idolatry. This was in compliance with a revelation in the Koran: "God hath sent his apostle with the direction, and the religion of truth, that he may exalt the same over every religion. Verily, they who swear fealty to him, swear fealty unto God; the hand of God is over their hands." In the midst of his triumph, however, he rejected all homage paid exclusively to himself; and all regal authority. "Why dost thou tremble?" said he, to a man who approached with timid and faltering steps. "Of what dost thou stand in awe? I am no king, but the son of a Koreishite woman, who ate flesh dried in the sun."

His lenity was equally conspicuous. The once haughty chiefs of the Koreishites appeared with abject countenances before the man they had persecuted, for their lives were in his power.

"What can you expect at my hands?" demanded he sternly.

"Mercy, oh generous brother! Mercy, oh son of a generous line!"

"Be it so!" cried he, with a mixture of scorn and pity. "Away! begone! ye are free!"

Some of his followers who had shared his persecutions, were disappointed in their anticipations of a bloody revenge, and murmured at his clemency; but he persisted in it, and established Mecca as an inviolable sanctuary, or place of refuge, so to continue until the final resurrection. He reserved to himself, however, the right on the present occasion, and during that special day to punish a few of the people of the city, who had grievously offended, and been expressly proscribed; yet even these, for the most part, were ultimately forgiven.

Among the Koreishite women who advanced to take the oath, he descried Henda, the wife of Abu Sofian; the savage woman who had animated the infidels at the battle of Ohod, and had gnawed the heart of Hamza, in revenge for the death of her father. On the present occasion she had disguised herself to escape detection; but seeing the eyes of the prophet fixed on her, she threw herself at his feet, exclaiming, "I am Henda: pardon! pardon!" Mahomet pardoned her – and was requited for his clemency by her making his doctrines the subject of contemptuous sarcasms.

Among those destined to punishment, was Wacksa, the Ethiopian, who had slain Hamza; but he had fled from Mecca on the entrance of the army. At a subsequent period he presented himself before the prophet, and made the profession of faith before he was recognized. He was forgiven, and made to relate the particulars of the death of Hamza; after which Mahomet dismissed him with an injunction, never again to come into his presence. He survived until the time of the Caliphat of Omar, during whose reign he was repeatedly scourged for drunkenness.

Another of the proscribed was Abdallah Ibn Saad, a young Koreishite, distinguished for wit and humor, as well as for warlike accomplishments. As he held the pen of a ready writer, Mahomet had employed him to reduce the revelations of the Koran to writing. In so doing, he had often altered and amended the text; nay, it was discovered that, through carelessness or design, he had occasionally falsified it, and rendered it absurd. He had even made his alterations and amendments matter of scoff and jest among his companions, observing that if the Koran proved Mahomet to be a prophet, he himself must be half a prophet. His interpolations being detected, he had fled from the wrath of the prophet, and returned to Mecca, where he relapsed into idolatry. On the capture of the city his foster-brother concealed him in his house, until the tumult had subsided, when he led him into the presence of the prophet, and supplicated for his pardon. This was the severest trial of the lenity of Mahomet. The offender had betrayed his confidence; held him up to ridicule; questioned his apostolic mission, and struck at the very foundation of his faith. For some time he maintained a stern silence; hoping, as he afterwards declared, some zealous disciple might strike off the offender's head. No one, however, stirred; so, yielding to the entreaties of Othman, he granted a pardon. Abdallah instantly renewed his profession of faith; and continued a good Musulman. His name will be found in the wars of the Caliphs. He was one of the most dexterous horsemen of his tribe, and evinced his ruling passion to the last, for he died repeating the hundredth chapter of the Koran, entitled "The war steeds." Perhaps it was one which had experienced his interpolations.

Another of the proscribed was Akrema Ibn Abu Jahl, who on many occasions had manifested a deadly hostility to the prophet, inherited from his father. On the entrance of Mahomet into Mecca, Akrema threw himself upon a fleet horse, and escaped by an opposite gate, leaving behind him a beautiful wife, Omm Hakem, to whom he was recently married. She embraced the faith of Islam, but soon after learnt that her husband, in attempting to escape by sea to Yemen, had been driven back to port. Hastening to the presence of the prophet, she threw herself on her knees before him, loose, dishevelled, and unveiled, and implored grace for her husband. The prophet, probably more moved by her beauty than her grief, raised her gently from the earth, and told her her prayer was granted. Hurrying to the seaport, she arrived just as the vessel in which her husband had embarked was about to sail. She returned, mounted behind him, to Mecca, and brought him, a true believer, into the presence of the prophet. On this occasion, however, she was so closely veiled that her dark eyes alone were visible. Mahomet received Akrema's profession of faith; made him commander of a battalion of Hawazenites, as the dower of his beautiful and devoted wife, and bestowed liberal donations on the youthful couple. Like many other converted enemies, Akrema proved a valiant soldier in the wars of the faith, and after signalizing himself on various occasions, fell in battle, hacked and pierced by swords and lances.

The whole conduct of Mahomet on gaining possession of Mecca, showed that it was a religious, more than a military triumph. His heart, too, softened toward his native place, now that it was in his power; his resentments were extinguished by success, and his inclinations were all toward forgiveness.

The Ansarians, or Auxiliaries of Medina, who had aided him in his campaign, began to fear that its success might prove fatal to their own interests. They watched him anxiously, as one day, after praying on the hill Al Safa, he sat gazing down wistfully upon Mecca, the scene of his early struggles and recent glory: "Verily," said he, "thou art the best of cities, and the most beloved of Allah! Had I not been driven out from thee by my own tribe, never would I have left thee!" On hearing this, the Ansarians said, one to another, "Behold! Mahomet is conqueror and master of his native city; he will, doubtless, establish

himself here, and forsake Medina!" Their words reached his ear, and
he turned to them with reproachful warmth: "No!" cried he, "when you
plighted to me your allegiance, I swore to live and die with you. I
should not act as the servant of God, nor as his ambassador, were I to
leave you."

He acted according to his words, and Medina, which had been his
city of refuge, continued to be his residence to his dying day.

Mahomet did not content himself with purifying the Caaba, and
abolishing idolatry from his native city; he sent forth his captains at
the head of armed bands, to cast down the idols of different tribes set
up in the neighboring towns and villages, and to convert their worshippers to his faith.

Of all these military apostles, none was so zealous as Khaled; whose
spirit was still fermenting with recent conversion. Arriving at Naklah,
the resort of the idolatrous Koreishites to worship at the shrine of
Uzza, he penetrated the sacred grove, laid waste the temple, and cast
the idol to the ground. A horrible hag, black and naked, with dishevelled hair, rushed forth, shrieking and wringing her hands; but
Khaled severed her through the middle with one blow of his scimetar.
He reported the deed to Mahomet, expressing a doubt whether she
were priestess or evil spirit. "Of a truth," replied the prophet, "it was
Uzza herself whom thou hast destroyed."

On a similar errand into the neighboring province of Tehama,
Khaled had with him three hundred and fifty men, some of them of the
tribe of Suleim, and was accompanied by Abda'lrahman, one of the
earliest proselytes of the faith. His instructions from the prophet were
to preach peace and good will, to inculcate the faith, and to abstain
from violence, unless assailed. When about two days' journey on his
way to Tehama, he had to pass through the country of the tribe of Jadsima. Most of the inhabitants had embraced the faith, but some were
still of the Sabean religion. On a former occasion this tribe had plundered and slain an uncle of Khaled, also the father of Abda'lrahman,
and several Suleimites, as they were returning from Arabia Felix.
Dreading that Khaled and his host might take vengeance for these misdeeds, they armed themselves on their approach.

Khaled was secretly rejoiced at seeing them ride forth to meet him in
this military array. Hailing them with an imperious tone, he demanded
whether they were Moslems or infidels. They replied, in faltering accents, "Moslems." "Why, then, come ye forth to meet us with weapons

in your hands?" "Because we have enemies among some of the tribes who may attack us unawares."

Khaled sternly ordered them to dismount and lay by their weapons. Some complied, and were instantly seized and bound; the rest fled. Taking their flight as a confession of guilt, he pursued them with great slaughter; laid waste the country, and in the effervescence of his zeal even slew some of the prisoners.

Mahomet, when he heard of this unprovoked outrage, raised his hands to heaven, and called God to witness that he was innocent of it. Khaled, when upbraided with it on his return, would fain have shifted the blame on Abda'lrahman, but Mahomet rejected indignantly an imputation against one of the earliest and worthiest of his followers. The generous Ali was sent forthwith to restore to the people of Jadsima what Khaled had wrested from them, and to make pecuniary compensation to the relatives of the slain. It was a mission congenial with his nature, and he executed it faithfully. Inquiring into the losses and sufferings of each individual, he paid him to his full content. When every loss was made good, and all blood atoned for, he distributed the remaining money among the people, gladdening every heart by his bounty. So Ali received the thanks and praises of the prophet, but the vindictive Khaled was rebuked even by those whom he had thought to please.

"Behold!" said he, to Abda'lrahman, "I have avenged the death of thy father." "Rather say," replied the other, indignantly, "thou hast avenged the death of thine uncle. Thou hast disgraced the faith by an act worthy of an idolater."

CHAPTER XXXI

*Hostilities in the mountains – Enemy's camp in the valley of Autas
– Battle at the pass of Honein – Capture of the enemy's camp – Interview of Mahomet with the nurse of his childhood – Division of
spoil – Mahomet at his mother's grave*

While the military apostles of Mahomet were spreading his doctrines
at the point of the sword in the plains, a hostile storm was gathering in
the mountains. A league was formed among the Thakefites, the Hawazins, the Joshmites, the Saadites, and several other of the hardy mountain tribes of Bedouins, to check a power which threatened to subjugate all Arabia. The Saadites, or Beni Sad, here mentioned, are the
same pastoral Arabs among whom Mahomet had been nurtured in his
childhood; and in whose valley, according to tradition, his heart had
been plucked forth and purified by an angel. The Thakefites, who were
foremost in the league, were a powerful tribe, possessing the strong
mountain town of Tayef and its productive territory. They were big-
oted idolaters; maintaining at their capital the far-famed shrine of the
female idol Al Lat. The reader will remember the ignominious treatment of Mahomet, when he attempted to preach his doctrines at Tayef;
being stoned in the public square, and ultimately driven with insult
from the gates. It was probably a dread of vengeance at his hands,
which now made the Thakefites so active in forming a league against
him.

Malec Ibn Auf, the chief of the Thakefites, had the general command of the confederacy. He appointed the valley of Autas, between
Honein and Tayef, as the place of assemblage and encampment; and
as he knew the fickle nature of the Arabs, and their proneness to return
home on the least caprice, he ordered them to bring with them their
families and effects. They assembled, accordingly, from various parts,
to the number of four thousand fighting men; but the camp was
crowded with women and children, and encumbered with flocks and
herds.

The expedient of Malec Ibn Auf to secure the adhesion of the warriors, was strongly disapproved by Doraid, the chief of the Joshmites.
This was an ancient warrior, upwards of a hundred years old; meagre
as a skeleton, almost blind, and so feeble that he had to be borne in a
litter on the back of a camel. Still, though unable to mingle in battle,
he was potent in council from his military experience. This veteran of

151

the desert advised that the women and children should be sent home forthwith, and the army relieved from all unnecessary incumbrances. His advice was not taken; and the valley of Autas continued to present rather the pastoral encampment of a tribe, than the hasty levy of an army.

In the meantime Mahomet, hearing of the gathering storm, had sallied forth to anticipate it, at the head of about twelve thousand troops, partly fugitives from Mecca, and auxiliaries from Medina, partly Arabs of the desert, some of whom had not yet embraced the faith.

In taking the field he wore a polished cuirass and helmet, and rode his favorite white mule Daldal, seldom mounting a charger, as he rarely mingled in actual fight. His recent successes and his superiority in numbers, making him confident of an easy victory, he entered the mountains without precaution, and pushing forward for the enemy's camp at Autas, came to a deep gloomy valley on the confines of Honein. The troops marched without order through the rugged defile, each one choosing his own path. Suddenly they were assailed by showers of darts, stones, and arrows, which laid two or three of Mahomet's soldiers dead at his feet, and wounded several others. Malec, in fact, had taken post with his ablest warriors about the heights commanding this narrow gorge. Every cliff and cavern was garrisoned with archers and slingers, and some rushed down to contend at close quarters.

Struck with a sudden panic, the Moslems turned and fled. In vain did Mahomet call upon them as their general, or appeal to them as the prophet of God. Each man sought but his own safety, and an escape from this horrible valley.

For a moment all seemed lost, and some recent but unwilling converts betrayed an exultation in the supposed reverse of fortune of the prophet.

"By heavens!" cried Abu Sofian, as he looked after the flying Moslems, "nothing will stop them until they reach the sea."

"Ay," exclaimed another, "the magic power of Mahomet is at an end!"

A third, who cherished a lurking revenge for the death of his father, slain by the Moslems in the battle of Ohod, would have killed the prophet in the confusion, had he not been surrounded and protected by a few devoted followers. Mahomet himself, in an impulse of desperation, spurred his mule upon the enemy; but Al Abbas seized the bridle, stayed him from rushing to certain death, and at the same time put up a shout that echoed through the narrow valley. Al Abbas was renowned for strength of lungs, and at this critical moment it was the salvation of the army. The Moslems rallied when they heard his well-known voice, and finding they were not pursued, returned to the combat. The enemy had descended from the heights, and now a bloody conflict ensued in the defile. "The furnace is kindling," cried Mahomet exultingly, as he saw the glitter of arms and flash of weapons. Stooping from his saddle, and grasping a handful of dust, he scattered it in the air toward the enemy. "Confusion on their faces!" cried he, "may this dust blind them!" They were blinded accordingly, and fled in confusion, say the Moslem writers; though their defeat may rather be attributed to the Moslem superiority of force, and the zeal inspired by the exclamations of the prophet. Malec and the Thakefites took refuge in the distant city of Tayef, the rest retreated to the camp in the valley of Autas.

While Mahomet remained in the valley of Honein, he sent Abu Amir with a strong force, to attack the camp. The Hawazins made a brave defence. Abu Amir was slain; but his nephew, Abu Musa, took the command, and obtained a complete victory, killing many of the enemy. The camp afforded great booty and many captives, from the unwise expedient of Malec Ibn Auf, in encumbering it with the families and effects, the flocks and herds of the confederates; and from his disregard of the sage advice of the veteran Doraid. The fate of that ancient warrior of the desert is worthy of mention. While the Moslem troops, scattered through the camp, were intent on booty, Rabia Ibn Rafi, a young Suleimite, observed a litter borne off on the back of a camel, and pursued it, supposing it to contain some beautiful female. On overtaking it and drawing the curtain, he beheld the skeleton form of the ancient Doraid. Vexed and disappointed, he struck at him with his sword, but the weapon broke in his hand. "Thy mother," said the old man sneeringly, "has furnished thee with wretched weapons; thou wilt find a better one hanging behind my saddle."

The youth seized it, but as he drew it from the scabbard, Doraid perceiving that he was a Suleimite, exclaimed, "Tell thy mother thou hast slain Doraid Ibn Simma, who has protected many women of her tribe in the day of battle." The words were ineffectual; the skull of the veteran was cloven with his own scimetar. When Rabia, on his return to Mecca, told his mother of the deed, "Thou hast indeed slain a benefactor of thy race," said she reproachfully. "Three women of thy family has Doraid Ibn Simma freed from captivity."

Abu Musa returned in triumph to Mahomet, making a great display of the spoils of the camp of Autas, and the women and children whom he had captured. One of the female captives threw herself at the feet of the prophet, and implored his mercy as his foster-sister Al Shima, the daughter of his nurse Halêma, who had nurtured him in the Saadite valley. Mahomet sought in vain to recognize in her withered features the bright playmate of his infancy, but she laid bare her back, and showed a scar where he had bitten her in their childish gambols. He no longer doubted; but treated her with kindness, giving her the choice either to remain with him and under his protection, or to return to her home and kindred.

A scruple rose among the Moslems with respect to their female captives. Could they take to themselves such as were married, without committing the sin of adultery? The revelation of a text of the Koran put an end to the difficulty. "Ye shall not take to wife free women who are married, unless your right hand shall have made them slaves." According to this all women taken in war may be made the wives of the captors, though their former husbands be living. The victors of Honein failed not to take immediate advantage of this law.

Leaving the captives and the booty in a secure place, and properly guarded, Mahomet now proceeded in pursuit of the Thakefites who had taken refuge in Tayef. A sentiment of vengeance mingled with his pious ardor as he approached this idolatrous place, the scene of former injury and insult, and beheld the gate whence he had once been ignominiously driven forth. The walls were too strong however to be stormed, and there was a protecting castle; for the first time, therefore, he had recourse to catapults, battering-rams, and other engines used in sieges, but unknown in Arabian warfare. These were prepared under the direction of Salmân al Farsi, the converted Persian.

The besieged, however, repulsed every attack, galling the assailants with darts and arrows, and pouring down melted iron upon the shields of bull-hides, under covert of which they approached the walls. Mahomet now laid waste the fields, the orchards, and vineyards, and proclaimed freedom to all slaves who should desert from the city. For twenty days he carried on an ineffectual siege – daily offering up prayers midway between the tents of his wives Omm Salama and Zeinab, to whom it had fallen by lot to accompany him in this campaign. His hopes of success began to fail, and he was further discouraged by a dream, which was unfavorably interpreted by Abu Beker, renowned for his skill in expounding visions. He would have raised the siege, but his troops murmured; whereupon he ordered an assault upon one of the gates. As usual, it was obstinately defended; numbers were slain on both sides; Abu Sofian, who fought valiantly on the occasion, lost an eye, and the Moslems were finally repulsed.

Mahomet now broke up his camp, promising his troops to renew the siege at a future day, and proceeded to the place where were collected the spoils of his expedition. These, say Arabian writers, amounted to twenty-four thousand camels, forty thousand sheep, four thousand ounces of silver, and six thousand captives.

In a little while appeared a deputation from the Hawazins, declaring the submission of their tribe, and begging the restoration of their families and effects. With them came Halêma, Mahomet's foster-nurse, now well stricken in years. The recollections of his childhood again pleaded with his heart. "Which is dearest to you," said he to the Hawazins, "your families or your goods?" They replied, "Our families."

"Enough," rejoined he, "as far as it concerns Al Abbas and myself, we are ready to give up our share of the prisoners; but there are others to be moved. Come to me after noontide prayer, and say, 'we implore the ambassador of God that he counsel his followers to return us our wives and children; and we implore his followers that they intercede with him in our favor.'"

The envoys did as he advised. Mahomet and Al Abbas immediately renounced their share of the captives; their example was followed by all excepting the tribes of Tamim and Fazara, but Mahomet brought them to consent by promising them a sixfold share of the prisoners taken in the next expedition. Thus the intercession of Halêma procured the deliverance of all the captives of her tribe. A traditional anecdote shows the deference with which Mahomet treated this humble protector of his infancy. "I was sitting with the prophet," said one of his disciples, "when all of a sudden a woman presented herself, and he rose and spread his cloth for her to sit down upon. When she went away, it was observed, 'that woman suckled the prophet.'"

Mahomet now sent an envoy to Malec, who remained shut up in Tayef, offering the restitution of all the spoils taken from him at Honein, and a present of one hundred camels, if he would submit and embrace the faith. Malec was conquered and converted by this liberal offer, and brought several of his confederate tribes with him to the standard of the prophet. He was immediately made their chief; and proved, subsequently, a severe scourge in the cause of the faith to his late associates the Thakefites.

The Moslems now began to fear that Mahomet, in these magnani-

mous impulses, might squander away all the gains of their recent battles; thronging round him, therefore, they clamored for a division of
the spoils and captives. Regarding them, indignantly, "Have you ever,"
said he, "found me avaricious, or false, or disloyal?" Then plucking a
hair from the back of a camel, and raising his voice, "By Allah!" cried
he, "I have never taken from the common spoil the value of that camel's hair more than my fifth; and that fifth has always been expended
for your good."

He then shared the booty as usual; four-fifths among the troops; but
his own fifth he distributed among those whose fidelity he wished to
insure. The Koreishites he considered dubious allies; perhaps he had
overheard the exultation of some of them in anticipation of his defeat;
he now sought to rivet them to him by gifts. To Abu Sofian he gave
one hundred camels and forty okks of silver, in compensation for the
eye lost in the attack on the gate of Tayef. To Akrema Ibn Abu Jahl,
and others of like note, he gave in due proportions, and all from his
own share.

Among the lukewarm converts thus propitiated, was Abbas Ibn Mar-
das, a poet. He was dissatisfied with his share, and vented his discontent in satirical verses. Mahomet overheard him. "Take that man
hence," said he, "and cut out his tongue." Omar, ever ready for rigorous measures, would have executed the sentence literally, and on the
spot; but others, better instructed in the prophet's meaning, led Abbas,
all trembling, to the public square where the captured cattle were collected, and bade him choose what he liked from among them.

"What!" cried the poet, joyously, relieved from the horrors of mutilation, "is this the way the prophet would silence my tongue? By Allah! I
will take nothing." Mahomet, however, persisted in his politic generosity, and sent him sixty camels. From that time forward the poet was
never weary of chanting the liberality of the prophet.

While thus stimulating the good-will of lukewarm proselytes of
Mecca, Mahomet excited the murmurs of his auxiliaries of Medina.
"See," said they, "how he lavishes gifts upon the treacherous Koreishites, while we, who have been loyal to him through all dangers, receive
nothing but our naked share. What have we done that we should be
thus thrown into the background?"

Mahomet was told of their murmurs, and summoned their leaders to
his tent. "Hearken, ye men of Medina," said he; "were ye not in discord
among yourselves, and have I not brought you into harmony? Were ye

not in error, and have I not brought you into the path of truth? Were ye not poor, and have I not made you rich?"

They acknowledged the truth of his words. "Look ye!" continued he, "I came among you stigmatized as a liar, yet you believed in me; persecuted, yet you protected me; a fugitive, yet you sheltered me; helpless, yet you aided me. Think you I do not feel all this? Think you I can be ungrateful? You complain that I bestow gifts upon these people, and give none to you. It is true, I give them worldly gear, but it is to win their worldy hearts. To you, who have been true, I give – myself! They return home with sheep and camels; ye return with the prophet of God among you. For, by him in whose hands is the soul of Mahomet, though the whole world should go one way and ye another, I would remain with you! Which of you, then, have I most rewarded?"

The auxiliaries were moved even to tears by this appeal. "Oh, prophet of God," exclaimed they, "we are content with our lot!"

The booty being divided, Mahomet returned to Mecca, not with the parade and exultation of a conqueror, but in pilgrim garb, to complete the rites of his pilgrimage. All these being scrupulously performed, he appointed Moad Ibn Jabal as imam, or pontiff, to instruct the people in the doctrines of Islam, and gave the government of the city into the hands of Otab, a youth but eighteen years of age; after which he bade farewell to his native place, and set out with his troops on the return to Medina.

Arriving at the village of Al Abwa, where his mother was buried, his heart yearned to pay a filial tribute to her memory, but his own revealed law forbade any respect to the grave of one who had died in unbelief. In the strong agitation of his feelings he implored from heaven a relaxation of this law. If there was any deception on an occasion of this kind, one would imagine it must have been self-deception, and that he really believed in a fancied intimation from heaven relaxing the law, in part, in the present instance, and permitting him to visit the grave. He burst into tears on arriving at this trying place of the tenderest affections; but tears were all the filial tribute he was permitted to offer. "I asked leave of God," said he, mournfully, "to visit my mother's grave, and it was granted; but when I asked leave to pray for her, it was denied me!"

CHAPTER XXXII

Death of the prophet's daughter Zeinab – Birth of his son Ibrahim –
Deputations from distant tribes – Poetical contest in presence of the
prophet – His susceptibility to the charms of poetry – Reduction of
the city of Tayef; destruction of its idols – Negotiation with Amir
Ibn Tufiel, a proud Bedouin chief; independent spirit of the latter –
Interview of Adi, another chief, with Mahomet

Shortly after his return to Medina, Mahomet was afflicted by the death
of his daughter Zeinab, the same who had been given up to him in exchange for her husband Abul Aass, the unbeliever, captured at the battle of Beder. The domestic affections of the prophet were strong, and
he felt deeply this bereavement; he was consoled, however, by the
birth of a son, by his favorite concubine Mariyah. He called the child
Ibrahim, and rejoiced in the hope, that this son of his old age, his only
male issue living, would continue his name to after generations.

His fame, either as a prophet or a conqueror, was now spreading to
the uttermost parts of Arabia, and deputations from distant tribes
were continually arriving at Medina, some acknowledging him as a
prophet and embracing Islamism; others submitting to him as a temporal sovereign, and agreeing to pay tribute. The talents of Mahomet
rose to the exigency of the moment; his views expanded with his fortunes, and he now proceeded with statesmanlike skill to regulate the
fiscal concerns of his rapidly growing empire. Under the specious appellation of alms, a contribution was levied on true believers, amounting to a tithe of the productions of the earth, where it was fertilized by
brooks and rain; and a twentieth part where its fertility was the result
of irrigation. For every ten camels, two sheep were required; for forty
head of cattle, one cow; for thirty head, a two years' calf; for every
forty sheep, one; whoever contributed more than at this rate, would be
considered so much the more devout, and would gain a proportionate
favor in the eyes of God.

The tribute exacted from those who submitted to temporal sway, but
continued in unbelief, was at the rate of one dinar in money or goods,
for each adult person, bond or free.

Some difficulty occurred in collecting the charitable contributions;
the proud tribe of Tamim openly resisted them, and drove away the
collector. A troop of Arab horse was sent against them, and brought
away a number of men, women and children, captives. A deputation of
the Tamimites came to reclaim the prisoners. Four of the deputies

were renowned as orators and poets, and instead of humbling themselves before Mahomet, proceeded to declaim in prose and verse, defying the Moslems to a poetical contest.

"I am not sent by God as a poet," replied Mahomet, "neither do I seek fame as an orator."

Some of his followers, however, accepted the challenge, and a war of ink ensued, in which the Tamimites acknowledged themselves vanquished. So well pleased was Mahomet with the spirit of their defiance, with their poetry, and with their frank acknowledgment of defeat, that he not merely gave them up the prisoners, but dismissed them with presents.

Another instance of his susceptibility to the charms of poetry, is recorded in the case of Caab Ibn Zohair, a celebrated poet of Mecca, who had made him the subject of satirical verses, and had consequently been one of the proscribed; but had fled on the capture of the sacred city. Caab now came to Medina to make his peace, and approaching Mahomet when in the mosque, began chanting his praises in a poem afterwards renowned among the Arabs as a master-piece. He concluded by especially extolling his clemency, "for with the prophet of God, the pardon of injuries is, of all his virtues, that on which one can rely with the greatest certainty."

Captivated with the verse, and soothed by the flattery, Mahomet made good the poet's words, for he not merely forgave him, but taking off his own mantle, threw it upon his shoulders. The poet preserved the sacred garment to the day of his death, refusing golden offers for it. The Caliph Moawyah purchased it of his heirs for ten thousand drachmas, and it continued to be worn by the Caliphs in processions and solemn ceremonials, until the thirty-sixth Caliphat, when it was torn from the back of the Caliph Al-Most'asem Billah, by Holâgu, the Tartar conqueror, and burnt to ashes.

While town after town, and castle after castle of the Arab tribes were embracing the faith, and professing allegiance to Mahomet, Tayef, the stronghold of the Thakefites, remained obstinate in the worship of its boasted idol Al Lat. The inhabitants confided in their mountain position, and in the strength of their walls and castle. But, though safe from assault, they found themselves gradually hemmed in and isolated by the Moslems, so that at length they could not stir beyond their walls without being attacked. Thus threatened and harassed, they sent ambassadors to Mahomet to treat for peace.

The prophet cherished a deep resentment against this stiff-necked and most idolatrous city, which had at one time ejected him from its gates, and at another time repulsed him from its walls. His terms were conversion and unqualified submission. The ambassadors readily consented to embrace Islamism themselves, but pleaded the danger of suddenly shocking the people of Tayef, by a demand to renounce their ancient faith. In their name, therefore, they entreated permission for three years longer, to worship their ancient idol Al Lat. The request was peremptorily denied. They then asked at least one month's delay, to prepare the public mind. This likewise was refused, all idolatry being incompatible with the worship of God. They then entreated to be excused from the observance of the daily prayers.

"There can be no true religion without prayer," replied Mahomet. In fine, they were compelled to make an unconditional submission.

Abu Sofian Ibn Harb, and Al Mogheira, were sent to Tayef, to destroy the idol Al Lat, which was of stone. Abu Sofian struck at it with a pick-axe, but missing his blow, fell prostrate on his face. The populace set up a shout, considering it a good augury, but Al Mogheira demolished their hopes, and the statue, at one blow of a sledge-hammer. He then stripped it of the costly robes, the bracelets, the necklace, the ear-rings, and other ornaments of gold and precious stones wherewith it had been decked by its worshippers, and left it in fragments on the ground, with the women of Tayef weeping and lamenting over it.*

Among those who still defied the power of Mahomet, was the Bedouin chief Amir Ibn Tufiel, head of the powerful tribe of Amir. He was renowned for personal beauty and princely magnificence; but was of a haughty spirit, and his magnificence partook of ostentation. At the great fair of Okaz, between Tayef and Naklah, where merchants, pilgrims, and poets were accustomed to assemble from all parts of Arabia; a herald would proclaim: "Whoso wants a beast of burden, let him come to Amir; is any one hungry, let him come to Amir, and he will be fed; is he persecuted, let him fly to Amir, and he will be protected."

Amir had dazzled every one by his generosity, and his ambition had

---

* The Thakefites continue a powerful tribe to this day; possessing the same fertile region on the eastern declivity of the Hedjas chain of mountains. Some inhabit the ancient town of Tayef, others dwell in tents and have flocks of goats and sheep. They can raise two thousand match-locks, and defended their stronghold of Tayef in the wars with the Wahábys. – *Burckhardt's Notes*, v. 2.

kept pace with his popularity. The rising power of Mahomet inspired him with jealousy. When advised to make terms with him; "I have sworn," replied he haughtily, "never to rest until I had won all Arabia; and shall I do homage to this Koreishite?"

The recent conquests of the Moslems, however, brought him to listen to the counsels of his friends. He repaired to Medina, and coming into the presence of Mahomet, demanded frankly, "Wilt thou be my friend?"

"Never, by Allah!" was the reply, "unless thou dost embrace the faith of Islam."

"And if I do; wilt thou content thyself with the sway over the Arabs of the cities, and leave to me the Bedouins of the deserts?"

Mahomet replied in the negative.

"What then will I gain by embracing thy faith?"

"The fellowship of all true believers."

"I covet no such fellowship!" replied the proud Amir; and with a warlike menace he returned to his tribe.

A Bedouin chieftain of a different character was Adi, a prince of the tribe of Taï. His father Hatim had been famous, not merely for warlike deeds, but for boundless generosity, insomuch that the Arabs were accustomed to say, "as generous as Hatim." Adi the son was a Christian; and however he might have inherited his father's generosity, was deficient in his valor. Alarmed at the ravaging expeditions of the Moslems, he ordered a young Arab, who tended his camels in the desert, to have several of the strongest and fleetest at hand, and to give instant notice of the approach of an enemy.

It happened that Ali, who was scouring that part of the country with a band of horsemen, came in sight, bearing with him two banners, one white, the other black. The young Bedouin beheld them from afar, and ran to Adi, exclaiming, "The Moslems are at hand. I see their banners at a distance!" Adi instantly placed his wife and children on the camels, and fled to Syria. His sister, surnamed Saffana, or the Pearl, fell into the hands of the Moslems, and was carried with other captives to Medina. Seeing Mahomet pass near to the place of her confinement, she cried to him:

"Have pity upon me, oh ambassador of God! My father is dead, and he who should have protected has abandoned me. Have pity upon me, oh ambassador of God, as God may have pity upon thee!"

"Who is thy protector?" asked Mahomet.

"Adi, the son of Hatim."

"He is a fugitive from God and his prophet," replied Mahomet, and passed on.

On the following day, as Mahomet was passing by, Ali, who had been touched by the woman's beauty and her grief, whispered to her to arise and entreat the prophet once more. She accordingly repeated her prayer. "Oh prophet of God! my father is dead; my brother, who should have been my protector, has abandoned me. Have mercy upon me, as God will have mercy upon thee."

Mahomet turned to her benignantly. "Be it so," said he; and he not only set her free, but gave her raiment and a camel, and sent her by the first caravan bound to Syria.

Arriving in presence of her brother, she upbraided him with his desertion. He acknowledged his fault, and was forgiven. She then urged him to make his peace with Mahomet; "he is truly a prophet," said she, "and will soon have universal sway; hasten, therefore, in time to win his favor."

The politic Adi listened to her counsel, and hastening to Medina, greeted the prophet, who was in the mosque. His own account of the interview presents a striking picture of the simple manners and mode of life of Mahomet, now in the full exercise of sovereign power, and the career of rapid conquest. "He asked me," says Adi, "my name, and when I gave it, invited me to accompany him to his home. On the way a weak emaciated woman accosted him. He stopped and talked to her of her affairs. This, thought I to myself, is not very kingly. When we arrived at his house, he gave me a leathern cushion stuffed with palm-leaves to sit upon, while he sat upon the bare ground. This, thought I, is not very princely!

"He then asked me three times to embrace Islamism. I replied, 'I have a faith of my own.' 'I know thy faith,' said he, 'better than thou dost thyself. As prince, thou takest one-fourth of the booty from thy people. Is this Christian doctrine?' By these words I perceived him to be a prophet, who knew more than other men.

" 'Thou dost not incline to Islamism,' continued he, 'because thou seest we are poor. The time is at hand when true believers will have more wealth than they will know how to manage. Perhaps thou art deterred, by seeing the small number of the Moslems in comparison with the hosts of their enemies. By Allah! in a little while a Moslem woman will be able to make a pilgrimage on her camel, alone and fearless, from Kadesia to God's temple at Mecca. Thou thinkest, probably, that the might is in the hands of the unbelievers; know that the time is not far off when we will plant our standards on the white castles of Babylon.' "*

The politic Adi believed in the prophecy, and forthwith embraced the faith.

* Weil's Mohammed, p. 247.

CHAPTER XXXIII

Preparations for an expedition against Syria – Intrigues of Abdallah Ibn Obba – Contributions of the faithful – March of the army – The accursed region of Hajar – Encampment at Tabuc – Subjugation of the neighboring provinces – Khaled surprises Okaïder and his castle – Return of the army to Medina

Mahomet had now, either by conversion or conquest, made himself sovereign of almost all Arabia. The scattered tribes, heretofore dangerous to each other, but by their disunion powerless against the rest of the world, he had united into one nation, and thus fitted for external conquest. His prophetic character gave him absolute control of the formidable power thus conjured up in the desert, and he was now prepared to lead it forth for the propagation of the faith, and the extension of the Moslem power in foreign lands.

His numerous victories, and the recent affair at Muta, had at length, it is said, roused the attention of the Emperor Heraclius, who was assembling an army on the confines of Arabia to crush this new enemy. Mahomet determined to anticipate his hostilities, and to carry the standard of the faith into the very heart of Syria.

Hitherto he had undertaken his expeditions with secrecy; imparting his plans and intentions to none but his most confidential officers, and beguiling his followers into enterprises of danger. The present campaign, however, so different from the brief predatory excursions of the Arabs, would require great preparations; an unusual force was to be assembled, and all kinds of provisions made for distant marches, and a long absence. He proclaimed openly, therefore, the object and nature of the enterprise.

There was not the usual readiness to flock to his standard. Many remembered the disastrous affair of Muta, and dreaded to come again in conflict with disciplined Roman troops. The time of year also was unpropitious for such a distant and prolonged expedition. It was the season of summer heat; the earth was parched, and the springs and brooks were dried up. The date-harvest too was approaching, when the men should be at home to gather the fruit, rather than abroad on predatory enterprises.

All these things were artfully urged upon the people by Abdallah Ibn Obba, the Khazradite, who continued to be the covert enemy of Mahomet, and seized every occasion to counteract his plans. "A fine season this," would he cry, "to undertake such a distant march in defiance of dearth and drought, and the fervid heat of the desert! Mahomet seems to think a war with Greeks quite a matter of sport; trust me, you will find it very different from a war of Arab against Arab. By Allah! methinks I already see you all in chains."

By these and similar scoffs and suggestions, he wrought upon the fears and feelings of the Khazradites, his partisans, and rendered the enterprise generally unpopular. Mahomet, as usual, had resort to revelation. "Those who would remain behind, and refuse to devote themselves to the service of God," said a timely chapter of the Koran, "allege the summer heat as an excuse. Tell them the fire of hell is hotter! They may hug themselves in the enjoyment of present safety, but endless tears will be their punishment hereafter."

Some of his devoted adherents manifested their zeal at this lukewarm moment. Omar, Al Abbas, and Abda'lrahman, gave large sums of money; several female devotees brought their ornaments and jewels. Othman delivered one thousand, some say ten thousand, dinars to Mahomet, and was absolved from his sins, past, present, or to come. Abu Beker gave four thousand drachmas; Mahomet hesitated to accept the offer, knowing it to be all that he possessed. "What will remain," said he, "for thee and thy family?" "God and his prophet," was the reply.

These devout examples had a powerful effect; yet it was with much difficulty that an army of ten thousand horse and twenty thousand foot was assembled. Mahomet now appointed Ali governor of Medina during his absence, and guardian of both their families. He accepted the trust with great reluctance, having been accustomed always to accompany the prophet, and share all his perils. All arrangements being completed, Mahomet marched forth from Medina on this momentous expedition. A part of his army was composed of Khazradites and their confederates, led by Abdallah Ibn Obba. This man, whom Mahomet had well denominated the Chief of the Hypocrites, encamped separately with his adherents at night, at some distance in the rear of the main army; and when the latter marched forward in the morning, lagged behind and led his troops back to Medina. Repairing to Ali, whose dominion in the city was irksome to him and his adherents, he endeavored to make him discontented with his position, alleging that Mahomet had left him in charge of Medina solely to rid himself of an incumbrance. Stung by the suggestion, Ali hastened after Mahomet, and demanded if what Abdallah and his followers said were true.

"These men," replied Mahomet, "are liars. They are the party of Hypocrites and Doubters, who would breed sedition in Medina. I left thee behind to keep watch over them, and to be a guardian to both our families. I would have thee to be to me what Aaron was to Moses; excepting that thou canst not be, like him, a prophet; I being the last of the prophets." With this explanation, Ali returned contented to Medina.

Many have inferred from the foregoing, that Mahomet intended Ali for his Caliph or successor; that being the signification of the Arabic word used to denote the relation of Aaron to Moses.

The troops who had continued on with Mahomet soon began to experience the difficulties of braving the desert in this sultry season. Many turned back on the second day; and others on the third and fourth. Whenever word was brought to the prophet of their desertion, "Let them go," would be the reply; "if they are good for any thing God will bring them back to us; if they are not, we are relieved from so many incumbrances."

While some thus lost heart upon the march, others who had remained at Medina repented of their faint-heartedness. One, named Abu Khaithama, entering his garden during the sultry heat of the day, beheld a repast of viands and fresh water spread for him by his two wives in the cool shade of a tent. Pausing at the threshold, "At this moment," exclaimed he, "the prophet of God is exposed to the winds and heats of the desert, and shall Khaithama sit here in the shade beside his beautiful wives? By Allah! I will not enter the tent!" He immediately armed himself with sword and lance, and, mounting his camel, hastened off to join the standard of the faith.

In the meantime the army, after a weary march of seven days, entered the mountainous district of Hajar, inhabited in days of old by the Thamudites, one of the lost tribes of Arabia. It was the accursed region, the tradition concerning which has already been related. The advance of the army, knowing nothing of this tradition, and being heated and fatigued, beheld, with delight, a brook running through a verdant valley, and cool caves cut in the sides of the neighboring hills, once the abodes of the heaven-smitten Thamudites. Halting along the brook, some prepared to bathe, others began to cook and make bread, while all promised themselves cool quarters for the night in the caves.

Mahomet, in marching, had kept, as was his wont, in the rear of the army to assist the weak; occasionally taking up a wayworn laggard be-

hind him. Arriving at the place where the troops had halted, he recollected it of old, and the traditions concerning it, which had been told
to him when he passed here in the days of his boyhood. Fearful of in-
curring the ban which hung over the neighborhood, he ordered his
troops to throw away the meat cooked with the water of the brook, to
give the bread kneaded with it to the camels, and to hurry away from
the heaven-accursed place. Then wrapping his face in the folds of his
mantle, and setting spurs to his mule, he hastened through that sinful
region; the army following him as if flying from an enemy.

The succeeding night was one of great suffering; the army had to encamp without water; the weather was intensely hot, with a parching
wind from the desert; an intolerable thirst prevailed throughout the
camp, as though the Thamudite ban still hung over it. The next day,
however, an abundant rain refreshed and invigorated both man and
beast. The march was resumed with new ardor, and the army arrived,
without further hardship, at Tabuc, a small town on the confines of the
Roman empire, about half way between Medina and Damascus, and
about ten days' journey from either city.

Here Mahomet pitched his camp in the neighborhood of a fountain,
and in the midst of groves and pasturage. Arabian traditions affirm that
the fountain was nearly dry; insomuch that, when a small vase was
filled for the prophet, not a drop was left: having assuaged his thirst,
however, and made his ablutions, Mahomet threw what remained in
the vase back into the fountain; whereupon a stream gushed forth sufficient for the troops and all the cattle.

From this encampment Mahomet sent out his captains to proclaim
and enforce the faith, or to exact tribute. Some of the neighboring
princes sent embassies, either acknowledging the divinity of his mission, or submitting to his temporal sway. One of these was Johanna Ibn
Ruba, prince of Eyla, a Christian city, near the Red Sea. This was the
same city about which the tradition is told, that in days of old, when
its inhabitants were Jews, the old men were turned into swine, and the
young men into monkeys, for fishing on the Sabbath, a judgment solemnly recorded in the Koran.

The prince of Eyla made a covenant of peace with Mahomet,
agreeing to pay an annual tribute of three thousand dinars or crowns
of gold. The form of the covenant became a precedent in treating with
other powers.

Among the Arab princes who professed the Christian faith, and refused to pay homage to Mahomet, was Okaïder Ibn Malec, of the tribe of Kenda. He resided in a castle at the foot of a mountain, in the midst of his domain. Khaled was sent with a troop of horse to bring him to terms. Seeing the castle was too strong to be carried by assault, he had recourse to stratagem. One moonlight night, as Okaïder and his wife were enjoying the fresh air on the terraced roof of the castle, they beheld an animal grazing, which they supposed to be a wild ass from the neighboring mountains. Okaïder, who was a keen huntsman, ordered horse and lance, and sallied forth to the chase, accompanied by his brother Hassan and several of his people. The wild ass proved to be a decoy. They had not ridden far before Khaled and his men rushed from ambush and attacked them. They were too lightly armed to make much resistance. Hassan was killed on the spot, and Okaïder taken prisoner; the rest fled back to the castle; which, however, was soon surrendered. The prince was ultimately set at liberty on paying a heavy ransom and becoming a tributary.

As a trophy of the victory, Khaled sent to Mahomet the vest stripped from the body of Hassan. It was of silk, richly embroidered with gold. The Moslems gathered round, and examined it with admiration. "Do you admire this vest?" said the prophet. "I swear by him in whose hands is the soul of Mahomet, the vest which Saad, the son of Maadi, wears at this moment in paradise, is far more precious." This Saad was the judge who passed sentence of death on seven hundred Jewish captives at Medina, at the conclusion of a former campaign.

His troops being now refreshed by the sojourn at Tabuc, and the neighboring country being brought into subjection, Mahomet was bent upon prosecuting the object of his campaign, and pushing forward into the heart of Syria. His ardor, however, was not shared by his followers. Intelligence of immense bodies of hostile troops, assembled on the Syrian borders, had damped the spirits of the army. Mahomet remarked the general discouragement, yet was loth to abandon the campaign when but half completed. Calling a council of war, he propounded the question whether or not to continue forward. To this Omar replied, dryly, "If thou hast the command of God to proceed further, do so." "If I had the command of God to proceed further," observed Mahomet, "I should not have asked thy counsel."

Omar felt the rebuke. He then, in a respectful tone, represented the impolicy of advancing in the face of the overwhelming force said to be collected on the Syrian frontier; he represented, also, how much Ma-

homet had already effected in this campaign. He had checked the
threatened invasion of the imperial arms, and had received the homage
and submission of various tribes and people, from the head of the Red
Sea to the Euphrates: he advised him, therefore, to be content for the
present year with what he had achieved, and to defer the completion
of the enterprise to a future campaign.

His counsel was adopted: for, whenever Mahomet was not under
strong excitement, or fancied inspiration, he was rather prone to yield
up his opinion in military matters to that of his generals. After a sojourn of about twenty days, therefore, at Tabuc, he broke up his camp,
and conducted his army back to Medina.

The entries of Mahomet into Medina on returning from his warlike triumphs, partook of the simplicity and absence of parade, which characterized all his actions. On approaching the city, when his household came forth with the multitude to meet him, he would stop to greet them, and take up the children of the house behind him on his horse. It was in this simple way he entered Medina, on returning from the campaign against Tabuc.

The arrival of an army laden with spoil, gathered in the most distant expedition ever undertaken by the soldiers of Islam, was an event of too great moment, not to be hailed with triumphant exultation by the community. Those alone were cast down in spirit, who had refused to march forth with the army, or had deserted it when on the march. All these were at first placed under an interdict; Mahomet forbidding his faithful followers to hold any intercourse with them. Mollified, however, by their contrition or excuses, he gradually forgave the greater part of them. Seven of those who continued under interdict, finding themselves cut off from communion with their acquaintance, and marked with opprobrium amid an exulting community, became desperate, and chained themselves to the walls of the mosque; swearing to remain there until pardoned. Mahomet, on the other hand, swore he would leave them there unless otherwise commanded by God. Fortunately he received the command in a revealed verse of the Koran; but, in freeing them from their self-imposed fetters, he exacted one-third of their possessions, to be expended in the service of the faith.

Among those still under interdict were Kaab Ibn Malec, Murara Ibn Rabia, and Hilal Ibn Omeya. These had once been among the most zealous of professing Moslems; their defection was, therefore, ten times more heinous in the eyes of the prophet, than that of their neighbors, whose faith had been lukewarm and dubious. Toward them, therefore, he continued implacable. Forty days they remained interdicted, and the interdict extended to communication with their wives.

The account given by Kaab Ibn Malec of his situation, while thus excommunicated, presents a vivid picture of the power of Mahomet over the minds of his adherents. Kaab declared that every body

shunned him, or regarded him with an altered mien. His two companions in disgrace did not leave their homes; he, however, went about
from place to place, but no one spake to him. He sought the mosque,
sat down near the prophet, and saluted him, but his salutation was not
returned. On the forty-first day came a command, that he should separate from his wife. He now left the city, and pitched a tent on the hill
of Safa, determined there to undergo in its severest rigor the punishment meted out to him. His heart, however, was dying away; the wide
world, he said, appeared to grow narrow to him. On the fifty-first day
came a messenger holding out the hope of pardon. He hastened to
Medina, and sought the prophet at the mosque, who received him with
a radiant countenance, and said that God had forgiven him. The soul
of Kaab was lifted up from the depths of despondency, and in the
transports of his gratitude, he gave a portion of his wealth in atonement of his error.

Not long after the return of the army to Medina, Abdallah Ibn
Obba, the Khazradite, "the chief of the Hypocrites," fell ill, so that his
life was despaired of. Although Mahomet was well aware of the perfidy
of this man, and the secret arts he had constantly practised against
him, he visited him repeatedly during his illness; was with him at his
dying hour, and followed his body to the grave. There, at the urgent
entreaty of the son of the deceased, he put up prayers that his sins
might be forgiven.

Omar privately remonstrated with Mahomet for praying for a hypocrite; reminding him how often he had been slandered by Abdallah;
but he was shrewdly answered by a text of the Koran: "Thou mayest
pray for the 'Hypocrites' or not, as thou wilt; but though thou should-
est pray seventy times, yet will they not be forgiven."

The prayers at Abdallah's grave, therefore, were put up out of policy, to win favor with the Khazradites, and the powerful friends of the
deceased; and in this respect the prayers were successful, for most of
the adherents of the deceased became devoted to the prophet, whose
sway was thenceforth undisputed in Medina. Subsequently he announced another revelation, which forbade him to pray by the death-
bed or stand by the grave of any one who died in unbelief.

But though Mahomet exercised such dominion over his disciples, and
the community at large, he had great difficulty in governing his wives,
and maintaining tranquillity in his harem. He appears to have acted
with tolerable equity in his connubial concerns, assigning to each of his

wives a separate habitation, of which she was sole mistress, and passing the twenty-four hours with them by turns. It so happened, that on
one occasion, when he was sojourning with Hafsa, the latter left her
dwelling to visit her father. Returning unexpectedly, she surprised the
prophet with his favorite and fortunate slave Mariyah, the mother of
his son Ibrahim. The jealousy of Hafsa was vociferous. Mahomet endeavored to pacify her, dreading lest her outcries should rouse his
whole harem to rebellion; but she was only to be appeased by an oath
on his part never more to cohabit with Mariyah. On these terms she
forgave the past and promised secrecy.

She broke her promise, however, and revealed to Ayesha the infidelity of the prophet; and in a little while it was known throughout the
harem. His wives now united in a storm of reproaches; until, his patience being exhausted, he repudiated Hafsa, and renounced all intercourse with the rest. For a month he lay alone on a mat in a separate
apartment; but Allah, at length, in consideration of his lonely state,
sent down the first and sixth chapters of the Koran, absolving him from
the oath respecting Mariyah, who forthwith became the companion of
his solitary chamber.

The refractory wives were now brought to a sense of their error, and
apprized by the same revelation, that the restrictions imposed on ordinary men did not apply to the prophet. In the end he took back Hafsa,
who was penitent; and he was reconciled to Ayesha whom he tenderly
loved, and all the rest were in due time received into favor; but he continued to cherish Mariyah, for she was fair to look upon, and was the
mother of his only son.

CHAPTER XXXV

Abu Beker conducts the yearly pilgrimage to Mecca – Mission of Ali to announce a revelation

The sacred month of yearly pilgrimage was now at hand, but Mahomet was too much occupied with public and domestic concerns to absent himself from Medina: he deputed Abu Beker, therefore, to act in his place as emir or commander of the pilgrims, who were to resort from Medina to the holy city. Abu Beker accordingly departed at the head of three hundred pilgrims, with twenty camels for sacrifice.

Not long afterwards Mahomet summoned his son-in-law and devoted disciple Ali, and, mounting him on Al Adha, or the slit-eared, the swiftest of his camels, urged him to hasten with all speed to Mecca, there to promulgate before the multitude of pilgrims assembled from all parts, an important sura, or chapter of the Koran, just received from heaven.

Ali executed his mission with his accustomed zeal and fidelity. He reached the sacred city in the height of the great religious festival. On the day of sacrifice, when the ceremonies of pilgrimage were completed by the slaying of the victims in the valley of Mina, and when Abu Beker had preached and instructed the people in the doctrines and rites of Islamism, Ali rose before an immense multitude assembled at the hill Al Akaba, and announced himself a messenger from the prophet, bearing an important revelation. He then read the sura, or chapter of the Koran, of which he was the bearer; in which the religion of the sword was declared in all its rigor. It absolved Mahomet from all truce or league with idolatrous and other unbelievers, should they in any wise have been false to their stipulations, or given aid to his enemies. It allowed unbelievers four months of toleration from the time of this announcement, during which months they might "go to and fro about the earth securely," but at the expiration of that time all indulgence would cease; war would then be made in every way, at every time and in every place, by open force or by stratagem, against those who persisted in unbelief: no alternative would be left them but to embrace the faith, or pay tribute. The holy months and the holy places would no longer afford them protection. "When the months wherein ye are not allowed to attack them shall be passed," said the revelation, "kill the idolatrous wherever ye shall find them, or take them prisoners; besiege them, or lay in wait for them." The ties of blood and friendship

173

were to be alike disregarded; the faithful were to hold no communion
with their nearest relatives and dearest friends, should they persist in
idolatry. After the expiration of the current year, no unbeliever was to
be permitted to tread the sacred bounds of Mecca, nor to enter the
temple of Allah, a prohibition which continues to the present day.

This stringent chapter of the Koran is thought to have been provoked, in a great measure, by the conduct of some of the Jewish and
idolatrous Arabs, with whom Mahomet had made covenants, but who
had repeatedly played him false, and even made treacherous attempts
upon his life. It evinces, however, the increased confidence he felt in
consequence of the death of his insidious and powerful foe, Abdallah
Ibn Obba, and the rapid conversion or subjugation of the Arab tribes.
It was, in fact, a decisive blow for the exclusive domination of his faith.

When Abu Beker and Ali returned to Mecca, the former expressed
surprise and dissatisfaction that he had not been made the promulgator
of so important a revelation, as it seemed to be connected with his recent mission, but he was pacified by the assurance that all new revelations must be announced by the prophet himself, or by some one of his
immediate family.

The promulgation of the last-mentioned chapter of the Koran, with the accompanying denunciation of exterminating war against all who should refuse to believe or submit, produced hosts of converts and trib-utaries; so that, towards the close of the month, and in the beginning of the tenth year of the Hegira, the gates of Medina were thronged with envoys from distant tribes and princes. Among those who bowed to the temporal power of the prophet was Farwa, lieutenant of Hera-clius, in Syria, and governor of Amon, the ancient capital of the Am-monites. His act of submission, however, was disavowed by the em-peror, and punished with imprisonment.

Mahomet felt and acted more and more as a sovereign, but his grand-est schemes as a conqueror were always sanctified by his zeal as an apostle. His captains were sent on more distant expeditions than for-merly, but it was always with a view to destroy idols, and bring idola-trous tribes to subjection; so that his temporal power but kept pace with the propagation of his faith. He appointed two lieutenants to gov-ern in his name in Arabia Felix; but a portion of that rich and impor-tant country having shown itself refractory, Ali was ordered to repair thither at the head of three hundred horsemen, and bring the inhabi-tants to reason.

The youthful disciple expressed a becoming diffidence to undertake a mission where he would have to treat with men far older and wiser than himself; but Mahomet laid one hand upon his lips, and the other upon his breast, and raising his eyes to heaven, exclaimed, "Oh, Allah! loosen his tongue and guide his heart!" He gave him one rule for his conduct as a judge. "When two parties come before thee, never pro-nounce in favor of one until thou hast heard the other." Then giving into his hands the standard of the faith, and placing the turban on his head, he bade him farewell.

When the military missionary arrived in the heretical region of Yemen, his men, indulging their ancient Arab propensities, began to sack, to plunder, and destroy. Ali checked their excesses, and arresting the fugitive inhabitants, began to expound to them the doctrines of Islam. His tongue, though so recently consecrated by the prophet, failed to carry conviction, for he was answered by darts and arrows; whereupon he returned to the old argument of the sword, which he urged with such efficacy, that, after twenty unbelievers had been slain, the rest avowed themselves thoroughly convinced. This zealous achievement was followed by others of a similar kind, after each of which he dispatched messengers to the prophet, announcing a new triumph of the faith.

While Mahomet was exulting in the tidings of success from every quarter, he was stricken to the heart by one of the severest of domestic bereavements. Ibrahim, his son, by his favorite concubine Mariyah, a child but fifteen months old, his only male issue, on whom reposed his hope of transmitting his name to posterity, was seized with a mortal malady, and expired before his eyes. Mahomet could not control a father's feelings as he bent in agony over this blighted blossom of his hopes. Yet even in this trying hour he showed that submission to the will of God which formed the foundation of his faith. "My heart is sad," murmured he, "and mine eyes overflow with tears at parting with thee, oh my son! And still greater would be my grief, did I not know that I must soon follow thee; for we are of God; from him we came, and to him we must return."

Abda'lrahman seeing him in tears, demanded: "Hast thou not forbidden us to weep for the dead?" "No," replied the prophet. "I have forbidden ye to utter shrieks and outcries, to beat your faces, and rend your garments; these are suggestions of the evil one; but tears shed for a calamity are as balm to the heart, and are sent in mercy."

He followed his child to the grave, where amidst the agonies of separation, he gave another proof that the elements of his religion were ever present to his mind. "My son! my son!" exclaimed he as the body was committed to the tomb, "say God is my Lord! the prophet of God was my father, and Islamism is my faith!" This was to prepare his child for the questioning by examining angels, as to religious belief, which, according to Moslem creed, the deceased would undergo while in the grave.*

* One of the funeral rites of the Moslems is for the Mulakken or priest, to address the deceased when in the grave, in the following words: "Oh servant of God! O son of a handmaid of God! know that, at this time, there will come down to thee two angels commissioned respecting thee and the like of thee; when they

An eclipse of the sun which happened about that time, was interpreted by some of his zealous followers as a celestial sign of mourning for the death of Ibrahim; but the afflicted father rejected such obsequious flattery. "The sun and the moon," said he, "are among the wonders of God, through which at times he signifies his will to his servants; but their eclipse has nothing to do either with the birth or death of any mortal."

The death of Ibrahim was a blow which bowed him toward the grave. His constitution was already impaired by the extraordinary excitements and paroxysms of his mind, and the physical trials to which he had been exposed; the poison too, administered to him at Khaïbar, had tainted the springs of life, subjected him to excruciating pains, and brought on a premature old age. His religious zeal took the alarm from the increase of bodily infirmities, and he resolved to expend his remaining strength in a final pilgrimage to Mecca; intended to serve as a model for all future observances of the kind.

The announcement of his pious intention brought devotees from all parts of Arabia, to follow the pilgrim-prophet. The streets of Medina were crowded with the various tribes from the towns and cities, from the fastnesses of the mountains, and the remote parts of the desert, and the surrounding valleys were studded with their tents. It was a striking picture of the triumph of a faith, these recently disunited, barbarous, and warring tribes brought together as brethren, and inspired by one sentiment of religious zeal.

Mahomet was accompanied on this occasion by his nine wives, who were transported on litters. He departed at the head of an immense train, some say of fifty-five, others ninety, and others a hundred and fourteen thousand pilgrims. There was a large number of camels also, decorated with garlands of flowers and fluttering streamers, intended to be offered up in sacrifice.

---

say to thee, 'Who is thy Lord?' answer them, 'God is my Lord,' in truth; and when they ask thee concerning thy prophet, or the man who hath been sent unto you, say to them, 'Mahomet is the apostle of God,' with veracity; and when they ask thee concerning thy religion, say to them, 'Islamism is my religion.' And when they ask thee concerning thy book of direction, say to them, 'the Koran is my book of direction, and the Moslems are my brothers;' and when they ask thee concerning thy Kebla, say to them, 'the Caaba is my Kebla, and I have lived and died in the assertion that there is no deity but God, and Mahomet is God's apostle,' and they will say, 'Sleep, O servant of God, in the protection of God!' " – See *Lane's Modern Egyptians,* vol. ii. p. 338.

The first night's halt was a few miles from Medina, at the village of Dhu'l Holaïfa, where, on a former occasion, he and his followers had laid aside their weapons, and assumed the pilgrim garb. Early on the following morning, after praying in the mosque, he mounted his camel Al Aswa, and entering the plain of Baïda, uttered the prayer or invocation called in Arabic Talbijah, in which he was joined by all his followers. The following is the import of this solemn invocation: "Here am I in thy service, oh God! Here am I in thy service! Thou hast no companion. To thee alone belongeth worship. From thee cometh all good. Thine alone is the kingdom. There is none to share it with thee."

This prayer, according to Moslem tradition, was uttered by the patriarch Abraham, when, from the top of the hill of Kubeis, near Mecca, he preached the true faith to the whole human race, and so wonderful was the power of his voice, that it was heard by every living being throughout the world; insomuch, that the very child in the womb responded, "Here am I in thy service, oh God!"

In this way the pilgrim host pursued its course, winding in a lengthened train of miles, over mountain and valley, and making the deserts vocal at times with united prayers and ejaculations. There were no longer any hostile armies to impede or molest it, for by this time the Islam faith reigned serenely over all Arabia. Mahomet approached the sacred city over the same heights which he had traversed in capturing it, and he entered through the gate Beni Scheiba, which still bears the name of The Holy.

A few days after his arrival, he was joined by Ali, who had hastened back from Yemen; and who brought with him a number of camels to be slain in sacrifice.

As this was to be a model pilgrimage, Mahomet rigorously observed all the rites which he had continued in compliance with patriarchal usage, or introduced in compliance with revelation. Being too weak and infirm to go on foot, he mounted his camel, and thus performed the circuits round the Caaba, and the journeyings to and fro, between the hills of Safa and Merwa.

When the camels were to be offered up in sacrifice, he slew sixty-three with his own hand, one for each year of his age, and Ali, at the same time, slew thirty-seven on his own account.

Mahomet then shaved his head, beginning on the right side and ending on the left. The locks thus shorn away were equally divided among his disciples, and treasured up as sacred relics. Khaled ever afterwards wore one in his turban, and affirmed that it gave him supernatural strength in battle.

Conscious that life was waning away within him, Mahomet, during this last sojourn in the sacred city of his faith, sought to engrave his doctrines deeply in the minds and hearts of his followers. For this purpose he preached frequently in the Caaba from the pulpit, or in the open air from the back of his camel. "Listen to my words," would he say, "for I know not whether, after this year, we shall ever meet here again. Oh, my hearers, I am but a man like yourselves; the angel of death may at any time appear, and I must obey his summons."

He would then proceed to inculcate not merely religious doctrines and ceremonies, but rules for conduct in all the concerns of life, public and domestic; and the precepts laid down and enforced on this occasion, have had a vast and durable influence on the morals, manners, and habitudes of the whole Moslem world.

It was doubtless in view of his approaching end, and in solicitude for the welfare of his relatives and friends after his death, and especially of his favorite Ali, who, he perceived, had given dissatisfaction in the conduct of his recent campaign in Yemen, that he took occasion, during a moment of strong excitement and enthusiasm among his hearers, to address to them a solemn adjuration.

"Ye believe," said he, "that there is but one God; that Mahomet is his prophet and apostle; that paradise and hell are truths; that death and the resurrection are certain; and that there is an appointed time when all who rise from the grave must be brought to judgment."

They all answered, "We believe these things." He then adjured them solemnly by these dogmas of their faith ever to hold his family, and especially Ali, in love and reverence. "Whoever loves me," said he, "let him receive Ali as his friend. May God uphold those who befriend him, and may he turn from his enemies."

It was at the conclusion of one of his discourses in the open air, from the back of his camel, that the famous verse of the Koran is said to have come down from heaven in the very voice of the Deity. "Evil to those, this day, who have denied your religion. Fear them not; fear me. This day I have perfected your religion, and accomplished in you my grace. It is my good pleasure that Islamism be your faith."

On hearing these words, say the Arabian historians, the camel Al

Kaswa, on which the prophet was seated, fell on its knees in adoration. These words, add they, were the seal and conclusion of the law, for after them there were no further revelations.

Having thus fulfilled all the rites and ceremonies of pilgrimage, and made a full exposition of his faith, Mahomet bade a last farewell to his native city, and, putting himself at the head of his pilgrim army, set out on his return to Medina.

As he came in sight of it, he lifted up his voice and exclaimed, "God is great! God is great! There is but one God; he has no companion. His is the kingdom. To him alone belongeth praise. He is almighty. He hath fulfilled his promise. He has stood by his servant, and alone dispersed his enemies. Let us return to our homes, and worship and praise him!"

Thus ended what has been termed the valedictory pilgrimage, being the last made by the prophet.

CHAPTER XXXVII

Of the two false prophets Al Aswad and Moseïlma

The health of Mahomet continued to decline after his return to Medina; nevertheless his ardor to extend his religious empire was unabated, and he prepared, on a great scale, for the invasion of Syria and Palestine. While he was meditating foreign conquest, however, two rival prophets arose to dispute his sway in Arabia. One was named Al Aswad, the other Moseïlma; they received from the faithful the well-merited appellation of "The two Liars."

Al Aswad, a quick-witted man, and gifted with persuasive eloquence, was originally an idolater, then a convert to Islamism, from which he apostatized to set up for a prophet, and establish a religion of his own. His fickleness in matters of faith gained him the appellation of Ailhala, or "The Weather-cock." In emulation of Mahomet he pretended to receive revelations from heaven through the medium of two angels. Being versed in juggling arts and natural magic, he astonished and confounded the multitude with spectral illusions, which he passed off as miracles, insomuch that certain Moslem writers believe he was really assisted by two evil genii or demons. His schemes, for a time, were crowned with great success, which shows how unsettled the Arabs were in those days in matters of religion, and how ready to adopt any new faith.

Budhân, the Persian whom Mahomet had continued as viceroy of Arabia Felix, died in this year; whereupon Al Aswad, now at the head of a powerful sect, slew his son and successor, espoused his widow after putting her father to death, and seized upon the reins of government. The people of Najran invited him to their city; the gates of Sanaa, the capital of Yemen, were likewise thrown open to him, so that, in a little while, all Arabia Felix submitted to his sway.

The news of this usurpation found Mahomet suffering in the first stages of a dangerous malady, and engrossed by preparations for the Syrian invasion. Impatient of any interruption to his plans, and reflecting that the whole danger and difficulty in question depended upon the life of an individual, he sent orders to certain of his adherents, who were about Al Aswad, to make way with him openly or by stratagem, either way being justifiable against enemies of the faith, according to the recent revelation promulgated by Ali. Two persons undertook the task, less, however, through motives of religion than revenge. One, named Rais, had received a mortal offence from the usurper; the other, named Firuz the Daïlemite, was cousin to Al Aswad's newly espoused wife and nephew of her murdered father. They repaired to the woman, whose marriage with the usurper had probably been compulsory, and urged upon her the duty, according to the Arab law of blood, of avenging the deaths of her father and her former husband. With much difficulty they prevailed upon her to facilitate their entrance at the dead of night into the chamber of Al Aswad, who was asleep. Firuz stabbed him in the throat with a poniard. The blow was not effectual. Al Aswad started up, and his cries alarmed the guard. His wife, however, went forth and quieted them. "The prophet," said she, "is under the influence of divine inspiration." By this time the cries had ceased, for the assassins had stricken off the head of their victim. When the day dawned the standard of Mahomet floated once more on the walls of the city, and a herald proclaimed, by sound of trumpet, the death of Al Aswad, otherwise called the Liar and Impostor. His career of power began, and was terminated, within the space of four months. The people, easy of faith, resumed Islamism with as much facility as they had abandoned it.

Moseïlma, the other impostor, was an Arab of the tribe of Honeifa, and ruled over the city and province of Yamama, situated between the Red Sea and the Gulf of Persia. In the ninth year of the Hegira he had come to Mecca at the head of an embassy from his tribe, and had made profession of faith between the hands of Mahomet; but, on returning to his own country, had proclaimed that God had gifted him likewise with prophecy, and appointed him to aid Mahomet in converting the human race. To this effect he likewise wrote a Koran, which he gave forth as a volume of inspired truth. His creed was noted for giving the soul a humiliating residence in the region of the abdomen.

Being a man of influence and address, he soon made hosts of converts among his credulous countrymen. Rendered confident by success, he addressed an epistle to Mahomet, beginning as follows:

"From Moseïlma the prophet of Allah, to Mahomet the prophet of Allah! Come, now, and let us make a partition of the world, and let half be thine and half be mine."

This letter came also to the hands of Mahomet, while bowed down by infirmities and engrossed by military preparations. He contented himself for the present with the following reply:

"From Mahomet the prophet of God, to Moseïlma the Liar! The earth is the Lord's, and he giveth it as an inheritance to such of his servants as find favor in his sight. Happy shall those be who live in his fear."

In the urgency of other affairs, the usurpation of Moseïlma remained unchecked. His punishment was reserved for a future day.

CHAPTER XXXVIII

An army prepared to march against Syria – Command given to Osama – The prophet's farewell address to the troops – His last illness – His sermons in the mosque – His death and the attending circumstances

It was early in the eleventh year of the Hegira that, after unusual preparations, a powerful army was ready to march for the invasion of Syria. It would almost seem a proof of the failing powers of Mahomet's mind, that he gave the command of such an army, on such an expedition, to Osama, a youth but twenty years of age, instead of some one of his veteran and well-tried generals. It seems to have been a matter of favor, dictated by tender and grateful recollections. Osama was the son of Zeid, Mahomet's devoted freedman, who had given the prophet such a signal and acceptable proof of devotion in relinquishing to him his beautiful wife Zeinab. Zeid had continued to the last the same zealous and self-sacrificing disciple, and had fallen bravely fighting for the faith in the battle of Muta.

Mahomet was aware of the hazard of the choice he had made, and feared the troops might be insubordinate under so young a commander. In a general review, therefore, he exhorted them to obedience, reminding them that Osama's father, Zeid, had commanded an expedition of this very kind, against the very same people, and had fallen by their hands; it was but a just tribute to his memory, therefore, to give his son an opportunity of avenging his death. Then placing his banner in the hands of the youthful general, he called upon him to fight valiantly the fight of the faith against all who should deny the unity of God. The army marched forth that very day, and encamped at Djorf, a few miles from Medina; but circumstances occurred to prevent its further progress.

That very night Mahomet had a severe access of the malady which for some time past had affected him, and which was ascribed by some to the lurking effects of the poison given to him at Khaïbar. It commenced with a violent pain in the head, accompanied by vertigo, and the delirium which seems to have mingled with all his paroxysms of illness. Starting up in the mid-watches of the night from a troubled dream, he called upon an attendant slave to accompany him; saying he was summoned by the dead who lay interred in the public burying-place of Medina to come and pray for them. Followed by the slave, he passed through the dark and silent city, where all were sunk in sleep, to the great burying-ground, outside of the walls.

Arrived in the midst of the tombs, he lifted up his voice and made a solemn apostrophe to their tenants. "Rejoice, ye dwellers in the grave!" exclaimed he. "More peaceful is the morning to which ye shall awaken, than that which attends the living. Happier is your condition than theirs. God has delivered you from the storms with which they are threatened, and which shall follow one another like the watches of a stormy night, each darker than that which went before."

After praying for the dead, he turned and addressed his slave. "The choice is given me," said he, "either to remain in this world to the end of time, in the enjoyment of all its delights, or to return sooner to the presence of God; and I have chosen the latter."

From this time his illness rapidly increased, though he endeavored to go about as usual, and shifted his residence from day to day, with his different wives, as he had been accustomed to do. He was in the dwelling of Maimuna, when the violence of his malady became so great, that he saw it must soon prove fatal. His heart now yearned to be with his favorite wife Ayesha, and pass with her the fleeting residue of life. With his head bound up, and his tottering frame supported by Ali and Fadhl, the son of Al Abbas, he repaired to her abode. She, likewise, was suffering with a violent pain in the head, and entreated of him a remedy.

"Wherefore a remedy?" said he. "Better that thou shouldst die before me. I could then close thine eyes; wrap thee in thy funeral garb; lay thee in the tomb, and pray for thee."

"Yes," replied she, "and then return to my house and dwell with one of thy other wives, who would profit by my death."

Mahomet smiled at this expression of jealous fondness, and resigned himself into her care. His only remaining child, Fatima, the wife of Ali, came presently to see him. Ayesha used to say that she never saw any one resemble the prophet more in sweetness of temper, than this his daughter. He treated her always with respectful tenderness. When she came to him, he used to rise up, go towards her, take her by the hand, and kiss it, and would seat her in his own place. Their meeting on this occasion is thus related by Ayesha, in the traditions preserved by Abulfeda.

" 'Welcome, my child,' said the prophet, and made her sit beside him. He then whispered something in her ear, at which she wept. Perceiving her affliction, he whispered something more, and her countenance brightened with joy. 'What is the meaning of this?' said I to Fatima. 'The prophet honors thee with a mark of confidence never bestowed on any of his wives.' 'I cannot disclose the secret of the prophet of God,' replied Fatima. Nevertheless, after his death she declared that at first he announced to her his impending death; but, seeing her weep, consoled her with the assurance that she would shortly follow him, and become a princess in heaven, among the faithful of her sex."

In the second day of his illness Mahomet was tormented by a burning fever, and caused vessels of water to be emptied on his head and over his body; exclaiming, amidst his paroxysms, "Now I feel the poison of Khaïbar rending my entrails."

When somewhat relieved, he was aided in repairing to the mosque, which was adjacent to his residence. Here, seated in his chair, or pulpit, he prayed devoutly; after which, addressing the congregation, which was numerous, "If any of you," said he, "have aught upon his conscience, let him speak out, that I may ask God's pardon for him."

Upon this a man, who had passed for a devout Moslem, stood forth and confessed himself a hypocrite, a liar, and a weak disciple. "Out upon thee!" cried Omar, "why dost thou make known what God had suffered to remain concealed?" But Mahomet turned rebukingly to Omar. "Oh son of Khattâb," said he, "better is it to blush in this world, than suffer in the next." Then lifting his eyes to heaven, and praying for the self-accused, "Oh God," exclaimed he, "give him rectitude and faith, and take from him all weakness in fulfilling such of thy commands as his conscience dictates."

Again addressing the congregation, "Is there any one among you," said he, "whom I have stricken; here is my back, let him strike me in return. Is there any one whose character I have aspersed; let him now cast reproach upon me. Is there any one from whom I have taken aught unjustly; let him now come forward and be indemnified."

Upon this, a man among the throng reminded Mahomet of a debt of three dinars of silver, and was instantly repaid with interest. "Much easier is it," said the prophet, "to bear punishment in this world than throughout eternity."

He now prayed fervently for the faithful, who had fallen by his side in the battle of Ohod, and for those who had suffered for the faith in other battles; interceding with them in virtue of the pact which exists between the living and the dead.

After this he addressed the Mohadjerins or Exiles, who had accompanied him from Mecca, exhorting them to hold in honor the Ansarians, or allies of Medina. "The number of believers," said he, "will increase, but that of the allies never can. They were my family with whom I found a home. Do good to those who do good to them, and break friendship with those who are hostile to them."

He then gave three parting commands:

First. – Expel all idolaters from Arabia.

Second. – Allow all proselytes equal privileges with yourselves.

Third. – Devote yourselves incessantly to prayer.

His sermon and exhortation being finished, he was affectionately supported back to the mansion of Ayesha, but was so exhausted on arriving there that he fainted.

His malady increased from day to day, apparently with intervals of delirium; for he spoke of receiving visits from the angel Gabriel, who came from God to inquire after the state of his health; and told him that it rested with himself to fix his dying moment; the angel of death being forbidden by Allah to enter his presence without his permission.

In one of his paroxysms he called for writing implements, that he might leave some rules of conduct for his followers. His attendants were troubled, fearing he might do something to impair the authority of the Koran. Hearing them debate among themselves, whether to comply with his request, he ordered them to leave the room, and when they returned said nothing more on the subject.

On Friday, the day of religious assemblage, he prepared, notwithstanding his illness, to officiate in the mosque, and had water again poured over him to refresh and strengthen him, but on making an effort to go forth, fainted. On recovering, he requested Abu Beker to perform the public prayers; observing, "Allah has given his servant the right to appoint whom he pleases in his place." It was afterwards maintained by some that he thus intended to designate this long tried friend and adherent as his successor in office; but Abu Beker shrank from construing the words too closely.

Word was soon brought to Mahomet, that the appearance of Abu Beker in the pulpit had caused great agitation, a rumor being circulated that the prophet was dead. Exerting his remaining strength, therefore, and leaning on the shoulders of Ali and Al Abbas, he made his way into the mosque, where his appearance spread joy throughout the congregation. Abu Beker ceased to pray, but Mahomet bade him proceed, and taking his seat behind him in the pulpit, repeated the prayers after him. Then addressing the congregation, "I have heard," said he, "that a rumor of the death of your prophet filled you with alarm; but has any prophet before me lived for ever, that ye think I would never leave you? Every thing happens according to the will of God, and has its appointed time, which is not to be hastened nor avoided. I return to him who sent me; and my last command to you is, that ye remain united; that ye love, honor, and uphold each other; that ye exhort each other to faith and constancy in belief, and to the performance of pious deeds; by these alone men prosper; all else leads to destruction."

In concluding his exhortation, he added, "I do but go before you; you will soon follow me. Death awaits us all; let no one then seek to turn it aside from me. My life has been for your good; so will be my death."

These were the last words he spake in public; he was again conducted back by Ali and Abbas to the dwelling of Ayesha.

On a succeeding day there was an interval during which he appeared so well that Ali, Abu Beker, Omar, and the rest of those who had been constantly about him, absented themselves for a time, to attend to their affairs. Ayesha alone remained with him. The interval was but illusive. His pains returned with redoubled violence. Finding death approaching, he gave orders that all his slaves should be restored to freedom, and all the money in the house distributed among the poor; then raising his eyes to heaven, "God be with me, in the death struggle," exclaimed he.

Ayesha now sent in haste for her father and Hafza. Left alone with Mahomet, she sustained his head on her lap, watching over him with tender assiduity, and endeavoring to soothe his dying agonies. From time to time he would dip his hand in a vase of water, and with it feebly sprinkle his face. At length raising his eyes and gazing upward for a time with unmoving eyelids, "Oh Allah!" ejaculated he, in broken accents, "be it so ! – among the glorious associates in paradise!"

"I knew by this," said Ayesha, who related the dying scene, "that his last moment had arrived, and that he had made choice of supernal existence."

In a few moments his hands were cold, and life was extinct. Ayesha laid his head upon the pillow, and beating her head and breast, gave way to loud lamentations. Her outcries brought the other wives of Ma-

homet, and their clamorous grief soon made the event known throughout the city. Consternation seized upon the people, as if some prodigy
had happened. All business was suspended. The army which had
struck its tents was ordered to halt, and Osama, whose foot was in the
stirrup for the march, turned his steed to the gates of Medina, and
planted his standard at the prophet's door.

The multitude crowded to contemplate the corpse, and agitation and
dispute prevailed even in the chamber of death. Some discredited the
evidence of their senses. "How can he be dead?" cried they. "Is he not
our mediator with God? How then can he be dead? Impossible! He is
but in a trance, and carried up to heaven like Isa (Jesus) and the other
prophets."

The throng augmented about the house, declaring with clamor that
the body should not be interred; when Omar, who had just heard the
tidings, arrived. He drew his scimetar, and pressing through the crowd,
threatened to strike off the hands and feet of any one who should affirm that the prophet was dead. "He has but departed for a time," said
he, "as Musa (Moses) the son of Amram went up forty days into the
mountain; and like him he will return again."

Abu Beker, who had been in a distant part of the city, arrived in
time to soothe the despair of the people and calm the transports of
Omar. Passing into the chamber he raised the cloth which covered the
corpse, and kissing the pale face of Mahomet, "Oh thou!" exclaimed he,
"who wert to me as my father and my mother; sweet art thou even in
death, and living odors dost thou exhale! Now livest thou in everlasting
bliss, for never will Allah subject thee to a second death."

Then covering the corpse he went forth, and endeavored to silence
Omar, but finding it impossible, he addressed the multitude: "Truly if
Mahomet is the sole object of your adoration, he is dead; but if it be
God you worship, he cannot die. Mahomet was but the prophet of
God, and has shared the fate of the apostles and holy men who have
gone before him. Allah, himself, has said in his Koran that Mahomet
was but his ambassador, and was subject to death. What then! will you
turn the heel upon him, and abandon his doctrine because he is dead?
Remember your apostasy harms not God, but insures your own con-
demnation; while the blessings of God will be poured out upon those
who continue faithful to him."

The people listened to Abu Beker with tears and sobbings, and as
they listened their despair subsided. Even Omar was convinced but not

consoled, throwing himself on the earth and bewailing the death of Mahomet, whom he remembered as his commander and his friend.

The death of the prophet, according to the Moslem historians Abulfeda and Al Jannabi, took place on his birthday, when he had completed his sixty-third year. It was in the eleventh year of the Hegira, and the 632d year of the Christian era.

The body was prepared for sepulture by several of the dearest relatives and disciples. They affirmed that a marvelous fragrance which, according to the evidence of his wives and daughters, emanated from his person during life, still continued; so that to use the words of Ali, "it seemed as if he were, at the same time, dead and living."

The body having been washed and perfumed, was wrapped in three coverings; two white, and the third of the striped cloth of Yemen. The whole was then perfumed with amber, musk, aloes, and odoriferous herbs. After this it was exposed in public, and seventy-two prayers were offered up.

The body remained three days unburied, in compliance with oriental custom, and to satisfy those who still believed in the possibility of a trance. When the evidences of mortality could no longer be mistaken, preparations were made for interment. A dispute now arose as to the place of sepulture. The Mohadjerins or disciples from Mecca contended for that city, as being the place of his nativity; the Ansarians claimed for Medina, as his asylum and the place of his residence during the last ten years of his life. A third party advised that his remains should be transported to Jerusalem, as the place of sepulture of the prophets. Abu Beker, whose word had always the greatest weight, declared it to have been the expressed opinion of Mahomet that a prophet should be buried in the place where he died. This in the present instance was complied with to the very letter, for a grave was digged in the house of Ayesha, beneath the very bed on which Mahomet had expired.

NOTE – The house of Ayesha was immediately adjacent to the mosque; which was at that time a humble edifice with clay walls, and a roof thatched with palm-leaves, and supported by the trunks of trees. It has since been included in a spacious temple, on the plan of a colonnade, inclosing an oblong square, 165 paces by 130, open to the heavens, with four gates of entrance. The colonnade, of several rows of pillars of various sizes covered with stucco, and gayly painted, supports a succession of small white cupolas on the four sides of the square. At the four corners are lofty and tapering minarets.

Near the southeast corner of the square is an inclosure, surrounded by an iron railing, painted green, wrought with filagree work and interwoven with brass and gilded wire; admitting no view of the interior excepting through small windows, about six inches square. This inclosure, the great resort of pilgrims, is called the Hadgïra, and contains the tombs of Mahomet, and his two friends and early successors, Abu Beker and Omar. Above this sacred inclosure rises a lofty dome surmounted with a gilded globe and crescent, at the first sight of which, pilgrims, as they approach Medina, salute the tomb of the prophet with profound inclinations of the body and appropriate prayers. The marvellous tale, so long considered veritable, that the coffin of Mahomet remained suspended in the air without any support, and which Christian writers accounted for by supposing that it was of iron, and dexterously placed midway between two magnets, is proved to be an idle fiction.

The mosque has undergone changes. It was at one time partially thrown down and destroyed in an awful tempest, but was rebuilt by the Soldan of Egypt. It has been enlarged and embellished by various Caliphs, and in particular by Waled I, under whom Spain was invaded and conquered. It was plundered of its immense votive treasures by the Wahábys when they took and pillaged Medina. It is now maintained, though with diminished splendor, under the care of about thirty Agas, whose chief is called Sheikh Al Haram, or chief of the Holy House. He is the principal personage in Medina. Pilgrimage to Medina, though considered a most devout and meritorious act, is not imposed on Mahometans, like pilgrimage to Mecca, as a religious duty, and has much declined in modern days.

The foregoing particulars are from Burckhardt, who gained admission into Medina, as well as into Mecca, in disguise and at great peril; admittance into those cities being prohibited to all but Moslems.

CHAPTER XXXIX

Person and character of Mahomet, and speculations on his prophetic career

Mahomet, according to accounts handed down by tradition from his contemporaries, was of the middle stature, square built and sinewy, with large hands and feet. In his youth he was uncommonly strong and vigorous; in the latter part of his life he inclined to corpulency. His head was capacious, well shaped and well set on a neck which rose like a pillar from his ample chest. His forehead was high, broad at the temples and crossed by veins extending down to the eyebrows, which swelled whenever he was angry or excited. He had an oval face, marked and expressive features, an aquiline nose, black eyes, arched eyebrows which nearly met, a mouth large and flexible, indicative of eloquence; very white teeth, somewhat parted and irregular; black hair which waved without a curl on his shoulders, and a long and very full beard.

His deportment, in general, was calm and equable; he sometimes indulged in pleasantry, but more commonly was grave and dignified; though he is said to have possessed a smile of captivating sweetness. His complexion was more ruddy than is usual with Arabs, and in his excited and enthusiastic moments there was a glow and radiance in his countenance, which his disciples magnified into the supernatural light of prophecy.

His intellectual qualities were undoubtedly of an extraordinary kind. He had a quick apprehension, a retentive memory, a vivid imagination, and an inventive genius. Owing but little to education, he had quickened and informed his mind by close observation, and stored it with a great variety of knowledge concerning the systems of religion current in his day, or handed down by tradition from antiquity. His ordinary discourse was grave and sententious, abounding with those aphorisms and apologues so popular among the Arabs; at times he was excited and eloquent, and his eloquence was aided by a voice musical and sonorous.

He was sober and abstemious in his diet, and a rigorous observer of fasts. He indulged in no magnificence of apparel, the ostentation of a petty mind; neither was his simplicity in dress affected; but the result of a real disregard to distinction from so trivial a source. His garments were sometimes of wool; sometimes of the striped cotton of Yemen, and were often patched. He wore a turban, for he said turbans were worn by the angels; and in arranging it he let one end hang down between his shoulders, which he said was the way they wore it. He forbade the wearing of clothes entirely of silk; but permitted a mixture of thread and silk. He forbade also red clothes and the use of gold rings. He wore a seal ring of silver, the engraved part under his finger close to the palm of his hand, bearing the inscription, "Mahomet the messenger of God." He was scrupulous as to personal cleanliness, and observed frequent ablutions. In some respects he was a voluptuary. "There are two things in this world," would he say, "which delight me, women and perfumes. These two things rejoice my eyes, and render me more fervent in devotion." From his extreme cleanliness, and the use of perfumes and of sweet-scented oil for his hair, probably arose that sweetness and fragrance of person, which his disciples considered innate and miraculous. His passion for the sex had an influence over all his affairs. It is said that when in the presence of a beautiful female, he was continually smoothing his brow and adjusting his hair, as if anxious to appear to advantage.

The number of his wives is uncertain. Abulfeda, who writes with more caution than other of the Arabian historians, limits it to fifteen, though some make it as much as twenty-five. At the time of his death he had nine, each in her separate dwelling, and all in the vicinity of the mosque at Medina. The plea alleged for his indulging in a greater number of wives than he permitted to his followers, was a desire to beget a race of prophets for his people. If such indeed were his desire, it was disappointed. Of all his children, Fatima the wife of Ali alone survived him, and she died within a short time after his death. Of her descendants, none excepting her eldest son Hassan ever sat on the throne of the Caliphs.

In his private dealings he was just. He treated friends and strangers, the rich and poor, the powerful and the weak, with equity, and was beloved by the common people for the affability with which he received them, and listened to their complaints.

He was naturally irritable, but had brought his temper under great control, so that even in the self-indulgent intercourse of domestic life he was kind and tolerant. "I served him from the time I was eight years old," said his servant Anas, "and he never scolded me for any thing, though things were spoiled by me."

The question now occurs, was he the unprincipled impostor that he

has been represented? Were all his visions and revelations deliberate
falsehoods, and was his whole system a tissue of deceit? In considering
this question we must bear in mind, that he is not chargeable with
many extravagancies which exist in his name. Many of the visions and
revelations handed down as having been given by him are spurious.
The miracles ascribed to him are all fabrications of Moslem zealots. He
expressly and repeatedly disclaimed all miracles excepting the Koran;
which, considering its incomparable merit, and the way in which it
had come down to him from heaven, he pronounced the greatest of
miracles. And here we must indulge a few observations on this famous
document. While zealous Moslems and some of the most learned doctors of the faith draw proofs of its divine origin from the inimitable
excellence of its style and composition, and the avowed illiteracy of
Mahomet, less devout critics have pronounced it a chaos of beauties
and defects; without method or arrangement; full of obscurities, incoherencies, repetitions, false versions of scriptural stories, and direct contradictions. The truth is that the Koran as it now exists is not the same
Koran delivered by Mahomet to his disciples, but has undergone many
corruptions and interpolations. The revelations contained in it were
given at various times, in various places, and before various persons;
sometimes they were taken down by his secretaries or disciples on
parchment, on palm-leaves, or the shoulder-blades of sheep, and thrown
together in a chest, of which one of his wives had charge; sometimes
they were merely treasured up in the memories of those who heard
them. No care appears to have been taken to systematize and arrange
them during his life; and at his death they remained in scattered fragments, many of them at the mercy of fallacious memories. It was not
until some time after his death that Abu Beker undertook to have them
gathered together and transcribed. Zeid Ibn Thabet, who had been one
of the secretaries of Mahomet, was employed for the purpose. He professed to know many parts of the Koran by heart, having written them
down under the dictation of the prophet; other parts he collected piecemeal from various hands, written down in the rude way we have
mentioned, and many parts he took down as repeated to him by various disciples who professed to have heard them uttered by the
prophet himself. The heterogeneous fragments thus collected were
thrown together without selection; without chronological order, and
without system of any kind. The volume thus formed during the Caliphat of Abu Beker was transcribed by different hands, and many pro-

fessed copies put in circulation and dispersed throughout the Moslem cities. So many errors, interpolations, and contradictory readings, soon crept into these copies, that Othman, the third Caliph, called in the various manuscripts, and forming what he pronounced the genuine Koran, caused all the others to be destroyed.

This simple statement may account for many of the incoherencies, repetitions, and other discrepancies charged upon this singular document. Mahomet, as has justly been observed, may have given the same precepts, or related the same apologue at different times, to different persons in different words; or various persons may have been present at one time, and given various versions of his words; and reported his apologues and scriptural stories in different ways, according to their imperfect memoranda or fallible recollections. Many revelations given by him as having been made in foregone times to the prophets, his predecessors, may have been reported as having been given as revelations made to himself. It has been intimated that Abu Beker, in the early days of his Caliphat, may have found it politic to interpolate many things in the Koran, calculated to aid him in emergencies, and confirm the empire of Islamism. What corruptions and interpolations may have been made by other and less scrupulous hands, after the prophet's death, we may judge by the daring liberties of the kind taken by Abdallah Ibn Saad, one of his secretaries, during his lifetime.

From all these circumstances it will appear, that even the documentary memorials concerning Mahomet abound with vitiations, while the traditional are full of fable. These increase the difficulty of solving the enigma of his character and conduct. His history appears to resolve itself into two grand divisions. During the first part, up to the period of middle life, we cannot perceive what adequate object he had to gain by the impious and stupendous imposture with which he stands charged. Was it riches? His marriage with Cadijah had already made him wealthy, and for years preceding his pretended vision he had manifested no desire to increase his store. Was it distinction? He already stood high in his native place, as a man of intelligence and probity. He was of the illustrious tribe of Koreish, and of the most honored branch of that tribe. Was it power? The guardianship of the Caaba, and with it the command of the sacred city, had been for generations in his immediate family, and his situation and circumstances entitled him to look forward with confidence to that exalted trust. In attempting to subvert the faith in which he had been brought up, he struck at the

root of all these advantages. On that faith were founded the fortunes
and dignities of his family. To assail it must draw on himself the hostility of his kindred, the indignation of his fellow-citizens, and the horror
and odium of all his countrymen, who were worshippers at the Caaba.

Was there any thing brilliant in the outset of his prophetic career to
repay him for these sacrifices, and to lure him on? On the contrary, it
was begun in doubt and secrecy. For years it was not attended by any
material success. In proportion as he made known his doctrines and
proclaimed his revelations, they subjected him to ridicule, scorn, oblo-
quy, and finally to an inveterate persecution; which ruined the fortunes
of himself and his friends; compelled some of his family and followers
to take refuge in a foreign land; obliged him to hide from sight in his
native city, and finally drove him forth a fugitive to seek an uncertain
home elsewhere. Why should he persist for years in a course of imposture which was thus prostrating all his worldly fortunes, at a time of life
when it was too late to build them up anew?

In the absence of sufficient worldly motives, we are compelled to
seek some other explanation of his conduct in this stage of his most
enigmatical history; and this we have endeavored to set forth in the
early part of this work; where we have shown his enthusiastic and visionary spirit gradually wrought up by solitude, fasting, prayer, and
meditation, and irritated by bodily disease into a state of temporary
delirium, in which he fancies he receives a revelation from heaven, and
is declared a prophet of the Most High. We cannot but think there was
self-deception in this instance; and that he believed in the reality of
the dream or vision; especially after his doubts had been combated by
the zealous and confiding Cadijah, and the learned and crafty Waraka.

Once persuaded of his divine mission to go forth and preach the
faith, all subsequent dreams and impulses might be construed to the
same purport; all might be considered intimations of the divine will,
imparted in their several ways to him as a prophet. We find him repeatedly subject to trances and ecstasies in times of peculiar agitation
and excitement, when he may have fancied himself again in communication with the Deity, and these were almost always followed by revelations.

The general tenor of his conduct up to the time of his flight from
Mecca, is that of an enthusiast acting under a species of mental delusion; deeply imbued with a conviction of his being a divine agent for
religious reform: and there is something striking and sublime in the lu-

minous path which his enthusiastic spirit struck out for itself through the bewildering maze of adverse faiths and wild traditions; the pure and spiritual worship of the one true God, which he sought to substitute for the blind idolatry of his childhood.

All the parts of the Koran supposed to have been promulgated by him at this time, incoherently as they have come down to us, and marred as their pristine beauty must be in passing through various hands, are of a pure and elevated character, and breathe poetical, if not religious, inspiration. They show that he had drunk deep of the living waters of Christianity, and if he had failed to imbibe them in their crystal purity, it might be because he had to drink from broken cisterns, and streams troubled and perverted by those who should have been their guardians. The faith he had hitherto inculcated was purer than that held forth by some of the pseudo Christians of Arabia, and his life, so far, had been regulated according to its tenets.

Such is our view of Mahomet and his conduct during the early part of his career, while he was a persecuted and ruined man in Mecca. A signal change, however, took place, as we have shown in the foregoing chapters, after his flight to Medina, when, in place of the mere shelter and protection which he sought, he finds himself revered as a prophet, implicitly obeyed as a chief, and at the head of a powerful, growing, and warlike host of votaries. From this time worldly passions and worldly schemes too often give the impulse to his actions, instead of that visionary enthusiasm which, even if mistaken, threw a glow of piety on his earlier deeds. The old doctrines of forbearance, long-suffering, and resignation, are suddenly dashed aside; he becomes vindictive towards those who have hitherto oppressed him, and ambitious of extended rule. His doctrines, precepts, and conduct, become marked by contradictions, and his whole course is irregular and unsteady. His revelations, henceforth, are so often opportune, and fitted to particular emergencies, that we are led to doubt his sincerity, and that he is any longer under the same delusion concerning them. Still, it must be remembered, as we have shown, that the records of these revelations are not always to be depended upon. What he may have uttered as from his own will, may have been reported as if given as the will of God. Often, too, as we have already suggested, he may have considered his own impulses as divine intimations; and that, being an agent ordained to propagate the faith, all impulses and conceptions toward that end might be part of a continued and divine inspiration.

If we are far from considering Mahomet the gross and impious impostor that some have represented him, so also are we indisposed to
give him credit for vast forecast, and for that deeply concerted scheme
of universal conquest which has been ascribed to him. He was, undoubtedly, a man of great genius and a suggestive imagination, but it
appears to us that he was, in a great degree, the creature of impulse
and excitement, and very much at the mercy of circumstances. His
schemes grew out of his fortunes, and not his fortunes out of his
schemes. He was forty years of age before he first broached his doctrines. He suffered year after year to steal away before he promulgated
them out of his own family. When he fled from Mecca thirteen years
had elapsed from the announcement of his mission, and from being a
wealthy merchant he had sunk to be a ruined fugitive. When he
reached Medina he had no idea of the worldly power that awaited
him; his only thought was to build a humble mosque where he might
preach; and his only hope that he might be suffered to preach with impunity. When power suddenly broke upon him, he used it for a time in
petty forays and local feuds. His military plans expanded with his resources, but were by no means masterly, and were sometimes unsuccessful. They were not struck out with boldness, nor executed with decision; but were often changed in deference to the opinions of warlike
men about him, and sometimes at the suggestion of inferior minds, who
occasionally led him wrong. Had he, indeed, conceived from the outset
the idea of binding up the scattered and conflicting tribes of Arabia
into one nation by a *brotherhood of faith,* for the purpose of carrying
out a scheme of external conquest, he would have been one of the first
of military projectors; but the idea of extended conquest seems to have
been an after-thought, produced by success. The moment he proclaimed the religion of the sword, and gave the predatory Arabs a taste
of foreign plunder, that moment he was launched in a career of conquest, which carried him forward with its own irresistible impetus. The
fanatic zeal with which he had inspired his followers did more for his
success than his military science; their belief in his doctrine of predestination produced victories which no military calculation could have anticipated. In his dubious outset, as a prophet, he had been encouraged
by the crafty counsels of his scriptural oracle Waraka; in his career as a
conqueror, he had Omar, Khaled, and other fiery spirits by his side to
urge him on, and to aid him in managing the tremendous power which
he had evoked into action. Even with all their aid, he had occasionally

to avail himself of his supernatural machinery as a prophet, and in so doing may have reconciled himself to the fraud by considering the pious end to be obtained.

His military triumphs awakened no pride nor vainglory, as they would have done had they been effected for selfish purposes. In the time of his greatest power, he maintained the same simplicity of manners and appearance as in the days of his adversity. So far from affecting regal state, he was displeased if, on entering a room, any unusual testimonial of respect were shown him. If he aimed at universal dominion, it was the dominion of the faith: as to the temporal rule which grew up in his hands, as he used it without ostentation, so he took no step to perpetuate it in his family.

The riches which poured in upon him from tribute and the spoils of war, were expended in promoting the victories of the faith, and in relieving the poor among its votaries; insomuch that his treasury was often drained of its last coin. Omar Ibn Al Hareth declares that Mahomet, at his death, did not leave a golden dinar nor a silver dirhem, a slave nor a slave girl, nor any thing but his gray mule Daldal, his arms, and the ground which he bestowed upon his wives, his children, and the poor. "Allah," says an Arabian writer, "offered him the keys of all the treasures of the earth; but he refused to accept them."

It is this perfect abnegation of self, connected with this apparently heartfelt piety, running throughout the various phases of his fortune, which perplex one in forming a just estimate of Mahomet's character. However he betrayed the alloy of earth after he had worldly power at his command, the early aspirations of his spirit continually returned and bore him above all earthly things. Prayer, that vital duty of Islamism, and that infallible purifier of the soul, was his constant practice. "Trust in God," was his comfort and support in times of trial and despondency. On the clemency of God, we are told, he reposed all his hopes of supernal happiness. Ayesha relates that on one occasion she inquired of him, "Oh prophet, do none enter paradise but through God's mercy?" "None – none – none!" replied he, with earnest and emphatic repetition. "But you, oh prophet, will not *you* enter excepting through his compassion?" Then Mahomet put his hand upon his head, and replied three times, with great solemnity, "Neither shall I enter paradise unless God cover me with his mercy!"

When he hung over the death-bed of his infant son Ibrahim, resignation to the will of God was exhibited in his conduct under this keenest of afflictions; and the hope of soon rejoining his child in paradise was his consolation. When he followed him to the grave, he invoked his spirit, in the awful examination of the tomb, to hold fast to the foundations of the faith, the unity of God, and his own mission as a prophet. Even in his own dying hour, when there could be no longer a worldly motive for deceit, he still breathed the same religious devotion, and the same belief in his apostolic mission. The last words that trembled on his lips ejaculated a trust of soon entering into blissful companionship with the prophets who had gone before him.

It is difficult to reconcile such ardent, persevering piety, with an incessant system of blasphemous imposture; nor such pure and elevated and benignant precepts as are contained in the Koran, with a mind haunted by ignoble passions, and devoted to the grovelling interests of mere mortality; and we find no other satisfactory mode of solving the enigma of his character and conduct, than by supposing that the ray of mental hallucination which flashed upon his enthusiastic spirit during his religious ecstasies in the midnight cavern of Mount Hara, continued more or less to bewilder him with a species of monomania to the end of his career, and that he died in the delusive belief of his mission as a prophet.

APPENDIX

APPENDIX

OF THE ISLAM FAITH

In an early chapter of this work we have given such particulars of the faith inculcated by Mahomet as we deemed important to the understanding of the succeeding narrative: we now, though at the expense of some repetition, subjoin a more complete summary, accompanied by a few observations.

The religion of Islam, as we observed on the before-mentioned occasion, is divided into two parts; FAITH and PRACTICE: – and first of Faith. This is distributed under six different heads, or articles, viz.: 1st, faith in God; 2d, in his angels; 3d, in his Scriptures or Koran; 4th, in his prophets; 5th, in the resurrection and final judgment; 6th, in predestination. Of these we will briefly treat in the order we have enumerated them.

FAITH IN GOD. – Mahomet inculcated the belief that there is, was, and ever will be, one only God, the creator of all things; who is single, immutable, omniscient, omnipotent, all merciful, and eternal. The unity of God was specifically and strongly urged, in contradistinction to the Trinity of the Christians. It was designated, in the profession of faith, by raising one finger, and exclaiming, "La illaha il Allah!" There is no God but God – to which was added, "Mohamed Resoul Allah!" Mahomet is the prophet of God.

FAITH IN ANGELS. – The beautiful doctrine of angels, or ministering spirits, which was one of the most ancient and universal of oriental creeds, is interwoven throughout the Islam system. They are represented as ethereal beings, created from fire, the purest of elements, perfect in form and radiant in beauty, but without sex; free from all gross or sensual passion, and all the appetites and infirmities of frail humanity; and existing in perpetual and unfading youth. They are various in their degrees and duties, and in their favor with the Deity. Some worship around the celestial throne; others perpetually hymn the praises of Allah; some are winged messengers to execute his orders, and others intercede for the children of men.

The most distinguished of this heavenly host are four Archangels. Gabriel, the angel of revelations, who writes down the divine decrees;

Michael, the champion, who fights the battles of the faith; Azraïl, the angel of death; and Israfil, who holds the awful commission to sound the trumpet on the day of resurrection. There was another angel named Azazil, the same as Lucifer, once the most glorious of the celestial band; but he became proud and rebellious. When God commanded his angels to worship Adam, Azazil refused, saying, "Why should I, whom thou hast created of fire, bow down to one whom thou hast formed of clay?" For this offence he was accursed and cast forth from paradise, and his name changed to Eblis, which signifies despair. In revenge of his abasement, he works all kinds of mischief against the children of men, and inspires them with disobedience and impiety.

Among the angels of inferior rank is a class called Moakkibat; two of whom keep watch upon each mortal, one on the right hand, the other on the left, taking note of every word and action. At the close of each day they fly up to heaven with a written report, and are replaced by two similar angels on the following day. According to Mahometan tradition, every good action is recorded ten times by the angel on the right; and if the mortal commit a sin, the same benevolent spirit says to the angel on the left, "Forbear for seven hours to record it; peradventure he may repent and pray and obtain forgiveness."

Beside the angelic orders Mahomet inculcated a belief in spiritual beings called Gins or Genii, who, though likewise created of fire, partake of the appetites and frailties of the children of the dust, and like them are ultimately liable to death. By beings of this nature, which haunt the solitudes of the desert, Mahomet, as we have shown, professed to have been visited after his evening orisons in the solitary valley of Al Naklah.

When the angel Azazil rebelled and fell and became Satan or Eblis, he still maintained sovereignty over these inferior spirits; who are divided by Orientalists into Dives and Peri: the former ferocious and gigantic; the latter delicate and gentle, subsisting on perfumes. It would seem as if the Peri were all of the female sex, though on this point there rests obscurity. From these imaginary beings it is supposed the European fairies are derived.

Besides these there are other demi-spirits called Tacwins or Fates; being winged females of beautiful forms, who utter oracles and defend mortals from the assaults and machinations of evil demons.

There is vagueness and uncertainty about all the attributes given by Mahomet to these half-celestial beings; his ideas on the subject having been acquired from various sources. His whole system of intermediate spirits has a strong, though indistinct infusion of the creeds and superstitions of the Hebrews, the Magians, and the Pagans or Sabeans.

The third article of faith is a belief in the KORAN, as a book of divine revelation. According to the Moslem creed a book was treasured up in the seventh heaven, and had existed there from all eternity, in which were written down all the decrees of God and all events, past, present, or to come. Transcripts from these tablets of the divine will were brought down to the lowest heaven by the angel Gabriel, and by him revealed to Mahomet from time to time, in portions adapted to some event or emergency. Being the direct words of God, they were all spoken in the first person.

Of the way in which these revelations were taken down or treasured up by secretaries and disciples, and gathered together by Abu Beker after the death of Mahomet, we have made sufficient mention. The compilation, for such in fact it is, forms the Moslem code of civil and penal as well as religious law, and is treated with the utmost reverence by all true believers. A zealous pride is shown in having copies of it splendidly bound and ornamented. An inscription on the cover forbids any one to touch it who is unclean, and it is considered irreverent, in reading it, to hold it below the girdle. Moslems swear by it, and take omens from its pages, by opening it and reading the first text that meets the eye. With all its errors and discrepancies, if we consider it mainly as the work of one man, and that an unlettered man, it remains a stupendous monument of solitary legislation.

Beside the Koran or written law, a number of precepts and apologues which casually fell from the lips of Mahomet were collected after his death from ear-witnesses, and transcribed into a book called the Sonna or Oral Law. This is held equally sacred with the Koran by a sect of Mahometans thence called Sonnites; others reject it as apocryphal; these last are termed Schiites. Hostilities and persecutions have occasionally taken place between these sects almost as virulent as those which, between Catholics and Protestants, have disgraced Christianity. The Sonnites are distinguished by white, the Schiites by red turbans; hence the latter have received from their antagonists the appellation of Kussilbachi, or Red Heads.

It is remarkable that circumcision, which is invariably practised by the Mahometans and forms a distinguishing rite of their faith, to which all proselytes must conform, is neither mentioned in the Koran nor the

Sonna. It seems to have been a general usage in Arabia, tacitly adopted from the Jews, and is even said to have been prevalent throughout the East before the time of Moses.

It is said that the Koran forbids the making of likenesses of any living thing, which has prevented the introduction of portrait-painting among Mahometans. The passage of the Koran, however, which is thought to contain the prohibition, seems merely an echo of the second commandment, held sacred by Jews and Christians, not to form images or pictures for worship. One of Mahomet's standards was a black eagle. Among the most distinguished Moslem ornaments of the Alhambra at Granada is a fountain supported by lions carved of stone, and some Moslem monarchs have had their effigies stamped on their coins.

Another and an important mistake with regard to the system of Mahomet, is the idea that it denies souls to the female sex, and excludes them from paradise. This error arises from his omitting to mention their enjoyments in a future state, while he details those of his own sex with the minuteness of a voluptuary. The beatification of virtuous females is alluded to in the 56th sura of the Koran, and also in other places, although from the vagueness of the language a cursory reader might suppose the Houris of paradise to be intended.

The fourth article of faith relates to the PROPHETS. Their number amounts to two hundred thousand, but only six are super-eminent, as having brought new laws and dispensations upon earth, each abrogating those previously received wherever they varied or were contradictory. These six distinguished prophets were Adam, Noah, Abraham, Moses, Jesus, and Mahomet.

The fifth article of Islam faith is on the RESURRECTION and the FINAL JUDGMENT. On this awful subject Mahomet blended some of the Christian belief with certain notions current among the Arabian Jews. One of the latter is the fearful tribunal of the Sepulchre. When Azraïl, the angel of death, has performed his office, and the corpse has been consigned to the tomb, two black angels, Munkar and Nakeer, of dismal and appalling aspect, present themselves as inquisitors; during whose scrutiny the soul is reunited to the body. The defunct, being commanded to sit up, is interrogated as to the two great points of faith, the unity of God and the divine mission of Mahomet, and likewise as to the deeds done by him during life; and his replies are recorded in books against the day of judgment. Should they be satisfactory, his soul is gently drawn forth from his lips, and his body left to its repose;

should they be otherwise, he is beaten about the brows with iron clubs, and his soul wrenched forth with racking tortures. For the convenience of this awful inquisition, the Mahometans generally deposit their dead in hollow or vaulted sepulchres; merely wrapped in funeral clothes, but not placed in coffins.

The space of time between death and resurrection is called Berzak, or the Interval. During this period the body rests in the grave, but the soul has a foretaste, in dreams or visions, of its future doom.

The souls of prophets are admitted at once into the full fruition of paradise. Those of martyrs, including all who die in battle, enter into the bodies or crops of green birds, who feed on the fruits and drink of the streams of paradise. Those of the great mass of true believers are variously disposed of, but, according to the most received opinion, they hover, in a state of seraphic tranquility, near the tombs. Hence the Moslem usage of visiting the graves of their departed friends and relatives, in the idea that their souls are the gratified witnesses of these testimonials of affection.

Many Moslems believe that the souls of the truly faithful assume the forms of snow-white birds, and nestle beneath the throne of Allah; a belief in accordance with an ancient superstition of the Hebrews, that the souls of the just will have a place in heaven under the throne of glory.

With regard to the souls of infidels, the most orthodox opinion is that they will be repulsed by angels both from heaven and earth, and cast into the cavernous bowels of the earth, there to await in tribulation the day of judgment.

THE DAY OF RESURRECTION will be preceded by signs and portents in heaven and earth. A total eclipse of the moon; a change in the course of the sun, rising in the west instead of the east; wars and tumults; a universal decay of faith; the advent of Antichrist; the issuing forth of Gog and Magog to desolate the world; a great smoke, covering the whole earth: these and many more prodigies and omens affrighting and harassing the souls of men, and producing a wretchedness of spirit and a weariness of life; insomuch that a man passing by a grave shall envy the quiet dead, and say, "Would to God I were in thy place!"

The last dread signal of the awful day will be the blast of a trumpet by the archangel Izrafil. At the sound thereof the earth will tremble; castles and towers will be shaken to the ground, and mountains levelled with the plains. The face of heaven will be darkened; the firmament will melt away, and the sun, the moon, and stars will fall into the sea. The ocean will be either dried up, or will boil and roll in fiery billows.

At the sound of that dreadful trump a panic will fall on the human race; men will fly from their brothers, their parents, and their wives; and mothers, in frantic terror, abandon the infant at the breast. The savage beasts of the forests, and the tame animals of the pasture, will forget their fierceness and their antipathies, and herd together in affright.

The second blast of the trumpet is the blast of extermination. At that sound, all creatures in heaven and on earth and in the waters under the earth, angels and genii and men and animals, all will die; excepting the chosen few especially reserved by Allah. The last to die will be Azraïl, the angel of death!

Forty days, or, according to explanations, forty years of continued rain will follow this blast of extermination; then will be sounded for the third time the trumpet of the archangel Izrafil; it is the call to judgment! At the sound of this blast, the whole space between heaven and earth will be filled with the souls of the dead flying in quest of their respective bodies. Then the earth will open; and there will be a rattling of dry bones, and a gathering of scattered limbs; the very hairs will congregate together, and the whole body be reunited, and the soul will re-enter it, and the dead will rise from mutilation, perfect in every part, and naked as when born. The infidels will grovel with their faces on the earth, but the faithful will walk erect; as to the truly pious, they will be borne aloft on winged camels, white as milk, with saddles of fine gold.

Every human being will then be put upon his trial as to the manner in which he has employed his faculties, and the good and evil actions of his life. A mighty balance will be poised by the angel Gabriel; in one of the scales, termed Light, will be placed his good actions; in the other, termed Darkness, his evil deeds. An atom or a grain of mustard-seed will suffice to turn this balance; and the nature of the sentence will depend on the preponderance of either scale. At that moment retribution will be exacted for every wrong and injury. He who has wronged a fellow-mortal will have to repay him with a portion of his own good deeds, or, if he have none to boast of, will have to take upon himself a proportionate weight of the other's sins.

The trial of the balance will be succeeded by the ordeal of the bridge. The whole assembled multitude will have to follow Mahomet across the bridge Al Serát, as fine as the edge of a scimetar, which crosses the gulf of Jehennam or Hell. Infidels and sinful Moslems will grope along it darkling and fall into the abyss; but the faithful, aided by a beaming light, will cross with the swiftness of birds and enter the realms of paradise. The idea of this bridge, and of the dreary realms of Jehennam, is supposed to have been derived partly from the Jews, but chiefly from the Magians.

Jehennam is a region fraught with all kinds of horrors. The very trees have writhing serpents for branches, bearing for fruit the heads of demons. We forbear to dwell upon the particulars of this dismal abode, which are given with painful and often disgusting minuteness. It is described as consisting of seven stages, one below the other, and varying in the nature and intensity of torment. The first stage is allotted to Atheists, who deny creator and creation, and believe the world to be eternal. The second for Manicheans and others that admit two divine principles; and for the Arabian idolaters of the era of Mahomet. The third is for the Brahmins of India; the fourth for the Jews; the fifth for Christians; the sixth for the Magians or Ghebers of Persia; the seventh for hypocrites, who profess without believing in religion.

The fierce angel Thabeck, that is to say, the Executioner, presides over this region of terror.

We must observe that the general nature of Jehennam, and the distribution of its punishments, have given rise to various commentaries and expositions among the Moslem doctors. It is maintained by some, and it is a popular doctrine, that none of the believers in Allah and his prophets will be condemned to eternal punishment. Their sins will be expiated by proportionate periods of suffering, varying from nine hundred to nine thousand years.

Some of the most humane among the Doctors contend against eternity of punishment to any class of sinners, saying that, as God is all merciful, even infidels will eventually be pardoned. Those who have an intercessor, as the Christians have in Jesus Christ, will be first redeemed. The liberality of these worthy commentators, however, does not extend so far as to admit them into paradise among true believers; but concludes that, after long punishment, they will be relieved from their torments by annihilation.

Between Jehennam and paradise is Al Araf or the Partition, a region destitute of peace or pleasure, destined for the reception of infants, lunatics, idiots, and such other beings as have done neither good nor evil. For such too whose good and evil deeds balance each other; though these may be admitted to paradise through the intercession of Mahomet, on performing an act of adoration, to turn the scales in their favor. It is said that the tenants of this region can converse with their neighbors on either hand, the blessed and the condemned; and that Al Araf appears a paradise to those in hell and a hell to those in paradise.

AL JANNAT, OR THE GARDEN. – When the true believer has passed through all his trials, and expiated all his sins, he refreshes himself at the Pool of the Prophet. This is a lake of fragrant water, a month's journey in circuit, fed by the river Al Cauther, which flows from paradise. The water of this lake is sweet as honey, cold as snow, and clear as crystal; he who once tastes of it will never more be tormented by thirst; a blessing dwelt upon with peculiar zest by Arabian writers, accustomed to the parching thirst of the desert.

After the true believer has drunk of this water of life, the gate of paradise is opened to him by the angel Rushvan. The same prolixity and minuteness which occur in the description of Jehennam, are lavished on the delights of paradise, until the imagination is dazzled and confused by the details. The soil is of the finest wheaten flour, fragrant with perfumes, and strewed with pearls and hyacinths instead of sands and pebbles.

Some of the streams are of crystal purity, running between green banks enamelled with flowers; others are of milk, of wine and honey; flowing over beds of musk, between margins of camphire, covered with moss and saffron! The air is sweeter than the spicy gales of Sabea, and cooled by sparkling fountains. Here, too, is Taba, the wonderful tree of life, so large that a fleet horse would need a hundred years to cross its shade. The boughs are laden with every variety of delicious fruit, and bend to the hand of those who seek to gather.

The inhabitants of this blissful garden are clothed in raiment sparkling with jewels; they wear crowns of gold enriched with pearls and diamonds, and dwell in sumptuous palaces or silken pavilions, reclining in voluptuous couches. Here every believer will have hundreds of attendants, bearing dishes and goblets of gold, to serve him with every variety of exquisite viand and beverage. He will eat without satiety, and drink without inebriation; the last morsel and the last drop will be equally relished with the first: he will feel no repletion, and need no evacuation.

The air will resound with the melodious voice of Izrafil, and the songs of the daughters of paradise; the very rustling of the trees will produce ravishing harmony, while myriads of bells, hanging among their branches, will be put in dulcet motion by airs from the throne of Allah.

Above all, the faithful will be blessed with female society to the full extent even of oriental imaginings. Beside the wives he had on earth, who will rejoin him in all their pristine charms, he will be attended by the Hûr al Oyûn, or Houris, so called from their large black eyes; re-splendent beings, free from every human defect or frailty; perpetually retaining their youth and beauty, and renewing their virginity. Seven-ty-two of these are allotted to every believer. The intercourse with them will be fruitful or not according to their wish, and the offspring will grow within an hour to the same stature with the parents.

That the true believer may be fully competent to the enjoyments of this blissful region, he will rise from the grave in the prime of man-hood, at the age of thirty, of the stature of Adam, which was thirty cubits; with all his faculties improved to a state of preternatural per-fection, with the abilities of a hundred men, and with desires and ap-petites quickened rather than sated by enjoyment.

These and similar delights are promised to the meanest of the faith-ful; there are gradations of enjoyment, however, as of merit; but, as to those prepared for the most deserving, Mahomet found the powers of description exhausted, and was fain to make use of the text from Scrip-ture, that they should be such things "as eye hath not seen, ear hath not heard, neither hath it entered into the heart of man to conceive."

The expounders of the Mahometan law differ in their opinions as to the whole meaning of this system of rewards and punishments; one set understanding every thing in a figurative, the other in a literal sense. The former insist that the prophet spake in parable, in a manner suited to the coarse perceptions and sensual natures of his hearers; and main-tain that the joys of heaven will be mental as well as corporeal; the resurrection being of both soul and body. The soul will revel in a su-pernatural development and employment of all its faculties; in a knowledge of all the arcana of nature; the full revelation of every thing past, present, and to come. The enjoyments of the body will be equally suited to its various senses, and perfected to a supernatural degree.

The same expounders regard the description of Jehennam as equally figurative; the torments of the soul consisting in the anguish of perpetual remorse for past crimes, and deep and ever increasing despair for the loss of heaven; those of the body in excruciating and never-ending pain.

The other doctors, who construe every thing in a literal sense, are considered the most orthodox, and their sect is beyond measure the most numerous. Most of the particulars in the system of rewards and punishments, as has been already observed, have close affinity to the superstitions of the Magians and the Jewish Rabbins. The Houri, or black-eyed nymphs, who figure so conspicuously in the Moslem's paradise, are said to be the same as the Huram Behest of the Persian Magi, and Mahomet is accused by Christian investigators of having purloined much of his description of heaven from the account of the New Jerusalem in the Apocalypse; with such variation as is used by knavish jewellers, when they appropriate stolen jewels to their own use.

The sixth and last article of the Islam faith is PREDESTINATION, and on this Mahomet evidently reposed his chief dependence for the success of his military enterprises. He inculcated that every event had been predetermined by God, and written down in the eternal tablet previous to the creation of the world. That the destiny of every individual, and the hour of his death, were irrevocably fixed, and could neither be varied nor invaded by any effort of human sagacity or foresight. Under this persuasion, the Moslems engaged in battle without risk; and, as death in battle was equivalent to martyrdom, and entitled them to an immediate admission into paradise, they had in either alternative, death or victory, a certainty of gain.

This doctrine, according to which men by their own free will can neither avoid sin nor avert punishment, is considered by many Musulmen as derogatory to the justice and clemency of God; and several sects have sprung up, who endeavor to soften and explain away this perplexing dogma; but the number of these doubters is small, and they are not considered orthodox.

The doctrine of Predestination was one of those timely revelations to Mahomet, that were almost miraculous from their seasonable occurrence. It took place immediately after the disastrous battle of Ohod, in which many of his followers, and among them his uncle Hamza, were slain. Then it was, in a moment of gloom and despondency, when his followers around him were disheartened, that he promulgated this law, telling them that every man must die at the appointed hour, whether in bed or in the field of battle. He declared, moreover, that the angel

Gabriel had announced to him the reception of Hamza into the seventh heaven, with the title of Lion of God and of the Prophet. He added, as he contemplated the dead bodies, "I am witness for these, and for all who have been slain for the cause of God, that they shall appear in glory at the resurrection, with their wounds brilliant as vermilion and odoriferous as musk."

What doctrine could have been devised more calculated to hurry forward, in a wild career of conquest, a set of ignorant and predatory soldiers, than this assurance of booty if they survived, and paradise if they fell?* It rendered almost irresistible the Moslem arms; but it likewise contained the poison that was to destroy their dominion. From the moment the successors of the prophet ceased to be aggressors and conquerors, and sheathed the sword definitively, the doctrine of predestination began its baneful work. Enervated by peace, and the sensuality permitted by the Koran – which so distinctly separates its doctrines from the pure and self-denying religion of the Messiah – the Moslem regarded every reverse as preordained by Allah, and inevitable; to be borne stoically, since human exertion and foresight were vain. "Help thyself and God will help thee," was a precept never in force with the followers of Mahomet, and its reverse has been their fate. The crescent has waned before the cross, and exists in Europe, where it was once so mighty, only by the suffrage, or rather the jealousy of the great Christian powers, probably ere long to furnish another illustration, that "they that take the sword shall perish with the sword."

RELIGIOUS PRACTICE

The articles of religious practice are fourfold: Prayer, including ablution, Alms, Fasting, Pilgrimage.

ABLUTION is enjoined as preparative to PRAYER, purity of body being considered emblematical of purity of soul. It is prescribed in the Koran with curious precision. The face, arms, elbows, feet, and a fourth part of the head, to be washed once; the hands, mouth and nostrils, three times; the ears to be moistened with the residue of the water used for the head, and the teeth to be cleaned with a brush. The ablution to

---

* The reader may recollect that a belief in predestination, or destiny, was encouraged by Napoleon, and had much influence on his troops.

commence on the right and terminate on the left; in washing the hands and feet to begin with the fingers and toes; where water is not to be had, fine sand may be used.

PRAYER is to be performed five times every day, viz.: the first in the morning before sunrise; the second at noon; the third in the afternoon before sunset; the fourth in the evening between sunset and dark; the fifth between twilight and the first watch, being the vesper prayer. A sixth prayer is volunteered by many between the first watch of the night and the dawn of day. These prayers are but repetitions of the same laudatory ejaculation, "God is great! God is powerful! God is all powerful!" and are counted by the scrupulous upon a string of beads. They may be performed at the mosque, or in any clean place. During prayer the eyes are turned to the Kebla, or point of the heaven in the direction of Mecca; which is indicated in every mosque by a niche called Al Mehrab, and externally by the position of the minarets and doors. Even the postures to be observed in prayer are prescribed, and the most solemn act of adoration is by bowing the forehead to the ground. Females in praying are not to stretch forth their arms, but to fold them on their bosoms. They are not to make as profound inflexions as the men. They are to pray in a low and gentle tone of voice. They are not permitted to accompany the men to the mosque, lest the minds of the worshippers should be drawn from their devotions. In addressing themselves to God, the faithful are enjoined to do so with humility; putting aside costly ornaments and sumptuous apparel.

Many of the Mahometan observances with respect to prayer were similar to those previously maintained by the Sabeans; others agreed with the ceremonials prescribed by the Jewish Rabbins. Such were the postures, inflexions and prostrations, and the turning of the face towards the Kebla, which, however, with the Jews was in the direction of the temple at Jerusalem.

Prayer, with the Moslem, is a daily exercise; but on Friday there is a sermon in the mosque. This day was generally held sacred among oriental nations as the day on which man was created. The Sabean idolaters consecrated it to Astarte, or Venus, the most beautiful of the planets and brightest of the stars. Mahomet adopted it as his Sabbath, partly perhaps from early habitude, but chiefly to vary from the Saturday of the Jews and Sunday of the Christians.

The *second article* of religious practice is CHARITY, or the giving of alms. There are two kinds of alms, viz.: those prescribed by law, called

Zacat, like tithes in the Christian church, to be made in specified proportions, whether in money, wares, cattle, corn, or fruit; and voluntary
gifts termed Sadakat, made at the discretion of the giver. Every Moslem is enjoined, in one way or the other, to dispense a tenth of his
revenue in relief of the indigent and distressed.

The *third article* of practice is FASTING, also supposed to have been
derived from the Jews. In each year for thirty days, during the month
Ramadan, the true believer is to abstain rigorously, from the rising to
the setting of the sun from meat and drink, baths, perfumes, the intercourse of the sexes, and all other gratifications and delights of the
senses. This is considered a great triumph of self-denial, mortifying
and subduing the several appetites, and purifying both body and soul.
Of these three articles of practice the Prince Abdalasis used to say,
"Prayer leads us half way to God; fasting conveys us to his threshold,
but alms conduct us into his presence."

PILGRIMAGE is the *fourth grand practical* duty enjoined upon Moslems. Every true believer is bound to make one pilgrimage to Mecca
in the course of his life, either personally or by proxy. In the latter
case, his name must be mentioned in every prayer offered up by his
substitute.

Pilgrimage is incumbent only on free persons of mature age, sound
intellect, and who have health and wealth enough to bear the fatigues
and expenses of the journey. The pilgrim before his departure from
home arranges all his affairs, public and domestic, as if preparing for
his death.

On the appointed day, which is either Tuesday, Thursday, or Saturday, as being propitious for the purpose, he assembles his wives, children, and all his household, and devoutly commends them and all his
concerns to the care of God during his holy enterprise. Then passing
one end of his turban beneath his chin to the opposite side of his head,
like the attire of a nun, and grasping a stout staff of bitter almonds, he
takes leave of his household, and sallies from the apartment, exclaiming, "In the name of God I undertake this holy work, confiding in his
protection. I believe in him, and place in his hands my actions and my
life."

On leaving the portal he turns his face toward the Kebla, repeats
certain passages of the Koran, and adds, "I turn my face to the Holy
Caaba, the throne of God, to accomplish the pilgrimage commanded
by his law, and which shall draw me near to him."

He finally puts his foot in the stirrup, mounts into the saddle, commends himself again to God, almighty, all wise, all merciful, and sets forth on his pilgrimage. The time of departure is always calculated so as to insure an arrival at Mecca at the beginning of the pilgrim month Dhu'l-hajji.

Three laws are to be observed throughout this pious journey.

1. To commence no quarrel.

2. To bear meekly all harshness and reviling.

3. To promote peace and good-will among his companions in the caravan.

He is, moreover, to be liberal in his donations and charities throughout his pilgrimage.

When arrived at some place in the vicinity of Mecca, he allows his hair and nails to grow, strips himself to the skin, and assumes the Ihram or pilgrim garb, consisting of two scarfs, without seams or decorations, and of any stuff excepting silk. One of these is folded round the loins, the other thrown over the neck and shoulders, leaving the right arm free. The head is uncovered, but the aged and infirm are permitted to fold something round it in consideration of alms given to the poor. Umbrellas are allowed as a protection against the sun, and indigent pilgrims supply their place by a rag on the end of a staff.

The instep must be bare; and peculiar sandals are provided for the purpose, or a piece of the upper leather of the shoe is cut out. The pilgrim, when thus attired, is termed Al Mohrem.

The Ihram of females is an ample cloak and veil, enveloping the whole person, so that, in strictness, the wrists, the ankles, and even the eyes should be concealed.

When once assumed, the Ihram must be worn until the pilgrimage is completed, however unsuited it may be to the season or the weather. While wearing it, the pilgrim must abstain from all licentiousness of language; all sensual intercourse; all quarrels and acts of violence; he must not even take the life of an insect that infests him; though an exception is made in regard to biting dogs, to scorpions, and birds of prey.

On arriving at Mecca, he leaves his baggage in some shop, and, without attention to any wordly concern, repairs straightway to the Caaba, conducted by one of the Metowefs or guides, who are always at hand to offer their services to pilgrims.

Entering the mosque by the Bab el Salam, or Gate of Salutation, he makes four prostrations, and repeats certain prayers as he passes under the arch. Approaching the Caaba, he makes four prostrations opposite the Black Stone, which he then kisses; or, if prevented by the throng, he touches it with his right hand, and kisses that. Departing from the Black Stone, and keeping the building on his left hand, he makes the seven circuits, the three first quickly, the latter four with slow and solemn pace. Certain prayers are repeated in a low voice, and the Black Stone kissed, or touched, at the end of every circuit.

The Towaf, or procession, round the Caaba was an ancient ceremony, observed long before the time of Mahomet, and performed by both sexes entirely naked. Mahomet prohibited this exposure, and prescribed the Ihram, or pilgrim dress. The female Hajji walk the Towaf generally during the night; though occasionally they perform it mingled with the men in the daytime.*

The seven circuits being completed, the pilgrim presses his breast against the wall between the Black Stone and the door of the Caaba, and with outstretched arms, prays for pardon of his sins.

He then repairs to the Makam, or station of Abraham, makes four prostrations, prays for the intermediation of the Patriarch, and thence to the well Zem Zem, and drinks as much of the water as he can swallow.

During all this ceremonial, the uninstructed Hajji has his guide or Metowef close at his heels, muttering prayers for him to repeat. He is now conducted out of the mosque by the gate Bab el Zafa to a slight ascent about fifty paces distant, called the Hill of Zafa, when, after uttering a prayer with uplifted hands, he commences the holy promenade, called the Saa or Say. This lies through a straight and level street, called Al Mesaa, six hundred paces in length, lined with shops like a bazaar, and terminating at a place called Merowa. The walk of the Say is in commemoration of the wandering of Hagar over the same ground, in search of water for her child Ishmael. The pilgrim, therefore, walks at times slowly, with an inquisitive air, then runs in a certain place, and again walks gravely, stopping at times and looking anxiously back.

Having repeated the walk up and down this street seven times, the Hajji enters a barber's shop at Merowa; his head is shaved, his nails pared, the barber muttering prayers and the pilgrim repeating them all

---

* Burckhardt's Travels in Arabia, vol. i. p. 260, Lond. edit., 1829.

the time. The paring and shearing are then buried in consecrated ground, and the most essential duties of the pilgrimage are considered as fulfilled.*

On the ninth of the month Al Dhu'l-hajji, the pilgrims make a hurried and tumultuous visit to Mount Arafat, where they remain until sunset; then pass the night in prayer at an Oratory, called Mozdalifa, and before sunrise next morning repair to the valley of Mena, where they throw seven stones at each of three pillars, in imitation of Abraham, and some say also of Adam, who drove away the devil from this spot with stones, when disturbed by him in his devotions.

Such are the main ceremonies which form this great Moslem rite of pilgrimage; but, before concluding this sketch of Islam faith, and closing this legendary memoir of its founder, we cannot forbear to notice one of his innovations, which has entailed perplexity on all his followers, and particular inconvenience on pious pilgrims.

The Arabian year consists of twelve lunar months, containing alternately thirty and twenty-nine days, and making three hundred and fifty-four in the whole, so that eleven days were lost in every solar year. To make up the deficiency, a thirteenth or wandering month was added to every third year, previous to the era of Mahomet, to the same effect as one day is added to the Christian calendar to every leap-year. Mahomet, who was uneducated and ignorant of astronomy, retrenched this thirteenth or intercalary month, as contrary to the divine order of revolutions of the moon, and reformed the calendar by a divine revelation during his last pilgrimage. This is recorded in the ninth sura or chapter of the Koran, to the following effect:

"For the number of months is twelve, as was ordained by Allah, and recorded on the eternal tables† on the day wherein he created the heaven and the earth."

* The greater part of the particulars concerning Mecca and Medina, and their respective pilgrimages, are gathered from the writings of that accurate and indefatigable traveller, Burckhardt; who, in the disguise of a pilgrim, visited these shrines, and complied with all the forms and ceremonials. His works throw great light upon the manners and customs of the East, and practice of the Mahometan faith.

The facts related by Burckhardt have been collated with those of other travellers and writers, and many particulars have been interwoven with them from other sources.

† The eternal tables or tablet was of white pearl, extended from east to west and from earth to heaven. All the decrees of God were recorded on it, and all events past, present, and to come, to all eternity. It was guarded by angels.

"Transfer not a sacred month unto another month, for verily it is an innovation of the infidels."

The number of days thus lost amount in 33 years to 363. It becomes necessary, therefore, to add an intercalary year at the end of each thirty-third year to reduce the Mahometan into the Christian era.

One great inconvenience arising from this revelation of the prophet is, that the Moslem months do not indicate the season; as they commence earlier by eleven days every year. This at certain epochs is a sore grievance to the votaries to Mecca, as the great pilgrim month Dhu'l-hajji, during which they are compelled to wear the Ihram, or half-naked pilgrim garb, runs the round of the seasons, occurring at one time in the depth of winter, at another in the fervid heat of summer.

Thus Mahomet, though according to legendary history he could order the moon from the firmament and make her revolve about the sacred house, could not control her monthly revolutions; and found that the science of numbers is superior even to the gift of prophecy, and sets miracles at defiance.

END OF VOL. I

MAHOMET AND
HIS SUCCESSORS

Volume II

PREFACE

It is the intention of the author in the following pages, to trace the progress of the Moslem dominion from the death of Mahomet, in A.D. 632, to the invasion of Spain, in A.D. 710. In this period, which did not occupy fourscore and ten years, and passed within the lifetime of many an aged Arab, the Moslems extended their empire and their faith over the wide regions of Asia and Africa, subverting the empire of the Khosrus; subjugating great territories in India; establishing a splendid seat of power in Syria; dictating to the conquered kingdom of the Pharaohs; overrunning the whole northern coast of Africa; scouring the Mediterranean with their ships; carrying their conquests in one direction to the very walls of Constantinople, and in another to the extreme limits of Mauritania; in a word, trampling down all the old dynasties which once held haughty and magnificent sway in the East. The whole presents a striking instance of the triumph of fanatic enthusiasm over disciplined valor, at a period when the invention of firearms had not reduced war to a matter of almost arithmetical calculation. There is also an air of wild romance about many of the events recorded in this narrative, owing to the character of the Arabs, and their fondness for stratagems, daring exploits, and individual achievements of an extravagant nature. These have sometimes been softened, if not suppressed, by cautious historians; but the author has found them so in unison with the people and the times, and with a career of conquest, of itself out of the bounds of common probability, that he has been induced to leave them in all their graphic force.

Those who have read the life of Mahomet, will find in the following pages most of their old acquaintances again engaged, but in a vastly grander field of action; leading armies, subjugating empires, and dictating from the palaces and thrones of deposed potentates.

In constructing his work, which is merely intended for popular use, the author has adopted a form somewhat between biography and chronicle, admitting of personal anecdote, and a greater play of familiar traits and peculiarities, than is considered admissible in the stately walk of history. His ignorance of the oriental languages has obliged him to take his materials at second-hand, where he could have wished to read them in the original; such, for instance, has been the case with

223

the accounts given by the Arabian writer, Al Wákidi, of the conquest of Syria, and especially of the siege of Damascus, which retain much of their dramatic spirit even in the homely pages of Ockley. To this latter writer, the author has been much indebted, as well as to the Abbé de Marigny's History of the Arabians, and to D'Herbelot's Bibliothèque Orientale. In fact, his pages are often a mere digest of facts already before the public, but divested of cumbrous diction and uninteresting details. Some, however, are furnished from sources recently laid open, and not hitherto wrought into the regular web of history.

In his account of the Persian conquest, the author has been much benefited by the perusal of the Gemäldesaal of the learned Hammer-Purgstall, and by a translation of the Persian historian Tabari, recently given to the public through the pages of the Journal of the American Oriental Society, by Mr. John P. Brown, dragoman of the United States legation at Constantinople.

In the account of the Moslem conquests along the northern coast of Africa, of which so little is known, he has gleaned many of his facts from Conde's Domination of the Arabs in Spain; and from the valuable work on the same subject, recently put forth under the sanction of the Oriental Translation Fund of Great Britain and Ireland, by his estimable friend, Don Pascual de Gayangos, formerly Professor of Arabic in the Athenæum of Madrid.

The author might cite other sources whence he has derived scattered facts; but it appears to him that he has already said enough on this point, about a work written more through inclination than ambition; and which, as before intimated, does not aspire to be consulted as authority, but merely to be read as a digest of current knowledge, adapted to popular use.

SUNNYSIDE, 1850.

CHAPTER I

The death of Mahomet left his religion without a head and his people without a sovereign; there was danger, therefore, of the newly formed empire falling into confusion. All Medina, on the day of his death, was in a kind of tumult, and nothing but the precaution of Osama Ibn Zeid in planting the standard before the prophet's door, and posting troops in various parts, prevented popular commotions. The question was, on whom to devolve the reins of government? Four names stood prominent as having claims of affinity; Abu Beker, Omar, Othman, and Ali. Abu Beker was the father of Ayesha, the favorite wife of Mahomet. Omar was father of Hafsa, another of his wives, and the one to whose care he had confided the coffer containing the revelations of the Koran. Othman had married successively two of his daughters, but they were dead, and also their progeny. Ali was cousin-german of Mahomet and husband of Fatima, his only daughter. Such were the ties of relationship to him of these four great captains. The right of succession, in order of consanguinity, lay with Ali; and his virtues and services eminently entitled him to it. On the first burst of his generous zeal, when Islamism was a derided and persecuted faith, he had been pronounced by Mahomet his brother, his vicegerent; he had ever since been devoted to him in word and deed, and had honored the cause by his magnanimity as signally as he had vindicated it by his valor. His friends, confiding in the justice of his claims, gathered round him in the dwelling of his wife Fatima, to consult about means of putting him quietly in possession of the government.

Other interests, however, were at work, operating upon the public mind. Abu Beker was held up, not merely as connected by marriage ties with the prophet, but as one of the first and most zealous of his disciples; as the voucher for the truth of his night journey; as his fellow-sufferer in persecution; as the one who accompanied him in his flight from Mecca; as his companion in the cave when they were miraculously saved from discovery; as his counsellor and co-operator in all his plans and undertakings; as the one in fact whom the prophet had plainly pointed out as his successor, by deputing him to officiate in his stead in the religious ceremonies during his last illness. His claims were strongly urged by his daughter Ayesha, who had great influence among the faithful; and who was stimulated not so much by zeal for her father, as by hatred of Ali, whom she had never forgiven for having inclined his ear to the charge of incontinence against her in the celebrated case entitled The False Accusation.

Omar also had a powerful party among the populace, who admired him for his lion-like demeanor; his consummate military skill; his straight-forward simplicity and dauntless courage. He also had an active female partisan in his daughter Hafsa.

While therefore Ali and his friends were in quiet council in the house of Fatima, many of the principal Moslems gathered together without their knowledge, to settle the question of succession. The two most important personages in this assemblage were Abu Beker and Omar. The first measure was to declare the supreme power not hereditary but elective; a measure which at once destroyed the claims of Ali on the score of consanguinity, and left the matter open to the public choice. This has been ascribed to the jealousy of the Koreishites of the line of Abd Schems; who feared, should Ali's claims be recognized, that the sovereign power, like the guardianship of the Caaba, might be perpetuated in the haughty line of Haschem. Some, however, pretend to detect in it the subtle and hostile influence of Ayesha.

A dispute now arose between the Mohadjerins or refugees from Mecca and the Ansarians or Helpers of Medina, as to the claims of their respective cities in nominating a successor to Mahomet. The former founded the claims of Mecca on its being the birth-place of the prophet, and the first in which his doctrines had been divulged; they set forward their own claims also as his townsmen, his relatives, and the companions of his exile. The Ansarians, on the other hand, insisted on the superior claims of Medina, as having been the asylum of the prophet, and his chosen residence; and on their own claims as having supported him in his exile, and enabled him to withstand and overcome his persecutors.

The dispute soon grew furious, and scimetars flashed from their scabbards, when one of the people of Medina proposed as a compromise, that each party should furnish a ruler and the government have two heads. Omar derided the proposition with scorn. "Two blades," said he, "cannot go into one sheath." Abu Beker also remonstrated against a measure calculated to weaken the empire in its very infancy. He conjured the Moslems to remain under one head, and named Omar and Abu Obeidah as persons worthy of the office, and between whom they should choose. Abu Obeidah was one of the earliest disciples of

Mahomet, he had accompanied him in his flight from Mecca, and adhered to him in all his fortunes.

The counsel of Abu Beker calmed for a time the turbulence of the
assembly, but it soon revived with redoubled violence. Upon this Omar
suddenly rose, advanced to Abu Beker and hailed him as the oldest,
best, and most thoroughly-tried of the adherents of the prophet, and
the one most worthy to succeed him. So saying, he kissed his hand in
token of allegiance, and swore to obey him as his sovereign.

This sacrifice of his own claims in favor of a rival struck the assembly with surprise, and opened their eyes to the real merits of Abu
Beker. They beheld in him the faithful companion of the prophet, who
had always been by his side. They knew his wisdom and moderation
and venerated his gray hairs. It appeared but reasonable that the man
whose counsels had contributed to establish the government, should be
chosen to carry it on. The example of Omar, therefore, was promptly
followed, and Abu Beker was hailed as chief.

Omar now ascended the pulpit. "Henceforth," said he, "if any one
shall presume to take upon himself the sovereign power without the
public voice, let him suffer death; as well as all who may nominate or
uphold him." This measure was instantly adopted, and thus a bar was
put to the attempts of any other candidate.

The whole policy of Omar in these measures, which at first sight appears magnanimous, has been cavilled at as crafty and selfish. Abu
Beker, it is observed, was well-stricken in years, being about the same
age with the prophet; it was not probable he would long survive. Omar
trusted, therefore, to succeed in a little while to the command. His last
measure struck at once at the hopes of Ali, his most formidable com-
petitor; who, shut up with his friends in the dwelling of Fatima, knew
nothing of the meeting in which his pretensions were thus demolished.
Craft, however, we must observe, was not one of Omar's characteristics, and was totally opposed to the prompt, stern, and simple course of
his conduct on all occasions; nor did he ever show any craving lust for
power. He seems ever to have been a zealot in the cause of Islam, and
to have taken no indirect measures to promote it.

His next movement was indicative of his straight-forward cut-and-
thrust policy. Abu Beker, wary and managing, feared there might be
some outbreak on the part of Ali and his friends when they should hear
of the election which had taken place. He requested Omar, therefore,
to proceed with an armed band to the mansion of Fatima, and main-

tain tranquillity in that quarter. Omar surrounded the house with his followers; announced to Ali the election of Abu Beker, and demanded his concurrence. Ali attempted to remonstrate, alleging his own claims; but Omar proclaimed the penalty of death, decreed to all who should attempt to usurp the sovereign power in defiance of public will; and threatened to enforce it by setting fire to the house and consuming its inmates.

"Oh son of Khattâb!" cried Fatima reproachfully, "thou wilt not surely commit such an outrage!"

"Aye will I in very truth!" replied Omar, "unless ye all make common cause with the people."

The friends of Ali were fain to yield, and to acknowledge the sovereignty of Abu Beker. Ali, however, held himself apart in proud and indignant reserve until the death of Fatima, which happened in the course of several months. He then paid tardy homage to Abu Beker, but, in so doing, upbraided him with want of openness and good faith in managing the election without his privity; a reproach which the reader will probably think not altogether unmerited. Abu Beker, however, disavowed all intrigue, and declared he had accepted the sovereignty merely to allay the popular commotion; and was ready to lay it down whenever a more worthy candidate could be found who would unite the wishes of the people.

Ali was seemingly pacified by this explanation; but he spurned it in his heart, and retired in disgust into the interior of Arabia, taking with him his two sons Hassan and Hosein; the only descendants of the prophet. From these have sprung a numerous progeny, who to this day are considered noble, and wear green turbans as the outward sign of their illustrious lineage.

CHAPTER II

On assuming the supreme authority, Abu Beker refused to take the title of king or prince; several of the Moslems hailed him as God's vicar on earth, but he rejected the appellation; he was not the vicar of God, he said, but of his prophet, whose plans and wishes it was his duty to carry out and fulfil. "In so doing," added he, "I will endeavor to avoid all prejudice and partiality. Obey me only so far as I obey God and the prophet. If I go beyond these bounds, I have no authority over you. If I err, set me right, I shall be open to conviction."

He contented himself, therefore, with the modest title of Caliph, that is to say, successor, by which the Arab sovereigns have ever since been designated. They have not all, however, imitated the modesty of Abu Beker, in calling themselves successors of the prophet; but many, in after times, arrogated to themselves the title of Caliphs and Vicars of God, and his Shadow upon Earth. The supreme authority, as when exercised by Mahomet, united the civil and religious functions: the Caliph was sovereign and pontiff.

It may be well to observe, that the original name of the newly elected Caliph was Abdallah Athek Ibn Abu Kahafa. He was also, as we have shown, termed Al Seddek, or The Testifier to the Truth; from having maintained the verity of Mahomet's nocturnal journey; but he is always named in Moslem histories, Abu Beker; that is to say, The Father of the Virgin; his daughter Ayesha being the only one of the prophet's wives that came a virgin to his arms; the others having previously been in wedlock.

At the time of his election Abu Beker was about sixty-two years of age; tall, and well formed, though spare; with a florid complexion and thin beard, which would have been gray, but that he tinged it after the oriental usage. He was a man of great judgment and discretion, whose wariness and management at times almost amounted to craft; yet his purposes appear to have been honest and unselfish; directed to the good of the cause, not to his own benefit. In the administration of his office he betrayed nothing of sordid worldliness. Indifferent to riches, and to all pomps, luxuries, and sensual indulgencies, he accepted no pay for his services but a mere pittance, sufficient to maintain an Arab establishment of the simplest kind, in which all his retinue consisted of a camel and a black slave. The surplus funds accruing to his treasury he dispensed every Friday; part to the meritorious, the rest to the poor; and was ever ready, from his own private means, to help the distressed. On entering office he caused his daughter Ayesha to take a strict account of his private patrimony, to stand as a record against him should he enrich himself while in office.

Notwithstanding all his merits, however, his advent to power was attended by public commotions. Many of the Arabian tribes had been converted by the sword, and it needed the combined terrors of a conqueror and a prophet to maintain them in allegiance to the faith. On the death of Mahomet, therefore, they spurned at the authority of his successor, and refused to pay the Zacat, or religious contributions of tribute, tithes, and alms. The signal of revolt flew from tribe to tribe, until the Islam empire suddenly shrank to the cities of Mecca, Medina, and Tayef.

A strong body of the rebels even took the field and advanced upon Medina. They were led on by a powerful and popular Sheikh named Malec Ibn Nowirah. He was a man of high birth and great valor, an excellent horseman, and a distinguished poet; all great claims on Arab admiration. To these may be added the enviable fortune of having for wife the most beautiful woman in all Arabia.

Hearing of the approach of this warrior poet and his army, Abu Beker hastened to fortify the city, sending the women and children, the aged and infirm, to the rocks and caverns of the neighboring mountains.

But though Mahomet was dead, the sword of Islam was not buried with him; and Khaled Ibn Waled now stood forward to sustain the fame acquired by former acts of prowess. He was sent out against the rebels at the head of a hasty levy of four thousand five hundred men and eleven banners. The wary Abu Beker, with whom discretion kept an equal pace with valor, had a high opinion of the character and talents of the rebel chief, and hoped, notwithstanding his defection, to conquer him by kindness. Khaled was instructed, therefore, should Malec fall into his power, to treat him with great respect; to be lenient to the vanquished, and to endeavor, by gentle means, to win all back to the standard of Islam.

Khaled, however, was a downright soldier, who had no liking for

gentle means. Having overcome the rebels in a pitched battle, he overran their country, giving his soldiery permission to seize upon the
flocks and herds of the vanquished, and make slaves of their children.

Among the prisoners brought into his presence were Malec and his
beautiful wife. The beauty of the latter dazzled the eyes even of the
rough soldier, but probably hardened his heart against her husband.

"Why," demanded he of Malec, "do you refuse to pay the Zacat?"

"Because I can pray to God without paying these exactions," was the
reply.

"Prayer, without alms, is of no avail," said Khaled.

"Does your master say so?" demanded Malec, haughtily.

"My master!" echoed Khaled, "and is he not thy master likewise? By
Allah, I have a mind to strike off thy head!"

"Are these also the orders of your master?" rejoined Malec, with a
sneer.

"Again!" cricd Khaled, in a fury – "smite off the head of this rebel."

His officers interfered, for all respected the prisoner; but the rage of
Khaled was not to be appeased.

"The beauty of this woman kills me," said Malec, significantly, pointing to his wife.

"Nay!" cried Khaled, "it is Allah who kills thee because of thine
apostasy."

"I am no apostate," said Malec, "I profess the true faith——"

It was too late; the signal of death had already been given. Scarce
had the declaration of faith passed the lips of the unfortunate Malec,
when his head fell beneath the scimetar of Derar Ibn al Azwar, a
rough soldier after Khaled's own heart.

This summary execution, to which the beauty of a woman was alleged as the main excitement, gave deep concern to Abu Beker, who
remarked, that the prophet had pardoned even Wacksa, the Ethiop,
the slayer of his uncle Hamza, when the culprit made profession of the
faith. As to Omar, he declared that Khaled, according to the laws of
the Koran, ought to be stoned to death for adultery, or executed for
the murder of a Moslem. The politic Abu Beker, however, observed
that Khaled had sinned through error rather than intention. "Shall I,"
added he, "sheathe the sword of God? The sword which he himself has
drawn against the unbelieving?"

So far from sheathing the sword, we find it shortly afterwards employed in an important service. This was against the false prophet

Moseïlma; who, encouraged by the impunity with which, during the
illness of Mahomet, he had been suffered to propagate his doctrines,
had increased greatly the number of his proselytes and adherents, and
held a kind of regal and sacerdotal sway over the important city and
fertile province of Yamama, between the Red Sea and the Gulf of Persia.

There is quite a flavor of romance in the story of this impostor.
Among those dazzled by his celebrity and charmed by his rhapsodical
effusions, was Sedjah, wife of Abu Cahdla, a poetess of the tribe of
Tamim, distinguished among the Arabs for her personal and mental
charms. She came to see Moseïlma in like manner as the Queen of
Sheba came to witness the wisdom and grandeur of King Solomon.
They were inspired with a mutual passion at the first interview, and
passed much of their time together in tender, if not religious intercourse. Sedjah became a convert to the faith of her lover, and caught
from him the imaginary gift of prophecy. He appears to have caught,
in exchange, the gift of poetry, for certain amatory effusions, addressed
by him to his beautiful visitant, are still preserved by an Arabian historian, and breathe all the warmth of the Song of Solomon.

This dream of poetry and prophecy was interrupted by the approach
of Khaled at the head of a numerous army. Moseïlma sallied forth to
meet him with a still greater force. A battle took place at Akreba, not
far from the capital city of Yamama. At the onset the rebels had a transient success, and twelve hundred Moslems bit the dust. Khaled, however, rallied his forces; the enemy were overthrown, and ten thousand
cut to pieces. Moseïlma fought with desperation, but fell covered with
wounds. It is said his death-blow was given by Wacksa, the Ethiopian,
the same who had killed Hamza, uncle of Mahomet, in the battle of
Ohod, and that he used the self-same spear. Wacksa, since his pardon
by Mahomet, had become a zealous Moslem.

The surviving disciples of Moseïlma became promptly converted to
Islamism under the pious but heavy hand of Khaled; whose late offence in the savage execution of Malec was completely atoned for by
his victory over the false prophet. He added other services of the same
military kind in this critical juncture of public affairs; reinforcing and
co-operating with certain commanders who had been sent in different
directions to suppress rebellions; and it was chiefly through his prompt
and energetic activity that, before the expiration of the first year of the

Caliphat, order was restored, and the empire of Islam re-established in Arabia.

It was shortly after the victory of Khaled over Moseïlma, that Abu Beker undertook to gather together, from written and oral sources, the precepts and revelations of the Koran, which hitherto had existed partly in scattered documents, and partly in the memories of the disciples and companions of the prophet. He was greatly urged to this undertaking by Omar, that ardent zealot for the faith. The latter had observed with alarm the number of veteran companions of the prophet who had fallen in the battle of Akreba. "In a little while," said he, "all the living testifiers to the faith, who bear the revelations of it in their memories, will have passed away, and with them so many records of the doctrines of Islam." He urged Abu Beker, therefore, to collect from the surviving disciples all that they remembered; and to gather together from all quarters whatever parts of the Koran existed in writing. The manner in which Abu Beker proceeded to execute this pious task has been noticed in the preceding volume; it was not, however, completed until under a succeeding Caliph.

CHAPTER III

*Campaign against Syria — Army sent under Yezed Ibn Abu Sofian —
Successes — Another army under Amru Ibn al Aass — Brilliant
achievements of Khaled in Irak*

The rebel tribes of Arabia being once more brought into allegiance, and tranquillity established at home, Abu Beker turned his thoughts to execute the injunction of the prophet, to propagate the faith throughout the world, until all nations should be converted to Islamism, by persuasion or the sword. The moment was auspicious for such a gigantic task. The long and desolating wars between the Persian and Byzantine emperors, though now at an end, had exhausted those once mighty powers, and left their frontiers open to aggression. In the second year of his reign, therefore, Abu Beker prepared to carry out the great enterprise contemplated by Mahomet in his latter days; the conquest of Syria.

Under this general name, it should be observed, were comprehended the countries lying between the Euphrates and the Mediterranean, including Phœnicia and Palestine.* These countries, once forming a system of petty states and kingdoms, each with its own government and monarch, were now merged into the great Byzantine empire, and acknowledged the sway of the emperor Heraclius at Constantinople.

Syria had long been a land of promise to the Arabs. They had known it for ages by the intercourse of the caravans, and had drawn from it their chief supplies of corn. It was a land of abundance. Part of it was devoted to agriculture and husbandry, covered with fields of grain, with vineyards and trees producing the finest fruits; with pastures well stocked with flocks and herds. On the Arabian borders it had cities, the rich marts of internal trade; while its seaports, though declined from the ancient splendor and pre-eminence of Tyre and Sidon, still were the staples of an opulent and widely extended commerce.

In the twelfth year of the Hegira, the following summons was sent by Abu Beker to the chiefs of Arabia Petrea, and Arabia Felix.

"In the name of the Most Merciful God! Abdallah Athek Ibn Abu Kahafa to all true believers, health, happiness, and the blessing of God. Praise be to God, and to Mahomet his prophet! This is to inform you that I intend to send an army of the faithful into Syria, to deliver that

---

* Syria, in its widest oriental acceptation, included Mesopotamia, Chaldea, and even Assyria, the whole forming what in Scriptural geography was denominated Aram.

country from the infidels, and I remind you that to fight for the true faith is to obey God!"

There needed no further inducement to bring to his standard every Arab that owned a horse or a camel, or could wield a lance. Every day brought some Sheikh to Medina at the head of the fighting men of his tribe, and before long the fields round the city were studded with encampments. The command of the army was given to Yezed Ibn Abu Sofian. The troops soon became impatient to strike their sunburnt tents and march. "Why do we loiter?" cried they; "all our fighting men are here; there are none more to come. The plains of Medina are parched and bare, there is no food for man or steed. Give us the word, and let us march for the fruitful land of Syria."

Abu Beker assented to their wishes. From the brow of a hill he reviewed the army on the point of departure. The heart of the Caliph swelled with pious exultation as he looked down upon the stirring multitude; the glittering array of arms; the squadrons of horsemen; the lengthening line of camels; and called to mind the scanty handful that used to gather round the standard of the prophet. Scarce ten years had elapsed since the latter had been driven a fugitive from Mecca, and now a mighty host assembled at the summons of his successor, and distant empires were threatened by the sword of Islam. Filled with these thoughts, he lifted up his voice and prayed to God to make these troops valiant and victorious. Then giving the word to march, the tents were struck, the camels laden, and in a little while the army poured in a long continuous train over hill and valley.

Abu Beker accompanied them on foot on the first day's march. The leaders would have dismounted and yielded him their steeds. "Nay," said he, "ride on. You are in the service of Allah. As for me, I shall be rewarded for every step I take in his cause."

His parting charge to Yezed, the commander of the army, was a singular mixture of severity and mercy.

"Treat your soldiers with kindness and consideration; be just in all your dealings with them, and consult their feelings and opinions. Fight valiantly, and never turn your back upon a foe. When victorious harm not the aged, and protect women and children. Destroy not the palm-tree, nor fruit-trees of any kind; waste not the cornfield with fire; nor kill any cattle excepting for food. Stand faithfully to every covenant and promise; respect all religious persons who live in hermitages, or convents, and spare their edifices. But should you meet with a class of unbelievers of a different kind, who go about with shaven crowns, and belong to the synagogue of Satan, be sure you cleave their skulls unless they embrace the true faith, or render tribute."

Having received this summary charge, Yezed continued his march toward Syria, and the pious Caliph returned to Medina.

The prayers which the latter had put up for the success of the army appeared to be successful. Before long a great cavalgada of horses, mules, and camels laden with booty poured into the gates of Medina. Yezed had encountered, on the confines of Syria, a body of troops detached by the emperor Heraclius to observe him, and had defeated them, killing the general and twelve hundred men. He had been equally successful in various subsequent skirmishes. All the booty gained in these actions had been sent to the Caliph, as an offering by the army of the first fruits of the harvest of Syria.

Abu Beker sent tidings of this success to Mecca, and the surrounding country, calling upon all true believers to press forward in the career of victory, thus prosperously commenced. Another army was soon set on foot, the command of which was given to Seid Ibn Khaled. This appointment, however, not being satisfactory to Omar, whose opinions and wishes had vast weight at Medina, Ayesha prevailed on her father to invite Seid to resign, and to appoint in his place Amru Ibn al Aass; the same who in the early days of the faith ridiculed Mahomet and his doctrines in satirical verses; but who, since his conversion to Islamism, had risen to eminence in its service and was one of its most valiant and efficient champions.

Such was the zeal of the Moslems in the prosecution of this holy war, that Seid Ibn Khaled cheerfully resigned his command and enlisted under the standard which he had lately reared.

At the departure of the army Abu Beker, who was excellent at counsel, and fond of bestowing it, gave Amru a code of conduct for his government; admonishing him to live righteously, as a dying man in the presence of God, and accountable for all things in a future state. That he should not trouble himself about the private concerns of others; and should forbid his men all religious disputes about events and doctrines of the "times of ignorance;" that is to say, the times antecedent to Mahomet; but should enforce the diligent reading of the Koran, which contained all that was necessary for them to know.

As there would now be large bodies of troops in Syria, and various

able commanders, Abu Beker in maturing the plan of his campaign assigned them different points of action. Amru was to draw toward Palestine; Abu Obeidah to undertake Emessa; Seid Ibn Abu Sofian, Damascus; and Serhil Ibn Hasan, the country about the Jordan. They were all
to act as much as possible in concert, and to aid each other in case of
need. When together they were all to be under the orders of Abu Obeidah, to whom was given the general command in Syria. This veteran
disciple of the prophet stood high, as we have shown, in the esteem
and confidence of Abu Beker, having been one of the two whom he
had named as worthy of the Caliphat. He was now about fifty years of
age; zealously devoted to the cause, yet one with whom the sword of
faith was sheathed in meekness and humanity; perhaps the cautious
Abu Beker thought his moderation would be a salutary check to the
headlong valor of the fanatical soldiers of Islam.

While this grand campaign was put in operation against the Roman
possessions in Syria, a minor force was sent to invade Irak. This province, which included the ancient Chaldea and the Babylonia of Ptolemy, was bounded on the east by Susiana or Khurzestan and the
mountains of Assyria and Medea, on the north by part of Mesopotamia,
on the west and south by the Deserts of Sham or Syria and by a part of
Arabia Deserta. It was a region tributary to the Persian monarch, and
so far a part of his dominions. The campaign in this quarter was confided to Khaled, of whose prowess Abu Beker had an exalted opinion,
and who was at this time at the head of a moderate force in one of the
rebellious provinces which he had brought into subjection. The Caliph's letter to him was to the following effect. "Turn thee toward Arabian Irak! The conquest of Hira and Cufa is intrusted to thee. After the
subjection of those lands, turn thee against Aila and subdue it with
God's help!"

Hira was a kingdom to the west of Babylonia, on the verge of the
Syrian Desert: it had been founded by a race of Arabs, descendants of
Kahtan, and had subsisted upwards of six hundred years; the greater
part of the time it had been under a line of princes of the house of
Mondar; who acknowledged allegiance to the kings of Persia, and
acted as their lieutenants over the Arabs of Irak.

During the early part of the third century many Jacobite Christians
had been driven, by the persecutions and disorders of the Eastern
Church, to take refuge among the Arabs of Hira. Their numbers had

been augmented in subsequent times by fugitives from various quarters, until, shortly before the birth of Mahomet, the king of Hira and all his subjects had embraced Christianity.

Much was said of the splendor of the capital, which bore the same name with the kingdom. Here were two palaces of extraordinary magnificence, the beauty of one of which, if Arabian legends speak true, was fatal to the architect; for the king, fearing that he might build one still more beautiful for some other monarch, had him thrown headlong from the tower.

Khaled acted with his usual energy and success in the invasion of this kingdom. With ten thousand men he besieged the city of Hira; stormed its palaces; slew the king in battle; subdued the kingdom; imposed on it an annual tribute of seventy thousand pieces of gold, the first tribute ever levied by Moslems on a foreign land, and sent the same, with the son of the deceased king, to Medina.

He next carried his triumphant arms against Aila, defeated Hormuz, the Persian governor, and sent his crown, with a fifth part of the booty, to the Caliph. The crown was of great value, being one of the first class of those worn by the seven vicegerents of the Persian "King of Kings." Among the trophies of victory sent to Medina was an elephant. Three other Persian generals and governors made several attempts, with powerful armies, to check the victorious career of Khaled, but were alike defeated. City after city fell into his hands; nothing seemed capable of withstanding his arms. Planting his victorious standard on the bank of the Euphrates, he wrote to the Persian monarch, calling upon him to embrace the faith or pay tribute. "If you refuse both," added he, "I will come upon you with a host who love death as much as you do life."

The repeated convoys of booty sent by Khaled to Medina after his several victories, the sight of captured crowns and captured princes, and of the first tribute imposed on foreign lands, had excited the public exultation to an uncommon degree. Abu Beker especially took pride in his achievements; considering them proofs of his own sagacity and foresight, which he had shown in refusing to punish him with death when strongly urged to do so by Omar. As victory after victory was announced, and train after train laden with spoils crowded the gates of Medina, he joyed to see his anticipations so far outstripped by the deeds of this headlong warrior. "By Allah," exclaimed he, in an ecstasy, "womankind is too weak to give birth to another Khaled."

CHAPTER IV

Incompetency of Abu Obeidah for the general command in Syria —
Khaled sent to supersede him — Peril of the Moslem army before
Bosra — Timely arrival of Khaled — His exploits during the siege —
Capture of Bosra

The exultation of the Caliph over the triumphs in Irak was checked by
tidings of a different tone from the army in Syria. Abu Obeidah, who
had the general command, wanted the boldness and enterprise requisite to an invading general. A partial defeat of some of his troops discouraged him, and he heard with disquiet of vast hosts which the emperor Heraclius was assembling to overwhelm him. His letters to the
Caliph partook of the anxiety and perplexity of his mind. Abu Beker,
whose generally sober mind was dazzled at the time by the daring exploits of Khaled, was annoyed at finding that, while the latter was
dashing forward in a brilliant career of conquest in Irak, Abu Obeidah
was merely standing on the defensive in Syria. In the vexation of the
moment, he regretted that he had intrusted the invasion of the latter
country to one who appeared to him a nerveless man; and he forthwith
sent missives to Khaled ordering him to leave the prosecution of the
war in Irak to his subordinate generals, and repair, in all haste, to aid
the armies in Syria, and take the general command there. Khaled
obeyed the orders with his usual promptness. Leaving his army under
the charge of Mosenna Ibn Haris, he put himself at the head of fifteen
hundred horse, and spurred over the Syrian borders to join the Moslem
host, which he learned, while on the way, was drawing toward the
Christian city of Bosra.

This city, the reader will recollect, was the great mart on the Syrian
frontier, annually visited by the caravans, and where Mahomet, when a
youth, had his first interview with Sergius, the Nestorian monk, from
whom he was said to have received instructions in the Christian faith.
It was a place usually filled with merchandise, and held out a promise
of great booty; but it was strongly walled, its inhabitants were inured
to arms, and it could at any time pour forth twelve thousand horse. Its
very name, in the Syrian tongue, signified a tower of safety. Against
this place Abu Obeidah had sent Serjabil Ibn Hasanah, a veteran secretary of Mahomet, with a troop of ten thousand horse. On his approach, Romanus, the governor of the city, notwithstanding the
strength of the place and of the garrison, would fain have paid tribute,

239

for he was dismayed by the accounts he had received of the fanatic zeal and irresistible valor of the Moslems, but his people were stout of heart, and insisted on fighting.

The venerable Serjabil, as he drew near to the city, called upon Allah to grant the victory promised in his name by his apostle; and to establish the truth of his unity by confounding its opposers. His prayers apparently were of no avail. Squadron after squadron of horsemen wheeled down from the gates of Bosra, attacked the Moslems on every side, threw them into confusion, and made great slaughter. Overwhelmed by numbers, Serjabil was about to order a retreat, when a great cloud of dust gave notice of another army at hand.

There was a momentary pause on both sides, but the shout of Allah Achbar! Allah Achbar! resounded through the Moslem host, as the eagle banner of Khaled was descried through the cloud. That warrior came galloping to the field, at the head of his troop of horsemen, all covered with dust. Charging the foe with his characteristic impetuosity, he drove them back to the city, and planted his standard before the walls.

The battle over, Serjabil would have embraced his deliverer, who was likewise his ancient friend, but Khaled regarded him reproachfully. "What madness possessed thee," said he, "to attack with thy handful of horsemen a fortress girt with stone walls and thronged with soldiers?"

"I acted," said Serjabil, "not for myself, but at the command of Abu Obeidah."

"Abu Obeidah," replied Khaled, bluntly, "is a very worthy man, but he knows little of warfare."

In effect the army of Syria soon found the difference between the commanders. The soldiers of Khaled, fatigued with a hard march, and harder combat, snatched a hasty repast, and throwing themselves upon the ground, were soon asleep. Khaled alone took no rest; but, mounting a fresh horse, prowled all night round the city and the camp, fearing some new irruption from the foe.

At daybreak he roused his army for the morning prayer. Some of the troops performed their ablutions with water, others with sand. Khaled put up the matin prayer: then every man grasped his weapon and sprang to horse, for the gates of Bosra were already pouring forth their legions. The eyes of Khaled kindled as he saw them prancing down into the plain, and glittering in the rising sun. "These infidels," said he, "think us weary and wayworn, but they will be confounded. Forward to the fight, for the blessing of Allah is with us!"

As the armies approached each other, Romanus rode in advance of his troops, and defied the Moslem chief to single combat. Khaled advanced on the instant. Romanus, however, instead of levelling his lance, entered into a parley in an under tone of voice. He declared that he was a Mahometan at heart, and had incurred great odium among the people of the place by endeavoring to persuade them to pay tribute. He now offered to embrace Islamism, and to return and do his best to yield the city into the hands of the Moslems, on condition of security for life, liberty, and property.

Khaled readily assented to the condition, but suggested that they should exchange a few dry blows, to enable Romanus to return to the city with a better grace, and prevent a suspicion of collusion. Romanus agreed to the proposal, but with no great relish, for he was an arrant craven. He would fain have made a mere feint and flourish of weapons; but Khaled had a heavy hand and a kindling spirit, and dealt such hearty blows, that he would have severed the other in twain, or cloven him to the saddle, had he struck with the edge instead of the flat of the sword.

"Softly, softly," cried Romanus. "Is this what you call sham fighting; or do you mean to slay me?"

"By no means," replied Khaled, "but we must lay on our blows a little roughly, to appear in earnest."

Romanus, battered and bruised, and wounded in several places, was glad to get back to his army with his life. He now extolled the prowess of Khaled, and advised the citizens to negotiate a surrender; but they upbraided him with his cowardice, stripped him of his command, and made him a prisoner in his own house: substituting in his place the general who had come to them with reinforcements from the emperor Heraclius.

The new governor, as his first essay in command, sallied in advance of the army, and defied Khaled to combat. Abda'lrahman, son of the Caliph, a youth of great promise, begged of Khaled the honor of being his champion. His request being granted, he rode forth, well armed, to the encounter. The combat was of short duration. At the onset the governor was daunted by the fierce countenance of the youthful Moslem, and confounded by the address with which he managed his horse and wielded his lance. At the first wound he lost all presence of mind, and turning the reins, endeavored to escape by dint of hoof. His steed was swiftest, and he succeeded in throwing himself into the midst of his forces. The impetuous youth spurred after him, cutting and slashing, right and left, and hewing his way with his scimetar.

Khaled, delighted with his valor, but alarmed at his peril, gave the signal for a general charge. To the fight! to the fight! Paradise! Paradise! was the maddening cry. Horse was spurred against horse; man grappled man. The desperate conflict was witnessed from the walls, and spread dismay through the city. The bells rang alarms, the shrieks of women and children mingled with the prayers and chants of priests and monks moving in procession through the streets.

The Moslems, too, called upon Allah for succor, mingling prayers and execrations as they fought. At length the troops of Bosra gave way: the squadrons that had sallied forth so gloriously in the morning, were driven back in broken and headlong masses to the city; the gates were hastily swung to and barred after them; and, while they panted with fatigue and terror behind their bulwarks, the standards and banners of the cross were planted on the battlements, and couriers were sent off imploring reinforcements from the emperor.

Night closed upon the scene of battle. The stifled groans of wounded warriors, mingled with the wailings of women, and the prayers of monks and friars, were heard in the once joyful streets of Bosra; while sentinels walked the rounds of the Arab camp to guard it against the desperation of the foe.

Abda'lrahman commanded one of the patrols. Walking his round beneath the shadow of the city walls, he beheld a man come stealthily forth, the embroidery of whose garments, faintly glittering in the starlight, betrayed him to be a person of consequence. The lance of Abda'lrahman was at his breast, when he proclaimed himself to be Romanus, and demanded to be led to Khaled. On entering the tent of that leader, he inveighed against the treatment he had experienced from the people of Bosra, and invoked vengeance. They had confined him to his house, but it was built against the wall of the city. He had caused his sons and servants, therefore, to break a hole through it, by which he had issued forth, and by which he offered to introduce a band of soldiers, who might throw open the city gates to the army.

His offer was instantly accepted, and Abda'lrahman was intrusted with the dangerous enterprise. He took with him a hundred picked men, and, conducted by Romanus, entered in the dead of night, by the breach in the wall, into the house of the traitor. Here they were refreshed with food, and disguised to look like the soldiers of the garrison. Abda'lrahman then divided them into four bands of twenty-five men each; three of which he sent in different directions, with orders to keep quiet until he and his followers should give the signal shout of Allah Achbar! He then requested Romanus to conduct him to the quarters of the governor, who had fled the fight with him that day. Under the guidance of the traitor, he and his twenty-five men passed with noiseless steps through the streets. Most of the unfortunate people of Bosra had sunk to sleep; but now and then the groan of some wounded warrior, or the lament of some afflicted woman, broke the stillness of the night and startled the prowlers.

Arrived at the gate of the citadel they surprised the sentinels, who mistook them for a friendly patrol, and made their way to the governor's chamber. Romanus entered first, and summoned the governor to receive a friend.

"What friend seeks me at this hour of the night?"

"Thy friend Abda'lrahman," cried Romanus with malignant triumph; "who comes to send thee to hell!"

The wretched poltroon would have fled. "Nay," cried Abda'lrahman, "you escape me not a second time!" and with a blow of his scimetar laid him dead at his feet. He then gave the signal shout of Allah Achbar! It was repeated by his followers at the portal; echoed by the other parties in different quarters; the city gates were thrown open, the legions of Khaled and Serjabil rushed in, and the whole city resounded with the cries of Allah Achbar! The inhabitants, startled from their sleep, hastened forth to know the meaning of the uproar, but were cut down at their thresholds, and a horrible carnage took place until there was a general cry for quarter. Then, in compliance with one of the precepts of Mahomet, Khaled put a stop to the slaughter, and received the survivors under the yoke.

The savage tumult being appeased, the unhappy inhabitants of Bosra inquired as to the mode in which they had been surprised. Khaled hesitated to expose the baseness of Romanus; but the traitor gloried in his shame, and in the vengeance he had wreaked upon former friends. " 'Twas I!" cried he with demoniac exultation. "I renounce ye both in this world and the next. I deny him who was crucified and despise his worshippers. I choose Islam for my faith; the Caaba for my temple; the Moslems for my brethren; Mahomet for my prophet; and I bear witness that there is but one only God, who has no partner in his power and glory."

Having made this full recantation of his old faith and profession of his new, in fulfilment of his traitorous compact the apostate departed from Bosra, followed by the execrations of its inhabitants, among whom he durst no longer abide; and Khaled, although he despised him in his heart, appointed a guard to protect his property from plunder.

CHAPTER V

Khaled lays siege to Damascus

The capture of Bosra increased the ambition and daring of the Moslems, and Khaled now aspired to the conquest of Damascus. This renowned and beautiful city, one of the largest and most magnificent of the East, and reputed to be the oldest in the world, stood in a plain of wonderful richness and fertility, covered with groves and gardens, and bounded by an amphitheatre of hills, the skirts of Mount Lebanon. A river called by the ancients Chrysorrhoa, or the stream of gold, flows through this plain, feeding the canals and water-courses of its gardens, and the fountains of the city.

The commerce of the place bespoke the luxuriance of the soil; dealing in wines, silks, wool, prunes, raisins, figs of unrivalled flavor, sweet-scented waters and perfumes. The fields were covered with odoriferous flowers, and the rose of Damascus has become famous throughout the world. This is one of the few, the very few, cities famous in ancient times, which still retain a trace of ancient delights. "The citron," says a recent traveller, "perfumes the air for many miles round the city; and the fig-trees are of vast size. The pomegranate and orange grow in thickets. There is the trickling of water on every hand. Wherever you go there is a trotting brook, or a full and silent stream beside the track; and you have frequently to cross from one vivid green meadow to another by fording, or by little bridges. These streams are all from the river beloved by Naaman of old. He might well ask whether the Jordan was better than Pharpar and Abana, the rivers of Damascus."

In this city too were invented those silken stuffs called damask from the place of their origin, and those swords and scimetars proverbial for their matchless temper.

When Khaled resolved to strike for this great prize, he had but fifteen hundred horse, which had followed him from Irak, in addition to the force which he found with Serjabil; having, however, the general command of the troops in Syria, he wrote to Abu Obeidah to join him with his army, amounting to thirty-seven thousand men.

The Moslems, accustomed to the aridity of the desert, gazed with wonder and delight upon the rich plain of Damascus. As they wound in lengthening files along the banks of the shining river, through verdant and flowery fields, or among groves and vineyards and blooming

gardens, it seemed as if they were already realizing the paradise promised by the prophet to true believers; but when the fanes and towers of
Damascus rose to sight from among tufted bowers, they broke forth
into shouts of transport.

Heraclius the emperor was at Antioch, the capital of his Syrian dominions, when he heard of the advance of the Arabs upon the city of
Damascus. He supposed the troops of Khaled, however, to be a mere
predatory band, intent as usual on hasty ravage, and easily repulsed
when satisfied with plunder; and he felt little alarm for the safety of
the city, knowing it to be very populous, strongly fortified, and well
garrisoned. He contented himself, therefore, with dispatching a general
named Caloüs with five thousand men to reinforce it.

In passing through the country, Caloüs found the people flying to
castles and other strongholds and putting them in a state of defence. As
he approached Baalbec, the women came forth with dishevelled hair,
wringing their hands and uttering cries of despair. "Alas!" cried they,
"the Arabs overrun the land, and nothing can withstand them. Aracah
and Sachnah, and Tadmor and Bosra, have fallen, and who shall protect Damascus!"

Caloüs inquired the force of the invaders.

They knew but of the troops of Khaled, and answered, "fifteen hundred horse."

"Be of good cheer," said Caloüs; "in a few days I will return with the
head of Khaled on the point of this good spear."

He arrived at Damascus before the Moslem army came in sight, and
the same self-confidence marked his proceedings. Arrogating to himself
the supreme command, he would have deposed and expelled the former governor Azraïl, a meritorious old soldier, well beloved by the
people. Violent dissensions immediately arose, and the city, instead of
being prepared for defence, was a prey to internal strife.

In the height of these tumults, the army of Khaled, forty thousand
strong, being augmented by that of Abu Obeidah, was descried marching across the plain. The sense of danger calmed the fury of contention, and the two governors sallied forth, with a great part of the garrison, to encounter the invaders.

Both armies drew up in battle array. Khaled was in front of the Moslem line, and with him was his brother in arms, Derar Ibn al Azwar.
The latter was mounted on a fine Arabian mare, and poised a ponderous lance, looking a warrior at all points. Khaled regarded him with

friendly pride, and resolved to give him an opportunity of distinguishing himself. For this purpose he detached him with a small squadron of horse to feel the pulse of the enemy. "Now is the time, Derar," cried he, "to show thyself a man, and emulate the deeds of thy father and other illustrious soldiers of the faith. Forward in the righteous cause, and Allah will protect thee."

Derar levelled his lance, and at the head of his handful of followers charged into the thickest of the foe. In the first encounter four horsemen fell beneath his arm; then wheeling off, and soaring as it were into the field to mark a different quarry, he charged with his little troop upon the foot soldiers, slew six with his own hand, trampled down others, and produced great confusion. The Christians, however, recovered from a temporary panic, and opposed him with overwhelming numbers and Roman discipline. Derar saw the inequality of the fight, and having glutted his martial fury, showed the Arab dexterity at retreat, making his way back safely to the Moslem army by whom he was received with acclamation.

Abda'lrahman gave a similar proof of fiery courage; but his cavalry was received by a battalion of infantry arranged in phalanx with extended spears, while stones and darts hurled from a distance galled both horse and rider. He also, after making a daring assault and sudden carnage, retired upon the spur and rejoined the army.

Khaled now emulated the prowess of his friends, and careering in front of the enemy, launched a general defiance to single combat.

The jealousies of the two Christian commanders continued in the field. Azraïl, turning to Caloüs, taunted him to accept the challenge as a matter of course; seeing he was sent to protect the country in this hour of danger.

The vaunting of Caloüs was at an end. He had no inclination for so close a fight with such an enemy, but pride would not permit him to refuse. He entered into the conflict with a faint heart, and in a short time would have retreated, but Khaled wheeled between him and his army. He then fought with desperation, and the contest was furious on both sides, until Caloüs beheld his blood streaming down his armor. His heart failed him at the sight; his strength flagged; he fought merely on the defensive. Khaled perceiving this, suddenly closed with him, shifted his lance to his left hand, grasped Caloüs with the right, dragged him out of the saddle, and bore him off captive to the Moslem host, who rent the air with triumphant shouts.

Mounting a fresh horse Khaled prepared again for battle.

"Tarry, my friend," cried Derar; "repose thyself for a time, and I will take thy place."

"Oh Derar," replied Khaled, "he who labors to-day shall rest to-morrow. There will be repose sufficient amidst the delights of paradise!"

When about to return to the field Caloüs demanded a moment's audience, and making use of the traitor Romanus as an interpreter, advised Khaled to bend all his efforts against Azraïl, the former governor of the city, whose death he said would be the surest means of gaining the victory. Thus a spirit of envy induced him to sacrifice the good of his country to the desire of injuring a rival.

Khaled was willing to take advice even from an enemy, especially when it fell in with his own humor; he advanced, therefore, in front, challenging Azraïl loudly by name. The latter quickly appeared, well armed and mounted, and with undaunted bearing.

The contest was long and obstinate. The combatants paused for breath. Khaled could not but regard his adversary with admiration.

"Thy name," said he, "is Azraïl? (This is the Arabic name for the angel of death.)

"Azraïl is my name," replied the other.

"By Allah!" replied Khaled, "thy namesake is at hand, waiting to carry thy soul to the fire of Jehennam!"

They renewed the fight. Azraïl, who was the more fleetly mounted, being sorely pressed, made use of an Arabian stratagem, and giving the reins to his steed pretended to fly the field. Having distanced his adversary and fatigued his horse, he suddenly wheeled about and returned to the charge. Khaled, however, was not to be outdone in stratagem. Throwing himself lightly from his saddle just as his antagonist came galloping upon him, he struck at the legs of his horse, brought him to the ground and took his rider prisoner.

The magnanimity of Khaled was not equal to his valor; or rather his fanatical zeal overcame all generous feelings. He admired Azraïl as a soldier; but detested him as an infidel. Placing him beside his late rival Caloüs, he called upon both to renounce Christianity and embrace the faith of Islam. They persisted in a firm refusal, upon which he gave the signal, and their heads were struck off and thrown over the walls into the city, a fearful warning to the inhabitants.

CHAPTER VI

Siege of Damascus continued – Exploits of Derar – Defeat of the imperial army

The siege of Damascus continued with increasing rigor. The inhabitants were embarrassed and dismayed by the loss of their two governors, and the garrison was thinned by frequent skirmishes, in which the bravest warriors were sure to fall. At length the soldiers ceased to sally forth, and the place became strictly invested. Khaled, with one half of the army, drew near to the walls on the east side; while Abu Obeidah, with the other half, was stationed on the west. The inhabitants now attempted to corrupt Khaled, offering him a thousand ounces of gold, and two hundred magnificent damask robes to raise the siege. His reply was, that they must embrace the Islam faith, pay tribute, or fight unto the death.

While the Arabs lay thus encamped round the city, as if watching its expiring throes, they were surprised one day by the unusual sound of shouts of joy within its walls. Sending out scouts, they soon learnt the astounding intelligence that a great army was marching to the relief of the place.

The besieged, in fact, in the height of their extremity, had lowered a messenger from the walls in the dead of the night, bearing tidings to the emperor at Antioch of their perilous condition, and imploring prompt and efficient succor. Aware for the first time of the real magnitude of the danger, Heraclius dispatched an army of a hundred thousand men to their relief, led on by Werdan, perfect of Emessa, an experienced general.

Khaled would at once have marched to meet the foe; alleging that so great a host could come only in divisions, which might be defeated in detail; the cautious and quiet Abu Obeidah, however, counselled to continue the siege, and send some able officer with a detachment to check and divert the advancing army. His advice was adopted, and Derar, the cherished companion in arms of Khaled, was chosen for the purpose. That fiery Moslem was ready to march at once and attack the enemy with any handful of men that might be assigned him; but Khaled rebuked his inconsiderate zeal. "We are expected," said he, "to fight for the faith, but not to throw ourselves away." Allotting to his friend, therefore, one thousand chosen horsemen, he recommended to him to hang on the flanks of the enemy and impede their march.

The fleetly mounted band of Derar soon came in sight of the van of Werdan's army, slowly marching in heavy masses. They were for hovering about it and harassing it in the Arab manner, but the impetuous valor of Derar was inflamed, and he swore not to draw back a step without hard fighting. He was seconded by Rafi Ibn Omeirah, who reminded the troops that a handful of the faithful was sufficient to defeat an army of infidels.

The battle cry was given. Derar, with some of his choicest troops, attacked the centre of the army, seeking to grapple with the general, whom he beheld there, surrounded by his guard. At the very onset he struck down the prefect's right-hand man, and then his standard-bearer. Several of Derar's followers sprang from their steeds to seize the standard, a cross richly adorned with precious stones, while he beat off the enemy, who endeavored to regain it. The captured cross was borne off in triumph; but at the same moment Derar received a wound in the left arm from a javelin, launched by a son of Werdan. Turning upon the youth, he thrust his lance into his body, but, in withdrawing it, the iron head remained in the wound. Thus left, unarmed, he defended himself for a time with the mere truncheon of the lance, but was overpowered and taken prisoner. The Moslems fought furiously to rescue him, but in vain, and he was borne captive from the field. They would now have fled, but were recalled by Rafi Ibn Omeirah. "Whoever flies," cried he, "turns his back upon God and his prophet. Paradise is for those who fall in battle. If your captain be dead, God is living, and sees your actions."

They rallied and stood at bay. The fortune of the day was against them; they were attacked by tenfold their number, and though they fought with desperation, they would soon have been cut to pieces, had not Khaled, at that critical moment, arrived at the scene of action with the greater part of his forces; a swift horseman having brought him tidings of the disastrous affray, and the capture of his friend.

On arriving, he stopped not to parley, but charged into the thickest of the foe, where he saw most banners, hoping there to find his captive friend. Wherever he turned he hewed a path before him, but Derar was not to be found. At length a prisoner told him that the captive had been sent off to Emessa under a strong escort. Khaled instantly dispatched Rafi Ibn Omeirah with a hundred horse in pursuit. They soon overtook the escort, attacked them furiously, slew several, and put the rest to flight, who left Derar, bound with cords, upon his charger.

By the time that Rafi and Derar rejoined the Moslem army, Khaled had defeated the whole forces of Werdan, division after division, as they arrived successively at the field of action. In this manner a hundred thousand troops were defeated, in detail, by less than a third of their number, inspired by fanatic valor, and led on by a skilful and intrepid chief. Thousands of the fugitives were killed in the pursuit; an immense booty in treasure, arms, baggage, and horses fell to the victors, and Khaled led back his army, flushed with conquest, but fatigued with fighting and burthened with spoils, to resume the siege of Damascus.

The tidings of the defeat of Werdan and his powerful army, made the emperor Heraclius tremble in his palace at Antioch, for the safety of his Syrian kingdom. Hastily levying another army of seventy thousand men, he put them under the command of Werdan, at Aiznadin, with orders to hasten to the relief of Damascus, and attack the Arab army, which must be diminished and enfeebled by the recent battle.

Khaled took counsel of Abu Obeidah how to avoid the impending storm. It was determined to raise the siege of Damascus, and seek the enemy promptly at Aiznadin. Conscious, however, of the inadequacy of his forces, Khaled sent missives to all the Moslem generals within his call.

"In the name of the most merciful God! Khaled Ibn al Walid to Amru Ibn al Aass, health and happiness. The Moslem brethren are about to march to Aiznadin to do battle with seventy thousand Greeks, who are coming to extinguish the light of God. But Allah will preserve his light in despite of all the infidels. Come to Aiznadin with thy troops; for, God willing, thou shalt find me there." These missives sent, he broke up his encampment before Damascus, and marched, with his whole force, toward Aiznadin. He would have placed Abu Obeidah at the head of the army; but the latter modestly remarked, that as Khaled was now commander-in-chief that station appertained to him. Abu Obeidah, therefore, brought up the rear, where were the baggage, the booty, the women, and the children.

When the garrison of Damascus saw their enemy on the march, they sallied forth under two brothers named Peter and Paul. The former led ten thousand infantry, the latter six thousand horse. Overtaking the rear of the Moslems, Paul with his cavalry charged into the midst of them, cutting down some, trampling others under foot, and spreading wide confusion. Peter in the meantime, with his infantry, made a sweep of the camp equipage, the baggage, and the accumulated booty, and capturing most of the women, made off with his spoils towards Damascus.

Tidings of this onset having reached Khaled in the van, he sent Derar, Abda'lrahman, and Rafi Ibn Omeirah, scouring back, each at the head of two hundred horse, while he followed with the main force.

Derar and his associates soon turned the tide of battle, routing Paul and his cavalry with such slaughter, that of the six thousand but a small part escaped to Damascus. Paul threw himself from his horse, and attempted to escape on foot, but was taken prisoner. The exultation of the victors, however, was damped by the intelligence that their women had been carried away captive, and great was the grief of Derar, on learning that his sister Caulah, a woman of great beauty, was among the number.

In the meantime, Peter and his troops, with their spoils and captives, had proceeded on the way to Damascus, but halted under some trees beside a fountain, to refresh themselves and divide their booty. In the division, Caulah the sister of Derar was allotted to Peter. This done, the captors went into their tents to carouse and make merry with the spoils, leaving the women among the baggage, bewailing their captive state.

Caulah, however, was the worthy sister of Derar. Instead of weeping and wringing her hands, she reproached her companions with their weakness. "What!" cried she, "shall we, the daughters of warriors and followers of Mahomet, submit to be the slaves and paramours of barbarians and idolaters? For my part, sooner will I die!"

Among her fellow-captives were Hamzarite women, descendants as it is supposed of the Amalekites of old, and others of the tribe of Hïmiar, all bold viragos, accustomed from their youth to mount the horse, ply the bow, and launch the javelin. They were roused by the appeal of Caulah. "What, however, can we do," cried they, "having neither sword nor lance nor bow?"

"Let us each take a tent pole," replied Caulah, "and defend ourselves to the utmost. God may deliver us; if not, we shall die and be at rest, leaving no stain upon our country." She was seconded by a resolute woman named Offeirah. Her words prevailed. They all armed themselves with tent poles, and Caulah placed them closely side by side in a circle. "Stand firm," said she. "Let no one pass between you; parry the weapons of your assailants, and strike at their heads."

With Caulah, as with her brother, the word was accompanied by the deed; for scarce had she spoken, when a Greek soldier happening to approach, with one blow of her staff she shattered his skull.

The noise brought the carousers from the tents. They surrounded the women, and sought to pacify them; but whoever came within reach of their staves was sure to suffer. Peter was struck with the matchless form and glowing beauty of Caulah, as she stood fierce and fearless, dealing her blows on all who approached. He charged his men not to harm her, and endeavored to win her by soothing words and offers of wealth and honor; but she reviled him as an infidel, a dog, and rejected with scorn his brutal love. Incensed at length by her taunts and menaces, he gave the word, and his followers rushed upon the women with their scimetars. The unequal combat would soon have ended, when Khaled and Derar came galloping with their cavalry to the rescue. Khaled was heavily armed; but Derar was almost naked, on a horse without a saddle, and brandishing a lance.

At sight of them Peter's heart quaked; he put a stop to the assault on the women, and would have made a merit of delivering them up unharmed. "We have wives and sisters of our own," said he, "and respect your courageous defence. Go in peace to your countrymen."

He turned his horse's head, but Caulah smote the legs of the animal and brought him to the ground; and Derar thrust his spear through the rider as he fell. Then alighting and striking off the head of Peter, he elevated it on the point of his lance. A general action ensued. The enemy were routed and pursued with slaughter to the gates of Damascus, and great booty was gained of horses and armor.

The battle over, Paul was brought a prisoner before Khaled, and the gory head of his brother was shown to him. "Such," cried Khaled, "will be your fate unless you instantly embrace the faith of Islam." Paul wept over the head of his brother, and said he wished not to survive him. "Enough," cried Khaled; the signal was given, and the head of Paul was severed from his body.

The Moslem army now retired to their old camp, where they found Abu Obeidah, who had rallied his fugitives and intrenched himself, for it was uncertain how near Werdan and his army might be. Here the weary victors reposed themselves from their dangers and fatigues; talked over the fortunes of the day, and exulted in the courage of their women.

CHAPTER VIII

Battle of Aiznadin

The army of the prefect Werdan, though seventy thousand in number, was for the most part composed of newly levied troops. It lay encamped at Aiznadin, and ancient historians speak much of the splendid appearance of the imperial camp, rich in its sumptuous furniture of silk and gold, and of the brilliant array of the troops in burnished armor, with glittering swords and lances.

While thus encamped, Werdan was surprised one day to behold clouds of dust rising in different directions, from which as they advanced broke forth the flash of arms and din of trumpets. These were in fact the troops which Khaled had summoned by letter from various parts, and which, though widely separated, arrived at the appointed time with a punctuality recorded by the Arabian chroniclers as miraculous.

The Moslems were at first a little daunted by the number and formidable array of the imperial host; but Khaled harangued them in a confident tone. "You behold," said he, "the last stake of the infidels. This army vanquished and dispersed, they can never muster another of any force, and all Syria is ours."

The armies lay encamped in sight of each other all night, and drew out in battle array in the morning.

"Who will undertake," said Khaled, "to observe the enemy near at hand, and bring me an account of the number and disposition of his forces?"

Derar immediately stepped forward. "Go," said Khaled, "and Allah go with thee. But I charge thee, Derar, not to strike a blow unprovoked, nor to expose thy life unnecessarily."

When Werdan saw a single horseman prowling in view of his army and noting its strength and disposition, he sent forth thirty horsemen to surround and capture him. Derar retreated before them until they became separated in the eagerness of pursuit, then suddenly wheeling, he received the first upon the point of his lance, and so another and another, thrusting them through or striking them from their saddles, until he had killed or unhorsed seventeen, and so daunted the rest, that he was enabled to make his retreat in safety.

Khaled reproached him with rashness and disobedience of orders.

"I sought not the fight," replied Derar. "They came forth against me, and I feared that God should see me turn my back. He doubtless aided me, and had it not been for your orders, I should not have desisted when I did."

Being informed by Derar of the number and positions of the enemy's troops, Khaled marshalled his army accordingly. He gave command of the right wing to Mead and Noman; the left to Saad Ibn Abu Wakkâs and Serjabil, and took charge of the centre himself, accompanied by Amru, Abda'lrahman, Derar, Kais, Rafi, and other distinguished leaders. A body of four thousand horse, under Yezed Ebn Abu Sofian, was posted in the rear to guard the baggage and the women.

But it was not the men alone that prepared for this momentous battle. Caulah and Offeirah, and their intrepid companions, among whom were women of the highest rank, excited by their recent success, armed themselves with such weapons as they found at hand, and prepared to mingle in the fight. Khaled applauded their courage and devotion, assuring them that, if they fell, the gates of paradise would be open to them. He then formed them into two battalions, giving command of one to Caulah, and of the other to Offeirah; and charged them, besides defending themselves against the enemy, to keep a strict eye upon his own troops; and whenever they saw a Moslem turn his back upon the foe, to slay him as a recreant and an apostate. Finally he rode through the ranks of his army, exhorting them all to fight with desperation, since they had wives, children, honor, religion, every thing at stake: and no place of refuge should they be defeated.

The war cries now arose from either army; the Christians shouting "for Christ and for the faith;" the Moslems, "La i'laha illa Allah, Mohammed Resoul Allah!" "There is but one God! Mahomet is the prophet of God!"

Just before the armies engaged, a venerable man came forth from among the Christians, and, approaching Khaled, demanded, "Art thou the general of this army?" "I am considered such," replied Khaled, "while I am true to God, the Koran, and the prophet."

"Thou art come unprovoked," said the old man, "thou and thy host, to invade this Christian land. Be not too certain of success. Others who have heretofore invaded this land, have found a tomb instead of a triumph. Look at this host. It is more numerous, and perhaps better disciplined than thine. Why wilt thou tempt a battle which may end in thy defeat, and must at all events cost thee most lamentable bloodshed? Retire, then, in peace, and spare the miseries which must otherwise fall upon either army. Shouldst thou do so, I am authorized to offer, for every soldier in thy host, a suit of garments, a turban, and a piece of gold; for thyself a hundred pieces and ten silken robes, and for thy Caliph, a thousand pieces and a hundred robes."

"You proffer a part," replied Khaled, scornfully, "to one who will soon possess the whole. For yourselves there are but three conditions; embrace the faith, pay tribute, or expect the sword." With this rough reply the venerable man returned sorrowfully to the Christian host.

Still Khaled was unusually wary. "Our enemies are two to one," said he, "we must have patience and outwind them. Let us hold back until nightfall, for that with the prophet was the propitious time of victory."

The enemy now threw their Armenian archers in the advance, and several Moslems were killed and wounded with flights of arrows. Still Khaled restrained the impatience of his troops, ordering that no man should stir from his post. The impetuous Derar at length obtained permission to attack the insulting band of archers, and spurred vigorously upon them with his troop of horse. They faltered, but were reinforced: troops were sent to sustain Derar; many were slain on both sides, but success inclined to the Moslems.

The action was on the point of becoming general, when a horseman from the advance army galloped up, and inquired for the Moslem general. Khaled, considering it a challenge, levelled his lance for the encounter. "Turn, thy lance aside, I pray thee," cried the Christian, eagerly; "I am but a messenger, and seek a parley."

Khaled quietly reined up his steed, and laid his lance athwart the pommel of his saddle: "Speak to the purpose," said he, "and tell no lies."

"I will tell the naked truth; dangerous for me to tell, but most important for thee to hear; but first promise protection for myself and family."

Having obtained this promise, the messenger, whose name was David, proceeded: "I am sent by Werdan to entreat that the battle may cease, and the blood of brave men be spared; and that thou wilt meet him to-morrow morning, singly, in sight of either army, to treat of terms of peace. Such is my message; but beware, oh Khaled! for treason lurks beneath it. Ten chosen men, well armed, will be stationed in the night close by the place of conference, to surprise and seize, or kill thee, when defenceless and off thy guard."

He then proceeded to mention the place appointed for the confer-

ence, and all the other particulars. "Enough," said Khaled. "Return to
Werdan, and tell him I agree to meet him."

The Moslems were astonished at hearing a retreat sounded, when
the conflict was inclining in their favor; they withdrew reluctantly from
the field, and Abu Obeidah and Derar demanded of Khaled the meaning of this conduct. He informed them of what had just been revealed
to him. "I will keep this appointment," said he. "I will go singly, and
will bring back the heads of all the assassins." Abu Obeidah, however, remonstrated against his exposing himself to such unnecessary danger.
"Take ten men with thee," said he, "man for man." "Why defer the
punishment of their perfidy until morning?" cried Derar. "Give me the
ten men, and I will counterplot these lurkers this very night."

Having obtained permission, he picked out ten men of assured cool-
ness and courage, and set off with them in the dead of the night for the
place of ambush. As they drew near Derar caused his companions to
halt, and, putting off his clothes to prevent all rustling noise, crept war-
ily with his naked scimetar to the appointed ground. Here he beheld
the ten men fast asleep, with their weapons beneath their heads. Returning silently, and beckoning his companions, they singled out each
his man, so that the whole were dispatched at a blow. They then
stripped the dead, disguised themselves in their clothes, and awaited
the coming day.

The rising sun shone on the two armies, drawn out in battle array,
and awaiting the parley of the chiefs. Werdan rode forth on a white
mule, and was arrayed in rich attire, with chains of gold and precious
stones. Khaled was clad in a yellow silk vest and green turban. He suffered himself to be drawn by Werdan towards the place of ambush;
then, alighting, and seating themselves on the ground, they entered
into a parley. Their conference was brief and boisterous. Each considered the other in his power, and conducted himself with haughtiness
and acrimony. Werdan spoke of the Moslems as needy spoilers, who
lived by the sword, and invaded the fertile territories of their neighbors in quest of plunder. "We, on the other hand," said he, "are
wealthy, and desire peace. Speak, what do you require to relieve your
wants and satisfy your rapacity?"

"Miserable infidel!" replied Khaled. "We are not so poor as to accept
alms at your hands. Allah provides for us. You offer us a part of what is
all our own; for Allah has put all that you have into our hands; even to

your wives and children. But do you desire peace? We have already told you our conditions. Either acknowledge that there is no other God but God, and that Mahomet is his prophet, or pay us such tribute as we may impose. Do you refuse? For what, then, have you brought me here? You knew our terms yesterday, and that all your propositions were rejected. Do you entice me here alone for single combat? Be it so, and let our weapons decide between us."

So saying, he sprang upon his feet. Werdan also rose, but expecting instant aid, neglected to draw his sword. Khaled seized him by the throat, upon which he called loudly to his men in ambush. The Moslems in ambush rushed forth, and, deceived by their Grecian dresses, Werdan for an instant thought himself secure. As they drew near, he discovered his mistake, and shrank with horror at the sight of Derar, who advanced, almost naked, brandishing a scimetar, and in whom he recognized the slayer of his son. "Mercy! Mercy!" cried he to Khaled, at finding himself caught in his own snare.

"There is no mercy," replied Khaled, "for him who has no faith. You came to me with peace on your lips, but murder in your heart. Your crime be upon your head."

The sentence was no sooner pronounced, than the powerful sword of Derar performed its office, and the head of Werdan was struck off at a blow. The gory trophy was elevated on the point of a lance and borne by the little band toward the Christian troops, who, deceived by the Greek disguises, supposed it the head of Khaled and shouted with joy. Their triumph was soon turned to dismay as they discovered their error. Khaled did not suffer them to recover from their confusion, but bade his trumpets sound a general charge. What ensued was a massacre rather than a battle. The imperial army broke and fled in all directions; some toward Cæsarea, others to Damascus, and others to Antioch. The booty was immense; crosses of silver and gold, adorned with precious stones, rich chains and bracelets, jewels of price, silken robes, armor and weapons of all kinds, and numerous banners, all which Khaled declared should not be divided until after the capture of Damascus.

Tidings of this great victory was sent to the Caliph at Medina, by his brave and well beloved son Abda'lrahman. On receiving it, Abu Beker prostrated himself and returned thanks to God. The news spread rapidly throughout Arabia. Hosts of adventurers hurried to Medina from all parts, and especially from Mecca. All were eager to serve in the cause of the faith, now that they found it crowned with conquest and rewarded with riches.

The worthy Abu Beker was disposed to gratify their wishes, but Omar on being consulted sternly objected. "The greater part of these fellows," said he, "who are so eager to join us now that we are successful, are those who sought to crush us when we were few and feeble. They care not for the faith, but they long to ravage the rich fields of Syria, and share the plunder of Damascus. Send them not to the army to make brawls and dissensions. Those already there are sufficient to complete what they have begun. They have won the victory; let them enjoy the spoils."

In compliance with this advice, Abu Beker refused the prayer of the applicants. Upon this the people of Mecca, and especially those of the tribe of Koreish, sent a powerful deputation, headed by Abu Sofian, to remonstrate with the Caliph. "Why are we denied permission," said they, "to fight in the cause of our religion? It is true, that in the days of darkness and ignorance we made war on the disciples of the prophet, because we thought we were doing God service. Allah, however, has blessed us with the light; we have seen and renounced our former errors. We are your brethren in the faith, as we have ever been your kindred in blood, and hereby take upon ourselves to fight in the common cause. Let there then no longer be jealousy and envy between us."

The heart of the Caliph was moved by these remonstrances. He consulted with Ali and Omar, and it was agreed that the tribe of Koreish should be permitted to join the army. Abu Beker accordingly wrote to Khaled congratulating him on his success, and informing him that a large reinforcement would join him conducted by Abu Sofian. This letter he sealed with the seal of the prophet, and dispatched it by his son Abda'lrahman.

CHAPTER IX

*Occurrences before Damascus – Exploits of Thomas – Abân Ibn
Zeid and his Amazonian wife*

The fugitives from the field of Aiznadin carried to Damascus the dismal tidings that the army was overthrown, and the last hope of succor destroyed. Great was the consternation of the inhabitants, yet they set to work, with desperate activity, to prepare for the coming storm. The fugitives had reinforced the garrison with several thousand effective men. New fortifications were hastily erected. The walls were lined with engines to discharge stones and darts, which were managed by Jews skilled in their use.

In the midst of their preparation, they beheld squadron after squadron of Moslem cavalry emerging from among distant groves, while a lengthening line of foot soldiers poured along between the gardens. This was the order of march of the Moslem host. The advance guard, of upwards of nine thousand horsemen, was led by Amru. Then came two thousand Koreishite horse, led by Abu Sofian. Then a like number under Serjabil. Then Omar Ibn Rabiyah with a similar division; then the main body of the army led by Abu Obeidah, and lastly the rearguard displaying the black eagle, the fateful banner of Khaled, and led by that invincible warrior.

Khaled now assembled his captains, and assigned to them their different stations. Abu Sofian was posted opposite the southern gate. Serjabil opposite that of St. Thomas. Amru before that of Paradise, and Kais Ibn Hobeirah before that of Kaisan. Abu Obeidah encamped at some distance, in front of the gate of Jabiyah, and was charged to be strict and vigilant, and to make frequent assaults, for Khaled knew his humane and easy nature. As to Khaled himself, he took his station and planted his black eagle before the eastern gate.

There was still a southern gate, that of St. Mark, so situated that it was not practicable to establish posts or engage in skirmishes before it; it was, therefore, termed the Gate of Peace. As to the active and impetuous Derar, he was ordered to patrol round the walls and scour the adjacent plain at the head of two thousand horse, protecting the camp from surprise and preventing supplies and reinforcements to the city. "If you should be attacked," said Khaled, "send me word, and I will come to your assistance." "And must I stand peaceably until you arrive?" said Derar, in recollection of former reproofs of his rash contests.

"Not so," rejoined Khaled, "but fight stoutly, and be assured I will not fail you." The rest of the army were dismounted to carry on the siege on foot.

The Moslems were now better equipped for war than ever, having supplied themselves with armor and weapons taken in repeated battles. As yet, however, they retained their Arab frugality and plainness, neglecting the delicate viands, the sumptuous raiment, and other luxurious indulgences of their enemies. Even Abu Obeidah, in the humility of his spirit, contented himself with his primitive Arab tent of camel's hair; refusing the sumptuous tents of the Christian commanders, won in the recent battle. Such were the stern and simple-minded invaders of the effeminate and sensual nations of the East.

The first assaults of the Moslems were bravely repelled, and many were slain by darts and stones hurled by the machines from the wall. The garrison even ventured to make a sally, but were driven back with signal slaughter. The siege was then pressed with unremitting rigor, until no one dared to venture beyond the bulwarks. The principal inhabitants now consulted together whether it were not best to capitulate, while there was yet a chance of obtaining favorable terms.

There was at this time living in Damascus, a noble Greek, named Thomas, who was married to a daughter of the emperor Heraclius. He held no post, but was greatly respected, for he was a man of talents and consummate courage. In this moment of general depression, he endeavored to rouse the spirits of the people; representing their invaders as despicable, barbarous, naked, and poorly armed, without discipline or military service, and formidable only through their mad fanaticism, and the panic they had spread through the country.

Finding all arguments in vain, he offered to take the lead himself, if they would venture upon another sally. His offer was accepted, and the next morning appointed for the effort.

Khaled perceived a stir of preparation throughout the night, lights gleaming in the turrets and along the battlements, and exhorted his men to be vigilant, for he anticipated some desperate movement. "Let no man sleep," said he. "We shall have rest enough after death, and sweet will be the repose that is never more to be followed by labor."

The Christians were sadly devout in this hour of extremity. At early dawn the bishop, in his robes, proceeded at the head of the clergy to the gate by which the sally was to be made; where he elevated the cross, and laid beside it the New Testament. As Thomas passed out at the gate, he laid his hand upon the sacred volume. "Oh God!" exclaimed he, "if our faith be true, aid us, and deliver us not into the hands of its enemies."

The Moslems, who had been on the alert, were advancing to attack just at the time of the sally, but were checked by a general discharge from the engines on the wall. Thomas led his troops bravely to the encounter, and the conflict was fierce and bloody. He was a dexterous archer, and singled out the most conspicuous of the Moslems, who fell one after another beneath his shafts. Among others he wounded Abân Ibn Zeid with an arrow tipped with poison. The latter bound up the wound with his turban, and continued in the field, but being overcome by the venom, was conveyed to the camp. He had but recently been married to a beautiful woman of the intrepid race of the Himiar; one of those Amazons accustomed to use the bow and arrow, and to mingle in warfare.

Hearing that her husband was wounded, she hastened to his tent, but before she could reach it he had expired. She uttered no lamentation, nor shed a tear, but, bending over the body, "Happy art thou, oh my beloved," said she, "for thou art with Allah, who joined us but to part us from each other. But I will avenge thy death, and then seek to join thee in paradise. Henceforth shall no man touch me more, for I dedicate myself to God!"

Then grasping her husband's bow and arrows, she hastened to the field in quest of Thomas, who, she had been told, was the slayer of her husband. Pressing toward the place where he was fighting, she let fly a shaft, which wounded his standard-bearer in the hand. The standard fell, and was borne off by the Moslems. Thomas pursued it, laying about him furiously, and calling upon his men to rescue their banner. It was shifted from hand to hand until it came into that of Serjabil. Thomas assailed him with his scimetar: Serjabil threw the standard among his troops and closed with him. They fought with equal ardor, but Thomas was gaining the advantage, when an arrow, shot by the wife of Abân, smote him in the eye. He staggered with the wound, but his men, abandoning the contested standard, rushed to his support, and bore him off to the city. He refused to retire to his home, and, his wound being dressed on the ramparts, would have returned to the conflict, but was overruled by the public. He took his station, however, at the city gate, whence he could survey the field and issue his orders. The battle continued with great fury; but such showers of stones and

darts and other missiles were discharged by the Jews from the engines
on the walls, that the besiegers were kept a distance. Night terminated
the conflict. The Moslems returned to their camp wearied with a long
day's fighting; and, throwing themselves on the earth, were soon buried
in profound sleep.

Thomas, finding the courage of the garrison roused by the stand they
had that day made, resolved to put it to further proof. At his suggestion, preparations were made in the dead of the night for a general
sally at daybreak from all the gates of the city. At the signal of a single
stroke upon a bell at the first peep of dawn, all the gates were thrown
open, and from each rushed forth a torrent of warriors upon the nearest encampment.

So silently had the preparations been made, that the besiegers were
completely taken by surprise. The trumpets sounded alarms, the Moslems started from sleep and snatched up their weapons, but the enemy
were already upon them, and struck them down before they had recovered from their amazement. For a time it was a slaughter rather than a
fight, at the various stations. Khaled is said to have shed tears at beholding the carnage. "Oh thou, who never sleepest!" cried he, in the
agony of his heart, "aid thy faithful servants; let them not fall beneath
the weapons of these infidels." Then, followed by four hundred horsemen, he spurred about the field wherever relief was most needed.

The hottest of the fight was opposite the gate whence Thomas had
sallied. Here Serjabil had his station, and fought with undaunted valor.
Near him was the intrepid wife of Abân, doing deadly execution with
her shafts. She had expended all but one, when a Greek soldier attempted to seize her. In an instant the arrow was sped through his
throat, and laid him dead at her feet; but she was now weaponless, and
was taken prisoner.

At the same time Serjabil and Thomas were again engaged hand to
hand with equal valor; but the scimetar of Serjabil broke on the buckler of his adversary, and he was on the point of being slain or captured,
when Khaled and Abda'lrahman galloped up with a troop of horse.
Thomas was obliged to take refuge in the city, and Serjabil and the
Amazonian widow were rescued.

The troops who sallied out at the gate of Jabiyah, met with the severest treatment. The meek Abu Obeidah was stationed in front of that
gate, and was slumbering quietly in his hair tent at the time of the
sally. His first care in the moment of alarm was to repeat the morning

prayer. He then ordered forth a body of chosen men to keep the enemy at bay, and while they were fighting, led another detachment, silently but rapidly, round between the combatants and the city. The Greeks thus suddenly found themselves assailed in front and rear; they fought desperately, but so successful was the stratagem, and so active the valor of the meek Abu Obeidah, when once aroused, that never a man, says the Arabian historian, that sallied from that gate, returned again.

The battle of the night was almost as sanguinary as that of the day; the Christians were repulsed in all quarters, and driven once more within their walls, leaving several thousand dead upon the field. The Moslems followed them to the very gates, but were compelled to retire by the deadly shower hurled by the Jews from the engines on the walls.

CHAPTER X

Surrender of Damascus – Disputes of the Saracen generals – Departure of Thomas and the exiles

For seventy days had Damascus been besieged by the fanatic legions of the desert: the inhabitants had no longer the heart to make further sallies, but again began to talk of capitulating. It was in vain that Thomas urged them to have patience until he should write to the emperor for succor; they listened only to their fears, and sent to Khaled begging a truce, that they might have time to treat of a surrender. That fierce warrior turned a deaf ear to their prayer: he wished for no surrender, that would protect the lives and property of the besieged; he was bent upon taking the city by the sword, and giving it up to be plundered by his Arabs.

In their extremity the people of Damascus turned to the good Abu Obeidah, whom they knew to be meek and humane. Having first treated with him by a messenger who understood Arabic, and received his promise of security, a hundred of the principal inhabitants, including the most venerable of the clergy, issued privately one night by the gate of Jabiyah, and sought his presence. They found this leader of a mighty force, that was shaking the empire of the Orient, living in a humble tent of hair-cloth, like a mere wanderer of the desert. He listened favorably to their propositions, for his object was conversion rather than conquest; tribute rather than plunder. A covenant was soon written, in which he engaged that hostilities should cease on their delivering the city into his hands; that such of the inhabitants as pleased might depart in safety with as much of their effects as they could carry, and those who remained as tributaries should retain their property, and have seven churches allotted to them. This covenant was not signed by Abu Obeidah, not being commander-in-chief, but he assured the envoys it would be held sacred by the Moslems.

The capitulation being arranged, and hostages given for the good faith of the besieged, the gate opposite to the encampment of Abu Obeidah was thrown open, and the venerable chief entered at the head of a hundred men to take possession.

While these transactions were taking place at the gate of Jabiyah, a different scene occurred at the eastern gate. Khaled was exasperated by the death of a brother of Amru, shot from the walls with a poisoned arrow. In the height of his indignation, an apostate priest, named Jo-

266

sias, undertook to deliver the gate into his hands, on condition of security of person and property for himself and his relatives.

By means of this traitor, a hundred Arabs were secretly introduced within the walls, who, rushing to the eastern gate, broke the bolts and bars and chains by which it was fastened, and threw it open with the signal shout of Allah Achbar!

Khaled and his legions poured in at the gate with sound of trumpet and tramp of steed; putting all to the sword, and deluging the streets with blood. "Mercy! Mercy!" was the cry. "No mercy for infidels!" was Khaled's fierce response.

He pursued his career of carnage into the great square before the church of the Virgin Mary. Here, to his astonishment, he beheld Abu Obeidah and his attendants, their swords sheathed, and marching in solemn procession with priests and monks and the principal inhabitants, and surrounded by women and children.

Abu Obeidah saw fury and surprise in the looks of Khaled, and hastened to propitiate him by gentle words. "Allah in his mercy," said he, "has delivered this city into my hands by peaceful surrender; sparing the effusion of blood and the necessity of fighting."

"Not so," cried Khaled in a fury. "I have won it with this sword, and I grant no quarter."

"But I have given the inhabitants a covenant written with my own hand."

"And what right had you," demanded Khaled, "to grant a capitulation without consulting me? Am not I the general? Yes, by Allah! and to prove it I will put every inhabitant to the sword."

Abu Obeidah felt that in point of military duty he had erred, but he sought to pacify Khaled, assuring him he had intended all for the best, and felt sure of his approbation; entreating him to respect the covenant he had made in the name of God and the prophet, and with the approbation of all the Moslems present at the transaction.

Several of the Moslem officers seconded Abu Obeidah, and endeavored to persuade Khaled to agree to the capitulation. While he hesitated, his troops, impatient of delay, resumed the work of massacre and pillage.

The patience of the good Abu Obeidah was at an end. "By Allah!" cried he, "my word is treated as nought, and my covenant is trampled under foot!"

Spurring his horse among the marauders, he commanded them, in the name of the prophet, to desist until he and Khaled should have time to settle their dispute. The name of the prophet had its effect; the soldiery paused in their bloody career, and the two generals with their officers retired to the church of the Virgin.

Here, after a sharp altercation, Khaled, callous to all claims of justice and mercy, was brought to listen to policy. It was represented to him that he was invading a country where many cities were yet to be taken; that it was important to respect the capitulations of his generals, even though they might not be altogether to his mind; otherwise the Moslem word would cease to be trusted, and other cities, warned by the fate of Damascus, instead of surrendering on favorable terms, might turn a deaf ear to all offers of mercy and fight to the last extremity.

It was with the utmost difficulty that Abu Obeidah wrung from the iron soul of Khaled a slow consent to his capitulation, on condition that the whole matter should be referred to the Caliph. At every article he paused and murmured. He would fain have inflicted death upon Thomas, and another leader named Herbis, but Abu Obeidah insisted that they were expressly included in the covenant.

Proclamation was then made that such of the inhabitants as chose to remain tributaries to the Caliph should enjoy the exercise of their religion; the rest were permitted to depart. The greater part preferred to remain; but some determined to follow their champion Thomas to Antioch. The latter prayed for a passport or a safe-conduct through the country controlled by the Moslems. After much difficulty, Khaled granted them three days' grace, during which they should be safe from molestation or pursuit; on condition they took nothing with them but provisions.

Here the worthy Abu Obeidah interfered, declaring that he had covenanted to let them go forth with bag and baggage. "Then," said Khaled, "they shall go unarmed." Again Abu Obeidah interfered, and Khaled at length consented that they should have arms sufficient to defend themselves against robbers and wild beasts; he, however, who had a lance, should have no sword; and he who had a bow, should have no lance.

Thomas and Herbis, who were to conduct this unhappy caravan, pitched their tents in the meadow adjacent to the city, whither all repaired who were to follow them into exile; each laden with plate, jewels, silken stuffs, and whatever was most precious and least burdensome. Among other things was a wardrobe of the emperor Heraclius, in which there were above three hundred loads of costly silks and cloth of gold.

All being assembled, the sad multitude set forth on their wayfaring. Those who from pride, from patriotism, or from religion, thus doomed themselves to poverty and exile, were among the noblest and most highly bred of the land; people accustomed to soft and luxurious life, and to the silken abodes of palaces. Of this number was the wife of Thomas, a daughter of the emperor Heraclius, who was attended by her maidens. It was a piteous sight to behold aged men, delicate and shrinking women, and helpless children, thus setting forth on a wandering journey through wastes and deserts, and rugged mountains, infested by savage hordes. Many a time did they turn to cast a look of fondness and despair on those sumptuous palaces and delightful gardens, once their pride and joy; and still would they turn and weep, and beat their breasts, and gaze through their tears on the stately towers of Damascus, and the flowery banks of the Pharpar.

Thus terminated the hard-contested siege of Damascus, which Voltaire has likened for its stratagems, skirmishes, and single combats, to Homer's siege of Troy. More than twelve months elapsed between the time the Saracens first pitched their tents before it and the day of its surrender.

CHAPTER XI

*Story of Jonas and Eudocea – Pursuit of the exiles – Death of the
Caliph Abu Beker*

It is recorded that Derar gnashed his teeth with rage at seeing the multitude of exiles departing in peace, laden with treasures, which he considered as so much hard-earned spoil, lost to the faithful; but what
most incensed him was, that so many unbelievers should escape the
edge of the scimetar. Khaled would have been equally indignant, but
that he had secretly covenanted with himself to regain this booty. For
this purpose he ordered his men to refresh themselves and their horses,
and be in readiness for action, resolving to pursue the exiles when the
three days of grace should have expired.

A dispute with Abu Obeidah concerning a quantity of grain, which
the latter claimed for the citizens, detained him one day longer, and he
was about to abandon the pursuit as hopeless, when a guide presented
himself who knew all the country, and the shortest passes through the
mountains. The story of this guide is worthy of notice, as illustrating
the character of these people and these wars.

During the siege, Derar, as has been related, was appointed to patrol
round the city and the camp, with two thousand horse. As a party of
these were one night going their rounds, near the walls, they heard the
distant neighing of a horse, and looking narrowly round, descried a
horseman coming stealthily from the gate Keisan. Halting in a shadowy
place, they waited until he came close to them, when, rushing forth,
they made him prisoner. He was a youthful Syrian, richly and gallantly
arrayed, and apparently a person of distinction. Scarcely had they
seized him when they beheld another horseman issuing from the same
gate, who in a soft voice called upon their captive, by the name of
Jonas. They commanded the latter to invite his companion to advance.
He seemed to reply, and called out something in Greek: upon hearing
which, the other turned bridle and galloped back into the city. The
Arabs, ignorant of Greek, and suspecting the words to be a warning,
would have slain their prisoner on the spot; but, upon second thoughts,
conducted him to Khaled.

The youth avowed himself a nobleman of Damascus, and betrothed
to a beautiful maiden named Eudocea; but her parents, from some ca-
pricious reason, had withdrawn their consent to his nuptials; whereupon the lovers had secretly agreed to fly from Damascus. A sum of

gold had bribed the sentinels who kept watch that night at the gate. The damsel, disguised in male attire, and accompanied by two domestics, was following her lover at a distance, as he sallied in advance. His reply in Greek, when she called upon him, was, "the bird is caught!" a warning at the hearing of which she had fled back to the city.

Khaled was not the man to be moved by a love tale; but he gave the prisoner his alternative. "Embrace the faith of Islam," said he, "and when Damascus falls into our power, you shall have your betrothed; refuse, and your head is forfeit."

The youth paused not between a scimetar and a bride. He made immediate profession of faith between the hands of Khaled, and thenceforth fought zealously for the capture of the city, since its downfall was to crown his hopes.

When Damascus yielded to its foes, he sought the dwelling of Eudocea, and learnt a new proof of her affection. Supposing, on his capture by the Arabs, that he had fallen a martyr to his faith, she had renounced the world, and shut herself up in a convent. With throbbing heart he hastened to the convent, but when the lofty-minded maiden beheld in him a renegade, she turned from him with scorn, retired to her cell, and refused to see him more. She was among the noble ladies who followed Thomas and Herbis into exile. Her lover, frantic at the thoughts of losing her, reminded Khaled of his promise to restore her to him, and entreated that she might be detained; but Khaled pleaded the covenant of Abu Obeidah, according to which all had free leave to depart.

When Jonas afterwards discovered that Khaled meditated a pursuit of the exiles, but was discouraged by the lapse of time, he offered to conduct him by short and secret passes through the mountains, which would insure his overtaking them. His offer was accepted. On the fourth day after the departure of the exiles, Khaled set out in pursuit, with four thousand chosen horsemen; who, by the advice of Jonas, were disguised as Christian Arabs. For some time they traced the exiles along the plains, by the numerous foot-prints of mules and camels, and by articles thrown away to enable them to travel more expeditiously. At length, the foot-prints turned towards the mountains of Lebanon, and were lost in their arid and rocky defiles. The Moslems began to falter. "Courage!" cried Jonas, "they will be entangled among the mountains. They cannot now escape."

They continued their weary course, stopping only at the stated hours of prayer. They had now to climb the high and cragged passes of Lebanon, along rifts and glens worn by winter torrents. The horses struck fire at every tramp; they cast their shoes, their hoofs were battered on the rocks, and many of them were lamed and disabled. The horsemen dismounted and scrambled up on foot, leading their weary and crippled steeds. Their clothes were worn to shreds, and the soles of their iron-shod boots were torn from the upper leathers. The men murmured and repined; never in all their marches had they experienced such hardships; they insisted on halting, to rest and to bait their horses. Even Khaled, whose hatred of infidels furnished an impulse almost equal to the lover's passion, began to flag, and reproached the renegade as the cause of all this trouble.

Jonas still urged them forward: he pointed to fresh foot-prints and tracks of horses that must have recently passed. After a few hours' refreshment they resumed the pursuit; passing within sight of Jabalah and Laodicea, but without venturing within their gates, lest the disguise of Christian Arabs, which deceived the simple peasantry, might not avail with the shrewder inhabitants of the towns.

Intelligence received from a country boor increased their perplexity. The emperor Heraclius, fearing that the arrival of the exiles might cause a panic at Antioch, had sent orders for them to proceed along the sea-coast to Constantinople. This gave their pursuers a greater chance to overtake them: but Khaled was startled at learning, in addition, that troops were assembling to be sent against him, and that but a single mountain separated him from them. He now feared they might intercept his return, or fall upon Damascus in his absence. A sinister dream added to his uneasiness, but it was favorably interpreted by Abda'lrahman, and he continued the pursuit.

A tempestuous night closed on them: the rain fell in torrents, and man and beast was ready to sink with fatigue: still they were urged forward: the fugitives could not be far distant, the enemy was at hand: they must snatch their prey and retreat. The morning dawned; the storm cleared up, and the sun shone brightly on the surrounding heights. They dragged their steps wearily, however, along the defiles, now swept by torrents or filled with mire, until the scouts in the advance gave joyful signal from the mountain brow. It commanded a grassy meadow, sprinkled with flowers, and watered by a running stream.

On the borders of the rivulet was the caravan of exiles, reposing in the sunshine from the fatigues of the recent storm. Some were sleeping on the grass, others were taking their morning repast; while the meadow was gay with embroidered robes and silks of various dyes spread out to dry upon the herbage. The weary Moslems, worn out with the horrors of the mountains, gazed with delight on the sweetness and freshness of the meadow; but Khaled eyed the caravan with an eager eye, and the lover only stretched his gaze to catch a glimpse of his betrothed among the females reclining on the margin of the stream.

Having cautiously reconnoitred the caravan without being perceived, Khaled disposed of his band in four squadrons; the first commanded by Derar, the second by Rafi Ibn Omeirah, the third by Abda'lrahman, and the fourth led by himself. He gave orders that the squadrons should make their appearance successively, one at a time, to deceive the enemy as to their force, and that there should be no pillaging until the victory was complete.

Having offered up a prayer, he gave the word to his division, "In the name of Allah and the prophet!" and led to the attack. The Christians were roused from their repose on beholding a squadron rushing down from the mountain. They were deceived at first by the Greek dresses, but were soon aware of the truth; though the small number of the enemy gave them but little dread. Thomas hastily marshalled five thousand men to receive the shock of the onset, with such weapons as had been left them. Another and another division came hurrying down from the mountain; and the fight was furious and well contested. Thomas and Khaled fought hand to hand; but the Christian champion was struck to the ground. Abda'lrahman cut off his head, elevated it on the spear of the standard of the cross which he had taken at Damascus, and called upon the Christians to behold the head of their leader.

Rafi Ibn Omeirah penetrated with his division into the midst of the encampment to capture the women. They stood courageously on the defensive, hurling stones at their assailants. Among them was a female of matchless beauty, dressed in splendid attire, with a diadem of jewels. It was the reputed daughter of the emperor, the wife of Thomas. Rafi attempted to seize her, but she hurled a stone that struck his horse in the head and killed him. The Arab drew his scimetar, and would have slain her, but she cried for mercy, so he took her prisoner, and gave her in charge to a trusty follower.

In the midst of the carnage and confusion, Jonas hastened in search of his betrothed. If she had treated him with disdain as a renegade, she

now regarded him with horror, as the traitor who had brought this destruction upon his unhappy countrymen. All his entreaties for her to
forgive and be reconciled to him, were of no avail. She solemnly vowed
to repair to Constantinople and end her days in a convent. Finding
supplication fruitless, he seized her, and after a violent struggle, threw
her on the ground and made her prisoner. She made no further resistance, but submitting to captivity, seated herself quietly on the grass.
The lover flattered himself that she relented; but, watching her opportunity, she suddenly drew forth a poniard, plunged it in her breast, and
fell dead at his feet.

While this tragedy was performing the general battle, or rather carnage, continued. Khaled ranged the field in quest of Herbis, but, while
fighting pell-mell among a throng of Christians, that commander came
behind him and dealt a blow that severed his helmet, and would have
cleft his skull but for the folds of his turban. The sword of Herbis fell
from his hand with the violence of the blow, and before he could recover it, he was cut in pieces by the followers of Khaled. The struggle
of the unhappy Christians was at an end: all were slain, or taken prisoners, except one, who was permitted to depart, and who bore the dismal tidings of the massacre to Constantinople.

The renegade Jonas was loud in his lamentations for the loss of his
betrothed, but his Moslem comrades consoled him with one of the doctrines of the faith he had newly embraced. "It was written in the book
of fate," said they, "that you should never possess that woman; but be
comforted, Allah has doubtless greater blessings in store for you;" and,
in fact, Rafi Ibn Omeirah, out of compassion for his distress, presented
him with the beautiful princess he had taken captive. Khaled consented to the gift, provided the emperor did not send to ransom her.

There was now no time to be lost. In this headlong pursuit they had
penetrated above a hundred and fifty miles into the heart of the enemy's country, and might be cut off in their retreat. "To horse and
away," therefore, was the word. The plunder was hastily packed upon
the mules, the scanty number of surviving exiles were secured, and the
marauding band set off on a forced march for Damascus. While on
their way they were one day alarmed by a cloud of dust, through
which their scouts descried the banner of the cross. They prepared for
a desperate conflict. It proved, however, a peaceful mission. An ancient
bishop, followed by a numerous train, sought from Khaled, in the emperor's name, the liberation of his daughter. The haughty Saracen re-

leased her without ransom. "Take her," said he, "but tell your master I intend to have him in exchange; never will I cease this war until I have wrested from him every foot of territory."

To indemnify the renegade for this second deprivation, a large sum of gold was given him, wherewith to buy a wife from among the captives; but he now disclaimed for ever all earthly love, and, like a devout Mahometan, looked forward for consolation among the black-eyed Houris of paradise. He continued more faithful to his new faith and new companions than he had been to the religion of his fathers and the friends of his infancy; and after serving the Saracens in a variety of ways, earned an undoubted admission to the paradise of the prophet, being shot through the breast at the battle of Yermouk.

Thus perished this apostate, says the Christian chronicler; but Al-wakedi, the venerable Cadi of Bagdad, adds a supplement to the story, for the encouragement of all proselytes to the Islam faith. He states that Jonas, after his death, was seen in a vision by Rafi Ibn Omeirah, arrayed in rich robes and golden sandals, and walking in a flowery mead; and the beatified renegade assured him that, for his exemplary services, Allah had given him seventy of the black-eyed damsels of paradise, each of resplendent beauty, sufficient to throw the sun and moon in the shade. Rafi related his vision to Khaled, who heard it with implicit faith. "This it is," said that Moslem zealot, "to die a martyr to the faith. Happy the man to whose lot it falls!"*

Khaled succeeded in leading his adventurous band safely back to Damascus, where they were joyfully received by their companions in arms, who had entertained great fears for their safety. He now divided the rich spoils taken in his expedition; four parts were given to the officers and soldiers, a fifth he reserved for the public treasury, and sent it off to the Caliph, with letters informing him of the capture of Damascus; of his disputes with Abu Obeidah as to the treatment of the city and its inhabitants, and lastly of his expedition in pursuit of the exiles, and his recovery of the wealth they were bearing away. These missives were sent in the confident expectation that his policy of the sword would far outshine, in the estimation of the Caliph, and of all true Moslems, the more peaceful policy of Abu Obeidah.

---

* The story of Jonas and Eudocea has been made the subject of an English tragedy by Hughes, entitled The Siege of Damascus; but the lover's name is changed to Phocyas, the incidents are altered, and the catastrophe is made entirely different.

It was written in the book of fate, say the Arabian historians, that the pious Abu Beker should die without hearing of the brightest triumph of the Islam faith; the very day that Damascus surrendered, the Caliph breathed his last at Medina. Arabian authors differ as to the cause of his death. Abulfeda asserts that he was poisoned by the Jews, in his frugal repast of rice; but his daughter Ayesha, with more probability, ascribes his death to bathing on an unusually cold day, which threw him into a fever. While struggling with his malady, he directed his chosen friend Omar to perform the religious functions of his office in his stead.

Feeling his end approaching, he summoned his secretary, Othman Ibn Affân, and in presence of several of the principal Moslems, dictated as follows: "I, Abu Beker Ibn Abu Kahafa, being on the point of leaving this world for the next, and at that moment when infidels believe, when the wicked cease to doubt, and when liars speak the truth, do make this declaration of my will to the Moslems. I nominate, as my successor,"—— Here he was overtaken with faintness so that he could not speak. Othman, who knew his intentions, added the name of Omar Ibn al Khattâb. When Abu Beker came to himself, and saw what his secretary had written, "God bless thee," said he, "for this foresight!" He then continued to dictate. "Listen to him, and obey him, for, as far as I know him, and have seen him, he is integrity itself. He is competent to every thing he undertakes. He will rule with justice; if not, God, who knows all secrets, will reward him according to his works. I mean all for the best, but I cannot see into the hidden thoughts of men. Farewell. Act uprightly, and the blessing of Allah be upon you."

He ordered this testament to be sealed with his seal, and copies of it to be sent to the principal authorities, civil and military. Then, having sent for Omar, he told him of his having nominated him as his successor.

Omar was a stern and simple-minded man, unambitious of posts and dignities. "Oh successor to the apostle of God!" said he, "spare me from this burthen. I have no need of the Caliphat." "But the Caliphat has need of you!" replied the dying Abu Beker.

He went on to claim his acceptance of the office as a proof of friendship to himself, and of devotion to the public good, for he considered him eminently calculated to maintain an undivided rule over the restless people so newly congregated into an empire. Having brought him to accept, he gave him much dying counsel, and after he had retired, prayed fervently for his success, and that the dominion of the faith might be strengthened and extended during his reign. Having thus provided for a quiet succession to his office, the good Caliph expired in the arms of his daughter Ayesha, in the sixty-fourth year of his age, having reigned two years, three months, and nine days. At the time of his death his father and mother were still living, the former ninety-seven years of age. When the ancient Moslem heard of the death of his son, he merely said, in Scriptural phrase: "The Lord hath given, and the Lord hath taken away. Blessed be the name of the Lord!"

Abu Beker had four wives; the last had been the widow of Jaafar, who fell in the battle of Muta. She bore him two sons after his sixtieth year. He does not appear, however, to have had the same fondness for the sex as the prophet, notwithstanding his experience in wedlock. "The women," he used to say, "are all an evil; but the greatest evil of all is, that they are necessary."

Abu Beker was universally lamented by his subjects, and he deserved their lamentations, for he had been an excellent ruler, just, moderate, temperate, frugal, and disinterested. His reign was too short to enable him to carry out any extensive schemes; but it was signalized by the promptness and ability with which, through the aid of the sword, he quelled the wide-spreading insurrections on the death of the prophet, and preserved the scarcely launched empire of Islam from perfect shipwreck. He left behind him a name dear to all true Moslems, and an example which, Omar used to say, would be a difficult pattern for his successors to imitate.

CHAPTER XII

*Election of Omar, second Caliph – Khaled superseded in command
by Abu Obeidah – Magnanimous conduct of those generals – Expedition to the convent of Abyla*

The nomination of Omar to the succession was supported by Ayesha,
and acquiesced in by Ali, who saw that opposition would be ineffectual. The election took place on the day of the decease of Abu Beker.
The character of the new Caliph has already, through his deeds, been
made known in some measure to the reader; yet a sketch of him may
not be unacceptable. He was now about fifty-three years of age; a tall
dark man, with a grave demeanor and a bald head. He was so tall, says
one of his biographers, that when he sat, he was higher than those who
stood. His strength was uncommon, and he used the left as adroitly as
the right hand. Though so bitter an enemy of Islamism at first as to
seek the life of Mahomet, he became from the moment of his conversion one of its most sincere and strenuous champions. He had taken an
active part in the weightiest and most decisive events of the prophet's
career. His name stands at the head of the weapon companions at
Beder, Ohod, Khaïbar, Honein, and Tabuc, at the defence of Medina,
and the capture of Mecca, and indeed he appears to have been the
soul of most of the early military enterprises of the faith. His zeal was
prompt and almost fiery in its operations. He expounded and enforced
the doctrines of Islam like a soldier; when a question was too knotty
for his logic, he was ready to sever it with the sword, and to strike off
the head of him who persisted in false arguing and unbelief.

In the administration of affairs, his probity and justice were proverbial. In private life he was noted for abstinence and frugality, and a
contempt for the false grandeur of the world. Water was his only beverage. His food a few dates, or a few bits of barley bread and salt; but
in time of penance, even salt was retrenched as a luxury. His austere
piety and self-denial, and the simplicity and almost poverty of his appearance, were regarded with reverence in those primitive days of
Islam. He had shrewd maxims on which he squared his conduct, of
which the following is a specimen. "Four things come not back: the
spoken word; the sped arrow; the past life, and the neglected opportunity."

During his reign mosques were erected without number for the instruction and devotion of the faithful, and prisons for the punishment

of delinquents. He likewise put in use a scourge with twisted thongs for the correction of minor offences, among which he included satire and scandal, and so potently and extensively was it plied, that the word went round, "Omar's twisted scourge is more to be feared than his sword."

On assuming his office, he was saluted as Caliph of the Caliph of the apostle of God, in other words, successor to the successor of the prophet. Omar objected, that such a title must lengthen with every successor, until it became endless; upon which it was proposed and agreed that he should receive the title of Emir-al-Moumenin, that is to say, Commander of the Faithful. This title altered into Miramamolin, was subsequently borne by such Moslem sovereigns as held independent sway, acknowledging no superior, and is equivalent to that of emperor.

One of the first measures of the new Caliph was with regard to the army in Syria. His sober judgment was not to be dazzled by daring and brilliant exploits in arms, and he doubted the fitness of Khaled for the general command. He acknowledged his valor and military skill, but considered him rash, fiery and prodigal; prone to hazardous and extravagant adventure, and more fitted to be a partisan than a leader. He resolved, therefore, to take the principal command of the army out of such indiscreet hands, and restore it to Abu Obeidah, who, he said, had proved himself worthy of it by his piety, modesty, moderation, and good faith. He accordingly wrote on a skin of parchment, a letter to Abu Obeidah, informing him of the death of Abu Beker, and his own elevation as Caliph, and appointing him commander-in-chief of the army of Syria.

The letter was delivered to Abu Obeidah at the time that Khaled was absent in pursuit of the caravan of exiles. The good Obeidah was surprised, but sorely perplexed by the contents. His own modesty made him unambitious of high command, and his opinion of the signal valor and brilliant services of Khaled made him loth to supersede him, and doubtful whether the Caliph would not feel disposed to continue him as commander-in-chief when he should hear of his recent success at Damascus. He resolved, therefore, to keep for the present, the contents of the Caliph's letter to himself; and accordingly on Khaled's return to Damascus continued to treat him as commander, and suffered him to write his second letter to Abu Beker, giving him an account of his recent pursuit and plundering of the exiles.

Omar had not been long installed in office, when he received the first letters of Khaled announcing the capture of Damascus. These tidings occasioned the most extravagant joy at Medina, and the valor of Khaled was extolled by the multitude to the very skies. In the midst of their rejoicings they learnt with astonishment, that the general command had been transferred to Abu Obeidah. The admirers of Khaled were loud in their expostulations. "What!" cried they, "dismiss Khaled when in the full career of victory? Remember the reply of Abu Beker, when a like measure was urged upon him. 'I will not sheathe the sword of God, drawn for the promotion of the faith.' "

Omar revolved their remonstrances in his mind, but his resolution remained unchanged. "Abu Obeidah," said he, "is tender and merciful; yet brave. He will be careful of his people, not lavishing their lives in rash adventures and plundering inroads; nor will he be the less formidable in battle for being moderate when victorious."

In the meantime came the second dispatches of Khaled, addressed to Abu Beker, announcing the success of his expedition in pursuit of the exiles; and requesting his decision of the matters in dispute between him and Abu Obeidah. The Caliph was perplexed by this letter, which showed that his election as Caliph was yet unknown to the army, and that Abu Obeidah had not assumed the command. He now wrote again to the latter reiterating his appointment; and deciding upon the matters in dispute. He gave it as his opinion, that Damascus had surrendered on capitulation, and had not been taken by the sword, and directed that the stipulations of the covenant should be fulfilled. He declared the pursuit of the exiles iniquitous and rash; and that it would have proved fatal, but for the mercy of God. The dismissal of the emperor's daughter free of ransom, he termed a prodigal action; as a large sum might have been obtained and given to the poor. He counselled Abu Obeidah, of whose mild and humane temper he was well aware, not to be too modest and compliant, but at the same time, not to risk the lives of the faithful in the mere hope of plunder. This latter hint was a reproof to Khaled.

Lest this letter should likewise be suppressed through the modesty of Abu Obeidah, he dispatched it by an officer of distinction, Shaded Ibn Aass, whom he appointed his representative in Syria, with orders to have the letter read in presence of the Moslems, and to cause him to be proclaimed Caliph at Damascus.

Shaded made good his journey, and found Khaled in his tent, still acting as commander-in-chief, and the army ignorant of the death of

Abu Beker. The tidings he brought struck every one with astonishment. The first sentiment expressed was grief at the death of the good Abu Beker, who was universally lamented as a father; the second was surprise at the deposition of Khaled from the command, in the very midst of such signal victories; and many of his officers and soldiers were loud in expressing their indignation.

If Khaled had been fierce and rude in his career of triumph, he proved himself magnanimous in this moment of adversity. "I know," said he, "that Omar does not love me; but since Abu Beker is dead, and has appointed him his successor, I submit to his commands." He accordingly caused Omar to be proclaimed Caliph at Damascus, and resigned his command to Abu Obeidah. The latter accepted it with characteristic modesty; but evinced a fear that Khaled would retire in disgust, and his signal services be lost to the cause of Islam. Khaled, however, soon let him know, that he was as ready to serve as to command, and only required an occasion to prove that his zeal for the faith was unabated. His personal submission extorted admiration even from his enemies, and gained him the fullest deference, respect, and confidence of Abu Obeidah.

About this time one of the Christian tributaries, a base-spirited wretch, eager to ingratiate himself with Abu Obeidah, came and informed him of a fair object of enterprise. "At no great distance from this, between Tripoli and Harran there is a convent called Daiz Abil Kodos, or the monastery of the Holy Father, from being inhabited by a Christian hermit, so eminent for wisdom, piety and mortification of the flesh, that he is looked up to as a saint; so that young and old, rich and poor, resort from all parts to seek his advice and blessing, and not a marriage takes place among the nobles of the country, but the bride and bridegroom repair to receive from him the nuptial benediction. At Easter there is an annual fair held at Abyla in front of the convent, to which are brought the richest manufactures of the surrounding country; silken stuffs, jewels of gold and silver, and other precious productions of art; and as the fair is a peaceful congregation of people, unarmed and unguarded, it will afford ample booty at little risk or trouble."

Abu Obeidah announced the intelligence to his troops. "Who," said he, "will undertake this enterprise?" His eye glanced involuntarily upon Khaled; it was just such a foray as he was wont to delight in; but Khaled remained silent. Abu Obeidah could not ask a service from one

so lately in chief command; and while he hesitated, Abdallah Ibn Jaafar, step-son to Abu Beker, came forward. A banner was given him,
and five hundred veteran horsemen, scarred in many a battle, sallied
with him from the gates of Damascus, guided by the traitor Christian.
They halted to rest before arriving at Abyla, and sent forward the
Christian as a scout. As he approached the place he was astonished to
see it crowded with an immense concourse of Greeks, Armenians,
Copts and Jews, in their various garbs; beside these there was a grand
procession of nobles and courtiers in rich attire, and priests in religious
dresses, with a guard of five thousand horse; all, as he learned, escorting the daughter of the prefect of Tripoli, who was lately married, and
had come with her husband to receive the blessing of the venerable
hermit. The Christian scout hastened back to the Moslems, and warned
them to retreat.

"I dare not," said Abdallah, promptly; "I fear the wrath of Allah,
should I turn my back. I will fight these infidels. Those who help me,
God will reward; those whose hearts fail them, are welcome to retire."
Not a Moslem turned his back. "Forward!" said Abdallah to the Christian, "and thou shalt behold what the companions of the prophet can
perform." The traitor hesitated, however, and was with difficulty persuaded to guide them on a service of such peril.

Abdallah led his band near to Abyla, where they lay close until
morning. At the dawn of day, having performed the customary prayer,
he divided his host into five squadrons of a hundred each; they were to
charge at once in five different places, with the shout of Allah Achbar!
and to slay or capture without stopping to pillage until the victory
should be complete. He then reconnoitred the place. The hermit was
preaching in front of his convent to a multitude of auditors; the fair
teemed with people in the variegated garbs of the Orient. One house
was guarded by a great number of horsemen, and numbers of persons,
richly clad, were going in and out, or standing about it. In this house
evidently was the youthful bride.

Abdallah encouraged his followers to despise the number of these
foes. "Remember," cried he, "the words of the prophet. 'Paradise is
under the shadow of swords!' If we conquer, we shall have glorious
booty; if we fall, paradise awaits us!"

The five squadrons charged as they had been ordered, with the
well-known war-cry. The Christians were struck with dismay, thinking
the whole Moslem army upon them. There was a direful confusion; the

multitude flying in all directions; women and children shrieking and crying; booths and tents overturned, and precious merchandise scattered about the streets. The troops, however, seeing the inferior number of the assailants, plucked up spirits and charged upon them. The merchants and inhabitants recovered from their panic and flew to arms, and the Moslem band, hemmed in among such a host of foes, seemed, say the Arabian writers, like a white spot on the hide of a black camel. A Moslem trooper, seeing the peril of his companions, broke his way out of the throng, and, throwing the reins on the neck of his steed, scoured back to Damascus for succor.

In this moment of emergency Abu Obeidah forgot all scruples of delicacy, and turned to the man he had superseded in office. "Fail us not," cried he, "in this moment of peril; but, for God's sake, hasten to deliver thy brethren from destruction."

"Had Omar given the command of the army to a child," replied the gracious Khaled, "I should have obeyed him; how much more thee, my predecessor in the faith of Islam!"

He now arrayed himself in a coat of mail, the spoil of the false prophet Moseïlma; he put on a helmet of proof, and over it a skull-cap, which he called the blessed cap, and attributed to it wonderful virtues, having received the prophet's benediction. Then springing on his horse, and putting himself at the head of a chosen band, he scoured off towards Abyla, with the bold Derar at his side.

In the meantime the troops, under Abdallah, had maintained throughout the day a desperate conflict; heaps of the slain testified their prowess; but their ranks were sadly thinned, scarce one of the survivors but had received repeated wounds, and they were ready to sink under heat, fatigue, and thirst. Towards sunset a cloud of dust is seen: is it a reinforcement of their enemies? A troop of horsemen emerge. They bear the black eagle of Khaled. The air resounds with the shout of Allah Achbar. The Christians are assailed on either side; some fly and are pursued to the river by the unsparing sword of Khaled; others rally round the monastery. Derar engages hand to hand with the prefect of Tripoli; they grapple; they struggle; they fall to the earth; Derar is uppermost, and, drawing a poniard, plunges it into the heart of his adversary. He springs upon his feet; vaults into the saddle of the prefect's horse, and, with the shout of Allah Achbar, gallops in quest of new opponents.

The battle is over. The fair is given up to plunder. Horses, mules, and asses are laden with silken stuffs, rich embroidery, jewels of gold and silver, precious stones, spices, perfumes, and other wealthy plunder of the merchants; but the most precious part of the spoil is the beautiful bride, with forty damsels, who formed her bridal train.

The monastery was left desolate, with none but the holy anchorite to inhabit it. Khaled called upon the old man, but received no answer; he called again, but the only reply was, to invoke the vengeance of heaven upon his head for the Christian blood he had spilt. The fierce Saracen paused as he was driving off the spoil, and laying his hand upon the hilt of his scimetar, looked back grimly upon the hermit. "What we have done," said he, "is in obedience to the law of God, who commands us to slay all unbelievers; and had not the apostle of God commanded us to let such men as thee alone, thou shouldst have shared the fate of thy fellow-infidels!"

The old man saw his danger in time, and discreetly held his peace, and the sword of Islam remained within its scabbard.

The conquerors bore their booty and their captives back in triumph to Damascus. One-fifth of the spoil was set apart for the public treasury: the rest was distributed among the soldiery. Derar, as a trophy of his exploit, received the horse of the prefect of Tripoli, but he made it a present to his Amazonian sister Caulah. The saddle and trappings were studded with precious stones; these she picked out and distributed among her female companions.

Among the spoils was a cloth curiously wrought with a likeness of the blessed Saviour; which, from the exquisite workmanship or the sanctity of the portrait, was afterwards sold in Arabia Felix for ten times its weight in gold.

Abdallah, for his part of the spoil, asked for the daughter of the prefect, having been smitten with her charms. His demand was referred to the Caliph Omar and granted, and the captive beauty lived with him many years. Obeidah, in his letters to the Caliph, generously set forth the magnanimous conduct and distinguished prowess of Khaled on this occasion; and entreated Omar to write a letter to that general expressive of his sense of his recent services; as it might soothe the mortification he must experience from his late deposition. The Caliph, however, though he replied to every other part of the letter of Obeidah, took no notice, either by word or deed, of that relating to Khaled, from which it was evident that, in secret, he entertained no great regard for the unsparing sword of Islam.

CHAPTER XIII

Moderate measures of Abu Obeidah – Reproved by the Caliph for his slowness

The alertness and hardihood of the Saracens in their rapid campaigns, have been attributed to their simple and abstemious habits. They knew nothing of the luxuries of the pampered Greeks, and were prohibited the use of wine. Their drink was water, their food principally milk, rice, and the fruits of the earth, and their dress the coarse raiments of the desert. An army of such men was easily sustained; marched rapidly from place to place; and was fitted to cope with the vicissitudes of war. The interval of repose, however, in the luxurious city of Damascus, and the general abundance of the fertile regions of Syria began to have their effect upon the Moslem troops, and the good Abu Obeidah was especially scandalized at discovering that they were lapsing into the use of wine, so strongly forbidden by the prophet. He mentioned the prevalence of this grievous sin in his letter to the Caliph, who read it in the mosque in presence of his officers. "By Allah," exclaimed the abstemious Omar; "these fellows are only fit for poverty and hard fare; what is to be done with these wine-bibbers?"

"Let him who drinks wine," replied Ali, promptly, "receive twenty bastinadoes on the soles of his feet."

"Good, it shall be so," rejoined the Caliph: and he wrote to that effect to the commander-in-chief. On receiving the letter, Abu Obeidah forthwith summoned the offenders, and had the punishment publicly inflicted for the edification of his troops; he took the occasion to descant on the enormity of the offence, and to exhort such as had sinned in private to come forward like good Moslems, make public confession, and submit to the bastinado in token of repentance; whereupon many, who had indulged in secret potations, moved by his paternal exhortation, avowed their crime and their repentance, and were set at ease in their consciences by a sound bastinadoing and the forgiveness of the good Abu Obeidah.

That worthy commander now left a garrison of five hundred horse at Damascus, and issued forth with his host to prosecute the subjugation of Syria. He had a rich field of enterprise before him. The country of Syria, from the amenity of its climate, tempered by the vicinity of the sea and the mountains, from the fertility of its soil, and the happy distribution of woods and streams, was peculiarly adapted for the vigorous support and prolific increase of animal life; it accordingly teemed with population, and was studded with ancient and embattled cities and fortresses. Two of the proudest and most splendid of these were Emessa (the modern Hems), the capital of the plains; and Baalbec, the famous city of the Sun, situated between the mountains of Lebanon.

These two cities, with others intermediate, were the objects of Abu Obeidah's enterprise, and he sent Khaled in advance, with Derar and Rafi Ibn Omeirah, at the head of a third of the army, to scour the country about Emessa. In his own slower march, with the main body of the army, he approached the city of Jusheyah, but was met by the governor, who purchased a year's truce with the payment of four hundred pieces of gold and fifty silken robes; and the promise to surrender the city at the expiration of a year, if in that interval Baalbec and Emessa should have been taken.

When Abu Obeidah came before Emessa he found Khaled in active operation. The governor of the place had died on the day on which the Moslem force appeared, and the city was not fully provisioned for a siege. The inhabitants negotiated a truce for one year by the payment of ten thousand pieces of gold and two hundred suits of silk, with the engagement to surrender at the end of that term, provided he should have taken Aleppo, Alhâdir, and Kennesrin, and defeated the army of the emperor. Khaled would have persevered in the siege, but Abu Obeidah thought it the wisest policy to agree to these golden terms, by which he provided himself with the sinews of war, and was enabled to proceed more surely in his career.

The moment the treaty was concluded, the people of Emessa threw open their gates; held a market or fair beneath the walls, and began to drive a lucrative trade; for the Moslem camp was full of booty, and these marauding warriors, flushed with sudden wealth, squandered plunder of all kinds, and never regarded the price of any thing that struck their fancy. In the meantime predatory bands foraged the country both far and near, and came driving in sheep and cattle, and horses and camels, laden with household booty of all kinds; besides multitudes of captives. The piteous lamentations of these people, torn from their peaceful homes and doomed to slavery, touched the heart of Abu Obeidah. He told them that all who would embrace the Islam faith should have their lives and property. On such as chose to remain in infidelity, he imposed a ransom of five pieces of gold a head, besides an annual tribute; caused their names and places of abode to be registered in a book, and then gave them back their property, their wives, and children, on condition that they should act as guides and interpreters to the Moslems in case of need.

The merciful policy of the good Abu Obeidah promised to promote the success of Islam, even more potently than the sword. The Syrian Greeks came in, in great numbers, to have their names enregistered in the book of tributaries; and other cities capitulated for a year's truce on the terms granted to Emessa. Khaled, however, who was no friend to truces and negotiations, murmured at these peaceful measures, and offered to take these cities in less time than it required to treat with them; but Abu Obeidah was not to be swerved from the path of moderation; thus, in a little time the whole territories of Emessa, Alhâdir and Kennesrin were rendered sacred from maraud. The predatory warriors of the desert were somewhat impatient at being thus hemmed in by prohibited boundaries, and on one occasion had well nigh brought the truce to an abrupt termination. A party of Saracen troopers, in prowling along the confines of Kennesrin, came to where the Christians, to mark their boundary, had erected a statue of the emperor Heraclius, seated on his throne. The troopers, who had a Moslem hatred of images, regarded this with derision, and amused themselves with careering round and tilting at it, until one of them, either accidentally or in sport, struck out one of the eyes with his lance.

The Greeks were indignant at this outrage. Messengers were sent to Abu Obeidah, loudly complaining of it as an intentional breach of the truce, and a flagrant insult to the emperor. Abu Obeidah mildly assured them that it was his disposition most rigorously to observe the truce; that the injury to the statue must have been accidental, and that no indignity to the emperor could have been intended. His moderation only increased the arrogance of the ambassadors; their emperor had been insulted; it was for the Caliph to give redress according to the measure of the law: "an eye for an eye, a tooth for a tooth." "What!" cried some of the over-zealous Moslems; "do the infidels mean to claim an eye from the Caliph?" In their rage they would have slain the messengers on the spot; but the quiet Abu Obeidah stayed their wrath. "They speak but figuratively," said he; then taking the messengers aside, he shrewdly compromised the matter, and satisfied their wounded loyalty, by agreeing that they should set up a statue of the Caliph, with glass eyes, and strike out one of them in retaliation.

While Abu Obeidah was pursuing this moderate course, and subduing the country by clemency rather than by force of arms, missives came from the Caliph, who was astonished at receiving no tidings of further conquests, reproaching him with his slowness, and with preferring worldly gain to the pious exercise of the sword. The soldiers when they heard of the purport of this letter, took the reproaches to themselves, and wept with vexation. Abu Obeidah himself was stung to the quick, and repented him of the judicious truces he had made. In the excitement of the moment, he held a council of war, and it was determined to lose not a day, although the truces had but about a month to run. He accordingly left Khaled with a strong force in the vicinity of Emessa to await the expiration of the truce, while he marched with the main host, against the city of Baalbec.

CHAPTER XIV

Siege and capture of Baalbec

Baalbec, so called from Baal, the Syrian appellation of the Sun, or Apollo, to which deity it was dedicated, was one of the proudest cities of ancient Syria. It was the metropolis of the great and fertile valley of Bekaa, lying between the mountains of Lebanon, and Anti Lebanon. During the Grecian domination it was called Heliopolis, which likewise means the City of the Sun. It was famous for its magnificent temple of Baal, which, tradition affirms, was built by Solomon the Wise, to please one of his wives, a native of Sidon and a worshipper of the Sun. The immense blocks of stone of which it was constructed, were said to have been brought by the genii, over whom Solomon had control by virtue of his talismanic seal. Some of them remain to this day objects of admiration to the traveller, and perplexity to the modern engineer.*

On his march against Baalbec, Abu Obeidah intercepted a caravan of four hundred camels laden with silks and sugars, on the way to that city. With his usual clemency he allowed the captives to ransom themselves; some of whom carried to Baalbec the news of his approach, and of the capture of the caravan. Herbis, the governor, supposing the Saracens to be a mere marauding party, sallied forth with six thousand horse and a multitude of irregular foot, in hope to recover the spoils, but found to his cost that he had an army to contend with, and was driven back to the city with great loss, after receiving seven wounds.

Abu Obeidah set himself down before the city, and addressed a letter to the inhabitants, reminding them of the invincible arms of the faithful, and inviting them to profess Islamism, or pay tribute. This letter he gave in charge to a Syrian peasant, and with it a reward of twenty pieces of silver, "for Allah forbid," said the conscientious general, "that I should employ thee without pay. The laborer is worthy of his hire."

The messenger was drawn up by a cord to the battlements, and delivered the letter to the inhabitants, many of whom, on hearing the contents, were inclined to surrender. Herbis, the governor, however, who was still smarting with his wounds, tore the letter in pieces, and dismissed the messenger without deigning a reply.

---

* Among these huge blocks some measure fifty-eight, and one sixty-nine feet in length.

Abu Obeidah now ordered his troops to the assault, but the garrison made brave defence, and did such execution with their engines from the walls, that the Saracens were repulsed with considerable loss. The weather was cold; so Abu Obeidah, who was ever mindful of the welfare of his men, sent a trumpeter round the camp next morning, forbidding any man to take the field until he had made a comfortable meal. All were now busy cooking, when, in the midst of their preparations, the city gates were thrown open, and the Greeks came scouring upon them, making great slaughter. They were repulsed with some difficulty, but carried off prisoners and plunder.

Abu Obeidah now removed his camp out of reach of the engines, and where his cavalry would have more room. He threw out detachments also, to distract the attention of the enemy and oblige them to fight in several places. Saad Ibn Zeid, with five hundred horse and three hundred foot, was to show himself in the valley opposite the gate looking towards the mountains; while Derar, with three hundred horse and two hundred foot, was stationed in front of the gate on the side toward Damascus.

Herbis, the governor, seeing the Saracens move back their tents, supposed them to be intimidated by their late loss. "These Arabs," said he, "are half-naked vagabonds of the desert, who fight without object; we are locked up in steel, and fight for our wives and children, our property and our lives." He accordingly roused his troops to make another sally, and an obstinate battle ensued. One of the Moslem officers, Sohail Ibn Sabah, being disabled by a sabre cut in the right arm, alighted from his horse, and clambered a neighboring hill which overlooked the field, the city and its vicinity. Here he sat watching the various fortunes of the field. The sally had been made through the gate before which Abu Obeidah was posted, who of course received the whole brunt of the attack. The battle was hot, and Sohail perceived from his hill that the Moslems in this quarter were hard pressed, and that the general was giving ground, and in imminent danger of being routed; while Derar and Saad remained inactive at their distant posts; no sally having been made from the gates before which they were stationed. Upon this Sohail gathered together some green branches, and set fire to them, so as to make a column of smoke; a customary signal by day among the Arabs, as fire was by night. Derar and Saad beheld the smoke and galloped with their troops in that direction. Their arrival changed the whole fortune of the field. Herbis, who had thought himself on the eve of victory, now found himself beset on each side and cut off from the city! Nothing but strict discipline and the impenetrable Grecian phalanx saved him. His men closed shield to shield, their lances in advance, and made a slow and defensive retreat, the Moslems wheeling around and charging incessantly upon them. Abu Obeidah, who knew nothing of the arrival of Derar and Saad, imagined the retreat of the Christians a mere feint, and called back his troops; Saad, however, who heard not the general's order, kept on in pursuit, until he drove the enemy to the top of a hill, where they ensconced themselves in an old deserted monastery.

When Abu Obeidah learnt the secret of this most timely aid, and that it was in consequence of a supposed signal from him, he acknowledged that the smoke was an apt thought, and saved his camp from being sacked; but he prohibited any man from repeating such an act without orders from the general.

In the meantime Herbis, the governor, finding the small number that invested the convent, sallied forth with his troops, in hopes of cutting his way to the city. Never did men fight more valiantly, and they had already made great havoc, when the arrival of a fresh swarm of Moslems drove them back to their forlorn fortress, where they were so closely watched, that not a Grecian eye could peer from the old walls without being the aim of a Moslem arrow.

Abu Obeidah now invested the city more closely than ever, leaving Saad, with his forces, to keep the governor encaged in the monastery. The latter perceived it would be impossible to hold out longer in this shattered edifice, destitute of provisions. His proud spirit was completely broken, and, throwing off his silken robes, and clothing him in a worn woollen garb, as suited to his humble situation, he sought a conference with Saad to treat on terms of capitulation. The Moslem captain replied, that he could only treat for the party in the convent, whom he would receive as brothers, if they would acknowledge God and the prophet, or would let them free on the pledge not to bear arms against the Moslems. He proffered to lead Herbis to the general, if he wished to treat for the city also; and added, that, should the negotiation fail, he and his Greeks might return into their convent, and let God and the sword decide.

Herbis was accordingly led through the besieging camp into the presence of Abu Obeidah, and gnawed his lip when he saw the inconsiderable number of the Moslem host. He offered, as a ransom for the city, one thousand ounces of gold, two thousand of silver, and one thousand silken robes; but Abu Obeidah demanded that he should double the amount, and add thereto one thousand sabres, and all the arms of the soldiers in the monastery; as well as engage in behalf of the city to pay an annual tribute; to engage to erect no more Christian churches, nor ever more act in hostility against the Moslem power.

These harsh terms being conceded, Herbis was permitted to enter the city alone, and submit them to the inhabitants, all his attendants being detained as hostages. The townsmen at first refused to capitulate, saying their city was the strongest in all Syria; but Herbis offered to pay down one-fourth of the ransom himself, and they at length complied. One point was conceded to the people of Baalbec to soothe their wounded pride. It was agreed that Rafi Ibn Abdallah, who was to remain with five hundred men, acting as lieutenant of Baalbec for Abu Obeidah, should encamp without the walls, and not enter the city. These matters being arranged, Abu Obeidah marched with his host on other enterprises.

The Saracen troops, under Rafi Ibn Abdallah, soon ingratiated themselves with the people of Baalbec. They pillaged the surrounding country, and sold their booty for low prices to the townsfolk, who thus grew wealthy on the spoils of their own countrymen. Herbis, the governor, felt a desire to participate in these profits. He reminded his fellow-citizens how much he had paid for their ransom, and what good terms he had effected for them; and then proposed that he should have one-tenth of what they gained in traffic with the Moslems, to reimburse him. They consented, though with extreme reluctance. In a few days he found the gain so sweet that he thirsted for more; he therefore told them that his reimbursement would be tedious at this rate, and proposed to receive one-fourth. The people, enraged at his cupidity, rushed on him with furious outcries, and killed him on the spot. The noise of the tumult reached the camp of Rafi Ibn Abdallah, and a deputation of the inhabitants coming forth, entreated him to enter the city and govern it himself. He scrupled to depart from the terms of the treaty until he had written to Abu Obeidah; but on receiving permission from the general, he entered and took command. Thus did the famous Baalbec, the ancient Heliopolis, or City of the Sun, fall under the Saracen sway on the 20th of January, A.D. 636, being the fifteenth year of the Hegira.

The year's truce with the city of Emessa having now expired, Abu Obeidah appeared before that place, and summoned it in the following form:

"In the name of the most merciful God. Abu Obeidah Ibn Aljerah, general of the armies of the Commander of the Faithful, Omar al Khattâb, to the people of Emessa. Let not the loftiness of your walls, the strength of your bulwarks, nor the robustness of your bodies, lead you into error. Allah hath conquered stronger places through the means of his servants. Your city would be of no more consideration against us than a kettle of pottage set in the midst of our camp.

"I invite you to embrace our holy faith, and the law revealed to our prophet Mahomet; and we will send pious men to instruct you, and you shall participate in all our fortunes.

"If you refuse, you shall still be left in possession of all your property on the payment of annual tribute. If you reject both conditions, come forth from behind your stone walls, and let Allah, the supreme judge, decide between us."

This summons was treated with scorn; and the garrison made a bold sally, and handled their besiegers so roughly, that they were glad when night put an end to the conflict. In the evening a crafty old Arab sought the tent of Abu Obeidah; he represented the strength of the place, the intrepidity of the soldiers, and the ample stock of provisions, which would enable it to stand a weary siege. He suggested a stratagem, however, by which it might be reduced: and Abu Obeidah adopted his counsel. Sending a messenger into the city, he offered to the inhabitants to strike his tents, and lead his troops to the attack of other places, provided they would furnish him provisions for five days' march. His offer was promptly accepted, and the provisions were furnished. Abu Obeidah now pretended that, as his march would be long, a greater supply would be necessary: he continued to buy, therefore, as long as the Christians had provisions to sell, and in this manner exhausted their magazines; and as the scouts from other cities beheld the people of Emessa throw open their gates and bring forth provisions, it became rumored throughout the country that the city had surrendered.

Abu Obeidah, according to promise, led his host against other places.

The first was Arrestan, a fortified city, well watered, provisioned, and garrisoned. His summons being repeated, and rejected, he requested the governor of the place to let him leave there twenty chests of cumbrous articles, which impeded him in his movements. The request was granted with great pleasure at getting clear so readily of such marauders. The twenty chests, secured with padlocks, were taken into the citadel, but every chest had a sliding bottom, and contained an armed man. Among the picked warriors thus concealed, were Derar, Abda'lrahman, and Abdallah Ibn Jaafar; while Khaled, with a number of troops, was placed in ambush to co-operate with those in the chests.

The Moslem host departed. The Christians went to church to return thanks for their deliverance, and the sounds of their hymns of triumph reached the ears of Derar and his comrades. Upon this they issued forth from their chests, seized the wife of the governor, and obtained from her the keys of the gates. Abdallah, with fourteen men, hastened to the church and closed the doors upon the congregation; while Derar, with four companions, threw open the gates with the cry of Allah Achbar; upon which Khaled and his forces rushed from their ambuscade, and the city was taken almost without bloodshed.

The city of Shaizar was next assailed, and capitulated on favorable terms; and now Abu Obeidah returned before Emessa, and once more summoned it to surrender. The governor remonstrated loudly, reminding the Moslem general of his treaty, by which he engaged to depart from Emessa, and carry the war against other places. "I engaged to depart," replied Abu Obeidah, "but I did not engage not to return. I have carried the war against other places, and have subdued Arrestan and Shaizar."

The people of Emessa now perceived how they had been circumvented. Their magazines had been drained of provisions, and they had not wherewithal to maintain them against a siege. The governor, however, encouraged them to try the chance of a battle as before. They prepared for the fight by prayers in the churches; and the governor took the sacrament in the church of St. George: but he sought to enhearten himself by grosser means, for we are told he ate the whole of a roasted kid for his supper, and caroused on wine until the crowing of the cock. In the morning, early, he arrayed himself in rich apparel, and sallied forth at the head of five thousand horsemen, all men of strength and courage, and well armed. They charged the besiegers so bravely, and their archers so galled them from the walls, that the Moslem force gave way.

Khaled now threw himself in front of the battle, and enacted wondrous feats to rally his soldiers and restore the fight. In an encounter, hand to hand, with a Greek horseman, his scimetar broke, and he was weaponless, but closing with his adversary, he clasped him in his arms, crushed his ribs, and drawing him from his saddle, threw him dead to the earth. The imminent peril of the fight roused a frantic valor in the Moslems. In the heat of enthusiasm Ikremah, a youthful cousin of Khaled, galloped about the field, fighting with reckless fury, and raving about the joys of paradise promised to all true believers who fell in the battles of the faith. "I see," cried he, "the black-eyed Houris of Paradise. One of them, if seen on earth, would make mankind die of love. They are smiling on us. One of them waves a handkerchief of green silk, and holds a cup of precious stones. She beckons me; come hither quickly, she cries, my well-beloved!" In this way he went, shouting Al Jennah! Al Jennah! Paradise! Paradise! charging into the thickest of the Christians, and making fearful havoc, until he reached the place where the governor was fighting, who sent a javelin through his heart, and dispatched him in quest of his vaunted Elysium.

Night alone parted the hosts, and the Moslems retired exhausted to their tents, glad to repose from so rude a fight. Even Khaled counselled Abu Obeidah, to have recourse to stratagem, and make a pretended flight the next morning; to draw the Greeks, confident through this day's success, into disorder; for while collected, their phalanx presented an impenetrable wall to the Moslem horsemen.

Accordingly, at the dawning of the day, the Moslems retreated; at first with a show of order; then with a feigned confusion, for it was an Arab stratagem of war to scatter and rally again in the twinkling of an eye. The Christians, thinking their flight unfeigned, broke up their steady phalanx, some making headlong pursuit, while others dispersed to plunder the Moslem camp.

Suddenly the Moslems faced about, surrounded the confused mass of Christians, and fell upon it, as the Arabian historian says, "like eagles upon a carcass." Khaled and Derar and other chiefs spirited them on with shouts of Allah Achbar, and a terrible rout and slaughter ensued. The number of Christian corpses on that field exceeded sixteen hundred. The governor was recognized among the slain by his enormous bulk, his bloated face, and his costly apparel, fragrant with perfumes.

The city of Emessa surrendered as a sequel to that fight, but the Moslems could neither stay to take possession, nor afford to leave a garrison. Tidings had reached them of the approach of an immense army, composed of the heavily armed Grecian soldiery and the light troops of the desert, that threatened completely to overwhelm them. Various and contradictory were the counsels in this moment of agitation and alarm. Some advised that they should hasten back to their native deserts, where they would be reinforced by their friends, and where the hostile army could not find sustenance; but Abu Obeidah objected that such a retreat would be attributed to cowardice. Others cast a wistful eye upon the stately dwellings, the delightful gardens, the fertile fields, and green pastures, which they had just won by the sword, and chose rather to stay and fight for this land of pleasure and abundance, than return to famine and the desert. Khaled decided the question. It would not do to linger there, he said; Constantine, the emperor's son, being not far off, at Cæsarea, with forty thousand men; he advised, therefore, that they should march to Yermouk, on the borders of Palestine and Arabia, where they would be within reach of assistance from the Caliph, and might await, with confidence, the attack of the Imperial army. The advice of Khaled was adopted.

CHAPTER XVI

Advance of a powerful Imperial army – Skirmishes of Khaled –
Capture of Derar – Interview of Khaled and Manuel

The rapid conquests of the Saracens, had alarmed the emperor Heraclius for the safety of his rich province of Syria. Troops had been levied both in Europe and Asia, and transported by sea and land to various parts of the invaded country. The main body, consisting of eighty thousand men, advanced to seek the Moslem host, under the command of a distinguished general, called Mahan, by the Arabian writers, and Manuel by the Greeks. On its way, the Imperial army was joined by Jabalah Ibn al Aynham, chief or king of the Christian tribe of Gassan. This Jabalah had professed the Mahometan faith, but had apostatized in consequence of the following circumstance. He had accompanied the Caliph Omar on a pilgrimage to Mecca, and was performing the religious ceremony of the Towaf, or sacred walk seven times round the Caaba, when an Arab of the tribe of Fezarah accidentally trod on the skirt of his Ihram or pilgrim scarf, so as to draw it from his shoulders. Turning fiercely upon the Arab, "Woe be unto thee," cried he, "for uncovering my back in the sacred house of God." The pilgrim protested it was an accident, but Jabalah buffeted him in the face, bruising him sorely, and beating out four of his teeth. The pilgrim complained to Omar, but Jabalah justified himself, stating the indignity he had suffered. "Had it not been for my reverence for the Caaba, and for the prohibition to shed blood within the sacred city, I would have slain the offender on the spot." "Thou hast confessed thy fault," said Omar, "and unless forgiven by thy adversary, must submit to the law of retaliation, 'an eye for an eye, and a tooth for a tooth.'" "I am a king," replied Jabalah, proudly, "and he is but a peasant." "Ye are both Moslems," rejoined Omar, "and in the sight of Allah, who is no respecter of persons, ye are equal." The utmost that Jabalah could obtain from the rigid justice of Omar was, that the execution of the sentence might be postponed until the next day. In the night he made his escape and fled to Constantinople, where he abjured Islamism, resumed the Christian faith, and went over to the service of the emperor Heraclius. He had now brought sixty thousand Arabs to the aid of Manuel. Such was the powerful host, the approach of which had compelled the Moslems to abandon Emessa on the very moment of surrender. They had marched to Yermouk, a place noted for its pleasant groves, and the sweet salubrity of its air, and lay encamped on the banks of a little stream of the same name, heretofore obscure, but now destined to become famous by a battle decisive of the fate of Syria.

Manuel advanced slowly and deliberately with his heavily armed Grecian soldiery; but he sent Jabalah in the advance, to scour the country with his light Arab troops, as best fitted to cope with the skirmishing warriors of the desert; thus, as he said, "using diamond to cut diamond." The course of these combined armies was marked with waste, rapine, and outrage, and they inflicted all kinds of injuries and indignities on those Christian places which had made treaties with or surrendered to the Moslems.

While Manuel with his main army was yet at a distance, he sent proposals of peace to Abu Obeidah, according to the commands of the emperor. His proposals were rejected; but Obeidah sent several messengers to Jabalah, reproaching him with his apostasy, and his warfare against his countrymen, and endeavoring to persuade him to remain neutral in the impending battle. Jabalah replied, however, that his faith was committed to the emperor, and he was resolved to fight in his cause.

Upon this Khaled came forward, and offered to take this apostate in his own hands: "He is far in the advance of the main army," said he, "let me have a small body of picked men chosen by myself, and I will fall upon him and his infidel Arabs before Manuel can come up to their assistance."

His proposal was condemned by many as rash and extravagant. "By no means," cried Khaled, with zealous zeal; "this infidel force is the army of the devil, and can do nothing against the army of Allah, who will assist us with his angels."

So pious an argument was unanswerable. Khaled was permitted to choose his men, all well-seasoned warriors whose valor he had proved. With them he fell upon Jabalah, who was totally unprepared for so hair-brained an assault, threw his host into complete confusion, and obliged him, after much slaughter, to retreat upon the main body. The triumph of Khaled, however, was damped by the loss of several valiant officers, among whom were Yezed, Rafi, and Derar, who were borne off captives by the retreating Christians.

In the meantime a special messenger, named Abdallah Ibn Kort, arrived at Medina, bringing letters to the Caliph from Abu Obeidah, describing the perilous situation of the Moslem army, and entreating reinforcements. The Caliph ascended the pulpit of Mahomet, and preached up the glory of fighting the good fight of faith for God and the prophet. He then gave Abdallah an epistle for Abu Obeidah, filled with edifying texts from the Koran, and ending with an assurance that he would pray for him, and would, moreover, send him a speedy reinforcement. This done, he pronounced a blessing on Abdallah, and bade him depart with all speed.

Abdallah was well advanced on his return, when he called to mind that he had omitted to visit the tomb of the prophet. Shocked at his forgetfulness, he retraced his steps, and sought the dwelling of Ayesha, within which the prophet lay interred. He found the beautiful widow reclining beside the tomb, and listening to Ali and Abbas, who were reading the Koran, while Hassan and Hosein, the two sons of Ali and grandsons of the prophet, were sitting on their knees.

Having paid due honors to the prophet's tomb, the considerate messenger expressed his fears that this pious visit might prevent his reaching the army before the expected battle; whereupon the holy party lifted up their hands to heaven, and Ali put up a prayer for his speedy journey. Thus inspirited, he set out anew, and travelled with such unusual and incredible speed, that the army looked upon it as miraculous, and attributed it to the blessing of Omar and the prayer of Ali.

The promised reinforcement was soon on foot. It consisted of eight thousand men under the command of Seid Ibn Amir; to whom the Caliph gave a red silk banner, and a word of advice at parting; cautioning him to govern himself as well as his soldiers, and not to let his appetites get the better of his self-command.

Seid, with Moslem frankness, counselled him, in return, to fear God and not man; to love all Moslems equally with his own kindred; to cherish those at a distance equally with those at hand; finally to command nothing but what was right and to forbid nothing but what was wrong. The Caliph listened attentively, his forehead resting on his staff and his eyes cast upon the ground. When Seid had finished, he raised his head and the tears ran down his cheek. "Alas!" said he, "who can do all this without the aid of God!"

Seid Ibn Amir led his force by the shortest route across the deserts, and hurrying forward with more rapidity than heed, lost his way. While he halted one night, in the vicinity of some springs, to ascertain his route, he was apprised by his scouts, that the prefect of Ammon, with five thousand men, was near at hand. He fell upon him instantly, and cut the infantry to pieces. The prefect fled with his cavalry, but encountered a foraging party from the Moslem camp, the leader of which, Zobeir, thrust a lance through his body, and between the two parties not a man of his troop escaped. The Moslems then placed the heads of the Christians on their lances, and arrived with their ghastly trophies at the camp; to the great encouragement of Abu Obeidah and his host.

The imperial army had now drawn near, and Manuel, the general, attempted again to enter into negotiations. Khaled offered to go and confer with him; but his real object was to attempt the release of his friends and brethren in arms, Abu Sofian, Derar, Rafi, and the two other officers captured in the late skirmish with the apostate Jabalah.

When Khaled reached the outpost of the Christian army, he was required to leave his escort of one hundred chosen warriors, and proceed alone to the presence of the general; but he refused. He equally refused a demand that he and his men should dismount and deliver up their scimetars. After some parley, he was permitted to enter into the presence of the general in his own way.

Manuel was seated in state on a kind of throne, surrounded by his officers, all splendidly arrayed, while Khaled entered with his hundred war-worn veterans, clad in the simplest guise. Chairs were set out for him and his principal companions, but they pushed them aside and seated themselves cross-legged on the ground, after the Arabic manner. When Manuel demanded the reason, Khaled replied by quoting a verse from the twentieth chapter of the Koran. "Of earth ye are created, from earth ye came, and unto earth ye must return." "God made the earth," added he, "and what God has made for man to sit upon, is more precious than your silken tapestries."

The conference was begun by Manuel, who expostulated on the injustice of the Moslems in making an unprovoked inroad into the territories of their neighbors, molesting them in their religious worship, robbing them of their wives and property, and seizing on their persons as slaves. Khaled retorted, that it was all owing to their own obstinacy, in refusing to acknowledge that there was but one God, without relation or associate, and that Mahomet was his prophet. Their discussion grew violent, and Khaled, in his heat, told Manuel that he should one day see him dragged into the presence of Omar with a halter round his neck, there to have his head struck off as an example to all infidels and for the edification of true believers.

Manuel replied in wrath, that Khaled was protected by his character of ambassador; but that he would punish his insolence by causing the five Moslem captives, his friends, to be instantly beheaded. Khaled defied him to execute his threat, swearing by Allah, by his prophet, and by the holy Caaba, that if a hair of their heads were injured, he would slay Manuel with his own hand on the spot, and that each of his Moslems present, should slay his man. So saying, he rose and drew his scimetar, as did likewise his companions.

The imperial general was struck with admiration at his intrepidity. He replied calmly, that what he had said was a mere threat, which his humanity and his respect for the mission of Khaled would not permit him to fulfil. The Saracens were pacified and sheathed their swords, and the conference went on calmly.

In the end, Manuel gave up the five prisoners to Khaled as a token of his esteem; and in return Khaled presented him with a beautiful scarlet pavilion, which he had brought with him, and pitched in the Christian camp, and for which Manuel had expressed a desire. Thus ended this conference, and both parties retired from it with soldier-like regard for each other.

CHAPTER XVII

The Battle of Yermouk

The great battle was now at hand that was to determine the fate of Syria, for the emperor had staked the fortunes of this favorite province on a single, but gigantic blow. Abu Obeidah, conscious of the momentous nature of the conflict, and diffident of his abilities in the field, gave a proof of his modesty and magnanimity, by restoring to Khaled the command of the whole army. For himself, he took his station with the women in the rear, that he might rally the Moslems should any of them be inclined to fly the field. Here he erected his standard, a yellow flag, given him by Abu Beker, being the same which Mahomet had displayed in the battle of Khaïbar.

Before the action commenced Khaled rode among his troops, making a short but emphatic speech. "Paradise," cried he, "is before you; the devil and hell behind. Fight bravely, and you will secure the one; fly, and you will fall into the other."

The armies closed, but the numbers of the Christians and the superiority of Greek and Roman discipline bore down the right wing of the Moslems. Those, however, who turned their backs and attempted to fly, were assailed with reproaches and blows by the women, so that they found it easier to face the enemy than such a storm. Even Abu Sofian himself received a blow over the face with a tent pole from one of those viragos, as he retreated before the enemy.

Thrice were the Moslems beaten back by the steady bearing of the Grecian phalanx, and thrice were they checked and driven back to battle by the women. Night at length brought a cessation of the bloody conflict; when Abu Obeidah went round among the wounded, ministering to them with his own hands, while the women bound up their wounds with tender care.

The battle was renewed on the following morning, and again the Moslems were sorely pressed. The Christian archers made fearful havoc, and such was their dexterity, that, among the great number of Moslems who suffered from their arrows on that day, seven hundred lost one or both eyes. Hence it was commemorated as "the Day of the Blinding;" and those who had received such wounds gloried in them, in after years, as so many trophies of their having struggled for the faith in that day of hard fighting. There were several single combats of note; among others, Serjabil was engaged hand to hand with a stout

Christian; but Serjabil, having signalized his piety by excessive watching and fasting, was so reduced in flesh and strength, that he was no match for his adversary, and would infallibly have been overpowered, had not Derar come behind the Christian, and stabbed him to the heart. Both warriors claimed the spoil, but it was adjudged to him who slew the enemy. In the course of this arduous day, the Moslems more then once wavered, but were rallied back by the valor of the women. Caulah, the heroic sister of Derar, mingling in the fight, was wounded and struck down; but Offeïrah, her female friend, smote off the head of her opponent, and rescued her. The battle lasted as long as there was light enough to distinguish friend from foe; but the night was welcome to the Moslems, who needed all their enthusiasm and reliance on the promises of the prophet to sustain them, so hard was the struggle and so overwhelming the numbers of the enemy. On this night, the good Abu Obeidah repeated at once the prayers belonging to two separate hours, that his weary soldiers might enjoy uninterrupted sleep.

For several successive days this desperate battle, on which hung the fate of Syria, was renewed with various fortunes. In the end the fanatic valor of the Moslems prevailed; the Christian host was completely routed and fled in all directions. Many were overtaken and slain in the difficult passes of the mountains; others perished in a deep part of the river to which they were decoyed by one of their own people, in revenge for an injury. Manuel, the imperial general, fell by the hand of a Moslem named Noman Ibn Alkamah.

Abu Obeidah went over the battle-field in person, seeing that the wounded Moslems were well taken care of, and the slain decently interred. He was perplexed for a time on finding some heads without bodies, to know whether they were Moslems or infidels, but finally prayed over them at a venture and had them buried like the rest.

In dividing the spoils, Abu Obeidah, after setting aside one-fifth for the Caliph and the public treasury, allotted to each foot soldier one portion and to each horseman three; two for himself and one for his steed; but for each horse of the pure Arabian breed, he allowed a double portion. This last allotment met with opposition, but was subsequently confirmed by the Caliph, on account of the superior value of true Arabian horses.

Such was the great battle fought on the banks of the Yermouk, near the city of that name, in the month of November, A.D. 636, and in the 15th year of the Hegira.

CHAPTER XVIII

Siege and capture of Jerusalem

The Moslem invaders reposed for a month at Damascus from the toil of conquest, during which time Abu Obeidah sent to the Caliph to know whether he should undertake the siege of Cæsarea, or Jerusalem. Ali was with Omar at the time, and advised the instant siege of the latter; for such, he said, had been the intention of the prophet. The enterprise against Jerusalem was as a holy war to the Moslems, for they reverenced it as an ancient seat of prophecy and revelation, connected with the histories of Moses, Jesus, and Mahomet, and sanctified by containing the tombs of several of the ancient prophets. The Caliph adopted the advice of Ali, and ordered Abu Obeidah to lead his army into Palestine, and lay siege to Jerusalem.

On receiving these orders, Abu Obeidah sent forward Yezed Abu Sofian, with five thousand men, to commence the siege, and for five successive days detached after him considerable reinforcements. The people of Jerusalem saw the approach of these portentous invaders, who were spreading such consternation throughout the East, but they made no sally to oppose them, nor sent out any one to parley, but planted engines on their walls, and prepared for vigorous defence. Yezed approached the city and summoned it by sound of trumpet, propounding the customary terms, profession of the faith or tribute: both were rejected with disdain. The Moslems would have made instant assault, but Yezed had no such instructions: he encamped, therefore, and waited until orders arrived from Abu Obeidah to attack the city, when he made the necessary preparations.

At cock-crow in the morning the Moslem host was marshalled, the leaders repeated the matin prayer each at the head of his battalion, and all, as if by one consent, with a loud voice gave the verse from the Koran:* "Enter ye, oh people! into the holy land which Allah hath destined for you."

For ten days they made repeated but unavailing attacks; on the eleventh day Abu Obeidah brought the whole army to their aid. He immediately sent a written summons requiring the inhabitants to believe in the unity of God, the divine mission of Mahomet, the resurrec-

---

* These words are from the fifth chapter of the Koran, where Mahomet puts them into the mouth of Moses, as addressed to the children of Israel.

tion and final judgment: or else to acknowledge allegiance, and pay tribute to the Caliph: "otherwise," concluded the letter, "I will bring men against you, who love death better than you love wine or swine's flesh; nor will I leave you, God willing, until I have destroyed your fighting men, and made slaves of your children."

The summons was addressed to the magistrates and principal inhabitants of Ælia, for so Jerusalem was named after the emperor Ælius Adrian, when he rebuilt that city.

Sophronius, the Christian patriarch, or bishop of Jerusalem, replied that this was the holy city, and the holy land, and that whoever entered either, for a hostile purpose, was an offender in the eyes of God. He felt some confidence in setting the invaders at defiance, for the walls and towers of the city had been diligently strengthened, and the garrison had been reinforced by fugitives from Yermouk, and from various parts of Syria. The city, too, was strong in its situation, being surrounded by deep ravines and a broken country; and above all there was a pious incentive to courage and perseverance in defending the sepulchre of Christ.

Four wintry months elapsed; every day there were sharp skirmishings; the besiegers were assailed by sallying parties, annoyed by the engines on the walls, and harassed by the inclement weather; still they carried on the siege with undiminished spirit. At length the Patriarch Sophronius held a parley from the walls with Abu Obeidah. "Do you not know," said he, "that this city is holy; and that whoever offers violence to it, draws upon his head the vengeance of heaven?"

"We know it," replied Abu Obeidah, "to be the house of the prophets, where their bodies lie interred; we know it to be the place whence our prophet Mahomet made his nocturnal ascent to heaven; and we know that we are more worthy of possessing it than you are, nor will we raise the siege until Allah has delivered it into our hands, as he has done many other places."

Seeing there was no further hope, the patriarch consented to give up the city, on condition that the Caliph would come in person to take possession and sign the articles of surrender.

When this unusual stipulation was made known to the Caliph, he held a council with his friends. Othman despised the people of Jerusalem, and was for refusing their terms, but Ali represented the sanctity and importance of the place in the eyes of the Christians, which might prompt them to reinforce it, and to make a desperate defence if treated with indignity. Besides, he added, the presence of the Caliph would cheer and inspirit the army in their long absence, and after the hardships of a wintry campaign.

The words of Ali had their weight with the Caliph: though certain Arabian writers pretend that he was chiefly moved by a tradition handed down in Jerusalem from days of yore, which said, that a man of his name, religion, and personal appearance, should conquer the holy city. Whatever may have been his inducements, the Caliph resolved to receive, in person, the surrender of Jerusalem. He accordingly appointed Ali to officiate in his place during his absence from Medina; then, having prayed at the mosque, and paid a pious visit to the tomb of the prophet, he set out on his journey.

The progress of this formidable potentate, who already held the destinies of empires in his grasp, and had the plunder of the Orient at his command, is characteristic of the primitive days of Mahometanism, and reveals, in some measure, the secret of its success. He travelled on a red or sorrel camel, across which was slung an alforja, or wallet, with a huge sack or pocket at each end, something like the modern saddlebags. One pocket contained dates and dried fruits, the other a provision called sawik, which was nothing more than barley, rice, or wheat, parched or sodden. Before him hung a leathern bottle, or sack, for water, and behind him a wooden platter. His companions, without distinction of rank, ate with him out of the same dish, using their fingers according to Oriental usage. He slept at night on a mat spread out under a tree, or under a common Bedouin tent of hair-cloth, and never resumed his march until he had offered up the morning prayer.

As he journeyed through Arabia in this simple way, he listened to the complaints of the people, redressed their grievances, and administered justice with sound judgment and a rigid hand. Information was brought to him of an Arab who was married to two sisters, a practice not unusual among idolaters, but the man was now a Mahometan. Omar cited the culprit and his two wives into his presence, and taxed him roundly with his offence; but he declared his ignorance that it was contrary to the law of the prophet.

"Thou liest!" said Omar, "thou shalt part with one of them instantly, or lose thy head."

"Evil was the day that I embraced such a religion," muttered the culprit. "Of what advantage has it been to me?"

"Come nearer to me," said Omar: and on his approaching, the Caliph bestowed two wholesome blows on his head with his walking-staff.

"Enemy of God and of thyself," cried he, "let these blows reform thy manners, and teach thee to speak with more reverence of a religion ordained by Allah, and acknowledged by the best of his creatures."

He then ordered the offender to choose between his wives, and finding him at a loss which to prefer, the matter was determined by lot, and he was dismissed by the Caliph with this parting admonition: "Whoever professes Islam, and afterwards renounces it, is punishable with death; therefore take heed to your faith. And as to your wife's sister, whom you have put away, if ever I hear that you have meddled with her, you shall be stoned."

At another place he beheld a number of men exposed to the burning heat of the sun by their Moslem conquerors, as a punishment for failing to pay their tribute. Finding, on inquiry, that they were entirely destitute of means, he ordered them to be released; and turning reproachfully to their oppressors, "Compel no men," said he, "to more than they can bear; for I heard the apostle of God say, he who afflicts his fellow-man in this world, will be punished with the fire of Jehennam."

While yet within a day's journey of Jerusalem, Abu Obeidah came to meet him and conduct him to the camp. The Caliph proceeded with due deliberation, never forgetting his duties as a priest and teacher of Islam. In the morning he said the usual prayers, and preached a sermon, in which he spoke of the security of those whom God should lead in the right way; but added, that there was no help for such as God should lead into error.

A gray-headed Christian priest, who sat before him, could not resist the opportunity to criticise the language of the Caliph preacher. "God leads no man into error," said he, aloud.

Omar deigned no direct reply, but, turning to those around, "Strike off that old man's head," said he, "if he repeats his words."

The old man was discreet, and held his peace. There was no arguing against the sword of Islam.

On his way to the camp Omar beheld a number of Arabs, who had thrown by the simple garb of their country, and arrayed themselves in the silken spoils of Syria. He saw the danger of this luxury and effeminacy, and ordered that they should be dragged with their faces in the dirt, and their silken garments torn from their backs.

When he came in sight of Jerusalem he lifted up his voice and exclaimed, "Allah Achbar! God is mighty! God grant us an easy conquest!" Then commanding his tent to be pitched, he dismounted from his camel and sat down within it on the ground. The Christians thronged to see the sovereign of this new and irresistible people, who were overrunning and subduing the earth. The Moslems, fearful of an attempt at assassination, would have kept them at a distance, but Omar rebuked their fears. "Nothing will befall us but what God hath decreed. Let the faithful trust in him."

The arrival of the Caliph was followed by immediate capitulation. When the deputies from Jerusalem were admitted to a parley, they were astonished to find this dreaded potentate a bald-headed man, simply clad, and seated on the ground in a tent of hair-cloth.

The articles of surrender were drawn up in writing by Omar, and served afterwards as a model for the Moslem leaders in other conquests. The Christians were to build no new churches in the surrendered territory. The church doors were to be set open to travellers, and free ingress permitted to Mahometans by day and night. The bells should only toll, and not ring, and no crosses should be erected on the churches, nor shown publicly in the streets. The Christians should not teach the Koran to their children; nor speak openly of their religion; nor attempt to make proselytes; nor hinder their kinsfolk from embracing Islam. They should not assume the Moslem dress, either caps, slippers, or turbans, nor part their hair like Moslems, but should always be distinguished by girdles. They should not use the Arabian language in inscriptions on their signets, nor salute after the Moslem manner, nor be called by Moslem surnames. They should rise on the entrance of a Moslem, and remain standing until he should be seated. They should entertain every Moslem traveller three days gratis. They should sell no wine, bear no arms, and use no saddle in riding; neither should they have any domestic who had been in Moslem service.

Such were the degrading conditions imposed upon the proud city of Jerusalem, once the glory and terror of the East, by the leader of a host of wandering Arabs. They were the conditions generally imposed by the Moslems in their fanatical career of conquest. Utter scorn and abhorrence of their religious adversaries formed one of the main pillars of their faith.

The Christians having agreed to surrender on these terms, the Caliph gave them, under his own hands, an assurance of protection in their lives and fortunes, the use of their churches, and the exercise of their religion.

Omar entered the once splendid city of Solomon on foot, in his simple Arab garb, with his walking-staff in his hand, and accompanied by the venerable Sophronius, with whom he talked familiarly, inquiring about the antiquities and public edifices. The worthy patriarch treated the conqueror with all outward deference, but, if we may trust the words of a Christian historian, he loathed the dirty Arab in his heart, and was particularly disgusted with his garb of coarse woollen, patched with sheep-skin. His disgust was almost irrepressible when they entered the church of the Resurrection, and Sophronius beheld the Caliph in his filthy attire, seated in the midst of the sacred edifice. "This, of a truth," exclaimed he, "is the abomination of desolation predicted by Daniel the prophet, standing in the holy place."

It is added that, to pacify the cleanly scruples of the patriarch, Omar consented to put on clean raiment which he offered him, until his own garments were washed.

An instance of the strict good faith of Omar is related as occurring on this visit to the Christian temples. While he was standing with the patriarch in the church of the Resurrection, one of the stated hours for Moslem worship arrived, and he demanded where he might pray. "Where you now are," replied the patriarch. Omar, however, refused, and went forth. The patriarch conducted him to the church of Constantine, and spread a mat for him to pray there; but again he refused. On going forth, he knelt, and prayed on the flight of steps leading down from the east gate of the church. This done, he turned to the patriarch, and gave him a generous reason for his conduct. "Had I prayed in either of the churches," said he, "the Moslems would have taken possession of it, and consecrated it as a mosque."

So scrupulous was he in observing his capitulations respecting the churches, that he gave the patriarch a writing, forbidding the Moslems to pray upon the steps where he had prayed, except one person at a time. The zeal of the faithful, however, outstripped their respect for his commands, and one-half of the steps and porch was afterwards included in a mosque built over the spot which he had accidentally sanctified.

The Caliph next sought the place where the temple of Solomon had stood, where he founded a mosque; which, in after times, being enlarged and enriched by succeeding Caliphs, became one of the noblest edifices of Islam worship, and second only to the magnificent mosque of Cordova.

The surrender of Jerusalem took place in the seventeenth year of the Hegira, and the six hundred and thirty-seventh year of the Christian era.

CHAPTER XIX

Progress of the Moslem arms in Syria – Siege of Aleppo – Obstinate defence by Youkenna – Exploit of Damâs – Capture of the castle – Conversion of Youkenna

The Caliph Omar remained ten days in Jerusalem, regulating the great scheme of Islam conquest. To complete the subjugation of Syria, he divided it into two parts. Southern Syria, consisting of Palestine and the maritime towns, he gave in charge to Yezed Ibn Abu Sofian, with a considerable portion of the army to enable him to master it; while Abu Obeidah, with a larger force, had orders promptly to reduce all Northern Syria, comprising the country lying between Hauran and Aleppo. At the same time, Amru Ibn al Aass, with a body of Moslem troops, was ordered to invade Egypt, which venerable and once mighty empire was then in a state of melancholy decline. Such were the great plans of Islam conquest in these regions; while at the same time, Saad Ibn Abu Wakkâs, another of Omar's generals, was pursuing a career of victories in the Persian territories.

The return of Omar to Medina was hailed with joy by the inhabitants, for they had regarded with great anxiety and apprehension his visit to Jerusalem. They knew the salubrity of the climate, the fertility of the country, and the sacred character of the city; containing the tombs of the prophets, and being the place, according to Moslem belief, where all mankind were to be assembled on the day of the resurrection. They had feared, therefore, that he would be tempted to fix his residence, for the rest of his days, in that consecrated city. Great was their joy, therefore, when they saw their Caliph re-enter their gates in his primitive simplicity, clad in his coarse Arab garb, and seated on his camel with his wallets of dried fruits and sodden corn; his leathern bottle and his wooden platter.

Abu Obeidah departed from Jerusalem shortly after the Caliph, and marched with his army to the north, receiving in the course of his progress through Syria, the submission of the cities of Kennesrin and Alhâdir, the inhabitants of which ransomed themselves and their possessions, for five thousand ounces of gold, the like quantity of silver, two thousand suits of silken raiment, and as much figs and aloes as would load five hundred mules; he then proceeded towards the city of Aleppo, which the Caliph had ordered him to besiege. The inhabitants of this place were much given to commerce, and had amassed great

311

wealth; they trembled, therefore, at the approach of these plundering sons of the desert, who had laid so many cities under contribution.

The city of Aleppo was walled and fortified; but it depended chiefly for defence upon its citadel, which stood without the walls and apart from the city, on an artificial hill or mound, shaped like a truncated cone or sugar-loaf, and faced with stone. The citadel was of great size, and commanded all the adjacent country; it was encompassed by a deep moat, which could be filled from springs of water, and was considered the strongest castle in all Syria. The governor, who had been appointed to this place by the emperor Heraclius, and who had held all the territory between Aleppo and the Euphrates, had lately died, leaving two sons, Youkenna and Johannas, who resided in the castle and succeeded to his command. They were completely opposite in character and conduct. Youkenna, the elder of the two, was a warrior and managed the government, while Johannas passed his life in almost monkish retirement, devoting himself to study, to religious exercises, and to acts of charity. On the approach of the Moslems Johannas sympathized with the fears of the wealthy merchants, and advised his brother to compound peaceably with the enemy for a ransom in money. "You talk like a monk," replied the fierce Youkenna; "you know nothing that is due to the honor of a soldier. Have we not strong walls, a brave garrison, and ample wealth to sustain us, and shall we meanly buy a peace without striking a blow? Shut yourself up with your books and beads; study and pray, and leave the defence of the place to me."

The next day he summoned his troops, distributed money among them, and having thus roused their spirit, "The Arabs," said he, "have divided their forces; some are in Palestine, some have gone to Egypt, it can be but a mere detachment that is coming against us; I am for meeting them on the way, and giving them battle before they come near to Aleppo." His troops answered his harangue with shouts, so he put himself at the head of twelve thousand men, and sallied forth to encounter the Moslems on their march.

Scarcely had this reckless warrior departed with his troops, when the timid and trading part of the community gathered together, and took advantage of his absence to send thirty of the most important and opulent of the inhabitants to Abu Obeidah, with an offer of a ransom for the city. These worthies, when they entered the Moslem camp, were astonished at the order and tranquillity that reigned throughout, under the wise regulations of the commander-in-chief. They were received by Abu Obeidah with dignified composure, and informed him that they had come without the knowledge of Youkenna, their warlike governor, who had sallied out on a foray, and whose tyranny they found insupportable. After much discussion, Abu Obeidah offered indemnity to the city of Aleppo, on condition that they should pay a certain sum of money, furnish provisions to his army, make discovery of every thing within their knowledge prejudicial to his interests, and prevent Youkenna from returning to the castle. They agreed to all the terms except that relating to the castle, which it was impossible for them to execute.

Abu Obeidah dispensed with that point, but exacted from them all an oath to fulfil punctually the other conditions; assuring them of his protection and kindness, should they observe it; but adding that, should they break it, they need expect no quarter. He then offered them an escort, which they declined, preferring to return quietly by the way they had come.

In the meantime Youkenna, on the day after his sallying forth, fell in with the advance guard of the Moslem army, consisting of one thousand men under Caab Ibn Damarrah. He came upon them by surprise while watering their horses, and resting themselves on the grass in negligent security. A desperate fight was the consequence; the Moslems at first were successful, but were overpowered by numbers. One hundred and seventy were slain, most of the rest wounded, and their frequent cries of "Ya Mahommed! Ya Mahommed!" (Oh Mahomet! Oh Mahomet!) showed the extremity of their despair. Night alone saved them from total massacre; but Youkenna resolved to pursue the work of extermination with the morning light. In the course of the night, however, one of his scouts brought him word of the peaceful negotiation carried on by the citizens of Aleppo during his absence. Boiling with rage, he gave up all further thought about Caab and his men, and hastening back to Aleppo, drew up his forces, and threatened to put every thing to fire and sword unless the inhabitants renounced the treaty, joined him against the Moslems and gave up the devisers of the late traitorous schemes. On their hesitating to comply with his demands, he charged on them with his troops, and put three hundred to the sword. The cries and lamentations of the multitude reached the pious Johannas in his retirement in the castle. He hastened to the scene of carnage, and sought by prayers and supplications, and pious remonstrances, to stay the fury of his brother. "What!" cried the fierce Youkenna, "shall I spare traitors who are leagued with the enemy, and selling us for gold?"

"Alas!" replied Johannas, "they have only sought their own safety; they are not fighting men."

"Base wretch!" cried Youkenna in a frenzy, "'tis thou hast been the contriver of this infamous treason."

His naked sword was in his hand; his actions were even more frantic than his words, and in an instant the head of his meek and pious brother rolled on the pavement.

The people of Aleppo were in danger of suffering more from the madness of the army than they had apprehended from the sword of the invader, when a part of the Moslem army appeared in sight led on by Khaled. A bloody battle ensued before the walls of the town, three thousand of Youkenna's troops were slain, and he was obliged to take refuge with a considerable number within the castle, where he placed engines on the walls, and prepared to defend himself to the last extremity.

A council was held in the Moslem camp. Abu Obeidah was disposed to besiege the citadel, and starve out the garrison, but Khaled, with his accustomed promptness, was for instant assault, before the emperor could send reinforcements and supplies. As usual his bold counsel prevailed: the castle was stormed, and he headed the assault. The conflict was one of the fiercest in the wars of Syria. The besieged hurled huge stones from the battlements; many of the assailants were slain, many maimed, and Khaled was compelled to desist from the attack.

In the dead of that very night, when the fires of the camp were extinguished, and the Moslems were sleeping after their hard-fought battle, Youkenna sallied forth with his troops, fell on the enemy sword in hand, killed sixty, and bore off fifty prisoners: Khaled, however, was hard on his traces, and killed above a hundred of his men before they could shelter themselves within the castle. On the next morning Youkenna paraded his fifty prisoners on the walls of the citadel, ordered them to be beheaded, and threw their heads among the besiegers.

Learning from his spies that a detachment of Moslems were foraging the country, Youkenna sent out, secretly, a troop of horse in the night, who fell upon the foragers, killed nearly sevenscore of them, slew or hamstrung their camels, mules, and horses, and then hid themselves in the recesses of the mountains, awaiting the night to get back to the castle.

Some fugitives carried tidings of this skirmish to the camp, and Khaled and Derar, with a troop of horse, were soon at the scene of combat. They found the ground strewed with the dead bodies of men and animals, learnt from some peasants whither the enemy had retreated, and were informed of a narrow defile by which they must return to the castle. Khaled and Derar stationed their troops in ambush in this defile. Late in the night they perceived the enemy advancing. They suffered them to get completely entangled in the defile, when, closing suddenly upon them on every side, they slew a number on the spot, and took three hundred prisoners. These were brought in triumph to the Moslem camp, where they would have redeemed themselves with ample ransom, but their heads were all stricken off in front of the castle, by way of retaliation.

For five months did the siege of this fortress continue; all the attacks of the Moslems were repulsed, all their stratagems discovered and circumvented; for Youkenna had spies in the very camp of the enemy, who gave him intelligence by word, or signal, of every plan and movement. Abu Obeidah despaired of reducing this impregnable castle, which impeded him in his career of conquest, and wrote to the Caliph, proposing to abandon the siege and proceed against Antioch. The Caliph, in reply, ordered him by no means to desist, as that would give courage to the enemy, but to press the siege hard, and trust the event to God. As an additional reliance, he sent him a reinforcement of horse and foot, with twenty camels to facilitate the march of the infantry. Notwithstanding all this aid, the siege was continued for seven-and-forty days, with no greater prospect of success.

While in this state of vexatious impediment and delay, Abu Obeidah was one day accosted by one of the newly arrived soldiers, who told him that, if he would give him thirty men, all strong and valiant, he would pledge his head to put him in possession of the castle. The man who made this singular application was named Damâs; he was of herculean strength and gigantic size, a brave soldier, and of great natural sagacity, although unimproved by education, as he was born a slave. Khaled backed his application, having heard of great exploits performed by him in Arabia. Abu Obeidah, in his perplexities, was willing to adopt any expedient to get possession of this obstinate castle, and

the Arabs were always prone to strange and extravagant stratagems in
their warfare. He accordingly placed thirty of his bravest men under
command of Damâs, charging them to obey him implicitly, notwithstanding his base condition; at the same time, in compliance with his
request, he removed with his army to the distance of a league, as
though about to abandon the siege.

It was now night, and Damâs concealed his thirty men near to the
castle, charging them not to stir, nor utter a sound. He then went out
alone and brought in six Christian prisoners, one after another. He
questioned them in Arabic, but they were ignorant of the language,
and replied in their own tongue. "The curse of Allah on these Christian
dogs and their barbarous jargon, which no man can understand," cried
the rude Arab, and in his rage he smote off their heads.

He went forth again, and saw a man sliding down the wall, whom he
seized the moment he touched the ground. He was a Christian Arab,
and was endeavoring to escape from the tyranny of Youkenna, and
from him Damâs obtained the information he desired. He instantly dispatched two men to Abu Obeidah, requesting him to send him some
horse about sunrise. He then took a goat-skin from his wallet, with
which he covered his back and shoulders, and a dry crust of bread in
his hand, and crept on all-fours close to the wall of the castle. His men
crept silently after him. When he heard a noise he gnawed his crust
with a sound like that of a dog gnawing a bone, and his followers remained motionless. In this way he reached a part of the castle wall
which was easiest of access. Then seating himself on the ground, he
made one of his men seat himself on his shoulders, and so on until
seven were thus mounted on each other. Then he who was uppermost
stood upright, and so did the others in succession, until Damâs rose
from the ground upon his feet, and sustained the whole by his wondrous strength, each rendering such aid as he could by bearing against
the wall. The uppermost man was now enabled to scramble upon the
battlement, where he found a Christian sentinel drunk and asleep. He
seized and threw him down to the Moslems below the wall, who instantly dispatched him. He then unfolded his turban and drew up the
man below him, and they two the next, and so on until Damâs was also
on the wall.

Damâs now enjoined silence on them all and left them. He found
two other sentinels sleeping, whom he dispatched with his dagger, and
then made his way to an aperture for the discharge of arrows, looking

through which he beheld Youkenna in a spacious chamber, richly clad, seated on tapestry of scarlet silk, flowered with gold, drinking and making merry with a large company; for it would seem as if, on the apparent departure of the besieging army, the whole castle had been given up to feasting and carousing.

Damâs considered the company too numerous to be attacked; returning to his men, therefore, he explored cautiously with them the interior of the castle. Coming suddenly upon the guards at the main entrance, who had no apprehension of danger from within, they killed them, threw open the gate, let down the draw-bridge, and were joined by the residue of their party. The castle was by this time alarmed: the garrison, half drunk and half asleep, came rushing from all quarters in wild confusion. The Moslems defended themselves stoutly on the draw-bridge and in the narrow pass of the barbican until the dawn of day, when a shout of Allah Achbar was heard, and Khaled, with a troop of horse, came thundering through the gate.

The Christians threw down their arms and cried for mercy. Khaled offered them their choice, death or the faith of Islam. Youkenna was the first to raise his finger and pronounce the formula; his example was followed by several of his leading men, whereupon their wives and children and property were secured to them. The castle having been taken by storm, was completely plundered, and the spoils were divided among the army, excepting the usual fifth part reserved for the Caliph. Damâs and his brave companions, who had been almost cut to pieces in the fight, were praised to the skies, nor would Abu Obeidah stir with his host until those of them who survived were out of danger from their wounds.

It is a circumstance worthy of remark in the history both of Mahomet and his successors, that the most inveterate enemies of the Islam faith, when once converted to it, even though their conversion were by the edge of the sword, that great Moslem instrument of persuasion, became its faithful defenders. Such was the case with Youkenna, who, from the time he embraced Islam with the Arab scimetar at his throat, became as determined a champion of its doctrines as he had before been an opponent. Like all new converts, he was anxious to give striking proofs of his zeal: he had slain a brother in supporting his old faith, he now proposed to betray a cousin in promoting the interests of the new. This cousin, whose name was Theodorus, was governor of an important town and fortress, named Aazaz, situated at no great distance from Aleppo, and which it was necessary for the Moslems to secure before they left that neighborhood. The castle was of great strength, and had a numerous garrison, but Youkenna offered to put it into the hands of Abu Obeidah by stratagem. His plan was, to have one hundred Moslems disguised as Christian soldiers: with these he would pretend to fly to the fortress of Aazaz for refuge; being pursued at a distance by a large body of Arabs, who, after coming in sight of the place, would appear to retire in despair, but would conceal themselves in the neighborhood. His cousin Theodorus, who knew nothing of his conversion, would receive him with perfect confidence: at a concerted hour of the night he and his men would fall suddenly upon the garrison, and at the same time throw open the gates to the party without the walls, and between them both, he had no doubt of carrying the place without difficulty.

Abu Obeidah held counsel with Khaled, who pronounced the stratagem apt and feasible, provided the sincerity of Youkenna's conversion might be depended upon. The new proselyte managed to obtain their confidence, and was dispatched on his enterprise with one hundred chosen men, selected by tens from ten tribes of Arabs. After they had departed a sufficient time, one thousand men were sent in pretended pursuit, headed by Malec Alashtar, who was instructed in the whole stratagem.

These Moslem wars were always a tissue of plot and counterplot, of which this whole story of Youkenna is a striking example. Scarce had this scheme of treachery been devised in the Moslem camp, when the distant governor of Aazaz was apprised of it, with a success and celerity that almost seemed like magic. He had at that time a spy in the Moslem camp, an Arab of the tribe of Gassan, who sent him a letter, tied under the wing of a carrier pigeon, informing him of the apostasy of Youkenna, and of his intended treachery; though the spy was ignorant of that part of the plan relating to the thousand men under Malec Alashtar. On receiving this letter, Theodorus put his town and castle in a posture of defence, called in the Christian Arabs of the neighboring villages capable of bearing arms, and dispatched a messenger named Tarik al Gassani to Lucas, the prefect of Arrawendân, urging him to repair with troops to his assistance.

Before the arrival of the latter, Youkenna appeared with his pretended fugitives before the gates of Aazaz, announcing that his castle was taken, and that he and his band were flying before pursuers. Theodorus sallied forth on horseback, at the head of many of his troops, as if to receive his cousin with all due honors. He even alighted from his steed, and, approaching Youkenna in a reverential manner, stooped as if to kiss his stirrup; but suddenly cutting the saddle girth, he pulled him with his face on the ground, and in an instant his hundred followers were likewise unhorsed and made prisoners. Theodorus then spat in the face of the prostrate Youkenna, and reproached him with his apostasy and treachery; threatening to send him to answer for his crimes before the emperor Heraclius, and to put all his followers to the sword.

In the meantime Tarik al Gassani, the Christian Arab, who had been sent by Theodorus to summon the prefect of Arrawendân to his aid, had executed his errand, but on the way back fell into the hands of Malec, who was lying in ambuscade with his thousand men. The sight of a naked scimetar drew from Tarik information that the plot of Youkenna had been discovered; that he had been sent after aid, and that Lucas, the perfect of Arrawendân, must be actually on his way with five hundred cavalry.

Profiting by this information, Malec placed his thousand men so advantageously, as completely to surprise and capture Lucas and his reinforcement, as they were marching in the night. He then devised a stratagem still to outwit the governor of Aazaz. First he disguised his five hundred men in dresses taken from their Christian prisoners, and gave them the Christian standard of the prefect of Arrawendân. Then sum-

moning Tarik the messenger before him, and again displaying the
scimetar, he exhorted him most earnestly to turn Mahometan. There
was no resisting his arguments, and Tarik made a full and hearty
profession of the faith. Malec then ordered him to prove his zeal for
the good cause by proceeding to Aazaz and informing Theodorus, that
the prefect of Arrawendân was at hand with a reinforcement of five
hundred men. The double-faced courier departed on his errand, accompanied by a trusty Moslem, who had secret orders to smite off his
head, if he should be found to waver; but there were still other plots at
work in this tissue of stratagems.

As Tarik and his companion approached Aazaz, they heard great
shouting and the sound of trumpets, and this was the cause of the
change. Theodorus, the governor, had committed Youkenna and his
men into the custody of his son Leon. Now it so happened, that the
youth having frequently visited his father's kinsmen at the castle of
Aleppo, had become violently enamored of the daughter of Youkenna,
but had met strong opposition to his love. The present breach between
his father and Youkenna, threatened to place an inseparable barrier between him and the gratification of his passion. Maddened by his desires, the youth now offered to Youkenna, if he would give him his
daughter to wife, to embrace Mahometanism, and to set him and his
companions at liberty. The offer was accepted. At the dead of the
night, when the prisoners were armed and liberated, they fell upon the
sleeping garrison; a tumultuous fight ensued, in the course of which
Theodorus was slain, by the hand, it is said, of his unnatural son.

It was in the height of this conflict, that Tarik and his companion
arrived at the place, and learning the situation of affairs, hastened back
to Malec Alashtar with the news. The latter hurried on with his troops
and came in time to complete the capture of the place. He bestowed
great praises on Youkenna, but the latter taking him by the hand, exclaimed, "Thank Allah and this youth." He then related the whole
story. The pious Malec lifted up his eyes and hands in wonder. "When
Allah wills a thing," exclaimed he, "he prepares the means."

Leaving Seid Ibn Amir in command of the place, with Youkenna's
band of a hundred men, as a garrison, Malec Alashtar returned to the
main army with great booty and many prisoners. Youkenna, however,
refused to accompany him. He was mortified at the questionable results of his undertaking against Aazaz, the place having been taken by
other means than his own, and vowed not to show himself in the Mos-

lem camp until he had retrieved his credit by some signal blow. Just at this time, there arrived at Aazaz, a foraging party of a thousand Moslems, that had been ravaging the neighboring country; among them were two hundred renegades, who had apostatized with Youkenna, and whose families and effects were in the castle of Aleppo. They were the very men for his purpose, and with these he marched off to execute one of his characteristic stratagems at Antioch.

CHAPTER XXI

Intrigues of Youkenna at Antioch – Siege of that city by the Moslems – Flight of the emperor to Constantinople – Surrender of Antioch

The City of Antioch was at that time the capital of Syria and the seat of the Roman government in the East. It was of great extent, surrounded by stone walls and numerous towers, and stood in the midst of a fertile country, watered by wells and fountains and abundant streams. Here Heraclius held his court, and here the Greeks, sunk in luxury and effeminacy, had lost all the military discipline and heroism that had made them conquerors in Asia.

Towards this capital Youkenna proceeded with his band of two hundred men; but in the second watch of the night he left them, after giving them orders to keep on in the high way of the caravans, and on arriving at Antioch, to give themselves out as fugitives from Aleppo. In the meantime, he with two of his relatives, struck into a by-road, and soon fell into the hands of one of the emperor's outposts. On announcing himself Youkenna, late governor of Aleppo, he was sent under a guard of horse to Antioch.

The emperor Heraclius, broken in spirit by his late reverses and his continual apprehensions, wept at the sight of Youkenna, and meekly upbraided him with his apostasy and treason, but the latter, with perfect self-possession and effrontery, declared that whatever he had done was for the purpose of preserving his life for the emperor's service; and cited the obstinate defence he had made at Aleppo, and his present voluntary arrival at Antioch, as proofs of his fidelity. The emperor was easily deceived by a man he had been accustomed to regard as one of his bravest and most devoted officers; and indeed the subtle apostate had the address to incline most of the courtiers in his favor. To console him for what was considered his recent misfortunes, he was put in command of the two hundred pretended fugitives of his former garrison, as soon as they arrived at Antioch; he had thus a band of kindred renegades, ready to aid him in any desperate treachery. Furthermore, to show his entire confidence in him, the emperor sent him with upwards of two thousand men, to escort his youngest daughter from a neighboring place to the court at Antioch. He performed his mission with correctness; as he and his troop were escorting the princess about midnight, the neighing of their horses put them on the alert, and sending out scouts they received intelligence of a party of Moslems asleep, with their horses grazing near them. They proved to be a body of a thousand Christian Arabs, under Haim, son of the apostate Jabalah Ibn al Ayam, who had made captives of Derar Ibn al Azwar and a foraging party of two hundred Moslems. They all proceeded together to Antioch, where the emperor received his daughter with great joy, and made Youkenna one of his chief counsellors.

Derar and his men were brought into the presence of the emperor, and commanded to prostrate themselves before him, but they held themselves erect and took no heed of the command. It was repeated more peremptorily. "We bow to no created being," replied Derar, "the prophet bids us to yield adoration to God alone."

The emperor, struck with this reply, propounded several questions touching Mahomet and his doctrines, but Derar, whose province did not lie in words, beckoned to Kais Ibn Amir, an old gray-headed Moslem, to answer them. A long and edifying conference ensued, in which, in reply to the searching questions of the emperor, the venerable Kais went into a history of the prophet, and of the various modes in which inspiration came upon him. Sometimes like the sound of a bell; sometimes in the likeness of an angel in human shape; sometimes in a dream; sometimes like the brightness of the dawning day; and that when it was upon him great drops of sweat rolled from his forehead, and a tremor seized upon his limbs. He furthermore descanted with eloquence upon the miracles of Mahomet, of his nocturnal journey to heaven, and his conversation with the Most High. The emperor listened with seeming respect to all these matters, but they roused the indignation of a bishop who was present, and who pronounced Mahomet an impostor. Derar took fire in an instant; if he could not argue, he could make use of a soldier's vocabulary, and he roundly gave the bishop the lie, and assailed him with all kinds of epithets. Instantly a number of Christian swords flashed from their scabbards, blows were aimed at him from every side; and according to Moslem accounts, he escaped death only by miracle; though others attribute it to the hurry and confusion of his assailants, and to the interference of Youkenna. The emperor was now for having him executed on the spot; but here the good offices of Youkenna again saved him, and his execution was deferred.

In the meantime Abu Obeidah, with his main army, was making his victorious approaches, and subjecting all Syria to his arms. The emperor, in his miserable imbecility and blind infatuation, put the treacherous Youkenna in full command of the city and army. He would again have executed Derar and his fellow-prisoners, but Youkenna suggested that they had better be spared to be exchanged for any Christians that might be taken by the enemy. They were then, by advice of the bishops, taken to one of the churches, and exhorted to embrace the Christian faith, but they obstinately refused. The Arabian writers, as usual, give them sententious replies to the questions put to them. "What hinders ye," demanded the patriarch, "from turning Christians?" "The truth of our religion," replied they. Heraclius had heard of the mean attire of the Caliph Omar, and asked them why, having gained so much wealth by his conquests, he did not go richly clad like other princes? They replied, that he cared not for this world, but for the world to come, and sought favor in the eyes of God alone. "In what kind of a palace does he reside?" asked the emperor. "In a house built of mud." "Who are his attendants?" "Beggars and the poor." "What tapestry does he sit upon?" "Justice and equity." "What is his throne?" "Abstinence and true knowledge." "What is his treasure?" "Trust in God." "And who are his guard?" "The bravest of the Unitarians."

Of all the prisoners one only could be induced to swerve from his faith; and he was a youth fascinated by the beauty and the unveiled charms of the Greek women. He was baptized with triumph; the bishops strove who most should honor him, and the emperor gave him a horse, a beautiful damsel to wife, and enrolled him in the army of Christian Arabs, commanded by the renegade Jabalah; but he was upbraided in bitter terms by his father, who was one of the prisoners, and ready to die in the faith of Islam.

The emperor now reviewed his army, which was drawn up outside of the walls, and at the head of every battalion was a wooden oratory with a crucifix; while a precious crucifix out of the main church, exhibited only on extraordinary occasions, was borne as a sacred standard, before the treacherous Youkenna. One of the main dependencies of Heraclius for the safety of Antioch, was in the Iron Bridge, so called from its great strength. It was a bridge of stone across the river Orontes, guarded by two towers and garrisoned by a great force, having not less than three hundred officers. The fate of this most important pass shows the degeneracy of Greek discipline and the licentiousness of the soldiery, to which in a great measure has been attributed the rapid successes of the Moslems. An officer of the court was charged to visit this fortress each day, and see that every thing was in order. On one of his visits, he found those who had charge of the towers, drinking and revelling, whereupon he ordered them to be punished with fifty stripes each. They treasured the disgrace in their hearts; the Moslem army approached to lay siege to that formidable fortress, and when the emperor expected to hear of a long and valiant resistance, he was astonished by the tidings that the Iron Bridge had been surrendered without a blow.

Heraclius now lost heart altogether. Instead of calling a council of his generals, he assembled the bishops and wealthiest citizens in the cathedral, and wept over the affairs of Syria. It was a time for dastard counsel; the apostate Jabalah proposed the assassination of the Caliph Omar, as a means of throwing the affairs of the Saracens into confusion. The emperor was weak enough to consent, and Vathek Ibn Mosapher, a bold young Arab of the tribe of Jabalah, was dispatched to Medina to effect the treacherous deed. The Arabian historians give a miraculous close to this undertaking. Arriving at Medina, Vathek concealed himself in a tree, without the walls, at a place where the Caliph was accustomed to walk after the hour of prayers. After a time Omar approached the place, and lay down to sleep near the foot of the tree. The assassin drew his dagger, and was descending, when he beheld a lion walking round the Caliph, licking his feet and guarding him as he slept. When he woke the lion went away, upon which Vathek, convinced that Omar was under the protection of heaven, hastened down from the tree, kissed his hand in token of allegiance, revealed his treacherous errand, and avowed his conversion to the Islam faith.

The surrender of the Iron Bridge had laid open Antioch to the approach of Abu Obeidah, and he advanced in battle array to where the Christian army was drawn up beneath its walls. Nestorius, one of the Christian commanders, sallied forth from among the troops and defied the Moslems to single combat. Damâs, the herculean warrior, who had taken the castle of Aleppo, spurred forward to meet him, but his horse stumbled and fell with him, and he was seized as the prisoner of Nestorius, and conveyed to his tent, where he was bound hand and foot. Dehac, another Moslem, took his place, and a brave fight ensued between him and Nestorius. The parties, however, were so well matched, that, after fighting for a long time until both were exhausted, they parted by mutual consent. While this fight was going on the soldiers, horse and foot, of either army, thronged to see it, and in the tumult the tent of Nestorius was thrown down. There were but three servants left in charge of it. Fearful of the anger of their master, they hastened to set it up again, and loosened the bands of Damâs that he might assist them; but the moment he was free, he arose in his giant strength, seized two of the attendants, one in each hand, dashed their heads against the head of the third, and soon laid them all lifeless on the ground. Then opening a chest, he arrayed himself in a dress belonging to Nestorius, armed himself with a sabre, sprang on a horse that stood ready saddled, and cut his way through the Christian Arabs of Jabalah to the Moslem host.

While these things were happening without the walls, treason was at work in the city. Youkenna, who commanded there, set free Derar and his fellow-prisoners, furnished them with weapons, and joined to them his own band of renegadoes. The tidings of this treachery, and the apprehension of revolt among his own troops, struck despair to the heart of Heraclius. He had been terrified by a dream, in which he had found himself thrust from his throne, and his crown falling from his head; the fulfilment appeared to be at hand. Without waiting to withstand the evil, he assembled a few domestics, made a secret retreat to the seashore, and set sail for Constantinople.

The generals of Heraclius, more brave than their emperor, fought a pitched battle beneath the walls; but the treachery of Youkenna, and the valor of Derar and his men, who fell on them unawares, rendered their gallant struggle unavailing; the people of Antioch seeing the battle lost, capitulated for the safety of their city at the cost of three hundred thousand golden ducats, and Abu Obeidah entered the ancient capital of Syria in triumph. This event took place on the 21st of August, in the year of redemption 638.

CHAPTER XXII

Expedition into the mountains of Syria – Story of a miraculous cap

The discreet Abu Obeidah feared to expose his troops to the enervating delights of Antioch, and to the allurements of the Greek women, and, after three days of repose and refreshment, marched forth from that luxurious city. He wrote a letter to the Caliph, relating his important conquest, and the flight of the emperor Heraclius; and added, that he discovered a grievous propensity among his troops to intermarry with the beautiful Grecian females, which he had forbidden them to do, as contrary to the injunctions of the Koran.

The epistle was delivered to Omar just as he was departing on a pilgrimage to Mecca, accompanied by the widows of the prophet. When he had read the letter he offered prayers and thanksgiving to Allah, but wept over Abu Obeidah's rigor to his soldiers. Seating himself upon the ground, he immediately wrote a reply to his general, expressing his satisfaction at his success, but exhorting him to more indulgence to his soldiers. Those who had fought the good fight ought to be permitted to rest themselves, and to enjoy the good things they had gained. Such as had no wives at home, might marry in Syria, and those who had a desire for female slaves, might purchase as many as they chose.

While the main army reposed after the taking of Antioch, the indefatigable Khaled, at the head of a detachment, scoured the country as far as to the Euphrates; took Membege, the ancient Hierapolis, by force, and Berah and Bales, and other places, by capitulation, receiving a hundred thousand pieces of gold by way of ransom, besides laying the inhabitants under annual tribute.

Abu Obeidah, in an assemblage of his officers, now proposed an expedition to subdue the mountains of Syria; but no one stepped forward to volunteer. The mountains were rugged and sterile, and covered with ice and snow for the greater part of the year, and the troops already began to feel the effects of the softening climate and delights of Syria. At length a candidate presented himself, named Meisara Ibn Mesroud; a numerous body of picked men was placed under his command, and a black flag was given him, bearing the inscription, "There is no God but God. Mahomet is the messenger of God." Damâs accompanied him at the head of one thousand black Ethiopian slaves. The detachment suffered greatly in the mountains, for they were men of sultry climates, unaccustomed to ice and snow, and they passed sud-

denly from a soft Syrian summer to the severity of frozen winter, and
from the midst of abundance to regions of solitude and sterility. The
inhabitants, too, of the scanty villages, fled at their approach. At length
they captured a prisoner, who informed them that an imperial army of
many thousand men was lying in wait for them in a valley about three
leagues distant, and that all the passes behind them were guarded. A
scout, dispatched in search of intelligence, confirmed this news: whereupon they intrenched themselves in a commanding position, and dispatched a fleet courier to Abu Obeidah, to inform him of their perilous
situation.

The courier made such speed, that when he reached the presence of
Obeidah, he fainted through exhaustion. Khaled, who had just returned from his successful expedition to the Euphrates, instantly hastened to the relief of Meisara with three thousand men, and was presently followed by Ayad Ibn Ganam, with two thousand more.

Khaled found Meisara and his men making desperate stand against
an overwhelming force. At the sight of this powerful reinforcement,
with the black eagle of Khaled in the advance, the Greeks gave over
the attack and returned to their camp, but secretly retreated in the
night, leaving their tents standing, and bearing off captive Abdallah
Ibn Hodafa, a near relative of the prophet, and a beloved friend of the
Caliph Omar, whom they straightway sent to the emperor at Constantinople.

The Moslems forbore to pursue the enemy through these difficult
mountains, and, after plundering the deserted tents, returned to the
main army. When the Caliph Omar received tidings from Abu Obeidah
of the capture of Abdallah Ibn Hodafa, he was grieved at heart, and
dispatched instantly an epistle to the emperor Heraclius at Constantinople.

"Bismillah! In the name of the all merciful God!

"Praise be to Allah, the Lord of this world, and of that which is to
come, who has neither companion, wife, nor son; and blessed be Mahomet his apostle. Omar Ibn al Khattâb, servant of God, to Heraclius,
emperor of the Greeks. As soon as thou shalt receive this epistle, fail
not to send to me the Moslem captive, whose name is Abdallah Ibn
Hodafa. If thou doest this, I shall have hope that Allah will conduct
thee in the right path. If thou dost refuse, I will not fail to send thee
such men as traffic and merchandise have not turned from the fear of
God. Health and happiness to all those who tread in the right way!"

In the meantime the emperor had treated his prisoner with great distinction, and as Abdallah was a cousin-german to the prophet, the son of one of his uncles, he was an object of great curiosity at Constantinople. The emperor proffered him liberty if he would only make a single sign of adoration to the crucifix, and magnificent rewards if he would embrace the Christian faith; but both proposals were rejected. Heraclius, say the Arab writers, then changed his treatment of him; shut him up for three days, with nothing to eat and drink but swine's flesh and wine, but on the fourth day found both untouched. The faith of Abdallah was put to no further proof, as by this time the emperor received the stern letter from the Caliph. The letter had its effect. The prisoner was dismissed, with costly robes and rich presents, and Heraclius sent to Omar a diamond of great size and beauty: but no jeweller at Medina could estimate its value. The abstemious Omar refused to appropriate it to his own use, though urged to do so by the Moslems. He placed it in the public treasury, of which, from his office, he was the guardian and manager. It was afterwards sold for a great sum.

A singular story is related by a Moslem writer, but not supported by any rumor or surmise among Christian historians. It is said that the emperor Heraclius wavered in his faith, if he did not absolutely become a secret convert of Mahometanism, and this is stated as the cause. He was afflicted with a violent pain in the head, for which he could find no remedy, until the Caliph Omar sent him a cap of mysterious virtue. So long as he wore this cap he was at ease, but the moment he laid it aside the pain returned. Heraclius caused the cap to be ripped open, and found within the lining a scrap of paper, on which was written, in Arabic character, Bismillah! Arrahmani Arrahimi! In the name of the all-merciful God. This cap is said to have been preserved among the Christians until the year 833, when it was given up by the governor of a besieged town to the Caliph Almotassem, on condition of his raising the siege. It was found still to retain its medicinal virtues, which the pious Arabians ascribed to the efficacy of the devout inscription. An unbelieving Christian will set it down among the charms and incantations which have full effect on imaginative persons inclined to credulity, but upon none others; such persons abounded among the Arabs.

CHAPTER XXIII

*Expedition of Amru Ibn al Aass against Prince Constantine in Syria
– Their conference – Capture of Tripoli and Tyre – Flight of Constantine – Death of Khaled*

The course of our history now turns to record the victories of Amru Ibn
al Aass, to whom, after the capture of Jerusalem, the Caliph had assigned the invasion and subjugation of Egypt. Amru, however, did not
proceed immediately to that country, but remained for some time with
his division of the army, in Palestine, where some places still held out
for the emperor. The natural and religious sobriety of the Arabs was
still sorely endangered among the temptations of Syria. Several of the
Moslem officers being seized while on the march, with chills and grip-
ing pains in consequence of eating unripe grapes, were counselled by a
crafty old Christian Arab, to drink freely of wine which he produced,
and which he pronounced a sovereign remedy. They followed his prescriptions so lustily, that they all came reeling into the camp to the
great scandal of Amru. The punishment for drunkenness, recommended
by Ali and adopted by the Caliph, was administered to the delinquents; who each received a sound bastinado on the soles of the feet.
This sobered them completely, but so enraged them with the old man
who had recommended the potations, that they would have put him to
death, had it not been represented to them that he was a stranger and
under Moslem protection.

Amru now advanced upon the city of Cæsarea, where Constantine,
son of the emperor, was posted with a large army. The Moslems were
beset by spies, sent by the Christian commander to obtain intelligence.
These were commonly Christian Arabs, whom it was almost impossible
to distinguish from those of the faith of Islam. One of these, however,
after sitting one day by the camp fires, as he rose trod on the end of
his own robe and stumbled; in his vexation, he uttered an oath "by
Christ!" He was immediately detected by his blasphemy to be a Christian and a spy, and was cut to pieces by the bystanders. Amru rebuked
them for their precipitancy, as he might have gained information from
their victim; and ordered that in future all spies should be brought to
him.

The fears of Constantine increased with the approach of the army,
and he now dispatched a Christian priest to Amru, soliciting him to
send some principal officer to confer amicably with him. An Ethiopian

negro named Belal Ibn Rebah, offered to undertake the embassy. He was a man of powerful frame and sonorous voice, and had been employed by Mahomet as a Muezzin or crier, to summon the people to prayers. Proud of having officiated under the prophet, he retired from office at his death, and had raised his voice but once since that event, and that was on the taking possession of Jerusalem, the city of the prophets, when at the Caliph Omar's command, he summoned the true believers to prayers with a force of lungs, that astonished the Jewish inhabitants.

Amru would have declined the officious offer of the vociferous Ethiopian, representing to him that such a mission required a smooth-spoken Arab, rather than one of his country; but, on Belal conjuring him in the name of Allah and the prophet, to let him go, he reluctantly consented. When the priest saw who was to accompany him back to Constantine, he objected stoutly to such an ambassador, and glancing contemptuously at the negro features of the Ethiopian, observed that Constantine had not sent for a slave but for an officer. The negro ambassador, however, persisted in his diplomatic errand, but was refused admission and returned mortified and indignant.

Amru now determined to undertake the conference in person. Repairing to the Christian camp, he was conducted to Constantine, whom he found seated in state, and who ordered a chair to be placed for him; but he put it aside, and seated himself cross-legged on the ground after the Arab fashion, with his scimetar on his thigh and his lance across his knees. The curious conference that ensued is minutely narrated by that pious Imam and Cadi, the Moslem historian Alwakedi, in his chronicle of the conquest of Syria.

Constantine remonstrated against the invasion, telling Amru that the Romans and Greeks and Arabs were brethren, as being all the children of Noah, although, it was true, the Arabs were misbegotten, as being the descendants of Ishmael, the son of Hagar, a slave and a concubine, yet being thus brethren, it was sinful for them to war against each other.

Amru replied that what Constantine had said was true, and that the Arabs gloried in acknowledging Ishmael as their progenitor, and envied not the Greeks their forefather Esau, who had sold his birthright for a mess of pottage. He added that their difference related to their religion, upon which ground even brothers were justified in warfare.

Amru proceeded to state that Noah, after the deluges, divided the earth into three parts, between his sons Shem, Ham, and Japhet, and that Syria was in the portion assigned to Shem, which continued down through his descendants Kahtan and Tesm, and Jodais to Amalek, the father of the Amalekite Arabs; but that the Arabs had been pushed from their fertile inheritance of Syria into the stony and thorny deserts of Arabia.

"We come now," continued Amru, "to claim our ancient inheritance, and resume the ancient partition. Take you the stones and the thorns and the barren deserts we have occupied, and give us back the pleasant land of Syria, with its groves, its pastures, its fair cities and running streams."

To this Constantine replied, that the partition was already made; that time and possession had confirmed it; and that the groves had been planted, and the cities built by the present inhabitants. Each, therefore, ought to be contented with the lot that had fallen to him.

"There are two conditions," rejoined Amru, "on which the land may remain with its present inhabitants. Let them profess the religion of Islam, or pay tribute to the Caliph, as is due from all unbelievers."

"Not so," said Constantine, "but let each continue to possess the land he has inhabited, and enjoy the produce of his own toil, and profess the faith which he believes, in his own conscience, to be true."

Upon this Amru sternly rose. "One only alternative," said he, "remains. Since you obstinately refuse the conditions I propose, even as your ancestor Esau refused obedience to his mother, let God and the sword decide between us."

As he was about to depart, he added: "We will acknowledge no kindred with you, while ye continue unbelievers. Ye are the children of Esau, we of Ishmael, through whom alone the seal and gift of prophecy descended from father to son, from our great forefather Adam, until it reached the prophet Mahomet. Now Ishmael was the best of the sons of his father, and made the tribe of Kenanah, the best tribe of Arabia; and the family of Koreish is the best of the tribe of Kenanah; and the children of Haschem are the best of the family of Koreish; and Abdallah Motâlleb, grandsire of Mahomet, was the best of the sons of Haschem; and Abdallah, the youngest and best of the thirteen sons of Abu Motâlleb, was the father of Mahomet, (on whom be peace!) who was the best and only issue of his sire; and to him the angel Gabriel descended from Allah, and inspired him with the gift of prophecy."

Thus terminated this noted conference, and Amru returned to his host. The armies now remained in sight of each other, prepared for

battle, but without coming to action. One day an officer richly arrayed
came forth from the Christian camp, defying the Moslems to single
combat. Several were eager to accept the challenge in hopes of gaining
such glittering spoil; but Amru rebuked their sordid motives. "Let no
man fight for gain," said he, "but for the truth. He who loses his life
fighting for the love of God, will have paradise as a reward; but he
who loses it fighting for any other object, will lose his life and all that
he fights for."

A stripling now advanced, an Arab from Yemen, or Arabia the
Happy, who had sought these wars not, as he said, for the delights of
Syria, or the fading enjoyments of this world, but to devote himself to
the service of God and his apostle. His mother and sister had in vain
opposed his leaving his peaceful home, to seek a life of danger. "If I
fall in the service of Allah," said he, "I shall be a martyr; and the
prophet has said, that the spirits of the martyrs shall dwell in the crops
of the green birds that eat of the fruits and drink of the rivers of paradise." Finding their remonstrances of no avail, his mother and sister
had followed him to the wars, and they now endeavored to dissuade
him from fighting with an adversary so much his superior in strength
and years; but the youthful enthusiast was not to be moved. "Farewell,
mother and sister!" cried he, "we shall meet again by that river of joy
provided in paradise, for the apostle and his followers."

The youth rushed to the combat, but obtained almost instantly the
crown of martyrdom he sought. Another, and another succeeded him,
but shared the same fate. Serjabil Ibn Hasanah stepped forth. As on a
former occasion, in purifying the spirit, he had reduced the flesh; and a
course of watching and fasting had rendered him but little competent
to face his powerful adversary. After a short combat the Christian bore
him to the earth, and setting his foot upon his breast, was about to take
his life, when his own hand was suddenly severed from his body. The
prostrate Serjabil looked up with surprise at his deliverer; for he was in
Grecian attire, and had come from the Grecian host. He announced
himself as the unhappy Tuleïa Ibn Chowailed, formerly a pretended
prophet and an associate of Moseïlma. After the death of that impostor,
he had repented of his false prophecies, and become a Moslem in
heart, and had sought an opportunity of signalizing his devotion to the
Islam cause.

"Oh brother!" cried Serjabil, "the mercy of Allah is infinite, and repentance wipes away all crimes."

Serjabil would now have taken him to the Moslem host, but Tuleïa hung back; and at length confessed that he would long since have joined the standard of Islam, but that he was afraid of Khaled, that terror and scourge of false prophets, who had killed his friend Moseïlma, and who might put him to death out of resentment for past misdeeds. Serjabil quieted his fears, by assuring him that Khaled was not in the Moslem camp; he then conducted him to Amru, who received him with great favor, and afterwards gave him a letter to the Caliph setting forth the signal service he had performed, and his sincere devotion to the cause of Islam. He was subsequently employed in the wars of the Moslems against the Persians.

The weather was cold and tempestuous, and the Christians disheartened by repeated reverses, began daily to desert their colors. The prince Constantine dreaded, with his diminished and discouraged troops, to encounter an enemy flushed with success, and continually augmenting in force. Accordingly, he took advantage of a tempestuous night, and abandoning his camp, to be plundered by the Moslems, retreated with his army to Cæsarea, and shut himself up within its walls. Hither he was soon followed by Amru, who laid close siege to the place, but the walls were strong, the garrison was numerous, and Constantine hoped to be able to hold out until the arrival of reinforcements. The tidings of further disasters and disgraces to the imperial cause, however, destroyed this hope; and these were brought about by the stratagems and treacheries of that arch deceiver Youkenna. After the surrender of Antioch, that wily traitor still kept up his pretended devotion to the Christian cause, and retreated with his band of renegadoes to the town of Tripoli, a seaport in Syria, situated on the Mediterranean. Here he was cordially admitted, as his treachery was still unknown. Watching his opportunity, he rose with his devoted band, seized on the town and citadel without noise or tumult, and kept the standard of the cross still flying, while he sent secret intelligence of his exploit to Abu Obeidah. Just at this time, a fleet of fifty ships from Cyprus and Crete put in there, laden with arms and provisions for Constantine's army. Before notice could be given of the posture of affairs, Youkenna gained possession of the ships, and embarked on board of them with his renegadoes and other troops, delivering the city of Tripoli into the hands of the force sent by Abu Obeidah to receive it.

Bent on new treacheries, Youkenna now sailed with the fleet to Tyre, displaying the Christian flag, and informing the governor that he was come with a reinforcement for the army of the emperor. He was kindly received, and landed with nine hundred of his troops, intending to rise on the garrison in the night. One of his own men, however, betrayed the plot, and Youkenna and his followers were seized and imprisoned in the citadel.

In the meantime Yezed Ibn Abu Sofian, who had marched with two thousand men against Cæsarea, but had left Amru to subdue it, came with his troops into the neighborhood of Tyre, in hopes to find it in possession of Youkenna. The governor of the city despising so slender a force, sallied forth with the greater part of his garrison, and the inhabitants mounted on the walls to see the battle.

It was the fortune of Youkenna, which he derived from his consummate skill in intrigue, that his failure and captivity on this occasion, as on a former one in the castle of Aazaz, served only as a foundation for his success. He contrived to gain over a Christian officer named Basil, to whose keeping he and the other prisoners were intrusted, and who was already disposed to embrace the Islam faith; and he sent information of his plan by a disguised messenger to Yezed, and to those of his own followers who remained on board of the fleet. All this was the work of a few hours, while the opposing forces were preparing for action.

The battle was hardly begun when Youkenna and his nine hundred men, set free by the apostate Basil, and conducted to the arsenal, armed themselves and separated in different parties. Some scoured the streets, shouting La ilaha Allah! and Allah Achbar! Others stationed themselves at the passages by which alone the guard could descend from the walls. Others ran to the port, where they were joined by their comrades from the fleet, and others threw wide the gates to a detachment of the army of Yezed. All this was suddenly effected, and with such co-operation from various points, that the place was presently in the hands of the Moslems. Most of the inhabitants embraced the Islam faith; the rest were pillaged and made slaves.

It was the tidings of the loss of Tripoli and Tyre, and of the capture of the fleet, with its munitions of war, that struck dismay into the heart of the prince Constantine, and made him quake within the walls of Cæsarea. He felt as if Amru and his besieging army were already within the walls, and, taking disgraceful counsel from his fears, and example from his father's flight from Antioch, he removed furtively from Cæsarea with his family and vast treasure, gained promptly a convenient port, and set all sail for Constantinople.

The people of Cæsarea finding one morning that the son of their sovereign had fled in the night, capitulated with Amru, offering to deliver up the city, with all the wealth belonging to the family of the late emperor, and two hundred thousand pieces of silver, as ransom for their own property. Their terms were promptly accepted, Amru being anxious to depart on the invasion of Egypt.

The surrender of Cæsarea was followed by the other places in the province which had still held out, and thus, after a war of six years, the Moslem conquest of Syria was completed, in the 5th year of the Caliph Omar, the 29th of the reign of the emperor Heraclius, the 17th of the Hegira, and the 639th year of our redemption.

The conquest was followed by a pestilence, one of the customary attendants upon war. Great numbers of the people of Syria perished, and with them twenty-five thousand of their Arabian conquerors. Among the latter was Abu Obeidah, the commander-in-chief, then fifty-eight years of age; also Yezed Ibn Abu Sofian, Serjabil, and other distinguished generals, so that the 18th year of the Hegira became designated as "The year of the mortality."

In closing this account of the conquest of Syria, we must note the fate of one of the most efficient of its conquerors, the invincible Khaled. He had never been a favorite of Omar, who considered him rash and headlong; arrogant in the exercise of command; unsparing in the use of the sword, and rapacious in grasping the spoils of victory. His brilliant achievements in Irak and Syria, and the magnanimity with which he yielded the command to Abu Obeidah, and zealously fought under his standard, had never sufficed to efface the prejudice of Omar.

After the capture of Emessa, which was mainly effected by the bravery of Khaled, he received congratulations on all hands as the victor. Eschaus, an Arabian poet, sang his exploits in lofty verse, making him the hero of the whole Syrian conquest. Khaled, who was as ready to squander as to grasp, rewarded the adulation of the poet with thirty thousand pieces of silver. All this, when reported to Omar, excited his quick disgust; he was indignant at Khaled for arrogating to himself, as he supposed, all the glory of the war; and he attributed the lavish reward of the poet to gratified vanity. "Even if the money came from his own purse," said he, "it was shameful squandering; and God, says the Koran, loves not a squanderer."

He now gave faith to a charge made against Khaled of embezzling the spoils set apart for the public treasury, and forthwith sent orders for him to be degraded from his command in presence of the assembled army; it is even said his arms were tied behind his back with his turban.

A rigid examination proved the charge of embezzlement to be unfounded, but Khaled was subjected to a heavy fine. The sentence causing great dissatisfaction in the army, the Caliph wrote to the commanders: "I have punished Khaled not on account of fraud or falsehood, but for his vanity and prodigality; paying poets for ascribing to him alone all the successes of the holy war. Good and evil come from God, not from Khaled!"

These indignities broke the heart of the veteran, who was already infirm from the wounds and hardships of his arduous campaigns, and he gradually sank into the grave, regretting in his last moments that he had not died in the field of battle. He left a name idolized by the soldiery, and beloved by his kindred; at his sepulture, all the women of his race cut off their hair in token of lamentation. When it was ascertained, at his death, that instead of having enriched himself by the wars, his whole property consisted of his war-horse, his arms, and a single slave, Omar became sensible of the injustice he had done to his faithful general, and shed tears over his grave.

CHAPTER XXIV

Invasion of Egypt by Amru – Capture of Memphis – Siege and surrender of Alexandria – Burning of the Alexandrian library

A proof of the religious infatuation, or the blind confidence in destiny, which hurried the Moslem commanders of those days into the most extravagant enterprises, is furnished in the invasion of the once proud empire of the Pharaohs, the mighty, the mysterious Egypt, with an army of merely five thousand men. The Caliph, himself, though he had suggested this expedition, seems to have been conscious of its rashness; or rather to have been chilled by the doubts of his prime counsellor Othman; for, while Amru was on the march, he dispatched missives after him to the following effect: "If this epistle reach thee before thou hast crossed the boundary of Egypt, come instantly back; but if it find thee within the Egyptian territory, march on with the blessing of Allah, and be assured I will send thee all necessary aid."

The bearer of the letter overtook Amru while yet within the bounds of Syria; that wary general either had secret information, or made a shrewd surmise, as to the purport of his errand, and continued his march across the border without admitting him to an audience. Having encamped at the Egyptian village of Arish, he received the courier with all due respect, and read the letter aloud in the presence of his officers. When he had finished, he demanded of those about him whether they were in Syria or Egypt. "In Egypt," was the reply. "Then," said Amru, "we will proceed, with the blessing of Allah, and fulfil the commands of the Caliph."

The first place to which he laid siege was Farwak, or Pelusium, situated on the shores of the Mediterranean, on the Isthmus which separates that sea from the Arabian Gulf, and connects Egypt with Syria and Arabia. It was therefore considered the key to Egypt. A month's siege put Amru in possession of the place; he then examined the surrounding country with more forethought than was generally manifested by the Moslem conquerors, and projected a canal across the Isthmus, to connect the waters of the Red Sea and the Mediterranean. His plan, however, was condemned by the Caliph, as calculated to throw open Arabia to a maritime invasion of the Christians.

Amru now proceeded to Misrah, the Memphis of the ancients, and residence of the early Egyptian kings. This city was at that time the strongest fortress in Egypt, except Alexandria, and still retained much of its ancient magnificence. It stood on the western bank of the Nile, above the Delta, and a little east of the Pyramids. The citadel was of great strength, and well garrisoned, and had recently been surrounded with a deep ditch, into which nails and spikes had been thrown, to impede assailants.

The Arab armies, rarely provided with the engines necessary for the attack of fortified places, generally beleagured them; cut off all supplies; attacked all foraging parties that sallied forth, and thus destroyed the garrison in detail, or starved it to a surrender. This was the reason of the long duration of their sieges. This of Misrah, or Memphis, lasted seven months: in the course of which the little army of Amru was much reduced by frequent skirmishings. At the end of this time he received a reinforcement of four thousand men, sent to him at his urgent entreaties by the Caliph. Still his force would have been insufficient for the capture of the place, had he not been aided by the treachery of its governor Mokawkas.

This man, an original Egyptian, or Copt, by birth, and of noble rank, was a profound hypocrite. Like most of the Copts, he was of the Jacobite sect, who denied the double nature of Christ. He had dissembled his sectarian creed, however, and deceived the emperor Heraclius by a show of loyalty; so as to be made prefect of his native province, and governor of the city. Most of the inhabitants of Memphis were Copts and Jacobite Christians; and held their Greek fellow-citizens, who were of the regular Catholic church of Constantinople, in great antipathy.

Mokawkas, in the course of his administration, had collected, by taxes and tribute, an immense amount of treasure, which he had deposited in the citadel. He saw that the power of the emperor was coming to an end in this quarter, and thought the present a good opportunity to provide for his own fortune. Carrying on a secret correspondence with the Moslem general, he agreed to betray the place into his hands, on condition of receiving the treasure as a reward for his treason. He accordingly, at an appointed time, removed the greater part of the garrison from the citadel to an island in the Nile. The fortress was immediately assailed by Amru, at the head of his fresh troops, and was easily carried by assault, the Copts rendering no assistance. The Greek soldiery, on the Moslem standard being hoisted on the citadel, saw through the treachery, and, giving up all as lost, escaped in their ships to the main land; upon which the prefect surrendered the place by capitulation. An annual tribute of two ducats a head was levied on all the inhabitants of the district, with the exception of old men, women, and boys under the age of sixteen years. It was further conditioned, that the Moslem army should be furnished with provisions, for which they would pay, and that the inhabitants of the country should, forthwith, build bridges over all the streams on the way to Alexandria. It was also agreed that every Musulman travelling through the country should be entitled to three days' hospitality, free of charge.

The traitor Mokawkas was put in possession of his ill-gotten wealth. He begged of Amru to be taxed with the Copts, and always to be en-rolled among them; declaring his abhorrence of the Greeks and their doctrines; urging Amru to persecute them with unremitting violence. He extended his sectarian bigotry even into the grave, stipulating that, at his death, he should be buried in the Christian Jacobite church of St. John, at Alexandria.

Amru, who was politic as well as brave, seeing the irreconcilable hatred of the Coptic or Jacobite Christians to the Greeks, showed some favor to that sect, in order to make use of them in his conquest of the country. He even prevailed upon their patriarch Benjamin to emerge from his desert and hold a conference with him; and subsequently de-clared that "he had never conversed with a Christian priest of more in-nocent manners or venerable aspect." This piece of diplomacy had its effect, for we are told that all the Copts above and below Memphis swore allegiance to the Caliph.

Amru now pressed on for the city of Alexandria, distant about one hundred and twenty-five miles. According to stipulation, the people of the country repaired the roads and erected bridges to facilitate his march; the Greeks, however, driven from various quarters by the prog-ress of their invaders, had collected at different posts on the island of the Delta, and the channels of the Nile, and disputed with desperate but fruitless obstinacy, the onward course of the conquerors. The se-verest check was given at Keram al Shoraik, by the late garrison of Memphis, who had fortified themselves there after retreating from the island of the Nile. For three days did they maintain a gallant conflict with the Moslems, and then retired in good order to Alexandria. With all the facilities furnished to them on their march, it cost the Moslems two-and-twenty days to fight their way to that great city.

Alexandria now lay before them, the metropolis of wealthy Egypt, the emporium of the East, a place strongly fortified, stored with all the munitions of war, open by sea to all kinds of supplies and reinforcements, and garrisoned by Greeks, aggregated from various quarters, who here were to make the last stand for their Egyptian empire. It would seem that nothing short of an enthusiasm bordering on madness, could have led Amru and his host on an enterprise against this powerful city.

The Moslem leader, on planting his standard before the place, summoned it to surrender on the usual terms, which being promptly refused, he prepared for a vigorous siege. The garrison did not wait to be attacked, but made repeated sallies, and fought with desperate valor. Those who gave greatest annoyance to the Moslems, were their old enemies, the Greek troops from Memphis. Amru, seeing that the greatest defence was from a main tower, or citadel, made a gallant assault upon it, and carried it sword in hand. The Greek troops, however, rallied to that point from all parts of the city; the Moslems, after a furious struggle, gave way, and Amru, his faithful slave Werdan, and one of his generals, named Moslema Ibn al Mokalled, fighting to the last, were surrounded, overpowered, and taken prisoners.

The Greeks, unaware of the importance of their captives, led them before the governor. He demanded of them, haughtily, what was their object in thus overrunning the world and disturbing the quiet of peaceable neighbors. Amru made the usual reply, that they came to spread the faith of Islam; and that it was their intention, before they laid by the sword, to make the Egyptians either converts or tributaries. The boldness of his answer, and the loftiness of his demeanor, awakened the suspicions of the governor, who, supposing him to be a warrior of note among the Arabs, ordered one of his guards to strike off his head. Upon this Werdan, the slave, understanding the Greek language, seized his master by the collar, and, giving him a buffet on the cheek, called him an impudent dog, and ordered him to hold his peace, and let his superiors speak. Moslema, perceiving the meaning of the slave, now interposed, and made a plausible speech to the governor; telling him that Amru had thoughts of raising the siege, having received a letter to that effect from the Caliph, who intended to send ambassadors to treat for peace, and assuring the governor that, if permitted to depart, they would make a favorable report to Amru.

The governor, who, if Arabian chronicles may be believed on this point, must have been a man of easy faith, ordered the prisoners to be set at liberty; but the shouts of the besieging army on the safe return of their general soon showed him how completely he had been duped.

But scanty details of the siege of Alexandria have reached the Christian reader, yet it was one of the longest, most obstinately contested and sanguinary, in the whole course of the Moslem wars. It endured fourteen months with various success; the Moslem army was repeatedly reinforced, and lost twenty-three thousand men; at length their irresistible ardor and perseverance prevailed; the capital of Egypt was conquered, and the Greek inhabitants were dispersed in all directions. Some retreated in considerable bodies into the interior of the country, and fortified themselves in strongholds; others took refuge in the ships, and put to sea.

Amru, on taking possession of the city, found it nearly abandoned; he prohibited his troops from plundering; and leaving a small garrison to guard the place, hastened with his main army in pursuit of the fugitive Greeks. In the meantime the ships which had taken off a part of the garrison were still lingering on the coast, and tidings reached them that the Moslem general had departed, and had left the captured city nearly defenceless. They immediately made sail back for Alexandria, and entered the port in the night. The Greek soldiers surprised the sentinels, got possession of the city, and put most of the Moslems they found there to the sword.

Amru was in full pursuit of the Greek fugitives, when he heard of the recapture of the city. Mortified at his own negligence in leaving so rich a conquest with so slight a guard, he returned in all haste, resolved to retake it by storm. The Greeks, however, had fortified themselves strongly in the castle, and made stout resistance. Amru was obliged, therefore, to besiege it a second time, but the siege was short. The castle was carried by assault; many of the Greeks were cut to pieces, the rest escaped once more to their ships, and now gave up the capital as lost. All this occurred in the nineteenth year of the Hegira, and the year 640 of the Christian era.

On this second capture of the city by force of arms, and without capitulation, the troops were clamorous to be permitted to plunder. Amru again checked their rapacity, and commanded that all persons and property in the place, should remain inviolate, until the will of the Caliph could be known. So perfect was his command over his troops, that not the most trivial article was taken. His letter to the Caliph shows what must have been the population and splendor of Alexandria, and the luxury and effeminacy of its inhabitants, at the time of the Moslem conquest. It states the city to have contained four thousand palaces;

five thousand baths; four hundred theatres and places of amusement; twelve thousand gardeners which supplied it with vegetables, and forty thousand tributary Jews. It was impossible, he said, to do justice to its riches and magnificence. He had hitherto held it sacred from plunder, but his troops having won it by force of arms, considered themselves entitled to the spoils of victory.

The Caliph Omar in reply, expressed a high sense of his important services, but reproved him for even mentioning the desire of the soldiery to plunder so rich a city, one of the greatest emporiums of the East. He charged him, therefore, most rigidly to watch over the rapacious propensities of his men; to prevent all pillage, violence and waste; to collect and make out an account of all moneys, jewels, household furniture, and every thing else that was valuable, to be appropriated towards defraying the expenses of this war of the faith. He ordered the tribute also, collected in the conquered country, to be treasured up at Alexandria, for the supplies of the Moslem troops.

The surrender of all Egypt followed the capture of its capital. A tribute of two ducats was laid on every male of mature age, besides a tax on all lands in proportion to their value, and the revenue which resulted to the Caliph is estimated at twelve millions of ducats.

We have shown that Amru was a poet in his youth; and throughout all his campaigns he manifested an intelligent and inquiring spirit, if not more highly informed, at least more liberal and extended in its views than was usual among the early Moslem conquerors. He delighted, in his hours of leisure, to converse with learned men, and acquire through their means such knowledge as had been denied to him by the deficiency of his education. Such a companion he found at Alexandria in a native of the place, a Christian of the sect of the Jacobites, eminent for his philological researches, his commentaries on Moses and Aristotle, and his laborious treatises of various kinds, surnamed Philoponus from his love of study, but commonly known by the name of John the Grammarian. An intimacy soon arose between the Arab conqueror and the Christian philologist; an intimacy honorable to Amru, but destined to be lamentable in its result to the cause of letters. In an evil hour, John the Grammarian, being encouraged by the favor shown him by the Arab general, revealed to him a treasure hitherto unnoticed, or rather unvalued by the Moslem conquerors. This was a vast collection of books or manuscripts, since renowned in history as the ALEXANDRIAN LIBRARY. Perceiving that in taking an account of every thing valuable in the city, and sealing up all its treasures, Amru had taken no notice of the books, John solicited that they might be given to him. Unfortunately, the learned zeal of the Grammarian gave a consequence to the books in the eyes of Amru, and made him scrupulous of giving them away without permission of the Caliph. He forthwith wrote to Omar, stating the merits of John, and requesting to know whether the books might be given to him. The reply of Omar was laconic, but fatal. "The contents of those books," said he, "are in conformity with the Koran, or they are not. If they are, the Koran is sufficient without them; if they are not, they are pernicious. Let them, therefore, be destroyed."

Amru, it is said, obeyed the order punctually. The books and manuscripts were distributed as fuel among the five thousand baths of the city; but so numerous were they that it took six months to consume them. This act of barbarism, recorded by Abulpharagius, is considered somewhat doubtful by Gibbon, in consequence of its not being mentioned by two of the most ancient chroniclers, Elmacin in his Saracenic history, and Eutychius in his annals, the latter of whom was patriarch of Alexandria, and has detailed the conquest of that city. It is inconsistent, too, with the character of Amru, as a poet and a man of superior intelligence; and it has recently been reported, we know not on what authority, that many of the literary treasures thus said to have been destroyed, do actually exist in Constantinople. Their destruction, however, is generally credited and deeply deplored by historians. Amru, as a man of genius and intelligence, may have grieved at the order of the Caliph; while, as a loyal subject and faithful soldier, he felt bound to obey it.*

The fall of Alexandria decided the fate of Egypt and likewise that of the emperor Heraclius. He was already afflicted with a dropsy, and took the loss of his Syrian, and now that of his Egyptian dominions, so much to heart, that he underwent a paroxysm, which ended in his

---

* The Alexandrian Library was formed by Ptolemy Soter, and placed in a building called the Bruchion. It was augmented in successive reigns to 400,000 volumes, and an additional 300,000 volumes were placed in a temple called the Serapeon. The Bruchion, with the books it contained, was burnt in the war of Cæsar, but the Serapeon was preserved. Cleopatra, it is said, added to it the library of Pergamas, given to her by Marc Antony, consisting of 200,000 volumes. It sustained repeated injuries during various subsequent revolutions, but was always restored to its ancient splendor, and numerous additions made to it. Such was its state at the capture of Alexandria by the Moslems.

death, about seven weeks after the loss of his Egyptian capital. He was succeeded by his son Constantine.

While Amru was successfully extending his conquests, a great dearth and famine fell upon all Arabia, insomuch that the Caliph Omar had to call upon him for supplies from the fertile plains of Egypt; whereupon Amru dispatched such a train of camels laden with grain, that it is said, when the first of the line had reached the city of Medina, the last had not yet left the land of Egypt. But this mode of conveyance proving too tardy, at the command of the Caliph, he dug a canal of communication from the Nile to the Red Sea, a distance of eighty miles; by which provisions might be conveyed to the Arabian shores. This canal had been commenced by Trajan, the Roman emperor.

The able and indefatigable Amru went on in this manner, executing the commands and fulfilling the wishes of the Caliph; and governed the country he had conquered, with such sagacity and justice, that he rendered himself one of the most worthily renowned among the Moslem generals.

CHAPTER XXV

Enterprises of the Moslems in Persia – Defence of the kingdom by
Queen Arzemia – Battle of the Bridge

For the sake of perspicuity, we have recorded the Moslem conquests in Syria and Egypt in a continued narrative, without pausing to notice events which were occurring at the same time in other quarters; we now recede several years, to take up the course of affairs in Persia, from the time that Khaled, in the thirteenth year of the Hegira, in obedience to the orders of Abu Beker, left his victorious army on the banks of the Euphrates, to take the general command in Syria. The victories of Khaled had doubtless been owing in part to the distracted state of the Persian empire. In the course of an inconsiderable number of years, the proud sceptre of the Khosrus had passed from hand to hand; Khosru II, surnamed Parviz, having been repeatedly defeated by Heraclius, was deposed in 628, by a party of his nobles, headed by his own son Siroes (or Shiruyah), and was put to death by the latter in a vault under the palace, among the treasures he had amassed. To secure possession of the throne, Siroes followed up the parricide by the massacre of seventeen of his brothers. It was not ambition alone that instigated these crimes. He was enamored of a sultana in the harem of his father; the matchless Shireen. While yet reeking with his father's blood, he declared his passion to her. She recoiled from him with horror, and when he would have used force, gave herself instant death to escape from his embraces. The disappointment of his passion; the upbraidings of his sisters for the murders of their father and their brothers; and the stings of his own conscience, threw Siroes into a moody melancholy, and either caused, or added acuteness to a malady, of which he died in the course of eight months.

His infant son, Ardisheer, was placed on the throne about the end of 628, but was presently slain, and the throne usurped by Sheriyar, a Persian noble, who was himself killed after a very short reign. Turan-Docht, a daughter of Khosru Parviz, was now crowned and reigned eighteen months, when she was set aside by her cousin Shah Shenandeh, who was himself deposed by the nobles, and Arzemi-Docht* or Arzemia, as the name is commonly given, another daughter of Khosru Parviz, was placed on the throne in the year 632 of the Christian era.

---

* Docht or Dokht, diminutive of dukhter, signifies the unmarried or maiden state.

The Persian seat of government, which had been often changed, was at this time held in the magnificent city of Madain or Madayn, on the Tigris, where was the ancient Ctesiphon.

Arzemia was distinguished alike for masculine talents and feminine beauty; she had been carefully instructed under her father Khosru, and had acquired sad experience, during the series of conspiracies and assassinations which had beset the throne for the last four years. Rejecting from her council the very traitors who had placed the crown upon her head, she undertook to wield the sceptre without the aid of a vizier, thereby giving mortal offence to the most powerful nobles of her realm. She was soon called upon to exert her masculine spirit by the continued aggressions of the Moslems.

The reader will recollect that the Moslem army on the Euphrates, at the departure of Khaled, was left under the command of Mosenna Ibn Haris (or Muthenna Ibn Hârith, as the name is sometimes rendered). On the accession of Omar to the Caliphat, he appointed Mosenna emir or governor of Sewad, the country recently conquered by Khaled, lying about the lower part of the Euphrates and the Tigris, forming a portion of the Persian province of Irak-Arabi. This was in compliance with the wishes and intentions of Abu Beker; though Omar does not appear to have had great confidence in the military talents of Mosenna, the career of conquest having languished in his hands since the departure of Khaled. He accordingly sent Abu Obeidah Sakfi, one of the most important disciples of the prophet, at the head of a thousand chosen men, to reinforce the army under Mosenna, and to take the lead in military enterprises.* He was accompanied by Sabit Ibn Kais, one of the veterans of the battle of Beder.

The Persian Queen, hearing of the advance of the Moslem army thus reinforced, sent an able general, Rustam Ibn Ferukh-Zad (or Feruchsad), with thirty thousand more, to repel them. Rustam halted on the confines of Irak, and sent forward strong detachments under a general named Dschaban, and a Persian prince named Narsi (or Narsis). These were so roughly handled by the Moslems, that Rustam found it necessary to hasten with his main force to their assistance. He arrived too late; they had been severally defeated and put to flight, and the whole country of Sewad was in the hands of the Moslems.

---

* This Abu Obeidah has sometimes been confounded with the general of the same name, who commanded in Syria; the latter, however, was Abu Obeidah *Ibn Aljerah* (the son of Aljerah).

Queen Arzemia, still more aroused to the danger of her kingdom, sent Rustam a reinforcement led by Behman Dschadu, surnamed the Veiled, from the shaggy eyebrows which overshadowed his visage. He brought with him three thousand men and thirty elephants. These animals, of little real utility in warfare, were formidable in the eyes of those unaccustomed to them, and were intended to strike terror into the Arabian troops. One of them was the white elephant Mahmoud, famous for having been ridden by Abraha, the Ethiopian king, in foregone times, when he invaded Mecca and assailed the Caaba. It was considered a harbinger of victory, all the enterprises in which it had been employed having proved successful.

With Behman, the heavy-browed, came also the standard of Kaoh, the sacred standard. It was originally the leathern apron of the blacksmith Kaoh, which he reared as a banner when he roused the people, and delivered Persia from the tyranny of Sohak. It had been enlarged from time to time, with costly silk, embroidered with gold, until it was twenty-two feet long and fifteen broad; and was decorated with gems of inestimable value. With this standard the fate of the kingdom was believed, by superstitious Persians, to be connected.

The Moslem forces, even with the reinforcement brought by Abu Obeidah Sakfi, did not exceed nine thousand in number; the Persians, encamped near the ruins of Babylon, were vastly superior. It was the counsel of Mosenna and the veteran Sabit, that they should fall back into the deserts, and remain encamped there until reinforcements could be obtained from the Caliph. Abu Obeidah, however, was for a totally different course. He undervalued the prowess of the Persians; he had heard Mosenna censured for want of enterprise, and Khaled extolled to the skies for his daring achievements in this quarter. He was determined to emulate them, to cross the Euphrates and attack the Persians in their encampment. In vain Mosenna and Sabit remonstrated. He caused a bridge of boats to be thrown across the Euphrates, and led the way to the opposite bank. His troops did not follow with their usual alacrity, for they felt the rashness of the enterprise. While they were yet crossing the bridge, they were severely galled by a body of archers, detached in the advance by Rustam; and were met at the head of the bridge by that warrior, with his vanguard of cavalry.

The conflict was severe. The banner of Islam passed from hand to hand of seven brave champions, as one after another fell in its defence. The Persians were beaten back, but now arrived the main body of the army with the thirty elephants. Abu Obeidah breasted fearlessly the storm of war which he had so rashly provoked. He called to his men not to fear the elephants, but to strike at their trunks. He himself severed, with a blow of his scimetar, the trunk of the famous white elephant, but in so doing his foot slipped, he fell to the earth, and was trampled to death by the enraged animal.

The Moslems, disheartened by his loss, and overwhelmed by numbers, endeavored to regain the bridge. The enemy had thrown combustibles into the boats on which it was constructed, and had set them on fire. Some of the troops were driven into the water and perished there; the main body retreated along the river, protected in the rear by Mosenna, who now displayed the skill of an able general, and kept the enemy at bay until a slight bridge could be hastily thrown across another part of the river. He was the last to cross the bridge, and caused it to be broken behind him.

Four thousand Moslems were either slain or drowned in this rash affair: two thousand fled to Medina, and about three thousand remained with Mosenna; who encamped and intrenched them, and sent a fleet courier to the Caliph, entreating instant aid. Nothing saved this remnant of the army from utter destruction but a dissension which took place between the Persian commanders; who, instead of following up their victory, returned to Madayn, the Persian capital.

This was the severest and almost the only severe check that Moslem audacity had for a long time experienced. It took place in the 13th year of the Hegira, and the year 634 of the Christian era; and was long and ruefully remembered by the Arabs as the battle of "El Jisir," or The Battle of the Bridge.

CHAPTER XXVI

Mosenna Ibn Haris ravages the country along the Euphrates –
Death of Arzemia – Yezdegird III raised to the throne – Saad Ibn
Abu Wakkâs given the general command – Death of Mosenna –
Embassy to Yezdegird – Its reception

Having received moderate reinforcements, Mosenna again took the field in Arab style, hovering about the confines of Babylonia, and sending detachments in different directions to plunder and lay waste the country bordering on the Euphrates. It was an instance of the vicissitude of human affairs, and the instability of earthly grandeur, that this proud region, which once held the world in awe, should be thus marauded and insulted by a handful of predatory Arabs.

To check their ravages, Queen Arzemia sent out a general named Mahran, with twelve thousand chosen cavalry. Mosenna, hearing of their approach, called in his plundering parties and prepared for battle. The two hosts met near Hirah, on the borders of the desert. Mosenna, who in the battle of the bridge had been the last man to retire, was now the foremost man to charge. In the fury of the fight he made his way, almost alone, into the heart of the Persian army, and with difficulty fought his way out again and back to his own men. The Persians, as we have noted, were chosen troops, and fought with unusual spirit. The Moslems, in some parts of the field, began to give way. Mosenna galloped up and threw himself before them; he expostulated, he threatened, he tore his beard in the agony of his feelings; he succeeded in leading them back to the fight; which endured from noon until sunset; and still continued doubtful. At the close of the day Mosenna encountered Mahran hand to hand, in the midst of his guards, and received a powerful blow, which might have proved fatal, but for his armor. In return he smote the Persian commander with his scimetar just where the neck joins to the shoulder, and laid him dead. The Persians, seeing their leader fall, took to flight, nor stopped until they reached Madayn.

The Moslems next made a plundering expedition to Bagdad, at that time a mere village, but noted for a great fair, the resort of merchants from various parts of the East. An Arab detachment pounced upon it at the time of the fair, and carried off many captives and immense booty.

The tidings of the defeat of Mahran, and the plundering of the fair, spread consternation in the Persian capital. The nobles and priests, who had hitherto stood in awe of the spirit of the queen, now raised a tumult. "These are the fruits," said they, "of having a woman to reign over us."

The fate of the beautiful Arzemia was hastened by private revenge. Faruch-Zad, one of the most powerful of her nobles, and governor of Khorassan, incited by love and ambition, had aspired to her hand. At first, it is said, she appeared to favor his addresses, fearing to provoke his enmity, but afterwards slighted them; whereupon he entered the palace by night, and attempted to get possession of her person. His attempt failed, and, by her command, he received instant death at the hands of her guards, accompanied by some indignities.

His son, Rustam, who had been left by him in the government of Khorassan, hastened, at the head of an armed force, to avenge his death. He arrived in the height of the public discontent; entered the city without opposition, stormed the palace, captured the young and beautiful queen, subjected her to degrading outrages, and put her to death in the most cruel manner. She was the sixth of the usurping sovereigns, and had not yet reigned a year.

A remaining son of Khosru Parviz was now brought forward and placed on the slippery throne, but was poisoned within forty days, some say by his courtiers, others by a slave.

The priests and nobles now elevated a youth about fifteen years of age to this perilous dignity. He was a grandson of Khosru Parviz, and had been secluded, during the late period of anarchy and assassination, in the city of Istakar, the ancient Persepolis. He is known by the name of Yezdegird III, though some historians call him Hermisdas IV, from his family, instead of his personal appellation. He was of a good natural disposition, but weak and irresolute, and apt, from his youth and inexperience, to become a passive instrument in the hands of the faction which had placed him on the throne.

One of the first measures of the new reign was to assemble a powerful army and place it under the command of Rustam, the same general who had so signally revenged the death of his father. It was determined, by a signal blow, to sweep the Arabian marauders from the land.

Omar, on his part, hearing of the changes and warlike preparations in the Persian capital, made a hasty levy of troops, and would have marched in person to carry the war into the heart of Persia. It was with great difficulty he was dissuaded from this plan by his discreet counsellors, Othman and Ali, and induced to send in his place Saad Ibn Abu Wakkâs. This was a zealous soldier of the faith who used to boast that he was the first who had shed the blood of the unbelieving: and, moreover, that the prophet, in the first holy war, had intrusted to him the care of his household during his absence; saying, "To you, oh Saad, who are to me as my father and my mother, I confide my family." To have been a favored and confidential companion of the prophet, was fast growing to be a title of great distinction among the faithful.

Saad was invested with the general command of the forces in Persia; and Mosenna, though his recent good conduct and signal success entitled him to the highest consideration, was ordered to serve under him.

Saad set out from Medina with an army of but six or seven thousand men; among these, however, were one thousand well-tried soldiers who had followed the prophet in his campaigns, and one hundred of the veterans of Beder. They were led on also by some of the most famous champions of the faith. The army was joined on its march by recruits from all quarters, so that by the time it joined the troops under Mosenna, it amounted to upwards of thirty thousand men.

Mosenna died three days after the arrival of his successor in the camp; the cause and nature of his death are not mentioned. He left behind him a good name, and a wife remarkable for her beauty. The widow was easily brought to listen to the addresses of Saad, who thus succeeded to Mosenna in his matrimonial as well as his military capacity.

The Persian force, under Rustam, lay encamped at Kadesia (or Khâdesîyah), on the frontier of Sawâd or Irak-Arabi, and was vastly superior in numbers to the Moslems. Saad sent expresses to the Caliph entreating reinforcements. He was promised them, but exhorted in the meantime to doubt nothing; never to regard the number of the foe, but to think always that he was fighting under the eye of the Caliph. He was instructed, however, before commencing hostilities, to send a delegation to Yezdegird inviting him to embrace the faith.

Saad accordingly sent several of his most discreet and veteran officers on this mission. They repaired to the magnificient city of Madayn, and were ushered through the sumptuous halls and saloons of the palace of the Khosrus, crowded with guards and attendants all richly arrayed, into the presence of the youthful monarch, whom they found seated in state on a throne, supported by silver columns, and surrounded by the dazzling splendor of an Oriental Court.

The appearance of the Moslem envoys, attired in simple Arab style, in the striped garments of Yemen, amidst the gorgeous throng of nobles arrayed in jewels and embroidery, was but little calculated to inspire deference in a young and inconsiderate prince, brought up in pomp and luxury, and accustomed to consider dignity inseparable from splendor. He had no doubt, also, been schooled for the interview by his crafty counsellors.

The audience opened by a haughty demand on his part, through his interpreter, as to the object of their embassy. Upon this, one of their number, Na'man Ibn Mukry, set forth the divine mission of the prophet and his dying command to enforce his religion by the sword, leaving no peaceable alternative to unbelievers, but conversion or tribute. He concluded by inviting the king to embrace the faith; if not, to consent to become a tributary; if he should refuse both, to prepare for battle.

Yezdegird restrained his indignation, and answered in words which had probably been prepared for him. "You Arabs," said he, "have hitherto been known to us by report, as wanderers of the desert; your food dates, and sometimes lizards and serpents; your drink brackish water; your garments coarse hair-cloth. Some of you, who by chance have wandered into our realms, have found sweet water, savory food, and soft raiment. They have carried back word of the same to their brethren in the desert, and now you come in swarms to rob us of our goods and our very land. Ye are like the starving fox, to whom the husbandman afforded shelter in his vineyard, and who in return, brought a troop of his brethren to devour his grapes. Receive from my generosity whatever your wants require; load your camels with corn and dates, and depart in peace to your native land; but if you tarry in Persia, beware the fate of the fox who was slain by the husbandman."

The most aged of the Arab envoys, the Sheikh Mukair Ibn Zarrarah, replied with great gravity and decorum, and an unaltered countenance. "Oh king! all thou hast said of the Arabs is most true. The green lizard of the desert was their sometime food; the brackish water of wells their drink; their garments were of hair-cloth, and they buried their infant daughters to restrain the increase of their tribes. All this was in the days of ignorance. They knew not good from evil. They were guilty, and they suffered. But Allah in his mercy sent his apostle Mahomet, and his sacred Koran among them. He rendered them wise and valiant. He commanded them to war with infidels until all should be converted to the true faith. On his behest we come. All we demand of thee is to acknowledge that there is no God but God, and that Mahomet is his apostle, and to pay from thy income the customary contribution of the Zacat, paid by all true believers, in charity to the poor, and for the support of the family of the prophet. Do this, and not a Moslem shall enter the Persian dominions, without thy leave; but if thou refuse it, and refuse to pay the tribute exacted from all unbelievers, prepare for the subjugation of the sword."

The forbearance of Yezdegird was at an end. "Were it not unworthy of a great Padischah," said he, "to put ambassadors to death, the sword should be the only tongue with which I would reply to your insolence. Away! ye robbers of the lands of others! take with ye a portion of the Persian soil ye crave." So saying, he caused sacks of earth to be bound upon their shoulders; to be delivered by them to their chiefs as symbols of the graves they would be sure to find at Kadesia.

When beyond the limits of the city, the envoys transferred the sacks of earth to the backs of their camels, and returned with them to Saad Ibn Abu Wakkâs; shrewdly interpreting into a good omen what had been intended by the Persian monarch as a scornful taunt. "Earth," said they, "is the emblem of empire. As surely, oh Saad, as we deliver thee these sacks of earth, so surely will Allah deliver the empire of Persia into the hands of true believers."

CHAPTER XXVII

The Battle of Kadesia

The hostile armies came in presence of each other on the plains of Kadesia (or Kâdesîyah), adjacent to a canal derived from the Euphrates. The huge mass of the Persian army would have been sufficient to bear down the inferior number of the Moslems, had it possessed the Grecian or Roman discipline; but it was a tumultuous multitude, unwieldy from its military pomp, and encumbered by its splendid trappings. The Arabs, on the contrary, were veteran skirmishers of the desert; light and hardy horsemen; dexterous with the bow and lance, and skilled to wheel and retreat, and to return again to the attack. Many individual acts of prowess took place between champions of either army, who dared each other to single combat in front of the hosts when drawn out in battle array. The costly armor of the Persians, wrought with gold, and their belts or girdles studded with gems, made them rich prizes to their Moslem victors; while the Persians, if victorious, gained nothing from the rudely clad warriors of the desert, but honor and hard blows.

Saad Ibn Abu Wakkâs was in an unfortunate plight for a leader of an army on such a momentous occasion. He was grievously afflicted with boils in his reins, so that he sat on his horse with extreme difficulty. Still he animated his troops by his presence, and gave the *tekbir* or battle-cry – Allah Achbar!

The Persian force came on with great shouts; their elephants in the van. The horses of the Moslem cavalry recoiled at sight of the latter, and became unmanageable. A great number of the horsemen dismounted; attacked the unwieldy animals with their swords, and drove them back upon their own host. Still the day went hard with the Moslems; their force being so inferior, and their general unable to take the lead and mingle in the battle. The arrival of a reinforcement from Syria, put them in new heart, and they fought on until the approach of night, when both parties desisted, and drew off to their encampments. Thus ended the first day's fight, which the Persians called the battle of Armâth; but the Moslems, The Day of Succor, from the timely arrival of reinforcements.

On the following morning the armies drew out again in battle array, but no general conflict took place. Saad was unable to mount his horse and lead his troops into action, and the Persians, aware of the reinforcements received by the Moslems, were not disposed to provoke a battle. The day passed in light skirmishes and single combats between the prime warriors of either host, who defied each other to trials of skill and prowess. These combats, of course, were desperate, and commonly cost the life of one, if not both of the combatants.

Saad overlooked the field from the shelter of a tent, where he sat at a repast with his beautiful bride beside him. Her heart swelled with grief at seeing so many gallant Moslems laid low; a thought of the valiant husband she had lost passed across her mind, and the unwary ejaculation escaped her, "Alas! Mosenna Ibn Haris, where art thou?" Saad was stung to the quick by what he conceived a reproach on his courage or activity, and, in the heat of the moment, struck her on the face with his dagger. "To-morrow," muttered he to himself, "I will mount my horse."

In the night he secretly sent out a detachment in the direction of Damascus, to remain concealed until the two armies should be engaged on the following day, and then to come with banners displayed, and a great sound of drum and tumpet, as though they were a reinforcement hurrying to the field of action.

The morning dawned, but still, to his great mortification, Saad was unable to sit upon his horse, and had to intrust the conduct of the battle to one of his generals. It was a day of bloody and obstinate conflict; and from the tremendous shock of the encountering hosts, was celebrated among the Arabs as "The day of the Concussion."

The arrival of the pretended reinforcement inspired the Moslems, who were ignorant of the stratagem, and dismayed the enemy. Rustam urged on his elephants to break down the Arab host, but they had become familiar with those animals, and attacked them so vigorously that, as before, they turned upon their own employers, and trampled them down in their unwieldy flight from the field.

The battle continued throughout the day with varying fortune; nor did it cease at nightfall, for Rustam rode about among his troops urging them to fight until morning. That night was called by some the night of delirium; for in the dark and deadly struggle the combatants struck at random, and often caught each other by the beard: by others it was called the night of howling and lamentation, from the cries of the wounded.

The battle ceased not even at the dawning, but continued until the heat of the day. A whirlwind of dust hid the armies from each other for a time, and produced confusion on the field, but it aided the Moslems, as it blew in the faces of the enemy. During a pause in the conflict, Rustam, panting with heat and fatigue, and half blinded with dust, took shelter from the sun under a tent which had been pitched near the water, and was surrounded by camels laden with treasure, and with the luxurious furniture of the camp. A gust of wind whirled the tent into the water. He then threw himself upon the earth in the shade of one of the camels. A band of Arab soldiers came upon him by surprise. One of them, Hellâl Ibn Alkameh by name, in his eagerness for plunder, cut the cords which bound the burthen on the camel. A package of silver fell upon Rustam and broke his spine. In his agony he fell, or threw himself into the water, but was drawn out by the leg, his head stricken off, and elevated on the lance of Hellâl. The Persians recognized the bloody features, and fled amain, abandoning to the victors their camp, with all its rich furniture and baggage, and scores of beasts of burden, laden with treasure and with costly gear. The amount of booty was incalculable.

The sacred standard, too, was among the spoils. To the soldier who had captured it, thirty thousand pieces of gold are said to have been paid at Saad's command; and the jewels, with which it was studded, were put with the other booty, to be shared according to rule. Hellâl, too, who brought the head of Rustam to Saad, was allowed as a reward, to strip the body of his victim. Never did Arab soldier make richer spoil. The garments of Rustam were richly embroidered, and he wore two gorgeous belts, ornamented with jewels, one worth a thousand pieces of gold, the other seventy thousand dirhems of silver.

Thirty thousand Persians are said to have fallen in this battle, and upwards of seven thousand Moslems. The loss most deplored by the Persians, was that of their sacred banner, with which they connected the fate of the realm.

This battle took place in the fifteenth year of the Hegira, and the six hundred and thirty-sixth year of the Christian era, and is said to be as famous among the Arabs as that of Arbela among the Greeks.

Complaints having circulated among the troops that Saad had not mingled in the fight, he summoned several of the old men to his tent, and, stripping himself, showed the boils by which he was so grievously afflicted; after which there were no further expressions of dissatisfaction. It is to be hoped he found some means, equally explicit, of excusing himself to his beautiful bride for the outrage he had committed upon her.

CHAPTER XXVIII

Founding of Bassora – Capture of the Persian capital – Flight of Yezdegird to Holwân

After the signal victory of Kadesia, Saad Ibn Abu Wakkâs, by command of the Caliph, remained for some months in the neighborhood, completing the subjugation of the conquered country, collecting tax and tribute, and building mosques in every direction for the propagation of the faith. About the same time Omar caused the city of Basra, or Bassora, to be founded in the lower part of Irak Arabi, on that great river formed by the junction of the Euphrates and the Tigris. This city was intended to protect the region conquered by the Moslems about the mouth of the Euphrates; to cut off the trade of India from Persia, and to keep a check upon Ahwâz (a part of Susiana or Khusestan), the prince or satrap of which, Hormusân by name, had taken an active part in the late battle of Kadesia. The city of Bassora was founded in the fourteenth year of the Hegira, by Orweh Ibn Otbeh. It soon gathered within its walls great numbers of inhabitants from the surrounding country; rose rapidly in importance, and has ever since been distinguished as a mart for the Indian commerce.

Having brought all the country in the neighborhood of Kadesia into complete subjection, Saad Ibn Abu Wakkâs, by command of the Caliph, proceeded in the conquest of Persia. The late victories, and the capture of the national banner, had struck despair into the hearts of the Persians. They considered the downfall of their religion and empire at hand, and for a time made scarcely any resistance to the invaders. Cities and strongholds surrendered almost without a blow. Babel is incidentally enumerated among the captured places; but the once all-powerful Babylon was now shrunk into such insignificance, that its capture seemed not worthy of a boast. Saad crossed the Tigris and advanced upon Madayn, the Persian capital. His army, on departing from Kadesia, had not exceeded twenty thousand men, having lost many by battle, and more by disease. Multitudes, however, from the subjugated cities, and from other parts, joined his standard while on the march, so that, as he approached Madayn, his forces amounted to sixty thousand men.

There was abundance of troops in Madayn, the wrecks of vanquished armies and routed garrisons, but there was no one capable or willing to take the general command. All seemed paralyzed by their

fears. The king summoned his counsellors about him, but their only advice was to fly. "Khorasan and Kerman are still yours," said they, "let
us depart while we may do so in safety; why should we remain here to
be made captives?"

Yezdegird hesitated to take this craven advice; but more from weakness and indecision of character than from any manly repugnance. He
wavered and lingered, until what might have been an orderly retreat
became a shameful flight. When the invaders were within one day's
march of his capital, he ordered his valuables to be packed upon beasts
of burthen, and set off, with a worthless retinue of palace minions, attendants, and slaves, male and female, for Holwân, at the foot of the
Medean hills. His example was followed throughout the city. There
was hurry and tumult in every part. Fortunate was he who had a
camel, or a horse, or an ass, to load with his most valuable effects; such
as were not so provided, took what they could on their shoulders; but,
in such a hasty and panic-stricken flight, where personal safety was the
chief concern, little could be preserved; the greater part of their riches
remained behind. Thus the wealthy Madayn, the once famous Ctesiphon, which had formerly repulsed a Roman army, though furnished
with battering-rams and other warlike engines, was abandoned without
a blow at the approach of these nomad warriors.

As Saad entered the deserted city, he gazed with wonder and admiration at its stately edifices, surrounded by vineyards and gardens, all
left to his mercy by the flying owners. In pious exultation he repeated
aloud a passage of the Koran, alluding to the abandonment by Pharaoh
and his troops of their habitations, when they went in pursuit of the
children of Israel. "How many gardens and fountains, and fields of
corn and fair dwellings, and other sources of delight did they leave behind them! Thus we dispossessed them thereof, and gave the same for
an inheritance to another people. Neither heaven nor earth wept for
them. They were unpitied."*

The deserted city was sacked and pillaged. One may imagine the
sacking of such a place by the ignorant hordes of the desert. The rude
Arabs beheld themselves surrounded by treasures beyond their conception; works of art, the value of which they could not appreciate, and
articles of luxury which moved their ridicule rather than their admiration. In roving through the streets they came to the famous palace of

* Koran, chapter xxiv.

the Khosrus, begun by Kobâd Ibn Firuz, and finished by his son Nu-shirwan, constructed of polished marble, and called the white palace, from its resplendent appearance. As they gazed at it in wonderment, they called to mind the prediction of Mahomet, when he heard that the haughty monarch of Persia had torn his letter: "Even so shall Allah rend his empire in pieces." "Behold the white palace of Khosru!" cried the Moslems to one another. "This is the fulfilment of the prophecy of the apostle of God!"

Saad entered the lofty portal of the palace with feelings of devotion. His first act was to make his salaam and prostrations, and pronounce the confession of faith in its deserted halls. He then took note of its contents, and protected it from the ravage of the soldiery, by making it his headquarters. It was furnished throughout with oriental luxury. It had wardrobes filled with gorgeous apparel. In the armory were weap-ons of all kinds, magnificently wrought: a coat of mail and sword, for state occasions, bedecked with jewels of incalculable value; a silver horseman on a golden horse, and a golden rider on a silver camel, all likewise studded with jewels.

In the vaults were treasures of gold and silver and precious stones; with money, the vast amount of which, though stated by Arabian histo-rians, we hesitate to mention.

In some of the apartments were gold and silver vessels filled with oriental perfumes. In the magazines were stored exquisite spices, odorif-erous gums, and medicinal drugs. Among the latter were quantities of camphor, which the Arabs mistook for salt, and mixed with their food.

In one of the chambers was a silken carpet of great size, which the king used in winter. Art and expense had been lavished upon it. It was made to represent a garden. The leaves of the plants were emeralds; the flowers were embroidered in their natural colors, with pearls and jew-els and precious stones; the fountains were wrought with diamonds and sapphires, to represent the sparkling of their waters. The value of the whole was beyond calculation.

The hall of audience surpassed every other part in magnificence. The vaulted roof, says D'Herbelot, resembled a firmament decked with golden spheres, each with a corresponding movement, so as to repre-sent the planets and the signs of the Zodiac. The throne was of prodi-gious grandeur, supported on silver columns. Above it was the crown of Khosru Nushirwan, suspended by a golden chain to bear the im-mense weight of its jewels, but contrived to appear as if on the head of the monarch when seated.

A mule is said to have been overtaken, on which a trusty officer of the palace was bearing away some of the jewels of the crown, the tiara or diadem of Yezdegird, with his belt and scimetar and bracelets.

Saad appointed Omar Ibn Mukry to take charge of all the spoils for regular distribution, and criers were sent about to make proclamation that the soldiers should render in their booty to that officer. Such was the enormous amount that, after a fifth had been set apart for the Caliph, the remainder, divided among sixty thousand men, gave each of them twelve hundred dirhems of silver.

It took nine hundred heavily laden camels to convey to Medina the Caliph's fifth of the spoil, among which the carpet, the clothing, and regalia of the king were included. The people of Medina, though of late years accustomed to the rich booty of the armies, were astonished at such an amount of treasure. Omar ordered that a mosque should be built of part of the proceeds. A consultation was held over the royal carpet, whether it should be stored away in the public treasury to be used by the Caliph on state occasions, or whether it should be included in the booty to be shared.

Omar hesitated to decide with his usual promptness, and referred the matter to Ali. "Oh prince of true believers!" exclaimed the latter; "how can one of thy clear perception doubt in this matter? In the world nothing is thine but what thou expendest in well-doing. What thou wearest will be worn out; what thou eatest will be consumed; but that which thou expendest in well-doing, is sent before thee to the other world."

Omar determined that the carpet should be shared among his chiefs. He divided it literally, with rigid equity, cutting it up without regard to the skill and beauty of the design, or its value as an entire piece of workmanship. Such was the richness of the materials, that the portion allotted to Ali alone, sold for eight thousand dirhems of silver.

This signal capture of the capital of Persia took place in the month Safar, in the sixteenth year of the Hegira, and the year 637 of the Christian era; the same year with the capture of Jerusalem. The fame of such immense spoil, such treasures of art in the hands of ignorant Arab soldiery, summoned the crafty and the avaricious from all quarters. All the world, it is said, flocked from the West, from Yemen, and from Egypt, to purchase the costly stuffs captured from the Persians. It was like the vultures, winging their way from all parts of the heavens, to gorge on the relics of a hunting camp.

CHAPTER XXIX

Capture of Jâlulâ – Flight of Yezdegird to Rei – Founding of Cufa – Saad receives a severe rebuke from the Caliph for his magnificence

Saab Ibn Abu Wakkâs would fain have pursued Yezdegird to Holwân, among the hills of ancient Media, where he had taken refuge; but he was restrained by the Caliph Omar, who kept a cautious check from Medina upon his conquering generals; fearful that in the flush and excitement of victory, they might hurry forward beyond the reach of succor. By the command of Omar, therefore, he remained with his main army in Madayn, and sent his brother Hashem with twelve thousand men in pursuit of the fugitive monarch. Hashem found a large force of Persians, relics of defeated armies, assembled in Jâlulâ, not far from Holwân, where they were disposed to make a stand. He laid siege to the place, but it was of great strength and maintained a brave and obstinate defence for six months, during which there were eighty assaults. At length, the garrison being reduced by famine and incessant fighting, and the commander slain, it surrendered.

Yezdegird on hearing of the capture of Jâlulâ abandoned the city of Holwân, leaving troops there under a general named Habesh, to check the pursuit of the enemy. The place of refuge which he now sought was the city of Rei, or Raï, the Rhages of Arrian; the Rhaga and Rhageia of the Greek geographers; a city of remote antiquity, contemporary, it is said, with Nineveh and Ecbatana, and mentioned in the book of Tobit; who, we are told, travelled from Nineveh to Rages, a city of Medea. It was a favorite residence of the Parthian kings in days of yore. In his flight through the mountains, the monarch was borne on a chair or litter between mules; travelling a station each day and sleeping in the litter. Habesh, whom he had left behind, was soon defeated, and followed him in his flight.

Saad again wrote to the Caliph, urging that he might be permitted to follow the Persian king to his place of refuge among the mountains, before he should have time to assemble another army; but he again met with a cautious check. "You have this year," said the Caliph, "taken Sawad and Irak; for Holwân is at the extremity of Irak. That is enough for the present. The welfare of true believers, is of more value than booty." So ended the sixteenth year of the Hegira.

The climate of Madayn proving unhealthy to his troops, and Saad wishing to establish a fortified camp in the midst of his victories, was

ordered by the Caliph to seek some favorable site on the western side
of the Euphrates, where there was good air, a well watered plain and
plenty of grass for the camels; things highly appreciated by the
Arabs.

Saad chose for the purpose the village of Cufa, which, according to
Moslem tradition, was the spot where Noah embarked in the Ark. The
Arabs further pretend that the serpent after tempting Eve was banished to this place. Hence, they say, the guile and treachery for which
the men of Cufa are proverbial. This city became so celebrated that
the Euphrates was at one time generally denominated Nahar Cufa, or
the river of Cufa. The most ancient characters of the Arabic alphabet
are termed Cufic to the present day.

In building Cufa, much of the stone, marble and timber for the
principal edifices were furnished from the ruins of Madayn; there
being such a scarcity of those materials in Babylonia and its vicinity,
that the houses were generally constructed of bricks baked in the sun
and cemented with bitumen. It used to be said, therefore, that the
army on its remove took with it all the houses of Sawad. Saad Ibn Abu
Wakkâs, who appears to have imbibed a taste for Persian splendor,
erected a sumptuous Kiosk or summer residence, and decorated it with
a grand portal taken from the palace of the Khosrus at Madayn. When
Omar heard of this he was sorely displeased, his great apprehension
being that his generals would lose the good old Arab simplicity of
manners in the luxurious countries they were conquering. He forthwith
dispatched a trusty envoy, Mahomet Ibn Muslemah, empowered to give
Saad a salutary rebuke. On arriving at Cufa, Mahomet caused a great
quantity of wood to be heaped against the door of the Kiosk, and set
fire to it. When Saad came forth in amazement at this outrage, Mahomet put into his hands, the following letter from the Caliph:

"I am told thou hast built a lofty palace, like to that of the Khosrus,
and decorated it with a door taken from the latter; with a view to have
guards and chamberlains stationed about it to keep off those who may
come in quest of justice or assistance, as was the practice of the Khosrus before thee. In so doing thou hast departed from the ways of the
prophet (on whom be benedictions), and hast fallen into the ways of
the Persian monarchs. Know that the Khosrus have passed from their
palace to the tomb; while the prophet, from his lowly habitation on
earth, has been elevated to the highest heaven. I have sent Mahomet
Ibn Muslemah to burn thy palace. In this world two houses are suffi-

cient for thee; one to dwell in, the other to contain the treasure of the Moslems."

Saad was too wary to make any opposition to the orders of the stern-minded Omar; so he looked on without a murmur as his stately Kiosk was consumed by the flames. He even offered Mahomet presents, which the latter declined, and returned to Medina. Saad removed to a different part of the city, and built a more modest mansion for himself, and another for the treasury.

In the same year with the founding of Cufa, the Caliph Omar married Omm Kolsam, the daughter of Ali and Fatima, and granddaughter of the prophet. This drew him in still closer bonds of friendship and confidence with Ali; who with Othman shared his counsels, and aided him in managing from Medina the rapidly accumulating affairs of the Moslem empire.

It must be always noted, that however stern and strict may appear the laws and ordinances of Omar, he was rigidly impartial in enforceing them; and one of his own sons, having been found intoxicated, received the twenty bastinadoes on the soles of the feet, which he had decreed for offences of the kind.

CHAPTER XXX

War with Hormuzân, the Satrap of Ahwâz – His subjugation and conversion

The founding of the city of Bassora had given great annoyance and uneasiness to Hormuzân, the satrap or viceroy of Ahwâz, or Susiana. His province lay between Babylonia and Farsistan, and he saw that this rising city of the Arabs was intended as a check upon him. His province was one of the richest and most important of Persia, producing cotton, rice, sugar, and wheat. It was studded with cities, which the historian Tabari compared to a cluster of stars. In the centre stood the metropolis Susa; one of the royal resorts of the Persian kings, celebrated in scriptural history, and said to possess the tomb of the prophet Daniel. It was once adorned with palaces and courts, and parks of prodigious extent, though now all is a waste, "echoing only to the roar of the lion, or yell of the hyæna."

Here Hormuzân, the satrap, emulated the state and luxury of a king. He was of a haughty spirit, priding himself upon his descent, his ancestors having once sat on the throne of Persia. For this reason his sons, being of the blood royal, were permitted to wear crowns, though of smaller size than those worn by kings, and his family was regarded with great deference by the Persians.

This haughty satrap, not rendered wary by the prowess of the Moslem arms, which he had witnessed and experienced at Kadesia, made preparations to crush the rising colony of Bassora. The founders of that city called on the Caliph for protection, and troops were marched to their assistance from Medina, and from the headquarters of Saad at Cufa. Hormuzân soon had reason to repent his having provoked hostilities. He was defeated in repeated battles, and at length was glad to make peace with the loss of half of his territories, and all but four of his cluster of cities. He was not permitted long to enjoy even this remnant of domain. Yezdegird, from his retreat at Rei, reproached Hormuzân and the satrap of the adjacent province of Farsistan, for not co-operating to withstand the Moslems. At his command they united their forces, and Hormuzân broke the treaty of peace which he had so recently concluded.

The devotion of Hormuzân to his fugitive sovereign ended in his ruin. The Caliph ordered troops to assemble from the different Moslem posts, and complete the conquest of Ahwâz. Hormuzân disputed his territory bravely, but was driven from place to place, until he made his last stand in the fortress of Ahwâz, or Susa. For six months he was beleaguered, during which time there were many sallies and assaults, and hard fighting on both sides. At length, Barâ Ibn Mâlek was sent to take command of the besiegers. He had been an especial favorite of the prophet, and there was a superstitious feeling concerning him. He manifested at all times an indifference to life or death; always pressed forward to the place of danger, and every action in which he served was successful.

On his taking the command, the troops gathered round him. "Oh Barâ! swear to overthrow these infidels, and the Most High will favor us."

Barâ swore that the place would be taken, and the infidels put to flight, but that he would fall a martyr.

In the very next assault, he was killed by an arrow sped by Hormuzân. The army took his death as a good omen. "One-half of his oath is fulfilled," said they, "and so will be the other."

Shortly afterward a Persian traitor came to Abu Shebrah, who had succeeded to the Moslem command, and revealed a secret entrance by a conduit under the castle, by which it was supplied with water. A hundred Moslems entered it by night, threw open the outward gates, and let in the army into the court-yards. Hormuzân was ensconced, however, in a strong tower, or keep, from the battlements of which he held a parley with the Moslem commander. "I have a thousand expert archers with me," said he, "who never miss their aim. By every arrow they discharge, you will lose a man. Avoid this useless sacrifice. Let me depart in honor; give me safe conduct to the Caliph, and let him dispose of me as he pleases."

It was agreed. Hormuzân was treated with respect as he issued from his fortress, and was sent under an escort to Medina. He maintained the air of one not conducted as a prisoner, but attended by a guard of honor. As he approached the city he halted, arrayed himself in sumptuous apparel, with his jewelled belt and regal crown, and in this guise entered the gates. The inhabitants gazed in astonishment at such unwonted luxury of attire.

Omar was not at his dwelling; he had gone to the mosque. Hormuzân was conducted thither. On approaching the sacred edifice, the Caliph's cloak was seen hanging against the wall, while he himself, arrayed in patched garments, lay asleep with his staff under his head.

The officers of the escort seated themselves at a respectful distance until he should awake. "This," whispered they to Hormuzân, "is the prince of true believers."

"This the Arab king!" said the astonished satrap; "and is this his usual attire?" "It is." "And does he sleep thus without guards?" "He does; he comes and goes alone; and lies down and sleeps where he pleases." "And can he administer justice, and conduct affairs without officers and messengers and attendants?" "Even so," was the reply. "This," exclaimed Hormuzân, at length, "is the condition of a prophet, but not of a king." "He is not a prophet," was the reply, "but he acts like one."

As the Caliph awoke he recognized the officers of the escort. "What tidings do you bring?" demanded he. – "But who is this so extravagantly arrayed?" rubbing his eyes as they fell upon the embroidered robes and jewelled crown of the satrap. "This is Hormuzân, the king of Ahwâz." "Take the infidel out of this place," cried he, turning away his head. "Strip him of his riches, and put on him the riches of Islam."

Hormuzân was accordingly taken forth, and in a little time was brought again before the Caliph, clad in a simple garb of the striped cloth of Yemen.

The Moslem writers relate various quibbles by which Hormuzân sought to avert the death with which he was threatened, for having slain Barâ Ibn Mâlek. He craved water to allay his thirst. A vessel of water was brought. Affecting to apprehend immediate execution: "Shall I be spared until I have drunk this?" Being answered by the Caliph in the affirmative, he dashed the vessel to the ground. "Now," said he, "you cannot put me to death, for I can never drink the water."

The straightforward Omar, however, was not to be caught by a quibble. "Your cunning will do you no good," said he. "Nothing will save you but to embrace Islamism." The haughty Hormuzân was subdued. He made the profession of faith in due style, and was at once enrolled among true believers.

He resided thenceforth in Medina; received rich presents from the Caliph, and subsequently gave him much serviceable information and advice in his prosecution of the war with Persia. The conquest of Ahwâz was completed in the nineteenth year of the Hegira.

CHAPTER XXXI

*Saad suspended from the command – A Persian army assembled at
Nehâvend – Council at the mosque of Medina – Battle of Nehâvend*

Omar, as we have seen, kept a jealous and vigilant eye upon his distant generals; being constantly haunted by the fear that they would become corrupted in the rich and luxurious countries they were invading, and lose that Arab simplicity which he considered inestimable in itself, and all-essential to the success of the cause of Islam. Notwithstanding the severe reproof he had given to Saad Ibn Abu Wakkâs in burning down his palace at Cufa, complaints still reached him that the general affected the pomp of a Caliph, that he was unjust and oppressive; unfair in the division of spoils, and slow in conducting military concerns. These charges proved, for the most part, unfounded, but they caused Saad to be suspended from his command until they could be investigated.

When the news reached Yezdegird at Rei that the Moslem general who had conquered at Kadesia, slain Rustam, captured Madayn, and driven himself to the mountains, was deposed from the command, he conceived fresh hopes, and wrote letters to all the provinces yet unconquered, calling on the inhabitants to take up arms and make a grand effort for the salvation of the empire. Nehâvend was appointed as the place where the troops were to assemble. It was a place of great antiquity, founded, says tradition, by Noah, and called after him, and was about fifteen leagues from Hamadân, the ancient Ecbatana. Here troops gathered together to the number of one hundred and fifty thousand.

Omar assembled his counsellors at the mosque of Medina, and gave them intelligence, just received, of this great armament. "This," said he, "is probably the last great effort of the Persians. If we defeat them now they will never be able to unite again." He expressed a disposition, therefore, to take the command in person. Strong objections were advanced. "Assemble troops from various parts," said Othman; "but remain, yourself, either at Medina, Cufa, or Holwân, to send reinforcements if required, or to form a rallying point for the Moslems, if defeated." Others gave different counsel. At length the matter was referred to Abbas Ibn Abd al Motâlleb, who was considered one of the sagest heads for counsel in the tribe of Koreish. He gave it as his opin-

ion that the Caliph should remain in Medina, and give the command
of the campaign to Nu'mân Ibn Mukry, who was already in Ahwâz,
where he had been ever since Saad had sent him thither from Irak. It
is singular to see the fate of the once mighty and magnificent empires
of the Orient, Syria, Chaldea, Babylonia, and the dominions of the
Medes and Persians, thus debated and decided in the mosque of Medina, by a handful of gray-headed Arabs, who but a few years previously had been homeless fugitives.

Orders were now sent to Nu'mân to march to Nehâvend, and reinforcements joined him from Medina, Bassora, and Cufa. His force,
when thus collected, was but moderate, but it was made up of men
hardened and sharpened by incessant warfare, rendered daring and
confident by repeated victory, and led by able officers. He was afterwards joined by ten thousand men from Sawad, Holwân, and other
places, many of whom were tributaries.

The Persian army now collected at Nchâvend was commanded by
Firuzân; he was old and infirm, but full of intelligence and spirit, and
the only remaining general considered capable of taking charge of such
a force, the best generals having fallen in battle. The veteran, knowing
the impetuosity of the Arab attack, and their superiority in the open
field, had taken a strong position, fortified his camp, and surrounded it
with a deep moat filled with water. Here he determined to tire out the
patience of the Moslems, and await an opportunity to strike a decisive
blow.

Nu'mân displayed his forces before the Persian camp, and repeatedly
offered battle, but the cautious veteran was not to be drawn out of his
intrenchments. Two months elapsed without any action, and the Moslem troops, as Firuzân had foreseen, began to grow discontented, and
to murmur at their general.

A stratagem was now resorted to by Nu'mân to draw out the enemy.
Breaking up his camp, he made a hasty retreat, leaving behind him
many articles of little value. The stratagem succeeded. The Persians
sallied, though cautiously, in pursuit. Nu'mân continued his feigned retreat for another day, still followed by the enemy. Having drawn them
to a sufficient distance from their fortified camp, he took up a position
at nightfall. "To-morrow," said he to his troops, "before the day red-
dens, be ready for battle. I have been with the prophet in many conflicts, and he always commenced battle after the Friday prayer."

The following day, when the troops were drawn out in order of battle, he made this prayer in their presence. "Oh Allah! sustain this day the cause of Islamism; give us victory over the infidels, and grant me the glory of martyrdom." Then turning to his officers, he expressed a presentiment that he should fall in the battle, and named the person who, in such case, should take the command.

He now appointed the signal for battle. "Three times," said he, "I will cry the tekbir, and each time will shake my standard. At the third time let every one fall on as I shall do." He gave the signal, Allah Achbar! Allah Achbar! Allah Achbar! At the third shaking of the standard, the tekbir was responded by the army, and the air was rent by the universal shout of Allah Achbar!

The shock of the two armies was terrific; they were soon enveloped in a cloud of dust, in which the sound of scimetars and battle-axes told the deadly work that was going on; while the shouts of Allah Achbar continued, mingled with furious cries and execrations of the Persians, and dismal groans of the wounded. In an hour the Persians were completely routed. "Oh Lord!" exclaimed Nu'mân in pious ecstasy, "my prayer for victory has been heard; may that for martyrdom be likewise favored!"

He advanced his standard in pursuit of the enemy, but at the same moment a Parthian arrow from the flying foe gave him the death he coveted. His body, with the face covered, was conveyed to his brother, and his standard given to Hadîfeh, whom he had named to succeed him in the command.

The Persians were pursued with great slaughter. Firuzân fled towards Hamadân, but was overtaken at midnight as he was ascending a steep hill, embarrassed among a crowd of mules and camels laden with the luxurious superfluities of a Persian camp. Here he and several thousand of his soldiers and camp-followers were cut to pieces. The booty was immense. Forty of the mules were found to be laden with honey; which made the Arabs say with a sneer, that Firuzân's army was clogged with its own honey, until overtaken by the true believers. The whole number of Persians slain in this battle, which sealed the fate of the empire, is said to have amounted to one hundred thousand. It took place in the twenty-first year of the Hegira, and the year 641 of the Christian era, and was commemorated among Moslems, as "The Victory of Victories."

On a day subsequent to the battle, a man mounted on an ass, rode into the camp of Hadîfeh. He was one who had served in the temples of the fire-worshippers, and was in great consternation, fearing to be sacrificed by the fanatic Moslems. "Spare my life," said he to Hadîfeh, "and the life of another person whom I shall designate, and I will deliver into your hands a treasure put under my charge by Yezdegird when he fled to Rei." His terms being promised, he produced a sealed box. On breaking the seal, Hadîfeh found it filled with rubies and precious stones of various colors, and jewels of great price. He was astonished at the sight of what appeared to him incalculable riches. "These jewels," said he, "have not been gained in battle, nor by the sword; we have, therefore, no right to any share in them." With the concurrence of his officers, therefore, he sent the box to the Caliph to be retained by himself or divided among the true believers as he should think proper. The officer who conducted the fifth part of the spoils to Medina, delivered the box, and related its history to Omar. The Caliph, little skilled in matters of luxury, and holding them in supreme contempt, gazed with an ignorant or scornful eye at the imperial jewels, and refused to receive them. "You know not what these things are," said he. "Neither do I; but they justly belong to those who slew the infidels, and to no one else." He ordered the officer, therefore, to depart forthwith and carry the box back to Hadîfeh. The jewels were sold by the latter to the merchants who followed the camp, and when the proceeds were divided among the troops, each horseman received for his share four thousand pieces of gold.

Far other was the conduct of the Caliph when he received the letter giving an account of the victory at Nehâvend. His first inquiry was after his old companion in the faith, Nu'mân. "May God grant you and him mercy!" was the reply. "He has become a martyr!"

Omar, it is said, wept. He next inquired who also were martyrs. Several were named with whom he was acquainted: but many who were unknown to him. "If I know them not," said he, piously quoting a text of the Koran, "God does!"

CHAPTER XXXII

Capture of Hamadân; of Rei – Subjugation of Tabaristan; of Azer-bîjân – Campaign among the Caucasian mountains

The Persian troops who had survived the signal defeat of Firuzân, assembled their broken forces near the city of Hamadân; but were soon routed again by a detachment sent against them by Hadîfeh, who had fixed his headquarters at Nehâvend. They then took refuge in Hamadân, and ensconced themselves in its strong fortress or citadel.

Hamadân was the second city in Persia for grandeur, and was built upon the site of Ecbatana, in old times the principal city of the Medes. There were more Jews among its inhabitants than were to be found in any other city of Persia, and it boasted of possessing the tombs of Esther and Mordecai. It was situated on a steep eminence, down the sides of which it descended into a fruitful plain, watered by streams gushing down from the lofty Orontes, now Mount Elwand. The place was commanded by Habesh, the same general who had been driven from Holwân after the flight of Yezdegird. Habesh sought an interview with Hadîfeh, at his encampment at Nehâvend, and made a treaty of peace with him; but it was a fraudulent one, and intended merely to gain time. Returning to Hamadân, he turned the whole city into a fortress, and assembled a strong garrison, being reinforced from the neighboring province of Azerbîjân.

On being informed of this want of good faith on the part of the governor of Hamadân, the Caliph Omar dispatched a strong force against the place, led by an able officer named Nu'haim Ibn Mukrin. Habesh had more courage than caution. Confident in the large force he had assembled, instead of remaining within his strongly fortified city, he sallied forth and met the Moslems in open field. The battle lasted for three days, and was harder fought than even that of Nehâvend, but ended in leaving the Moslems triumphant masters of the once formidable capital of Media.

Nu'haim now marched against Rei, late the place of refuge of Yezdegird. That prince, however, had deserted it on the approach of danger, leaving it in charge of a noble named Siyâwesh Ibn Barham. Hither the Persian princes had sent troops from the yet unconquered provinces, for Siyâwesh had nobly offered to make himself as a buckler to them, and conquer or fall in their defence. His patriotism was unavailing; treachery and corruption were too prevalent among the Persians. Zain, a powerful noble resident in Rei, and a deadly enemy of Siyâwesh, con-

spired to admit two thousand Moslems in at one gate of the city, at the
time when its gallant governor was making a sally by another. A scene
of tumult and carnage took place in the streets, where both armies engaged in deadly conflict. The patriot Siyâwesh was slain with a great
part of his troops; the city was captured and sacked, and its citadel destroyed, and the traitor Zain was rewarded for his treachery by being
made governor of the ruined place.

Nu'haim now sent troops in different directions against Kumish, and
Dameghân, and Jurgan (the ancient Hircania), and Tabaristan. They
met with feeble resistance. The national spirit was broken; even the national religion was nearly at an end. "This Persian religion of ours has
become obsolete," said Farkham, a military sage, to an assemblage of
commanders, who asked his advice; "the new religion is carrying every
thing before it; my advice is to make peace and pay tribute." His advice was adopted. All Tabaristan became tributary in the annual sum
of five hundred thousand dirhems, with the condition that the Moslems
should levy no troops in that quarter.

Azerbîjân was next invaded; the country which had sent troops to
the aid of Hamadân. This province lay north of Rei and Hamadân, and
extended to the Rocky Caucasus. It was the stronghold of the Magians
or Fire-worshippers, where they had their temples, and maintained
their perpetual fire. Hence the name of the country, Azer signifying
fire. The princes of the country made an ineffectual stand; their army
was defeated; the altars of the fire-worshippers were overturned; their
temples destroyed, and Azerbîjân won.

The arms of Islam had now been carried triumphantly to the very
defiles of the Caucasus; those mountains were yet to be subdued. Their
rocky sierras on the east separated Azerbîjân from Haziz and the shores
of the Caspian, and on the north from the vast Sarmatian regions. The
passes through these mountains were secured of yore, by fortresses and
walls and iron gates, to bar against irruptions from the shadowy land
of Gog and Magog, the terror of the olden time, for by these passes
had poured in the barbarous hordes of the north, "a mighty host all
riding upon horses," who lived in tents, worshipped the naked sword
planted in the earth, and decorated their steeds with the scalps of their
enemies slain in battle.*

---

* By some Gog and Magog are taken in an allegorical sense, signifying the
princes of heathendom, enemies of saints and the church.

According to the prophet Ezekiel, Gog was the king of Magog; Magog signifying the people, and Gog the king of the country. They are names that loom

Detachments of Moslems under different leaders penetrated the defiles of these mountains and made themselves masters of the Derbends, or mountain barriers. One of the most important, and which cost the greatest struggle, was a city or fortress called by the Persians Derbend; by the Turks Demir-Capi or the Gate of Iron, and by the Arabs Bab-el-abwâb (the Gate of Gates). It guards a defile between a promontory of Mount Caucasus and the Caspian Sea. A superstitious belief is still connected with it by the Moslems. Originally it had three gates; two only are left; one of these has nearly sunk into the earth; they say when it disappears the day of judgment will arrive.

---

vaguely and fearfully in the dark denunciations of the prophets; and in the olden time inspired awe throughout the eastern world.

The Arabs, says Sale, call Gog and Magog, Yâjûj and Mâjûj, and say they are two nations or tribes descended from Japhet, the son of Noah; or, as others write, Gog is a tribe of the Turks, and Magog those of Gilan; the Geli and the Gelæ of Ptolemy and Strabo. They made their irruptions into the neighboring countries in the spring, and carried off all the fruits of the earth. – *Sale's Koran*, note to ch. 18.

According to Moslem belief, a great irruption of Gog and Magog is to be one of the signs of the latter days, forerunning the resurrection and final judgment. They are to come from the north in a mighty host, covering the land as a cloud; so that when subdued, their shields and bucklers, their bows and arrows and quivers, and the staves of their spears, shall furnish the faithful with fuel for seven years. – All which is evidently derived from the book of the prophet Ezekiel; with which Mahomet had been made acquainted by his Jewish instructors.

The Koran makes mention of a wall built as a protection against these fearful people of the north by Dhu'lkarneim, or the Two Horned; by whom some suppose is meant Alexander the Great, others a Persian king of the first race, contemporary with Abraham.

And they said, O Dhu'lkarneim, verily Gog and Magog waste the land. . . . He answered, I will set a strong wall between you and them. Bring me iron in large pieces, until it fill up the space between the two sides of these mountains. And he said to the workmen, Blow with your bellows until it make the iron red hot; and bring me molten brass, that I may pour upon it. Wherefore, when this wall was finished, Gog and Magog could not scale it, neither could they dig through it. – *Sale's Koran*, chap. 18.

The Czar Peter the Great, in his expedition against the Persians, saw in the neighborhood of the city of Derbend, which was then besieged, the ruins of a wall which went up hill and down dale, along the Caucasus, and was said to extend from the Euxine to the Caspian. It was fortified from place to place, by towers or castles. It was eighteen Russian stades in height; built of stones laid up dry; some of them three ells long and very wide. The color of the stones, and the traditions of the country, showed it to be of great antiquity. The Arabs and Persians said that it was built against the invasions of Gog and Magog. – See *Travels in the East, by Sir William Ouseley*.

Abda'lrahman Ibn Rabïah, one of the Moslem commanders who penetrated the defiles of the Caucasus, was appointed by Omar to the command of the Derbends or passes, with orders to keep vigilant watch over them; for the Caliph was in continual solicitude about the safety of the Moslems on these remote expeditions, and was fearful that the Moslem troops might be swept away by some irruption from the north.

Abda'lrahman, with the approbation of the Caliph, made a compact with Shahr-Zad, one of the native chiefs, by which the latter, in consideration of being excused from paying tribute, undertook to guard the Derbends against the northern hordes. The Arab general had many conversations with Shahr-Zad about the mountains, which are favored regions of Persian romance and fable. His imagination was fired with what he was told about the people beyond the Derbends, the Allâni and the Rus; and about the great wall or barrier of Yâjûj and Mâjûj, built to restrain their inroads.

In one of the stories told by Shahr-Zad, the reader will perceive the germ of the Arabian tales of Sindbad the Sailor. It is recorded to the following purport, by Tabari, the Persian historian: "One day as Abda'lrahman was seated by Shahr-Zad, conversing with him, he perceived upon his finger a ring decorated with a ruby, which burned like fire in the daytime, but at night was of dazzling brilliancy. 'It came,' said Shahr-Zad, 'from the wall of Yâjûj and Mâjûj; from a king whose dominion between the mountains is traversed by the wall. I sent him many presents, and asked but one ruby in return.' Seeing the curiosity of Abda'lrahman aroused, he sent for the man who had brought the ring, and commanded him to relate the circumstances of his errand.

" 'When I delivered the presents and the letter of Shahr-Zad to that king,' said the man, 'he called his chief falconer, and ordered him to procure the jewel required. The falconer kept an eagle for three days without food, until he was nearly starved; he then took him up into the mountains near the wall, and I accompanied him. From the summit of one of these mountains, we looked down into a deep dark chasm like an abyss. The falconer now produced a piece of tainted meat; threw it into the ravine, and let loose the eagle. He swept down after it; pounced upon it as it reached the ground, and returning with it, perched upon the hand of the falconer. The ruby which now shines in that ring was found adhering to the meat.'

"Abda'lrahman asked an account of the wall. 'It is built,' replied the man, 'of stone, iron, and brass, and extends down one mountain and up another.' 'This,' said the devout and all-believing Abda'lrahman, 'must be the very wall of which the Almighty makes mention in the Koran.'

"He now inquired of Shahr-Zad what was the value of the ruby. 'No one knows its value,' was the reply; 'though presents to an immense amount had been made in return for it.' Shahr-Zad now drew the ring from his finger, and offered it to Abda'lrahman, but the latter refused to accept it, saying that a gem of that value was not suitable to him. 'Had you been one of the Persian kings,' said Shahr-Zad, 'you would have taken it from me by force; but men who conduct like you will conquer all the world.'"

The stories which he had heard, had such an effect upon Abda'lrahman, that he resolved to make a foray into the mysterious country beyond the Derbends. Still it could only be of a partial nature, as he was restrained from venturing far by the cautious injunctions of Omar. "Were I not fearful of displeasing the Caliph," said he, "I would push forward even to Yâjûj and Mâjûj, and make converts of all the infidels."

On issuing from the mountains, he found himself among a barbarous people, the ancestors of the present Turks, who inhabited a region of country between the Euxine and the Caspian seas. A soldier who followed Abda'lrahman in this foray gave the following account of these people to the Caliph on his return to Medina. "They were astonished," said he, "at our appearance, so different from their old enemies the Persians, and asked us, 'Are you angels, or the sons of Adam?' to which we replied, 'We are sons of Adam; but the angels of heaven are on our side and aid us in our warfare.'"

The infidels forbore to assail men thus protected; one, however, more shrewd or dubious than the rest, stationed himself behind a tree, sped an arrow and slew a Moslem. The delusion was at an end; the Turks saw that the strangers were mortal, and from that time there was hard fighting. Abda'lrahman laid siege to a place called Belandscher, the city or stronghold of the Bulgarians or Huns, another semi-barbarous and warlike people like the Turks, who, like them had not yet made themselves world-famous by their conquering migrations. The Turks came to the aid of their neighbors; a severe battle took place, the Moslems were defeated, and Abda'lrahman paid for his daring enterprise and romantic curiosity with his life. The Turks, who still appear to have retained a superstitious opinion of their unknown invaders, preserved the body of the unfortunate general as a relic, and erected a shrine in honor of it, at which they used to put up their prayers for rain in time of drought.

The troops of Abda'lrahman retreated within the Derbends; his brother Selman Ibn Rabïah was appointed to succeed him in the command of the Caucasian passes, and thus ended the unfortunate foray into the land of Gog and Magog.

CHAPTER XXXIII

The Caliph Omar assassinated by a fire-worshipper – His character
– Othman elected Caliph

The life and reign of the Caliph Omar, distinguished by such great and striking events, were at length brought to a sudden and sanguinary end. Among the Persians who had been brought as slaves to Medina, was one named Firuz, of the sect of the Magi, or fire-worshippers. Being taxed daily by his master two pieces of silver out of his earnings, he complained of it to Omar as an extortion. The Caliph inquired into his condition, and, finding that he was a carpenter, and expert in the construction of windmills, replied, that the man who excelled in such a handicraft could well afford to pay two dirhems a day. "Then," muttered Firuz, "I'll construct a windmill for you that shall keep grinding until the day of judgment." Omar was struck with his menacing air. "The slave threatens me," said he, calmly. "If I were disposed to punish any one on suspicion, I should take off his head;" he suffered him, however, to depart without further notice.

Three days afterwards, as he was praying in the mosque, Firuz entered suddenly and stabbed him thrice with a dagger. The attendants rushed upon the assassin. He made furious resistance, slew some and wounded others, until one of his assailants threw his vest over him and seized him, upon which he stabbed himself to the heart and expired. Religion may have had some share in prompting this act of violence; perhaps revenge for the ruin brought upon his native country. "God be thanked," said Omar, "that he by whose hand it was decreed I should fall, was not a Moslem!"

The Caliph gathered strength sufficient to finish the prayer in which he had been interrupted; "for he who deserts his prayers," said he, "is not in Islam." Being taken to his house, he languished three days without hope of recovery, but could not be prevailed upon to nominate a successor. "I cannot presume to do that," said he, "which the prophet himself did not do." Some suggested that he should nominate his son Abdallah. "Omar's family," said he, "has had enough in Omar, and needs no more." He appointed a council of six persons to determine as to the succession after his decease; all of whom he considered worthy of the Caliphat; though he gave it as his opinion that the choice would be either Ali or Othman. "Shouldst thou become Caliph," said he to Ali, "do not favor thy relatives above all others, nor place the house of Haschem on the neck of all mankind;" and he gave the same caution to Othman in respect to the family of Omeya.

Calling for ink and paper, he wrote a letter, as his last testament, to whosoever might be his successor, full of excellent counsel for the upright management of affairs, and the promotion of the faith. He charged his son Abdallah in the most earnest manner, as one of the highest duties of Islamism, to repay eighteen thousand dirhems which he had borrowed out of the public treasury. All present protested against this as unreasonable, since the money had been expended in relief of the poor and destitute, but Omar insisted upon it as his last will. He then sent to Ayesha and procured permission of her to be buried next to her father Abu Beker.

Ibn Abbas and Ali now spoke to him in words of comfort, setting forth the blessings of Islam, which had crowned his administration, and that he would leave no one behind him who could charge him with injustice. "Testify this for me," said he, earnestly, "at the day of judgment." They gave him their hands in promise: but he exacted that they should give him a written testimonial, and that it should be buried with him in the grave.

Having settled all his worldly affairs, and given directions about his sepulture, he expired, the seventh day after his assassination, in the sixty-third year of his age, after a triumphant reign of ten years and six months.

His death was rashly and bloodily revenged. Mahomet Ibn Abu Beker, the brother of Ayesha, and imbued with her mischief-making propensity, persuaded Abdallah, the son of Omar, that his father's murder was the result of a conspiracy; Firuz having been instigated to the act by his daughter Lulu, a Christian named Dschofeine, and Hormuzân, the once haughty and magnificent Satrap of Susiana. In the transport of his rage, and instigated by the old Arab principle of blood revenge, Abdallah slew all three of the accused; without reflecting on the improbability of Hormuzân, at least, being accessory to the murder; being, since his conversion, in close friendship with the late Caliph; and his adviser, on many occasions, in the prosecution of the Persian war.

The whole history of Omar shows him to have been a man of great powers of mind, inflexible integrity, and rigid justice. He was, more than any one else, the founder of the Islam empire; confirming and carrying out the inspirations of the prophet; aiding Abu Beker with his

counsels during his brief Caliphat; and establishing wise regulations
for the strict administration of the laws throughout the rapidly-extend-
ing bounds of the Moslem conquests. The rigid hand which he kept
upon his most popular generals in the midst of their armies, and in the
most distant scenes of their triumphs, give signal evidence of his extraordinary capacity to rule. In the simplicity of his habits, and his contempt for all pomp and luxury, he emulated the example of the
prophet and Abu Beker. He endeavored incessantly to impress the
merit and policy of the same in his letters to his generals. "Beware," he
would say, "of Persian luxury both in food and raiment. Keep to the
simple habits of your country, and Allah will continue you victorious;
depart from them, and he will reverse your fortunes." It was his strong
conviction of the truth of this policy, which made him so severe in
punishing all ostentatious style and luxurious indulgence in his officers.

Some of his ordinances do credit to his heart as well as his head. He
forbade that any female captive who had borne a child should be sold
as a slave. In his weekly distributions of the surplus money of his treasury, he proportioned them to the wants, not the merits of the applicants. "God," said he, "has bestowed the good things of this world to
relieve our necessities, not to reward our virtues: those will be rewarded in another world."

One of the early measures of his reign was the assigning pensions to
the most faithful companions of the prophet, and those who had signalized themselves in the early service of the faith. Abbas, the uncle of the
prophet, had a yearly pension of 200,000 dirhems; others of his relatives in graduated proportions; those veterans who had fought in the
battle of Beder 5000 dirhems; pensions of less amount to those who had
distinguished themselves in Syria, Persia, and Egypt. Each of the
prophet's wives was allowed ten thousand dirhems yearly, and Ayesha
twelve thousand. Hassan and Hosein, the sons of Ali and grandsons of
the prophet, had each a pension of five thousand dirhems. On any one
who found fault with these disbursements out of the public wealth,
Omar invoked the curse of Allah.

He was the first to establish a chamber of accounts or exchequer; the
first to date events from the Hegira or flight of the prophet; and the
first to introduce a coinage into the Moslem dominions; stamping the
coins with the name of the reigning Caliph, and the words, "There is
no God but God."

During his reign, we are told, there were thirty-six thousand towns, castles, and strongholds taken; but he was not a wasteful conqueror. He founded new cities; established important marts; built innumerable mosques, and linked the newly acquired provinces into one vast empire by his iron inflexibility of purpose. As has well been observed, "his Caliphat, crowned with the glories of its triple conquest of Syria, Persia, and Egypt, deserves to be distinguished as the heroic age of Saracen history. The gigantic foundations of the Saracenic power were perfected in the short space of less than ten years." Let it be remembered, moreover, that this great conqueror, this great legislator, this magnanimous sovereign, was originally a rude half-instructed Arab of Mecca. Well may we say in regard to the early champions of Islam, "there were giants in those days."

After the death of Omar, the six persons met together whom he had named as a council to elect his successor. They were Ali, Othman, Telha, Ibn Obeid'allah (Mahomet's son-in-law), Zobeir, Abda'lrahman Ibn Awf, and Saad Ibn Abu Wakkâs. They had all been personally intimate with Mahomet, and were therefore styled THE COMPANIONS.

After much discussion and repeated meetings the Caliphat was offered to Ali, on condition that he would promise to govern according to the Koran and the traditions of Mahomet, and the regulations established by the two seniors or elders; meaning the two preceding Caliphs Abu Beker and Omar.

Ali replied, that he would govern according to the Koran and the authentic traditions; but would, in all other respects, act according to his own judgment, without reference to the example of the seniors. This reply not being satisfactory to the council, they made the same proposal to Othman Ibn Affân, who assented to all the conditions, and was immediately elected, and installed three days after the death of his predecessor. He was seventy years of age at the time of his election. He was tall and swarthy, and his long gray beard was tinged with henna. He was strict in his religious duties; fasting, meditating, and studying the Koran; not so simple in his habits as his predecessors, but prone to expense and lavish of his riches. His bountiful spirit, however, was evinced at times in a way that gained him much popularity. In a time of famine he had supplied the poor of Medina with corn. He had purchased at great cost the ground about the mosque of Medina, to give room for houses for the prophet's wives. He had contributed six hundred and fifty camels and fifty horses for the campaign against Tabuc.

He derived much respect among zealous Moslems for having married two of the prophet's daughters; and for having been in both of the Hegiras, or flights, the first into Abyssinia, the second, the memorable flight to Medina. Mahomet used to say of him, "Each thing has its mate, and each man his associate: my associate in paradise is Othman."

Scarcely was the new Caliph installed in office, when the retaliatory punishment prescribed by the law was invoked upon Obeid'allah, the son of Omar, for the deaths so rashly inflicted on those whom he had suspected of instigating his father's assassination. Othman was perplexed between the letter of the law and the odium of following the murder of the father by the execution of the son. He was kindly relieved from his perplexity by the suggestion, that as the act of Obeid'allah took place in the interregnum between the Caliphats of Omar and Othman, it did not come under the cognizance of either. Othman gladly availed himself of the quibble; Obeid'allah escaped unpunished, and the sacrifice of the once magnificent Hormuzân and his fellow-victims remained unavenged.

CHAPTER XXXIV

Conclusion of the Persian conquest – Flight and death of Yezdegird

The proud empire of the Khosrus had received its death-blow during the vigorous Caliphat of Omar; what signs of life it yet gave were but its dying struggles. The Moslems, led by able generals, pursued their conquests in different directions. Some, turning to the west, urged their triumphant way through ancient Assyria; crossed the Tigris by the bridge of Mosul, passing the ruins of mighty Nineveh as unheedingly as they had passed those of Babylon; completed the subjugation of Mesopotamia, and planted their standards beside those of their brethren who had achieved the conquest of Syria.

Others directed their course into the southern and eastern provinces, following the retreating steps of Yezdegird. A fiat issued by the late Caliph Omar had sealed the doom of that unhappy monarch. "Pursue the fugitive king wherever he may go, until you have driven him from the face of the earth!"

Yezdegird, after abandoning Rei, had led a wandering life, shifting from city to city and province to province, still flying at the approach of danger. At one time we hear of him in the splendid city of Ispahan; next among the mountains of Farsistan, the original Persis, the cradle of the conquerors of Asia; and it is another of the lessons furnished by history, to see the last of the Khosrus a fugitive among those mountains whence, in foregone times, Cyrus had led his hardy but frugal and rugged bands to win, by force of arms, that vast empire which was now falling to ruin through its effeminate degeneracy.

For a time the unhappy monarch halted in Istakar, the pride of Persia, where the tottering remains of Persepolis, and its hall of a thousand columns, speak of the ancient glories of the Persian kings. Here Yezdegird had been fostered and concealed during his youthful days, and here he came near being taken among the relics of Persian magnificence.

From Farsistan he was driven to Kerman, the ancient Carmania; thence into Korassan; in the northern part of which vast province he took breath at the city of Merv, or Merou, on the remote boundary of Bactriana. In all his wanderings he was encumbered by the shattered pageant of an oriental court, a worthless throng which had fled with him from Madayn, and which he had no means of supporting. At Merv he had four thousand persons in his train; all minions of the palace, useless hangers-on, porters, grooms, and slaves; together with his wives and concubines, and their female attendants.

In this remote halting-place he devoted himself to building a fire-temple; in the meantime he wrote letters to such of the cities and provinces as were yet unconquered, exhorting his governors and generals to defend, piece by piece, the fragments of empire which he had deserted.

The city of Ispahan, one of the brightest jewels of his crown, was well garrisoned by wrecks of the army of Nehâvend, and might have made brave resistance; but its governor, Kadeskan, staked the fortunes of the place upon a single combat with the Moslem commander who had invested it, and capitulated at the first shock of lances; probably through some traitorous arrangement.

Ispahan has never recovered from that blow. Modern travellers speak of its deserted streets, its abandoned palaces, its silent bazaars. "I have ridden for miles among its ruins," says one, "without meeting any living creature, excepting, perhaps, a jackal peeping over a wall, or a fox running into his hole. Now and then an inhabited house was to be seen, the owner of which might be assimilated to Job's forlorn man dwelling in desolate cities, and in houses which no man inhabiteth; which are ready to become heaps."

Istakar made a nobler defence. The national pride of the Persians was too much connected with this city, once their boast, to let it fall without a struggle. There was another gathering of troops from various parts; one hundred and twenty thousand are said to have united under the standard of Shah-reg, the patriotic governor. It was all in vain. The Persians were again defeated in a bloody battle; Shah-reg was slain, and Istakar, the ancient Persepolis, once almost the mistress of the Eastern world, was compelled to pay tribute to the Arabian Caliph.

The course of Moslem conquest now turned into the vast province of Khorassan; subdued one part of it after another, and approached the remote region where Yezdegird had taken refuge. Driven to the boundaries of his dominions, the fugitive monarch crossed the Oxus (the ancient Gihon) and the sandy deserts beyond, and threw himself among the shepherd hordes of Scythia. His wanderings are said to have extended to the borders of Tshin, or China, from the emperor of which he sought assistance.

Obscurity hangs over this part of his story: it is affirmed that he succeeded in obtaining aid from the great Khan of the Tartars, and, re-crossing the Gihon, was joined by the troops of Balkh or Bactria, which province was still unsubdued and loyal. With these he endeavored to make a stand against his unrelenting pursuers. A slight reverse, or some secret treachery, put an end to the adhesion of his barbarian ally. The Tartar chief returned with his troops to Turkestan.

Yezdegird's own nobles, tired of following his desperate fortunes, now conspired to betray him and his treasures into the hands of the Moslems as a price for their own safety. He was at that time at Merv, or Merou, on the Oxus, called Merou al Roud, or 'Merou of the River,' to distinguish it from Merou in Khorassan. Discovering the intended treachery of his nobles, and of the governor of the place, he caused his slaves to let him down with cords from a window of his palace, and fled, alone and on foot, under cover of the night. At the break of day he found himself near a mill, on the banks of the river, only eight miles from the city, and offered the miller his ring and bracelets, enriched with gems, if he would ferry him across the stream. The boor, who knew nothing of jewels, demanded four silver oboli, or drachms, the amount of a day's earnings, as a compensation for leaving his work. While they were debating, a party of horsemen, who were in pursuit of the king, came up and clove him with their scimetars. Another account states that, exhausted and fatigued with the weight of his embroidered garments, he sought rest and concealment in the mill, and that the miller spread a mat, on which he lay down and slept. His rich attire, however, his belt of gold studded with jewels, his rings and bracelets, excited the avarice of the miller, who slew him with an axe while he slept, and, having stripped the body, threw it into the water. In the morning several horsemen, in search of him, arrived at the mill, where discovering, by his clothes and jewels, that he had been murdered, they put the miller to death.

This miserable catastrophe to a miserable career is said to have occurred on the 23d August, in the year 651 of the Christian era. Yezdegird was in the thirty-fourth year of his age; having reigned nine years previous to the battle of Nehâvend, and since that event having been ten years a fugitive. History lays no crimes to his charge, yet his hard fortunes and untimely end have failed to awaken the usual interest and sympathy. He had been schooled in adversity from his early youth, yet he failed to profit by it. Carrying about with him the wretched relics of an effeminate court, he sought only his personal safety, and wanted the courage and magnanimity to throw himself at the head of his armies, and battle for his crown and country like a great sovereign and a patriot prince.

Empires, however, like all other things, have their allotted time, and die, if not by violence, at length of imbecility and old age. That of Persia had long since lost its stamina, and the energy of a Cyrus would have been unable to infuse new life into its gigantic but palsied limbs. At the death of Yezdegird it fell under the undisputed sway of the Caliphs, and became little better than a subject province.*

* According to popular traditions in Persia, Yezdegird, in the course of his wanderings, took refuge for a time in the castle of Fahender, near Schiraz, and buried the crown jewels and treasures of Nushirwan, in a deep pit or well under the castle, where they still remain guarded by a talisman, so that they cannot be found or drawn forth. Others say that he had them removed and deposited in trust with the Khacan, or emperor of Chin or Tartary. After the extinction of the royal Persian dynasty, those treasures and the crown remained in Chin. – *Sir William Ouseley's Travels in the East,* vol. ii. p. 34.

CHAPTER XXXV

*Amru displaced from the government of Egypt – Revolt of the in-
habitants – Alexandria retaken by the imperialists – Amru reinstated
in command – Retakes Alexandria, and tranquillizes Egypt – Is again
displaced – Abdallah Ibn Saad invades the north of Africa*

"In the conquests of Syria, Persia, and Egypt," says a modern writer,
"the fresh and vigorous enthusiasm of the personal companions and
proselytes of Mahomet was exercised and expended, and the generation
of warriors whose simple fanaticism had been inflamed by the preaching of the pseudo prophet, was in a great measure consumed in the
sanguinary and perpetual toils of ten arduous campaigns."

We shall now see the effect of those conquests on the national character and habits; the avidity of place and power and wealth, superseding religious enthusiasm; and the enervating luxury and soft voluptuousness of Syria and Persia sapping the rude but masculine simplicity of the Arabian desert. Above all, the single-mindedness of Mahomet
and his two immediate successors is at an end. Other objects beside the
mere advancement of Islamism distract the attention of its leading professors; and the struggle for wordly wealth and wordly sway, for the
advancement of private ends, and the aggrandizement of particular
tribes and families, destroy the unity of the empire, and beset the Caliphat with intrigue, treason, and bloodshed.

It was a great matter of reproach against the Caliph Othman that he
was injudicious in his appointments, and had an inveterate propensity
to consult the interests of his relatives and friends before that of the
public. One of his greatest errors in this respect was the removal of
Amru Ibn Al Aass from the government of Egypt, and the appointment
of his own foster brother Abdallah Ibn Saad in his place. This was the
same Abdallah who, in acting as amanuensis to Mahomet, and writing
down his revelations, had interpolated passages of his own, sometimes
of a ludicrous nature. For this, and for his apostasy, he had been pardoned by Mahomet at the solicitation of Othman, and had ever since
acted with apparent zeal; his interest coinciding with this duty.

He was of a courageous spirit, and one of the most expert horsemen
of Arabia; but what might have fitted him to command a horde of the
desert, was insufficient for the government of a conquered province.
He was new and inexperienced in his present situation; whereas Amru
had distinguished himself as a legislator as well as a conqueror, and
had already won the affections of the Egyptians by his attention to

their interests, and his respect for their customs and habitudes. His dismission was, therefore, resented by the people, and a disposition was manifested to revolt against the new governor.

The emperor Constantine, who had succeeded to his father Heraclius, hastened to take advantage of these circumstances. A fleet and army were sent against Alexandria under a prefect named Manuel. The Greeks in the city secretly co-operated with him, and the metropolis was, partly by force of arms, partly by treachery, recaptured by the imperialists without much bloodshed.

Othman, made painfully sensible of the error he had commited, hastened to revoke the appointment of his foster brother, and reinstated Amru in the command in Egypt. That able general went instantly against Alexandria with an army, in which were many Copts, irreconcilable enemies of the Greeks. Among these was the traitor Makawkas, who, from his knowledge of the country, and his influence among its inhabitants, was able to procure abundant supplies for the army.

The Greek garrison defended the city bravely and obstinately. Amru, enraged at having thus again to lay siege to a place which he had twice already taken, swore, by Allah, that if he should master it a third time, he would render it as easy of access as a brothel. He kept his word, for when he took the city he threw down the walls and demolished all the fortifications. He was merciful, however, to the inhabitants, and checked the fury of the Saracens, who were slaughtering all they met. A mosque was afterwards erected on the spot at which he stayed the carnage, called the Mosque of Mercy. Manuel, the Greek general, found it expedient to embark with all speed with such of his troops as he could save, and make sail for Constantinople.

Scarce, however, had Amru quelled every insurrection and secured the Moslem domination in Egypt, when he was again displaced from the government, and Abdallah Ibn Saad appointed a second time in his stead.

Abdallah had been deeply mortified by the loss of Alexandria, which had been ascribed to his incapacity; he was emulous too of the renown of Amru, and felt the necessity of vindicating his claims to command by some brilliant achievement. The north of Africa presented a new field for Moslem enterprise. We allude to that vast tract extending west from the desert of Libya or Barca, to Cape Non, embracing more than two thousand miles of sea-coast; comprehending the ancient divisions of Mamarica, Cyrenaica, Carthage, Numidia, and Mauritania; or, according to modern geographical designations, Barca, Tripoli, Tunis, Algiers, and Morocco.

A few words respecting the historical vicissitudes of this once powerful region may not be inappropriate. The original inhabitants are supposed to have come at a remote time from Asia; or rather, it said that an influx of Arabs drove the original inhabitants from the sea-coast to the mountains, and the borders of the interior desert, and continued their nomad and pastoral life along the shores of the Mediterranean. About nine hundred years before the Christian era, the Phœnicians of Tyre founded colonies along the coast; of these Carthage was the greatest. By degrees it extended its influence along the African shores and the opposite coast of Spain, and rose in prosperity and power until it became a rival republic to Rome. On the wars between Rome and Carthage it is needless to dilate. They ended in the downfall of the Carthaginian republic and the domination of Rome over Northern Africa.

This domination continued for about four centuries, until the Roman prefect Bonifacius invited over the Vandals from Spain to assist him in a feud with a political rival. The invitation proved fatal to Roman ascendency. The Vandals, aided by the Moors and Berbers, and by numerous Christian sectarians recently expelled from the Catholic church, aspired to gain possession of the country, and succeeded. Genseric, the Vandal general, captured and pillaged Carthage, and having subjugated Northern Africa, built a navy, invaded Italy and sacked Rome. The domination of the Vandals by sea and land lasted above half a century. In 533 and 534, Africa was regained by Belisarius for the Roman empire, and the Vandals were driven out of the land. After the departure of Belisarius, the Moors rebelled and made repeated attempts to get the dominion, but were as often defeated with great loss, and the Roman sway was once more established.

All these wars and changes had a disastrous effect on the African provinces. The Vandals had long disappeared; many of the Moorish families had been extirpated; the wealthy inhabitants had fled to Sicily and Constantinople, and a stranger might wander whole days over regions, once covered with towns and cities, and teeming with population, without meeting a human being.

For near a century the country remained sunk in apathy and inaction, until now it was to be roused from its torpor by the all-pervading armies of Islam.

Soon after the reappointment of Abdallah to the government of Egypt, he set out upon the conquest of this country, at the head of forty thousand Arabs. After crossing the western boundary of Egypt he had to traverse the desert of Libya, but his army was provided with camels accustomed to the sandy wastes of Arabia, and, after a toilsome march, he encamped before the walls of Tripoli; then as now, one of the most wealthy and powerful cities of the Barbary coast. The place was well fortified and made good resistance. A body of Greek troops which were sent to reinforce it, were surprised by the besiegers on the sea-coast, and dispersed with great slaughter.

The Roman prefect Gregorius having assembled an army of one hundred and twenty thousand men, a great proportion of whom were the hastily levied and undisciplined tribes of Barbary, advanced to defend his province. He was accompanied by an Amazonian daughter of wonderful beauty, who had been taught to manage the horse, to draw the bow and wield the scimetar, and who was always at her father's side in battle.

Hearing of the approach of this army, Abdallah suspended the siege and advanced to meet it. A brief parley took place between the hostile commanders. Abdallah proposed the usual alternatives, profession of Islamism, or payment of tribute. Both were indignantly rejected. The armies engaged before the walls of Tripoli. Abdallah, whose fame was staked on this enterprise, stimulated his troops by word and example, and charged the enemy repeatedly at the head of his squadrons. Wherever he pressed, the fortune of the day would incline in favor of the Moslems; but on the other hand Gregorius fought with desperate bravery, as the fate of the province depended on this conflict; and wherever he appeared, his daughter was at his side, dazzling all eyes by the splendor of her armor and the heroism of her achievements. The contest was long, arduous, and uncertain. It was not one pitched battle, but a succession of conflicts, extending through several days, beginning at early dawn, but ceasing toward noon, when the intolerable heat of the sun obliged both armies to desist, and seek the shade of their tents.

The prefect Gregorius was exasperated at being in a manner held at bay by an inferior force, which he had expected to crush by the superiority of numbers. Seeing that Abdallah was the life and soul of his army, he proclaimed a reward of one hundred thousand pieces of gold and the hand of his daughter to the warrior who should bring him his head.

The excitement caused among the Grecian youth by this tempting prize, made the officers of Abdallah tremble for his safety. They represented to him the importance of his life to the army and the general cause, and prevailed upon him to keep aloof from the field of battle. His absence, however, produced an immediate change, and the valor of his troops, hitherto stimulated by his presence, began to languish.

Zobeir, a noble Arab of the tribe of Koreish, arrived at the field of battle with a small reinforcement, in the heat of one of the engagements. He found the troops fighting to a disadvantage, and looked round in vain for the general. Being told that he was in his tent, he hastened thither and reproached him with his inactivity. Abdallah blushed, but explained the reason of his remaining passive. "Retort on the infidel commander his perfidious bribe," cried Zobeir; "proclaim that his daughter as a captive, and one hundred thousand pieces of gold, shall be the reward of the Moslem who brings his head." The advice was adopted, as well as the following stratagem suggested by Zobeir. On the next morning, Abdallah sent forth only sufficient force to keep up a defensive fight; but, when the sun had reached its noontide height, and the panting troops retired as usual to their tents, Abdallah and Zobeir sallied forth at the head of the reserve, and charged furiously among the fainting Greeks. Zobeir singled out the prefect, and slew him after a well contested fight. His daughter pressed forward to avenge his death, but was surrounded and made prisoner. The Grecian army was completely routed, and fled to the opulent town of Safetula, which was taken and sacked by the Moslems.

The battle was over, Gregorius had fallen, but no one came forward to claim the reward set upon his head. His captive daughter, however, on beholding Zobeir, broke forth into tears and exclamations, and thus revealed the modest victor. Zobeir refused to accept the maiden or the gold. He fought, he said, for the faith, not for earthly objects; and looked for his reward in paradise. In honor of his achievements, he was sent with tidings of this victory to the Caliph; but when he announced it, in the great mosque at Medina, in presence of the assembled people, he made no mention of his own services. His modesty enhanced his merits in the eyes of the public, and his name was placed by the Moslems beside those of Khaled and Amru.

Abdallah found his forces too much reduced and enfeebled by battle and disease to enable him to maintain possession of the country he had subdued; and, after a campaign of fifteen months, he led back his victorious, but diminished army into Egypt, encumbered with captives and laden with booty.

He afterwards, by the Caliph's command, assembled an army in the Thebaid or Upper Egypt, and thence made numerous successful excursions into Nubia, the Christian king of which was reduced to make a humiliating treaty, by which he bound himself to send annually to the Moslem commander in Egypt a great number of Nubian or Ethiopian slaves by way of tribute.

CHAPTER XXXVI

Moawyah, Emir of Syria – His naval victories – Othman loses the prophet's ring – Suppresses erroneous copies of the Koran – Conspiracies against him – His death

Among the distinguished Moslems who held command of the distant provinces during the Caliphat of Othman, was Moawyah Ibn Abu Sofian. As his name denotes, he was the son of Abu Sofian, the early foe and subsequent proselyte of Mahomet. On his father's death he had become chief of the tribe of Koreish, and head of the family of Omeya or Ommiah. The late Caliph Omar, about four years before his death, had appointed him emir, or governor of Syria, and he was continued in that office by Othman. He was between thirty and forty years of age, enterprising, courageous, of quick sagacity, extended views, and lofty aims. Having the maritime coast and ancient ports of Syria under his command, he aspired to extend the triumphs of the Moslem arms by sea as well as land. He had repeatedly endeavored, but in vain, to obtain permission from Omar to make a naval expedition, that Caliph being always apprehensive of the too wide and rapid extension of the enterprises of his generals. Under Othman he was more successful, and in the twenty-seventh year of the Hegira was permitted to fit out a fleet, with which he launched forth on the Sea of Tarshish, or the Phœnician Sea, by both which names the eastern part of the Mediterranean Sea was designated in ancient times.

His first enterprise was against the island of Cyprus, which was still held in allegiance to the emperor of Constantinople. The Christian garrison was weak and the inhabitants of the island soon submitted to pay tribute to the Caliph.

His next enterprise was against the island of Aradus, where he landed his troops and besieged the city or fortress; battering it with military engines. The inhabitants made vigorous resistance, repelled him from the island, and it was only after he had come a second time, with superior force that he was able to subdue it. He then expelled the natives, demolished the fortifications, and set fire to the city.

His most brilliant achievement, however, was a battle with a large fleet, in which the emperor was cruising in the Phœnician Sea. It was called in Arab history The Battle of Masts, from the forest of masts in the imperial fleet. The Christians went into action singing psalms and elevating the cross; the Moslems repeating texts of the Koran, shouting

Allah Achbar, and waving the standard of Islam. The battle was severe; the imperial fleet dispersed, and the emperor escaped by dint of sails and oars.

Moawyah now swept the seas victoriously, made landings on Crete and Malta, captured the island of Rhodes, demolished its famous colossal statue of brass, and, having broken it to pieces, transported the fragments to Alexandria, where they were sold to a Jewish merchant of Edissa, and were sufficient to load nine hundred camels. He had another fight with a Christian fleet in the bay of Feneke, by Castel Rosso, in which both parties claimed the victory. He even carried his expeditions along the coasts of Asia Minor and to the very port of Constantinople.

These naval achievements, a new feature in Arab warfare, rendered Moawyah exceedingly popular in Syria, and laid the foundation for that power and importance to which he subsequently attained.

It is worthy of remark how the triumphs of an ignorant people, who had heretofore dwelt obscurely in the midst of their deserts, were overrunning all the historical and poetical regions of antiquity. They had invaded and subdued the once mighty empires on land, they had now launched forth from the old Scriptural ports of Tyre and Sidon, swept the Sea of Tarshish, and were capturing the isles rendered famous by classic fable.

In the midst of these foreign successes an incident, considered full of sinister import, happened to Othman. He accidentally dropped in a brook a silver ring, on which was inscribed, "Mahomet the apostle of God." It had originally belonged to Mahomet, and since his death had been worn by Abu Beker, Omar and Othman, as the symbol of command, as rings had been considered throughout the East from the earliest times. The brook was searched with the most anxious care, but the ring was not to be found. This was an ominous loss in the eyes of the superstitious Moslems.

It happened about this time that, scandalized by the various versions of the Koran, and the disputes that prevailed concerning their varying texts, he decreed, in a council of the chief Moslems, that all copies of the Koran which did not agree with the genuine one in the hands of Hafza, the widow of Mahomet, should be burnt. Seven copies of Hafza's Koran were accordingly made; six were sent to Mecca, Yemen, Syria, Bahrein, Bassora, and Cufa, and one was retained in Medina. All copies varying from these were to be given to the flames. This measure caused Othman to be called the Gatherer of the Koran. It, at any rate, prevented any further vitiation of the sacred Scripture of Islam, which has remained unchanged from that time to the present. Besides this pious act, Othman caused a wall to be built round the sacred house of the Caaba, and enlarged and beautified the mosque of the prophet in Medina.

Notwithstanding all this, disaffection and intrigue were springing up round the venerable Caliph in Medina. He was brave, open-handed, and munificent, but he wanted shrewdness and discretion; was prone to favoritism; very credulous and easily deceived.

Murmurs rose against him on all sides, and daily increased in virulence. His conduct, both public and private, was reviewed, and circumstances, which had been passed by as trivial, were magnified into serious offences. He was charged with impious presumption in having taken his stand, on being first made Caliph, on the uppermost step of the pulpit, where Mahomet himself used to stand, whereas Abu Beker had stood one step lower, and Omar two. A graver accusation, and one too well merited, was that he had displaced men of worth, eminent for their services, and given their places to his own relatives and favorites. This was especially instanced in dismissing Amru Ibn al Aass from the government of Egypt, and appointing in his stead his own brother Abdallah Ibn Saad, who had once been proscribed by Mahomet. Another accusation was, that he had lavished the public money upon parasites, giving one hundred thousand dinars to one, four hundred thousand to another, and no less than five hundred and four thousand upon his secretary of state, Merwân Ibn Hakem, who had, it was said, an undue ascendency over him, and was, in fact, the subtle and active spirit of his government.The last sum, it was alleged, was taken out of a portion of the spoils of Africa, which had been set apart for the family of the prophet.

The ire of the old Caliph was kindled at having his lavish liberality thus charged upon him as a crime. He mounted the pulpit and declared that the money in the treasury belonged to God, the distribution to the Caliph at his own discretion, as successor to the prophet; and he prayed God to confound whoever should gainsay what he had set forth.

Upon this Ammar Ibn Yaser, one of the primitive Moslems, of whom Mahomet himself had said that he was filled with faith from the crown of his head to the sole of his foot, rose and disputed the words of Othman, whereupon some of the Caliph's kindred of the house of Ommiah fell upon the venerable Ammar and beat him until he fainted.

The outrage offered to the person of one of the earliest disciples and especial favorites of the prophet was promulgated far and wide, and contributed to the general discontent which now assumed the aspect of rebellion. The ringleader of the disaffected, was Ibn Caba, formerly a Jew. This son of mischief made a factious tour from Yemen to Hidschaf, thence to Bassora, to Cufa, to Syria and Egypt, decrying the Caliph and the emirs he had appointed; declaring that the Caliphat had been usurped by Othman from Ali, to whom it rightly belonged, as the nearest relative of the prophet, and suggesting by word of mouth and secret correspondence, that the malcontents should assemble simultaneously in various parts under pretext of a pilgrimage to Mecca.

The plot of the renegade Jew succeeded. In the fulness of time deputations arrived from all parts. One amounting to a hundred and fifty persons from Bassora; another of two hundred under Malec Alashtar from Cufa; a third of six hundred from Egypt headed by Mahomet, the son of Abu Beker, and brother of Ayesha, together with numbers of a sect of zealots called Karigites, who took the lead. These deputies encamped like an army within a league of Medina, and summoned the Caliph by message either to redress their grievances or to abdicate.

Othman in consternation applied to Ali to go forth and pacify the multitude. He consented on condition that Othman would previously make atonement for his errors from the pulpit. Harassed and dismayed, the aged Caliph mounted the pulpit, and with a voice broken by sobs and tears, exclaimed, "My God, I beg pardon of thee, and turn to thee with penitence and sorrow." The whole assemblage were moved and softened, and wept with the Caliph.

Merwân, the intriguing and well-paid secretary of Othman, and the soul of his government, had been absent during these occurrences, and on returning reproached the Caliph with what he termed an act of weakness. Having his permission, he addressed the populace in a strain that soon roused them to tenfold ire. Ali, hereupon, highly indignant, renounced any further interference in the matter.

Naile, the wife of Othman, who had heard the words of Merwân, and beheld the fury of the people, warned her husband of the storm gathering over his head, and prevailed upon him again to solicit the mediation of Ali. The latter suffered himself to be persuaded and went forth, among the insurgents. Partly by good words and liberal donations from the treasury, partly by a written promise from the Caliph to redress all their grievances, the insurgents were quieted, all but the deputies from Egypt who came to complain against the Caliph's foster-brother Abdallah Ibn Saad, who they said had oppressed them with exactions, and lavished their blood in campaigns in Barbary, merely for his own fame and profit, without retaining a foothold in the country. To pacify these complainants, Othman displaced Abdallah from the government, and left them to name his successor. They unanimously named Mahomet, the brother of Ayesha; who had in fact been used by that intriguing woman as a firebrand to kindle this insurrection; her object being to get Telha appointed to the Caliphat.

The insurgent camp now broke up. Mahomet with his followers set out to take possession of his post, and the aged Caliph flattered himself he would once more be left in peace.

Three days had Mahomet and his train been on their journey, when they were overtaken by a black slave on a dromedary. They demanded who he was, and whither he was travelling so rapidly. He gave himself out as a slave of the secretary Merwân bearing a message from the Caliph to his emir in Egypt. "I am the emir," said Mahomet. "My errand," said the slave, "is to the emir Abdallah Ibn Saad." He was asked if he had a letter, and on his prevaricating was searched. A letter was found concealed in a water-flask. It was from the Caliph, briefly ordering the emir, on the arrival of Mahomet Ibn Abu Beker, to make way with him secretly, destroy his diploma, and imprison, until further orders, those who had brought complaints to Medina.

Mahomet Ibn Abu Beker returned furious to Medina, and showed the perfidious letter to Ali, Zobeir, and Telha, who repaired with him to Othman. The latter denied any knowledge of the letter. It must then, they said, be a forgery of Merwân's, and requested that he might be summoned. Othman would not credit such treason on the part of his secretary, and insisted it must have been a treacherous device of one of his enemies. Medina was now in a ferment. There was a gathering of the people. All were incensed at such an atrocious breach of faith, and insisted that if the letter originated with Othman, he should resign the Caliphat, if with Merwân, that he should receive the merited punishment. Their demands had no effect upon the Caliph.

Mahomet Ibn Abu Beker now sent off swift messengers to recall the recent insurgents from the provinces, who were returning home, and to call in aid from the neighboring tribes. The dwelling of Othman was beleaguered; the alternative was left him to deliver up Merwân or to abdicate. He refused both. His life was now threatened. He barricadoed himself in his dwelling. The supply of water was cut off. If he made his appearance on the terraced roof, he was assailed with stones. Ali, Zobeir, and Telha, endeavored to appease the multitude, but they were deaf to their entreaties. Saad Ibn al Aass advised the Caliph, as the holy month was at hand, to sally forth on a pilgrimage to Mecca, as the piety of the undertaking and the sanctity of the pilgrim garb would protect him. Othman rejected the advice. "If they seek my life," said he, "they will not respect the pilgrim garb."

Ali, Zobeir, and Telha, seeing the danger imminent, sent their three sons, Hassan, Abdallah, and Mahomet, to protect the house. They stationed themselves by the door, and for some time kept the rebels at bay; but the rage of the latter knew no bounds. They stormed the house; Hassan was wounded in its defence. The rebels rushed in; among the foremost was Mahomet, the brother of Ayesha, and Ammer Ibn Yaser, whom Othman had ordered to be beaten. They found the venerable Caliph seated on a cushion, his beard flowing on his breast; the Koran open on his lap, and his wife Naile beside him.

One of the rebels struck him on the head, another stabbed him repeatedly with a sword, and Mahomet Ibn Abu Beker thrust a javelin into his body after he was dead. His wife was wounded in endeavoring to protect him, and her life was only saved through the fidelity of a slave. His house was plundered, as were some of the neighboring houses, and two chambers of the treasury.

As soon as the invidious Ayesha heard that the murder was accomplished, she went forth in hypocritical guise loudly bewailing the death of a man to whom she had secretly been hostile, and joining with the Ommiah family in calling for blood revenge.

The noble and virtuous Ali with greater sincerity, was incensed at his sons for not sacrificing their lives in defence of the Caliph, and reproached the sons of Telha and Zobeir with being lukewarm. "Why are you so angry, father of Hassan?" said Telha; "had Othman given up Merwân this evil would not have happened."

In fact it has been generally affirmed that the letter really was written by Merwân without the knowledge of the Caliph, and was intended to fall into the hands of Mahomet, and produce the effect which resulted from it. Merwân, it is alleged, having the charge of the correspondence of the Caliphat, had repeatedly abused the confidence of the weak and superannuated Othman in like manner, but not with such a nefarious aim. Of late he had secretly joined the cabal against the Caliph.

The body of Othman lay exposed for three days, and was then buried in the clothes in which he was slain, unwashed and without any funeral ceremony. He was eighty-two years old at the time of his death, and had reigned nearly twelve years. The event happened in the thirty-fifth year of the Hegira, in the year 655 of the Christian era. Notwithstanding his profusion and the sums lavished upon his favorites, immense treasures were found in his dwelling, a considerable part of which he had set apart for charitable purposes.

CHAPTER XXXVII

*Candidates for the Caliphat – Inauguration of Ali, fourth Caliph –
He undertakes measures of reform – Their consequences – Conspiracy of Ayesha – She gets possession of Bassora*

We have already seen that the faith of Islam had begun to lose its influence in binding together the hearts of the faithful, and uniting their feelings and interests in one common cause. The factions which sprang up at the very death of Mahomet, had increased with the election of every successor, and candidates for the succession multiplied as the brilliant successes of the Moslem arms elevated victorious generals to popularity and renown. On the assassination of Othman, four candidates were presented for the Caliphat; and the fortuitous assemblage of deputies from the various parts of the Moslem empire threatened to make the election difficult and tumultuous.

The most prominent candidate was Ali, who had the strongest natural claim, being cousin and son-in-law of Mahomet, and his children by Fatima being the only posterity of the prophet. He was the noblest branch of the noble race of Koreish. He possessed the three qualities most prized by Arabs: courage, eloquence, and munificence. His intrepid spirit had gained him from the prophet, the appellation of The Lion of God; specimens of his eloquence remain in some verses and sayings preserved among the Arabs; and his munificence was manifested in sharing among others, every Friday, what remained in the treasury. Of his magnanimity, we have given repeated instances; his noble scorn of every thing false and mean, and the absence in his conduct of every thing like selfish intrigue.

His right to the Caliphat was supported by the people of Cufa, the Egyptians, and a great part of the Arabs who were desirous of a line of Caliphs of the blood of Mahomet. He was opposed, however, as formerly, by the implacable Ayesha, who, though well-stricken in years, retained an unforgiving recollection of his having once questioned her chastity.

A second candidate was Zobeir, the same warrior who distinguished himself by his valor, in the campaign of Barbary, by his modesty in omitting to mention his achievements, and in declining to accept their reward. His pretensions to the Caliphat were urged by the people of Bassora.

A third candidate was Telha, who had been one of the six electors of Othman, and who had now the powerful support of Ayesha.

A fourth candidate was Moawyah, the military governor of Syria, and popular from his recent victories by sea and land. He had, moreover, immense wealth to back his claims, and was head of the powerful tribe of Koreish; but he was distant from the scene of election, and in his absence, his partisans could only promote confusion and delay.

It was a day of tumult and trouble in Medina. The body of Othman was still unburied. His wife Naile, at the instigation of Ayesha, sent off his bloody vest to be carried through the distant provinces, a ghastly appeal to the passions of the inhabitants.

The people, apprehending discord and disunion, clamored for the instant nomination of a Caliph. The deputations, which had come from various parts with complaints against Othman became impatient. There were men from Babylonia, and Mesopotamia, and other parts of Persia; from Syria and Egypt, as well as from the three divisions of Arabia; these assembled tumultuously, and threatened the safety of the three candidates, Ali, Telha, and Zobeir, unless an election were made in four-and-twenty hours.

In this dilemma, some of the principal Moslems repaired to Ali, and entreated him to accept the office. He consented with reluctance, but would do nothing clandestinely, and refused to take their hands, the Moslem mode at that time of attesting fealty, unless it were in public assembly at the mosque; lest he should give cause of cavil or dispute to his rivals. He refused, also, to make any promises or conditions. "If I am elected Caliph," said he, "I will administer the government with independence, and deal with you all according to my ideas of justice. If you elect another, I will yield obedience to him, and be ready to serve him as his vizier." They assented to every thing he said, and again entreated him to accept, for the good of the people and of the faith.

On the following morning there was a great assemblage of the people at the mosque, and Ali presented himself at the portal. He appeared in simple Arab style, clad in a thin cotton garb girded round his loins, a coarse turban, and using a bow as a walking-staff. He took off his slippers in reverence of the place, and entered the mosque bearing them in his left hand.

Finding that Telha and Zobeir were not present, he caused them to be sent for. They came, and knowing the state of the public mind, and that all immediate opposition would be useless, offered their hands in token of allegiance. Ali paused, and asked them if their hearts went with their hands; "speak frankly," said he; "if you disapprove of my election, and will accept the office, I will give my hand to either of you." They declared their perfect satisfaction, and gave their hands. Telha's right arm had been maimed in the battle of Ohod, and he stretched it forth with difficulty. The circumstance struck the Arabs as an evil omen. "It is likely to be a lame business, that is begun with a lame hand," muttered a bystander. Subsequent events seemed to justify the foreboding.

Moawyah, the remaining candidate, being absent at his government in Syria, the whole family of Ommiah, of which he was the head, withdrew from the ceremony. This, likewise, boded future troubles.

After the inauguration, Telha and Zobeir, with a view, it is said, to excite disturbance, applied to Ali to investigate and avenge the death of Othman. Ali, who knew that such a measure would call up a host of enemies, evaded the insidious proposition. It was not the moment, he said, for such an investigation. The event had its origin in old enmities and discontents instigated by the devil, and when the devil once gained a foothold, he never relinquished it willingly. The very measure they recommended was one of the devil's suggesting, for the purpose of fomenting disturbances. "However," added he, "if you will point out the assassins of Othman, I will not fail to punish them according to their guilt."

While Ali thus avoided the dangerous litigation, he endeavored to cultivate the good will of the Koreishites, and to strengthen himself against apprehended difficulties with the family of Ommiah. Telha and Zobeir, being disconcerted in their designs, now applied for important commands. Telha for the government of Cufa, and Zobeir for that of Bassora; but Ali again declined complying with their wishes; observing that he needed such able counsellors at hand in his present emergencies. They afterwards separately obtained permission from him to make a pilgrimage to Mecca; and set off on that devout errand with piety on their lips, but crafty policy in their breasts; Ayesha had already repaired to the holy city, bent upon opposition to the government of the man she hated.

Ali was now Caliph, but did not feel himself securely fixed in his authority. Many abuses had grown up during the dotage of his predecessor, which called for redress, and most of the governments of provinces were in the hands of persons in whose affection and fidelity he felt no confidence. He determined upon a general reform; and as a first step, to remove from office all the governors who had been appointed by the superannuated Othman. This measure was strongly opposed by some of his counsellors. They represented to him that he was not yet sufficiently established to venture upon such changes; and that he would make powerful enemies of men, who, if left in office, would probably hasten to declare allegiance to him, now that he was Caliph.

Ali was not to be persuaded. "Sedition," he said, "like fire, is easily extinguished at the commencement; but the longer it burns the more fiercely it blazes."

He was advised, at least, to leave his formidable rival Moawyah, for the present, in the government of Syria, as he was possessed of great wealth and influence, and a powerful army, and might rouse that whole province to rebellion; and in such case might be joined by Telha and Zobeir, who were both disappointed and disaffected men. He had recently shown his influence over the feelings of the people under his command; when the bloody vest of Othman arrived in the province, he had displayed it from the pulpit of the mosque in Damascus. The mosque resounded with lamentations mingled with clamors for the revenge of blood; for Othman had won the hearts of the people of Syria by his munificence. Some of the noblest inhabitants of Damascus swore to remain separate from their wives, and not to lay their heads on a pillow until blood for blood had atoned for the death of Othman. Finally the vest had been hoisted as a standard, and had fired the Syrian army with a desire for vengeance.

Ali's counsellor represented all these things to him. "Suffer Moawyah, therefore," added he, "to remain in command until he has acknowledged your government, and then he may be displaced without turmoil. Nay, I will pledge myself to bring him bound hand and foot into your presence."

Ali spurned at this counsel, and swore he would practise no such treachery, but would deal with Moawyah with the sword alone. He commenced immediately his plan of reform, with the nomination of new governors devoted to his service. Abdallah Ibn Abbas was appointed to Arabia Felix, Ammar Ibn Sahel to Cufa, Othman Ibn Hanif to Bassora, Sahel Ibn Hanif to Syria, and Saad Ibn Kais to Egypt. These generals lost no time in repairing to their respective governments, but the result soon convinced Ali that he had been precipitate.

Jaali, the governor of Arabia Felix, readily resigned his post to Abdallah Ibn Abbas, and retired to Mecca; but he took with him the public treasure, and delivered it into the hands of Ayesha, and her confederates Telha and Zobeir, who were already plotting rebellion.

Othman Ibn Hanif on arriving at Bassora to take the command, found the people discontented and rebellious, and having no force to subjugate them, esteemed himself fortunate in escaping from their hands and returning to the Caliph.

When Ammar Ibn Sahel reached the confines of Cufa, he learnt that the people were unanimous in favor of Abu Musa Alashari, their present governor, and determined to support him by fraud or force. Ammar had no disposition to contend with them, the Cufians being reputed the most treacherous and perfidious people of the East; so he turned the head of his horse, and journeyed back mortified and disconcerted to Ali.

Saad Ibn Kais was received in Egypt with murmurs by the inhabitants, who were indignant at the assassination of Othman, and refused to submit to the government of Ali, until justice was done upon the perpetrators of that murder. Saad prudently, therefore, retraced his steps to Medina.

Sahel Ibn Hanif had no better success in Syria; he was met at Tabuc, by a body of cavalry, who demanded his name and business. "For my name," said he, "I am Sahel, the son of Hanif; and for my business, I am governor of this province, as lieutenant of the Caliph Ali, Commander of the Faithful." They assured him in reply, that Syria had already an able governor in Moawyah, son of Abu Sofian, and that to their certain knowledge there was not room in the province for the sole of his foot; so saying, they unsheathed their scimetars.

The new governor, who was not provided with a body of troops sufficient to enforce his authority, returned also to the Caliph with this intelligence. Thus of the five governors, so promptly sent forth by Ali in pursuance of his great plan of reform, Abdallah Ibn Abbas was the only one permitted to assume his post.

When Ali received tidings of the disaffection of Syria, he wrote a letter to Moawyah, claiming his allegiance, and transmitted it by an especial messenger. The latter was detained many days by the Syrian commander, and then sent back, accompanied by another messenger, bearing a sealed letter superscribed, "From Moawyah to Ali." The two couriers arrived at Medina in the cool of the evening, the hour of concourse, and passed through the multitude bearing the letter aloft on a staff, so that all could see the superscription. The people thronged after the messengers into the presence of Ali. On opening the letter it was found to be a perfect blank, in token of contempt and defiance.

Ali soon learned that this was no empty bravado. He was apprised by his own courier that an army of sixty thousand men was actually on foot in Syria, and that the bloody garment of Othman, the standard of rebellion, was erected in the mosque at Damascus. Upon this he solemnly called Allah and the prophet to witness that he was not guilty of that murder; but made active preparations to put down the rebellion by force of arms; sending missives into all the provinces, demanding the assistance of the faithful.

The Moslems were now divided into two parties: those who adhered to Ali, among whom were the people of Medina generally; and the Motazeli, or Separatists, who were in the opposition. The latter were headed by the able and vindictive Ayesha, who had her headquarters at Mecca, and with the aid of Telha and Zobeir, was busy organizing an insurrection. She had induced the powerful family of Ommiah to join her cause, and had sent couriers to all the governors of provinces whom Ali had superseded, inviting them to unite in the rebellion. The treasure brought to her by Jaali, the displaced governor of Arabia Felix, furnished her with the means of war, and the bloody garment of Othman proved a powerful auxiliary.

A council of the leaders of this conspiracy was held at Mecca. Some inclined to join the insurgents in Syria, but it was objected, that Moawyah was sufficiently powerful in that country without their aid. The intrepid Ayesha was for proceeding immediately to Medina and attacking Ali in his capital, but it was represented that the people of Medina were unanimous in his favor, and too powerful to be assailed with success. It was finally determined to march for Bassora, Telha assuring them that he had a strong party in that city, and pledging himself for its surrender.

A proclamation was accordingly made by sound of trumpet through the streets of Mecca to the following effect:

"In the name of the most high God. Ayesha, Mother of the Faithful, accompanied by the chiefs Telha and Zobeir, is going in person to Bassora. All those of the faithful who burn with a desire to defend the faith and avenge the death of the Caliph Othman, have only to present themselves and they shall be furnished with all necessaries for the journey."

Ayesha sallied forth from one of the gates of Mecca, borne in a litter placed on the back of a strong camel named Alascar. Telha and Zobeir attended her on each side, followed by six hundred persons of some note, all mounted on camels, and a promiscuous multitude of about six thousand on foot.

After marching some distance, the motley host stopped to refresh themselves on the bank of a rivulet near a village. Their arrival aroused the dogs of the village, who surrounded Ayesha and barked at her most clamorously. Like all Arabs, she was superstitious, and considered this an evil omen. Her apprehensions were increased on learning that the name of the village was Jowab. "My trust is in God," exclaimed she, solemnly. "To him do I turn in time of trouble," – a text from the Koran, used by Moslems in time of extreme danger. In fact, she called to mind some proverb of the prophet about the dogs of Jowab, and a prediction that one of his wives would be barked at by them when in a situation of imminent peril. "I will go no further," cried Ayesha, "I will halt here for the night." So saying, she struck her camel on the leg to make him kneel that she might alight.

Telha and Zobeir, dreading any delay, brought some peasants whom they had suborned to assign a different name to the village, and thus quieted her superstitious fears. About the same time some horsemen, likewise instructed by them, rode up with a false report that Ali was not far distant with a body of troops. Ayesha hesitated no longer, but mounting nimbly on her camel, pressed to the head of her little army, and they all pushed forward with increased expedition towards Bassora. Arrived before the city, they had hoped, from the sanguine declarations of Telha, to see it throw open its gates to receive them; the gates, however, remained closely barred. Othman Ibn Hanef, whom Ali had sent without success to assume the government of Cufa, was now in command at Bassora, whither he had been invited by a part of the inhabitants.

Ayesha sent a summons to the governor to come forth and join the standard of the faithful, or at least to throw open his gates; but he was a timid, undecided man, and confiding the defence of the city to his lieutenant Ammar, retired in great tribulation within his own dwelling in the citadel, and went to prayers.

Ammar summoned the people to arms, and called a meeting of the principal inhabitants in the mosque. He soon found out, to his great discouragement, that the people were nearly equally divided into two factions, one for Ali, since he was regularly elected Caliph, the other composed of partisans of Telha. The parties, instead of deliberating, fell to reviling, and ended by throwing dust in each others' faces.

In the meantime Ayesha and her host approached the walls, and many of the inhabitants went forth to meet her. Telha and Zobeir alternately addressed the multitude, and were followed by Ayesha, who harangued them from her camel. Her voice, which she elevated that it might be heard by all, became shrill and sharp, instead of intelligible, and provoked the merriment of some of the crowd. A dispute arose as to the justice of her appeal; mutual revilings again took place between the parties; they gave each other the lie, and again threw dust in each others' faces. One of the men of Bassora then turned and reproached Ayesha. "Shame on thee, oh Mother of the Faithful!" said he. "The murder of the Caliph was a grievous crime, but was a less abomination than thy forgetfulness of the modesty of thy sex. Wherefore dost thou abandon thy quiet home, and thy protecting veil, and ride forth like a man barefaced on that accursed camel, to foment quarrels and dissensions among the faithful?"

Another of the crowd scoffed at Telha and Zobeir. "You have brought your mother with you," cried he, "why did you not also bring your wives?"

Insults were soon followed by blows, swords were drawn, a skirmish ensued, and they fought until the hour of prayer separated them.

Ayesha sat down before Bassora with her armed host, and some days passed in alternate skirmishes and negotiations. At length a truce was agreed upon, until deputies could be sent to Medina to learn the cause of these dissensions among the Moslems, and whether Telha and Zobeir agreed voluntarily to the election of Ali, or did so on compulsion: if the former, they should be considered as rebels; if the latter, their partisans in Bassora should be considered justified in upholding them.

The insurgents, however, only acquiesced in this agreement to get the governor in their power, and so gain possession of the city. They endeavored to draw him to their camp by friendly messages, but he apparently suspected their intentions, and refused to come forth until the answer should be received from Medina. Upon this Telha and Zobeir, taking advantage of a stormy night, gained an entrance into the city with a chosen band, and surprised the governor in the mosque, where they took him prisoner, after killing forty of his guard. They sent to Ayesha to know what they should do with their captive. "Let him be put to death," was her fierce reply. Upon this one of her women interceded. "I adjure thee," said she, "in the name of Allah and the

companions of the apostle, do not slay him." Ayesha was moved by this
adjuration, and commuted his punishment into forty stripes and imprisonment. He was doomed, however, to suffer still greater evils before he
escaped from the hands of his captors. His beard was plucked out hair
by hair, one of the most disgraceful punishments that can be inflicted
on an Arab. His eyebrows were served in the same manner, and he was
then contemptuously set at liberty.

The city of Bassora was now taken possession of without further resistance. Ayesha entered it in state, supported by Telha and Zobeir,
and followed by her troops and adherents. The inhabitants were
treated with kindness, as friends who had acted through error; and
every exertion was made to secure their good-will, and to incense them
against Ali, who was represented as a murderer and usurper.

CHAPTER XXXVIII

Ali defeats the rebels under Ayesha – His treatment of her

When Ali heard of the revolt at Mecca, and the march against Bassora, he called a general meeting in the mosque, and endeavored to stir up the people to arm and follow him in pursuit of the rebels: but, though he spoke with his usual eloquence, and was popular in Medina, a coldness and apathy pervaded the assembly. Some dreaded a civil war; others recollected that the leader of the rebels, against whom they were urged to take up arms, was Ayesha, the favorite wife of the prophet, the Mother of the Faithful; others doubted whether Ali might not, in some degree, be implicated in the death of Othman, which had been so artfully charged against him.

At length a Moslem of distinction, Ziyad Ibn Hantelah, rose with generous warmth, and, stepping up to Ali, "Let whosoever will, hold back," cried he, "we will go forward."

At the same time two Ansars, or doctors of the law, men of great weight, pronounced with oracular voice, "The Imam Othman, master of the two testimonies, did not die by the hand of the master of the two testimonies;"* that is to say, "Othman was not slain by Ali."

The Arabs are a mercurial people, and acted upon by sudden impulses. The example of Ziyad, and the declaration of the two Ansars, caused an immediate excitement. Abu Kotada, an Ansar of distinction, drew his sword. "The apostle of God," said he, "upon whom be peace, girt me with this sword. It has long been sheathed. I now devote it to the destruction of these deceivers of the faithful."

A matron in a transport of enthusiasm exclaimed, "Oh Commander of the Faithful, if it were permitted by our law, I myself would go with thee; but here is my cousin, dearer to me than my own life, he shall follow thee and partake of thy fortunes."

Ali profited by the excitement of the moment, and making a hasty levy, marched out of Medina at the head of about nine hundred men, eager to overtake the rebels before they should reach Bassora. Hearing, however, that Ayesha was already in possession of that city, he halted at a place called Arrabdah until he should be joined by reinforcements: sending messengers to Abu Musa Alashari, governor of Cufa, and to

---

* The two testimonies mean the two fundamental beliefs of the Moslem creed: "There is but one God. Mahomet is the apostle of God." The Caliph, as Imam or pontiff of the Musulman religion, is master of the two testimonies.

various other commanders, ordering speedy succor. He was soon joined by his eldest son Hassan, who undertook to review his conduct, and lecture him on his policy. "I told you," said he, "when the Caliph Othman was besieged, to go out of the city, lest you should be implicated in his death. I told you not to be inaugurated until deputies from the Arabian tribes were present. Lastly, I told you when Ayesha and her two confederates took the field, to keep at home until they should be pacified; so that, should any mischief result, you might not be made responsible. You have not heeded my advice, and the consequence is that you may now be murdered to-morrow, with nobody to blame but yourself."

Ali listened with impatience to this filial counsel, or rather, censure: when it was finished, he replied, "Had I left the city when Othman was besieged, I should myself have been surrounded. Had I waited for my inauguration until all the tribes came in, I should have lost the votes of the people of Medina, the 'Helpers,' who have the privilege of disposing of the government. Had I remained at home after my enemies had taken the field, like a wild beast lurking in its hole, I should like a wild beast have been digged out and destroyed. If I do not look after my own affairs, who will look after them? If I do not defend myself, who will defend me? Such are my reasons for acting as I have acted; and now, my son, hold your peace." We hear of no further counsels from Hassan.

Ali had looked for powerful aid from Abu Musa Alashari, governor of Cufa, but he was of a lukewarm spirit, and cherished no good will to the Caliph, from his having sent Othman Ibn Hanef to supplant him, as has been noticed. He therefore received his messengers with coldness, and sent a reply full of evasions. Ali was enraged at this reply; and his anger was increased by the arrival about the same time of the unfortunate Othman Ibn Hanef, who had been so sadly scourged and maltreated and ejected from his government at Bassora. What most grieved the heart of the ex-governor was the indignity that had been offered to his person. "Oh Commander of the Faithful," said he, mournfully, "when you sent me to Bassora I had a beard, and now, alas, I have not a hair on my chin!"

Ali commiserated the unfortunate man who thus deplored the loss of his beard more than of his government; but comforted him with the assurance that his sufferings would be counted to him as merits. He then spoke of his own case; the Caliphs, his predecessors, had reigned without opposition; but, for his own part, those who had joined in electing him, had proved false to him. "Telha and Zobeir," said he, "have submitted to Abu Beker, Omar, and Othman, why have they arrayed themselves against me? By Allah they shall find that I am not one jot inferior to my predecessors!"

Ali now sent more urgent messages to Abu Musa, governor of Cufa, by his son Hassan and Ammar Ibn Yaser, his general of the horse, a stern old soldier, ninety years of age, the same intrepid spokesman who, for his hardihood of tongue, had been severely maltreated by order of the Caliph Othman. They were reinforced by Alashtar, a determined officer, who had been employed in the previous mission, and irritated by the prevarications of Abu Musa.

Hassan and Ammar were received with ceremonious respect by the governor, and their mission was discussed, according to usage, in the mosque, but Alashtar remained with the guard that had escorted them. The envoys pressed their errand with warmth, urging the necessity of their sending immediate succor to the Caliph. Abu Musa, however, who prided himself more upon words than deeds, answered them by an evasive harangue; signifying his doubts of the policy of their proceeding; counselling that the troops should return to Medina, that the whole matter in dispute should be investigated, and the right to rule amicably adjusted. "It is a bad business," added he, "and he that meddles least with it, stands less chance of doing wrong. For what says the prophet touching an evil affair of the kind? He who sleepeth in it is more secure than he that waketh; he that lyeth than he that sitteth; he that sitteth than he that standeth; he that standeth than he that walketh; and he that walketh than he that rideth. Sheathe, therefore, your swords, take the heads from your lances, and the strings from your bows, and receive him that is injured into your dwellings, until all matters are adjusted and reconciled."

The ancient general, Ammar, replied to him tartly, that he had misapplied the words of the prophet, which were meant to rebuke such servants as himself, who were better sitting than standing, and sleeping than awake. Abu Musa would have answered him with another long harangue in favor of non-resistance, but was interrupted by the sudden entrance of a number of his soldiers, bearing evidence of having been piteously beaten. While Abu Musa had been holding forth at the mosque, Alashtar, the hardy officer who remained with the escort, had seized upon the castle of Cufa, caused the garrison to be soundly scourged, and sent them to the mosque to cut short the negotiation. This prompt measure of Alashtar placed the cold-spirited conduct of Abu Musa in so ridiculous a light that the feelings of the populace were instantly turned against him. Hassan, the son of Ali, seized upon the moment to address the assembly. He maintained the innocence of his father in regard to the assassination of Othman. His father, he said, had either done wrong, or had suffered wrong. If he had done wrong, God would punish him. If he had suffered wrong, God would help him. The case was in the hand of the Most High. Telha and Zobeir, who were the first to inaugurate him, were the first to turn against him. What had he done, as Caliph, to merit such opposition? What injustice had he committed? What covetous or selfish propensity had he manifested? "I am going back to my father," added Hassan, "those who are disposed to render him assistance, may follow me."

His eloquence was powerfully effective, and the people of Cufa followed him to the number of nearly nine thousand. In the meantime the army of Ali had been reinforced from other quarters, and now amounted to thirty thousand men, all of whom had seen service. When he appeared with his force before Bassora, Ayesha and her confederates were dismayed, and began to treat of conciliation. Various messages passed between the hostile parties, and Telha and Zobeir, confiding in the honorable faith of Ali, had several interviews with him.

When these late deadly enemies were seen walking backward and forward together, in sight of either army, and holding long conversations, it was confidently expected that a peace would be effected; and such would have been the case had no malign influence interfered; for Ali, with his impressive eloquence, touched the hearts of his opponents when he reproached them with their breach of faith, and warned them against the judgments of heaven. "Dost thou not remember," said he to Zobeir, "how Mahomet once asked thee if thou didst not love his dear son Ali? and when thou answered yea, dost thou not remember his reply: 'Nevertheless a day will come when thou wilt rise up against him, and draw down miseries upon him and upon all the faithful?'"

"I remember it well," replied Zobeir, "and had I remembered it before, never would I have taken up arms against you."

He returned to his camp determined not to fight against Ali, but was overruled by the vindictive Ayesha. Every attempt at pacification was defeated by that turbulent woman, and the armies were at length brought to battle. Ayesha took the field on that memorable occasion, mounted in a litter on her great camel Alascar, and rode up and down among her troops, animating them by her presence and her voice. The fight was called, from that circumstance, The Battle of the Camel, and also The Battle of Karibah, from the field on which it was fought.

It was an obstinate and bloody conflict, for Moslem was arrayed against Moslem, and nothing is so merciless and unyielding as civil war. In the heat of the fight Merwân Ibn Hakem, who stood near Ali, noticed Telha endeavoring to goad on the flagging valor of his troops. "Behold the traitor Telha," cried he, "but lately one of the murderers of Othman, now the pretended avenger of his blood." So saying, he let fly an arrow and wounded him in the leg. Telha writhed with the pain, and at the same moment his horse reared and threw him. In the dismay and anguish of the moment, he imprecated the vengeance of Allah upon his own head for the death of Othman. Seeing his boot full of blood, he made one of his followers take him up behind him on his horse and convey him to Bassora. Finding death approaching, he called to one of Ali's men who happened to be present, "Give me your hand," said the dying penitent, "that I may put mine in it, and thus renew my oath of fealty to Ali." With these words he expired. His dying speech was reported to Ali, and touched his generous heart. "Allah," said he, "would not call him to heaven until he had blotted out his first breach of his word by his last vow of fidelity."

Zobeir, the other conspirator, had entered into the battle with a heavy heart. His previous conversation with Ali had awakened compunction in his bosom. He now saw that old Ammar Ibn Yaser, noted for probity and rectitude, was in the Caliph's host; and he recollected hearing Mahomet say that Ammar Ibn Yaser would always be found on the side of truth and justice. With a boding spirit he drew out of the battle and took the road towards Mecca. As he was urging his melancholy way, he came to a valley crossed by the brook Sabaa, where Hanef Ibn Kais was encamped with a horde of Arabs, awaiting the issue of the battle, ready to join the conqueror and share the spoil. Hanef knew him at a distance. "Is there no one," said he, "to bring me tidings of Zobeir?" One of his men, Amru Ibn Jarmuz, understood the hint, and spurred to overtake Zobeir. The latter, suspecting his intentions, bade him keep at a distance. A short conversation put them on friendly terms, and they both dismounted and conversed together. The hour of prayers arrived. "Salat" (to prayers!) cried Zobeir. "Salat," replied Amru; but as Zobeir prostrated himself in supplication, Amru struck off his head, and hastened with it, as a welcome trophy, to Ali. That generous conqueror shed tears over the bleeding head of one who was once his friend. Then turning to his slayer, "Hence, miscreant!" cried he, "and carry thy tidings to Ben Safiah in hell." So unexpected a malediction, where he expected a reward, threw Amru into a transport of rage and desperation; he uttered a rhapsody of abuse upon Ali, and then, drawing his sword, plunged it into his own bosom.

Such was the end of the two leaders of the rebels. As to Ayesha, the implacable soul of the revolt, she had mingled that day in the hottest of the fight. Tabari, the Persian historian, with national exaggeration, declares that the heads of threescore and ten men were cut off that held the bridle of her camel, and that the inclosed litter in which she rode, was bristled all over with darts and arrows. At last her camel was hamstrung, and sank with her to the ground, and she remained there until the battle was concluded.

Ayesha might have looked for cruel treatment at the hands of Ali, having been his vindictive and persevering enemy, but he was too magnanimous to triumph over a fallen foe. It is said some reproachful words passed between them, but he treated her with respect; gave her an attendance of forty females, and sent his sons Hassan and Hosein to escort her a day's journey toward Medina, where she was confined to her own house, and forbidden to intermeddle any more with affairs of state. He then divided the spoils among the heirs of his soldiers who were slain, and appointed Abdallah Ibn Abbas governor of Bassora. This done, he repaired to Cufa, and in reward of the assistance he had received from its inhabitants, made that city the seat of his Caliphat. These occurrences took place in the thirty-fifth year of the Hegira, the 655th of the Christian era.

CHAPTER XXXIX

Battles between Ali and Moawyah – Their claims to the Caliphat left to arbitration; the result – Decline of the power of Ali – Loss of Egypt

The victory at Karibah had crushed the conspiracy of Ayesha, and given Ali quiet dominion over Egypt, Arabia, and Persia; still his most formidable adversary remained unsubdued. Moawyah Ibn Abu Sofian held sway over the wealthy and populous province of Syria; he had immense treasures and a powerful army at his command; he had the prejudices of the Syrians in his favor, who had been taught to implicate Ali in the murder of Othman, and refused to acknowledge him as Caliph. Still further to strengthen himself in defiance of the sovereign power, he sought the alliance of Amru, who had been displaced from the government of Egypt by Ali, and was now a discontented man in Palestine. Restoration to that command, was to be the reward of his successful co-operation with Moawyah in deposing Ali: the terms were accepted: Amru hastened to Damascus at the head of a devoted force; and finding the public mind ripe for his purpose, gave the hand of allegiance to Moawyah in presence of the assembled army, and proclaimed him Caliph, amid the shouts of the multitude.

Ali had in vain endeavored to prevent the hostility of Moawyah, by all conciliatory means; when he heard of this portentous alliance, he took the field and marched for Syria, at the head of ninety thousand men. The Arabians, with their accustomed fondness for the marvellous, signalize his entrance into the confines of Syria with an omen. Having halted his army in a place where there was no water, he summoned a Christian hermit, who lived in a neighboring cave, and demanded to be shown a well. The anchorite assured him that there was nothing but a cistern, in which there were scarce three buckets of rain water. Ali maintained that certain prophets of the people of Israel had abode there in times of old, and had digged a well there. The hermit replied, that a well did indeed exist there, but it had been shut up for ages, and all traces of it lost, and it was only to be discovered and reopened by a predestined hand. He then, says the Arabian tradition, produced a parchment scroll written by Simeon ben Safa (Simon Cephas), one of the greatest apostles of Jesus Christ, predicting the coming of Mahomet, the last of the prophets, and that this well would be discovered and reopened by his lawful heir and successor.

415

Ali listened with becoming reverence to this prediction; then turning to his attendants and pointing to a spot, "Dig there," said he. They digged, and after a time came to an immense stone, which having been removed with difficulty, the miraculous well stood revealed, affording a seasonable supply to the army, and an unquestionable proof of the legitimate claim of Ali to the Caliphat. The venerable hermit was struck with conviction; he fell at the feet of Ali, embraced his knees, and never afterwards would leave him.

It was on the first day of the thirty-seventh year of the Hegira (18th June, A.D. 657), that Ali came in sight of the army of Moawyah, consisting of eighty thousand men, encamped on the plain of Seffein, on the banks of the Euphrates, on the confines of Babylonia and Syria. Associated with Moawyah was the redoubtable Amru, a powerful ally both in council and in the field. The army of Ali was superior in number; in his host, too, he had several veterans who had fought under Mahomet in the famous battle of Beder, and thence prided themselves in the surname of Shahabah; that is to say, Companions of the Prophet. The most distinguished of these was old Ammar Ibn Yaser, Ali's general of horse, who had fought repeatedly by the side of Mahomet. He was ninety years of age, yet full of spirit and activity, and idolized by the Moslem soldiery.

The armies lay encamped in sight of each other, but as it was the first month of the Moslem year, a sacred month, when all warfare is prohibited, it was consumed in negotiations; for Ali still wished to avoid the effusion of kindred blood. His efforts were in vain, and in the next month hostilities commenced; still Ali drew his sword with an unwilling hand; he charged his soldiers never to be the first to fight; never to harm those who fled, and never to do violence to a woman. Moawyah and Amru were likewise sensible of the unnatural character of this war; the respective leaders, therefore, avoided any general action, and months passed in mere skirmishings. These, however, were sharp and sanguinary, and in the course of four months Moawyah is said to have lost five-and-forty thousand men, and Ali more than half that number.

Among the slain on the part of Ali, were five-and-twenty of the Shahabah, the veterans of Beder, and companions of the prophet. Their deaths were deplored even by the enemy; but nothing caused greater grief than the fall of the brave old Ammar Ibn Yaser, Ali's general of horse, and the patriarch of Moslem chivalry. Moawyah and Amru beheld him fall. "Do you see," cried Moawyah, "what precious lives are lost in our dissensions?" "See," exclaimed Amru; "would to God I had died twenty years since!"

Ali forgot his usual moderation on beholding the fate of his brave old general of the horse; and putting himself at the head of twelve thousand cavalry, made a furious charge to avenge his death. The ranks of the enemy were broken by the shock; but the heart of Ali soon relented at the sight of carnage. Spurring within call of Moawyah, "How long," cried he, "shall Moslem blood be shed like water in our strife? Come forth, and let Allah decide between us. Which ever is victor in the fight, let him be ruler."

Amru was struck with the generous challenge, and urged Moawyah to accept it; but the latter shunned an encounter with an enemy surnamed "The Lion," for his prowess, and who had always slain his adversary in single fight. Amru hinted at the disgrace that would attend his refusal; to which Moawyah answered with a sneer, "You do wisely to provoke a combat that may make you governor of Syria."

A desperate battle at length took place, which continued throughout the night. Many were slain on both sides; but most on the part of the Syrians. Alashtar was the hero of this fight; he was mounted upon a piebald horse, and wielded a two-edged sword; every stroke of that terrible weapon clove down a warrior, and every stroke was accompanied by the shout of Allah Achbar! He was heard to utter that portentous exclamation, say the Arabian historians, four hundred times during the darkness of the night.

The day dawned disastrously upon the Syrians. Alashtar was pressing them to their very encampment, and Moawyah was in despair; when Amru suggested an expedient, founded on the religious scruples of the Moslems. On a sudden, the Syrians elevated the Koran on the points of their lances. "Behold the book of God," cried they. "Let that decide our differences." The soldiers of Ali instantly dropped the points of their weapons. It was in vain Ali represented that this was all a trick, and endeavored to urge them on. "What!" cried they, "do you refuse to submit to the decision of the book of God!"

Ali found that to persist would be to shock their bigot prejudices, and to bring a storm upon his own head; reluctantly, therefore, he sounded a retreat; but it required repeated blasts to call off Alashtar, who came, his scimetar dripping with blood, and murmuring at being, as he said, tricked out of so glorious a victory.

Umpires were now appointed to settle this great dispute according to the dictates of the Koran. Ali would have nominated on his part Abdallah Ibn Abbas, but he was objected to, as being his cousin-german. He then named the brave Alashtar, but he was likewise set aside, and Abu Musa pressed upon him; an upright, but simple and somewhat garrulous man, as has already been shown. As to Moawyah, he managed on his part to have Amru Ibn al Aass appointed, the shrewdest and most sagacious man in all Arabia. The two rival leaders then retired, Ali to Cufa, and Moawyah to Damascus, leaving generals in command of their respective armies.

The arbitrators met several months afterwards at Jumat al Joudel, in presence of both armies, who were pledged to support their decision. Amru, who understood the weak points of Musa's character, treated him with great deference, and after having won his confidence, persuaded him that, to heal these dissensions, and prevent the shedding of kindred blood, it would be expedient to set aside both candidates and let the faithful elect a third. This being agreed upon, a tribunal was erected between the armies, and Amru, through pretended deference, insisted that Musa should be the first to ascend it and address the people. Abu Musa accordingly ascended, and proclaimed with a loud voice, "I depose Ali and Moawyah from the office to which they pretend, even as I draw this ring from my finger." So saying he descended.

Amru now mounted in his turn. "You have heard," said he, "how Musa on his part has deposed Ali; I on my part depose him also; and I adjudge the Caliphat to Moawyah, and invest him with it, as I invest my finger with this ring: and I do it with justice, for he is the rightful successor and avenger of Othman."

Murmurs succeeded from the partisans of Ali, and from Abu Musa, who complained of the insincerity of Amru. The Syrians applauded the decision, and both parties, being prevented from hostilities by a solemn truce, separated without any personal violence; but with mutual revilings and augmented enmity. A kind of religious feud sprang up, which continued for a long time between the house of Ali and that of Ommiah; they never mentioned each other without a curse, and pronounced an excommunication upon each other whenever they harangued the people in the mosque.

The power of Ali now began to wane; the decision pronounced against him influenced many of his own party, and a revolt was at length stirred up among his followers, by a sect of fanatic zealots called

Karigites or seceders; who insisted that he had done wrong in referring to the judgment of men what ought to be decided by God alone; and that he had refused to break the truce and massacre his enemies when in his power, though they had proved themselves to be the enemies of God; they therefore renounced allegiance to him; appointed Abdallah Ibn Waheb as their leader, and set up their standard at Naharwan, a few miles from Bagdad, whither the disaffected repaired from all quarters, until they amounted to twenty-five thousand.

The appearance of Ali with an army brought many of them to their senses. Willing to use gentle measures, he caused a standard to be erected outside of his camp, and proclaimed a pardon to such of the malcontents as should rally round it. The rebel army immediately began to melt away, until Abdallah Ibn Waheb was left with only four thousand adherents. These, however, were fierce enthusiasts, and their leader was a fanatic. Trusting that Allah and the prophet would render him miraculous assistance, he attacked the army of Ali with his handful of men, who fought with such desperation that nine only escaped. These served as firebrands to enkindle future mischief.

Moawyah had now recourse to a stratagem to sow troubles in Egypt, and ultimately to put it in the hands of Amru. Ali, on assuming the Caliphat, had appointed Saad Ibn Kais to the government of that province, who administered its affairs with ability. Moawyah now forged a letter from Saad to himself, professing devotion to his interests, and took measures to let it fall into the hands of Ali. The plan was successful. The suspicions of Ali were excited; he recalled Saad and appointed in his place Mahomet, son of Abu Beker, and brother of Ayesha. Mahomet began to govern with a high hand; proscribing and exiling the leaders of the Othman faction, who made the murder of the late Caliph a question of party. This immediately produced commotions and insurrections, and all Egypt was getting into a blaze. Ali again sought to remedy the evil by changing the governor, and dispatched Malec Shutur, a man of prudence and ability, to take the command. In the course of his journey Malec lodged one night at the house of a peasant, on the confines of Arabia and Egypt. The peasant was a creature of Moawyah's, and poisoned his unsuspecting guest with a pot of honey. Moawyah followed up this treacherous act by sending Amru with six thousand horse to seize upon Egypt in its present stormy state. Amru hastened with joy to the scene of his former victories, made his way rapidly to Alexandria, united his force with that of Ibn Sharig, the

leader of the Othman party, and they together routed Mahomet Ibn
Abu Beker and took him prisoner. The avengers of Othman reviled
Mahomet with his assassination of that Caliph, put him to death, en-
closed his body in the carcass of an ass, and burnt both to ashes. Then
Amru assumed the government of Egypt as lieutenant of Moawyah.

When Ayesha heard of the death of her brother, she knelt down in
the mosque, and in the agony of her heart invoked a curse upon
Moawyah and Amru, an invocation which she thenceforth repeated at
the end of all her prayers. Ali, also, was afflicted at the death of Mahomet, and exclaimed, "The murderers will answer for this before
God."

CHAPTER XL

Preparations of Ali for the invasion of Syria – His assassination

The loss of Egypt was a severe blow to the fortunes of Ali, and he had the mortification subsequently to behold his active rival make himself master of Hejaz, plant his standard on the sacred cities of Mecca and Medina, and ravage the fertile province of Yemen. The decline of his power affected his spirits, and he sank at times into despondency. His melancholy was aggravated by the conduct of his own brother Okail, who, under pretence that Ali did not maintain him in suitable style, deserted him in his sinking fortunes, and went over to Moawyah, who rewarded his unnatural desertion with ample revenues.

Still Ali meditated one more grand effort. Sixty thousand devoted adherents pledged themselves to stand by him to the death, and with these he prepared to march into Syria. While preparations were going on, it chanced that three zealots, of the sect of Karigites, met as pilgrims in the mosque of Mecca, and fell into conversation about the battle of Naharwan, wherein four thousand of their brethren had lost their lives. This led to lamentations over the dissensions and dismemberment of the Moslem empire, all which they attributed to the ambition of Ali, Moawyah, and Amru. The Karigites were a fanatic sect, and these men were zealots of that dangerous kind who are ready to sacrifice their lives in the accomplishment of any bigot plan. In their infuriate zeal they determined that the only way to restore peace and unity to Islam, would be to destroy those three ambitious leaders, and they devoted themselves to the task, each undertaking to dispatch his victim. The several assassinations were to be effected at the same time, on Friday, the seventeenth of the month Ramadan, at the hour of prayer; and that their blows might be infallibly mortal, they were to use poisoned weapons.

The names of the conspirators were Barak Ibn Abdallah, Amru Ibn Asi, and Abda'lrahman Ibn Melgem. Barak repaired to Damascus and mingled in the retinue of Moawyah on the day appointed, which was the Moslem Sabbath; then, as the usurper was officiating in the mosque as pontiff, Barak gave him what he considered a fatal blow. The wound was desperate, but the life of Moawyah was saved by desperate remedies; the assassin was mutilated of hands and feet and suffered to live; but was slain in after years by a friend of Moawyah.

Amru Ibn Asi, the second of these fanatics, entered the mosque in

Egypt on the same day and hour, and with one blow killed Karijah the Imam, who officiated, imagining him to be Amru Ibn al Aass, who was prevented from attending the mosque through illness. The assassin being led before his intended victim, and informed of his error, replied with the resignation of a predestinarian: "I intended Amru; but Allah intended Karijah." He was presently executed.

Abda'lrahman, the third assassin, repaired to Cufa, where Ali held his court. Here he lodged with a woman of the sect of the Karigites, whose husband had been killed in the battle of Naharwan. To this woman he made proposals of marriage, but she replied she would have no man who could not bring her, as a dowry, three thousand drachms of silver, a slave, a maid-servant, and the head of Ali. He accepted the conditions, and joined two other Karigites, called Derwan and Shabib, with him in the enterprise. They stationed themselves in the mosque to await the coming of the Caliph.

Ali had recently been afflicted with one of his fits of despondency, and had uttered ejaculations which were afterwards considered presages of his impending fate. In one of his melancholy moods he exclaimed, with a heavy sigh, "Alas, my heart! there is need of patience, for there is no remedy against death!" In parting from his house to go to the mosque, there was a clamor among his domestic fowls, which he interpreted into a fatal omen. As he entered the mosque the assassins drew their swords, and pretended to be fighting among themselves; Derwan aimed a blow at the Caliph, but it fell short, and struck the gate of the mosque; a blow from Abda'lrahman was better aimed, and wounded Ali in the head. The assassins then separated and fled. Derwan was pursued and slain at the threshold of his home; Shabib distanced his pursuers and escaped. Abda'lrahman, after some search, was discovered hidden in a corner of the mosque, his sword still in his hand. He was dragged forth and brought before the Caliph. The wound of Ali was pronounced mortal; he consigned his murderer to the custody of his son Hassan, adding, with his accustomed clemency, "Let him want for nothing; and, if I die of my wound, let him not be tortured; let his death be by a single blow." His orders, according to the Persian writers, were strictly complied with, but the Arabians declare that he was killed by piecemeal; and the Moslems opposed to the sect of Ali hold him up as a martyr.

The death of Ali happened within three days after receiving his wound: it was in the fortieth year of the Hegira, A.D. 660. He was about sixty-three years of age, of which he had reigned not quite five. His remains were interred about five miles from Cufa; and, in after times, a magnificent tomb, covered by a mosque, with a splendid dome, rose over his grave, and it became the site of a city called Meshed Ali, or, the Sepulchre of Ali, and was enriched and beautified by many Persian monarchs.

We make no concluding comments on the noble and generous character of Ali, which has been sufficiently illustrated throughout all the recorded circumstances of his life. He was one of the last and worthiest of the primitive Moslems, who imbibed his religious enthusiasm from companionship with the prophet himself; and who followed, to the last, the simplicity of his example. He is honorably spoken of as the first Caliph who accorded some protection to Belles-Lettres. He indulged in the poetic vein himself, and many of his maxims and proverbs are preserved, and have been translated into various languages. His signet bore this inscription: "The kingdom belongs to God." One of his sayings shows the little value he set upon the transitory glories of this world. "Life is but the shadow of a cloud; the dream of a sleeper."

By his first wife, Fatima, the daughter of Mahomet, he had three sons, Mohassan, who died young, and Hassan and Hosein, who survived him. After her death he had eight other wives, and his issue, in all, amounted to fifteen sons and eighteen daughters. His descendants, by Fatima, are distinguished among Moslems as descendants of the prophet, and are very numerous, being reckoned both by the male and female line. They wear turbans of a peculiar fashion, and twist their hair in a different manner from other Moslems. They are considered of noble blood, and designated in different countries by various titles, such as Sheriffs, Fatimites, and Emirs. The Persians venerate Ali as next to the prophet, and solemnize the anniversary of his martyrdom. The Turks hold him in abhorrence, and for a long time, in their prayers, accompanied his name with execrations; but subsequently abated in their violence. It is said that Ali was born in the Caaba, or holy temple of Mecca, where his mother was suddenly taken in labor, and that he was the only person of such distinguished birth.

CHAPTER XLI

*Succession of Hassan, fifth Caliph — He abdicates in favor of
Moawyah*

In his dying moments Ali had refused to nominate a successor, but his
eldest son Hassan, then in his 37th year, was elected without opposition. He stood high in the favor of the people, partly from his having
been a favorite with his grandfather, the prophet, to whom in his features he bore a strong resemblance; but chiefly from the moral excellence of his character, for he was upright, sincere, benevolent and devout. He lacked, however, the energy and courage necessary to a sovereignty, where the sceptre was a sword; and he was unfitted to command in the civil wars which distracted the empire, for he had a horror
of shedding Moslem blood. He made a funeral speech over his father's
remains, showing that his death was coincident with great and solemn
events. "He was slain," said he, "on the same night of the year, in
which the Koran was transmitted to earth; in which Isa (Jesus) was
taken up to heaven, and in which Joshua, the son of Nun, was killed.
By Allah! none of his predecessors surpassed him, nor will he ever be
equalled by a successor."

Then Kais, a trusty friend of the house of Ali, commenced the inauguration of the new Caliph. "Stretch forth thy hand," said he to Hassan, "in pledge that thou wilt stand by the book of God, and the tradition of the apostle, and make war against all opposers." Hassan complied with the ceremonial, and was proclaimed Caliph, and the people
were called upon to acknowledge allegiance to him, and engage to
maintain peace with his friends, and war with his enemies. Some of the
people, however, with the characteristic fickleness of Babylonians, murmured at the suggestion of further warfare, and said, we want no fighting Caliph.

Had Hassan consulted his own inclination, he would willingly have
clung to peace, and submitted to the usurpations of Moawyah; but he
was surrounded by valiant generals eager for action, and stimulated by
his brother Hosein, who inherited the daring character of their father;
beside, there were sixty thousand fighting men, all ready for the field,
and who had been on the point of marching into Syria under Ali. Unwillingly, therefore, he put himself at the head of this force and commenced his march. Receiving intelligence that Moawyah had already
taken the field and was advancing to meet him, he sent Kais in the ad-

vance, with 12,000 light troops, to hold the enemy in check, while he
followed with the main army. Kais executed his commission with spirit,
had a smart skirmish with the Syrians, and having checked them in
their advance, halted and put himself in a position to await the coming
of the Caliph.

Hassan, however, had already become sensible of his incompetency
for military command. There was disaffection among some of his troops,
who were people of Irak or Babylonia, disinclined to this war. On
reaching the city of Madayn, an affray took place among the soldiers in
which one was slain; a fierce tumult succeeded; Hassan attempted to
interfere, but was jostled and wounded in the throng, and obliged to
retire into the citadel. He had taken refuge from violence, and was in
danger of treason, for the nephew of the governor of Madayn proposed
to his uncle, now that he had Hassan within his castle, to make him his
prisoner, and send him in chains to Moawyah. "A curse upon thee for a
traitor and an infidel!" cried the honest old governor; "wouldst thou betray the son of the daughter of the Apostle of God!"

The mild-tempered Caliph, who had no ambition of command, was
already disheartened by its troubles. He saw that he had an active and
powerful enemy to contend with, and fickleness and treachery among
his own people; he sent proposals to Moawyah, offering to resign the
Caliphat to him, on condition that he should be allowed to retain the
money in the public treasury at Cufa, and the revenues of a great estate in Persia, and that Moawyah would desist from all evil-speaking
against his deceased father. Moawyah assented to the two former of
these stipulations, but would only consent to refrain from speaking evil
of Ali in presence of Hassan; and indeed, such was the sectarian hatred
already engendered against Ali, that, under the sway of Moawyah, his
name was never mentioned in the mosques without a curse, and such
continued to be the case for several generations under the dominion of
the house of Ommiah.

Another condition exacted by Hassan, and which ultimately proved
fatal to him, was that he should be entitled to resume the Caliphat on
the death of Moawyah, who was above a score of years his senior.
These terms being satisfactorily adjusted, Hassan abdicated in favor of
Moawyah, to the great indignation of his brother Hosein, who considered the memory of their father Ali dishonored by this arrangement.
The people of Cufa refused to comply with that condition relative to
the public treasury; insisting upon it that it was their property. Moa-

wyah, however, allowed Hassan an immense revenue, with which he retired with his brother to Medina, to enjoy that ease and tranquillity
which he so much prized. His life was exemplary and devout, and the
greater part of his revenue was expended in acts of charity.

Moawyah seems to have been well aware of the power of gold in
making the most distasteful things palatable. An old beldame of the
lineage of Haschem, and branch of Ali, once reproached him with having supplanted that family, who were his cousins, and with having
acted toward them as Pharaoh did toward the children of Israel.
Moawyah gently replied, "May Allah pardon what is past," and inquired what were her wants. She said two thousand pieces of gold for
her poor relations, two thousand as a dower for her children, and two
thousand as a support for herself. The money was given instantly, and
the tongue of the clamorous virago was silenced.

CHAPTER XLII

*Reign of Moawyah I, sixth Caliph – Account of his illegitimate
brother Ziyad – Death of Amru*

Moawyah now, in the forty-first year of the Hegira, assumed legitimate
dominion over the whole Moslem empire. The Karigites, it is true, a
fanatic sect opposed to all regular government, spiritual or temporal,
excited an insurrection in Syria, but Moawyah treated them with more
thorough rigor than his predecessors, and finding the Syrians not sufficient to cope with them, called in his new subjects, the Babylonians, to
show their allegiance by rooting out this pestilent sect; nor did he stay
his hand, until they were almost exterminated.

With this Caliph commenced the famous dynasty of the Ommiades
or Omeyades, so called from Ommiah his great-grandfather; a dynasty
which lasted for many generations, and gave some of the most brilliant
names to Arabian history. Moawyah himself gave indications of intellectual refinement. He surrounded himself with men distinguished in
science or gifted with poetic talent, and from the Greek provinces and
islands which he had subdued, the Greek sciences began to make their
way, and under his protection to exert their first influence on the Arabs.

One of the measures adopted by Moawyah to strengthen himself in
the Caliphat excited great sensation, and merits particular detail. At
the time of the celebrated flight of Mahomet, Abu Sofian, father of
Moawyah, at that time chief of the tribe of Koreish, and as yet an inveterate persecutor of the prophet, halted one day for refreshment at
the house of a publican in Tayef. Here he became intoxicated with
wine, and passed the night in the arms of the wife of a Greek slave,
named Somyah, who in process of time made him the father of a male
child. Abu Sofian, ashamed of this amour, would not acknowledge the
child, but left him to his fate; hence he received the name of Ziyad Ibn
Abihi, that is to say, Ziyad the son of nobody.

The boy, thus deserted, gave early proof of energy and talent. When
scarce arrived at manhood, he surprised Amru Ibn al Aass, by his eloquence and spirit in addressing a popular assembly. Amru, himself illegitimate, felt a sympathy in the vigor of this spurious offset. "By the
prophet!" exclaimed he, "if this youth were but of the noble race of
Koreish, he would drive all the tribes of Arabia before him with his
staff!"

Ziyad was appointed cadi or judge, in the reign of Omar, and was

427

distinguished by his decisions. On one occasion, certain witnesses came
before him accusing Mogeirah Ibn Seid, a distinguished person of un-
blemished character, with incontinence, but failed to establish the
charge; whereupon, Ziyad dismissed the accused with honor, and
caused his accusers to be scourged with rods for bearing false witness.
This act was never forgotten by Mogeirah, who, becoming afterwards
one of the counsellors of the Caliph Ali, induced him to appoint Ziyad
lieutenant or governor of Persia, an arduous post of high trust, the duties of which he discharged with great ability.

After the death of Ali and the abdication of Hassan, events which
followed hard upon each other, Ziyad, who still held sway over Persia,
hesitated to acknowledge Moawyah as Caliph. The latter was alarmed
at this show of opposition, fearing lest Ziyad should join with the family
of Haschem, the kindred of the prophet, who desired the elevation of
Hosein; he, therefore, sent for Mogeirah, the former patron of Ziyad,
and prevailed upon him to mediate between them. Mogeirah repaired
to Ziyad in person, bearing a letter of kindness and invitation from the
Caliph, and prevailed on him to accompany him to Cufa. On their arrival Moawyah embraced Ziyad, and received him with public demon-
strations of respect and affection, as his brother by the father's side.
The fact of their consanguinity was established on the following day,
in full assembly, by the publican of Tayef, who bore testimony to the
intercourse between Abu Sofian and the beautiful slave.

This decision, enforced by the high hand of authority, elevated
Ziyad to the noblest blood of Koreish, and made him eligible to the
highest offices; though in fact, the strict letter of the Mahometan law
would have pronounced him the son of the Greek slave, who was husband of his mother.

The family of the Ommiades were indignant at having the base-born
offspring of a slave, thus introduced among them; but Moawyah disregarded these murmurs; he had probably gratified his own feelings of
natural affection, and he had firmly attached to his interest, a man of
extensive influence, and one of the ablest generals of the age.

Moawyah found good service in his valiant, though misbegotten
brother. Under the sway of incompetent governors the country round
Bassora had become overrun with thieves and murderers, and disturbed by all kinds of tumults. Ziyad was put in the command, and
hastened to take possession of his turbulent post. He found Bassora a
complete den of assassins; not a night but was disgraced by riot and

bloodshed, so that it was unsafe to walk the streets after dark. Ziyad
was an eloquent man, and he made a public speech terribly to the
point. He gave notice that he meant to rule with the sword, and to
wreak unsparing punishment on all offenders; he advised all such,
therefore, to leave the city. He warned all persons from appearing in
public after evening prayers, as a patrol would go the rounds and put
every one to death who should be found in the streets. He carried this
measure into effect. Two hundred persons were put to death by the patrol during the first night, only five during the second, and not a drop
of blood was shed afterwards, nor was there any further tumult or disturbance.

Moawyah then employed him to effect the same reforms in Korassan
and many other provinces, and the more he had to execute, the more
was his ability evinced; until his mere name would quell commotion,
and awe the most turbulent into quietude. Yet he was not sanguinary
nor cruel, but severely rigid in his discipline, and inflexible in the dis-
pensation of justice. It was his custom, wherever he held sway, to order
the inhabitants to leave their doors open at night, with merely a hurdle
at the entrance to exclude cattle, engaging to replace any thing that
should be stolen: and so effective was his police, that no robberies
were committed.

Though Ziyad had whole provinces under his government, he felt
himself not sufficiently employed; he wrote to the Caliph, therefore,
complaining that, while his left hand was occupied in governing Babylonia, his right hand was idle; and he requested the government of Arabia Petrea also, which the Caliph gladly granted him, to the great terror of its inhabitants, who dreaded so stern a ruler. But the sand of
Ziyad was exhausted. He was attacked with the plague when on the
point of setting out for Arabia. The disease made its appearance with
an ulcer in his hand, and the agony made him deliberate whether to
smite it off. As it was a case of conscience among predestinarians, he
consulted a venerable cadi. "If you die," said the old expounder of the
law, "you go before God without that hand, which you have cut off to
avoid appearing in his presence. If you live, you give a by-name to your
children, who will be called the sons of the cripple. I advise you, therefore, to let it alone." The intensity of the pain, however, made him determine on amputation, but the sight of the fire and cauterizing irons
again deterred him. He was surrounded by the most expert physicians,
but, say the Arabians, "It was not in their power to reverse the sealed

decree." He died in the forty-fifth year of the Hegira and of his own age, and the people he had governed with so much severity, considered his death a deliverance. His son Obeid'allah, though only twenty-five years of age, was immediately invested by the Caliph with the government of Korassan, and gave instant proofs of inheriting the spirit of his father. On his way to his government he surprised a large Turkish force, and put them to such sudden flight, that their queen left one of her buskins behind, which fell into the hands of her pursuers, and was estimated, from the richness of its jewels, at two thousand pieces of gold.

Ziyad left another son named Salem, who was, several years afterwards, when but twenty-four years of age, appointed to the government of Korassan, and rendered himself so beloved by the people, that upwards of twenty thousand children were named after him. He had a third son called Kameil, who was distinguished for sagacity and ready wit, and he furthermore left from his progeny a dynasty of princes in Arabia Felix, who ruled under the denomination of the children of Ziyad.

The wise measures of Moawyah produced a calm throughout his empire, although his throne seemed to be elevated on the surface of a volcano. He had reinstated the famous Amru Ibn al Aass in the government of Egypt, allowing him to enjoy the revenues of that opulent province, in gratitude for his having proclaimed him Caliph during his contest with Ali; but stipulating that he should maintain the forces stationed there. The veteran general did not long enjoy this post, as he died in the forty-third year of the Hegira, A.D. 663, as full of honors as of years. In him the cause of Islam lost one of its wisest men and most illustrious conquerors. "Show me," said Omar to him on one occasion, "the sword with which you have fought so many battles and slain so many infidels." The Caliph expressed surprise when he unsheathed an ordinary scimetar. "Alas!" said Amru, "the sword, without the arm of the master, is no sharper nor heavier than the sword of Farezdak the poet."

Mahomet, whose death preceded that of Amru upwards of thirty years, declared that there was no truer Moslem than he would prove to be; nor one more steadfast in the faith. Although Amru passed most of his life in the exercise of arms, he found time to cultivate the softer arts which belong to peace. We have already shown that he was an orator and a poet. The witty lampoons, however, which he wrote against the prophet in his youth, he deeply regretted in his declining age. He sought the company of men of learning and science, and delighted in the conversation of philosophers. He has left some proverbs distinguished for pithy wisdom, and some beautiful poetry, and his dying advice to his children was celebrated for manly sense and affecting pathos.

CHAPTER XLIII

Siege of Constantinople – Truce with the emperor – Murder of Hassan – Death of Ayesha

The Caliph Moawyah being thoroughly established in his sovereignty, was ambitious of foreign conquests, which might shed lustre on his name, and obliterate the memory of these civil wars. He was desirous, also, of placing his son Yezid in a conspicuous light, and gaining for him the affections of the people; for he secretly entertained hopes of making him his successor. He determined, therefore, to send him with a great force to attempt the conquest of Constantinople, at that time the capital of the Greek and Roman empire. This indeed was a kind of holy war; for it was fulfilling one of the most ardent wishes of Mahomet; who had looked forward to the conquest of the proud capital of the Cæsars as one of the highest triumphs of Islam; and had promised full pardon of all their sins to the Moslem army that should achieve it.

The general command of the army in this expedition was given to a veteran named Sophian, and he was accompanied by several of those old soldiers of the faith, battered in the wars, and almost broken down by years, who had fought by the side of the prophet at Beder and Ohod, and were, therefore, honored by the title of "Companions," and who now showed, among the ashes of age, the sparks of youthful fire, as they girded on their swords for this sacred enterprise.

Hosein, the valiant son of Ali, also accompanied this expedition; in which, in fact, the flower of Moslem chivalry engaged. Great preparations were made by sea and land, and sanguine hopes entertained of success; the Moslem troops were numerous and hardy, inured to toil and practised in warfare, and they were animated by the certainty of paradise, should they be victorious. The Greeks, on the other hand, were in a state of military decline, and their emperor, Constantine, a grandson of Heraclius, disgraced his illustrious name by indolence and incapacity.

It is singular and to be lamented, that of this momentous expedition we have very few particulars, notwithstanding that it lasted long, and must have been checkered by striking vicissitudes. The Moslem fleet passed without impediment through the Dardanelles, and the army disembarked within seven miles of Constantinople. For many days they pressed the siege with vigor, but the city was strongly garrisoned by fugitive troops from various quarters, who had profited by sad experience in the defence of fortified towns; the walls were strong and high; and the besieged made use of Greek fire, to the Moslems a new and terrific agent of destruction.

Finding all their efforts in vain, the Moslems consoled themselves by ravaging the neighboring coasts of Europe and Asia, and on the approach of winter retired to the island of Cyzicus, about eighty miles from Constantinople, where they had established their headquarters.

Six years were passed in this unavailing enterprise; immense sums were expended; thousands of lives were lost by disease; ships and crews, by shipwreck and other disasters, and thousands of Moslems were slain, gallantly fighting for paradise under the walls of Constantinople. The most renowned of these was the venerable Abu Ayub, in whose house Mahomet had established his quarters when he first fled to Medina, and who had fought by the side of the prophet at Beder and Ohod. He won an honored grave; for though it remained for ages unknown, yet nearly eight centuries after this event, when Constantinople was conquered by Mahomet II, the spot was revealed in a miraculous vision, and consecrated by a mausoleum and mosque, which exist to this day, and to which the grand seigniors of the Ottoman empire repair to be belted with the scimetar on their accession to the throne.

The protracted war with the Greeks revived their military ardor, and they assailed the Moslems in their turn. Moawyah found the war which he had provoked threatening his own security. Other enemies were pressing on him; age, also, had sapped his bodily and mental vigor, and he became so anxious for safety and repose, that he in a manner purchased a truce of the emperor for thirty years, by agreeing to pay an annual tribute of three thousand pieces of gold, fifty slaves, and fifty horses of the noblest Arabian blood.

Yezid, the eldest son of Moawyah, and his secretly-intended successor, had failed to establish a renown in this enterprise, and if Arabian historians speak true, his ambition led him to a perfidious act sufficient to stamp his name with infamy. He is accused of instigating the murder of the virtuous Hassan, the son of Ali, who had abdicated in favor of Moawyah, but who was to resume the Caliphat on the death of that potentate. It is questionable whether Hassan would ever have claimed this right, for he was of quiet, retired habits, and preferred the security and repose of a private station. He was strong, however, in the affection of the people, and to remove out of the way so dangerous a rival, Yezid, it is said, prevailed upon one of his wives to poison him, promising to marry her in reward of her treason. The murder took place in the forty-ninth year of the Hegira, A.D. 669, when Hassan was forty-seven years of age. In his last agonies, his brother Hosein inquired at whose instigation he supposed himself to have been poisoned, that he might avenge his death, but Hassan refused to name him. "This world," said he, "is only a long night; leave him alone until he and I shall meet in open daylight, in the presence of the Most High."

Yezid refused to fulfil his promise of taking the murderess to wife, alleging that it would be madness to intrust himself to the embraces of such a female; he, however, commuted the engagement for a large amount in money and jewels. Moawyah is accused, of either countenancing, or being pleased with a murder, which made his son more eligible to the succession, for it is said that when he heard of the death of Hassan, "he fell down and worshipped."

Hassan had been somewhat uxorious; or rather, he had numerous wives, and was prone to change them when attracted by new beauties. One of them was the daughter of Yezdegird, the last king of the Persians, and she bore him several children. He had, altogether, fifteen sons and five daughters, and contributed greatly to increase the race of Sheriffs, or Fatimites, descendants from the prophet. In his testament he left directions that he should be buried by the sepulchre of his grandsire Mahomet; but Ayesha, whose hatred for the family of Ali went beyond the grave, declared that the mansion was hers, and refused her consent; he was, therefore, interred in the common burial-ground of the city.

Ayesha, herself, died some time afterwards, in the fifty-eighth year of the Hegira, having survived the prophet forty-seven years. She was often called the Prophetess, and generally denominated the Mother of the Faithful, although she had never borne any issue to Mahomet, and had employed her widowhood in intrigues to prevent Ali and his children, who were the only progeny of the prophet, from sitting on the throne of the Caliphs. All the other wives of Mahomet who survived him, passed the remainder of their lives in widowhood; but none, save her, seem to have been held in especial reverence.

CHAPTER XLIV

Moslem conquests in Northern Africa – Achievements of Acbah; his death

The conquest of Northern Africa, so auspiciously commenced by Abdallah Ibn Saad, had been suspended for a number of years by the pressure of other concerns, and particularly by the siege of Constantinople, which engrossed a great part of the Moslem forces; in the meantime Cyrene had shaken off the yoke, all Cyrenaica was in a state of insurrection, and there was danger that the places which had been taken, and the posts which had been established by the Arab conquerors would be completely lost.

The Caliph Moawyah now looked round for some active and able general, competent to secure and extend his sway along the African sea-coast. Such a one he found in Acbah Ibn Nafe el Fehri, whom he dispatched from Damascus with ten thousand horse. Acbah made his way with all speed into Africa, his forces augmenting as he proceeded, by the accession of barbarian troops. He passed triumphantly through Cyrenaica; laid close siege to the city of Cyrene, and retook it, notwithstanding its strong walls and great population; but in the course of the siege many of its ancient and magnificent edifices were destroyed.

Acbah continued his victorious course westward, traversing wildernesses sometimes barren and desolate; sometimes entangled with forests, and infested by serpents and savage animals, until he reached the domains of ancient Carthage, the present territory of Tunis. Here he determined to found a city to serve as a stronghold, and a place of refuge in the heart of these conquered regions. The site chosen was a valley closely wooded, and abounding with lions, tigers, and serpents. The Arabs give a mavellous account of the founding of the city. Acbah, say they, went forth into the forest, and adjured its savage inhabitants. "Hence! avaunt! wild beasts and serpents! Hence, quit this wood and valley!" This solemn adjuration he repeated three several times, on three several days, and not a lion, tiger, leopard, nor serpent, but departed from the place.

Others, less poetic, record that he cleared away a forest which had been a lurking place not merely for wild beasts and serpents, but for rebels and barbarous hordes; that he used the wood in constructing walls for his new city, and when these were completed, planted his lance in the centre, and exclaimed to his followers, "This is your Caravan." Such was the origin of the city of Kairwan or Caerwan, situated thirty-three leagues southeast of Carthage, and twelve from the sea on the borders of the great desert. Here Acbah fixed his seat of government, erecting mosques and other public edifices, and holding all the surrounding country in subjection.

While Acbah was thus honorably occupied, the Caliph Moawyah, little aware of the immense countries embraced in these recent conquests, united them with Egypt under one command, as if they had been two small provinces, and appointed Muhegir Ibn Omm Dinar, one of the Ansari, as emir or governor. Muhegir was an ambitious, or rather an envious and perfidious man. Scarce had he entered upon his government, when he began to sicken with envy of the brilliant fame of Acbah and his vast popularity, not merely with the army, but throughout the country; he accordingly made such unfavorable reports of the character and conduct of that general, in his letters to the Caliph, that the latter was induced to displace him from the command of the African army, and recall him to Damascus.

The letter of recall being sent under cover to Muhegir, he transmitted it by Muslama Ibn Machlad, one of his generals, to Acbah, charging his envoy to proceed with great caution, and to treat Acbah with profound deference, lest the troops, out of their love for him, should resist the order for his deposition. Muslama found Acbah in his camp at Cyrene, and presented him the Caliph's letter of recall, and a letter from Muhegir as governor of the province, letting him know that Muslama and the other generals were authorized to arrest him should he hesitate to obey the command of the Caliph.

There was no hesitation on the part of Acbah. He at once discerned whence the blow proceeded. "Oh God!" exclaimed he, "spare my life until I can vindicate myself from the slanders of Muhegir Ibn Omm Dinar." He then departed instantly, without even entering his house; made his way with all speed to Damascus, and appeared before Moawyah in the presence of his generals and the officers of his court. Addressing the Caliph with noble indignation, "I have traversed deserts," said he, "and encountered savage tribes; I have conquered towns and regions, and have brought their infidel inhabitants to the knowledge of God and his law. I have built mosques and palaces, and fortified our dominion over the land, and in reward I have been degraded from my post, and summoned hither as a culprit. I appeal to your justice, whether I have merited such treatment?"

Moawyah felt rebuked by the magnanimous bearing of his general, for he was aware that he had been precipitate in condemning him on false accusations. "I am already informed," said he, "of the true nature of the case. I now know who is Muhegir, and who is Acbah; return to the command of the army, and pursue your glorious career of conquest."

Although it was not until the succeeding Caliphat, that Acbah resumed the command in Africa, we will anticipate dates in order to maintain unbroken the thread of his story. In passing through Egypt he deposed Muslama from a command, in which he had been placed by Muhegir, and ordered him to remain in one of the Egyptian towns a prisoner at large.

He was grieved to perceive the mischief that had been done in Africa, during his absence, by Muhegir, who, out of mere envy and jealousy, had endeavored to mar and obliterate all traces of his good deeds; dismantling the cities he had built; destroying his public edifices at Caerwan, and transferring the inhabitants to another place. Acbah stripped him of his command, placed him in irons, and proceeded to remedy the evils he had perpetrated. The population was restored to Caerwan; its edifices were rebuilt, and it rose from its temporary decline more prosperous and beautiful than ever. Acbah then left Zohair Ibn Kais in command of this metropolis, and resumed his career of western conquest, carrying Muhegir with him in chains. He crossed the Kingdom of Numidia, now Algiers, and the vast regions of Mauritania, now Morocco, subduing their infidel inhabitants or converting them with the sword, until coming to the western shores of Africa, he spurred his charger into the waves of the Atlantic, until they rose to his saddle girths; then raising his scimetar toward heaven, "Oh Allah!" cried the zealous Moslem, "did not these profound waters prevent me, still further would I carry the knowledge of thy law, and the reverence of thy holy name!"

While Acbah was thus urging his victorious way to the uttermost bounds of Mauritania, tidings overtook him that the Greeks and barbarians were rising in rebellion in his rear; that the mountains were pouring down their legions, and that his city of Caerwan was in imminent danger. He had in fact incurred the danger against which the late Caliph Omar had so often cautioned his too adventurous generals. Turning his steps he hastened back, marching at a rapid rate. As he passed through Zab or Numidia, he was harassed by a horde of Ber-

bers or Moors, headed by Aben Cahina, a native chief of daring prowess, who had descended from the fastnessess of the mountains, in
which he had taken refuge from the invaders. This warrior, with his
mountain band, hung on the rear of the army, picking off stragglers,
and often carrying havoc into the broken ranks, but never venturing on
a pitched battle. He gave over his pursuit as they crossed the bounds
of Numidia.

On arriving at Caerwan, Acbah found every thing secure; the rebellion having been suppressed by the energy and bravery of Zohair,
aided by an associate warrior, Omar Ibn Ali, of the tribe of Koreish.

Acbah now distributed a part of his army about the neighborhood,
formed of the residue a flying camp of cavalry, and leaving Zohair and
his brave associate to maintain the safety of the metropolis, returned to
scour the land of Zab, and take vengeance on the Berber chief, who
had harassed and insulted him when on the march.

He proceeded without opposition as far as a place called Téhuda;
when in some pass or defile, he found himself surrounded by a great
host of Greeks and Berbers, led on by the mountain chief Aben Cahina. In fact, both Christians and Moors, who had so often been in
deadly conflict in these very regions, had combined to drive these new
intruders from the land.

Acbah scanned the number and array of the advancing enemy, and
saw there was no retreat, and that destruction was inevitable. He marshalled his little army of horsemen, however, with great calmness; put
up the usual prayers, and exhorted his men to fight valiantly. Summoning Muhegir to his presence, "This," said he, "is a day of liberty and
gain for all true Moslems, for it is a day of martyrdom. I would not
deprive you of so great a chance for paradise." So saying, he ordered
his chains to be taken off.

Muhegir thanked him for the favor, and expressed his determination
to die in the cause of the faith. Acbah then gave him arms and a horse,
and both of them drawing their swords, broke the scabbards in token
that they would fight until victory or death. The battle was desperate,
and the carnage terrible. Almost all the Moslems fought to the very
death, asking no quarter. Acbah was one of the last of his devoted band,
and his corpse was found scimetar in hand, upon a heap of the enemy
whom he had slain.

CHAPTER XLV

Moawyah names his successor – His last acts and death – Traits of his character

Moawyah was now far advanced in years, and aware that he had not long to live; he sought therefore, to accomplish a measure which he had long contemplated, and which was indicative of his ambitious character and his pride of family. It was to render the Caliphat hereditary, and to perpetuate it in his line. For this purpose he openly named his son Yezid as his successor, and requested the different provinces to send deputies to Damascus to perform the act of fealty to him. The nomination of a successor was what the prophet himself had not done, and what Abu Beker, Omar, and Othman had therefore declined to do; the attempt to render the Caliphat hereditary was in direct opposition to the public will manifested repeatedly in respect to Ali; Yezid, to whom he proposed to bequeath the government, was publicly detested, yet, notwithstanding all these objections, such influence had Moawyah acquired over the public mind, that delegates arrived at Damascus from all parts, and gave their hands to Yezid in pledge of future fealty. Thus was established the dynasty of the Ommiades, which held the Caliphat for nearly a hundred years. There were fourteen Caliphs of this haughty line, known as the Pharaohs of the house of Omaya (or rather Ommiah). The ambition of rule manisfested in Moawyah, the founder of the dynasty, continued even among his remote descendants, who exercised sovereignty nearly four centuries afterwards in Spain. One of them, anxious to ascend the throne in a time of turbulence and peril, exclaimed: "Only make me king to-day, and you may kill me to-morrow!"

The character of the Caliphat had much changed in the hands of Moawyah, and in the luxurious city of Damascus assumed more and more the state of the oriental sovereigns which it superseded. The frugal simplicity of the Arab, and the stern virtues of the primitive disciples of Islam, were softening down and disappearing among the voluptuous delights of Syria. Moawyah, however, endeavored to throw over his favorite city of Damascus some of the sanctity with which Mecca and Medina were invested. For this purpose he sought to transfer to it, from Medina, the pulpit of the prophet, as also his walking-staff; "for such precious relics of the apostle of God," said he, "ought not to remain among the murderers of Othman."

The staff was found after great search, but when the pulpit was about to be removed, there occurred so great an eclipse of the sun, that the stars became visible. The superstitious Arabs considered this a signal of divine disapprobation, and the pulpit was suffered to remain in Medina.

Feeling his end approaching, Moawyah summoned his son Yezid to his presence, and gave advice full of experience and wisdom. "Confide in the Arabs," said he, "as the sure foundation of your power. Prize the Syrians, for they are faithful and enterprising, though prone to degenerate when out of their own country. Gratify the people of Irak in all their demands, for they are restless and turbulent, and would unsheath a hundred thousand scimetars against thee on the least provocation."

"There are four rivals, my son," added he, "on whom thou must keep a vigilant eye; the first is Hosein, the son of Ali, who has great influence in Irak, but he is upright and sincere, and thy own cousin; treat him, therefore, with clemency, if he fall within thy power. The second is Abdallah Ibn Omar; but he is a devout man, and will eventually come under allegiance to thee. The third is Abda'lrahman; but he is a man of no force of mind, and merely speaks from the dictates of others; he is, moreover, incontinent, and a gambler; he is not a rival to be feared. The fourth is Abdallah Ibn Zobeir; he unites the craft of the fox with the strength and courage of the lion. If he appear against thee, oppose him valiantly; if he offer peace, accept it, and spare the blood of thy people. If he fall within your power, cut him to pieces!"

Moawyah was gathered to his fathers in the sixtieth year of the Hegira, A.D. 679, at the age of seventy, or, as some say, seventy-five years, of which he had reigned nearly twenty. He was interred in Damascus, which he had made the capital of the Moslem empire, and which continued to be so during the dynasty of the Ommiades. The inscription of his signet was "Every deed hath its meed;" or, according to others, "All power rests with God."

Though several circumstances in his reign savor of crafty, and even treacherous policy, yet he bears a high name in Moslem history. His courage was undoubted, and of a generous kind; for though fierce in combat, he was clement in victory. He prided himself greatly upon being of the tribe of Koreish, and was highly aristocratical before he attained to sovereign power; yet he was affable and accessible at all times, and made himself popular among his people. His ambition was tempered with some considerations of justice. He assumed the throne, it is true, by the aid of the scimetar, without regular election; but he subsequently bought off the right of his rival Hassan, the legitimate Caliph; and transcended munificently all the stipulations of his purchase, presenting him, at one time, with four million pieces of gold. One almost regards with incredulity the stories of immense sums passing from hand to hand among these Arab conquerors, as freely as bags of dates in their native deserts; but it must be recollected they had the plundering of the rich empires of the East, and as yet were flush with the spoils of recent conquests.

The liberality of Moawyah is extolled as being beyond all bounds; one instance on record of it, however, savors of policy. He gave Ayesha a bracelet valued at a hundred thousand pieces of gold, that had formerly, perhaps, sparkled on the arm of some Semiramis; but Ayesha, he knew, was a potent friend and a dangerous enemy.

Moawyah was sensible to the charms of poetry, if we may judge from the following anecdotes:

A robber, who had been condemned by the Cadi to have his head cut off, appealed to the Caliph in a copy of verses, pleading the poverty and want by which he had been driven. Touched by the poetry, Moawyah reversed the sentence, and gave the poet a purse of gold, that he might have no plea of necessity for repeating the crime.

Another instance was that of a young Arab, who had married a beautiful damsel, of whom he was so enamored, that he lavished all his fortune upon her. The governor of Cufa happening to see her, was so struck with her beauty, that he took her from the youth by force. The latter made his complaint to the Caliph in verse, poured forth with Arab eloquence, and with all the passion of a lover, praying redress or death. Moawyah, as before, was moved by the poetic appeal, and sent orders to the governor of Cufa to restore the wife to her husband. The governor, infatuated with her charms, entreated the Caliph to let him have the enjoyment of her for one year, and then to take his head. The curiosity of the Caliph was awakened by this amorous contest, and he caused the female to be sent to him. Struck with her ravishing beauty, with the grace of her deportment, and the eloquence of her expressions, he could not restrain his admiration; and in the excitement of the moment told her to choose between the young Arab, the governor of

Cufa, and himself. She acknowledged the honor proffered by the Caliph to be utterly beyond her merit; but avowed that affection and duty
still inclined her to her husband. Her modesty and virtue delighted
Moawyah even more than her beauty; he restored her to her husband,
and enriched them both with princely munificence.

CHAPTER XLVI

Succession of Yezid, seventh Caliph – Final fortunes of Hosein, the son of Ali

Yezid, the son of Moawyah, succeeded to the Caliphat without the ceremony of an election. His inauguration took place in the new moon of the month Rajeb, in the sixtieth year of the Hegira; coincident with the seventh day of April, in the year of our Lord, 680. He was thirty-four years of age, and is described as tall and thin; with a ruddy countenance pitted with the small-pox, black eyes, curled hair, and a comely beard. He was not deficient in talent, and possessed the popular gift of poetry. The effect of his residence among the luxuries and refinements of Syria, was evinced in a fondness for silken raiment and the delights of music; but he was stigmatized as base-spirited, sordid and covetous; grossly sensual, and scandalously intemperate.

Notwithstanding all this, he was readily acknowledged as Caliph throughout the Moslem empire, excepting by Mecca, Medina, and some cities of Babylonia. His first aim was to secure undisputed possession of the Caliphat. The only competitors from whom he had danger to apprehend, were Hosein, the son of Ali, and Abdallah, the son of Zobeir. They were both at Medina, and he sent orders to Waled Ibn Otbah, the governor of that city, to exact from them an oath of fealty. Waled, who was of an undecided character, consulted Merwân Ibn Hakem, formerly secretary of Othman, and suspected of forging the letter which effected the ruin of that Caliph. He was in fact one of the most crafty, as well as able men of the age. His advice to the governor was to summon Hosein and Abdallah to his presence, before they should hear of the death of Moawyah, and concert any measures of opposition; then to tender to them the oath of fealty to Yezid, and, should they refuse, to smite off their heads.

Hosein and Abdallah discovered the plot in time to effect their escape with their families to Mecca; where they declared themselves openly in opposition to Yezid. In a little while Hosein received secret messages from the people of Cufa, inviting him to their city, assuring him not merely of protection, but of joyful homage as the son of Ali, the legitimate successor of the prophet. He had only, they said, to show himself in their city, and all Babylonia would rise in arms in his favor.

Hosein sent his cousin, Muslim Ibn Okail, to ascertain the truth of these representations, and to foment the spirit of insurrection should it

really exist among the people of Cufa. Muslim made his way, almost un-
attended, and with great peril and hardship across the deserts of Irak.
On arriving at Cufa, he was well received by the party of Hosein; they
assured him that eighteen thousand men were ready to sacrifice their
blood and treasure in casting down the usurper and upholding the legitimate Caliph. Every day augmented the number of apparent zealots
in the cause, until it amounted to one hundred and forty thousand. Of
all this, Muslim sent repeated accounts to Hosein; urging him to come
on, and assuring him that the conspiracy had been carried on with
such secrecy, the Nu'mân Ibn Baschir, the governor of Cufa, had no
suspicion of it.

But though the conspiracy had escaped the vigilance of Nu'mân, intimation of it had reached the Caliph Yezid at Damascus, who sent instant orders to Obeid'allah, the emir of Bassora, to repair with all
speed to Cufa, displace its negligent governor, and take that place likewise under his command.

Obeid'allah was the son of Ziyad, and inherited all the energy of his
father. Aware that the moment was critical, he set off from Bassora
with about a score of fleet horsemen. The people of Cufa were on the
look out for the arrival of Hosein, which was daily expected, when Obei-
d'allah rode into the city in the twilight at the head of his troopers.
He wore a black turban, as was the custom likewise with Hosein. The
populace crowded round him, hailing the supposed grandson of the
prophet.

"Stand off!" cried the horsemen fiercely. "It is the emir Obei-
d'allah."

The crowd shrank back abashed and disappointed, and the emir
rode on to the castle. The popular chagrin increased when it was
known that he had command of the province; for he was reputed a second Ziyad in energy and decision. His measures soon proved his claims
to that character. He discovered and disconcerted the plans of the conspirators; drove Muslim to a premature outbreak; dispersed his hasty
levy, and took him prisoner. The latter shed bitter tears on his capture;
not on his own account, but on the account of Hosein, whom he feared
his letters and sanguine representations had involved in ruin, by induc-
ing him to come on to Cufa. The head of Muslim was struck off and
sent to the Caliph.

His letters had indeed produced the dreaded effect. On receiving
them Hosein prepared to comply with the earnest invitation of the peo-

ple of Cufa. It was in vain his friends reminded him of the proverbial faithlessness of these people; it was in vain they urged him to wait until they had committed themselves, by openly taking the field. It was in vain that his near relative Abdallah Ibn Abbas urged him at least, to leave the females of his family at Mecca; lest he should be massacred in the midst of them, like the Caliph Othman. Hosein in the true spirit of a Moslem and predestinarian declared he would leave the event to God; and accordingly set out with his wives and children, and a number of his relatives, escorted by a handful of Arab troops.

Arrived in the confines of Babylonia, he was met by a body of a thousand horse, led on by Harro, an Arab of the tribe of Temimah. He at first supposed them to be a detachment of his partisans sent to meet him, but was soon informed by Harro, that he came from the emir Obeid'allah to conduct him and all the people with him to Cufa.

Hosein haughtily refused to submit to the emir's orders; and represented that he came in peace, invited by the inhabitants of Cufa, as the rightful Caliph. He set forth at the same time, the justice of his claims, and endeavored to enlist Harro in his cause, but the latter, though in no wise hostile to him, avoided committing himself, and urged him to proceed quietly to Cufa under his escort.

While they were yet discoursing, four horsemen rode up accompanied by a guide. One of these named Thirmah was known to Hosein, and was reluctantly permitted by Harro to converse with him apart. Hosein inquired about the situation of things at Cufa. "The nobles," replied the other, "are now against you to a man; some of the common people are still with you; by to-morrow, however, not a scimetar but will be unsheathed against you."

Hosein inquired about Kais, a messenger whom he had sent in advance to apprise his adherents of his approach. He had been seized on suspicion; ordered as a test by Obeid'allah to curse Hosein and his father Ali, and on his refusing had been thrown headlong from the top of the citadel.

Hosein shed tears at hearing the fate of his faithful messenger. "There be some," said he, in the words of the Koran, "who are already dead, and some who living expect death. Let their mansions, Oh God, be in the gardens of paradise, and receive us with them to thy mercy."

Thirmah represented to Hosein that his handful of followers would be of no avail against the host prepared to oppose him in the plains of Cufa, and offered to conduct him to the impregnable mountains of Aja, in the province of Naja, where ten thousand men of the tribe of Tay might soon be assembled to defend him. He declined his advice, however, and advanced towards Kadesia, the place famous for the victory over the Persians. Harro and his cavalry kept pace with him, watching every movement, but offering no molestation. The mind of Hosein, however, was darkened by gloomy forebodings. A stupor at times hung over his faculties as he rode slowly along; he appeared to be haunted with a presentiment of death. "We belong to God and to God we must return," exclaimed he as he roused himself at one time from a dream or reverie. He had beheld in his phantasy, a horseman who had addressed him in warning words, "men travel in the night, and their destiny travels in the night to meet them." This he pronounced a messenger of death.

In this dubious and desponding mood he was brought to a halt, near the banks of the Euphrates, by the appearance of four thousand men, in hostile array, commanded by Amar Ibn Saad. These, likewise, had been sent out by the emir Obeid'allah, who was full of uneasiness lest there should be some popular movement in favor of Hosein. The latter, however, was painfully convinced by this repeated appearance of hostile troops, without any armament in his favor, that the fickle people of Cufa were faithless to him. He held a parley with Amar, who was a pious and good man, and had come out very unwillingly against a descendant of the prophet, stated to him the manner in which he had been deceived by the people of Cufa, and now offered to return to Mecca. Amar dispatched a fleet messenger to apprise the emir of this favorable offer, hoping to be excused from using violence against Hosein. Obeid'allah wrote in reply: "Get between him and the Euphrates; cut him off from the water as he did Othman; force him to acknowledge allegiance to Yezid, and then we will treat of terms."

Amar obeyed these orders with reluctance, and the little camp of Hosein suffered the extremities of thirst. Still he could not be brought to acknowledge Yezid as Caliph. He now offered three things, either to go to Damascus and negotiate matters personally with Yezid; to return into Arabia; or to repair to some frontier post in Khorassan and fight against the Turks. These terms were likewise transmitted by Amar to Obeid'allah.

The emir was exasperated at these delays, which he considered as intended to gain time for tampering with the public feeling. His next letter to Amar was brief and explicit. "If Hosein and his men submit and take the oath of allegiance, treat them kindly; if they refuse, slay them – ride over them – trample them under the feet of thy horses!" This letter was sent by Shamar, a warrior of note, and of a fierce spirit. He had private instructions. "If Amar fail to do as I have ordered, strike off his head and take command of his troops." He was furnished also with a letter of protection, and passports for four of the sons of Ali, who had accompanied their brother Hosein.

Amar, on receiving the letter of the emir, had another parley with Hosein. He found him in front of his tent conversing with his brother Al Abbas, just after the hour of evening prayer, and made known to him the peremptory demand of the emir and its alternative. He also produced the letter of protection and the passports for his brothers, but they refused to accept them.

Hosein obtained a truce until the morning to consider the demand of the emir; but his mind was already made up. He saw that all hope of honorable terms was vain, and he resolved to die.

After the departure of Amar, he remained seated alone at the door of his tent, leaning on his sword, lost in gloomy cogitation on the fate of the coming day. A heaviness again came over him, with the same kind of portentous fantasies that he had already experienced. The approach of his favorite sister, Zeinab, roused him. He regarded her with mournful signficance. "I have just seen," said he, "in a dream, our grandsire the prophet, and he said, 'Thou wilt soon be with me in paradise.'"

The boding mind of Zeinab interpreted the portent. "Woe unto us and our family," cried she, smiting her breast; "our mother Fatima is dead, and our father Ali and our brother Hassan! Alas for the desolation of the past and the destruction that is to come!" So saying her grief overcame her, and she fell into a swoon. Hosein raised her tenderly, sprinkled water in her face, and restored her to consciousness. He entreated her to rely with confidence on God, reminding her that all the people of the earth must die, and every thing that exists must perish, but that God, who created them, would restore them and take them to himself. "My father, and my mother, and my brother," said he, "were better than I, yet they died, and every Moslem has had an example in the death of the apostle of God." Taking her then by the hand, he led her into the tent, charging her, in case of his death, not to give way thus to immoderate sorrow.

He next addressed his friends and followers. "These troops by whom we are surrounded," said he, "seek no life but mine, and will be contented with my death. Tarry not with me, therefore, to your destruction, but leave me to my fate."

"God forbid," cried Al Abbas, "that we should survive your fall;" and his words were echoed by the rest.

Seeing his little band thus determined to share his desperate fortunes, Hosein prepared to sell their lives dear, and make their deaths a memorable sacrifice. By his orders all the tents were disposed in two lines, and the cords interwoven so as to form barriers on both sides of the camp, while a deep trench in the rear was filled with wood, to be set on fire in case of attack. It was assailable, therefore, only in front. This done, the devoted band, conscious that the next day was to be their last, passed the night in prayer; while a troop of the enemy's horse kept riding round to prevent their escape.

When the morning dawned, Hosein prepared for battle. His whole force amounted only to twoscore foot soldiers, and two-and-thirty horse; but all were animated with the spirit of martyrs. Hosein and several of his chief men washed, anointed, and perfumed themselves; "for in a little while," said they, "we shall be with the blackeyed Houris of paradise."

His steadfastness of soul, however, was shaken by the loud lamentations of his sisters and daughters, and the thought of the exposed and desolate state in which his death would leave them. He called to mind, too, the advice which he had neglected of Abdallah Ibn Abbas, to leave his women in safety at Mecca. "God will reward thee, Abdallah!" exclaimed he in the fulness of his feelings.

A squadron of thirty horse, headed by Harro, now wheeled up, but they came as friends and allies. Harro repented him of having given the first check to Hosein, and now came in atonement to fight and die for him. "Alas for you, men of Cufa!" cried he, as Amar and his troops approached; "you have invited the descendant of the prophet to your city, and now you come to fight against him. You have cut off from him and his family the waters of the Euphrates, which are free even to infidels and the beasts of the field, and have shut him up like a lion in the toils."

Amar began to justify himself and to plead the orders of the emir; but the fierce Shamar cut short all parley by letting fly an arrow into the camp of Hosein; calling all to witness that he struck the first blow. A skirmish ensued, but the men of Hosein kept within their camp, where they could only be reached by the archers. From time to time there were single combats in defiance, as was customary with the Arabs. In these the greatest loss was on the side of the enemy, for Hosein's men fought with the desperation of men resolved on death.

Amar now made a general assault, but the camp being open only in front, was successfully defended. Shamar and his followers attempted to pull down the tents, but met with vigorous resistance. He thrust his lance through the tent of Hosein, and called for fire to burn it. The women ran out shrieking. "The fire of Jehennam be thy portion!" cried Hosein, "wouldst thou destroy my family?"

Even the savage Shamar stayed his hand at the sight of defenceless women, and he and his band drew off with the loss of several of their number.

Both parties desisted from the fight at the hour of noontide prayer; and Hosein put up the prayer of Fear, which is only used in time of extremity.

When the prayers were over the enemy renewed the assault, but chiefly with arrows from a distance. The faithful followers of Hosein were picked off one by one, until he was left almost alone; yet no one ventured to close upon him. An arrow from a distance pierced his little son Abdallah, whom he had upon his knee. Hosein caught his blood in the hollow of his hand and threw it toward heaven. "Oh God," exclaimed he, "if thou withholdest help from us, at least take vengeance on the wicked for this innocent blood."

His nephew, a beautiful child with jewels in his ears, was likewise wounded in his arms. "Allah will receive thee, my child," said Hosein; "thou wilt soon be with thy forefathers in paradise."

At this moment Zeinab rushed forth imprecating the vengeance of Heaven upon the murderers of her family. Her voice was overpowered by the oaths and curses of Shamar, who closed with his men upon Hosein. The latter fought desperately, and laid many dead around him, but his strength was failing him; it became a massacre rather than a fight; he sank to the earth, and was stripped ere life was extinct. Thirty wounds were counted in his body, and four-and-thirty bruises. His head was then cut off to be sent to Obeid'allah, and Shamar, with his troops, rode forward and backward over the body, as he had been ordered, until it was trampled into the earth.

Seventy-two followers of Hosein were slain in this massacre; seventeen of whom were descendants from Fatima. Eighty-eight of the enemy were killed, and a great number wounded. All the arms and furniture of Hosein and his family were taken as lawful spoils, although against the command of Amar.

Shamar dispatched one of his troopers to bear the head of Hosein to the emir Obeid'allah. He rode with all speed, but arrived at Cufa after the gates of the castle were closed. Taking the gory trophy to his own house until morning, he showed it with triumph to his wife; but she shrank from him with horror, as one guilty of the greatest outrage to the family of the prophet; and from that time forward renounced all intercourse with him.

When the head was presented to Obeid'allah, he smote it on the mouth with his staff. A venerable Arab present was shocked at his impiety. "By Allah!" exclaimed he, "I have seen those lips pressed by the sacred lips of the prophet!"

As Obeid'allah went forth from the citadel, he beheld several women, meanly attired and seated disconsolately on the ground at the threshold. He had to demand three times who they were, before he was told that it was Zeinab, sister of Hosein, and her maidens. "Allah be praised," cried he with ungenerous exultation, "who has brought this proud woman to shame, and wrought death upon her family." "Allah be praised," retorted Zeinab haughtily, "who hath glorified our family by his holy apostle Mahomet. As to my kindred, death was decreed to them, and they have gone to their resting-place; but God will bring you and them together, and will judge between you."

The wrath of the emir was inflamed by this reply, and his friends, fearful he might be provoked to an act of violence, reminded him that she was a woman and unworthy of his anger.

"Enough," cried he, "let her revile; Allah has given my soul full satisfaction in the death of her brother, and the ruin of her rebellious race."

"True!" replied Zeinab, "you have indeed destroyed our men, and cut us up root and branch. If that be any satisfaction to your soul, you have it."

The emir looked at her with surprise. "Thou art indeed," said he, "a worthy descendant of Ali, who was a poet and a man of courage."

"Courage," replied Zeinab, "is not a woman's attribute; but what my heart dictates, my tongue shall utter."

The emir cast his eyes on Ali, the son of Hosein, a youth just approaching manhood, and ordered him to be beheaded. The proud heart of Zeinab now gave way. Bursting into tears she flung her arms round her nephew. "Hast thou not drunk deep enough of the blood of our family?" cried she to Obeid'allah; "and dost thou thirst for the blood of this youth? Take mine too with it, and let me die with him."

The emir gazed on her again, and with greater astonishment; he mused for awhile, debating with himself, for he was disposed to slay the lad; but was moved by the tenderness of Zeinab. At length his better feelings prevailed, and the life of Ali was spared.

The head of Hosein was transmitted to the Caliph Yezid, at Damascus, in charge of the savage-hearted Shamar; and with it were sent Zeinab and her women, and the youth Ali. The latter had a chain round his neck, but the youth carried himself proudly, and would never vouchsafe a word to his conductors.

When Shamar presented the head with the greetings of Obeid'allah, the Caliph shed tears, for he recalled the dying counsel of his father with respect to the son of Ali. "Oh Hosein!" ejaculated he, "hadst thou fallen into my hands thou wouldst not have been slain." Then giving vent to his indignation against the absent Obeid'allah, "The curse of God," exclaimed he, "be upon the son of Somyah."*

He had been urged by one of his courtiers to kill Ali, and extinguish the whole generation of Hosein, but milder counsels prevailed. When the women and children were brought before him, in presence of the Syrian nobility, he was shocked at their mean attire, and again uttered a malediction on Obeid'allah. In conversing with Zeinab, he spoke with disparagement of her father Ali and her brother Hosein, but the proud heart of this intrepid woman again rose to her lips, and she replied with a noble scorn and just invective, that shamed him to silence.

Yezid now had Zeinab and the other females of the family of Hosein treated with proper respect; baths were provided for them, and apparel suited to their rank; they were entertained in his palace, and the widowed wives of his father Moawyah came and kept them company, and joined with them in mourning for Hosein. Yezid acted also with great kindness toward Ali and Amru, the sons of Hosein, taking them with him in his walks. Amru was as yet a mere child. Yezid asked him one day jestingly, "Wilt thou fight with my son Khaled?" The urchin's eye flashed fire. "Give him a knife," cried he, "and give me one!" "Be-

---

* A sneer at Obeid'allah's illegitimate descent from Somyah, the wife of a Greek slave.

ware of this child," said a crafty old courtier who stood by, and who was
an enemy to the house of Ali. "Beware of this child, depend upon it,
one serpent is the parent of another."

After a time when the family of Hosein wished to depart for Medina,
Yezid furnished them abundantly with every comfort for the journey,
and a safe convoy under a careful officer, who treated them with all
due deference. When their journey was accomplished, Zeinab and Fatima, the young daughter of Hosein, would have presented their conductor with some of their jewels, but the worthy Syrian declined their
offer. "Had I acted for reward," said he, "less than these jewels would
have sufficed; but what I have done, was for the love of God, and for
the sake of your relationship to the prophet."

The Persians hold the memory of Hosein in great veneration, enti-
tling him Shahed or the Martyr, and Seyejed or Lord; and he and his
lineal descendants for nine generations are enrolled among the twelve
Imams or Pontiffs of the Persian creed. The anniversary of his martyrdom is called Rus Hosein (the day of Hosein), and is kept with great
solemnity. A splendid monument was erected in after years on the spot
where he fell, and was called in Arabic Meshed Hosein, The Sepulchre
of Hosein. The Shyites, or sectaries of Ali, relate divers prodigies as
having signalized his martyrdom. The sun withdrew his light, the stars
twinkled at noonday and clashed against each other, and the clouds
rained showers of blood. A supernatural light beamed from the head of
the martyr, and a flock of white birds hovered around it. These miracles, however, are all stoutly denied by the sect of Moslems called
Sonnites, who hold Ali and his race in abomination.

The death of Hosein had removed one formidable rival of Yezid; but gave strength to the claims of another, who was scarcely less popular. This was Abdallah, the son of Zobeir; honored for his devotion to the faith; beloved for the amenity of his manners, and of such adroit policy, that he soon managed to be proclaimed Caliph, by the partisans of the house of Haschem, and a large portion of the people of Medina and Mecca. The martyrdom, as he termed it, of Hosein furnished him a theme for public harangues, with which, after his inauguration, he sought to sway the popular feelings. He called to mind the virtues of that grandson of the prophet, his pious watchings, fastings, and prayers; the perfidy of the people of Cufa, to which he had fallen a victim; the lofty heroism of his latter moments, and the savage atrocities which had accompanied his murder. The public mind was heated by these speeches; the enthusiasm awakened for the memory of Hosein was extended to his politic eulogist. An Egyptian soothsayer, famed for skill in divination, and who had studied the prophet Daniel, declared that Abdallah would live and die a king; and this operated powerfully in his favor among the superstitious Arabs, so that his party rapidly increased in numbers.

The Caliph Yezid, although almost all the provinces of the empire were still in allegiance to him, was alarmed at the movements of this new rival. He affected, however to regard him with contempt, and sent a silver collar to Merwân Ibn Hakem, then governor of Medina, directing him to put it round the neck of the "mock Caliph," should he persist in his folly, and send him in chains to Damascus. Merwân, however, who was of a wily character himself, and aware of the craft and courage of Abdallah, and his growing popularity in Medina, evaded the execution of the order.

Yezid had no better success in his endeavors to crush the rising power of Abdallah at Mecca. In vain he repeatedly changed his governors of that city; each in his turn was outwitted by the superior sagacity of Abdallah, or overawed by the turbulent discontent of the people.

Various negotiations took place between Yezid and these disaffected cities, and dispatches were sent from the latter to Damascus; but these only rendered the schism in the Caliphat more threatening. The deputies brought back accounts of the dissolute life of Yezid, which shocked the pious and abstemious Arabs of the sacred cities. They represented him as destitute of religion and morality; neglectful of the hours of worship; a gross sensualist addicted to wine and banqueting; an effeminate voluptuary, passing his time amid singing and dancing women, listening to music and loose minstrelsy, and surrounded by dogs and eunuchs.

The contempt and loathing caused by their representations were fomented by the partisans of Abdallah Ibn Zobeir, and extended to the whole house of Ommiah, of which Yezid was a member. Open rebellion at length broke out in a manner characteristic of the Arabs. During an assemblage in the mosque of Medina, one of the conspirators threw his turban on the ground, exclaiming, "I cast off Yezid as I cast off this turban." Another seconded him with the exclamation, "I cast off Yezid as I cast off this shoe." Heaps of shoes and turbans soon showed that the feeling was unanimous.

The next move was to banish the house of Ommiah and all its dependents; but these, to the number of a thousand, took refuge in the palace of Merwân Ibn Hakem, the governor, who was of that race. Here they were closely besieged and sent off to Yezid, imploring instant succor.

It was with difficulty Yezid could prevail upon any of his generals to engage in so unpopular a cause. Meslem Ibn Okbah, a stout-hearted but infirm old general, at length undertook it; but observed, with contempt, that a thousand men who suffered themselves to be cooped up like fowls, without fighting, scarce deserved assistance.

When the troops were about to depart, Yezid rode about among them, his scimetar by his side, and an Arab bow across his shoulder, calling upon them to show their loyalty and courage. His instructions to Meslem were to summon the city of Medina, three days in succession, before he made any assault; if it refused to surrender, he should, after taking it, give it up to three days' pillage. He charged him, however, to be careful of the safety of the youth Ali, son of Hosein, who was in the city, but had taken no part in the rebellion.

Meslem departed at the head of twelve thousand horse and five thousand foot. When he arrived before Medina he found a huge trench digged round the city, and great preparations made for defence. On three successive days he summoned it to surrender, and on each day re-

ceived a refusal. On the fourth day he attacked it by storm, making
his assault on the east side, that the besieged might be blinded by the
rising sun. The city held out until most of its prime leaders were slain;
it would then have capitulated, but the stern old general compelled an
unconditional surrender.

Meslem entered the city sword in hand, and sent instantly for Ali,
the youthful son of Hosein, whom he placed on his own camel, and
furnished with a trusty guard. His next care was to release the thousand
men of the house of Ommiah from confinement, lest they should be involved in the sacking of the city; this done, he abandoned the place for
three days to his soldiery, and a scene of slaughter, violence, and rapine
ensued, too horrible to be detailed. Those of the inhabitants who survived the massacre were compelled to submit as slaves and vassals of
Yezid. The rigid severity of old Meslem, which far surpassed his orders,
gained him the appellation of Musreph, or, The Extortionate. His
memory has ever been held in odium by the Moslems, for the outrages
which he permitted in this sacred city. This capture of Medina took
place at night, in the sixty-third year of the Hegira, and the year 682 of
the Christian era.

The old general now marched on to wreak the same fate upon Mecca;
but his fires were burnt out; he died on the march of fatigue, infirmity,
and old age, and the command devolved on a Syrian general named
Hozein Ibn Thamir. The latter led his force up to the walls of Mecca,
where Abdallah Ibn Zobeir commanded in person. For the space of
forty days he besieged the city: battering the walls with engines brought
from Syria. In the course of the siege a part of the Caaba was beaten
down and the rest burnt. Some ascribe the fire to the engines of the
besiegers; and others affirm that Abdallah, hearing a shouting in the
night, caused a flaming brand to be elevated on a lance to discover the
cause, and that the fire communicated to the veil which covered the
edifice.

Mecca was reduced to extremity, and the inhabitants began to dread
the fate of Medina, when a swift messenger brought to Abdallah Ibn
Zobeir the joyful tidings of the death of Yezid. He immediately mounted
the walls and demanded of the besiegers why they continued to fight,
seeing that their master Yezid was no more. They regarded his words
as a mere subterfuge, and continued the attack with increased vigor.
The intelligence, however, was speedily confirmed.

Hozein now held a conference with Abdallah; he expressed an ardent desire to put an end to all further effusion of kindred blood; and proffered the allegiance of himself and his army, in which were some of the leading men of Syria. Abdallah, for once, was too cautious for his own good. He shrank from trusting himself with Hozein and his army; he permitted them, however, at their earnest request, to walk in religious procession round the ruins of the Caaba, of course without arms; after which Hozein and his host departed on the march homeward; and the late beleaguered family of Ommiah accompanied them to Syria.

The death of the Caliph Yezid took place at Hawwarin, in Syria, in the sixty-fourth year of the Hegira, A.D. 683, in the thirty-ninth year of his age, after a reign of three years and six months. He was cut down in the flower of his days, say the Moslem writers, in consequence of his impiety in ordering the sacking of Medina, the burial-place of the prophet; for the latter had predicted, "Whoever injureth Medina, shall melt away even as salt melteth in water." The Persian writers also, sectarians of Ali, hold the memory of Yezid in abhorrence, charging him with the deaths of Hassan and Hosein, and accompany his name with the imprecation, "May he be accursed of God!"

CHAPTER XLVIII

Inauguration of Moawyah II, eighth Caliph – His abdication and death – Merwân Ibn Hakem and Abdallah Ibn Zobeir, rival Caliphs – Civil wars in Syria

On the death of Yezid, his son, Moawyah II, was proclaimed at Damascus, being the third Caliph of the house of Ommiah. He was in the twenty-first year of his age, feeble in mind and body, and swayed in his opinions and actions by his favorite teacher Omar Almeksus, of the sect of the Kadarii, who maintain the free-will of men, and that a contrary opinion would make God the author of sin.

Moawyah assumed the supreme authority with extreme reluctance, and felt his incompetency for its duties; for the state of his health obliged him to shun daylight, and keep in darkened rooms; whence the Arabs, in their propensity to by-names, gave him the derisive appellation of Abuleilah, "Father of the Night."

He abdicated at the end of six months, alleging his incompetency. The Ommiades were indignant at his conduct; they attributed it, and probably with reason, to the counsels of the sage Omar Almeksus, on whom they are said to have wreaked their rage by burying him alive.

Moawyah refused to nominate a successor. His grandfather Moawyah, he said, had wrested the sceptre from the hands of a better man; his father Yezid had not merited so great a trust, and he himself, being unworthy and unfit to wield it, was equally unworthy to appoint a successor; he left the election, therefore, to the chiefs of the people. In all which he probably spake according to the dictates of the sage Omar Almeksus.

As soon as he had thrown off the cares of government, he shut himself up in the twilight gloom of his chamber, whence he never stirred until his death; which happened soon after: caused, some say, by the plague, others by poison. His own diseased frame and morbid temperament, however, account sufficiently for his dissolution.

The election of a Caliph again distracted the Moslem empire. The leading men at Damascus determined upon Merwân Ibn Hakem, of the family of Ommiah, and once the secretary of state of Othman, who had so craftily managed the correspondence of that unfortunate Caliph. He was now well stricken in years; tall and meagre, with a pale face and yellow beard, doubtless tinged according to oriental usage. Those who elected him took care to stipulate that he should not nominate any of

457

his posterity as his successor; but should be succeeded by Khaled, the son of Yezid; as yet a minor. Merwân, in his eagerness for power, pledged himself without hesitation; how faithfully he redeemed his pledge will be seen hereafter.

While this election was held at Damascus, Abdallah Ibn Zobeir was acknowledged as Caliph in Mecca, Medina, and throughout Arabia, as also in Korassan, in Babylonia, and in Egypt.

Another candidate for the supreme power unexpectedly arose in Obeid'allah Ibn Ziyad; the emir of Bassora; the same who had caused the massacre of Hosein. He harangued an assemblage of the people of Bassora on the state of the contending factions in Syria and Arabia; the importance of their own portion of the empire, so capable of sustaining itself in independence, and the policy of appointing some able person as a protector to watch over the public weal, until these dissensions should cease, and a Caliph be unanimously appointed. The assembly was convinced by his reasoning, and urged him to accept the appointment. He declined it repeatedly with politic grace, but was at length prevailed upon; and the leaders gave him their hands, promising allegiance to him as a provisional chief, until a Caliph should be regularly elected. His authority, however, was but of short duration. The people of Cufa, who had experienced his tyranny as governor, rejected with scorn his election as protector; their example reacted upon the fickle Bassorians, who suddenly revoked their late act of allegiance, rose in tumultuous opposition to the man they had so recently honored, and Obeid'allah was fain to disguise himself in female attire, and take refuge in the house of an adherent. During his sway, however, he had secured an immense amount of gold from the public treasury. This he now shared among his partisans, and distributed by handsful among the multitude: but though he squandered in this way above two hundred thousand pieces of gold upon the populace, and raised a few transient tumults in his favor, he was ultimately obliged to fly for his life, and his effects were pillaged by the rabble. So fared it with the temporary tyrant who smote the gory head of the virtuous Hosein.

He fled by night at the head of only a hundred men; after a time weariness compelled him to exchange the camel on which he was mounted for an ass. In this humble plight, with drooping head, and legs dangling to the ground, journeyed the imperious Obeid'allah, who, but the day before, was governor of Babylonia, and aspired to the throne of the Caliphs. One of his attendants noticing his dejection, and hearing him mutter to himself, supposed him smitten with contrition, and upbraiding himself with having incurred these calamities, as a judgment for the death of Hosein: he ventured to suggest his thoughts and to offer consolation; but Obeid'allah quickly let him know that his only repentance and self-reproach were for not having attacked the faithless Bassorians, and struck off their heads at the very outbreak of their revolt. Obeid'allah effected his escape into Syria, and arrived at Damascus in time to take an active part in the election of Merwân to the Caliphat: in the meantime Bassora declared its allegiance to Abdallah Ibn Zobeir.

The claims of Merwân to the Caliphat were acknowledged in Syria alone, but Syria, if undivided, was an empire in itself. It was divided, however. A powerful faction headed by Dehac Ibn Kais, late governor of Cufa, disputed the pretensions of Merwân, and declared for Abdallah. They appeared in arms in the plain near Damascus. Merwân took the field against them in person; a great and sanguinary battle took place; Dehac and fourscore of the flower of Syrian nobility were slain, and an immense number of their adherents. Victory declared for Merwân. IIe called off his soldiers from the pursuit, reminding them that the fugitives were their brethren.

When the head of Dehac was brought to him he turned from it with sorrow. "Alas!" exclaimed he, "that an old and worn-out man like myself, should occasion the young and vigorous to be cut to pieces!"

His troops hailed him as Caliph beyond all dispute; and bore him back in triumph to Damascus. He took up his abode in the palace of his predecessors Moawyah and Yezid; but now came a harder part of his task. It had been stipulated that at his death, Khaled the son of Yezid should be his successor; it was now urged that he should marry the widow of Yezid, the mother of the youth, and thus make himself his legitimate guardian.

The aged Merwân would fain have evaded this condition, but it was forced upon him as a measure of policy, and he complied; no sooner, however, was the marriage solemnized than he left his capital and his bride, and set off with an army for Egypt, to put down the growing ascendency of Abdallah in that region. He sent in advance, Amru Ibn Saad, who acted with such promptness and vigor, that while the Caliph was yet on the march, he received tidings that the lieutenant of Abdallah had been driven from the province, and the Egyptians brought under subjection; whereupon, Merwân turned his face again toward Damascus.

Intelligence now overtook him that an army under Musab, brother of Abdallah, was advancing upon Egypt. The old Caliph again faced about, and resumed his march in that direction, but again was anticipated by Amru, who routed Musab in a pitched battle, and completely established the sway of Merwân over Egypt. The Caliph now appointed his son Abd'alaziz to the government of that important country, and once more returned to Damascus, whither he was soon followed by the victorious Amru.

CHAPTER XLIX

State of affairs in Khorassan – Conspiracy at Cufa – Faction of the Penitents; their fortunes – Death of the Caliph Merwân

In the present divided state of the Moslem empire, the people of Khorassan remained neuter, refusing to acknowledge either Caliph. They appointed Salem, the son of Ziyad, to act as regent, until the unity of the Moslem government should be restored. He continued for a length of time in this station, maintaining the peace of the province, and winning the hearts of the inhabitants by his justice, equity, and moderation.

About this time, there was a sudden awakening among the sect of Ali, in Babylonia. The people of Cufa, proverbially fickle and faithless, were seized with tardy remorse for the fate of Hosein, of which they were conscious of being the cause. Those who had not personally assisted in his martyrdom, formed an association to avenge his death. Above a hundred of the chief men of the country joined them; they took the name of The Penitents, to express their contrition for having been instrumental in the death of the martyr, and they chose for their leader one of the veteran companions of the prophet, the venerable Solyman Ibn Sorâd, who devoted his gray hairs to this pious vengeance.

The awakening spread far and wide; in a little while upwards of sixteen thousand names were enrolled; a general appeal to arms was anticipated throughout the country, and the verteran Solyman called upon all true Moslems disposed to prosecute this "holy war," to assemble at a place called Nochaila. Before the appointed time, however, the temporary remorse of the people of Cufa had subsided; the enthusiasm for the memory of Hosein had cooled throughout the province; intriguing meddlers, jealous of the appointment of Solyman, had been at work, and when the veteran came to the place of assemblage, he found but an inconsiderable number prepared for action.

He now dispatched two horsemen to Cufa, who arrived there at the hour of the last evening prayer, galloped through the streets to the great mosque, rousing the Penitents with the war cry of "Vengeance for Hoscin." The call was not lost on the real enthusiasts; a kind of madness seized upon many of the people, who thronged after the couriers, echoing the cry of vengeance. The cry penetrated into the depths of the houses. One man tore himself from the arms of a beautiful and tenderly beloved wife, and began to arm for battle. She asked him if

461

he were mad. "No!" cried he, "but I hear the summons of the herald of God, and I fly to avenge the death of Hosein." "And in whose protection do you leave our child?" "I commend him and thee to the protection of Allah!" So saying he departed.

Another called for a lance and steed; told his daughter that he fled from crime to penitence; took a hurried leave of his family and galloped to the camp of Solyman.

Still, when the army of Penitents was mustered on the following day it did not exceed four thousand. Solyman flattered himself, however, that reinforcements, promised him from various quarters, would join him when on the march. He harangued his scanty host, roused their ardor, and marched them to the place of Hosein's murder, where they passed a day and night in prayer and lamentation. They then resumed their march. Their intention was to depose both Caliphs, Merwân and Abdallah; to overthrow the family of Ommiah, and restore the throne to the house of Ali; but their first object was vengeance on Obeid'allah, the son of Ziyad, to whom they chiefly ascribed the murder of Hosein. The aged Solyman led his little army of enthusiasts through Syria, continually disappointed of recruits, but unabated in their expectation of aid from heaven, until they were encountered by Obeid'allah with an army of twenty thousand horsemen, and cut in pieces.

In the midst of these internal feuds and dissensions, a spark of the old Saracen spirit was aroused by the news of disastrous reverses in Northern Africa. We have recorded in a former chapter, the heroic but disastrous end of Acbah on the plains of Numidia, where he and his little army were massacred by a Berber host, led on by Aben Cahina. That Moorish chieftain, while flushed with victory, had been defeated by Zohair before the walls of Caerwan, and the spirits of the Moslems had once more revived; especially on the arrival of reinforcements sent by Abd'alaziz from Egypt. A sad reverse, however, again took place. A large force of imperialists, veteran and well armed soldiers from Constantinople, were landed on the African coast to take advantage of the domestic troubles of the Moslems, and drive them from their African possessions. Being joined by the light troops of Barbary, they attacked Zobeir in open field. He fought long and desperately, but being deserted by the Egyptian reinforcements, and overpowered by numbers, was compelled to retreat to Barca, while the conquering foe marched on to Caerwan, captured that city, and made themselves masters of the surrounding country.

It was the tidings of this disastrous reverse, and of the loss of the great outpost of Moslem conquest in Northern Africa, that roused the Saracen spirit from its domestic feuds. Abd'almâlec, the eldest son of the Caliph Merwân, who had already served in Africa, was sent with an army to assist Zobeir. He met that general in Barca, where he was again collecting an army. They united their forces; retraced the westward route of victory, defeated the enemy in every action, and replaced the standard of the faith on the walls of Caerwan. Having thus wiped out the recent disgraces, Abd'almâlec left Zobeir in command of that region, and returned covered with glory to sustain his aged father in the Caliphat at Damascus.

The latter days of Merwân had now arrived. He had been intriguing and faithless in his youth; he was equally so in his age. In his stipulations on receiving the Caliphat, he had promised the succession to Khaled, the son of Yezid; he had since promised it to his nephew Amru, who had fought his battles and confirmed his power; in his latter days he caused his own son Abd'almâlec, fresh from African exploits, to be proclaimed his successor, and allegiance to be sworn to him. Khaled, his step-son, reproached him with his breach of faith; in the heat of reply, Merwân called the youth by an opprobrious epithet; which brought in question the chastity of his mother. This unlucky word, is said to have caused the sudden death of Merwân. His wife, the mother of Khaled, is charged with having given him poison; others say that she threw a pillow on his face while he slept, and sat on it until he was suffocated. He died in the 65th year of the Hegira, A.D. 684, after a brief reign of not quite a year.

On the death of Merwân, his son Abd'almâlec was inaugurated Caliph at Damascus, and acknowledged throughout Syria and Egypt, as well as in the newly-conquered parts of Africa. He was in the full vigor of life, being about forty years of age; his achievements in Africa testify his enterprise, activity, and valor, and he was distinguished for wisdom and learning. From the time of his father's inauguration he had been looking forward to the probability of becoming his successor, and ambition of sway had taken place of the military ardor of his early youth. When the intelligence of his father's death reached him, he was sitting cross-legged, in oriental fashion, with the Koran open on his knees. He immediately closed the sacred volume and rising exclaimed, "Fare thee well, I am called to other matters."

The accession to sovereign power is said to have wrought a change in his character. He had always been somewhat superstitious; he now became attentive to signs, omens and dreams, and grew so sordid and covetous, that the Arabs, in their propensity to give characteristic and satirical surnames, used to call him Rafhol Hejer, that is to say, Sweat-Stone; equivalent to our vulgar epithet of skin-flint.

Abdallah Ibn Zobeir was still acknowledged as Caliph by a great portion of the Moslem dominions, and held his seat of government at Mecca; this gave him great influence over the true believers, who resorted in pilgrimage to the Caaba. Abd'almâlec determined to establish a rival place of pilgrimage within his own dominions. For this purpose he chose the temple of Jerusalem, sacred in the eyes of the Moslems, as connected with the acts and revelations of Moses, of Jesus, and of Mahomet, and as being surrounded by the tombs of the prophets. He caused this sacred edifice to be enlarged so as to include within its walls the steps upon which the Caliph Omar prayed on the surrender of that city. It was thus converted into a mosque, and the venerable and sanctified stone called Jacob's pillow, on which the patriarch is said to have had his dream, was presented for the kisses of pilgrims, in like manner as the black stone of the Caaba.

There was at this time a general of bold, if not ferocious character, who played a sort of independent part in the troubles and commotions of the Moslem empire. He was the son of Abu Obeidah, and was some-

times called Al Thakifi, from his native city Tayef, but won for himself
the more universal appellation of Al Moktâr, or the Avenger. The first
notice we find of him is during the short reign of Hassan, the son of
Ali, being zealously devoted to the family of that Caliph. We next find
him at Cufa, harboring and assisting Muslem, the emissary of Hosein,
and secretly fomenting the conspiracy in favor of the latter. When the
emir Obeid'allah came to Cufa, he was told of the secret practices of Al
Moktâr, and questioned him on the subject. Receiving a delusive reply,
he smote him over the face with his staff and struck out one of his eyes.
He then cast him into prison, where he lay until the massacre of Hosein. Intercessions were made in his favor with the Caliph Yezid, who
ordered his release. The emir executed the order, but gave Al Moktâr
notice, that if, after the expiration of three days, he were found within
his jurisdiction, his life should be forfeit.

Al Moktâr departed, uttering threats and maledictions. One of his
friends who met him, inquired concerning the loss of his eye. "It was
the act of that son of a wanton, Obeid'allah," said he, bitterly, "but
may Allah confound me if I do not one day cut him in pieces." Blood
revenge for the death of Hosein became now his ruling thought. "May
Allah forsake me," he would say, "if I do not kill as many in vengeance
of that massacre, as were destroyed to avenge the blood of John, the
son of Zacharias, on whom be peace!"

He now repaired to Mecca, and presented himself before Abdallah
Ibn Zobeir, who had recently been inaugurated; but he would not take
the oath of allegiance until the Caliph had declared his disposition to
revenge the murder of Hosein. "Never," said he, "will the affairs of Abdallah prosper, until I am at the head of his army taking revenge for
that murder."

Al Moktâr fought valiantly in defence of the sacred city while besieged; but when the siege was raised in consequence of the death of
Yezid, and Abdallah became generally acknowledged, he found the
Caliph growing cold towards him, or towards the constant purpose of
his thoughts; he left him therefore, and set out for Cufa, visiting all the
mosques on the way, haranguing the people on the subject of the
death of Hosein, and declaring himself his avenger.

On arriving at Cufa, he found his self-appointed office of avenger
likely to be forestalled by the veteran Solyman, who was about to depart on his mad enterprise with his crazy Penitents. Calling together the
sectaries of Ali, he produced credentials from Mahomet, the brother of

Hosein, which gained for him their confidence; and then represented to them the rashness and futility of the proposed expedition; and to his opposition may be ascribed the diminished number of volunteers that assembled at the call of Solyman.

While thus occupied he was arrested on a charge of plotting an insurrection with a view to seize upon the province, and was thrown into the same prison in which he had been confined by Obeid'allah. During his confinement he kept up a correspondence with the sectaries of Ali by letters conveyed in the lining of a cap. On the death of the Caliph Merwân he was released from prison, and found himself head of the Alians, or powerful sect of Ali; who even offered their adhesion to him as Caliph, on condition that he would govern according to the Koran, and the Sonna or traditions, and would destroy the murderers of Hosein and his family.

Al Moktâr entered heartily upon the latter part of his duties, and soon established his claim to the title of Avenger. The first on whom he wreaked his vengeance was the ferocious Shamar, who had distinguished himself in the massacre of Hosein. Him he overcame and slew. The next was Caulah, who cut off the head of Hosein and conveyed it to the emir Obeid'allah. Him he beleaguered in his dwelling, and killed, and gave his body to the flames. His next victim was Amar Ibn Saad, the commander of the army that surrounded Hosein; with him he slew his son; and sent both of their heads to Mahomet, the brother of Hosein. He then seized Adi Ibn Hathem, who had stripped the body of Hosein while the limbs were yet quivering with life. Him he handed over to some of the sect of Ali, who stripped him, set him up as a target, and discharged arrows at him until they stood out from his body like the quills of a porcupine. In this way Al Moktâr went on, searching out the murderers of Hosein wherever they were to be found, and inflicting on them a diversity of deaths.

Sustained by the Alians, or sect of Ali, he now maintained a military sway in Cufa, and held, in fact, a sovereign authority over Babylonia; he felt, however, that his situation was precarious; an army out of Syria, sent by Abd'almâlec, was threatening him on one side; and Musab, brother of the Caliph Abdallah, was in great force at Bassora menacing him on the other. He now had recourse to stratagems to sustain his power, and accomplish his great scheme of vengeance. He made overtures to Abdallah, offering to join him with his forces. The wary Caliph suspected his sincerity, and required, as proofs of it, the oath of allegiance from himself and his people, and a detachment to proceed against the army of Abd'almâlec.

Al Moktâr promptly sent off an officer, named Serjabil, with three thousand men, with orders to proceed to Medina. Abdallah, still wary and suspicious, dispatched a shrewd general, Abbas Ibn Sahel, with a competent force to meet Serjabil and sound his intentions, and if he were convinced there was lurking treachery, to act accordingly.

Abbas and Serjabil encountered at the head of their troops on the highway to Medina. They had an amicable conference, in which Abbas thought he discovered sufficient proof of perfidy. He took measures accordingly. Finding the little army of Serjabil almost famished for lack of provisions, he killed a great number of fat sheep and distributed them among the hungry troops. A scene of hurry and glad confusion immediately took place. Some scattered themselves about the neighborhood in search of fuel; some were cooking, some feasting. In this unguarded moment Abbas set upon them with his troops, slew Serjabil, and nearly four hundred of his men; but gave quarter to the rest, most of whom enlisted under his standard.

Al Moktâr, finding that his good faith was doubted by Abdallah, wrote privately to Mahomet, brother of Hosein, who was permitted by the Caliph to reside in Mecca, where he led a quiet, inoffensive life, offering to bring a powerful army to his assistance if he would take up arms. Mahomet sent a verbal reply, assuring Al Moktâr of his belief in the sincerity of his offers; but declining all appeal to arms, saying he was resolved to bear his lot with patience, and leave the event to God. As the messenger was departing he gave him a parting word: "Bid Al Moktâr fear God and abstain from shedding blood."

The pious resignation and passive life of Mahomet were of no avail. The suspicious eye of Abdallah was fixed upon him. The Cufians of the sect of Ali, and devotees to the memory of Hosein, who yielded allegiance to neither of the rival Caliphs, were still permitted to make their pilgrimages to the Caaba, and when in Mecca, did not fail to do honor to Mahomet Ibn Ali and his family. The secret messages of Al Moktâr to Mahomet were likewise known. The Caliph Abdallah, suspecting a conspiracy, caused Mahomet and his family, and seventeen of the principal pilgrims from Cufa, to be arrested, and confined in the edifice by the sacred well Zem Zem, threatening them with death, unless by a certain time they gave the pledge of allegiance.

From their prison they contrived to send a letter to Al Moktâr, ap-

prising him of their perilous condition. He assembled the Alians, or
sect of Ali, at Cufa, and read the letter. "This comes," said he, "from
Mahomet, the son of Ali and brother of Hosein. He and his family, the
purest of the house of your prophet, are shut up like sheep destined for
the slaughter. Will you desert them in their extremity, and leave them
to be massacred as you did the martyr Hosein and his family?"

The appeal was effectual; the Alians cried out to be led to Mecca. Al
Moktâr marshalled out seven hundred and fifty men, bold riders, hard
fighters, well armed and fleetly mounted, arranged them in small
troops to follow each other at considerable intervals, troop after troop
like the waves of the sea; the leader of the first troop, composed of a
hundred and fifty men, was Abu Abdallah Aljodali. He set off first; the
others followed at sufficient distance to be out of sight, but all spurred
forward, for no time was to be lost.

Abu Abdallah was the first to enter Mecca. His small troop awakened no alarm. He made his way to the well of Zem Zem, crying "Vengeance for Hosein;" drove off the guard and broke open the prison
house, whence he liberated Mahomet Ibn Ali and his family.

The tumult brought the Caliph and his guard. Abu Abdallah would
have given them battle, but Mahomet interfered, and represented that
it was impious to fight within the precincts of the Caaba. The Caliph,
seeing the small force that was with Abdallah, would on his part have
proceeded to violence, when lo, the second troop of hard riders spurred
up; then the third, and presently all the rest; shouting "Allah Achbar,"
and "Vengeance for Hosein."

The Caliph, taken by surprise, lost all presence of mind. He knew
the popularity of Mahomet Ibn Ali and his family, and dreaded an insurrection. Abu Abdallah in the moment of triumph would have put
him to death, but his hand was stayed by the pious and humane Mahomet. The matter was peaceably adjusted. The Caliph was left unmolested; Mahomet distributed among his friends and adherents a great
sum of money, which had been sent to him by Al Moktâr, and then
with his family departed in safety from Mecca.

Al Moktâr had now to look to his safety at home; his old enemy
Obeid'allah, former emir of Cufa, was pressing forward at the head of an
army of the Caliph Abd'almâlec, to recover that city, holding out to his
troops a promise of three days' sack and pillage. Al Moktâr called on
the inhabitants to take arms against their former tyrant and the murderer of Hosein. A body of troops sallied forth headed by Ibrahim, the

son of Alashtar. To give a mysterious sanctity to the expedition, Al Moktâr caused a kind of throne covered with a veil to be placed on a mule, and led forth with the army; to be to them what the ark was to the children of Israel, a sacred safeguard. On going into battle, the following prayer was to be offered up at it: "Oh God! keep us in obedience to thee; and help us in our need." To which all the people were to respond, "Amen!"

The army of Ibrahim encountered the host of Obeid'allah on the plains, at some distance from Cufa. They rushed forward with a holy enthusiasm inspired by the presence of their ark: "Vengeance for Hosein!" was their cry, and it smote upon the heart of Obeid'allah. The battle was fierce and bloody; the Syrian force, though greatly superior, was completely routed; Obeid'allah was killed, fighting with desperate valor, and more of his soldiers were drowned in the flight than were slaughtered in the field. This signal victory was attributed, in a great measure, to the presence of the ark or veiled throne, which thenceforward was regarded almost with idolatry.

Ibrahim caused the body of Obeid'allah to be burnt to ashes, and sent his head to Al Moktâr. The gloomy heart of the Avenger throbbed with exultation, as he beheld this relic of the man who had oppressed, insulted, and mutilated him; he recollected the blow over the face which had deprived him of an eye, and smote the gory head of Obeid'allah, even as he had been smitten.

Thus, says the royal and pious historian Abulfeda, did Allah make use of the deadly hate of Al Moktâr, to punish Obeid'allah, the son of Ziyad, for the martyrdom of Hosein.

The triumph of Al Moktâr was not of long duration. He ruled over a fickle people, and he ruled them with a rod of iron. He persecuted all who were not, or whom he chose to consider as not, of the Hosein party, and he is charged with fomenting an insurrection of the slaves against the chief men of the city of Cufa. A combination was at length formed against him, and an invitation was sent to Musab Ibn Zobeir, who had been appointed emir of Bassora, by his brother, the Caliph Abdallah.

The invitation was borne by one Shebet, an enthusiast who made his entrance into Bassora on a mule with cropt ears and tail, his clothes rent, exclaiming with a loud voice, "Ya gautha! Ya gautha! Help! help!" He delivered his message in a style suited to his garb, but accompanied it by letters from the chief men of Cufa, which stated their grievances in a more rational manner. Musab wrote instantly to Al Mohalleb, the emir of Persia, one of the ablest generals of the time, to come to his aid with men and money; and on his arrival, joined forces with him to attack the Avenger in his seat of power.

Al Moktâr did not wait to be besieged. He took the field with his accustomed daring, and gave battle beneath the walls of his capital. It was a bloody fight; the presence of the mysterious throne had its effect upon the superstitious minds of the Cufians, but Al Moktâr had become hateful from his tyranny, and many of the first people were disaffected to him. His army was routed; he retreated into the royal citadel of Cufa, and defended it bravely and skilfully, until he received a mortal wound. Their chief being killed, the garrison surrendered at discretion, and Musab put every man to the sword, to the number of seven thousand.

Thus fell Al Moktâr Ibn Abu Obeidah, in his sixty-seventh year, after having defeated the ablest generals of three Caliphs, and by the sole power of his sword, made himself the independent ruler of all Babylonia. He is said never to have pardoned an enemy; to have persecuted with inveterate hate all who were hostile to the family of Ali, and in vengeance of the massacre of Hosein, to have shed the blood of nearly fifty thousand men, exclusive of those who were slain in battle. Well did he merit the title of the Avenger.

CHAPTER LI

Musab Ibn Zobeir takes possession of Babylonia – Usurpation of Amru Ibn Saad; his death – Expedition of Abd'almâlec against Musab – The result – Omens; their effect upon Abd'almâlec – Exploits of Al Mohalleb

The death of Al Moktâr threw the province of Babylonia, with its strong capital, Cufa, into the hands of Musab Ibn Zobeir, brother to the Caliph Abdallah. Musab was well calculated to win the favor of the people. He was in the flower of his days, being but thirty-six years of age, comely in person, engaging in manners, generous in spirit, and of consummate bravery, though not much versed in warfare. He had been an intimate friend of Abd'almâlec before the latter was made Caliph, but he was brother to the rival Caliph, and connected by marriage with families in deadly opposition to the house of Ommiah. Abd'almâlec, therefore, regarded him as a formidable foe, and warned by the disasters of his army under Obeid'allah, resolved now to set out at the head of a second expedition in person, designed for the invasion of Babylonia.

In setting forth on this enterprise, he confided the government of Damascus to his cousin, Amru Ibn Saad; he did this in consideration of the military skill of Amru, though secretly there was a long nourished hate between them. The origin of this hatred shows the simplicity of Saracen manners in those days. When boys, Abd'almâlec and Amru were often under the care of an old beldame of their family, who used to prepare their meals, and produce quarrels between them in the allotment of their portions. These childish disputes became fierce quarrels and broils as they grew up together, and were rivals in their youthful games and exercises. In manhood they ripened into deadly jealousy and envy, as they became conquering generals; but the elevation of Abd'almâlec to the Caliphat, sank deep into the heart of Amru, as a flagrant wrong; the succession having been promised to him by his uncle, the late Caliph Merwân, as a reward for having subjugated Egypt. As soon, therefore, as Abd'almâlec had departed from Damascus, Amru, not content with holding the government of the city, aspired to the sovereignty of Syria, as his rightful dominion.

Abd'almâlec heard of the usurpation while on the march, returned rapidly in his steps, and a bloody conflict ensued between the forces of the rival cousins in the streets of Damascus. The women rushed be-

471

tween them; held up their children and implored the combatants to desist from this unnatural warfare. Amru laid down his arms and articles of reconciliation were drawn up and signed by the cousins.

Abd'almâlec proved faithless to his engagements. Getting Amru into his power by an artful stratagem, he struck off his head; put to death the principal persons who had supported him in his usurpation, and banished his family. As the exiles were about to depart, he demanded of the widow of Amru, the written articles of pacification which he had exchanged with her husband. She replied that she had folded them up in his winding sheet, to be at hand at the final day of judgment.

Abd'almâlec now resumed his march for Babylonia. He had sent agents before him to tamper with the fidelity of the principal persons. One of these, Ibrahim Ibn Alashtar, he had offered to make emir if he would serve his cause. Ibrahim, who was of incorruptible integrity, showed the letter to Musab, warned him that similar attempts must have been made to sap the fidelity of other persons of importance and advised him to use the scimetar freely, wherever he suspected disaffection; but Musab was too just and merciful to act thus upon mere suspicion. The event showed that Ibrahim understood the fickle and perfidious nature of the people of Irak.

A battle took place on the margin of the desert, not far from Palmyra. It commenced with a gallant charge of cavalry, headed by Ibrahim Ibn Alashtar, which broke the ranks of the Syrians and made great havoc. Abd'almâlec came up with a reinforcement, and rallied his scattered troops. In making a second charge, however, Ibrahim was slain, and now the perfidy of the Cufians became apparent. Musab's general of horse wheeled round and spurred ignominiously from the field; others of the leaders refused to advance. Musab called loudly for Ibrahim; but seeing his lifeless body on the ground, "Alas!" he exclaimed, "there is no Ibrahim for me this day."

Turning to his son Isa, a mere stripling, yet who had fought with manly valor by his side, "Fly, my son," cried he; "fly to thy uncle Abdallah at Mecca; tell him of my fate, and of the perfidy of the men of Irak." Isa, who inherited the undaunted spirit of the family of Zobeir, refused to leave his father. "Let us retreat," said he, "to Bassora, where you will still find friends, and may thence make good your return to Mecca."

"No, my son!" replied Musab, "never shall it be said among the men of Koreish, that I fled the field of battle, or entered the temple of Mecca, a vanquished general!"

During an interval of the battle, Abd'almâlec sent Musab an offer of his life. His reply was, he had come to conquer or to die. The conflict was soon at an end. The troops who adhered to Musab were cut to pieces, his son Isa was slain by his side, and he himself, after being repeatedly wounded with arrows was stabbed to the heart, and his head struck off.

When Abd'almâlec entered Cufa in triumph, the fickle inhabitants thronged to welcome him and take the oath of allegiance, and he found himself in quiet possession of both Babylonia and Persian Irak. He distributed great sums of money to win the light affections of the populace, and gave a sumptuous banquet in the citadel to which all were welcome.

In the height of the banquet, when all was revelry, a thought passed through the mind of the Caliph, as to the transient duration of all human grandeur. "Alas!" he ejaculated, "how sweetly we might live, if a shadow would but last!" The same vein of melancholy continued when the banquet was over, and he walked about the castle with an old gray-headed inhabitant, listening to his account of its antiquities and traditions. Every reply of the old man to his questions about things or persons, began with the words, "This was, – That was, – He was."

"Alas!" sighed the Caliph, repeating a verse from an Arabian poet; "every thing new soon runneth to decay, and of every one that is, it is soon said, He was!"

While thus conversing, the head of Musab was brought to him, and he ordered a thousand dinars of gold to the soldier who brought it, but he refused the reward. "I slew him," he said, "not for money, but to avenge a private wrong." The old chronicler of the castle now broke forth on the wonderful succession of events. "I am fourscore and ten years old," said he, "and have outlived many generations. In this very castle I have seen the head of Hosein presented to Obeid'allah, the son of Ziyad; then the head of Obeid'allah to Al Moktâr; then the head of Al Moktâr to Musab, and now that of Musab to yourself." The Caliph was superstitious, and the words of the old man sounded ominously as the presage of a brief career to himself. He determined that his own head should not meet with similar fate within that castle's walls, and gave orders to raze the noble citadel of Cufa to the foundation.

Abd'almâlec now appointed his brother Besher Ibn Merwân to the government of Babylonia; and as he was extremely young, he gave him, as chief counsellor, or vizier, a veteran named Musa Ibn Nosseyr, who had long enjoyed the confidence of the family of Merwân, as had his father before him. It is said by some that his father Nosseyr was a liberated slave of the Caliph's brother Abd'alaziz, and employed by him in high functions. So great was the confidence of the Caliph in Musa, that he intrusted him with all the military rolls of the province, and signified to him that in future the responsibility would rest upon him. On taking possession of his government, Besher delivered his seal of office into the hands of Musa, and intrusted him with the entire management of affairs. This Musa, it will be found, rose afterwards to great renown.

The Caliph also appointed Khaled Ibn Abdallah to the command at Bassora, after which he returned to his capital of Damascus. The province of Babylonia, however, was not destined to remain long at peace. There was at this time a powerful Moslem sect in Persia, a branch of the Motazelites, called Azarakites from the name of their founder Ibn Al Azarak, but known also by the name of Separatists. They were enemies of all regular government, and fomenters of sedition and rebellion. During the sway of the unfortunate Musab, they had given him great trouble by insurrections in various parts of the country, accompanied by atrocious cruelties. They had been kept in check, however, by Mohalleb, the lieutenant of Musab, and one of the ablest generals of the age, who was incessantly on the alert at the head of the army, and never allowed their insurrections to come to any head.

Mohalleb was on a distant command at the time of the invasion and conquest. As soon as he heard of the defeat and death of Musab, and the change in the government of Irak, he hastened to Bassora to acknowledge allegiance to Abd'almâlec. Khaled accepted his services, in the name of the Caliph, but instead of returning him to the post he had so well sustained at the head of the army, appointed him supervisor or collector of tributes, and gave the command of the forces to his own brother, named Abd'alaziz. The change was unfortunate. The Azarakites had already taken breath, and acquired strength during the temporary absence of their old adversary, Mohalleb; but as soon as they heard he was no longer in command, they collected all their forces and made a rapid inroad into Irak.

Abd'alaziz advanced to meet them; but he was new to his own

troops, being a native of Mecca, and he knew little of the character of the enemy. He was entirely routed, and his wife, a woman of great beauty, taken captive. A violent dispute arose among the captors as to the ransom of their prize, some valuing her at one hundred thousand dinars: until a furious zealot, indignant that her beauty should cause dissension among them, struck off her head.

The Caliph Abd'almâlec was deeply grieved when he heard of this defeat, and wrote to Khaled, emir of Bassora, reproving him for having taken the command of the army from Mohalleb, a man of penetrating judgment, and hardened in war, and given it to Abd'alaziz, "a mere Arab of Mecca." He ordered him, therefore, to replace Mohalleb forthwith, and wrote also to his brother, Besher, emir of Babylonia, to send the general reinforcements.

Once more Mohalleb proved his generalship, by defeating the Azarakites in a signal and bloody battle near the city of Ahwâz; nor did he suffer them to rally, but pursued them over the borders and into the heart of the mountains, until his troops lost almost all their horses, and returned crowned with victory, but wayworn and almost famished.

The effect of all these internal wars was to diminish, for a time, the external terror of the Moslem name. The Greek emperor, during the recent troubles, had made successful incursions into Syria; and Abd'almâlec, finding enemies enough among those of his own faith, had been fain to purchase a humiliating truce of the Christian potentate by an additional yearly tribute of fifty thousand ducats.

CHAPTER LII

Abd'almâlec makes war upon his rival Caliph in Mecca – Siege of the sacred city – Death of Abdallah – Demolition and reconstruction of the Caaba

Abd'almâlec, by his recent victories, had made himself sovereign of all the eastern part of the Moslem dominions; he had protected himself also from the Christian emperor by a disgraceful augmentation of tribute; he now determined to carry a war against his rival, Abdallah, to the very gates of Mecca; and make himself sovereign of an undivided empire.

The general chosen for this important enterprise was Al Hejagi (or Hedjadgi) Ibn Yusef, who rose to renown as one of the ablest and most eloquent men of that era. He set off from Damascus with but two thousand men; but was joined by Taric Ibn Amar with five thousand more. Abd'almâlec had made proclamations beforehand, promising protection and favor to such of the adherents of Abdallah as should come unto his allegiance, and he trusted that many of the inhabitants of Mecca would desert to the standard of Al Hejagi.

Abdallah sent forth troops of horse to waylay and check the advance of the army, but they were easily repulsed, and Al Hejagi arrived without much difficulty before the sacred city. Before proceeding to hostilities he discharged arrows over the walls carrying letters, in which the inhabitants were assured that he came merely to release them from the tyranny of Abdallah; and were invited to accept the most favorable terms, and abandon a man who would fain die with the title of Caliph, though the ruins of Mecca should be his sepulchre.

The city was now assailed with battering-rams and catapults; breaches were made in the walls; the houses within were shattered by great stones, or set on fire by flaming balls of pitch and naphtha.

A violent storm of thunder and lightning killed several of the besiegers, and brought them to a pause. "Allah is wreaking his anger upon us," said they, "for assailing his holy city." Al Hejagi rebuked their superstitious fears and compelled them to renew the attack; setting them an example by discharging a stone with his own hands.

On the following day there was another storm which did most injury to the garrison. "You perceive," said Al Hejagi, "the thunder strikes your enemies as well as yourselves."

The besieged held out valiantly, and repulsed every assault. Abdal-

lah, though now aged and infirm, proved himself a worthy son of Zobeir. During the early part of the siege, he resided chiefly in the Caaba;
that sacred edifice, therefore, became an object of attack; a part of it
was battered down by stones, and it was set on fire repeatedly by the
balls of naphtha. He therefore abandoned it, and retired to his own
dwelling. He was sustained throughout all this time of peril by the
presence and counsels of his mother; a woman of masculine spirit and
unfailing energy, though ninety years of age. She was the granddaughter of Abu Beker, and proved herself worthy of her descent. She accompanied her son to the ramparts; caused refreshments to be distributed among the fighting men; was consulted in every emergency and
present in every danger.

The siege continued with unremitting strictness; many of Abdallah's
most devoted friends were killed; others became disheartened; nearly
ten thousand of the inhabitants deserted to the enemy; even two of the
Caliph's sons, Hamza and Koheib, forsook him, and made terms for
themselves with the besiegers.

In this forlorn state, his means of defence almost exhausted, and
those who ought to have been most faithful deserting him; Abdallah
was tempted by an offer of his own terms on condition of surrender.

He turned to his aged mother for advice. "Judge for yourself, my
son," said the resolute descendant of Abu Beker. "If you feel that your
cause is just, persevere. Your father Zobeir died for it, as did many of
your friends. Do not bend your neck to the scorn of the haughty race
of Ommiah. How much better an honorable death, than a dishonored
life for the brief term you have yet to live."

The Caliph kissed her venerable forehead. "Thy thoughts are my
own," said he, "nor has any other motive than zeal for God induced me
thus far to persevere. From this moment, consider thy son as dead; and
refrain from immoderate lamentation." "My trust is in God," replied
she, "and I shall have comfort in thee, my son, whether I go before or
follow thee."

As she took a parting embrace, she felt a coat of mail under the
outer garments of Abdallah, and told him to put it off, as unsuited to a
martyr prepared to die. "I have worn it," replied he, "that I might be
the better able to defend thee, my mother." He added that he had little
fear of death, but a horror of the insults and exposures to which his
body might be subjected after death.

"A sheep once killed, my son, feels not the flaying." With these words she gave him, to rouse his spirits, a cordial draught in which was a strong infusion of musk, and Abdallah went forth a self-devoted martyr.

This last sally of the veteran Caliph struck terror and astonishment into the enemy. At the head of a handful of troops he repulsed them from the breach; drove them into the ditch, and slew an incredible number with his own hand; others, however, thronged up in their place: he fought until his followers were slain, his arrows expended, and he had no weapon but sword and lance. He now retreated, step by step, with his face to the foe, disputing every inch of ground, until he arrived in a narrow place where he could only be assailed in front. Here he made his last stand. His opponents, not daring to come within reach of his weapons, assailed him from a distance with darts and arrows, and when these missiles were expended, with bricks, and tiles and stones. A blow on the head from a stone made him totter, and the blood streamed down his face and beard. His assailants gave a shout; but he recovered himself and uttered a verse of a poet, "The blood of our wounds falls on our instep, not on our heels;" implying that he had not turned his back upon the foe. At length he sank under repeated wounds and bruises, and the enemy closing upon him cut off his head. Thus died Abdallah the son of Zobeir, in the seventy-third year of the Hegira, and the seventy-second year of his own age, after a stormy and disastrous reign of nine years.

Taric Ibn Amar, struck with admiration of his persevering valor, exclaimed, "Never did woman bear a braver son!" "How is this," cried Al Hejagi, "do you speak thus of an enemy of the Commander of the Faithful?" But Abd'almâlec, when the speech was reported to him, concurred in the praise of his fallen rival. "By Allah!" exclaimed he, "what Taric hath spoken is the truth." When the tidings of Abdallah's death were brought to his aged mother, she experienced a revulsion of nature which she had not known for fifty years, and died of hemorrhage.

Abdallah was said to unite the courage of the lion with the craftiness of the fox. He was free from any glaring vice, but reputed to be sordidly covetous and miserly, insomuch that he wore the same garment for several years. It was a saying in Arabia, that he was the first example of a man being at the same time brave and covetous; but the spoils of foreign conquest were fast corrupting the chivalrous spirit of the Arab conquerors. He was equally renowned for piety, being according to tradition so fixed and immovable in prayer, that a pigeon once perched upon his head mistaking him for a statue.

With the death of Abdallah ended the rival Caliphat, and the conquering general received the oaths of allegiance of the Arabs for Abd'almâlec. His conduct, however, toward the people of Mecca and Medina, was as cruel and oppressive as his military operations had been brilliant. He inflicted severe punishments for trivial offences, sometimes on mere suspicion; and marked many with stamps of lead upon the neck, to disgrace them in the public eye. His most popular act was the reconstruction of the dilapidated Caaba on the original form which it had borne before the era of the prophet.

For a time the people of Mecca and Medina groaned under his tyranny, and looked back with repining to the gentler sway of Abdallah; and it was a cause of general joy throughout those cities, when the following circumstances caused him to be removed from their government and promoted to a distant command.

Though the death of Abdallah had rendered Abd'almâlec sole sovereign of the Moslem empire, the emir of Khorassan, Abdallah Ibn Hazem, who had been appointed by his rival, hesitated to give in his allegiance. His province, so distant and great in extent, might make him a dangerous rebel; Abd'almâlec, therefore, sent a messenger, claiming his oath of fealty, and proffering him in reward, the government of Khorassan for seven years, with the enjoyment of all its revenues; at the same time, he sent him the head of the deceased Caliph, to intimate the fate he might expect should he prove refractory.

The emir, instead of being intimidated, was filled with horror, and swore never to acknowledge Abd'almâlec as Commander of the Faithful. He reverently washed and embalmed the head, folded it in fine linen, prayed over it, and sent it to the family of the deceased Caliph at Medina. Then summoning the messenger, he made him eat the epistle of Abd'almâlec in his presence, and dismissed him with the assurance that his sacred character of herald alone saved his head.

It was to go against this refractory but high-minded emir, that Al Hejagi was called off from his command in Arabia. He entered Khorassan with a powerful army, defeated the emir in repeated battles, and at length slew him and reduced the province to obedience.

The vigor, activity, and indomitable courage displayed by Al Hejagi in these various services, pointed him out as the very man to take

charge of the government of Babylonia, or Irak, recently vacated by
the death of the Caliph's brother Besher; and he was accordingly sent
to break that refractory province into more thorough obedience.

The province of Babylonia, though formerly a part of the Persian
empire, had never been really Persian in character. Governed by viceroys, it had partaken of the alien feeling of a colony; forming a frontier
between Persia and Arabia, and its population made up from both
countries, it was deficient in the virtues of either. The inhabitants had
neither the simplicity and loyalty of the Arabs of the desert, nor the
refinement and cultivation of the Persians of the cities. Restless, turbulent, factious, they were ever ready to conspire against their rulers; to
desert old faiths, and to adopt new sects and heresies. Before the conquest by the Moslems, when Irak was governed by a Persian satrap,
and Syria by an imperial prefect, a spirit of rivalry and hostility existed
between these frontier provinces; the same had revived during the division of the Caliphat; and while Syria was zealous in its devotion to
the house of Ommiah, Irak had espoused the cause of Ali. Even since
the reunion and integrity of the Caliphat, it still remained a restless,
unsteady part of the Moslem empire; the embers of old seditions still
lurked in its bosom, ready at any moment once more to burst forth into
flame. We shall see how Al Hejagi fared in his government of that most
combustible province.

CHAPTER LIII

Administration of Al Hejagi as emir of Babylonia

Al Hejagi, aware of the nature of the people over whom he was to rule, took possession of his government in military style. Riding into Cufa at the head of four thousand horse, he spurred on to the mosque, alighted at the portal, and ascending the pulpit, delivered an harangue to the multitude, that let them know the rigorous rule they were to expect. He had come, he said, "to make the wicked man bear his own burden, and wear his own shoe;" and, as he looked round on the densely-crowded assemblage, he intimated he saw before him turbaned heads ripe for mowing, and beards which required to be moistened with blood.

His sermon was carried out in practice; he ruled with a rigorous hand, swearing he would execute justice in a style that should put to shame all who had preceded, and serve as an example to all who might follow him. He was especially severe, and even cruel, towards all who had been in any way implicated in the assassination of the Caliph Othman. One person, against whom he came prepared to exercise the utmost severity, was the veteran Musa Ibn Nosseyr, who had officiated as prime minister to the deceased emir Basher. He had been accused of appropriating and squandering the taxes collected in the province, and the Caliph had lent a too ready ear to the accusation. Fortunately, the following letter, from a friend in Damascus, apprised Musa in time of his danger:

"Thy deposition is signed; orders have been despatched to Al Hejagi to seize on thy person and inflict on thee the most severe punishment: so away! away! thy safety depends on the fleetness of thy horse. If thou succeed in placing thyself under the protection of Abd'alaziz Ibn Merwân, all will go well with thee."

Musa lost no time, but mounted his steed and fled to Damascus, where Abd'alaziz was then sojourning, having arrived with the tribute of Egypt. Abd'alaziz received with protecting kindness the veteran adherent of the family, and accompanied him before the Caliph. "How darest thou show thy beard here?" exclaimed Abd'almâlec." "Why should I hide it?" replied the veteran; "what have I done to offend the Commander of the Faithful?" "Thou hast disobeyed my orders, and squandered my treasures." "I did no such thing," replied Musa, firmly; "I have always acted like a faithful subject; my intentions have been pure; my actions true." "By Allah," cried the Caliph, "thou shalt make thy defalcation good fifty times over." The veteran was about to make an angry reply, but at a sign from Abd'alaziz, he checked himself, and bowing his head, "Thy will be done," said he, "oh, Commander of the Faithful." He was fined fifty thousand dinars of gold; which, however, Abd'alaziz enabled him to pay; and, on his return to his government in Egypt, took his old favorite with him. How he further indemnified Musa for his maltreatment will be shown hereafter.

To resume the affairs of Al Hejagi in Irak. Having exercised the rod of government in Cufa, he proceeded to Bassora, where he was equally sharp with his tongue, and heavy with his hand. The consequence was, as usual, an insurrection. This suited his humor. He was promptly in the field; defeated the rebels in a pitched battle; sent the heads of eighteen of their leaders to the Caliph, and then returned to the administration of affairs at Bassora. He afterwards sent two of his lieutenants to suppress a new movement among the Azarakite sectaries, who were defeated and driven out of the province.

In the 76th year of the Hegira, a conspiracy was formed against the life of Abd'almâlec, by two Karigite fanatics, named Shebib Ibn Zeid and Saleh Ibn Mari. Their conspiracy was discovered and defeated, but they made their escape and repaired to the town of Daras, in Mesopotamia, where they managed to get together adherents to the number of one hundred and twenty men. Saleh was smooth-tongued and seductive; having a melodious voice and a great command of figurative language. He completely fascinated and bewildered his companion Shebib, and their infatuated followers, mingling his inflammatory harangues with pious precepts and expositions of the Koran. In the end he was hailed Commander of the Faithful by the motley crew, and gravely accepted the office. His men were all armed, but most of them were on foot; he therefore, led them, to a neighboring village, where they seized upon the best horses in the name of Allah and the prophet, to whom they referred the owners for payment.

Mahomet, brother of Abd'almâlec, who was at that time emir of Mesopotamia, was moved to laughter when he heard of this new Caliph and his handful of rabble followers; and ordered Adi, one of his officers, to take five hundred men and sweep them from the province.

Adi shook his head doubtfully. "One madman," said he, "is more dangerous than five soldiers in their senses."

"Take one thousand, then," said the emir; and with that number well armed and mounted, Adi set out in quest of the fanatics. He found them and their pseudo Caliph living in free quarters on the fat of the land, and daily receiving recruits in straggling parties of two, and three, and four at a time, armed with such weapons as they could catch up in their haste. On the approach of Adi they prepared for battle, having full confidence that a legion of angels would fight on their side.

Adi held a parley, and endeavored to convince them of the absurdity of their proceedings, or to persuade them to carry their marauding enterprises elsewhere; but Saleh, assuming the tone of Caliph as well as sectarian, admonished Adi and his men to conform to his doctrines, and come into his allegiance. The conference ended while it was yet the morning hour. Adi still forbore to attack such a handful of misguided men, and paid dearly for his forbearance. At noontide, when he and his men were engaged in the customary prayer, and their steeds were feeding, the enthusiast band charged suddenly upon them with the cry of Allah Achbar! Adi was slain in the onset, and his body was trampled under foot; his troops were slaughtered or dispersed, and his camp and horses, with a good supply of arms, became welcome booty to the victors.

The band of sectarians increased in numbers and in daring after this signal exploit. Al Hejagi sent five thousand veteran troops against them, under Al Hareth Alamdani. These came by surprise upon the two leaders, Saleh and Shebib, with a party of only ninety men, at a village on the Tigris not far from Mousul, the capital of Mesopotamia. The fanatic chiefs attacked the army with a kind of frantic courage, but Saleh, the mock Caliph, was instantly killed, with a score of his followers. Shebib was struck from his horse, but managed to keep together the remnant of his party; made good his retreat with them into Montbagi, a dismantled fortress, and swung to and secured the ponderous gate.

The victors kindled a great fire against the gate, and waited patiently until it should burn down, considering their prey secure.

As the night advanced, Shebib, who from his desolate retreat watched anxiously for some chance of escape, perceived, by the light of the fire, that the greater part of the besiegers, fatigued by their march, were buried in deep sleep. He now exacted from his men an oath of implicit obedience, which they took between his hands. He then caused them to steep most of their clothing in a tank of water within the castle, after which, softly drawing the bolts of the flaming gate, they threw it down on the fire kindled against it; flung their wet garments on the burning bridge thus suddenly formed, and rushed forth scimetar in hand.

Instead of contenting themselves with an escape, the crazy zealots charged into the very heart of the sleeping camp, and wounded the general before an alarm was given. The soldiers started awake in the midst of havoc and confusion; supposing themselves surprised by a numerous army, they fled in all directions, never ceasing their flight until they had taken refuge in Mosul or Jukhi, or some other walled city.

Shebib established himself amid the abundance of the deserted camp; scarce any of his men had been killed or wounded in this midnight slaughter; he considered himself therefore invincible; proclaimed himself Commander of the Faithful, and partisans crowded to his standard. Strengthened by numbers, he led his fanatic horde against Cufa, and had the address and good fortune to make himself master of it, Al Hejagi, the emir, being absent at Bassora. He was soon joined by his wife Gazala; established himself as Caliph with some ceremonial, and doubtless his vagabond sway was more acceptable to the people of Cufa, than the iron rule of Al Hejagi.

The mock Caliphat, however, was of brief duration. Al Hejagi, reinforced by troops from Syria, marched in person against Cufa. He was boldly met in the plains near that city by Shebib, at the head of four thousand men. The fanatics were defeated, and Gazala, the wife of the mock Caliph, who had accompanied her husband to the field, was slain. Shebib with a remnant of his force cut his way through the Syrian army; crossed and recrossed the Tigris, and sought refuge and reinforcements in the interior of Persia. He soon returned into Irak, with a force inconsiderable in numbers, but formidable for enthusiasm and desperate valor. He was encountered at the bridge of Dojail al Ahwâz. Here a sudden and unexpected end was put to his fanatic career. His horse struck his forefeet on some loose stones on the margin of the bridge, and threw his rider into the stream. He rose twice to the surface, and each time uttered a pious ejaculation. "What God decrees is just!" was the first exclamation. "The will of God be done!" was the second, and the waters closed over him. His followers cried with loud lamentations, "The Commander of the Faithful is no more!" and every man betook himself to flight. The water was dragged with a net, the body was found and decapitated, and the head sent to Al Hejagi, who transmitted it to the Caliph. The heart of this enthusiast was also taken out of his breast, and is said to have been as hard as stone. He was assuredly a man of extraordinary daring.

Arabian writers say that the manner of Shebib's death was predicted before his birth. His mother was a beautiful Christian captive, purchased at a public sale by Yezid Ibn Naim for his harem. Just before she gave birth to Shebib, she had a dream that a coal of fire proceeded from her, and, after enkindling a flame over the firmament, fell into the sea and was extinguished. This dream was interpreted that she would give birth to a man-child, who would prove a distinguished warrior, but would eventually be drowned. So strong was her belief in this omen, that when she heard, on one occasion, of his defeat and of his alleged death on the battle-field, she treated the tidings as an idle rumor, saying it was by water only her son would die. At the time of Shebib's death he had just passed his fiftieth year.

The emir Al Hejagi was destined to have still farther commotions in his turbulent and inconstant province. A violent feud existed between him and Abda'lrahman Ibn Mohammed, a general subject to his orders. To put an end to it, or to relieve himself from the presence of an enemy, he sent him on an expedition to the frontiers against the Turks. Abda'lrahman set out on his march, but when fairly in the field, with a force at his command, conceived a project either of revenge or ambition.

Addressing his soldiers in a spirited harangue, he told them that their numbers were totally inadequate to the enterprise; that the object of Al Hejagi in sending him on such a dangerous service with such incompetent means, was to effect his defeat and ruin, and that they had been sent to be sacrificed with him.

The harangue produced the desired effect. The troops vowed devotion to Abda'lrahman and vengeance upon the emir. Without giving their passion time to cool, he led them back to put their threats in execution. Al Hejagi heard of the treason, and took the field to meet them, but probably was not well seconded by the people of Babylonia, for he was defeated in a pitched battle. Abda'lrahman then marched to the city of Bassora; the inhabitants welcomed him as their deliverer from a tyrant, and, captivated by his humane and engaging manners, hailed him as Caliph. Intoxicated by his success, he gravely assumed the title, and proceeded toward Cufa. Encountering Al Hejagi on the way, with a hastily levied army, he gave him another signal defeat, and then entered Cufa in triumph, amid the shouts of its giddy populace, who were delighted with any change that released them from the yoke of Al Hejagi.

Abda'lrahman was now acknowledged Caliph throughout the territories bordering on the Euphrates and the Tigris, a mighty empire in ancient days, and still important from its population, for he soon had on foot an army of one hundred thousand men.

Repeated defeat had but served to rouse the energy of Al Hejagi. He raised troops among such of the people of Irak as remained faithful to Abd'almâlec; received reinforcements from the Caliph, and by dint of indefatigable exertions was again enabled to take the field.

The two generals, animated by deadly hate, encamped their armies at places not far apart. Here they remained between three and four months, keeping vigilant eye upon each other, and engaged in incessant conflicts, though never venturing upon a pitched battle.

The object of Al Hejagi was to gain an advantage by his superior military skill, and he succeeded. By an artful manœuvre he cut off Abda'lrahman, with a body of five thousand men, from his main army; compelled him to retreat, and drove him to take refuge in a fortified town; where, being closely besieged, and having no hope of escape, he threw himself headlong from a lofty tower, rather than fall into the hands of his cruel enemy.

Thus terminated the rebellion of this second mock Caliph, and Al Hejagi, to secure the tranquillity of Irak, founded a strong city on the Tigris, called Al Wazab, or the Centre, from its lying at equal distance from Cufa, Bassora, Bagdad, and Ahwâz, about fifty leagues from each.

Al Hejagi, whom we shall have no further occasion to mention, continued emir of Irak until his death, which took place under the reign of the next Caliph, in the ninety-fifth year of the Hegira, and the fifty-fourth of his own age. He is said to have caused the death of one hundred and twenty thousand persons, independent of those who fell in battle, and that, at the time of his death, he left fifty thousand confined in different prisons. Can we wonder that he was detested as a tyrant?

In his last illness, say the Arabian historians, he sent for a noted astrologer, and asked him whether any great general was about to end his days. The learned man consulted the stars, and replied, that a great captain named Kotaib, or 'The Dog,' was at the point of death. "That," said the dying emir, "is the name my mother used to call me when a child." He inquired of the astrologer if he was assured of his prediction. The sage, proud of his art, declared that it was infallible. "Then," said the emir, "I will take you with me, that I may have the benefit of your skill in the other world." So saying, he caused his head to be struck off.

The tyranny of this general was relieved at times by displays of great magnificence and acts of generosity, if not clemency. He spread a thousand tables at a single banquet, and bestowed a million dirhems of silver at a single donation.

On one occasion, an Arab, ignorant of his person, spoke of him, in his presence, as a cruel tyrant. "Do you know me?" said Al Hejagi, sternly. "I do not," replied the Arab. "I am Al Hejagi!" "That may be," replied the Arab, quickly; "but do you know me? I am of the family of Zobeir, who are fools in the full of the moon; and if you look upon the heavens you will see that this is my day." The emir laughed at his ready wit, and dismissed him with a present.

On another occasion, when separated from his party while hunting, he came to a spring where an Arab was feeding his camels, and demanded drink. The Arab bade him, rudely, to alight and help himself. It was during the rebellion of Abda'lrahman. After he had slaked his thirst, he demanded of the Arab whether he was for the Caliph Abd'almâlec. The Arab replied "no; for the Caliph had sent the worst man in the world to govern the province." Just then a bird, passing over head, uttered a croaking note. The Arab turned a quick eye upon the emir: "Who art thou?" cried he, with consternation. "Wherefore the question?" "Because I understand the language of birds, and he says that thou art chief of yon horsemen that I see approaching."

The emir smiled, and when his attendants came up, bade them to bring the camel-driver with them. On the next day, he sent for him; had meat set before him, and bade him eat. Before he complied, the Arab uttered a grace, "Allah grant that the end of this meal be as happy as the beginning."

The emir inquired if he recollected their conversation of yesterday. "Perfectly! but I entreat thee to forget it, for it was a secret which should be buried in oblivion."

"Here are two conditions for thy choice," said the emir; "recant what thou hast said and enter unto my service, or abide the decision of the Caliph, to whom thy treasonable speech shall be repeated." "There is a third course," replied the Arab, "which is better than either. Send me to my own home, and let us be strangers to each other as heretofore."

The emir was amused by the spirit of the Arab, and dismissed him with a thousand dirhems of silver.

There were no further troubles in Irak during the lifetime of Al Hejagi, and even the fickle, turbulent and faithless people of Cufa became submissive and obedient. Abulfaragius says that this general died of eating dirt. It appears that he was subject to dyspepsia or indigestion, for which he used to eat Terra Lemnia, and other medicinal or absorbent earths. Whether he fell a victim to the malady, or the medicine, is not clearly manifest.

CHAPTER LIV

*Renunciation of tribute to the emperor – Battles in Northern Africa
– The prophet queen Cahina; her achievements and fate*

The seventy-second year of the Hegira, saw the Moslem dominions at length free from rebellion and civil war, and united under one Caliph. Abd'almâlec now looked abroad, and was anxious to revive the foreign glories of Islam, which had declined during the late vicissitudes. His first movement was to throw off the galling tribute to the Greek emperor. This, under Moawyah I, had originally been three thousand dinars of gold, but had been augmented to three hundred and sixty-five thousand; being one thousand for every day in the Christian year. It was accompanied by three hundred and sixty-five female slaves, and three hundred and sixty-five Arabian horses of the most generous race.

Not content with renouncing the payment of tribute, Abd'almâlec sent Alid one of his generals on a ravaging expedition into the imperial dominions, availing himself of a disaffection evinced to the new emperor Leontius. Alid returned laden with spoils. The cities of Lazuca and Baruncium were likewise delivered up to the Moslems through the treachery of Sergius, a Christian general.

Abd'almâlec next sought to vindicate the glory of the Moslem arms along the northern coast of Africa. There, also, the imperialists had taken advantage of the troubles of the Caliphat, to reverse the former successes of the Moslems, and to strengthen themselves along the seacoast, of which their navy aided them to hold possession. Zohair, who had been left by Abd'almâlec in command of Barca, had fallen into an ambush and been slain with many of his men, and the posts still held by the Moslems were chiefly in the interior.

In the seventy-seventh year of the Hegira, therefore, Abd'almâlec sent Hossán Ibn An-no'mán, at the head of forty thousand choice troops, to carry out the scheme of African conquest. That general pressed forward at once with his troops against the city of Carthage, which, though declined from its ancient might and glory, was still an important seaport, fortified with lofty walls, haughty towers and powerful bulwarks, and had a numerous garrison of Greeks and other Christians. Hossán proceeded according to the old Arab mode; beleaguering it and reducing it by a long siege; he then assailed it by storm, scaled its lofty walls with ladders, and made himself master of the place. Many of the inhabitants fell by the edge of the sword; many escaped by sea to Sicily and Spain. The walls were then demolished; the city was given up to be plundered by the soldiery, the meanest of whom was enriched by booty. Particular mention is made among the spoils of victory of a great number of female captives of rare beauty.

The triumph of the Moslem host was suddenly interrupted. While they were revelling in the ravaged palaces of Carthage, a fleet appeared before the port; snapped the strong chain which guarded the entrance, and sailed into the harbor. It was a combined force of ships and troops from Constantinople and Sicily; reinforced by Goths from Spain; all under the command of the prefect John, a patrician general of great valor and experience.

Hossán felt himself unable to cope with such a force; he withdrew, however, in good order, and conducted his troops laden with spoils to Tripoli and Caerwan, and having strongly posted them, he awaited reinforcements from the Caliph. These arrived in the course of time, by sea and land. Hossán again took the field; encountered the prefect John, not far from Utica, defeated him in a pitched battle, and drove him to embark the wrecks of his army, and make all sail for Constantinople.

Carthage was again assailed by the victors, and now its desolation was complete, for the vengeance of the Moslems gave that majestic city to the flames. A heap of ruins and the remains of a noble aqueduct, are all the relics of a metropolis that once valiantly contended for dominion with Rome, the mistress of the world.

The imperial forces were now expelled from the coasts of Northern Africa, but the Moslems had not yet achieved the conquest of the country. A formidable enemy remained in the person of a native and heroic queen, who was revered by her subjects as a saint or prophetess. Her real name was Dhabbá, but she is generally known in history by the surname, given to her by the Moslems, of Cahina or the Sorceress. She has occasionally been confounded with her son Aben, or rather Ibn Cahina, of whom mention has been made in a previous chapter.

Under the sacred standard of this prophet queen were combined the Moors of Mauritania and the Berbers of the mountains, and of the plains bordering on the interior deserts. Roving and independent tribes, which had formerly warred with each other, now yielded implicit obedience to one common leader, whom they regarded with religious reverence. The character of marabout or saint has ever had vast

influence over the tribes of Africa. Under this heroic woman the combined host had been reduced to some degree of discipline, and inspired
with patriotic ardor, and were now prepared to make a more effective
struggle for their native land than they had yet done under their generals.

After repeated battles, the emir Hossán was compelled to retire with
his veteran but diminished army to the frontiers of Egypt. The patriot
queen was not satisfied with this partial success. Calling a council of
war of the leaders and principal warriors of the different hordes: "This
retreat of the enemy," said she, "is but temporary; they will return in
greater force. What is it that attracts to our land these Arab spoilers?
The wealth of our cities; the treasures of silver and gold digged from
the bowels of the earth; the fruits of our gardens and orchards; the
produce of our fields. Let us demolish our cities; return these accursed
treasures into the earth; fell our fruit-trees; lay waste our fields, and
spread a barrier of desolation between us and the country of these robbers!"

The words of the royal prophetess were received with fanatic enthusiasm by her barbarian troops; the greater part of whom, collected
from the mountains and from distant parts, had little share in the property to be sacrificed. Walled towns were forthwith dismantled; majestic
edifices were tumbled into ruins; groves of fruit-trees were hewn down,
and the whole country from Tangiers to Tripoli was converted from a
populous and fertile region into a howling and barren waste. A short
time was sufficient to effect a desolation, which centuries have not sufficed to remedy.

This sacrificial measure of Queen Cahina, however patriotic its intention, was fatal in the end to herself. The inhabitants of the cities and
the plains, who had beheld their property laid waste by the infuriated
zeal of their defenders, hailed the return of the Moslem invaders as
though they had been the saviours of the land.

The Moslems, as Cahina predicted, returned with augmented forces:
but when she took the field to oppose them, the ranks of her army were
thinned; the enthusiasm which had formerly animated them was at an
end: they were routed, after a sanguinary battle, and the heroine fell
into the hands of the enemy. Those who captured her spared her life,
because she was a woman and a queen. When brought into the presence of Hossán she maintained her haughty and fierce demeanor. He

proposed the usual conditions, of conversion or tribute. She refused both with scorn, and fell a victim to her patriotism and religious constancy, being beheaded in presence of the emir.

Hossán Ibn An-no'mán now repaired to Damascus, to give the Caliph an account of his battles and victories; bearing an immense amount of booty, and several signal trophies. The most important of the latter was a precious box, containing the embalmed head of the slaughtered Cahina. He was received with great distinction, loaded with honors, and the government of Barca was added to his military command.

This last honor proved fatal to Hossán. Abd'alaziz Ibn Merwân, the Caliph's brother, was at that time emir of Egypt, and considered the province of Barca a part of the territories under his government. He had, accordingly, appointed one of his officers to command it as his lieutenant. He was extremely displeased and disconcerted, therefore, when he was told that Hossán had solicited and obtained the government of that province. Sending for the latter, as he passed through Egypt on his way to his post, he demanded whether it was true that in addition to his African command, he was really appointed governor of Barca. Being answered in the affirmative, he appeared still to doubt; whereupon Hossán produced the mandate of the Caliph. Finding it correct, Abd'alaziz urged him to resign the office. "Violence only," said Hossán, "shall wrest from me an honor conferred by the Commander of the Faithful." "Then I deprive thee of both governments," exclaimed the emir, in a passion, "and will appoint a better man in thy stead; and my brother will soon perceive the benefit he derives from the change." So saying, he tore the diploma in pieces.

It is added that, not content with depriving Hossán of his command, he despoiled him of all his property, and carried his persecution so far, that the conqueror of Carthage, the slayer of the patriot queen, within a brief time after her death, and almost amid the very scenes of his triumphs, died of a broken heart. His cruel treatment of the heroic Cahina reconciles us to the injustice wreaked upon himself.

CHAPTER LV

Musa Ibn Nosseyr made emir of Northern Africa – His campaigns
against the Berbers

The general appointed by the Caliph's brother, Abd'alaziz Ibn Merwân, to the command in Northern Africa, was Musa Ibn Nosseyr, the same old adherent of the Merwân family that had been prime counsellor of the Caliph's brother Besher, when emir of Irak, and had escaped by dint of hoof from the clutches of Al Hejagi, when the latter was about to arrest him on a charge of squandering the public funds. Abd'alaziz, it will be remembered, assisted him to pay the fifty thousand dinars of gold, in which he was mulcted by the Caliph, and took him with him to Egypt; and it may have been with some view to self-reimbursement, that the Egyptian emir now took the somewhat bold step of giving him the place assigned to Hossán, by Abd'almâlec.

At the time of his appointment, Musa was sixty years of age. He was still active and vigorous; of noble presence, and concealed his age by tinging his hair and beard with henna. He had three brave sons who aided him in his campaigns, and in whom he took great pride. The eldest he had named Abd'alaziz, after his patron; he was brave and magnanimous, in the freshness of his youth and his father's right hand in all his enterprises. Another of his sons, he had called Merwân, the family name of Abd'alaziz and the Caliph.

Musa joined the army at its African encampment, and addressed his troops in frank and simple language. "I am a plain soldier like yourselves," said he; "whenever I act well, thank God, and endeavor to imitate me. When I do wrong, reprove me, that I may amend; for we are all sinners and liable to err. If any one has at any time a complaint to make, let him state it frankly, and it shall be attended to. I have orders from the emir Abd'alaziz (to whom God be bountiful!) to pay you three times the amount of your arrears. Take it, and make good use of it." It is needless to say, that the address, especially the last part, was received with acclamations.

While Musa was making his harangue, a sparrow fluttered into his bosom. Interpreting it as a good omen, he called for a knife; cut off the bird's head; besmeared the bosom of his vest with the blood, and scattering the feathers in the air above his head – "Victory! Victory!" he cried, "by the master of the Caaba, victory is ours!"

It is evident that Musa understood the character and foibles of his troops; he soon won their favor by his munificence, and still more by his affability; always accosting them with kind words and cheerful looks; carefully avoiding the error of those reserved commanders, shut up in the fancied dignity of station, who looked, he said, "as if God had tied a knot in their throats, so that they could not utter a word."

"A commander," he used to say, "ought to consult wise and experienced men in every undertaking; but when he has made up his mind, he should be firm and steady of purpose. He should be brave, adventurous, at times even rash, confiding in his good fortune, and endeavoring to do more than is expected of him. He should be doubly cautious after victory; doubly brave after defeat."

Musa found a part of Eastern Africa,* forming the present states of Tunis and Algiers, in complete confusion and insurrection. A Berber chief, Warkattáf by name, scoured night and day the land between Zaghwan and Caerwan. The Berbers had this advantage; if routed in the plains they took refuge in the mountains, which ran parallel to the coast, forming part of the great chain of Atlas; in the fastnesses of these mountains they felt themselves secure; but should they be driven out of these, they could plunge into the boundless deserts of the interior, and bid defiance to pursuit.

The energy of Musa rose with the difficulty of his enterprise. "Take courage," would he say to his troops. "God is on our side, and will enable us to cope with our enemies, however strong their holds. By Allah! I'll carry the war into yon haughty mountains, nor cease until we have seized upon their passes, surmounted their summits, and made ourselves masters of the country beyond."

His words were not an empty threat. Having vanquished the Berbers in the plains, he sent his sons Abd'alaziz and Merwân with troops in different directions, who attacked the enemy in their mountain-holds, and drove them beyond to the borders of the Southern desert. Warkattáf was slain with many of his warriors, and Musa had the gratification of seeing his sons return triumphant from their different expeditions, bringing to the camp thousands of captives and immense booty. Indeed the number of prisoners of both sexes, taken in these campaigns, is said to have amounted to three hundred thousand; of whom one-fifth, or sixty thousand, formed the Caliph's share.

---

* Northern Africa, extending from Egypt to the extremity of Mauritania, was subdivided into Eastern and Western Africa.

Musa hastened to write an account of his victories to his patron Abd'alaziz Ibn Merwân, and as he knew covetousness to be the prime failing of the emir, he sent him, at the same time, a great share of the spoils, with choice horses and female slaves of surpassing beauty.

The letter and the present came most opportunely. Abd'alaziz had just received a letter from his brother, the Caliph, rebuking him for having deposed Hossán, a brave, experienced and fortunate officer, and given his office to Musa, a man who had formerly incurred the displeasure of the government; and he was ordered forthwith to restore Hossán to his command.

In reply, Abd'alaziz transmitted the news of the African victories. "I have just received from Musa," writes he, "the letter which I inclose, that thou mayest peruse it, and give thanks to God."

Other tidings came to the same purport, accompanied by a great amount of booty. The Caliph's feelings toward Musa immediately changed. He at once saw his fitness for the post he occupied, and confirmed the appointment of Abd'alaziz, making him emir of Africa. He, moreover, granted yearly pensions of two hundred pieces of gold to himself and one hundred to each of his sons, and directed him to select from among his soldiers five hundred of those who had most distinguished themselves in battle, or received most wounds, and give them each thirty pieces of gold. Lastly, he revoked the fine formerly imposed upon him of fifty thousand dinars of gold, and authorized him to reimburse himself out of the Caliph's share of the spoil.

This last sum Musa declined to receive for his own benefit, but publicly devoted it to the promotion of the faith and the good of its professors. Whenever a number of captives were put up for sale after a victory, he chose from among them those who were young, vigorous, intelligent, of noble origin, and who appeared disposed to be instructed in the religion of Islam. If they were converted, and proved to have sufficient talent, he gave them their liberty, and appointed them to commands in his army; if otherwise, he returned them to the mass of captives, to be disposed of in the usual manner.

The fame of Musa's victories, and of the immense spoil collected by his troops, brought recruits to his standard from Egypt and Syria, and other distant parts; for rapine was becoming more and more the predominant passion of the Moslems. The army of Musa was no longer composed, like the primitive armies of the faith, merely of religious zealots. The campaigns in foreign countries, and the necessity, at distant points, of recruiting the diminished ranks from such sources as were at hand, had relaxed the ancient scruples, as to unity of faith, and men of different creeds now fought under the standard of Islam without being purified by conversion. The army was, therefore, a motley host of every country and kind; Arabs and Syrians, Persians and Copts, and nomadic Africans; arrayed in every kind of garb, and armed with every kind of weapon. Musa had succeeded in enlisting in his service many of the native tribes; a few of them were Christians, a greater proportion idolaters, but the greatest number professed Judaism. They readily amalgamated with the Arabs, having the same nomad habits, and the same love of war and rapine. They even traced their origin to the same Asiatic stock. According to their traditions five colonies, or tribes, came in ancient times from Sabæa, in Arabia the Happy; being expelled thence with their king Ifrique. From these descended the five most powerful Berber tribes, the Zenhagians, Muzamudas, Zenetes, Gomeres and Hoares.

Musa artfully availed himself of these traditions; addressed the conquered Berbers as Aulad-Arabi (sons of the Arabs), and so soothed their pride by this pretended consanguinity, that many readily embraced the Moslem faith, and thousands of the bravest men of Numidia enrolled themselves, of their own free will, in the armies of Islam.

Others, however, persisted in waging stubborn war with the invaders of their country, and among these, the most powerful and intrepid, were the Zenetes. They were a free, independent and haughty race. Marmol, in his description of Africa, represents them as inhabiting various parts of the country; some leading a roving life about the plains, living in tents like the Arabs; others having castles and strongholds in the mountains; others, very troglodytes, infesting the dens and caves of Mount Atlas, and others wandering on the borders of the Libyan desert.

The Gomeres were also a valiant and warlike tribe, inhabiting the mountains of the lesser Atlas, in Mauritania, bordering the frontiers of Ceuta, while the Muzamudas lived in the more western part of that extreme province, where the great Atlas advances into the Atlantic Ocean.

In the eighty-third year of the Hegira, Musa made one of his severest campaigns against a combined force of these Berber tribes, collected under the banners of their several princes. They had posted themselves in one of the fastnesses of the Atlas mountains, to which the only approach was through different gorges and defiles. All these were defended with great obstinacy, but were carried, one after the other, after several days of severe fighting.

The armies at length found themselves in presence of each other, when a general conflict was unavoidable. As they were drawn out, regarding each other with menacing aspect, a Berber chief advanced, and challenged any one of the Moslem cavaliers to single combat. There was a delay in answering to the challenge; whereupon Musa turned to his son Merwân, who had charge of the banners, and told him to meet the Berber warrior. The youth handed his banner to his brother Abd'alaziz, and stepped forward with alacrity. The Berber, a stark and seasoned warrior of the mountains, regarded with surprise and almost scorn, an opponent scarce arrived at manhood. "Return to the camp," cried he, "I would not deprive thine aged father of so comely a son." Merwân replied but with his weapon, assailing his adversary so vigorously, that he retreated and sprang upon his horse. He now urged his steed upon the youth, and made a thrust at him with a javelin, but Merwân seized the weapon with one hand, and with the other thrust his own javelin through the Berber's side, burying it in the flanks of the steed; so that both horse and rider were brought to the ground and slain.

The two armies now closed in a general struggle; it was bloody and desperate, but ended in the complete defeat of the Berbers. Kasleyah, their king, fell, fighting to the last. A vast number of captives were taken; among them were many beautiful maidens, daughters of princes and military chiefs. At the division of the spoil, Musa caused these high-born damsels to stand before him, and bade Merwân, his son, who had so recently distinguished himself, to choose among them. The youth chose one who was a daughter of the late king Kasleyah. She appears to have found solace for the loss of her father in the arms of a youthful husband; and ultimately made Merwân the father of two sons, Musa and Abd'almâlec.

CHAPTER LVI

Naval enterprises of Musa – Cruisings of his son Abdolola – Death of Abd'almâlec

The bold and adventurous spirit of Musa Ibn Nosseyr was not content with victories on land. "Always endeavor to do more than is expected of thee," was his maxim, and he now aspired to achieve triumphs on the sea. He had ports within his province, whence the Phœnicians and Carthaginians, in the days of their power, had fitted out maritime enterprises. Why should he not do the same?

The feelings of the Arab conquerors had widely changed in regard to naval expeditions. When Amru, the conqueror of Egypt, was at Alexandria, the Caliph Omar required of him a description of the Mediterranean. "It is a great pool," replied Amru, "which some foolhardy people furrow; looking like ants on logs of wood." The answer was enough for Omar, who was always apprehensive that the Moslems would endanger their conquests by rashly-extended enterprises. He forbade all maritime expeditions. Perhaps he feared that the inexperience of the Arabs would expose them to defeat from the Franks and Romans, who were practised navigators.

Moawyah, however, as we have shown, more confident of the Moslem capacity for nautical warfare, had launched the banner of Islam on the sea from the ancient ports of Tyre and Sidon, and had scoured the eastern waters of the Mediterranean. The Moslems now had armaments in various ports of Syria and Egypt, and warred with the Christians by sea as well as by land. Abd'almâlec had even ordered Musa's predecessor, Hossán, to erect an arsenal at Tunis; Musa now undertook to carry those orders into effect; to found dock-yards, and to build a fleet for his proposed enterprise.

At the outset he was surrounded by those sage doubters who are ever ready to chill the ardor of enterprise. They pronounced the scheme rash and impracticable. A gray-headed Berber, who had been converted to Islam, spoke in a different tone. "I am one hundred and twenty years old," said he, "and I well remember hearing my father say, that when the Lord of Carthage thought of building his city, the people all, as at present, exclaimed against it as impracticable; one alone rose and said, oh king, put thy hand to the work and it will be achieved; for the kings thy predecessors persevered and achieved every thing they undertook, whatever might be the difficulty. And I say to thee, oh emir, put thy hand to this work, and God will help thee!"

Musa did put his hand to the work, and so effectually, that by the conclusion of the eighty-fourth year of the Hegira, A.D. 703, the arsenal and dock-yard were complete, and furnished with maritime stores, and there was a numerous fleet in the port of Tunis.

About this time a Moslem fleet, sent by Abd'alaziz, the emir of Egypt, to make a ravaging descent on the coast of Sardinia, entered the port of Susa, which is between Caerwan and Tunis. Musa sent provisions to the fleet, but wrote to the commander, Attá Ibn Rafi, cautioning him that the season was too late for his enterprise, and advising him to remain in port until more favorable time and weather.

Attá treated his letter with contempt, as the advice of a landsman: and having refitted his vessels, put to sea. He landed on an island, called by the Arab writers, Salsalah, probably Linosa or Lampedosa; made considerable booty of gold, silver, and precious stones, and again set sail on his plundering cruise. A violent storm arose, his ships were dashed on the rocky coast of Africa, and he and nearly all his men were drowned.

Musa, hearing of the disaster, dispatched his son, Abd'alaziz, with a troop of horse to the scene of the shipwreck, to render all the assistance in his power; ordering that the vessels and crews which survived the storm, should repair to the port of Tunis; all which was done. At the place of the wreck Abd'alaziz found a heavy box cast up on the sea-shore; on being opened, its contents proved to be the share of spoil of one of the warriors of the fleet, who had perished in the sea.

The author of the tradition from which these facts are gleaned, adds, that one day he found an old man sitting on the sea-shore with a reed in his hand, which he attempted to take from him. A scuffle ensued; he wrested the reed from his hands, and struck him with it over his head; when lo, it broke, and out fell gold coins and pearls and precious stones. Whether the old man, thus hardly treated, was one of the wrecked cruisers, or a wrecker, seeking to profit by their misfortunes, is not specified in the tradition. The anecdote shows in what a random way the treasures of the earth were in those days scattered about the world by the predatory hosts of Islam.

The surviving ships having been repaired, and added to those recently built at Tunis, and the season having become favorable, Musa, early in the eighty-fifth year of the Hegira, declared his intention to undertake, in person, a naval expedition. There was a universal eagerness among the troops to embark; Musa selected about a thousand of the choicest of his warriors, especially those of rank and family, so that the enterprise was afterwards designated The Expedition of the Nobles. He did not, however, accompany it as he had promised; he had done so merely to enlist his bravest men in the undertaking; the command was given to his son, Abdolola, to give him an opportunity to distinguish himself; for the reputation of his sons was as dear to Musa as his own.

It was, however, a mere predatory cruise; a type of the ravaging piracies from the African ports in after ages. Abdolola coasted the fair island of Sicily with his ships, landed on the western side, and plundered a city which yielded such abundant spoil, that each of the thousand men embarked in the cruise received one hundred dinars of gold for his share. This done, the fleet returned to Africa.

Soon after the return of his ships, Musa received news of the death of his patron Abd'alaziz, which was followed soon after by tidings of the death of the Caliph. On hearing of the death of the latter, Musa immediately sent a messenger to Damascus to take the oath of allegiance, in his name, to the new Caliph; to inform him of the naval achievements of his son Abdolola, and to deliver to him his share of the immense booty gained. The effect of course was to secure his continuance in office as emir of Africa.

The malady which terminated in the death of Abd'almâlec is supposed to have been the dropsy. It was attended in its last stages with excessive thirst, which was aggravated by the prohibition of his physicians that any water should be given to him, lest it should cause certain death. In the paroxysms of his malady the expiring Caliph demanded water of his son Waled; it was withheld through filial piety. His daughter, Fatima, approached with a flagon, but Waled interfered and prevented her; whereupon the Caliph threatened him with disinheritance and his malediction. Fatima handed to him the flagon, he drained it at a draught, and almost instantly expired. He was about sixty years old at the time of his death, and had reigned about twenty years. Abulfeda gives him a character for learning, courage, and foresight. He certainly showed ability and management in reuniting, under his sway, the dismembered portions of the Moslem empire, and quelling the various sects that rose in arms against him. His foresight with regard to his family also, was crowned with success, as four of his sons succeeded him, severally, in the Caliphat.

He evinced an illiberal spirit of hostility to the memory of Ali, carrying it to such a degree that he would not permit the poet Ferazdak to celebrate in song the virtues of any of his descendants. Perhaps this may have gained for Abd'almâlec another by-name with which some of the Arab writers have signalized his memory, calling him the "Father of Flies;" for so potent, say they, was his breath, that any fly which alighted on his lips died on the spot.

CHAPTER LVII

Inauguration of Waled, 12th Caliph – Revival of the arts under his reign – His taste for architecture – Erection of mosques – Conquests of his generals

Waled, the eldest son of Abd'almâlec, was proclaimed Caliph at Damascus immediately on the death of his father, in the eighty-sixth year of the Hegira, and the year 705 of the Christian era. He was about thirty-eight years of age; and is described as being tall and robust, with a swarthy complexion, a face much pitted with the small-pox, and a broad flat nose; in other respects, which are left to our conjecture, he is said to have been of a good countenance. His habits were indolent and voluptuous, yet he was of a choleric temper, and somewhat inclined to cruelty.

During the reign of Waled the arts began to develope themselves under the Moslem sway; finding a more genial home in the luxurious city of Damascus, than they had done in the holy cities of Mecca or Medina. Foreign conquests had brought the Arabs in contact with the Greeks and the Persians. Intercourse with them, and residence in their cities, had gradually refined away the gross habits of the desert; had awakened thirst for the sciences, and a relish for the elegancies of cultivated life. Little skilled in the principles of government, accustomed in their native deserts to the patriarchal rule of separate tribes, without any extended scheme of policy, or combined system of union, the Arabs, suddenly masters of a vast and continually widening empire, had to study the art of governing in the political institutions of the countries they conquered. Persia, the best organized monarchy in Asia, held out a model by which they were fain to profit; and in their system of emirs vested with the sway of distant and powerful provinces, but strictly responsible to the Caliph, we see a copy of the satraps or viceroys, the provincial depositaries of the power of the Khosrus.

Since Moawyah had moved the seat of the Caliphat to Damascus, a change had come over the style of the Moslem court. It was no longer, as in the days of Omar, the conference of a poorly clad Arab chieftain with his veteran warriors and gray-beard companions, seated on their mats in the corner of a mosque: the Moslem Caliph at Damascus had now his divan, in imitation of the Persian monarch; and his palace began to assume somewhat of oriental state and splendor.

In nothing had the Moslem conquerors showed more ignorance of

affairs than in financial matters. The vast spoils acquired in their conquests, and the tribute and taxes imposed on subjugated countries, had
for a time been treated like the chance booty caught up in predatory
expeditions in the deserts. They were amassed in public treasuries
without register or account, and shared and apportioned without judgment and often without honesty. Hence continual frauds and pecula-
tions; hence those charges so readily brought and readily believed,
against generals and governors in distant stations, of enormous frauds
and embezzlements, and hence that grasping avarice, that avidity of
spoil and treasure, which were more and more destroying the original
singleness of purpose of the soldiers of Islam.

Moawyah was the first of the Caliphs who ordered that registers of
tribute and taxes, as well as of spoils, should be kept in the Islamite
countries, in their respective languages; that is to say, in the Greek language in Syria, and in the Persian language in Irak; but Abd'almâlec
went further, and ordered that they should all be kept in Arabic. Nothing, however, could effectually check the extortion and corruption which
was prevailing more and more in the administration of the conquered
provinces. Even the rude Arab soldier, who in his desert would have
been content with his tent of hair-cloth, now aspired to the possession
of fertile lands, or a residence amid the voluptuous pleasures of the
city.

Waled had grown up amid the refinements and corruptions of the
transplanted Caliphat. He was more of a Greek and Persian than an
Arab in his tastes; and the very opposite of that primitive Moslem,
Omar, in most of his habitudes. On assuming the sovereign power, he
confirmed all the emirs or governors of provinces, and also the generals
appointed by his father. On these he devolved all measures of government and warlike duties; for himself, he led a soft luxurious life
amidst the delights of his harem. Yet, though he had sixty-three wives,
he does not appear to have left any issue. Much of his time was devoted to the arts, and especially the art of architecture, in which he left
some noble monuments to perpetuate his fame.

He caused the principal mosque at Cairo to be demolished, and one
erected of greater majesty, the pillars of which had gilded capitals. He
enlarged and beautified the grand mosque erected on the site of the
temple of Solomon, for he was anxious to perpetuate the pilgrimage to
Jerusalem established by his father. He gave command that the bounds
of the mosque at Medina should be extended; so as to include the

tomb of the prophet, and the nine mansions of his wives. He furthermore ordered, that all the buildings round the Caaba at Mecca should
be thrown down, and a magnificent quadrangular mosque erected,
such as is to be seen at the present day. For this purpose, he sent a
body of skilful Syrian architects from Damascus.

Many of the faithful were grieved, particularly those well-stricken in
years, the old residents of Mecca, to see the ancient simplicity established by the prophet, violated by the splendor of this edifice; especially
as the dwellings of numerous individuals were demolished to furnish a
vast square for the foundations of the new edifice; which now inclosed
within its circuit, the Caaba, the well of Zem Zem, and the stations of
different sects of Moslems, which came in pilgrimage.

All these works were carried on under the supervision of his emirs,
but the Caliph attended in person to the erection of a grand mosque in
his capital of Damascus. In making arrangements for this majestic pile
he cast his eyes on the superb church of St. John the Baptist, which
had been embellished by the Roman emperors during successive ages,
and enriched with the bones and relics of saints and martyrs. He offered the Christians forty thousand dinars of gold for this holy edifice;
but they replied, gold was of no value in comparison with the sacred
bones enshrined within its walls.

The Caliph, therefore, took possession of the church on his own authority, and either demolished or altered it, so as to suit his purpose in
the construction of his mosque, and did not allow the Christian owners
a single dirhem of compensation. He employed twelve thousand workmen constantly, in this architectural enterprise, and one of his greatest
regrets in his last moments was that he should not live to see it completed.

The architecture of these mosques was a mixture of Greek and Persian, and gave rise to the Saracenic style, of which Waled may be said
to be founder. The slender and graceful palm-tree, may have served as
a model for its columns; as the clustering trees and umbrageous forests
of the north are thought to have thrown their massive forms and shadowy glooms into Gothic architecture. These two kinds of architecture
have often been confounded, but the Saracenic takes the precedence;
the Gothic borrowed graces and embellishments from it in the times of
the Crusades.

While the Caliph Waled lived indolently and voluptuously at Damascus, or occupied himself in erecting mosques, his generals extended

his empire in various directions. Moslema Ibn Abd'almâlec, one of his fourteen brothers, led an army into Asia Minor, invaded Cappadocia, and laid siege to Tyana, a strong city garrisoned with imperial troops. It was so closely invested, that it could receive no provisions; but the besiegers were equally in want of supplies. The contest was fierce on both sides, for both were sharpened and irritated by hunger, and it became a contest which could hold out longest against famine.

The duration of the siege enabled the emperor to send reinforcements to the place, but they were raw undisciplined recruits, who were routed by the hungry Moslems, their camp captured and their provisions greedily devoured. The defeat of these reinforcements rendered the defence of the city hopeless, and the pressure of famine hastened a capitulation, the besieged not being aware that the besiegers were nearly as much famished as themselves. Moslema is accused by Christian writers, of having violated the conditions of surrender; many of the inhabitants were driven forth into the deserts, and many of the remainder were taken for slaves. In a subsequent year Moslema made a successful incursion into Pontus and Armenia, a great part of which he subjugated, and took the city of Amasia, after a severely contested siege. He afterwards made a victorious campaign into Galatia, ravaging the whole province, and bearing away rich spoils and numerous captives.

While Moslema was thus bringing Asia Minor into subjection, his son Khatiba, a youth of great bravery, was no less successful in extending the empire of the faith toward the East. Appointed to the government of Khorassan, he did not content himself with attending to the affairs of his own province, but crossing the Oxus, ravaged the provinces of Turkistan, defeated a great army of Turks and Tartars, by which he had been beleaguered and reduced to great straits, and took the capital city of Bochara, with many others of inferior note.

He defeated also Magourek, the Khan of Charism, and drove him to take refuge in the great city of Samarcand. This city, anciently called Marcanda, was one of the chief marts of Asia, as well for the wares imported from China and Tangut across the desert of Gobi, as of those brought through the mountains of the great Tibet, and those conveyed from India to the Caspian Sea. It was, therefore, a great resort and resting-place for caravans from all quarters. The surrounding country was renowned throughout the East for fertility, and ranked among the paradises, or gardens, of Asia.

To this city Khatiba laid siege, but the inhabitants set him at defiance, being confident of the strength of their walls, and aware that the Arabs had no battering-rams, nor other engines necessary for the attack of fortified places. A long and close siege, however, reduced the garrison to great extremity, and finding that the besiegers were preparing to carry the place by storm, they capitulated, agreeing to pay an annual tribute of one thousand dinars of gold and three thousand slaves.

Khatiba erected a magnificent mosque in that metropolis, and officiated personally in expounding the doctrines of Islam, which began soon to supersede the religion of the Magians, or Ghebers.

Extensive victories were likewise achieved in India during the reign of Waled, by Mohamed Ibn Casem, a native of Tayef, one of his generals, who conquered the kingdom of Sindia, or Sinde, killed its sovereign in battle, and sent his head to the Caliph; overran a great part of Central India, and first planted the standard of Islam on the banks of the Ganges, the sacred river of the Hindoos.

CHAPTER LVIII

Further triumphs of Musa Ibn Nosseyr – Naval enterprises – Descents in Sicily, Sardinia, and Mallorca – Invasion of Tingitania – Projects for the invasion of Spain – Conclusion

To return to affairs in Africa. During the first years of the Caliphat of Waled, the naval armaments fitted out by Musa in the ports of Eastern Africa, continued to scour the Mediterranean, and carry terror and devastation into its islands. One of them coasted the island of Sicily in the eighty-sixth year of the Hegira, and attacked the city of Syracuse; but the object appears to have been mere plunder, not to retain possession. Another ravaged the island of Sardinia, sacked its cities, and brought off a vast number of prisoners and immense booty. Among the captives were Christian women of great beauty, and highly prized in the Eastern harems. The command of the sea was ultimately given by Musa to his son Abdolola, who added to his nautical reputation by a descent upon the island of Mallorca.

While Abdolola was rejoicing his father's heart by exploits and triumphs on the sea, Abd'alaziz contributed no less to his pride and exultation by his achievements on land. Aided by this favorite son, Musa carried the terror of the Moslem arms to the western extremity of Mount Atlas, subduing Fez, Duquella, Morocco, and Sus. The valiant tribes of the Zenetes at length made peace, and entered into compact with him; from other tribes Musa took hostages; and by degrees the sway of the Caliph was established throughout western Almagreb to Cape Non on the Atlantic.

Musa was not a ferocious conqueror. The countries subjected by his arms became objects of his paternal care. He introduced law and order; instructed the natives in the doctrines of Islam, and defended the peaceful cultivators of the fields and residents in the cities against the incursions of predatory tribes. In return they requited his protection by contributing their fruits and flocks to the support of the armies, and furnishing steeds matchless for speed and beauty.

One region, however, yet remained to be subjugated before the conquest of Northern Africa would be complete; the ancient Tingis, or Tingitania, the northern extremity of Almagreb. Here the continent of Africa protruded boldly to meet the continent of Europe; a narrow strait intervened; the strait of Hercules, the gate of the Mediterranean Sea. Two rocky promontories appeared to guard it on each side, the

far-famed pillars of Hercules. Two rock-built cities, Ceuta and Tangiers, on the African coast, were the keys of this gate, and controlled
the neighboring seaboard. These had been held in ancient times by the
Berber kings, who made this region their stronghold, and Tangiers
their seat of power; but the keys had been wrested from their hands at
widely-separated periods, first by the Vandals, and afterwards by the
Goths, the conquerors of the opposite country of Spain; and the Gothic
Spaniards had now held military possession for several generations.

Musa seems to have reserved this province for his last African campaign. He stationed his son Merwân, with ten thousand men, in a fortified camp on the frontier, while Taric Ibn Zeyad, a veteran general
scarred in many a battle, scoured the country from the fountains or
head waters of the river Moluya, to the mountains of Aldaran. The
province was bravely defended by a Gothic noble, Count Julian by
name; but he was gradually driven to shut himself up in Ceuta. Meantime Tangiers yielded to the Moslem arms after an obstinate defence,
and was strongly garrisoned by Arab and Egyptian troops, and the
command given to Taric. An attempt was made to convert the Christian inhabitants to the faith of Islam; the Berber part easily conformed,
but the Gothic persisted in unbelief, and rather than give up their religion, abandoned their abodes, and crossed over to Andaluz with the
loss of all their property.

Musa now advanced upon Ceuta, into which Count Julian had
drawn all his troops. He attempted to carry it by storm, but was gallantly repulsed, with the loss of many of his best troops. Repeated assaults were made with no better success; the city was situated on a
promontory, and strongly fortified. Musa now laid waste the surrounding country, thinking to reduce the place by famine, but the proximity
of Spain enabled the garrison to receive supplies and reinforcements
across the straits.

Months were expended in this protracted and unavailing siege. According to some accounts Musa retired personally from the attempt,
and returned to his seat of government at Caerwan, leaving the army
and province in charge of his son Merwân, and Taric in command of
Tangiers.

And now occurred one of the most memorable pieces of treason in
history. Count Julian, who had so nobly defended his post, and
checked the hitherto irresistible arms of Islam, all at once made secret
offers, not merely to deliver up Ceuta to the Moslem commander, but

to betray Andaluz itself into his hands. The country he represented as rife for a revolt against Roderick the Gothic king, who was considered a usurper; and he offered to accompany and aid the Moslems in a descent upon the coast, where he had numerous friends ready to flock to his standard.

Of the private wrongs received by Count Julian from his sovereign, which provoked him to this stupendous act of treason, we shall here say nothing. Musa was startled by his proposition. He had long cast a wistful eye at the mountains of Andaluz, brightening beyond the strait, but hitherto the conquest of Northern Africa had tasked all his means. Even now he feared to trust too readily to a man whose very proposition showed an utter want of faith. He determined, therefore, to dispatch Taric Ibn Zeyad on a reconnoitring expedition to coast the opposite shores, accompanied by Count Julian, and ascertain the truth of his representations.

Taric accordingly embarked with a few hundred men in four merchant vessels, crossed the straits under the guidance of Count Julian, who, on landing, dispatched emissaries to his friends and adherents, summoning them to a conference at Jesirah al Khadra, or the Green Island, now Algeziras. Here, in presence of Taric, they confirmed all that Julian had said of the rebellious disposition of the country, and of their own readiness to join the standard of an invader. A plundering cruise along the coast convinced Taric of the wealth of the country, and he returned to the African shores with ample spoils and female captives of great beauty.

A new career of conquest seemed thus opening upon Musa. His predecessor, Acbah, had spurred his steed into the waves of the Atlantic, and sighed that there were no further lands to conquer; but here was another quarter of the world inviting the triumphs of Islam. He forthwith wrote to the Caliph, giving a glowing account of the country thus held out for conquest; a country abounding in noble monuments and wealthy cities; rivalling Syria in the fertility of its soil and the beauty of its climate; Yemen, or Arabia the Happy, in its temperature; India in its flowers and spices; Hegiaz in its fruits and productions; Cathay in its precious and abundant mines; Aden in the excellence of its ports and harbors. "With the aid of God," added he, "I have reduced to obedience the Zenetes and the other Berber tribes of Zab and Derâr, Zaara, Mazamuda, and Sus: the standard of Islam floats triumphant on the walls of Tangiers; thence to the opposite coast of Andaluz is but a space of twelve miles. Let but the Commander of the Faithful give the word, and the conquerors of Africa will cross into that land, there to carry the knowledge of the true God and the law of the Koran."

The Arab spirit of the Caliph was roused by this magnificent prospect of new conquests. He called to mind a tradition that Mahomet had promised the extension of his law to the uttermost regions of the West; and he now gave full authority to Musa to proceed in his pious enterprise, and carry the sword of Islam into the benighted land of Andaluz.

We have thus accomplished our self-allotted task. We have set forth, in simple and succinct narrative, a certain portion of this wonderful career of fanatical conquest. We have traced the progress of the little cloud which rose out of the deserts of Arabia, "no bigger than a man's hand," until it has spread out and overshadowed the ancient quarters of the world and all their faded glories. We have shown the handful of proselytes of a pseudo prophet, driven from city to city, lurking in dens and caves of the earth; but at length rising to be leaders of armies and mighty conquerors; overcoming in pitched battle the Roman cohort, the Grecian phalanx, and the gorgeous hosts of Persia; carrying their victories from the gates of the Caucasus, to the western descents of Mount Atlas; from the banks of the Ganges to the Sus, the ultimate river in Mauritania; and now planting their standard on the pillars of Hercules, and threatening Europe with like subjugation.

Here, however, we stay our hand. Here we lay down our pen. Whether it will ever be our lot to resume this theme, to cross with the Moslem hosts the strait of Hercules, and narrate their memorable conquest of Gothic Spain, is one of those uncertainties of mortal life and aspirations of literary zeal, which beguile us with agreeable dreams, but too often end in disappointment.

THE END

EDITORIAL APPENDIX

*Historical Note by
E. N. Feltskog*

*Textual Commentary,
Discussions, and Lists by
Henry A. Pochmann*

The establishment of the text and the preparation of the textual commentary and lists were the primary responsibility of Henry A. Pochmann, and the writing of the historical note the responsibility of E. N. Feltskog; but in reality the points at which Irving's numerous variants and inconsistencies impinged on both areas required a true collaboration almost from the beginning in a manner to unite the two areas originally envisaged as distinct.

ACKNOWLEDGMENTS

We are indebted to many persons and institutions. We are under particular obligation to Mrs. A. Duer Irving, of Wilmington, Delaware, and to Mr. Washington Irving, of Providence, Rhode Island, for granting permission on behalf of the heirs of Washington Irving to publish parts of Irving's manuscripts. We offer grateful thanks to the Graduate Research Committee of the University of Wisconsin for providing free time for the editors, and money to pay for hourly help for the machine, as well as the sight, collations; to the Center for Editions of American Authors for financial support derived chiefly from the National Endowment for the Humanities (National Foundation on the Arts and Humanities); and to The New York Public Library, Astor, Lenox and Tilden Foundations, to the Museum of the City of New York, to the Historical Society of Pennsylvania, and to the library of the University of Virginia for making available their manuscripts bearing on *Mahomet and His Successors*. We are indebted to numerous libraries and several individuals, named in the Textual Commentary, who supplied us with copies essential for the collations.

Among individuals, especial thanks are owing to Mr. John R. Murray, the current head of the house of Murray, at 50 Albemarle Street, for supplying us with data from the Murray archives before they became more generally accessible, as they now are; to Mr. James W. Henderson, Chief of The Research Libraries, and Dr. Lola L. Szladits, Curator of The Berg Collection, both of The New York Public Library, as well as Dr. A. K. Baragwanath, Senior Curator of the Museum of the City of New York, for numerous courtesies; to Professor James F. Beard and Professor Ralph M. Aderman for the gift and loan of copies of *Mahomet* hard to come by; to Professor G. Thomas Tanselle, for expert advice on bibliographical problems; to Mrs. Jacqueline S. Kelly, Chief of the Interlibrary Loan Section, and to Dr. Felix Pollak, Curator of the Rare Book Room, of the University of Wisconsin Libraries, for cheerful responses to many requests.

H. A. P.
E. N. F.

University of Wisconsin
October 1, 1969

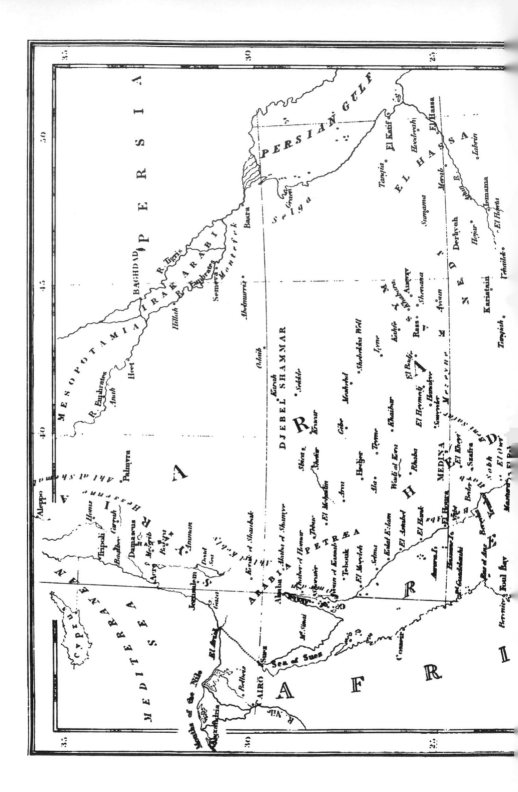

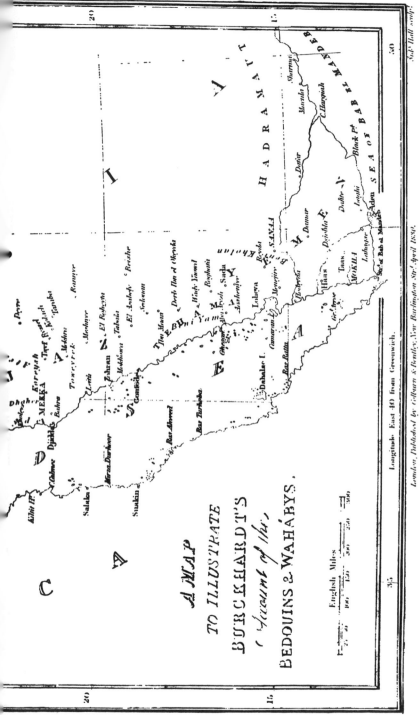

Map of Arabia, from one of Irving's sources for *Mahomet and His Successors*: John Lewis Burckhardt, *Notes on the Bedouins and Wahábys* (London, 1830).

HISTORICAL NOTE

On July 26, 1848, after more than three months of desultory negotiations, Washington Irving signed an agreement with George Palmer Putnam, the rising publisher, for a new edition of his complete works. Irving had been contemplating such a venture since at least as early as 1842, when he approached Lea and Blanchard of Philadelphia with a proposal for a large and expensive edition of all his books,[1] and early in 1847, only shortly after his second return from Spain, his nephew, Pierre M. Irving, wrote to revive his interest in the project and to chide him for his idle rummaging in his old portfolios of moribund and abortive manuscripts while grander opportunities were slipping away: "You lost the Conquest of Mexico [to W. H. Prescott] by not acting upon the motto of *Carpe diem;* and I am a little afraid you may let slip the present opportunity for a favorable sale of a uniform edition of your works, by suffering your pen to be diverted in a new direction. A literary harvest is before you from this source, on which you could reckon with confidence *now.*"[2]

And Pierre Irving, ever ambitious for his uncle's literary and financial success, had good cause for concern. Ever since Washington Irving's return from his four years of service as American ambassador to the turbulent Spanish court, he had done very little more than potter about Sunnyside, promenade Broadway, and turn over, rather wistfully, the faded pages of Spanish romance and Moorish legend written during his first Spanish sojourn twenty-odd years before. Some of this material, Irving thought, might pay for the alterations he was making at Sunnyside, for, as he wrote to his nephew about this same time, "That you may not be frightened at my extravagance, and cut off supplies, I must tell you that I have lately been working up some old stuff which had lain for years lumbering like rubbish in one of my trunks, and which, I trust, will more than pay the expense of my new building."[3]

Whether Irving ever intended any of this "old stuff" to form a vol-

1. Stanley T. Williams, *The Life of Washington Irving* (New York, 1935), II, 215; hereafter cited as STW.
2. Pierre M. Irving, *The Life and Letters of Washington Irving* (New York, 1862–1864), IV, 14; hereafter cited as PMI.
3. PMI, III, 401–2.

ume or volumes in the uniform edition which his nephew had – none too gently – urged him to undertake is uncertain, although on April 14, 1847, he wrote once again to assure Pierre Irving, "I am not letting my pen be diverted in a new direction. I am, by a little agreeable exertion, turning to account a mass of matter that has been lying like lumber in my trunks for years." These manuscripts, Irving continued, dated from the time of his composition of *The Conquest of Granada,* and it was with some pride that he announced, "In a word, I have now complete, though not thoroughly finished off, The Chronicle of Pelayo; the Chronicle of Count Fernan Gonzales; the Chronicle of the Dynasty of the Ommiades in Spain . . . ; also the Chronicle of Fernando the Saint, with the reconquest of Seville."[4]

Although most of these chronicles were not published in their entirety until the posthumous *Spanish Papers* of 1866, and although Irving seems to have made no particular effort to have them included in the Putnam edition of his complete works, still he recognized that these gleanings from his first Spanish manuscripts had a particularly restorative value after the revisions he had reluctantly begun in his published works to meet Pierre Irving's plans for a uniform edition: "You see, all this has cost me but a very few weeks of amusing occupation, and has put me quite in heart again, as well as in literary vein. The poring over my published works was rather muddling me, and making me feel as if the true literary vein was extinct. I think, therefore, you will agree with me that my time for the last five weeks has been well employed. I have secured the frame and part of the finish of an entire new work, and can now put it by to be dressed off at leisure."[5] Perhaps the state of Irving's mind and the height of his literary ambition in early 1847 can best be judged from his confident assumption that the fragments of Spanish legend and Moorish history so long laid by in his trunk could be revived as "an entire new work," whether or not it finally received his customary careful toning of time-long romance. At least these manuscripts were in Irving's once-familiar manner; he had not worked extensively at Spanish materials since the publication of his "Spanish sketch book," *The Alhambra,* in 1832; and if he had not published anything of significance for the past six or seven years, still a doting public both in America and throughout Europe might confi-

4. PMI, IV, 14–15.
5. PMI, IV, 16.

dently be expected to welcome yet another volume of easy history from Fray Antonio Agapida.

For in 1847 Washington Irving was an international institution, proudly recognized and celebrated as a literary ambassador from the New World to the Old, a confidant of Spanish queens and German princelings and the genial idler of literary salons in Paris and London and Madrid. As Jonathan Oldstyle or Diedrich Knickerbocker or Geoffrey Crayon or Fray Antonio Agapida, he was equally at home at Cockloft Hall or Bracebridge Hall or Newstead Abbey or the Alhambra itself. With Sir Walter Scott he could savor the romance of border chivalry, with Mateo Ximénez he could stroll the Moorish courts of timeless Granada, with the Comte de Pourtalès and Tonish he could resume his rambles on the boundless prairies of the Far West. His literary reputation was secure, constantly reinforced, moreover, by admiring magazine essays, by Irving Societies and Irving Literary Institutes, by Knickerbocker steamboats and hotels, by disciples and imitators, the generous praises of Prescott, Longfellow, and Hawthorne, the friendly visits of Dickens and Thackeray, and even by the recurrent piracy of his books in England and throughout the rest of the literary world.

Thus his return to his familiar manuscripts and his well-wrought themes in early 1847, thus his renewed overtures to Lea and Blanchard in early 1848[6] for a collected edition of his works, and thus, finally, his eager acceptance of the onerous task of completely revising all of his slow books for their republication in Putnam's Author's Revised Edition can be explained not so much by Irving's sudden access of artistic inspiration and vigor after the tedious hiatus of his diplomatic mission to Spain or by any decline in his literary reputation as by a quite legitimate desire to have his long and impressive career fittingly memorialized by the ranked volumes of his collected works. Geoffrey Crayon would be a certified classic, the acknowledged *arbiter elegantiarum* of America's middle style.

The Works of Washington Irving appeared in fifteen volumes between September 1848 and August 1850, sometimes at the rate of a volume a month, and most of these books Irving retouched and toned

6. STW, II, 215. Carey had originally made overtures to Irving in Paris for an American edition of his works as early as 1825 (see Washington Irving, *Journals and Notebooks,* Vol. III (Madison: University of Wisconsin Press, 1970), entries for August 11, 15, 17, 18, 1825).

and proofread with at least as much care and attention as he usually gave
to his work in its original progress through the press. Moreover, at least
three volumes in the series were new books – *The Life of Oliver Goldsmith* (August? 1849), and *Mahomet and His Successors* (Volume I,
December 1849; Volume II, April 1850), the former a hasty expansion of
hack work done for the Parisian publisher Galignani as early as 1824, the
latter a more recent retrieval from the manuscript lumber of his traveling trunk. To his niece, Mrs. Sarah Storrow, Irving confided on July 5,
1849, "For upward of a year past I have been very much from home,
obliged to be for the most of the time in the city, superintending the
publication of a new and revised edition of my works, making researches for other works on which I am employed,[7] and attending to
the settlement of Mr. Astor's estate, and the organization of the Astor
Library. Althogether, I have had more toil of head and fagging of the
pen for the last eighteen months, than in any other period of my life,
and have been once or twice fearful my health might become de-
ranged, but it has held out marvellously; and now I hope to be able to
ease off in my toils, and to pass my time at home as usual."[8]

By such careworn labor was *Mahomet and His Successors* brought to
life. Like *Goldsmith* and *Washington* it was first planned during Irving's European *Wanderjähre* in the 1820's, and like those books its subjects and its themes are closely connected with his earliest literary ambitions. The Tripolitanian Mustapha of *Salmagundi* may have been
only a vapid imitation of Goldsmith's Citizen of the World, but Irving
later became sufficiently interested in the then comparatively romantic
subjects of Islam and its Prophet to accept an article on both for publication in the *Analectic Review* during his editorship of the magazine in
1813–1815. Indeed, Irving seems to have undertaken his first casual
study of the history and religions of the Near East at almost the very
moment when, through and by the example of the German Romantic
historians and philosophers, Islamic and Koranic scholarship began to
assume both a discipline and a critical responsibility of its own, when,
that is, Mahomet and his creed could at last be studied and judged as
something more than evidences of God's punishment of Christian heresies and the mutability of human history. Although Irving never read

7. That is, gathering materials and resuming his work on *The Life of George
Washington* and probably, though by no means exclusively, writing the second, or
Successors, volume of *Mahomet and His Successors*.
8. PMI, IV, 52.

carefully or systematically in the increasingly significant canons of Oriental travel, literature, and history, still, like other educated men of his generation, he knew about the extraordinary discoveries (and subsequent publications) of the French Academy's savants in Egypt in 1798 and 1799 – discoveries which substantially transformed intellectual Europe's conceptions of Pharaohnic Egypt and which gave renewed emphasis to the early-nineteenth-century vision of the ancient Near East as wonderfully and timelessly romantic. Irving undoubtedly felt the full impression of Germany's particular passion for Orientalia during his extended visits to the Rhineland and Dresden in 1822–1823, but even before he left England he was well prepared by personal observation and literary ambition to follow the lines of popular success and imagination. To James Kirke Paulding on May 27, 1820, and to Henry Brevoort on August 15 Irving wrote that one of the high points of the year had been his encounter, at John Murray's, with Giovanni Battista Belzoni, perhaps the most flamboyant and daring Egyptologist of the age: "I have been very much pleased also with Belzoni, the traveller, who is just bringing out a personal narrative of his researches, illustrated with very extraordinary plates. There is the interior of a temple, excavated in a hill, which he discovered & opened; which had the effect on me of an Arabian tale. There are rows of gigantic statues, thirty feet high, cut out of the calcareous rock, in perfect preservation. I have been as much delighted in conversing with him, & getting from him an account of his adventures & feelings, as was ever one of Sindbad's auditors."[9]

That Geoffrey Crayon, the genteel sentimentalist of *The Sketch Book*, could ever turn any of the contemporary historical or literary passion for Oriental subjects and themes to advantage (as his friend Tom Moore had done with *Lalla Rookh* in 1817) may seem doubtful in retrospect, but in November 1823, after his rambles in Germany, Irving wrote to his publisher, John Murray II, to propose a collection of Arabian tales, a project which apparently received no real encouragement.[10]

9. Irving to Brevoort, *Letters of Washington Irving to Henry Brevoort*, ed. George S. Hellman (New York, 1918), p. 344.

10. Ben Harris McClary, ed., *Washington Irving and the House of Murray* (Knoxville: University of Tennessee Press, 1969), pp. 47–48. From Paris on February 2, 1825, Irving wrote again to Murray to ask, "Have you ever heard any thing about the MSS. of the Arabian Tales?" – presumably a reference to the manuscripts for a five-volume edition of *The Arabian Nights* which John Murray II purchased from the publisher William Miller in 1802 (McClary, pp. 69 and 48, n. 69).

Tales of a Traveller and most of a year's sojourn in France in 1825 – when, as his journal shows, Irving continued to "Read in Hist of Arabs"[11] – intervened before he began his first Spanish residence from 1826 to 1829, the years that opened to him new scenes and new areas of literary activity, years that brought him more substantial fame and some fortune as the historian of Columbus and his companions, as Fray Antonio Agapida, the chronicler of the Christian reconquest of Moorish Granada, and as the solitary rambler among the courts of the Alhambra. Even these subjects did not exhaust his imagination and his ambition; he sketched out scenes of the wars of the Saracens and Goths and made tentative notes toward "The Legendary Life of Mahomet," the bookish and unassimilated beginnings of what, some twenty years later, would be *Mahomet and His Successors*.

It was in Madrid, between 1826 and 1828, that Irving researched and wrote *The Life and Voyages of Christopher Columbus,* and his extant journals from these years record his daily visits to the Jesuits' Library at the Convent of San Isidro or to the magnificent collections of his friend, Obadiah Rich, the American bibliophile, and in intervals of boredom or blockage with *Columbus* he turned eagerly to collateral researches for *The Conquest of Granada,* for the "Chronicle of the Ommiades," and, in late 1827, for the life of Mahomet. On November 16, 1827, there appears Irving's first terse journal entry "Mahomet," followed, next day, by "all the morng writing at Mahomet," and, on November 18, "all day writing legend of Mahomet." Similar entries run through November 20, but on November 21 he resumed his "Moorish hist." – the "Chronicle of the Ommiades."[12] He took up the "life of Mahomet" again on January 7, 1828, after having finished the "dynasty of the Omeyas" on January 5 and writing "a little at Crusade of Master of Calatrava" on January 6. Almost every day for the next two weeks (through January 23) his journal records "Jesuits Library. life of Mahomet" or "write a little at Mahomet," but on Thursday, January 24, he resumed work "at last chaps of Conquest of Granada," and it was not until Monday, January 28, that he wrote "Library notes about Mahomet." Similar entries conclude the month and run through the first ten days of February. On February 14 he seems to have concluded his research at Madrid with the laconic note "at the library for a short time

11. Irving, *Journals and Notebooks,* Vol. III, entry for April 11, 1825.
12. Andrew B. Myers, ed., "Washington Irving's Madrid Journal 1827–1828 and Related Letters," *Bulletin of the New York Public Library,* LXII (1958), 408.

but could not work."[13] On March 1 he set off for the south, for Cordova, Seville, and Granada, his portfolio fully replenished by two years of toilsome scholarship in the libraries of Madrid.[14]

It would seem that the manuscript of the "legend of Mahomet" was not a complete or finished work; it may indeed have been intended only as a kind of general prologue to the series "illustrative of the domination of the Arabs in Spain" of which Irving speaks in his preface to the first volume of *Mahomet and His Successors* and which Pierre Irving describes as "materials on hand for easy arrangement" in 1829: "a Sketch of the Life of Mahomet, prepared while at Madrid, and intended as introductory to other writings, which he had in contemplation connected with the Moorish domination in Spain; Legends of the Conquest of Spain; Chronicles of Don Pelayo, and the successors of Don Pelayo; Chronicles of the Ommiades (or the house of Omeya, one of the two lines descended from Mahomet), Chronicle of Don Fernando Gonzales, Count of Castile; Don Garcia Fernandez (his successor); the Seven Sons of Lara; and Chronicle of Fernando el Santo (the Conqueror of Seville)."[15] Within such a context the life of Mahomet – so far, at least, as Irving had planned and written it in late 1827 and early 1828 – would doubtless have been as legendary and romantic as *The Conquest of Granada* itself, but for reasons which are not yet clear Irving laid the manuscript aside for the rest of his Spanish sojourn and turned instead to a revision of his *Columbus,* to the polishing of *The Conquest of Granada,* and to the completion of *The Voyages and Discoveries of the Companions of Columbus.*

Irving returned to England in September 1829 to take up his duties as secretary of the American legation in London and to resume the literary friendships and alliances forged during Geoffrey Crayon's triumphs in 1819–1820. Though his work at the legation kept him extremely busy, still he mingled in the salons of aristocratic and literary London, dined with duchesses and Samuel Rogers, saw the *Companions of Columbus* through Murray's press, and worked desultorily at his "Spanish sketch book" and the manuscript of the life of Mahomet. Only shortly after his return to England, in fact, Irving had proposed both the *Companions of Columbus* and the life of Mahomet to Murray; Mc-

13. *Ibid.,* pp. 412–14.
14. *Journal of Washington Irving 1828 and Miscellaneous Notes on Moorish Legend and History,* ed. Stanley T. Williams (New York, 1937), p. 1.
15. PMI, II, 373.

Clary notes that "The proposed study of the voyages of Columbus' companions and the life of Mahomet the publisher viewed favorably as possible volumes for his Family Library."[16] With the *Companions of Columbus* finally published by Murray in late 1830, Irving was free to spend what time he could snatch from legation duties at the life of Mahomet and *The Alhambra,* his "Spanish sketch book," works which apparently proceeded in tandem, so that on September 28, 1831, he called upon John Murray II to announce that a manuscript now provisionally entitled "The Legendary Life of Mahomet" would be ready for the printer in a few days and that the "Spanish sketch book" might be expected before the end of the year. For the first volume Irving would modestly settle for five hundred guineas, but another prospective *Sketch Book* – and Murray had badly misjudged the success of the first – should certainly command a thousand guineas! "Let me see the manuscripts," Murray replied, and after some further discussion Irving departed, with Murray's assurance, "Yes, I'll write you!" – feeling that his literary interests were still in capable hands.[17]

Irving wasted no time in writing to Colonel Thomas Aspinwall, his agent in former negotiations with Murray and now a colleague in the American legation, "I have made a bargain with the Murray for a brace of volumes I am preparing for the press, but will get you to call on him and arrange the terms of payment &c.&c. and the legal writings &c. when I have my batch of MS. ready for delivery."[18] From Birmingham on October 4 Irving sent to Aspinwall twenty-one chapters of "The Legendary Life of Mahomet" and a covering letter urging Aspinwall to drive a shrewd bargain with Murray. On the same day he himself wrote to the publisher, "I have . . . requested my friend & agent Col. Aspinwall to call upon you and arrange in my name the terms of payment, and reduce the whole to writing." Recalling Murray's wish to see the manuscripts, Irving could only promise, "Col. Aspinwall will hand you the first 21 chapters of Mahomet. There will be about 70 chapters in all and the rest will be forwarded as fast as you can need them." Irving's "about 70 chapters" must have roused Murray's apprehensions almost at once, for, though he had once purchased *Tales of a Traveller* sight unseen, still the book market in 1831 was depressed, and, as Irving was soon to discover, he had never been one of Murray's most

16. McClary, *Irving and the House of Murray,* p. 126.
17. *Ibid.,* p. 156.
18. *Ibid.,* p. 157.

profitable authors. Thus, "about 70 chapters" might mean that Irving himself had no idea how long his "Legendary Life of Mahomet" might be; indeed, Murray might justifiably have supposed that Irving was again about to feed a manuscript piecemeal through the press, altering and revising and toning it as it returned to him in proof. In fact, Irving's next two sentences seemed almost to admit that the manuscript was far from being either complete or perfected: "I will thank you to have the work put to press as soon as possible and furnish proof in slips, as I may wish to make occasional alteration & additions. I will commence sending MS. of the miscellaneous volume [the "Spanish sketch book"] shortly, so that both works may be out before Christmas."[19]

Murray did not reply to this letter, and Irving appears to have rested secure in his assumption that the fragment of one manuscript now in his publisher's hands and at least the certain *promise* of another – and his moderate prices for both – could not fail of a quick acceptance. Only such confidence in his own popularity and in his publisher's forbearance can explain Irving's direction to Colonel Aspinwall on October 14, "Tell him [Murray] if he would prefer it, I may be able to make the Miscellaneous work a couple of light volumes of about three hundred and twenty pages each, instead of one volume of about 400 pages – but then I should ask 1600 guineas instead of 1000. I am anxious to have the arrangement made and the works put to press immediately, and printed *rapidly* so as to have them in type by the end of next month, that I may be *free*."[20]

But Aspinwall's negotiations had neither failed nor succeeded; he had not been able to see Murray at all, and Irving's gathering impatience broke out in a letter to Aspinwall on October 22, in which he fairly accused his publisher of ingratitude, and in another letter of the same date to Murray himself. What motives of artistic overconfidence or financial insecurity inspired his disastrous letter to Murray can never be known, but Irving's hectoring tone and whining petulance were alike unsupportable:

Sheffield, Oct. 22d 1831.

Dear Sir,
    I wrote to you between two and three weeks since wishing the

19. *Ibid.*, pp. 157–58.
20. STW, II, 21–22.

arrangement to be closed with my agent Col. Aspinwall about the publication of the two works which I have ready for the press and which for various urgent reasons I wish to have published immediately. I have since authorized Col. Aspinwall to make further propositions to you concerning one of these works. I find however by a letter from him dated the 21st that he has not been able to see you on the business. As this delay is excessively annoying to me and impedes all my plans and movements, and as it is very probable that you may not be desirous of publishing at this moment, I am perfectly willing that what has passed between us on the subject should be considered as null and void, and in such case will thank you to return to Col. Aspinwall the MS. already left with you. Should you still be disposed however to publish that work (Mahomet) and to put it to press forthwith it is at your service at the price agreed upon (though it rather exceeds the quantity of MS. I mentioned). As to the other work, I do not think there is any likelihood of your being able to get it out as early as I wish. I trust, therefore, you will not take it amiss if I seek some other person or mode to publish it. Nothing but the peculiar circumstances which hurry me at this time would make me quit my usual channel; but time is every thing with me now.

I am my dear Sir
Very truly yours,
Washington Irving.[21]

Such a letter to a publisher of Murray's quality and character was not only tactless; it was impudent, especially in view of Murray's earlier open and generous acceptance of Irving both as a writer and as a man, his munificent payments, and his uncomplaining acceptance of ever more careless manuscripts for books with an ever smaller popular market and critical esteem. "The Legendary Life of Mahomet," incomplete as it probably was,[22] must have been the least promising manuscript Murray had ever received from Irving's hands, and probably the most carelessly and incompetently written. Only two years before, moreover, Murray had published Sir John Malcolm's revised two-volume edition of *The History of Persia, from the Most Early Period to the*

21. McClary, *Irving and the House of Murray*, p. 159.

22. It should be noted, however, that in his letter of October 22 to Aspinwall Irving claimed, "The Mahomet is entirely ready, and the other [the 'Spanish Sketch Book'] I can furnish as fast as it could be wanted" (*ibid.*, p. 158).

Present Time, a monument of contemporary Eastern scholarship, and he thus had a sure knowledge of the salability of Orientalia (even in the Family Library) and as a matter of course recognized Irving's confused superficiality in "The Legendary Life of Mahomet." Under the circumstances Murray's reply to Irving's letter of October 22 was a model of civil restraint:

Albemarle Street
Octr. 25, 1831.

My Dear Sir,

My reply was "Yes, I'll write to you," and the cause of my not having done so earlier, is one for which I am sure you will make allowances [Murray had been ill]. You told me upon our former negociations, and you repeated it recently, that you would not suffer me to be a loser by any of your Works; and the state of matters in this respect, I am exceedingly unwilling because it is contrary to my nature to submit to you, and in doing so at length, you will I am sure do me the justice to believe that I have no other expectations than those which are founded upon your own good feelings. The publication of Columbus cost me. Paper – Print – Advertising – Author, £5,700 and it has produced but £4,700 – Grenada cost £3,073 and its sale has produced but £1,830, making my gross loss of £2,250. – I have thought it better to communicate with yourself direct, than through the medium of Mr. Aspinwall. –

Let me have time to read the two new MSS – and then we shall not differ I think about terms.

With sincere regard,
I remain,
My Dear Sir,
faithfully yours,
(signed)   John Murray[23]

Irving could not misunderstand this letter: Murray would not accept *The Alhambra* sight unseen; he might not accept "The Legendary Life of Mahomet" at all; and in the context his emphasis upon conditional "terms" was in every way a shock and an affront, as Irving made clear in his letter to the publisher from Barlborough Hall, Chesterfield, on October 29. His first paragraph recapitulated his understanding of "your offer of 500 guineas for 'Mahomet' & . . . 1000 guineas for the

---

23. *Ibid.,* p. 160.

miscellaneous volume of Spanish Tales and Sketches." Even now Irving seems not to have understood how seriously his relations with his
publisher had deteriorated, for his second paragraph makes no apology
for the manuscript fragment of "The Legendary Life of Mahomet" already in Murray's hands and assumes, more than gratuitously, that
Murray could have no objection to his extensive revisions in proof: "I
accordingly sent you a portion of the MS. of Mahomet, anticipating a
prompt return of proof sheets. By your letter of the 25th however I find
you do not consider any arrangement existing between us. You now say
'let me have time to read the new MSS. & then we shall not differ I think
about the terms.' No stipulation of the kind was ever hinted at when
we made our bargain; and depending on the indulgence to be given me
of having my works printed on slips, I left my manuscripts in the rough
intending to make final corrections in the proof sheets. I could not prepare them for critical examination without a loss of time that would
alter all my plans [for his return to America]. As it is the delay that
has already occurred will oblige me to change my scheme of publication."[24]

The baffled assurance of this passage is pathetic enough, as is Irving's next paragraph describing (from his point of view) the profits his
assured literary reputation and future productions would bring to the
firm of John Murray. Somewhat stiffly he closed this very curious letter
by assuring his publisher, "I shall be happy to hear from you," if Murray finally determined to publish both manuscripts on the terms Irving
had originally offered. The whole imbroglio ended in bluster and confusion, and Irving's subsequent account of the affair to Charles Leslie
betrayed an uncharacteristic stuffiness and pique: "All this Statement,
as I observed is merely to let you know how I am situated in regard to
Mr Murray, in case he should refer to the past – I do not wish you to
say any thing on the subject to him. neither am I desirous of renewing
my literary connexion with him – *I am tired of him.*"[25]

That Irving had been just neither to his own ambition nor to his publisher's reputation the extant manuscript of "The Legendary Life of
Mahomet" makes perfectly clear, and there is thus an unintended irony
in the fact that the first new volumes in the Putnam Author's Revised
Edition to be printed in England were *Mahomet and His Successors,*

24. *Ibid.,* pp. 161–62.
25. Irving to Leslie, "Newstead Abbey Jany 9th. 1832," Berg Collection, New
York Public Library.

published from American plates by the firm of John Murray at 50 Albe-marle Street. Although Colburn and Bentley brought out *The Alham-bra* in 1832, Irving seems to have made no further effort to place "The Legendary Life of Mahomet" during his last months in England. At present the first manuscript of *Mahomet* (hereafter referred to as MSa), still in a remarkably good state of preservation, indicates that the book, whenever and wherever it was finished, had but sixty-five chapters (paged from 1 to 558), of which Chapters 61–64 and four or five scattered leaves have disappeared.[26]

So far as MSa and the first volume of *Mahomet and His Successors* bear thematic comparison at all, both versions share a rough chrono-logical order tracing the rise of Islam through the developing character and self-consciousness of the Prophet himself, themselves the indices of his prophetic mission. It is thus a fair generalization that the first vol-ume of *Mahomet and His Successors* is only an expansion and an elab-oration of the historical materials first worked out in MSa, though of course in his second version Irving took considerable pains to develop more fully traits of Mahomet's character and ambition, establish more strikingly thematic juxtapositions and contrasts, and, most important, to emphasize more clearly than in MSa the identification of Mahomet himself and the religion he proclaimed. Both MSa and the first volume of *Mahomet and His Successors* conclude their accounts of the Proph-et's career with a survey of the faith of Islam and a brief analysis of its sectarian divisions, and both contain a concluding chapter on the rules and ceremonies of Pilgrimage. Both versions show a pronounced ten-dency to equate Islam and Mahomet with the geography of Arabia and the fanaticisms of the desert tribes and to contrast these vigorous pair-ings with the effete Byzantine Christianity of Heraclius and the deca-dent Persian Zoroastrianism of the Khosrus, all of which rested upon a simplistic environmentalism and a cyclic theory of historical progres-sion which most serious Orientalists of the period had already dis-carded. MSa is far more romantic (not to say diffuse) than the first volume of *Mahomet and His Successors* in its exposition of Eastern leg-end and myth, and in later chapters Irving was rather too much given to ponderous moralizings on the decline and fall of the Eastern Empire and to heavy-handed ridicule of the credulity of the Prophet's disciples and wives. MSa makes no pretensions to an informed analysis of Islam

26. See the Textual Commentary, pages 561–576, below, for further descriptive analyses of MSa.

and its founder, to any comprehension of the internal dynamics of Mahomet's urbanizing mission, or to any clear-cut distinctions between Mahomet as inspired religionist and Mahomet as a historical personality. Finally, there is no evidence in MSa that Irving had it in mind in 1831 or earlier to write a continuation of the book to include the lives of the successors of the Prophet, and thus the second volume of *Mahomet and His Successors* was almost certainly new composition for the Putnam Author's Revised Edition.

Physically MSa – at least through Chapter 33 and page 261 – shows clearly the probable stages of Irving's composition of "The Legendary Life of Mahomet." Especially in the earliest chapters of MSa, Irving incorporated, with appropriately ballooned bridges and transitions, very carefully written pages of clear extracts and paraphrases from Abulfeda, the Syrian historian and geographer whose Arabic codex, generally known as the *Annales Moslemici*,[27] Jean Gagnier had abridged and translated into Latin as *De Vita et Rebus Gestis Mohammedis, Moslemicae Religionis Auctoris, et Imperii Saracenici Fundatoris* and published at Oxford in 1723. It is presumably to this volume that Irving refers in his preface to the first volume of *Mahomet and His Successors* when he speaks of "Gagnier's translation of the Arabian historian Abulfeda, a copy of which the author found in the Jesuits' Library of the Convent of St. Isidro, at Madrid." It may be assumed that Irving's excerpts from Gagnier's redaction of the *De Vita et Rebus Gestis Mohammedis* incorporated in the earliest chapters of "The Legendary Life of Mahomet" were part of his earliest research (1827–1828) in Spain, and these passages from Abulfeda and others from such diverse sources as Bleda's *Coronica de los Moros de España*, Ockley's *History of the Saracens*, Marigny's *History of the Arabians*, D'Herbelot's *Bibliothèque Orientale*, Gibbon's *Decline and Fall of the Roman Empire*, Gagnier's *Vie de Mahomet*, and even *An Universal History, from the Earliest Account of Time*, Irving copied out on the right-hand two-thirds of the pages of his manuscript notes and memoranda, leaving the left-hand third of these leaves clear for authorial commentary and expansion. His extant notebooks and loose memoranda for *Mahomet* contain a considerable number of similar pages which Irving apparently could not fit into the scheme of the book as he planned it for Murray in 1831, but it is a sufficient indication of the extreme haste with which at

27. Not published in full until J. J. Reiske's translation (Leipzig, 1754).

least the first third or half of "The Legendary Life of Mahomet" was prepared for publication that Irving simply incorporated these library jottings (some of which may have been made in England) into his printer's copy more or less *en bloc*, while making only the slightest effort to fit these heterogeneous materials into some kind of congruent form and unity. Certainly Irving relied on Murray's usual forbearance to bring these short and poorly assimilated chapters up to the standards of his earlier historical works.

Genetically MSa is of considerable interest and importance for the elucidation of Irving's sources both for the manuscript itself (and thus for a general description of the extent of his interest in and knowledge of Eastern sources) and for the first volume of *Mahomet and His Successors* as well as for his methods of composition in general. Unlike *Mahomet and His Successors*, MSa is heavily documented (although many of Irving's footnotes here are simply his own ascriptions for the manuscript notes he made in a number of libraries), so that it would appear that he had meant to erect a careful façade of Islamic scholarship and factual reliability around the shaky structure of his narrative. That Irving was cooking his research even for MSa will be shown hereafter, but at this point it is enough to say that MSa, had it ever been published, would have made the same claims to historical breadth and painstaking research that Irving had risked in his preface to *Columbus:* even a volume for Murray's very popular Family Library, in other words, was a serious intellectual exercise, and Irving's jerry-built scaffolding of obscure Spanish chronicles and forgotten Arabian and Persian histories laboriously cited in latinate footnotes would not dispel the illusion that the historian of Columbus had once again ransacked whole libraries for his narrative of the conquering triumphs of Islam and its Prophet.

Murray would have had only to glance at the manuscript of "The Legendary Life of Mahomet," of course, to discover at once how specious Irving's pretensions to Oriental scholarship and research really were. The merely physical condition of MSa shows at once that Irving had been muddling with many of these chapters, indeed that he had never been quite sure just how the book ought to be put together, and that at least the first twenty-one chapters submitted to Murray's judgment were an uneasy compromise among as many as four or five different schemes of narrative development. Almost all of the first twenty-one chapters in "The Legendary Life of Mahomet" show at

least two foliations, one in the final sequence 1–558 firmly marked in
Irving's hand in the center of each page, and another (and sometimes
two or three or four) in the upper right corner – clearly an indication
that Irving had concocted these sections of the narrative separately and
perhaps in isolation from one another and then had tried to find some
logical sequence in which they might be finally organized for the book.
Frequently these right-corner foliations are simply in the sequence 1, 2,
3, 4 to the end of the chapter, but in several instances Irving rearranged the order of a whole block of chapters, so that any given section
of MSa may be found to have not only the 1, 2, 3 foliation by chapter
but also a superscript sequence 79, 80, 81 and so on – in addition, of
course, to Irving's final pagination 1–558. Other chapters contain
pasted-up irregular leaves, again showing that Irving was economically
saving time and material by fitting scraps and tags of historical facts
and personal anecdote wherever they might find a tenuous relevance.
Even with these curious shifts and changes, the first twenty-one chapters of MSa (which may be all that Murray ever saw) remain a clumsy
pastiche of undigested generalities and outright plagiarisms from other
writers. Chapter 2, "Varieties of religion at the Era of Mahomet. Of the
Sabians or Worshippers of Stars. Of the Egyptian Theology" (pages
10–14a of MSa); Chapter 3, "Modifications of the Sabean Idolatry.
Heathen Mythology of Greece and Rome. Superstitions of the Scythian
Goths. Of the Hindoo Gentio or Brachman Theology" (pages 15–21);
Chapter 4, "Of the Magians or Fire Worshippers of Persia" (pages
22–24); Chapter 5, "State of the Jews at the Era of Mahomet" (pages
25–29); and Chapter 6, "State of Christianity in the East" (pages
30–38), indicate merely by their synoptic headings how awkwardly
and how superficially Irving had organized his introductory survey of
his subject, for these chapters seem more or less irrelevant where they
are and in fact redundant to the historically naive and personal emphases of the rest of MSa. Clearly these chapters were miscellaneous
gleanings which Irving was unwilling to waste, and so they were incorporated into "The Legendary Life of Mahomet," almost certainly as
mere filler, although Irving managed to salvage much of this miscellaneous material by redistributing it as appropriate historical example
and analogy throughout the first volume of *Mahomet and His Successors*.

But this alteration and expansion of the crabbed and chaotic manuscript of "The Legendary Life of Mahomet" (itself perhaps an expan-

sion of the "legend of Mahomet" prologue to the remainder of his "Spanish Suite"), with a great many other revisions and rediscoveries, Irving waited almost twenty years to accomplish, and the rejected volume returned with him to America in 1832, when it was superseded by his new American interests and books – *A Tour on the Prairies* (1835), *Astoria* (1836), *The Adventures of Captain Bonneville* (1837), and the *Biography and Poetical Remains of the Late Margaret Miller Davidson* (1841) – and by some thirty essays, sketches, and tales written for the *Knickerbocker Magazine* between March 1839 and October 1841. Apparently Irving tried unsuccessfully to place "The Legendary Life of Mahomet" with Marsh, Capen, Lyon, and Webb in 1839,[28] but no evidence survives to indicate that during the 1830's he revised MSa in any meaningful way. Like *The Life of George Washington*, another book first conceived during the 1820's, "The Legendary Life of Mahomet" was a part of Irving's literary deposits, to be drawn upon at need, though he undoubtedly added notes to the memoranda for each during the whole decade.

Irving's appointment as ambassador to Spain in 1842, however, seemed to promise "abundant leisure . . . for literary occupation,"[29] but revolution and counterrevolution, the exigencies of his post, and the renewal of old friendships in Madrid kept him from his writing desk. Only a recurrence of his old "inflammatory disease of the skin" in 1843–1844 gave him an enforced rest from his diplomatic obligations, as Irving's own preface to the first volume of *Mahomet and His Successors* makes clear: "During his last residence in Spain, the author beguiled the tediousness of a lingering indisposition, by again revising the manuscript, profiting in so doing by recent lights thrown on the subject by different writers, and particularly by Dr. Gustav Weil."

What precisely Irving meant by "revising the manuscript" is debatable (especially since most of the printer's copy for *Mahomet and His Successors* has disappeared), but no reference to Weil's *Mohammed der Prophet, sein Leben und sein Lehre*[30] appears in MSa, and in any case Irving was also at work on *Washington* during this period,[31] so that it seems safe to assume that in 1843–1844 Irving merely "dressed off" parts of "The Legendary Life of Mahomet," read over once again

28. STW, II, 393.
29. Irving to Mrs. Paris, August 3, 1842 (PMI, III, 224).
30. Leipzig, 1843.
31. PMI, III, 277.

his bundles of memoranda, and annotated Weil. He seems to have returned briefly to both manuscripts in late 1845 and early 1846, when, as
Stanley T. Williams remarks, "his literary passions had atrophied,"[32]
but Irving seems to have had no idea of rewriting MSa or of originat-
ing a second, *Successors,* volume until the fall of 1848, when the Putnam Author's Revised Edition was well under way. Pierre M. Irving
records, "Late in October [1848] I called on Mr. Irving, then in New
York, and found him engaged on his Life of Mahomet, evidently somewhat fagged. I told him I saw Putnam had advertised its appearance
for the 1st of January. Yes, he said; he was afraid it would hurry him to
get ready; he gave him [Putnam] a negligent answer, and he fixed
a day. Was a good deal bothered in his anxiety to finish this and the
Life of Washington. Hoped he would not drop in harness. I told him the
uniform edition was doing so well, he could afford to take his ease, and
not to drudge. 'Yes,' said he; 'but I know my nature. I must get through
with the work I have cut out for myself. I must weave my web, and then
die.' "[33] Pierre M. Irving makes no further mention of the progress of
Mahomet or its lack of progress until 1849, when he notes:

> On the 19th of September, I stopped in at Putnam's, who told
> me he had already disposed of the first edition of Goldsmith of
> 2,500, and was now busy on a second of 2,000. I wrote to Mr. Irving
> to that effect, and added that it had increased his publisher's im-
> patience for the appearance of Mahomet. In his reply of the 21st,
> he says:
> "I am getting on very well, but am not yet in a mood to take up
> my pen; so Mr. Putnam must stay his stomach with Goldsmith a
> little longer. I suppose, because I knocked off that work in such an
> offhand manner, he thinks it a very easy matter with me 'to blow
> up a dog.' "[34]

Thus *The Life of Oliver Goldsmith* had absorbed part of Irving's energies in 1849, although that book, according to Putnam's own later
recollections, was written in only sixty days.[35] By the end of the year,
however, the first volume of *Mahomet and His Successors* had passed
through Putnam's presses, and, some four months later, in April 1850,

32. STW, II, 197.
33. PMI, IV, 47–48.
34. *Ibid.,* p. 59.
35. "Recollections of Irving," *Atlantic Monthly,* VI (1860), 605.

the second volume appeared. The *Successors* was strictly a rush order, a book blown up almost as quickly as *Goldsmith,* but the first volume had been maturing in Irving's mind for nearly a quarter of a century, he had among his memoranda a full budget of miscellaneous information and extracts from writers useful for his own peculiar kind of romantic historiography, and at Sunnyside and at the Astor Library he had all the books he needed for the literary joinery required for the transformation of MSa, "The Legendary Life of Mahomet," into the first volume of *Mahomet and His Successors.* While *Mahomet* follows the general historical outlines and reflects some of the romantic emphases of MSa, the book as it presently stands in Irving's canon demonstrates not only the interests and values of his literary maturity but also and more importantly than does "The Legendary Life of Mahomet" Irving's prescriptions for a romantic historiography as he explained them in an analysis of *The Conquest of Granada* in a letter of October 21, 1828, to Alexander H. Everett: "It [*The Conquest of Granada*] is in the form of a Chronicle, made up from all the old Spanish historians I could lay my hands on, colored and tinted by the imagination so as to have a romantic air, without destroying the historical basis or the chronological order of events. I fancy it is as near the truth as any of the chronicles from which it is digested, and has the advantage of containing the striking facts and achievements, true or false, of them all. Of course it will have no pretensions as a grave historical production, or a work of authority, but I cannot help thinking it will present a lively picture of the war, and one somewhat characteristic of the times, so much of the materials having been drawn from contemporary historians."[36]

This passage demonstrates Irving's comparative indifference to modern source materials and methods of research in favor of "contemporary historians" and "histories colored and tinted by the imagination." History was thus "striking facts or achievements, true or false," an exercise of the romantic imagination in its less lofty flights, and "a lively picture." It is therefore not surprising to find Abulfeda most frequently cited in Irving's subscripted notes for "The Legendary Life of Mahomet," particularly the *De Vita et Rebus Gestis Mohammedis* and Gagnier's *La Vie de Mahomet* (largely based on Abulfeda), but there is at least one possible reference to the *Annales Moslemici,* and Irving

36. PMI, II, 348.

must be credited with considerable acumen or remarkably good luck in discovering and utilizing one of the most reliable Islamic historians. From *La Vie de Mahomet,* however, Irving also took extensive passages of paraphrase from "Al Jannabi" and "Abu Horaira," and occasionally he did not acknowledge these authors "apud Gagnier," thus allowing the assumption that these citations were discoveries or redactions of his own. The case is the same with his references to "Al Hafedh" and "Al Ishailius," subscripted on two successive pages of "The Legendary Life of Mahomet," but Irving gives the game away on the *next* page by footnoting "Al Hafedh quoted by Abulfeda Cap. 1," a reference which he later scored over. From either the *Annales Moslemici* or the *De Vita et Rebus Gestis Mohammedis,* or even from *La Vie de Mahomet,* Irving might have gathered several of his references to "Ahmed Ben Joseph" and "Ebn Isaac" in his account in MSa of Mahomet's "Night Journey" (otherwise indebted to Prideaux), but the precise provenance of many of the extracts loosely incorporated in "The Legendary Life of Mahomet" might equally well have come from any one of a number of contemporary European historians or Islamic scholars. Thus, Irving might have picked up his passing reference to "Al Gazali," the Persian historian, and to "Alwakidi" from any of a number of comparatively modern sources – though their direct provenance seems to be from Simon Ockley's *History of the Saracens,* and his own copy of George Sale's translation of the Koran furnished him with a good deal of reliable Saracenic culture and history. Thus we find Irving using "contemporary historians" as far as they were available to him in translation and manufacturing appropriate citations from earlier European writers who themselves had the first-hand knowledge of the original Arabian and Persian sources which he lacked. Still, Irving did show considerable initiative in his single reference to "Abul Faragius apud Pocock: Oxon. Pocock Spec. Hist. Arab. Ox [Oxford?] 1806 P. 13," from which he drew a Latin footnote for his account of the false prophet Moseïlma: Edward Pococke's *Specimen Historiae Arabum, sive Gregorii Abu'l Faragii Malatiensis de Origine et Moribus Arabum Succincta Narratio* had been a standard reference for some hundred and fifty years.

As might be expected, "The Legendary Life of Mahomet" shows some – but, under the circumstances, not much – borrowing from sources not entirely contemporary. Irving put D'Herbelot's massive six-volume *Bibliothèque Orientale* under contribution for the dressing and toning of his adaptations of Gagnier's several versions of Abulfeda, and certain specific passages in MSa seem to be drawn from both Gibbon and *An Universal History,* a compendium which his "pioneer" and critic, his brother Peter Irving, especially depended upon for his "Remarks" and interleaved comments. There is one definite reference to Bleda,[37] and, oddly enough, two or three direct citations from Humphrey Prideaux (one of which reappears at page 66 in *Mahomet and His Successors*), whose only value to Irving seems to have been that the highly controversial *The Life of Mahomet,* a monument of the *odium theologicum,* was nevertheless founded upon a sturdy basis of Arabian and Persian history and buttressed by a whole library of Jewish and Christian chroniclers and commentators. Of modern Eastern travelers Irving cited only Burckhardt and his *Travels in Arabia* and made but passing reference to Heron's translation of Niebuhr's *Travels.*

This brief account of the identifiable sources for "The Legendary Life of Mahomet" which Irving himself acknowledged does not, of course, exhaust the problems of documentation that the manuscript presents, particularly since most of the second half of MSa is more nearly fair printer's copy and thus does not contain the pages of extracts and digests which so disfigure the earlier chapters of "The Legendary Life of Mahomet." Irving also inked out a number of footnotes, and some are simply irrecoverable, as in his reference to "Houssan Vaez[?], Cap. Amram. Ebn Isaac." It is certainly possible that Irving may have searched out the collateral Latin or French translations of the sources upon which, for instance, D'Herbelot or Ockley or Prideaux based their narratives, but as between an Arabian or Persian history or commentary translated or footnoted in a modern source and a French or Latin redaction of an original Oriental source, Irving – like Emerson, for that matter – did not often discriminate, and when he returned to Mahomet and Islam during the 1840's he continued to rely upon those reference materials ready to his hand in languages which he could read.

Thus, "The Legendary Life of Mahomet" and the first volume of *Mahomet and His Successors* show decided similarities in derivation and consequently in their general thematic developments and emphases. But the *Mahomet* of 1849–1850, besides being almost twice the length of MSa, shows a far greater control of its materials and a more equable

---

37. Irving's reference is specifically to "Bleda. Hist. de Mahoma. c.3," a work which I have been unable to identify, though Irving had a copy of Bleda's *Coronica de los Moros de España* at Sunnyside.

balance between the values of historicity and the interests of personal anecdote, despite all of Irving's sweeping expansions and amplifications of incident, social color, and political and moral contrasts and comparisons. Where "The Legendary Life of Mahomet" flounders in the morass of schismatic theology or muddles through a confused account of the origin of religion itself, where it retards the movement of the narrative with a ponderous disquisition on the "Fundamental principles of the Religion of Mahomet" or frankly titillates the presumptive reader with the story "Of the loves of Mahomet & Zeinab," the printed version of *Mahomet* moves forward with a kind of awkward but determined authority, suppressing nearly all irrelevancies and concentrating upon Mahomet as inspired Prophet and Great Man. All other matters, all accounts of battles won and lost, of wives and concubines taken in wedlock or in battle, and of comrades victorious or defeated, are subordinated to Irving's insistent emphasis upon Mahomet and his conquering mission. *Mahomet* in its final form thus has a focus of interest and meaning which the hasty and loosely anecdotal "Legendary life of Mahomet" never pretended to, and the reasons for Irving's success with the book in 1849–1850, where he had failed in 1831 and earlier, are not to be explained so much by his subsequent twenty-five years of desultory reading and writing on Islam and Mahomet or by his greater maturity as by his belated recognition of the kind of book he finally meant to write, by his fortuitous discovery of a number of modern volumes of relevant Saracenic history and commentary, by his judiciously sustained use of the small library of Orientalia which he had patiently gathered at Sunnyside, and, particularly, by the pressure of Putnam's Author's Revised Edition and his own determination to dispose of *Mahomet* at last. All of these reasons, of course, are interconnected, and together they describe and explain the genesis of *Mahomet and His Successors* as both volumes stand in Irving's canon today.

In the first place, Irving had been adding sporadic installments to his memoranda for *Mahomet* since 1831, so that, in addition to the abortive manuscript previously submitted to Murray, with its full weight of undigested source materials, Irving had all the manuscript notes, extracts, and digests which he had not been able to use for the book that Murray refused, together with his accumulated casual jottings for almost twenty years thereafter. These materials – loose sheets and gatherings and notebooks of verbatim transcripts or general paraphrase from various primary and secondary sources – are of considerable interest for a genetic study of both MSa and the final Putnam version of the first volume of *Mahomet and His Successors*, for Irving's usual practice seems to have been to destroy those of his notes not actually incorporated into his manuscript or at least to separate them in some way from his working memoranda after he had completed the page or the chapter of which they had been the basis. Almost all of the extant memoranda for *Mahomet* represent materials for which Irving could find no real use, and although these notes, extracts, and digests are themselves of some importance in showing how far and how deeply Irving researched both versions of the book, they do not begin to suggest how MSa became the first volume of Putnam's *Mahomet and His Successors*. Moreover, manuscript notes among Irving's memoranda for *Mahomet* are of no particular help in determining when Irving may have read any given primary or secondary source. Citations in *Mahomet and His Successors* for books unmentioned in "The Legendary Life of Mahomet" may seem to indicate that Irving read these materials after 1831, but, because of his wholesale cancellations of his working notes, only publication dates of modern books that are specifically cited in either volume of *Mahomet and His Successors* are a reliable guide in discovering at which stage of his work Irving may have read and annotated any given source.

Thus, he did not encounter Weil's *Mohammed der Prophet* before 1843 or Sir Austen Henry Layard's famous *Nineveh and Its Remains* before 1849 or the Reverend Samuel Green's *The Life of Mahomet* before 1840 or John P. Brown's translation of Tabary's *Conquest of Persia by the Arabs* before late 1849 or early 1850, but as in the case of such a work as A. N. Matthews' translation of the *Mischcât-ul-Masâbih* (Calcutta, 1809), cited on page 25, above, in *Mahomet and His Successors* (if Irving did in fact see Matthews' comparatively rare two volumes and was not cribbing this citation from some other writer), it is simply impossible to say, on the basis of the extant memoranda, when and how Irving may have accumulated some of his information. About all that can safely be inferred or conjectured about Irving's knowledge, in 1831 or earlier, of Matthews and of similar recondite materials is that he may have read and annotated them but could not find a use for such highly specialized studies in the comparatively restricted development of "The Legendary Life of Mahomet." Similar problems surround Irving's expanded borrowings in 1848–1850 from Upham, Gibbon, Prideaux, Niebuhr, Conde, D'Herbelot, Ockley, Marigny, Gagnier, Burckhardt, and similar other early sources, for it is by no means clear from *Mahomet and His Successors* whether Irving indeed returned to the very books he had originally read when planning and writing "The Legendary Life of Mahomet" or whether he simply picked and chose among the extracts and digests from these sources among his memoranda. The latter assumption seems the more probable in view of the fact that almost all of the significant expansions of MSa into the first volume of *Mahomet and His Successors* Irving might have accomplished from his elbowchair at Sunnyside, where he had at his fingertips a two-volume edition of Gagnier's *La Vie de Mahomet* (1748), a four-volume edition of Marigny's *The History of the Arabians* (1758), a two-volume edition of George Sale's translation of the Koran (1825), Lane's *Selections from the Kur-an* (1843), Ockley's *History of the Saracens* (1757) – although it is almost certain that Irving had also read the carefully annotated Bohn "fourth edition" (1847) of Ockley – and Charles Mills's *An History of Muhammedanism* (1818).[38]

For example, Chapter I of *Mahomet and His Successors,* the "Preliminary Notice of Arabia and the Arabs," fills seventeen pages of type in the 1849–1850 Author's Revised Edition text and rests in part upon the nine manuscript pages of Irving's MSa Chapter 1, "Of Arabia and the Arabs"; the six pages of Chapter 2, "Varieties of religion at the Era of Mahomet. Of the Sabians or Worshippers of Stars. Of the Egyptian Theology"; the seven pages of Chapter 3, "Modifications of the Sabean Idolatry. Heathen Mythology of Greece and Rome. Superstitions of the Scythian Goths. Of the Hindoo Gentio or Brachman Theology"; and the three pages of Chapter 4, "Of the Magians or Five Worshippers of Persia," for a total of twenty-five manuscript pages or some twenty-five hundred words. Since a good deal of the rather heterogeneous materials of these chapters does not appear in the final "Preliminary Notice of Arabia and the Arabs" and since that chapter now contains almost forty-five hundred words, it is clear that in the re-creation of that body of introductory materials for *Mahomet and His Successors* Irving expanded the relevant parts of the first four chapters of "The Legendary Life of Mahomet" by somewhat more than three hundred percent, assuming (very generously) that some one thousand words in the corresponding section of MSa can be identified as old composition in the

38. And also the third volume of Morier's *The Adventures of Hajji Baba, of Ispahan, in England.*

present form of the "Preliminary Notice of Arabia and the Arabs." The sources for this careful expansion and refinement of Irving's introductory chapter can easily be seen, of course, in his lengthy footnote allusions to and citations from Layard on page 8 (by implication) and on page 9, above, and from *"Burckhardt, Notes on Bedouins,"* on pages 8–9 above. Almost as easily identifiable (although unacknowledged) are the extensive borrowings which Irving made from Sale's "Preliminary Discourse" (or from some other unidentifiable source dependent upon Sale) for his resumé of the general history and geography of pre-Islamic Arabia and for his descriptions of Arabian tribal and religious divisions, customs, and myths. All of this amplification from Sale indicates that the "Preliminary Discourse" was open before him as Irving toiled away at this chapter of *Mahomet and His Successors;* further source-hunting is of no great advantage here because the generalizing exposition of the "Preliminary Notice of Arabia and the Arabs" effectively obliterated Irving's specific obligations to D'Herbelot, Ockley, Marigny, Gibbon, and a good many other sources antecedent even to the composition of "The Legendary Life of Mahomet."

If specific sources and references for the "Preliminary Notice of Arabia and the Arabs" are in most cases irrecoverable, Irving's consistent thematic emphases may still be discerned, particularly in contrast to the original "legendary" qualities of MSa and *its* emphasis upon the romantic narrative of Mahomet's life and conquests. The concluding paragraph of the first chapter of *Mahomet and His Successors* is one long and intense sentence summarizing the meanings of Mahomet's life and career within a broadly thematic context: "The time at length arrived when its [Arabia's] discordant tribes were to be united in one creed, and animated by one common cause; when a mighty genius was to arise, who should bring together these scattered limbs, animate them with his own enthusiastic and daring spirit, and lead them forth, a giant of the desert, to shake and overturn the empires of the earth." That is to say, the hero of *Mahomet and His Successors* was a representative man and the story of his life would be representative or emblematic history. From this point of view *Mahomet and His Successors* would recapitulate many of the intellectual attitudes of Irving's earlier works like *Columbus* and would also look forward to the exemplary narrative of *Washington.* In this carefully climactic paragraph, moreover, Irving restated the dominant themes and syntheses of Carlyle's famous revisionist appreciation of Mahomet as "The Hero as Prophet," so that thematically much of the first volume of *Mahomet and His Successors* reflects Irving's decision to depersonalize "The Legendary Life of Mahomet" in favor of and in response to Carlyle's sweeping final generalization of Mahomet as the Great Man and historical archetype:

> To the Arab Nation it [Islam] was as a birth from darkness into light; Arabia first became alive by means of it. A poor shepherd people, roaming unnoticed in its deserts since the creation of the world: a Hero-Prophet was sent down to them with a word they could believe: see, the unnoticed becomes world-notable, the small has grown world-great; within one century afterwards, Arabia is at Grenada on this hand, at Delhi on that; – glancing in valour and splendour and the light of genius, Arabia shines through long ages over a great section of the world. Belief is great, life-giving. The history of a Nation becomes fruitful, soul-elevating, great, so soon as it believes. These Arabs, the man Mahomet, and that one century, – is it not as if a spark had fallen, one spark, on a world of what seemed black unnoticeable sand; but lo, the sand proves explosive powder, blazes heaven-high from Delhi to Grenada! I said, the Great Man was always as lightning out of heaven; the rest of men waited for him like fuel, and then they too would flame.[39]

That Irving was not consistently able to adhere to so sweeping a view of Mahomet and his historical mission may account for the curiously fluctuating tone of much of the first volume of *Mahomet and His Successors*, especially in respect to the almost mechanical alterations of historical fact and personal anecdote. It is in this regard that "The Legendary Life of Mahomet" most clearly influenced *Mahomet and His Successors* as it finally came to be written.

As might be expected, Irving's "Preliminary Notice of Arabia and the Arabs" shows his most careful expansions and revisions of the roughly corresponding chapters of "The Legendary Life of Mahomet," for in the rest of the first volume of *Mahomet and His Successors* Irving was largely content either to pad out the relevant chapters in the original manuscript with material drawn from the few sources ready to hand, or, in the case of such new materials as the present Chapter II, "Traditions Concerning Mecca and the Caaba," to return to the notes in his

---

39. *On Heroes, Hero-Worship and the Heroic in History,* World's Classics Series (London: Oxford University Press, 1968), p. 101.

memoranda, to widely scattered passages from "The Legendary Life of Mahomet," and particularly to Sale's notes and the fourth section of his "Preliminary Discourse." Sale also provided Irving with some of the material for his expansion of Chapter XXXVII, "Of the Two False Prophets Al Aswad and Moseïlma," and most of what is now the Appendix of the first volume, though the surviving final chapters of "The Legendary Life of Mahomet," which also deal with the ritual and doctrine of Islam, themselves also depend heavily upon Sale. Again, Chapter 22 of "The Legendary Life of Mahomet," "Nocturnal Journey of Mahomet to the Seven Heavens," is with its twenty-seven manuscript pages (most of which are clear printer's copy) and almost twenty-six hundred words much the longest chapter in the original manuscript. Incorporated pages of extracts and footnote citations suggest that the chapter rested originally upon Abulfeda's *De Vita et Rebus Gestis Mohammedis,* Gagnier's *La Vie De Mahomet,* Prideaux's *The Life of Mahomet,* and D'Herbelot's *Bibliothèque Orientale,* and these sources remain the basis for the present Chapter XII, "Night Journey of the Prophet from Mecca to Jerusalem; and Thence to the Seventh Heaven," which, legendary and romantic as it is, is only a thousand words longer than the corresponding Chapter 22 of "The Legendary Life of Mahomet." Irving did not need to expand *this* kind of material substantially, and thus several other more factual chapters of the first volume of *Mahomet and His Successors* are now considerably longer than the present Chapter XII, which itself also received some enlargement in 1848–1849 from Gagnier's *La Vie de Mahomet.* No comparison between "The Legendary Life of Mahomet" and the Author's Revised Edition text of *Mahomet and His Successors* shows more clearly the distinctive differences between the kind of history Irving judged appropriate for Murray's Family Library in 1831 and the comparatively sober and restrained narrative he wrote some twenty years later, after the experience and the discipline of his years of work preparatory to the more strictly scientific *Life of Washington.*

Similarly detailed analyses of other representative chapters of the first volume of *Mahomet and His Successors* would confirm the genetic and intellectual development of the text and would demonstrate with greater emphasis Irving's general if somewhat casual awareness of the extraordinary progress made in Oriental studies and in comparative religion during the twenty-odd years between 1828 and 1850. For example, he seems to have read carefully Weil's revisionistic *Mohammed der*

Prophet, sein Leben und seine Lehre and praised the book – perhaps a shade too ostentatiously – in his preface to the first volume of *Mahomet and His Successors*, and he cited Weil twice in the text. Williams found definite parallels between Irving and Weil,[40] but a closer examination of Irving's sources seems to indicate that these correspondences are more apparent than real and that Irving may have used Weil only as a supplement to a number of sources dating as far back as the original composition of "The Legendary Life of Mahomet." A more probable source, in the light of Irving's expanded discussion of the contrasts between Islam and Christianity, is Weil's *The Bible, the Koran, and the Talmud; or, Biblical Legends of the Mussulmans* (1846), an extremely important study of comparative Eastern religions and the sources of the Koran.[41]

These demonstrable exceptions apart, however, it is extremely difficult to show conclusively when any separate Oriental primary source or modern secondary materials and Koranic commentary first entered either Irving's memoranda or *Mahomet and His Successors* in either of its extant forms, or even whether Irving himself had read – in Latin or French, or, less probably, German or Spanish redactions – some of the Arabian, Syrian, or Persian sources (for example, page 47, "Al Maalem, an Arabian writer") which he cites so confidently in these pages. In the case of the second, or *Successors*, volume, however, there is really very little doubt at all about how the book was written and which sources Irving drew upon for it, and the contrast between the twenty-five years of leisurely research and writing which Irving was able to devote to the first volume and the very few hasty months he gave to the *Successors* volume could hardly be more striking.

Even Irving's manuscript memoranda show evident signs of the speed with which he researched and wrote the second volume of the book. Scattered leaves show the predictable extracts from Gibbon and Ockley and even from Sir William Ouseley's *Travels in Various Countries of the East,* and the manuscript notes confirm Irving's citation in the preface to the *Successors* volume of Joseph von Hammer-Purgstall's six-volume *Gemäldesaal der Lebensbeschreibungen grosser Moslimischer Herrscher der ersten sieben Jahrhunderte der Hidschret* (1837–1839). There are no identifiable references in the memoranda to the earlier vol-

40. STW, II, 396.
41. The *Biblical Legends* is the only Weil title among Irving's books at Sunnyside.

umes of Weil's massive five-volume *Geschichte der Chalifen* (1846–1862), but there is a remote possibility that Irving may have at least looked into this source at some time antecedent to the extremely hurried months in which he put together the *Successors* volume. Though Pierre M. Irving gives no details of the composition of the second volume, there is every indication that Irving must have written most of its five hundred pages (in the Author's Revised Edition) after completing the first volume in the early fall of 1849. Since the *Successors* volume was first published in April 1850, Irving may not in fact have had more than four or five months in which to drive his laboring pen over some 1500 of his usual pages of crabbed manuscript; and the *Successors* volume does indeed show numerous signs of extreme haste and unusual carelessness in its composition.

Indeed, a great part of the second volume of *Mahomet and His Successors* can be ascribed directly to three sources, Ockley's *History of the Saracens* (and especially to the Bohn "fourth edition" of 1847), the Abbé de Marigny's four-volume *History of the Arabians, Under the Government of the Caliphs,* and Brown's translation of Tabary's *Conquest of Persia by the Arabians.*[42] Brown provided Irving with much of the substance of Chapters XXVI, XXVII, XXVIII, XXIX, XXX, XXXI, XXXII, XXXIII, but even this consecutive block of narrative shows Irving's reliance upon Ockley and Marigny and, to a lesser degree, Hammer-Purgstall. The later chapters dealing with Moslem conquests in Northern Africa and the invasion of Spain come in large measure from Conde and De Gayangos, both of whom Irving acknowledged in his preface to the second volume, but only Brown's Tabary and De Gayangos were in any sense contemporary sources which Irving read and annotated specifically for the *Successors* volume; and as for the rest of the book it is not too much to say that very large parts of it are a mere pastiche of adaptations and transcriptions from Ockley and Marigny. In some passages, indeed, Irving did not bother even to paraphrase his authors but simply copied them *verbatim et literatim,* so much so that his reliance upon these two sources may properly be regarded as slavish. Irving is less than scrupulously accurate when in the preface to the *Successors* volume he acknowledges that he is "much indebted" to

42. *Journal of the American Oriental Society,* I (1851), 435–505. Since the *Journal* was published by Putnam, it is more than possible that Irving saw the translation of Tabary in Brown's manuscript before its publication. I have not discovered an earlier printing of Brown's Tabary.

Ockley "as well as to the Abbé de Marigny's History of the Arabians, and to D'Herbelot's Bibliothèque Orientale" but neglects to mention his heavy indebtedness to Gibbon and especially to Gibbon's organization of his separate narratives of the Arabian conquests of Syria, Iraq, Persia, Egypt, and Northern Africa. Irving's brief account, in Chapter XLIII, of the Arabs' first siege of Constantinople seems to owe much to Chapter LII of *The Decline and Fall of the Roman Empire,* but Irving's hasty summary lacks both the weight of Gibbon's scholarship and the clear coherence of his narrative. Indeed, Irving is often driven, from chapter to chapter, to such awkward transitions between chronological and geographical schemes of organization as "In the midst of these feuds and dissensions, a spark of the old Saracen spirit was aroused by the news of disastrous reverses in Northern Africa," so that much of the *Successors* volume becomes a farrago of confused dynastic struggle and local conquest and defeat.

Indeed, toward the middle of the second volume of *Mahomet and His Successors* Irving appears fundamentally to have lost control of his materials, so that the more or less chronological history of the separate caliphates (essentially based on Ockley and Marigny) gives over to what might be called a spatial or geographical narrative emphasis, and for the remainder of the book Irving alternates confusingly between the political histories of the successive caliphates and the tenuously related accounts of the progress of Moslem arms in the Near East and Africa. Even in a volume "merely to be read as a digest of current knowledge, adapted to popular use" (and Irving's "current knowledge" is certainly gratuitous), his failures of organization and assimilation of his materials in the *Successors* volume seem the result of haste and even a downright unfamiliarity with his sources. As with *Goldsmith,* so with *Mahomet and His Successors* Irving was trying to keep up with Putnam's demands for new copy for the Author's Revised Edition, and the confusions of his narrative, his obvious errors of fact and interpretation, and his outright plagiarisms from Marigny and Ockley show that the *Successors* volume was finally only a listless piece of literary hack work. Even the final version of *The Life of Oliver Goldsmith,* itself a comparable compilation of extracts and digests from recent lives of the poet *and* also a book on which Irving had been working for almost thirty years, had at least the clear distinction of Irving's mellow style and tone. Perhaps, as Stanley T. Williams observes, the worst effect of Irving's frantic efforts to turn the earlier versions of both

Goldsmith and *Mahomet* into substantial volumes for the Putnam Author's Revised Edition was that these nondescript compilations hastened his death, especially in view of the enormous efforts he must have made to complete the *Successors* volume – to order, as it were.[43] Even with Gibbon and Ockley and Brown and Marigny open before him on his writing desk, a daily stint of ten or a dozen of his usual hundred-word pages of manuscript must have been a severe trial, and it may well have been that the second volume of *Mahomet and His Successors* cost Irving too high a price in diminished vitality and in debased literary standards for its meager results, even though it was in the main favorably received both by the critics and by the public at large. We may be sure that such a volume coming from an author with a smaller reputation than Irving's would have been roundly damned.

Even Irving's extant memoranda for *Mahomet,* which of course do not include the extracts and digests that in one way or another found their way into both volumes of the book, show that most of his research centered upon source materials originally intended only for a life of the Prophet himself. These miscellaneous loose sheets, sewn and unsewn gatherings, and separate notebooks apparently extend over a period of more than a quarter of a century, for Irving economically transferred unused jottings for his *Columbus* to the memoranda for *Mahomet,* so that, mingled confusedly with his notes on Islamic subjects, there are scattered citations from Pierre Bergeron and other writers on Prester John and library extracts about Marco Polo. Even a cursory examination of these memoranda, however, does show that, whatever Irving's intentions may finally have been for the book and whatever compromises with his material he had perforce to make, initially he approached his subject with high ambitions and a laudable determination to research Islam and Mahomet as fully and as circumstantially as he (with his brother's assistance) could.[44]

Indeed, only such an explanation seems to account for the almost palpably obscure nature of the some of the works which he read and annotated for these working memoranda. Thus, besides the remaining

---

43. STW, II, 216: "So he danced about, revising the *Works,* writing a chapter or two on Washington, polishing sections of the *Mahomet;* during one period he found himself wrestling with no less than five different books. It was a pathetic higgledy-piggledy; and it may have cost him a year or two of his life."

44. The memoranda for *Mahomet and His Successors* are to be found in the Berg Collection of the New York Public Library.

but unused extracts from such familiar and acknowledged sources as
Sale, D'Herbelot, Hammer-Purgstall, Ockley, and Burckhardt, Irving
also included extensive observations from Sismondi on the literature
and historiography of Arabia, materials which he might profitably have
used in filling out his extremely sketchy account of Arabian culture at
the beginning of Mahomet's mission. Other memoranda passages seem
less relevant, notably Irving's many pages of direct transcriptions from
a source he identified as the "Dream of Saurid – origin of the Pyramids. In Mustadi – translated by Davies, p. 36 &c." – pages which also
include "The Annals of Two Coptite Brothers" and "Stories of the Pyramids." Besides these legendary tales, however, there are long pages of
extracts (perhaps in Peter Irving's or a copyist's hand) from such very
diverse and recondite sources as "A Needful Caveat or Admonition, for
them who desire to know what use may be made of, or if there be danger in reading the Alcoran by Alexander Ross (published in the
English translation of Ryers Alcoran 1649)," from "*Paradiso* Extract
from Confusione della Setta Macomettana di Giona Andrea Chap. 9,"
and from "The Life and Death of Mahumed &c. by Lancelot Addison
D.D." Other notes more briefly explain the "Twelve Articles of Mahometan Faith as reduced by Elmacinus," the "Articles of Mahomedan
Religion from Hottinger's Oriental History," and the "Five Fundamental Articles of Turkish Religion From Sir Paul Bryants History of the
present state of the Ottoman Empire. London, 1696."

From the point of view of Irving's own continuing interest in Islamic
history and culture (and perhaps of his frustrated plans to visit Northern Africa in 1829), perhaps the most interesting item among the
memoranda surviving for *Mahomet and His Successors* is a handsome
leather notebook, fifty pages of which are covered, partially or wholly,
with rudimentary illustrations of the Arabic alphabet and syllabary,
with detailed analyses of Arabic accents and vowel systems, and with
phonetic transcriptions of the language itself. This notebook is not certainly in Irving's hand and may have belonged to John Nalder Hall,
the young English painter whom he befriended at Seville in 1828.[45]
The important point, however, is that Irving carefully preserved among
his materials for *Mahomet* these unpromising and unfulfilled beginnings of his or Hall's study of Arabic, and the inference is surely al-

45. See Elsie L. West's "Gentle Flute: Washington Irving as Biographer" (Ph.D.
diss., Columbia University, 1965), pp. 154–55.

lowable that he may have long harbored the hope of finding the time and the occasion to continue his study of the language.

Thus, *Mahomet and His Successors* has an origin more complex than has been generally recognized, and the several stages of its composition introduced collateral expansions and refinements of theme and meaning in Irving's increasingly elaborate presentation of the history of Islam and its Prophet. Even as early as "The Legendary Life of Mahomet" Irving had made his crucial decision against a narrowly sectarian or polemical interpretation of Islamic history, and perhaps the most nearly modern aspect of *Mahomet and His Successors* is the basic fairmindedness of Irving's early chapters on the religions of the East and the Prophet's early stirrings of reformative enthusiasm. In this respect, at least, Irving differed from most of his sources (except Weil and Carlyle), for even in Gibbon he might have found so typical a judgment of Mahomet's life and mission as the summary generalization that "Of his last years ambition was the ruling passion; and a politician will suspect that he secretly smiled (the victorious impostor!) at the enthusiasm of his youth, and the credulity of his proselytes."[46] But Irving's fine impartiality toward Mahomet both as man and as Prophet in part militated against the sharp contrasts and the high coloring of his earlier histories, so that *Mahomet and His Successors* was never amenable to the rhetorical and thematic contrasts which he analyzed in a letter to Pierre M. Irving describing his own abortive plans for a history of the Conquest of Mexico: "My intention also was, to study the different characters of the *dramatis personae,* so as to bring them out in strong relief, and to have kept them, as much as possible, in view throughout the work. It is surprising how quickly distinctive characteristics may be caught from a few incidental words in old documents, letters, &c., and how the development of them and the putting them in action gives life and reality to a narrative."[47]

Mahomet and His Successors, however, could be neither the inspiring history of a hero-saint like Columbus nor the hortatory exemplum of the degeneration of empire like the life of Boabdil "El Chico" – men whose destinies gained an added dimension of glory or infamy through the contrasted characters of their enemies or friends. In the case of the Prophet of Islam Irving had of necessity to turn first to an identification

46. *The Decline and Fall of the Roman Empire* (New York, 1932), III, 115.
47. Washington Irving to Pierre M. Irving, Madrid, March 24, 1844 (PMI, III, 145).

of Mahomet with the history and geography of Arabia and then to a simplistic equation of Mahomet as equally and at all times both Koreishite prince and inspired, even fanatical, religious leader. Both indentifications, of course, meant that Mahomet's character was finally only inferable, emphatically not demonstrable, through the external actions and events of his biography and the Koran itself. While uncomplicated figures like Omar or Abu Beker seem to provide effective if limited contrasts to Mahomet himself, Irving initially did not proceed beyond a Carlylean conception of Mahomet as the Great Man of Arabian history and culture, the incorporation of Arabia's latent energies and strengths, and the epitome of her genius. As his narrative moves forward, however, Irving begins to probe more deeply at Mahomet's personality and character and finally proceeds beyond Carlyle's interpretation of the Prophet and his mission to demonstrate that Mahomet's earliest enthusiasm had been – by inference, at least – corrupted by "worldly passions and worldly interests," which in their turn led to the debasement of Islam itself:

> He now arrived at point where he completely diverged from the celestial spirit of the Christian doctrines, and stamped his religion with the alloy of fallible mortality. His human nature was not capable of maintaining the sublime forbearance he had hitherto inculcated . . . . He had come to Medina a fugitive seeking an asylum, and craving merely a quiet home. In a little while, and probably to his own surprise, he found an army at his command: for among the many converts daily made in Medina, – the fugitives flocking to him from Mecca, and proselytes from the tribes of the desert, – were men of resolute spirit, skilled in the use of arms, and fond of partisan warfare. Human passions and mortal resentments were awakened by this sudden access of power. They mingled with that zeal for religious reform, which was still his predominant motive. In the exaltations of his enthusiastic spirit, he endeavored to persuade himself, and perhaps did so effectually, that the power thus placed within his reach was a means of effecting his great purpose, and that he was called upon by divine command to use it.[48]

Irving proceeds to develop this rather simplistic interpretation of

48. See above, page 87.

Islam as a perverted religion of the sword through the rest of *Mahomet and His Successors* and insists that "The moment he proclaimed the religion of the sword, and gave the predatory Arabs a taste of foreign plunder, that moment he was launched in a career of conquest, which carried him forward with its own irresistible impetus."[49] Thus Mahomet in Irving's view became the victim of the irreconcilable conflict between his mission as inspired Prophet and the exigencies of his temporal sway over all Arabia; thus Islam was early tainted with bloodshed and rapine, and thus Mahomet compromised his originally pure religious fervor with "that worldly alloy which at times was debasing his spirit, now that he had become the Apostle of the Sword."[50]

It is clear that these inherent and nearly fatal contradictions in Islam and in Mahomet himself, at least as Irving chose to emphasize them, provided a central thematic coherence for the confused narrative of the first twelve Caliphs in the *Successors* volume, which itself begins with a carefully organized contrast between the simple Arabs of the desert, fired with a fanatical and plundering zeal, and the luxurious Greeks and Persians, torn by unending internal and external conflicts and sunk in a religious apathy. This contrast Irving emphasizes again and again in his descriptions of the decadent courts and gorgeous cities of the Eastern empires and the rugged simplicities of the Arabian chieftains in the crude mosque at Medina or before the besieged walls of some Syrian city: "Even Abu Obeidah, in the humility of his spirit, contented himself with his primitive Arab tent of camel's hair; refusing the sumptuous tents of the Christian commanders, won in the recent battle. Such were the stern and simple-minded invaders of the effeminate and sensual nations of the East."[51]

The remainder of the *Successors* volume then demonstrates how the Arabian conquerors of the East lapsed, in their turn, into the vices of their new subjects, how Islam itself, already much vitiated by the Prophet's own exigent secularizations of his originally lofty religious feelings, degenerated into factional strife, impiety, and luxury: "The character of the Caliphat had much changed in the hands of Moawyah, and in the luxurious city of Damascus assumed more and more the state of the oriental sovereigns which it superseded. The frugal simplicity of the Arab and the stern virtues of the primitive disciples of Islam, were

49. See above, page 198.
50. See above, page 123.
51. See above, page 262.

softening down and disappearing among the voluptuous delights of Syria."[52] In Irving's view the Prophet's own fateful determination to propagate his faith by the sword had led to those very triumphs of Islam which in turn completed the cycle of religious birth, maturity, and decay: "We shall now see the effect of those conquests on the national character and habits; the avidity of place and power and wealth, superseding religious enthusiasm; and the enervating luxury and soft voluptuousness of Syria and Persia sapping the rude but masculine simplicity of the Arabian desert. Above all, the single-mindedness of Mahomet and his two immediate successors is at an end."[53]

The oversimplifications of Irving's cyclical interpretations of Islamic history and Arabian civilization, of course, do not begin to explain the extraordinary triumphs of Saracenic arms and art in that part of Europe which he knew best, the Spanish peninsula, and Irving seems to have been content with a conception of Islam corrupt and imbecile in heart and head while full of vigorous and triumphant life in all its extremities, so that the concluding chapter of the book is only a factitious effort to reconcile the fundamental contradictions of his narrative and of his theme. There is, however, a tenuous thematic connection between *Mahomet and His Successors* and *The Conquest of Granada* in that the roles of conqueror and conquered have been reversed from book to book, and Ferdinand and Isabella and their Christian knights are the simple and pious warriors of a faith that in history's regular cycle now triumphs over Islam's luxurious and outworn creed. But *Mahomet and His Successors* shows that very absence of Irving's personal interest in, and involvement with, his central figures that make his other histories more than merely factual narratives. Particularly in the *Successors* volume Irving's customary tone is missing; his apposite philosophical generalizations and his easy moralizations on character and incident, his flowing style and his well-developed sense of history's romance of time and its mutability have seemingly all been defeated by the intractability of his materials, by his dreary extracts and digests of forgotten battles and palace intrigues.

Perhaps the real reason for the comparative insipidity and dullness of much of *Mahomet and His Successors* may finally be found in Irving's failure to project a recognizable *persona* for the separate strands

52. See above, page 439.
53. See above, page 387.

of his narrative: there is no Diedrich Knickerbocker here to mock – by his own example – the pretensions of history and historians, there is no Geoffrey Crayon to moralize upon the ruins of time, there is no Fray Antonio Agapida to dramatize the inescapable ironies of human existence; the only voice in the narrative is Irving's own – calm, judicious, and completely detached. Very occasionally Irving permits himself a mild pleasantry at the Prophet's timely revelations at moments of spiritual or amatory crisis, and there are dim echoes of Knickerbocker's old mordant mockery when Irving describes the credulity of the Prophet's disciples[54] or the delights of a Musulman's Paradise, but such passages are few and far beyond "the stately walk of history" as Irving paced it in *Mahomet and His Successors*.

Yet even this deficiency in tone, in felicitous style and substance, seems to have been no great obstacle to the book's critical and popular success and esteem. The critics were surprisingly generous to *Mahomet and His Successors*, although some of the tributes were more obviously offered to Irving as America's greatest living author than as objective evaluations of his latest book. As early as December 1847, an anonymous spokesman for American culture observed in *The United States Magazine* that "the literary world are now in impatient expectation" of the rumored publication of Irving's life of Mahomet, especially since his survey of Irving's earlier histories and popularizations had convinced this commentator that Irving was almost the only American writer capable of doing justice to such a mighty theme: "The life of Mohammed by Washington Irving! What visions of delight flood the mind at the thought! What stores of long-buried lore, rescued from the dust of ages by so experienced a literary delver, may we not reasonably hope to see!"[55] Nor were these expectations disappointed when in January 1850, among its "Notices of New Books," the same journal carried an enthusiastic paragraph of praise for the first volume of *Mahomet and His Successors*: "It is scarcely necessary to add, that the romantic story of the founders of the Moslem faith, is here told with a perspicuity and grace which has seldom been equalled. The demand for the

54. For example, see Irving's note, page 129, above: " 'Abu Rafe,' observes Gibbon, 'was an eye-witness; but who is to be witness to Abu Rafe?' We join with the distinguished historian in his doubt; yet if we scrupulously question the testimony of an eye-witness, what will become of history?"

55. "Washington Irving," *The United States Magazine and Democratic Review*, XXI (December 1847), 492.

work is of course such as the announcement of a new production by the distinguished author would not fail to produce."⁵⁶ In May 1850, the magazine more briefly noticed the *Successors* volume and limited its praise to the restrained observation, "It is one of the most attractive books of the season."⁵⁷ The *Literary Gazette* found the *Successors* volume "thoroughly redolent of the East" and considered that "For variety, adventure, and characteristic traits of a singular people, and the wonderful imposition of a strange religion upon the world, it is hardly possible to imagine a more stirring narrative. The essence of Romance pervades the solid structure of History."⁵⁸

A similar tone of approval marks the more or less official judgments of *Mahomet and His Successors* in the *Literary World* and the *North American Review*. The *Literary World* devoted parts of three separate issues in December 1849 to the book, excerpting "Mahomet's Night Journey" on December 8 and printing extensive appreciations of the book on December 22 and December 29. The *Literary World's* reviewer recognized at the beginning of the first critique that Irving's intention in *Mahomet and His Successors* was "to feed his taste for the picturesque in the survey of that shadowy Orientalism, the mixed history and legend, the fact and fable, the truth and error which are inextricably confounded in Islam."⁵⁹ Discerning Irving's predilection for "picturesque associations,"⁶⁰ the critic was able to conclude his first essay with the graceful observation that "The reflections on the character of Mahomet, Irving shares in common with many writers; but these graceful narratives, so delicately touched, will be found in his pages alone."⁶¹ The *Literary World's* second review, however, was considerably less generous; perhaps the reviewer had had second thoughts, or the "picturesque associations" had vanished, leaving Irving's intellectual confusions and vagaries only too apparent:

> We hardly know how to characterize Irving's description of these extraordinary scenes. As a chapter of history it falls below

56. "Irving's Works – Mahomet and His Successors," *ibid.*, XXVI (January, 1850), 96.

57. "The Works of Washington Irving – Mahomet and His Successors," *ibid.*, XXVI (May 1850), 476.

58. STW, II, 226.

59. "Irving's Mahomet," *Literary World*, No. 151 (December 22, 1849), 537.

60. *Ibid.*, p. 538.

61. *Ibid.*, p. 539. The critic was especially appreciative of Irving's account of "Habib the Wise" and the miraculous cure of his daughter.

the dignity and weight of the subject. It is painted in water colors, while it should be cast in bronze. At times even a humorous cast is given to the story as if it were a mere Arabian tale of pleasing character and wonderment . . . . Still the topic was grave and weighty, and needed a certain severity of treatment – more of the tragic element. But we are not disposed to press this as a defect of a work which has given us so much pleasure in the perusal, and which in its simple transparent style is the vehicle of so much information gracefully and truthfully conveyed. The general estimate of Mahomet appears to us a just one, distinguished by the good sense which marks all the writings of Irving. It is far removed from the vulgar portraits of the man. It rests upon a liberal view of human nature – a genial observation which, as with its Mahometan recording angels, has ten entries of a virtue to one of a vice.[62]

Perhaps more typical of the general appreciations of *Mahomet and His Successors* was the leading essay in the *North American Review* for October 1850 – a critique which again exhibits the pronounced tendency of most sympathetic reviewers to praise Irving's genial good sense and fair-mindedness and then to proceed to a long discussion of Islam itself, a discussion which in most cases clearly implied Irving's own failures of organization and perspicacity. Thus the critic of the *North American Review* set the tone of his essay by observing initially, "We are glad to see the theme in the impartial and generous hands of Mr. Irving" who "possesses the rare power – fruit of genial sympathy and most honest intent – of throwing his own mind into the mind he contemplates, so as to see with its eyes, understand with its understanding, and feel with its passions."[63] Indeed, Irving's own distance from his material the reviewer accounted a positive virtue, for "if we miss the imposing strength imparted by partisan bias or sectarian malignity, we are also protected from the prejudices which are so apt to cloud the vision of those who look at men and events with the mental eye ever so little inflamed."[64]

Other critics, however, were less generous. "C.A.W." in the *Southern Quarterly Review* simply reversed the usual order of general praise

62. "Irving's Mahomet," *ibid.*, No. 152 (December 29, 1849), 560–61.
63. "Mahomet and His Successors. By Washington Irving," *North American Review*, LXXI (October 1850), 273–74.
64. *Ibid.*, p. 274.

for Irving and a concluding historical survey of, and polemical commentary upon, Islam by first giving a detailed analysis of the historical
and moral ambiguities of Mahomet and his religion and by then demon-
strating how Irving had failed to meet his responsibilities either as religious historian or cultural analyst: "It remains to us to say of these
volumes that, without affording us any new materials, they present us
with a very graceful compilation from the old."[65] Indeed, "C.A.W."
implicitly condemned Irving for the crude anachronisms of his historical
method and for the moral timidity of his judgments and concluded that
"a life of Mahomet, such as is worthy of his powers and pretensions, has
yet to be written. To do this well, requires a genius,"[66] which Irving
apparently did not possess. Some of the religious journals, on the other
hand, censured Irving for his evasion of theological controversy, and
The Christian Observer in June 1851 came remarkably close to a proper
appraisal of *Mahomet and His Successors:* "We do not think the book
. . . contributes to throw any important new light upon the character
either of Mahomet or his religion. Mr. Washington Irving is a pleasant
writer, but not, we think, a very deep or acute thinker. He is possessed
of what must be termed a bright, though sometimes too florid, imagination."[67] Moreover, *The Christian Observer* continued, "We do not think
that Islamism is a subject altogether adapted to Mr. Irving's cast of
mind,"[68] a generalization which the reviewer proceeded to demonstrate
with his own very lengthy analysis of Mahomet and Islam and the leading points of contemporary religious controversy.

Even with the preponderance of ecclesiastical journalism opposed to
the romantic and theologically restrained tone of *Mahomet and His
Successors*, the book during the remainder of Irving's lifetime enjoyed
a moderate success – as the Textual Commentary for the Wisconsin
edition amply illustrates – both as Volumes XII and XIII of the Author's Revised Edition and in its own right, although its popularity
never remotely approached that of *The Sketch Book* or even that of
The Conquest of Granada, its closest analogue in Irving's canon and its
nearest contemporary in point of original composition as "The Legendary Life of Mahomet." Like *The Life of George Washington, Ma-*

65. "Islamism," *The Southern Quarterly Review*, n.s. IV (July 1851), 205.
66. *Ibid.*, p. 206.
67. "Lives of Mahomet and His Successors," *The Christian Observer*, n.s. 162
(June 1851), 378.
68. *Ibid.*, p. 379.

homet and His Successors holds the middle rank of popular success and esteem, and, barring the differences in the dates of their first appearances from Putnam's press, both books show similar patterns of publication and republication in America and translations and reprintings in Europe, although *Washington,* unlike *Mahomet and His Successors,* was never a *cause célèbre* in transatlantic literacy piracy and evolving copyright law.

Like *Washington,* again, *Mahomet and His Successors* seems to have remained almost constantly in print during the nineteenth century, though Putnam usually issued it as part of one or another special so-called edition of Irving's complete works and sometimes in conjunction with one or more of the legends or chronicles of the Christian reconquest of Spain. After its appearance in the enlarged twenty-eight volume Sunnyside Edition by Putnam in 1860, *Mahomet and His Successors* was subsequently reprinted in various formats and/or combinations of volumes in such various Putnam impressions as the Kinderhook Edition (ca. 1868), the Knickerbocker Edition (1868–1869), the People's Edition and the Riverside Edition (both 1869), another Knickerbocker Edition (1896), the Author's Autograph Edition (1896–1897), the Hudson Edition (1902), and a New Knickerbocker Edition (precise date unknown), in addition, of course, to various re-issues of various dates of all these separate editions – a bibliographic tangle of staggering complexity. In the late 1860's and early 1870's, moreover, J. B. Lippincott & Company of Philadelphia also began publication – sometimes in conjunction with Putnam and apparently sometimes alone – of various cumulative "editions" of Irving's works, in which *Mahomet and His Successors* was regularly included, although there seems to be no evidence that any of the separate sets of the book with the Lippincott imprint were anything more than different impressions of the same plates used in one or another of the Lippincott editions – as is true, for that matter, of later Putnam sets from various subsequent editions. Throughout the rest of the nineteenth century, after Putnam's copyright had expired, other and smaller houses (such as P. F. Collier, A. L. Burt, T. Y. Crowell, J. B. Alden, De Fau & Co., F. F. Lovell) also reprinted the book alone or as part of one or another aptly titled editions (for example, Alden's Rip Van Winkle Edition of 1887), so that, in addition to being in print almost constantly for more than fifty years, *Mahomet and His Successors* was, in one form or another, in press on the average of once or more every five years. Such seeming popularity, of course, may be ascribed to the fact that *Mahomet and His Successors* was a part of Irving's complete works and was thus reprinted as a matter of course with other and immensely more popular works like *The Sketch Book* or *Tales of a Traveller*. *Mahomet and His Successors* was in fact not often reprinted alone, though it did from time to time appear in a separate volume or set with *Goldsmith* or with one or another of the Spanish legends or chronicles, almost always from the smaller reprint houses.

Mahomet and His Successors was much less successful in England and on the Continent during the nineteenth century than it had been in America. Both Bohn and Routledge attempted to pirate the book from Murray in 1850, and, although Murray finally secured Bohn's acknowledgment of his prior rights to the book, it was in fact Bohn who published the cheap reprints of the book (in the Shilling Series, the Cheap Series, or the Shilling Library) after Murray's sales of the first English edition had been ruined or at least substantially reduced following Bohn's first piracy, and it was Bohn who in fact kept the book intermittently in print in England throughout the rest of the nineteenth century. J. M. Dent and Sons in London and E. P. Dutton in New York kept the book in print in the twentieth century, and primarily through the Everyman's Library series, in which *Mahomet and His Successors* was last reprinted in 1949.

As might be expected, the book was even less successful in Continental Europe, although a German translation, *Das Leben Mohammed's, von Washington Irving*, was published almost at once in Leipzig, in 1850, and the *Geschichte der Kalifen, vom Tode Mohammed's bis zum Einfall in Spanien, von Washington Irving* appeared in 1854, again in Leipzig. Extracts from both volumes appeared in the *Magazin für die Literatur des Auslandes* in 1850 and 1851, and new editions of both volumes appeared in 1865 and again in 1874. The first (and apparently only) French translation, the *Vie de Mahomet*, was made in 1865; a Polish translation in 1858 of the first volume; a Russian translation, again of the first volume, in 1898; a Spanish translation, the *Historia de Mahoma*, in Mexico in 1857; an Italian *Vita di Maometto* in 1854 (and a subsequent annotated edition in two volumes in 1928); a Greek translation in 1866; and an Icelandic translation of selections in 1853–1861.[69]

69. Further details of the vogue of *Mahomet and His Successors* may be found in Stanley T. Williams and Mary Ellen Edge, *A Bibliography of the Writings of Washington Irving: A Check List* (New York, 1936), pp. 2–6, 93–97.

From this summary account of the printing history of *Mahomet and His Successors* it may be inferred that the book stood highest in public favor when literary judgment depended upon the entire range of Irving's literary achievement; modern criticism has been more discriminating, if less inclusive, and Irving's modern position as an American classic depends less upon his more ambitious and scholarly works like *Columbus, Washington,* or even *Mahomet and His Successors,* than upon his miscellanies and travel books, *The Sketch Book, Bracebridge Hall,* and *Tales of a Traveller.* Yet Irving's particular kind of historiography was almost as gladly received by his contemporaries as were his lighter entertainments, and if contemporary criticism and scholarship have emphasized Irving's charm and his tone as the predominant elements of his final achievement and enduring value, the literary historian will recognize that Irving's chronicles and legends and lives were as complete a realization of his ambition and attitudes and accomplishment as his biography attests. The last ten years of his life he gave to *Washington,* the work he himself regarded as the perdurable monument of his literary career. With the earlier *Columbus, Mahomet and His Successors* was a crucial preparation for the *Life of George Washington,* the introductory statement of Irving's major theme, the Great Man as molder and model of history as romantic art.

TEXTUAL COMMENTARY

In the effort to arrive at a critical text of *Mahomet and His Successors* that will come as near as possible to reproducing Irving's intention, W. W. Greg's theory of copy-text[1] is adopted as a useful device on the basis of which to construct a rationale for making editorial decisions on both substantives and accidentals.[2] Ideally, the manuscript that was used as printer's copy (or author-corrected proof sheets, if they survive) provides copy-text; when neither is extant, the printed version nearest the author's manuscript is chosen. In the case of *Mahomet* the printed version becomes the inevitable choice because we have only 43 pages of manuscript from which the book was set in type. Another manuscript of 558 pages, complete enough in itself, is pre-copy-text, large portions of which were prepared some twenty years before the manuscript that served as printer's copy was written. For the sake of convenience the earlier manuscript is designated as MSa, and the 43-page fragment, MSb. MSa is significant for a genetic study of *Mahomet,* but it has little utility for the textual editor who is primarily concerned with the author's latest wishes rather than his earlier aims, or the process by which the manuscript was written. MSb may be used, as far as it goes, for making editorial decisions covering substantives; but because of its fragmentary nature (representing less than three per cent of the whole – 6,500 of some 228,000 words) and because of Irving's extraordinary carelessness in punctuation, hyphenation, capitalization, and spelling in general, it does not provide sufficiently conclusive data on the basis of which its authority (assuming that it could be ascertained) can be imposed on the entire book in the matter of accidentals.

---

1. The theory is explained in "The Rationale of Copy-Text," *Studies in Bibliography,* III (1950–1951), 19–36, and is applied to editions of nineteenth-century American authors by the *Statement of Editorial Principles* . . . prepared by the Center for Editions of American Authors, Modern Language Association of America, July 1967. The terminology used is Fredson Bowers' as set forth in his *Principles of Bibliographical Description* (Princeton, 1949).

2. Here and in the sequel, textual variants are classified as substantives when they affect meaning (i.e., word change) and as accidentals when they affect form (e.g., spelling and punctuation).

THE MANUSCRIPTS

The composition of MSa was a long-drawn-out process, extending from Irving's first through his last period of residence in Spain — all told some twenty years. The result was a manuscript of sixty-five chapters, paged continuously in Irving's firm hand from 1 to 558, presumably in 1831 when he prepared to submit it to John Murray for publication. MSb, on the other hand, while following the general outline and organization of MSa, was an entirely new, much enlarged, fair-copy manuscript, prepared during 1848–1849 specifically for George P. Putnam, utilizing not even a single page of the older manuscript.[3]

3. While only 43 pages of MSb have been located, the whole of MSa remains intact, in 558 pages, in the Berg Collection of the New York Public Library, except for the following: (1) Chapters 3–5, pp. 15–29, (2) pp. 384 and 385 forming the second and fourth pages of Chapter 49; (3) Chapters 61–64, pp. 506–544; and (4) the first portion of Chapter 65, pp. 546–550. Chapters 3–5, missing from the NYPL manuscript, are in the Barrett Collection of the University of Virginia.

Written at different times, in different places, under varying circumstances and conditions, and much revised, the physical features exhibit the expected characteristics: paper in loose sheets as well as in loosely stitched gatherings of various colors and grades (wove and laid, watermarked and unmarked) in all sizes, different inks, marginal additions as well as textual insertions and cancellations (some in his brother Peter's handwriting) in both pen and pencil, repeated renumbering of pages or sections of pages as they were shifted about, and numerous sheets of unusual length as a result of the scissors-and-paste-pot method of composition and revision.

In the dovetailing and piecing together that MSa underwent, individual chapters or segments of chapters were first given internal numbers and then repaged, often three, four, and even five times, before they found their place in the over-all foliation. While there is not enough of MSb to justify a broad generalization for the whole, it is noteworthy that although 32 of the 43 extant pages (or sheets) were repaged, no pages were renumbered more than once, or disturbed in the over-all foliation once they were given subnumbers such as 437/2, 437/3, and 437/4 to indicate insertions or interpolations. These circumstances suggest that whereas MSa was subjected to repeated revision and rearrangement, the composition of MSb was much more regular, doubtless because it was more continuous and concentrated.

Moreover, the fragments of MSb that survive in 43 pages (all but two of which are in the library of the Museum of the City of New York) are all written in the same color of ink on wove, unmarked, white sheets of paper of like quality and uniform size (although more than half of the sheets have been subjected to irregular trimming so that they vary roughly from 7⅝ x 4¾ to 8¼ x 5⅝ inches). They exhibit little of the kind of joinery so apparent in MSa. Paste-ons, for example, and interlinear additions are relatively rare.

One sheet lacking in the manuscript of the Museum of the City of New York is in the library of the Historical Society of Pennsylvania. It was numbered 438 by Irving, and it fits into, and supplies the missing page for, the fourth of the

In and of itself, MSa has little relevance for the textual editor of *Mahomet*, except in so far as an occasional passage invites comparison with the printed text derived from MSb, especially where it affords a check on a spelling, a point of fact, or a difference in the use or meaning of a word. But because MSa is properly a part of the genetic history of *Mahomet,* a brief account of its origins and vicissitudes is in order.

Conceived early during the first period of residence in Spain as an introductory but integral part of an ambitious history of the "domination of the Arabs in Spain," it remained, when Irving left for England to become secretary of the American legation in London, what Pierre Munro Irving called a "sketch of the Life of Mahomet" among a larger miscellaneous collection of notes, memoranda, and sizable extracts from available books and manuscripts dealing with Mahomet and Arabian history in general.

Apart from these voluminous and miscellaneous notes, written in pen and pencil, on various kinds and sizes of sheets, as well as into bound

---

sequences listed below. The other odd sheet, in the Berg Collection of the New York Public Library, stands alone. It carries Irving's number 265 in the upper right-hand corner and 310 at the top, center — without indication as to which is the correct number in the sequence from which the printer set type.

These 43 pages represent six segments of MSb that provided printer's copy for the first Putnam impression of Volumes I and II of *Mahomet and His Successors* in the following order:

MSb pages	Putnam, 1850	Wisconsin ed.	
295–296	I, 267.23–269.9	155.15–156.8	"Enough . . . good."
299–321	I, 270.16–287.21	156.37–167.9	"Mahomet . . . enemy."
265(310)	II, 297.26–298.18	390.12–390.28	"twenty . . . he."
437/3–446	II, 456.21–463.14	484.10–488.10	"Shebib . . . manifest."
447/3	II, 465.21–466.18	489.33–490.16	"and . . . land."
448–451	II, 467.25–470.20	491.6–492.31	"After . . . heart."

It might be presumed that the pages of manuscript now missing from MSa could have been transferred to MSb and thus provided text for the printed version. The evidence is all to the contrary. What precedes and follows the larger of these lacunae (pp. 506–544 and 546–550) makes it clear that the 44 missing pages dealt with the Doctrine of Predestination as promulgated by Mahomet and with the Rules of Pilgrimage, which together occupy 8½ pages in the printed text, in which the entire treatment of the Faith of Islam is drastically shortened – one of the very few sections in MSb that shows diminution, rather than elaboration, of MSa. This is obviously not enough space into which to compress 44 pages of MSa. The missing pages must therefore be considered lost on their own account – not as part of the losses sustained by MSb.

notebooks, there are two kinds of pages that together make up MSa. First, and by far the greater number, are the pages of connected and more or less finished writing which, wherever derived, represent nonetheless Irving's own composition; second, there are a number of pages consisting of extracts copied or only slightly modified from various printed sources and intended for future incorporation wherever they might fit, with a minimum of rewriting or revision. The first are readily distinguished from the latter by the editor who has any familiarity with the differences in handwriting that appear in Irving's journals and in his notebooks. The former are written in a flowing, often slurred script while his hand hurried to keep up with his thoughts; in the latter, the script is precise, regular, clear, even, and unhurried, each letter neatly formed. Whether copied verbatim or modified slightly in the process, these pages were designed for future use and therefore written with care. The two kinds of pages are further distinguished from each other by the circumstance that the pages of Irving's own composition are written solidly, left to right from margin to margin, and top to bottom; while the handwriting of the pages of extracts covers only about two-thirds of the right-hand side of the page, the extra-wide margin to the left and the liberal spaces at the top and bottom of the page apparently being designed to leave room for making revisions, identifying sources, incorporating insertions, or adding links, for and aft, wherever they could be incorporated into the running narrative. These two-thirds pages, interspersed as they now are among the full pages, appear in fifteen segments varying in length from 1 to 8 pages, each segment with its own pagination sequence, subsequently canceled when the entire manuscript was repaged (in Irving's own bold numerals), and the inserted segments were fitted into the over-all foliation. Some (in most cases, all) of these characteristics are observable in these interpolated pages, most of which also show more revisions (both cancellations and insertions) than do the full pages. Precisely how many of these interpolated segments there were when Murray looked at and rejected MSa cannot now be determined, but there were enough for him to sense the piecemeal nature of the manuscript. That Irving subsequently removed any of these passages is doubtful because the over-all page sequence of 1831 remains undisturbed. Even if he did, the following remain in MSa today and were presumably present in the first twenty-one chapters that Irving left for Murray's inspection: four pages (now numbered 51–54, originally 9–12) provide the conclusion of Chapter 8; two pages (71–72,

originally number 9–10 and then changed to 32–33) are inserted before the last paragraph of Chapter 10; Chapter 11 contains two such
pages, originally numbered 3–4, then 12–13, next 35–36, and finally 74–
75; another sequence of eight pages, originally 39–46 and renumbered
79–86, straddles Chapters 13 and 14; and finally, there are four pages,
originally numbered 69, 69/2, 69/3, and 69/4, repaged 144–147, that
form the opening of Chapter 20. If Murray saw no more than these
first twenty-one chapters (155 pages) – and there is nothing to indicate that he was able to extract any more from Irving, though he tried
– he saw enough to convince him that he was being asked to accept
something less than a book – to buy a pig in a poke – and that Irving's
offering it to him in that state was in fact an affront to his sagacity as a
publisher.[4]

The fact that beginning with Chapter 50 (page 391), the concluding
167 pages of MSa contain no such two-thirds-page inserts suggests that
this is the point where the portion written in Spain ended and the London beginning was made. While the kind and size of paper, color of
ink used, and other external evidence, in and of themselves, yield no
conclusive data to support this theory, there is the further circumstance
that, contrary to the practice observable in earlier chapters, where
chapter heads were obviously scribbled in after the chapters were written, arranged in sequence, and numbered, such titles or synoptic headings appear now to have been written at the time the chapter was begun or while it was in process of composition: the ink and hand are the
same as in the text, and the spacing is neatly apportioned. And this
firming-up process in both planning and execution is accentuated by
the further fact that each such heading is identified, in the left-hand
margin, by dates: first the Moslem year, followed by the Christian year.[5]

Whether everything preceding page 391 was written in Spain and

4. Other such segments of two-thirds-covered pages supply the following sections in the over-all foliation: 172–179 (originally 82–89), 189–190 (96–97),
209–213 (no canceled pagination), 217–220 (110–113), 224 (earlier pagination
illegible), 226–227 (12–13), 254–256 (135–137 and [138]), 285–291 (152–158),
323–328 (1–6), and 390 (80?).

5. To be observed, also, is the circumstance that although the over-all foliation
for the entire 558 leaves is correct (except for pp. 474–481, which Irving erroneously numbered 274–281), only the first 49 chapters (through p. 390) show more
than one foliation – all of them canceled, of course, in favor of the overriding 1–558
sequence; while those beginning with Chapter 50 (p. 391) show only the one
over-all sequence of page numbers.

everything that follows was composed in London during hours snatched from his "hand-gallop" work as secretary of the American legation does not matter very much, because (except for the differences noted) the whole was pretty much of a piece, and was doubtless considered so by Irving when, after paging in a firm hand the sheets from 1 to 558, he offered the whole of it as a "Legendary Life of Mahomet," along with a "Spanish sketch book" (*The Alhambra*), to Murray in September of 1831.[6]

The kind of joinery that was all too evident represents, of course, nothing more than a time-and-labor-saving device adopted while preparing a first draft, but the patchwork result did not escape Murray's practiced eye. And so Colonel Aspinwall was asked to sell *The Alhambra* to Colburn and Bentley, while *Mahomet* went back into Irving's traveling trunk for storage. So ended the uneasy connection of thirteen years with Murray, the erstwhile "Prince of Booksellers" now become "the most difficult being on earth to please."[7]

6. On submitting the first 21 chapters to Murray, Irving promised to supply the remaining chapters to the number of "about 70" as needed. Since the 65th or last chapter of MSa rounds out the narrative precisely as does the concluding chapter of the version printed in 1850, it may be presumed that 65 chapters were all he had in hand at the time, or indeed, planned, unless he intended to subdivide some or interpolate others to make 70.

7. "The Legendary History of Mahomet" had in fact been advertised in the *Literary Gazette* on September 10, 1831, as "in press" and as part of Murray's popular Family Library series, and as "forthcoming" in the *Athenaeum* for September 17; but it was no longer included in Murray's list of Irving's works in the *Athenaeum* for December 31.

Except for Murray's issuing in 1835 an English edition of *The Crayon Miscellany* (which naturally enough he was persuaded by Lockhart to accept in deference to Scott and Byron) the break lasted nearly two decades. When Irving was next published at 50 Albemarle Street, it was ironic but altogether fitting that the ill-fated *Mahomet,* mainly responsible for the break in the first place, should become one of the chief means for reestablishing the old relationship on a firm footing at the same time that it provided a much desired clarification, and inaugurated a new phase in the history, of international copyright. Although *Mahomet* itself turned out to be of no great pecuniary value for John Murray, it provided the *cause célèbre* by which he brought to bay the pirates Bohn and Routledge so that it became possible for him henceforth to pursue with assurance an arrangement that he made with Putnam to publish in London any volumes he considered promising of the Author's Revised Edition as they appeared in New York. By this arrangement *Mahomet* became the first of Irving's new books to appear under the Murray imprint, although among the older volumes *The Sketch Book, Columbus,* and the revised and enlarged *Goldsmith* had already appeared during 1849, while *Granada* followed hard upon *Mahomet* the next year. Why *Knickerbocker* was not published

In fairness to Irving it should be observed that there is no dearth of extended passages intended as fair copy that are in fact just what the term implies. There are many pages and some entire sections of manuscript that show almost no cancellations, overwriting, or other revisions, that is to say, portions of manuscript which Murray would have found acceptable enough. But there are also numerous sections, ranging from a page or two to thirty, forty, and more pages that were not only heavily revised but were also shifted repeatedly from one position to another and repaged – in a manner to suggest less a rearrangement than a reshuffling of materials. It is these interpolations into earlier sequences where the marks of joint carpentry in terms of links, cancellations, and rewritings of transitional sentences and paragraphs to accommodate the insertions become painfully apparent. This kind of readjustment of materials, not entirely without precedent in Irving's earlier books, naturally enough first becomes marked in his biographical and historical books, such as *Columbus* and *Granada,* and even more pronounced during the last decade of his life, that produced, among a few more original works, his biographies of Goldsmith, Mahomet, and Washington – books concocted of materials drawn in large measure from printed sources.

This plan or procedure of writing, which depends largely on transcription and compilation, is observed as early as 1829, when, on leaving Spain, Irving told himself that for the life of Mahomet he had "the materials on hand for easy arrangement," and it is recognizable again in September of 1834 when, while planning *Astoria,* he summoned Pierre M. Irving from Illinois "to collate the various documents [Astor's], collect verbal information, and reduce the whole to such form that I might be able to dress it up advantageously, and with little labor, for the press."

Despite a resolve during the next decade to rehabilitate his ill-fated bantling, the manuscript lay on the shelf gathering dust, and there is

---

by Murray at this time remains unexplained. Although Murray paid Putnam £ 67 8s. 6d. in March of 1849 for the plates, they were never used and were finally melted in 1910, very much as the remaining 86 copies of an impression of 1,000 copies of *Mahomet and His Companions* were "wasted" in 1912 (Letter from John R. Murray to Henry A. Pochmann, August 30, 1968).

Irving saw John Murray II for the last time while en route to Spain in May 1842. Murray died the next year. After 1835 Irving's communications with the house of Murray were chiefly with the younger John Murray III.

nothing to suggest that he did anything more than take it down on occasions, correct the spelling of a proper name here, insert a phrase
there, and then wistfully lay it aside to gather another layer of dust
while he turned to more pressing and palatable matters, such as the
new western books. Even during the ambassadorship in Spain, where
he hoped that he would have abundant leisure, he found time only to
haul the manuscript from his trunk and finger the pages while thumb-
ing through and making what in the end proved more useful, copious
notes on and extracts from the newly published multivolume works on
Mahomet and his successors by men like Joseph von Hammer-Purgstall and Gustav Weil, as well as of Spanish manuscripts which would
not be available to him once he left Spain.

William H. Prescott's virtually writing out from under him the Spanish conquest of Mexico, which Irving had planned as the capstone for
"a suite of works" that were to form his "Spanish histories," shocked
him into the realization that unless he proceeded with alacrity he
might well lose what he had planned as introductory just as he had
already lost to Prescott the climax. The flood of new books on Spain
and the Moors, betokening an interest that he had himself been one of
the first to arouse, provided a further incentive to capture his rightful
share of the rewards before it would be too late. And, overriding all
other considerations was the compulsion he felt himself under increasingly since returning from Madrid that, in order to meet his growing
obligations, he must replenish his literary capital, and that in the process he could ill afford to leave unsalvaged anything in which he already had any considerable investment. Although he was already absorbed in the life of Washington, which would be his last and crown-
ing achievement, he naturally resorted to his earlier versions of *Goldsmith* and *Mahomet* as material that could be turned to more immediate profit. These could be finished out of hand, while the biography of
Washington would take years. Moreover, once Putnam began to print
the Author's Revised Edition of his collected works, issuing the first ten
volumes of old titles between September 1848 and June 1849, Putnam's
call for new titles to provide leaven for the old became increasingly
insistent. The endless hours devoted to revising, correcting, and proofing of the old texts left little time and less energy for the basic research and original composition required for *Washington;* so it made
good sense to drop the life of Washington, re-dress and expand his latest version of *Goldsmith,* and resume work on *Mahomet,* but on a

larger scale so as to incorporate the fruits of the recently published findings on the careers of the twelve caliphs who succeeded the founder of Islam, thus bringing his account to the verge of the Moorish conquest of Spain and completing at least this unit of his series of Spanish histories.

So it happened that the old manuscript, while kept within easy reach for reference, was in fact scrapped, because for the more elaborate scale on which MSb was planned MSa had only supplementary usefulness, chiefly by way of keeping him on course, as it were, when the abundance of new-found materials threatened to divert his narrative into byways. Even so, the more involved narrative structure of MSb resulted in a complication of lines of action, of plots and subplots, that could not be carried forward either simultaneously or in parallel, so that there is in it a good deal more yawing back and forth, dropping of one thread while pursuing another to its conclusion, and then backtracking to pick up action suspended earlier, than there is in MSa, which in this respect is more straightforward, because less complicated. Otherwise Irving found useful and adaptable a few passages which in the earlier version were already sufficiently elaborated to fit into the much enlarged scheme of things – among them battle scenes, records of various pilgrimages, the account of Mahomet's visit to the Seventh Heaven, and especially expository portions, such as the Faith of Islam, ultimately relegated to the appendix at the end of the first volume. Other materials that he found readily usable were segments that reported conversation in direct discourse,[8] but here again he had merely to follow his original sources a second time. For the rest, he salvaged whatever else he could find, chiefly notes,[9] most of which were little more than transcriptions from his historical sources in the first place, and now needed only recopying. But there was no interleafing from one manuscript into the other. The manuscript from which type was set was rewritten from beginning to end. While the subject matter followed the order of the old manuscript, there is seldom more than a paragraph or two sufficiently close to make collating corresponding

8. The more extensive use of direct discourse in the later manuscript is one of its distinguishing features, apparently adopted to elaborate narrative passages and to enhance their dramatic effectiveness.

9. Noteworthy examples occur in Volume I on pp. 6, 8–9, 33, 34, 40, 41–42, 43–44, 56, 61–62, 66, 78, 99, 129, 130, 135, 160, 176–177, 190–191, and 218 of the Wisconsin text.

passages anything more than a frustrating academic exercise. Relatively few topics treated in MSa are omitted in MSb, but many new subjects are added. That is, changes are all on the side of expansion, so much so that the original 56,000 words covering the life of Mahomet are expanded to some 97,000, plus 131,000 more on the lives of Mahomet's successors – some 228,000 in all.

This disproportion explains why MSa has little utility, except in a very supplementary way, for arriving at an authoritative text for *Mahomet and His Successors*, quite apart from the fact that it was written while Irving was still observing what have been termed his English forms of spelling and expression, whereas MSb was composed more than a decade after he had consciously adopted American modes and forms – forms which he had chosen during the early thirties as more consonant with his new western subjects, and which were now reenforced by the requirements of the Putnam house style.

Unfortunately MSb, aside from the difficulty inherent in the effort to impose forms barely indicated, or not indicated at all, in a fragment of 6,500 words upon a printed text of approximately 228,000, is an unreliable guide. Although it formed a part of what must be termed fair copy in the sense that it was so intended, that it was legible, and that it did in fact serve as printer's copy , its faulty (largely omitted) punctuation and other idiosyncrasies of form make it neither a clear nor an accurate guide on the basis of which to reach editorial decisions.

As a matter of fact, Irving had by now a long record of being slipshod in preparing printer's copy and careless about punctuation, hyphenation, and spelling while attending to the proof sheets of his books. Although we know little about the care he took with his earliest manuscripts or the opportunities he had for proofing *Oldstyle* and *Salmagundi* when they first appeared, there is ample evidence that the text of *Knickerbocker* (1809) was carelessly prepared or worse printed, though it is apparent that for the edition of 1812, which he supervised, he sought to correct misprints and spellings and to improve punctuation and diction.[10] His short term as editor of the *Analectic Magazine* could have taught him something of the methods and conventions of the printing business. At any rate, by 1819, when he was ready to put before the British and American public *The Sketch Book,* on the

---

10. *Diedrich Knickerbocker's History of New York,* ed. by Stanley Williams and Tremaine McDowell (New York, 1927), pp. liii–lix.

strength of which he knew very well he might rise or fall as a professional writer, he appears to have taken some care to prepare good copy and to pay more than common attention to the proof sheets, although he had perforce to delegate to Henry Brevoort the supervision of the American edition while he looked after the London edition. After the appearance of the first number in New York he wrote to Brevoort mildly remonstrating against liberties he felt had been taken with his punctuation, while admitting that he did not know precisely what they were, or indeed, whether the high pointing was owing to his own carelessness in preparing the manuscript or "the scrupulous precision of the Printer." In time he came to depend more on making revisions and alterations in the proof sheets than on preparing polished printer's copy in the first place. This becomes apparent in the small amount of time he devoted to preparing copy in comparison with the attention he gave the proofs while supervising Galignani's Paris edition of *Salmagundi*[11] in 1824, and it is clear enough that under Murray's pressure for promised manuscript he took progressively less care to present flawless copy for *Bracebridge Hall, Tales of a Traveller, Granada, Columbus,* and *The Companions of Columbus.* One example among many of this kind of inattention to final details occurs in a letter to Ebenezer on January 29, 1822, in which he instructed his brother to put Volume I of *Bracebridge Hall* to press at once (to assure copyright protection), preferably in a "rather small" first edition, and then to "put another to press the moment I furnish you with proof sheets of the English edition, in which there will doubtless be many alterations, as I have not had time to revise some parts of the work sufficiently, and am apt to make alterations to the last moment." And by way of final fillip, the long list of particulars ends with this instruction: "I have not had time to page the work, but must beg you to do it."

This procedure backfired in 1831 when Murray, long suffering from the patchwork copy that Irving sent and the extensive and expensive author's alterations that followed as the inevitable consequence, peremptorily rejected *Mahomet* because he recognized it for what is was – little more than a first draft. Doubtless Irving felt that he was no more to blame than Murray himself, who up to this point had always seemed eager to regularize, correct, and otherwise edit Irving's slipshod manu-

11. See *Journals and Notebooks,* Vol. III, entries for January 7–February 26, 1824.

scripts rather than wait longer for perfected copy. Knowing his manuscripts to be in good hands, sure to get the attention he had neither the time nor the inclination to bestow on them, he relied on Murray or his staff of craftsmen to supply acceptable forms wherever they were lacking, and grew more slack with each succeeding volume until Murray felt himself forced to tell him that his literary promises were no longer marketable.[12]

During the thirties, when Irving was adapting his western books to American forms and expressions and preparing them for relatively untried publishers, he appears to have been somewhat more attentive to supplying good copy and checking the proofs with an eye to accidentals as well as substantives, doubtless as much as a check on himself as on the printers; but when once again he found himself securely in the hands of an established, reliable publisher, and bolstered by a long-term contract – once he had himself revised the texts and read the proofs of the first ten volumes of the Author's Revised Edition and so come to know Putnam's house style as thoroughly as the compositors and proofreaders themselves – he proceeded to let the house of Putnam supply any nonsubstantive details that he found it easier not to bother with. Only so is it that we can explain his extraordinary inattention to the essentials of punctuation, his failure to supply quotation marks and parentheses in pairs, to distinguish between lower- and upper-case forms of letters, to insert hyphens in compounds, to underscore words

12. Only thus can we explain the habitually gentle Irving's complaint in a letter to Leslie at the time that Murray was "either inexcusably remiss or very deficient in good faith in business – and either is enough to unfit him for a publisher," adding, "I am determined to have nothing more to do with him" (January 9, 1832, Ben Harris McClary, ed., *Washington Irving and the House of Murray*, Knoxville: University of Tennessee Press, 1969, pp. 165–66).

How much the rebuff rankled through the years is suggested by the length to which he went in 1848, while preparing for Putnam the text of *The Sketch Book* by which it was to be known during the next century and more, to add the new preface for which he rummaged his files for the letter that Murray had written him on October 27, 1819, respectfully declining to publish the book that soon turned out to be Irving's major English success, and playfully, nonetheless gratuitously, quoting the whole of it. It was nothing less than a subtle form of revenge and not at all in character, explicable only as Irving's way of finally trading a resentment, long harbored, for whatever cathartic effect he felt at having the last word and telling the world how wrong Murray had been in the first place. It is to be noted, however, that by now he was prepared to let bygones be bygones, for the preface of 1848 ended with his testimony that Murray had conducted himself "in all his dealings with that fair, open, and liberal spirit" for which he was ready to re-enthrone him to the position of "the Prince of Booksellers."

to be italicized, to indicate indentations for paragraphs, and his use of contractions and abbreviations instead of full forms in a book like *Mahomet and His Successors* for which he had to furnish complete handwritten copy, as distinct from *Goldsmith,* for which he could use extracts for portions from earlier printed versions. Inconsistencies in spelling, too, did not much trouble him, unless they involved a proper name – a special problem in a book like *Mahomet,* whose Arabian names caused him much trouble both while preparing copy and later while "correcting" the proofs.

It does not follow that Irving approved every detail of the Putnam house style or that, if he had been required to present perfect copy, he would have used precisely the forms adopted by the printers. But not having this information in hand and knowing that while reading proofs Irving had ample opportunity to make alterations if he had wished to, we must conclude that he either made what changes he wanted to in the proofs, or that he acquiesced in the alterations made by Putnam's editors or printers – assuming that he noticed them at all. As between Irving's nonpunctuation and what can properly be called Putnam's overpointing, the editor has no choice but to play the odds by sticking close to Putnam's forms rather than take the risk of making unwarranted guesses of what Irving might have done in every instance – thus having at least the assurance of knowing that he is following what Irving did not disapprove rather than trying to guess what Irving's preferences might have been if the choices had been left entirely up to him. The alternative, the attempt to follow Irving's erratic and uncharted course, would be to enter a labyrinth which, once entered, leads to blind alleys from which there is no exit. In short, the editor has, in a measure, to emulate the procedure of the compositors who read Irving's manuscript according to either what they knew was Irving's intent, or what they considered it should have been, when his manuscript did not square with their own guidelines. This procedure is most readily checked by the manner in which they read his lower-case and upper-case forms. The result was that, Irving's erratic manuscripts to the contrary, they produced printed versions which did not differ materially from the accepted forms that marked Irving's other books of the period, nor from books by other authors currently issuing from Putnam's or comparable presses. There is no doubt that in so doing they introduced a degree of regularization and perhaps of overpointing that a textual editor may deplore as misrepresenting Irving's intention in some details; but lacking, as he does, reliable information about what Irving's intention in every instance was, the editor has no choice but to follow the forms of the copy-text.

To illustrate the wide discrepancies that prevent the editor's acceptance either of the manuscripts as his sole authority, or even the two together, corresponding passages of MSa, MSb, and the printed version are arranged on facing pages. Any number of other passages might have been selected that would have accentuated and actually represented the extent of these discrepancies more accurately. The particular passage chosen is the only one among the forty-three pages of MSb that has a corresponding passage in MSa, so that while it does not portray as faithfully as others might the variations between MSb and the printed version, it serves the useful purpose of pointing out the even larger differences between MSa and MSb, and so does dual service by providing a double comparison. (See pages 574–579.)

It will be noted that whereas the chief differences between the two manuscripts are substantive, those between the printer's copy and the printed version are almost exclusively accidentals.

To indicate the eccentric forms that Irving's punctuation takes within the narrow limits of the 43-page fragment of MSb, the following are enumerated: (1) Irving both uses and omits the comma separating coordinate clauses joined by a simple conjunction, besides occasionally using a semicolon; (2) he both uses and omits the comma to set off introductory dependent clauses, or phrases that contain a verb form, although the omissions are relatively rare; (3) he generally uses, but occasionally omits, commas to set off nonrestrictive modifiers, whether phrases or clauses; (4) he is as likely as not to use commas to separate restrictive modifiers, whether clauses or phrases, and while he normally uses commas to set off modifying (often participial) constructions, whether restrictive or not, he sometimes (though rarely) omits the first or last of intended pairs, (5) he often uses semicolons where modern usage finds commas sufficient, and occasionally a comma where a semicolon is indicated; (6) he appears to use semicolons and colons interchangeably in some cases; (7) he both uses and omits the comma before the conjunction in an *a*, *b*, and *c* series; (8) he is inconsistent in using the comma to designate coordinate adjectives modifying the same noun; (9) he does, and he does not, use the comma to separate compound verbs whether separated by intervening sentence elements or not; (10) he usually employs a semicolon to separate coordinate

On her return he received a ʌ suspension from the people of Taïef, who dreaded another invasion. They sued for peace and for permission, during three years longer, to serve their idol ʌAllat ~~abolished~~, their most renowned in all Arabia.

Mahomet sternly ~~refused~~ denied their ~~prayer~~ request. They asked for at least one month. This was equally refused. They entreated to be spared the necessity of praying. "There is no good in a religion," replied Mahomet, "in which there is not prayer." They were obliged to bow their poun and embrace the faith of Islam. Abu Sofian and al Mogheirah ʌTaïef to were sent to destroy the idol, which was a female statue of stone. Abu struck at it with a pick axe but missing his blow fell headlong on his face. The Taïfites shouted with

The prophet cherished a bitter grudge against this stiffnecked and most idolatrous city, which had at one time ejected him from its gates, and at another time repulsed him from its walls. His terms were conversion and unqualified submission. The ambassadors readily consented to embrace Islamism themselves, but pleaded the danger of suddenly shocking the people of Tayef by a demand to renounce their ancient faith. In their name, therefore, they entreated permission for three years longer to worship their ancient idol Al Lat. The request was peremptorily denied. They then asked at least one month's delay, to prepare the public mind. This likewise was refused, all idolatry being

incompatible with the worship of God.

They then entreated to be excused from the observance of the daily prayers. "There can be no true religion without prayer," replied Mahomet. In fine they were compelled to make an unconditional submission.

Abu Sofian Ibn Harb and Al Mogheira were sent to Tayef, to destroy the idol Al Lat, which was of stone. Abu Sofian struck at it with a pick axe but missing his blow fell prostrate on his face. The populace set up a shout

[MSa 412]

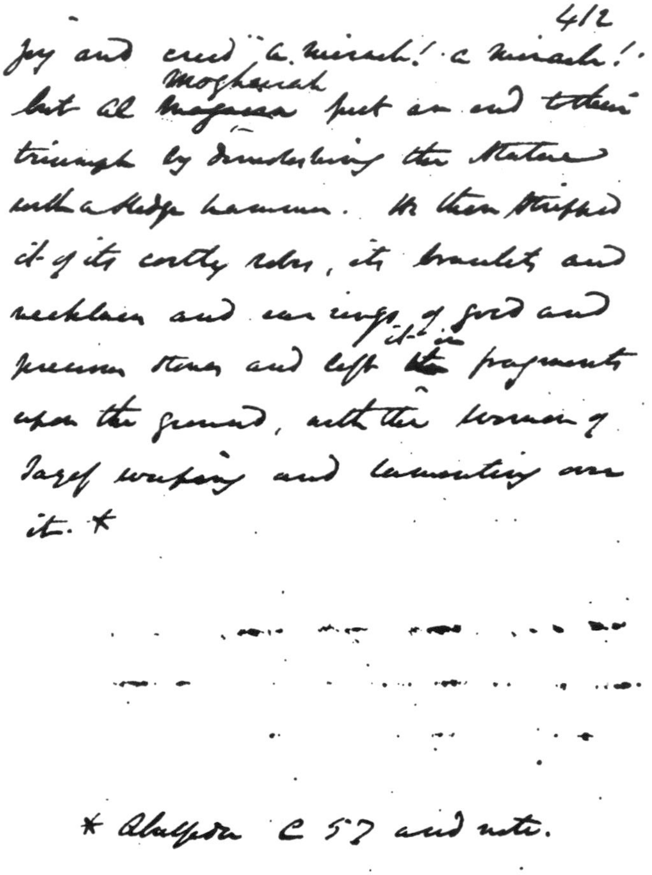
412

joy and cried "a miracle! a miracle!" but Al ~~Magassa~~ Moghasrah put an end to their triumph by demolishing the Statue with a sledge hammer. He then stripped it of its costly robes, its bracelets and necklaces and ear rings of gold and precious stones and left ~~the~~ it in fragments upon the ground, with the women of Tayef weeping and lamenting over it. *

* Abulfeda c 57 and note.

[handwritten text]

considering it a good augury but al
Mogheira demolished their hopes and
the statue at one blow of a sledge ham-
-mer. He then stripped it of the costly
robes, the bracelets, the necklace, the
ear rings and other ornaments of
gold and precious stones wherewith it had
been decked by its worshipers, and left
it in fragments on the ground, with
the women of Tayef weeping and
lamenting over it. *

[handwritten text]

* The Thakifites continue a powerful
tribe to this day; possessing
the same fertile region on the eastern
declivity of the Hejaz chain of mountains. Some the ancient town of
Tayef others dwell in tents and have
flocks of goats and sheep. They can raise
two thousand match locks, and defended
to them strong hold of Tayef on the
way with the Wahabys.
Burckhardt. notes V. 2.

The pages of MSb are reproduced by permission of the Museum of
the City of New York.

The prophet cherished a ⟨bitter grudge⟩↑deep resentment↓/ against this stiff necked and most idolatrous/ city, which had at one time ejected him/ from its gates and at another time/ repulsed him from its walls. His terms/ were conversion and unqualified sub-/ mission. The ambassadors readily/ consented to embrace Islamism them-/ selves, but pleaded the danger of sud-/ denly shocking the people of Tayef by a/ demand to renounce their ancient faith./ In their name, therefore, they entreated/ remission for three years longer to worship/ their ancient idol Al Lat. The/ request was peremptorily denied. They/ then asked at least one months delay,/ to prepare the public mind. This like-/ wise was refused, all idolatry being/ incompatible with the worship of God.

They then entreated to be excused from/ the observance of the daily prayers.

"There can be no true religion without/ prayer." replied Mahomet. In fine they were/ compelled to make an unconditional/submission.

Abu Sofian Ibn Harb and Al Mog-/ heira were sent to Tayef to destroy/ the idol Al Lat, which was of stone./ Abu Sofian struck at it with a pick axe/ but missing his blow fell prostrate/ on his face. The populace set up a shout/ considering it a good augury but Al/ Mogheira demolished their hopes and/ the statue at one blow of a sledge ham-/ mer. He then stripped it of the costly/ robes, the bracelets, the neck lace, the/ ear rings and other ornaments of/ gold and precious stones wherewith it had/ been decked by its worshippers, and left/ it in fragments on the ground, with/ the women of Tayef weeping and/ lamenting over it.*

* The Thakefites continue a powerful/ ⟨mountain⟩ tribe to this day; possessing/ the same fertile region on the eastern/ declivity of the Hedjas chain of mount-/ ains. Some ⟨dwell in⟩↑inhabit↓ the ancient town of/ Tayef others dwell in tents and have/ flocks of goats and sheep. They can raise/ two thousand match locks, and defended/ ⟨Th⟩ their strong hold of Tayef in the/ wars with the Wahabys.

Burkhardt. Notes V. 2.

Editorial symbols used above: ⟨ ⟩ restored cancellations; ↑ ↓ interlinear insertions; / end of line in manuscript.

[Copy-text I, 276.15–26]

The prophet cherished a deep resentment against this stiff-necked and most idolatrous city, which had at one time ejected him from its gates, and at another time repulsed him from its walls. His terms were conversion and unqualified submission. The ambassadors readily consented to embrace Islamism themselves, but pleaded the danger of suddenly shocking the people of Tayef, by a demand to renounce their ancient faith. In their name, therefore, they entreated permission for three years longer, to worship their ancient idol Al Lat. The request was peremptorily denied. They then asked at least one month's delay, to prepare the public mind. This likewise was refused, all idolatry being incompatible with the worship of

[Copy-text I, 277]

God. They then entreated to be excused from the observance of the daily prayers.

"There can be no true religion without prayer," replied Mahomet. In fine, they were compelled to make an unconditional submission.

Abu Sofian Ibn Harb, and Al Mogheira, were sent to Tayef, to destroy the idol Al Lat, which was of stone. Abu Sofian struck at it with a pick-axe, but missing his blow fell prostrate on his face. The populace set up a shout, considering it a good augury, but Al Mogheira demolished their hopes, and the statue, at one blow of a sledge-hammer. He then stripped it of the costly robes, the bracelets, the necklace, the ear-rings, and other ornaments of gold and precious stones wherewith it had been decked by its worshippers, and left it in fragments on the ground, with the women of Tayef weeping and lamenting over it.*

Among those who still defied the power of Mahomet, was the Bedouin chief Amir Ibn Tufiel, head of the powerful tribe of Amir. He was renowned for personal beauty and princely magnificence ; but was of a haughty spirit, and his magnificence partook of ostentation. At the great fair of Okaz, be-

---

* The Thakefites continue a powerful tribe to this day ; possessing the same fertile region on the eastern declivity of the Hedjas chain of mountains. Some inhabit the ancient town of Tayef, others dwell in tents and have flocks of goats and sheep. They can raise two thousand match-locks, and defended their stronghold of Tayef in the wars with the Wahabys.— *Burckhardt's Notes*, v. 2.

clauses that are involved or have internal comma division, but not consistently; (11) he does, and he does not, use a comma to separate a long and internally divided subject from the predicate, especially when the subject is a noun close or a gerundive construction; (12) he does, and he does not, use the comma to separate the verb from its complement or the object following it, especially when it takes the form of a noun clause; (13) he is far from scrupulous about setting off absolute constructions; (14) he is inconsistent in his use of commas in connection with parenthetical expressions; (15) he both uses and omits commas to set off appositives; (16) he appears not to discriminate between commas and exclamation points when indicating mild interjections, and occasionally omits both; (17) he both employs and omits commas to set off indirect, as well as direct, discourse; (18) he both uses and omits quotation marks (double and single) to indicate direct quotations, and sometimes leaves such punctuation open-ended; (19) generally he is chary in his use of hyphens, but occasionally he inserts them in words not commonly hyphenated, and often hyphens that should appear at the end of the line are placed at the beginning of the next; and (20) he both uses and omits apostrophes to indicate possessives or contractions, and occasionally he falters where, in Arabian names, the apostrophe is indicated.[13] In short, his practice is guided less by grammatical rules or

13. Besides these, there are a half-dozen or more lesser eccentricities of form: (1) he fails sometimes distinctly to indent new paragraph beginnings, (2) *i*'s are left undotted and *t*'s uncrossed, (3) diacritical marks are sometimes omitted or added gratuitously; (4) commas, semicolons, and quotation marks are often turned in the wrong direction; (5) commas are often indistinguishable from dashes; (6) he often places marks of punctuation above the line or below it; (7) he appears uncertain whether to place terminal marks of punctuation inside or outside quotation marks; and (8) he often uses a lower-case form for the first word of a quotation.

The data here presented, as well as those immediately following, apply in very nearly the same degree to the manuscript of the five-volume *Life of Washington*, which was prepared over a period of years encompassing the preparation of the manuscript for *Mahomet and His Successors* – roughly 1846–1859 – so that the irregularities observed are not peculiar to *Mahomet* but are part of the general writing habits of Irving during the last decade of his life. As will be indicated later, his proofing habits, too, were of a piece for the entire period of his association with the firm of George P. Putnam. Lists of memoranda prepared for his own convenience while reading proof for *Mahomet* and correction lists sent to Putnam, ranging from 1848 to 1859, plus six author-corrected page-proof sheets of *Washington*, all fall into a similar pattern, betokening a strict attention to substantive corrections and virtually no concern with accidentals, except in so far as he was

syntactical principles than by what seems to be a kind of half-visual, half-oral sense for supplying punctuation wherever this delicate sixth sense suggests the desirability of indicating a pause, placing a shade of emphasis, or supplying a special nuance of meaning whether covered by the rules or not.

Collating MSb with the first American edition (first impression, Putnam, 1850), which serves as copy-text, reveals the fact that in setting the 43 pages of MSb in type 480 alterations were made – an average of approximately 11 for each manuscript page. Of these, only 22 are substantive changes, the accidentals numbering 458 – a ratio of nearly 1 to 21 – a circumstance accounted for mainly by the necessity under which the printer was to add missing, or to correct faulty, punctuation, and to correct other details classifiable as accidentals.

Broken down, the substantive changes include the addition of 5 phrases (of two, three, four, five, and fifteen words), 2 deletions of one and two words, and 15 substitutions of a word each. Apart from the fact that all but one of these are alterations of a kind that an author, rather than the compositor, would make, our knowledge of Irving's practice, in correcting proof, of making substantive changes while largely ignoring accidentals permits us to ascribe responsibility for all but one of the substantive changes to Irving. The doubtful one is the substitution of "war of ink" for "war of wit" (159.7),[14] which is discussed below, pages 598–599, 623.

Among accidentals there are 36 altered spellings, capitalizations, and word divisions, and among additions, 6 accents, 5 apostrophes, 2 circumflexes, 10 hyphens, 1 exclamation point, 1 italics, 12 periods (as against 1 omission), and 5 new indentations (as against 1 in the manuscript that is ignored). The greatest discrepancy occurs in the use of commas, 293 being added and 12 omitted. Thirty-two quotation marks (double and single) are added and only 1 omitted. Beyond this, 1 semicolon is added and 2 are dropped, 1 dash is changed to a semicolon, 2 semicolons to colons, 1 dash to a comma, 6 semicolons to commas, 4 commas to semicolons, 1 period to a semicolon, and 1 needed question mark is substituted for a period. One lower-case form is changed to a

---

alert to errors or inconsistencies in the spelling of names, both of persons and of places.

14. All page and line references are to the text of the Wisconsin edition, unless otherwise indicated as either ARE (Putnam) or E (Murray).

capital, and 21 capitals to lower case. The count does not include un-dotted *i*'s and uncrossed *t*'s.[15]

The compositors' names that appear on the printer's copy afford no light on why the incidence of variants should be so high. Three names appear (Wood twice, Lanius twice, and Gage once); however, all stints but one (Lanius's first stint) are short, and the breaks in the manuscript intrude so often between signatures that no meaningful con-clusions can be drawn as to the compositorial habits or peculiarities among the three. Indeed, no noticeable differences in their methods ap-pear, each of them apparently following consistently the prescribed house style of George P. Putnam, or of John F. Trow, who did the printing for Putnam.[16] The conclusion is inescapable that while some of these numerous alterations are owing to house style, which Irving would not have followed in all particulars, if he had indeed taken the trouble to attend to these details, so long as the editor cannot know what Irving would have done in every case, he is not at liberty to make emendations except for the most compelling, readily substantiated rea-sons.

For the rest, the six surviving portions of MSb are regular enough, written in Irving's hand, the paper and ink uniform throughout. Most of the pages show two sequences of foliation, indicating some rear-

---

15. The figures given here and in other statistical summations derived from collations (whether in precise or approximate figures) are intended only as sug-gestive summaries of information. Readers wishing to work out for themselves other relationships based on lists of emendations and of variants by tabulating these data may not always arrive at the same totals because certain variants can be classified and counted in more than one way. Substitutions, for example, may be longer or shorter than the word or words they replace, and consequently may be counted differently. Also, it is not always possible strictly to decide whether a misprint or faulty impression is owing to broken, damaged, or dropped type or to faulty inking, or whether an irregularity represents an error of commission (authorial or compositorial) or ordinary plate wear and damage.

All over-all figures cited, it should be noted, include both the table of contents and the preface, as well as running heads, synoptic chapter headings, footnotes, and the appendix.

16. This observation holds also for the much more extensive sections of manu-script for Volumes III–V of *Washington* that survive. Here the several compositorial stints (as marked by signatures, usually with accompanying notations "Comm[ence] Slip" or "End of Slip," plus the number of the type-set page) are regularly indi-cated, but they provide no index to any appreciable variations as to the compara-tive accuracy or the individual peculiarities of the six compositors – none of whose names appear on the printer's copy of *Mahomet*.

rangement of materials: 24 of 27 pages belonging to Volume I show two number sequences (in Irving's hand), while 8 of the 16 pages belonging to Volume II show a similar repagination.

The pages for Volume I include two chapter beginnings (page 302 and page 314), complete with synoptic chapter headings. The first Irving originally numbered "Chap 31," then renumbered "28," before it became "CHAPTER XXXII" in print; the second, originally "Chap 32," was renumbered "29," and finally became "CHAPTER XXXIII." So little of MSb exists that we can only conjecture about what happened. It would seem that somewhere in the process of writing Volume I, three chapters (corresponding to Chapters 3–5, pages 16–29, of MSa, that drearily presented historical and religious background material for the rise of Islam) were either scrapped or severely shortened and scattered about (a paragraph or so at a time) in appropriate places or relegated to the appendix at the end of Volume I. Then, apparently, four additional chapters providing more detailed information on the early career of Mahomet before he actively assumed his mission were written and inserted to bring the over-all numbering into line with the sequence observed in print. These deletions and additions appear to have been made sometime after typesetting had already begun and certainly before the compositor reached page 293 of the manuscript, where the repaging first occurs in the fragment of MSb that we have. It is noteworthy that (contrary to the usual practice in John F. Trow's shop) the chapter numbers as they stand in print were never entered on the printer's copy – leaving conjectural the question of whether the compositor mentally made the necessary adjustments in the chapter numbering as he went along or inserted them afterwards in the proofs.

THE TEXTS

The following identifying symbols are adopted as convenient shortened forms of reference in the discussion that follows:

MSa   1828–1831 manuscript, 558 pages (all in the New York Public Library except 14 pages in the library of the University of Virginia)

MSb   1848–1849 manuscript, 43 pages (41 pages in the Museum of the City of New York, one in the Historical Society of Pennsylvania, and one in the New York Public Library)

ARE   Author's Revised Edition (50 through 60 as listed below)

50[17]   First American impression (Putnam, 1850)
  50a   Earlier state of variant sheets within 50
  50b   Later state of variant sheets within 50

51 ⎫
52 ⎪
53 ⎬   Reimpressions of ARE
54 ⎪
55 ⎭

57   Reimpression of ARE, except that 229 pages of Volume I and
        8 pages of Volume II are reset

59 ⎫
60 ⎭   Reimpressions of 57, without further alterations

E   First (and only) English impression (Murray, 1850), printed
        from a duplicate set of 50 plates; Preface and Contents reset
        and reversed, and plates otherwise mended in various details

W   University of Wisconsin Press edition

Because the manuscript from which the first edition of *Mahomet and
His Successors* was set in type has very limited authority, and because
no author-corrected proof sheets survive,[18] Putnam's first impression
(Volume I, December 1849, and Volume II, April 1850) provides copy-
text. The type was set and immediately stereotyped for Putnam by

17. Because the sequence of editions and impressions is very regular, numerals
50, 51, 52, etc., signifying 1850, 1851, 1852, etc., are used as providing a more
immediate identification than the designations 1A1, 1A2, 1E, and 2A used elsewhere
in the volumes of the Wisconsin edition. Since there was only one English impression that carried any kind of authority or relevance, E provides a sufficient identification. All editions or impressions identified by numerals from 50 to 60 are by
Putnam, no others (American or foreign) except E having any relevance.

18. The old Putnam firm virtually came to an end after the death of George
Haven Putnam on February 22, 1930, and the departure from the business of
George Palmer Putnam on August 15 of the same year. According to Mr. Walter
G. Minton, currently president of G. P. Putnam's Sons, there are no manuscripts,
letters, contracts, or manufacturing records that relate to Irving's books during the
nineteenth century.

John F. Trow ("Printer and Stereotyper, 49 and 51 Ann-st., New York"), a duplicate set of plates being made at the time, promptly shipped to John Murray, and printed for Murray by Bradbury and Evans of Whitefriars, London. Both Volumes I and II, in both the London and New York impressions, were dated 1850 on the title page.[19] Whether Murray did in fact publish Volume I before it appeared in New York, as was customary, seems to be settled by information furnished by Mr. John R. Murray, the present head of the firm at 50 Albemarle Street, to the effect that of the first and only printing (1000 copies of each volume, 86 of which remained in stock as late as 1912), the first copies of Volume I were moved from the stock room on January 7, 1850, and that therefore the official publication must have been after that date.[20]

19. The argument advanced by William R. Langfeld that because Murray's "List of Books," dated January 1850, advertised Volume I of *Mahomet* as "now ready," it was in fact published in 1849 overlooks the fact that announcements of this kind were often anticipatory, as well as the possibility that the volume may have been published between January 1 and 31 – as it very probably was. H. G. Bohn provides supporting evidence. In an advertisement, dated February 21, 1850, prefixed to his pirated one-volume *Life of Mahomet,* Bohn explains that he has been "goaded . . . in self defence, to adopt measures of reprisal" against American pirates, meanwhile excusing his infringements on Murray's rights as inconsequential because, as he goes on to argue, "no one [obviously Murray] can reasonably complain of a competition" because the book "was published in New York in December last, imported and sold here in January, more than a fortnight before any English edition appeared."

Murray did more than complain, for when Routledge brought out an unauthorized edition in 1850, he took Bohn to court and drew up a bill of complaint against Routledge – measures that brought both to heel and greatly clarified British copyright law, but ruined all future value of the book for Murray.

Bohn's statement clearly means that the first Putnam edition appeared before Murray's. This unusual reversal of the customary order can best be explained by the circumstance that when Murray received notice from Putnam in December 1849 about needed revisions to be made in the plates, these corrections and certain revisions that Murray undertook to make on his own account (as the sequel will show) delayed Murray's publication beyond the usual term.

20. John R. Murray to Henry A. Pochmann, June 18 and August 20, 1968.

The London *Publishers' Circular and Booksellers' Record* for January 1, 1850, advertised Volume I as "to appear shortly"; in the *Athenaeum* for January 12 it was announced as for "next week"; and it was reviewed in the *Literary Gazette* for January 26. Volume II was listed in the *Literary Gazette* on April 6, 1850, and reviewed on April 13.

Final substantiation for 1850 as the date of publication for both volumes appears in photocopy of two copies of the Form of Requiring Entry of Proprietorship in the

For the history of the text, two kinds of changes in the Putnam and Murray plates are to be noted. The first were probably made before any sheets were printed from them; at any rate, no bound uncorrected Putnam copies have been found, although one of these errors remained undetected and uncorrected in the Murray printing and so was perpetuated in that edition. This is the misspelling of "Burkhardt" for "Burckhardt." It was one of the names that Irving had trouble with in both MSa and MSb; hence the error – in four out of eleven instances where the word is used – must be presumed to have been Irving's rather than the compositor's. The name occurs in Volume I only: by page and line reference, ARE 19.23 (W 8.32), ARE 20.13 (W 9.26), ARE 34.26 (W 17.39), ARE 159.15 (W 91.32), ARE 160.26 (W 91.38), ARE 173.26 (W 99.41), ARE 277.27 (W 160.38), ARE 326.28 (W 191.23), ARE 369.25 (W 217.38), ARE 371.21 (W 218.23), ARE 371.25 (W 218.36) – always in footnotes. A comparison on the Hinman collating machine of the first Putnam impression with the Murray impression reveals (1) that in four occurences of "Burckhardt" – ARE 20.13 (W 9.26), ARE 159.15 (W 91.32), ARE 160.26 (W 91.38), and ARE 173.26 (W 99.41) – there are irregularities between the Putnam and Murray impressions, both between varying degrees of jamming together of letters and the spacings before and after the word in order to make room for the missing "c," and (2) that in the Murray plates the misspelling at ARE 159.15 (W 91.32) was overlooked. Whether the mending was done in Putnam's shop before the plates were shipped to Murray, or done separately, cannot now be ascertained. The oversight could have occured in either shop, though with less likilehood at Putnam's where the workman would have had both sets of plates before him, and where he did in fact correct all the errors in the Putnam set, and with more likelihood in Murray's, especially if it is assumed, as is likely, that the errors were reported to Murray as occuring in footnotes on pages ARE 19–20 (W 8–9), ARE 159–160 (W 91), and ARE 173 (W 99), without specifying that in the first two passages the word occurs both at the beginning of the note as well as in the reference at the end – that is, at ARE 19.23

Register Book of the Stationers' Company that were received from the Public Record Office after these passages were written. On January 26, 1850, John Murray affixed his witnessed signature to the first of these forms, testifying that the date of first publication for Volume I was January 26, 1850, and on April 2, 1850, he testified that Volume II was published on March 28, 1850.

(W 8.32), ARE 20.13 (W 9.26), ARE 159.15 (W 91.32), and ARE 160.26 (W 91.38). After correcting the error at ARE 20.13 (W 9.26), where it occurs only at the end of the footnote, the workman might naturally enough mend the error in the reference at the end of the next footnote (ARE 160.26; W 91.38) without noticing the earlier occurence in the opening sentence of the note itself (ARE 159.15; W 91.32). So it might come to pass that all misspellings of "Burckhardt" were mended in both sets except at ARE 159.15 (W 91.32) in the Murray set.

This kind of prepublication alteration does not serve to distinguish among possible American impressions in 1850. However, variations do exist among copies with Putnam 1850 title pages. In the copies examined, such variations have been noted in seven gatherings. In six of the gatherings the variations are textual: thus, in gathering 2, where some copies have the word "Ararat" (ARE 37.10; W 19.9), others read "Arafat"; in gathering 8, the variants are "Jaffar"/"Jaafar" (ARE 175.5; W 100.34) and "Kaled"/"Khaled" (ARE 182.1); W 105.18); in gathering 9, "Hoyai"/"Hoya" (ARE 209.1; W 121.4) and "of the"/"of the Sword" (ARE 212.12; W 123.6); in gathering 10, "eyes Mahomet"/"eyes of Mahomet" (ARE 225.13; W 131.9); in gathering 12, "Amir"/"Musa" (ARE 265.10; W 153.40); and in gathering 14, "IMPORTANCE"/ "IMPOSTURE" in the running head of two pages (ARE 333; W 195 and ARE 335; W 197). In the remaining gathering which shows variation, the differences involve imposition: in some copies, no leaves of publisher's advertisements are integral with gathering 16; in others, one leaf of advertisements is integral; and in still others, three leaves are integral (and this variety itself takes several forms, according to the particular advertisements which appear). Although it is difficult to determine the order of these variations in imposition, the order of the textual variations is indicated by noting which version remains through later impressions (in each pair of readings above, the one mentioned second is later). All these differences might seem to suggest that more than one 1850 impression exists; but the copies examined reveal no regular pattern in their combinations of these variant gatherings and yield no conclusive evidence to show that more than one distinct impression of the entire book occurred. In the light of this situation, the best copy to select for printer's copy for this edition would theoretically be one that contains the earliest ascertainable state of each of the variant gatherings; for practical purposes, however, since such copies are difficult to locate (and since only nine textual variants are involved), a copy with mixed sheets can serve as printer's copy.[21]

21. For further bibliographical comment on the first volume of the 1850 *Mahomet,* see Jacob Blanck's *Bibliography of American Literature,* V, 52, no. 10175. The BAL discussion postulates three impressions on the basis of the number of leaves in the final gathering; but it does not report the variety in which the six pages of integral advertisements are numbered 17A, 18, 19, 20, 21, 22, or the one in which they are numbered 34, 35, 36, 37, 38, 39, nor does it cite the various mixtures of sheets as revealed by a check of variant readings (only extensive collations, such as BAL could hardly undertake for all volumes, would reveal the last). The copy used for printer's copy for this edition (in the University of Texas library, call no. Ir81m/1850a/v.1) corresponds with the second variety of BAL 10175 but contains the earlier form of all but one (212.12) of the variant readings. This copy collates as follows: Vol. I, 12° (7⁷⁄₁₆ × 5⅛): ⟨ ⟩², 1–15¹² 16¹⁰, plus ⟨17¹² 18⁶⟩ [leaves 1 and 5 signed, 5 with added asterisk, but signature mark 1 wanting, 1* on 3 instead of 4, and 2* on 4ᵛ instead of 5], 192 leaves, pp. ⟨i series title⟩ ⟨ii blank⟩ ⟨iii title⟩ ⟨iv copyright⟩, ⟨i contents⟩ ii–vii ⟨viii blank⟩ ⟨ix preface⟩ x–xi ⟨xii blank⟩, ⟨13 text⟩ 14–341 ⟨342 blank⟩, ⟨343 appendix half-title⟩ ⟨344 blank⟩ ⟨345 appendix⟩ 346–373 ⟨374 blank⟩, 6 pp. advertisements, paged 16, 15, 19, 20, 22, 7; plus 36 pp. publisher's catalog, paged 1–36. Vol. II, 12° (7⁷⁄₁₆ × 5⅛): ⟨ ⟩², 1–20¹² 21¹⁰ [leaves 1 and 5 signed regularly, 5 with added asterisk], 252 leaves, pp. ⟨i series title⟩ ⟨ii blank⟩ ⟨iii title⟩ ⟨iv copyright⟩, ⟨i contents⟩ ii–viii ⟨ix preface⟩ x–xii, ⟨13 text⟩ 14–500.

While there is some variation in the signatures among 50a and 50b Putnam copies, all Murray copies examined collate identically as follows: Vol. I, 12° (8⅜ × 5¼): ⟨A⟩⁸ B–I⁸ K–U⁸ X–Z⁸ AA⁵(AA⁴⁺¹) [leaves 1 and 2 signed, 2 with added 2, supplementary signature mark wanting in AA], 189 leaves, pp. ⟨i title⟩ ⟨ii blank⟩ ⟨iii vol. title⟩ ⟨iv printer⟩ ⟨v preface⟩ vi–vii ⟨viii blank⟩ ⟨ix contents⟩ x–xv ⟨xvi blank⟩ ⟨13 text⟩ 14–341 ⟨342 blank⟩ ⟨343 appendix half-title⟩ ⟨344 blank⟩ ⟨345 appendix⟩ 346–373 ⟨374 notice for Vol. II⟩. Vol. II, 12° (8⅜ × 5¼): ⟨a⟩⁴ b⁴ A² B–I⁸ K–U⁸ X–Z⁸ 2A–2H⁸ 2I² [leaves 1 and 2 signed, 2 with added 2, supplementary signature marks wanting in b, A, and 2I], 252 leaves, pp. ⟨i vol. title⟩ ⟨ii blank⟩ ⟨iii title⟩ ⟨iv printer⟩ ⟨v preface⟩ vi–viii ⟨ix contents⟩ x–xvi ⟨13 text⟩ 14–500.

Among seven copies of the 1850 Putnam impression examined, the following combinations of variations exist: (1) Texas, Ir81m/1850a/v.1 – all early readings but one (ARE 212.12; W 123.6), with the last gathering corresponding to the second variety of BAL 10175; (2) American Antiquarium Society, G526/I72/M850(1) – all early readings but one (ARE 212.12; W 123.6), with the last gathering corresponding to the first variety of BAL 10175; (3) New York Public Library, accession no. 157101B – all early readings but one (ARE 37.10; W 19.9), with the last gathering corresponding to the first variety of BAL 10175; (4) Harvard, AL/1968/110/(12) – all early readings but two (ARE 37.10; W 19.9 and ARE 212.12; W 123.6), with the last gathering corresponding to the second variety of BAL 10175; (5) Texas, Ir81m/1850b/v.1 – all late readings but one (ARE 212.12; W 123.6), with the last gathering corresponding to an unrecorded form of the second variety of BAL 10175; (6) Univ. of Virginia library, Barrett/*PS2072/.M2/1850/580642/v.1 – all late readings, with the last gathering corresponding to the third variety of BAL 10175; (7) Ralph M. Aderman, uncatalogued, "Robert E. Living-

Oddly enough, among the copies of Volume II that have been examined, no evidence of plate correction or resetting between the first and
second printing has been discovered, though the first printing, too,
contained errors of various sorts that might have been rectified. Indeed,
Volume II appears to have been given short shrift, as when in 1857
both volumes were corrected prior to reprinting, and 229 pages of the
first volume were reset, while 8 were deemed sufficient for the second.

We do not know how many copies Putnam printed during 1850, but
we may infer, from the fact that the year before he printed an edition
of 2,500 of *Goldsmith* and before the year was out was "busy on a second 2,000," that *Mahomet* may have been printed and reprinted in approximately the same numbers.

Following 1850, *Mahomet and His Successors* was reprinted (one
volume or both) every year until 1860 except for 1856 and 1858, but
Volumes I and II were sold both in sets and separately (as well as in
the collected edition, where they formed Volumes XII and XIII), so
that seemingly uniform sets[22] bear varying combinations of dates 1850,

---

ston" written in pencil at the top of the half-title page — all late readings, with
the last gathering an unrecorded form of the second variety of BAL 10175. Considering the indiscriminate way in which the corrected and uncorrected sheets
were bound, there may well be more copies showing still other combinations of
variants than those that were found.

The chore of finding and correcting errors in the first Putnam impression appears
to have been referred to Irving himself. In the process he prepared a list of names
of persons and places. Seven pages of this list survive among Irving's "Memoranda
& Notes for Mahomet and his Successors" in the Berg Collection of the New York
Public Library. The pages record 110 names roughly in the order of their appearance (with pages of the Putnam text noted and often with brief identifying remarks) — all apparently names the spelling of which he wished to check. Among
them are "175 Jaffar (Jaafar)," "182 Kaled instead of Khaled," and "209 Hoyah
Ibn Ahktab (Hoya p. 225)." (Irving's page references are to Volume I of the ARE.)
Even with these precautionary aids to his memory, he overlooked errors and
inconsistencies. For example, at I, 209.1 (W 121.4) he correctly changed "Hoyai
Ibn Ahktab" to "Hoya Ibn Ahktab," but at I, 225.9 (W 131.5) he neglected to
change "Akhtab" to "Ahktab."

These pages are not correction sheets given to the printer, but merely Irving's
memoranda on the basis of which he could check on himself as he looked for
errors or inconsistencies to be corrected. However diligently he may have worked,
his corrections were far from thorough. Some that he overlooked were found later
and corrected in subsequent impressions; others were never found.

22. Here called sets because all outward signs (except dates) correspond as
regards bindings, inscribed names of erstwhile owners or bookplates, general
arrangement of half-title and title pages, library call numbers, etc.

1851, 1852, and so on, in turn suggesting that different impressions of the two volumes were variously combined, or stocks of one impression or another were bound separately and dated variously, or if already bound and dated, were mixed up so that Volume I might bear the date 1852 and Volume II, 1851. For example, there appears to have been no impression in 1851 of Volume I.[23] All 1853 and 1854 copies that were examined bear the same date for both volumes, but in 1855 the dates were again mixed up, the 1854 impression of Volume I being coupled with the 1855 of Volume II.[24] There appears to have been no new impression during 1856, probably in anticipation of the necessity of a new printing in 1857, for which extensive resetting was undertaken.

This mismatching is one of externals only, and does not matter very much so far as the text is concerned, because during Irving's lifetime and well beyond, all authorized printings of *Mahomet and His Successors* were in the hands of George P. Putnam and John Murray, and both used identical plates, so that after the first year (when both made individual changes so as to create differences between the Putnam and Murray texts, as well as within the first Putnam impression), nothing but occasional mendings of shopworn or damaged plates was attempted until 1857, when Putnam overhauled both volumes by reset-

23. There are many sets in which both Volumes I and II bear the date 1850, but for 1851 and 1852 these dates are variously combined: I, 1850, with II, 1851; I, 1850, with II, 1852; and I, 1852, with II, 1851; but never with a Volume I dated 1851. Despite an extensive search well beyond the locations listed in the Library of Congress National Union Catalog, no set bearing 1851 for both volumes has been found. It is possible that during 1850, Volume I (*Mahomet*) outsold Volume II (*Mahomet's Successors*, as it was labeled on the spine of the collected edition) by so many copies that a new impression of Volume I was called for long before the bound stock of Volume II was exhausted, and that then enough copies of Volume I were printed so that no new impression of it was needed during 1851 to match the demands that year for Volume II. In any case, a thorough search has failed to locate a copy of Volume I bearing the date 1851 – which is not to say that one will not turn up tomorrow, or years after these words appear in print.

24. To be sure, the date on the title page of a given volume is not conclusive evidence that the book itself was printed or bound in that year. As stock piles for the two volumes varied, the sheets might be bound up as needed, regardless of the date on the title page, resulting in a mismatching of dates during 1851–1852 and again during 1854–1855.

Data derived from title pages alone may make the printing history of a book appear very simple, when in reality an examination of gatherings and the superimposition of text on text by means of the Hinman collating machine may show it to be very complicated, *Mahomet and His Successors* being a case in point. *Salmagundi* is an extreme example.

ting 229 pages of the first volume and 8 pages of the second.[25] This disproportion of pages in the two volumes requiring replating bears out the suggestion that the demand for Volume I (*Mahomet*) exceeded that for Volume II (*Mahomet's Successors*).

Apparently no new printing was called for in 1858; those for 1857, 1859, and 1860 bear matching dates for both volumes, and exhibit no alterations or variants except those attributable to ordinary wear and tear of reprinting. This carries us well beyond the printings relevant to the problem in hand, all editions after 1859 being beyond Irving's possible direction. Indeed, preoccupied as he was with the last volumes of *The Life of George Washington*, it is questionable that he had either the time or the energy to devote any attention to the alterations made in the 1857 impression. Pierre M. Irving was still occupied in the city, so that he could not be counted on for prolonged assistance. Moreover, virtually all the changes made in the 1857 printing are accidentals bearing the marks of compositor's alterations, as distinct from what the author's more extended substantive corrections would doubtless have been. It is to be noted further that no concerted or organized effort was made to correct the pages not reset, so that many of the damaged or dropped characters as well as textual errors on the 636 pages not reset were simply perpetuated. Even for the 237 reset pages the new errors outnumber the corrections made by 192 to 141. Hence the 1857 impression inspires little confidence as a source for emendations.

Nonetheless, the resettings for the 1857 impression had become necessary because practically no mending of plates had been undertaken in the Putnam line of impressions after the corrections made in 1850, so that, except for sporadic tinkering, cumulative corruption in terms of smudged, blurred, broken, or dropped characters was both marked and constant, showing most clearly in 1854–1855.

Although not unlikely, it cannot be assumed that an 1854–1855 copy was used in making the new plates for the 1857 impression. An earlier one could have served as well. However that may be, it is apparent that the 1857 impression presents faults of its own that make it no bet-

25. The reset (replated) pages of Volume I (ARE) are i–vii, ix–xi, 13–48, 58, 110, and 193–373. All of these are 27-line pages except the following thirteen: 35, 58, 110, 262, 283, 301, 302, 306, 346, 352, 356, 359, and 364 – which are the regular 26-line pages characteristic of the original plates. In Volume II (ARE) the following pages are reset, all of them in the usual 26-line pages: vii, 171, 189, 241, 308, 366, 437, and 453.

ter than the 1854–1855, which it was designed to correct, if not to perfect. Aside from the fact that very little effort was made to mend the imperfections of the 636 pages that were not reset, the 237 that were reset are replete with old and new errors and imperfections. Apart from the 13 emendations (all of them accidentals) that were adopted for the Wisconsin edition from the 1857 impression, and the 6 substantive variants rejected, the 1857 impression shows a great number of alterations among accidentals of various kinds that break down into the following three categories: (1) there are 141 corrections, chiefly of damaged or dropped characters, that can be regarded as improvements; (2) 25 others, doubtless designed to be refinements, are unacceptable because they are not in full accord with Irving's practice in *Mahomet* or in other books of the period; and worst of all (3) 192 new errors are introduced, most of them typographical. Besides these, there are 93 flaws in the 1854–1855 impression that were overlooked and so merely perpetuated.[26] The record being what it is, the inference is inescapable

26. To provide a better overview of the entire sorry history of progressive plate deterioration, a complete list was made of all post-copy-text variations among accidentals. Because this compilation is bulky and very little to the immediate purpose of this edition, it is not reproduced, but is deposited in the library of the University of Texas along with all other collation data, and is available to anyone minded to examine it for a variety of textual and stylistic analyses for which these data supply the basic information. Combined with the lists accompanying the Textual Commentary, this extended compilation of variants among accidentals in the Putnam line between the 1857 impression and all earlier and later ones through 1860, provides in effect a historical collation of all relevant impressions that appeared during Irving's lifetime.

For the record it is to be noted that in addition to the resettings undertaken for the 1857 impression, the following words, passages, or pages were reset (in impressions as indicated below) to correct plate damage, but none of these resulted in any textual change (since these have no textual but only bibliographical significance for the W edition, only the ARE page and line references are given): I, 65.15 "his wife and his brother-in-law" in E; I, 132, in 50b; I, 144.10 "it quenches" in E; I, 146.15 "Biased" in E; I, 151.5 "day" in 52; I, 167.1 in E; I, 254.13 "interpolations" in E; I, 255.4 "hundredth chapter of the" in E; I, 280.1 "Hatim" in E; I, 297.2 "Mission of Ali to" in E; I, 323.3 "discredited the" in E; II, 20.2 "Reb" in 57; II, 24.22 "Al Azwar, a" in E; II, 45. 1–12 in 51; II, 93.1 "on . . . bait" in 57; II, 233.23–26, in 57; II, 252.12 "of the stone, marble and" in E; II, 267.11 "in the faith" in E; II, 271.3 "and Azerbîjân won" in E; II, 271.21 "denunciations of" in E; II, 273.9 "they say when it disappears" in E; II, 274.4, "and the Rus" in E; II, 280.4 "tes-" in E; II, 280.5 "soever" in E; II, 291.11 "other things" in E; II, 301.1–9 in E; II, 316.12 "deputations" in E; II, 328.1 "disgraceful" in E; II, 329.15 in E; II, 338.21 "Hosein to" in E; II, 349.8 "this before God" in 57; II, 362.33 in E; II, 364.6 "indignant at having" in 57; II, 378.18–19 leading between these two

that the alterations were executed solely in Putnam's shop, without benefit of authorial supervision, either direct or delegated, and in all probability, without the author's having any knowledge of it – as often happens in such cases. It was undertaken primarily to supply new plates for some that had become too shopworn to make good impressions. Inevitable as it was, in a resetting of so many pages, that a number of changes would be made in the text (both corrections and alteration for the worse), the 1857 impression was not intended to be a new or revised edition, and was not so in fact.

The two manuscripts and all authorized editions (Putnam and Murray) published during Irving's lifetime were collated according to the following pattern:

1. One sight collation[27] of MSa with corresponding passages of Volume I of the first Putnam impression (50)
2. Three sight collations of MSb with corresponding passages in Volumes I and II of 50
3. Two machine collations of 50 with E, the first (and only) Murray impression
4. Two machine collations of 50 with the 1852 impression of Volume I and the 1851 impression of Volume II (no matching copies of both volumes for either 1851 or 1852 being available then or later)
5. One machine collation of 50 with 53
6. One collation, partly by machine and partly by sight (for the 237 reset pages), of 53 with 60
7. One machine collation of 57 with 60
8. One machine collation of two copies of 50

---

lines in E much heavier than in the Putnam impressions; II, 422.4 in E; II, 429.3 "quarter to the rest" in E; II, 435.5 "Al" in E; II, 435.5 "Mohalleb" in E; II, 437.16 "warned" in E; II, 438.14 "may" in E; II, 445.3 "therefore abandoned it" in E; II, 454.6 "therefore led them" in E; II, 472.4–6 "mag- . . . hand" in E; II, 475.17–26 in E; II, 491.4 "These" in E; and II, 493.17 "by Mohamed Ibn Casem, a" in E. Bibliographically interesting as are these mendings (detected by the Hinman collating machine), their textual significance is slight beyond pointing up the resettings that Putnam made (one, each, in 50b, 51, 52, and five in the 57) and the 38 that Murray felt compelled to make – most of them apparently to correct plate damage sustained in shipping.

27. Sight collations (as distinct from machine collations, with the aid of the Hinman collating machine) are required when two editions (different settings of type) are involved. Impressions of the same edition are more expeditiously and accurately collated by machine.

9. One machine collation of two copies of E

10. One machine collation of Volume I of 50 with Volume I of 54, and of Volume II of 50 with Volume II of 55

11. One machine collation for substantives of 59 with 60[28]

28. Copies for these collations are recorded by library name and call number, or name of the present owner, together with whatever identifying marks can be noted: (1) NYPL (543 pages) and Univ. of Virginia (15 pages) vs. Henry A. Pochmann's copy of the 1852 impression of Vol. I, uncatalogued, with the name of "Geo. H. Ford" written in ink on the recto of the second flyleaf; (2) Museum of the City of New York (41 pages), the Hist. Soc. of Penna. (1 page), and the NYPL (1 page) vs. Texas Ir81m/1850a/v.1&2; (3) Texas Ir81m/1850b/v.1&2 vs. Texas Ir81m/1850j/v.1&2; (4) Texas Ir81m/1850a/v.1&2 vs. Henry A. Pochmann's copy of Vol. I, 1852, and Vol. II, 1851, uncatalogued, with the name of "Geo. H. Ford" written in ink on the recto of the second flyleaf of each volume; (5) Texas Ir81m/1850a/v.1&2 vs. Allegheny College T/922/M27/1853/v.1&2; (6) Allegheny College T/922/M27/1853/v.1&2 vs. Univ. of Virginia PS/2050/1860/v.12&13/copy 1; (7) Univ. of Illinois 297/M72Wi/1857/v.1&2 vs. Univ. of Virginia PS2050/1860/v.12&13/copy 1; (8) Texas Ir81m/1850a/v.1&2 vs. Texas Ir81m/1850b/v.1&2; (9) Texas Ir81m/1850j/v.1&2 vs. Texas Ir81m/1850k/v.1&2; (10) Texas Ir81m/1850a/v.1 vs. Case Western Reserve 297/M95vi/v.1 and Texas Ir81m/1850a/v.2 vs. Case Western Reserve 297/M95vi/v.2; (11) Univ. of Missouri BP/75/1859/v.1&2 vs. Univ. of Virginia PS/2050/1860/v.12&13/copy 1. The particular combinations of variant sheets found in the copies of 50 reported here are specified in footnote 21.

Collations 3–7 are full-scale collations noting and recording all variants, including damaged and dropped characters, as well as misalignments and resettings of type, whether these created any textual variants or not. Collations 8–11, devoted mainly to checking cruces (substantives as well as accidentals) already noted in 2–7, revealed no significant variations beyond the expected imperfections owing to progressive plate deterioration, but they served to establish continuity between the earlier collations and to check against possible hidden variants. Since the plates throughout all the steps remained basically the same, one collation for steps 5–11 sufficed to make cross checks, each on the other. All collations were for record, and the complete data are deposited in the University of Texas library.

In the course of the collations enumerated, various odd copies that became available were spot-checked against corresponding or near copies already collated for record, among them (1) Volumes I and II of E, Ralph M. Aderman, with the Ralph M. Aderman bookplate pasted on the inside front cover of both volumes; (2) Volume I, 50, and Volume II, 51, Harvard KD/47395/(12)&(13); (3) Volume II of 51, Duke Univ. Div. S./922.97/M9521/v.2; (4) Volume II of 52, Girard College B/M721/v.2; (5) Volume II of 54, Texas Ir81m/1854/v.2; (6) Volumes I and II of 61, Harvard AL/1968/571.15v.1&2; and (7) Volume I of 68 and Volume II of 69, Drexel Institute 818/Ir8/v.12&13. None of them revealed any significant variants not already noted.

All copies of Volume I of the first impression (Putnam, 1850) that were scrutinized are identified in footnote 21 above.

No further effort is made here to identify or describe the various impressions or printings of *Mahomet and His Successors* because the essentials are reported by

TREATMENT OF SUBSTANTIVES

Almost from the beginning of Irving's long literary career he held to the practice of making last-minute alterations in the proofs. This is what he called correcting the proof sheets, including what he also called re-dressing, that is, more than merely substituting the single word, which he said had sometimes great effect, however "hard to hit" it might be, but altering and inserting new matter. In 1831 he gave orders that he wanted the manuscript of *Mahomet*, though admittedly still "in the rough," put "to press forthwith," and that he wanted proof slips, as he often called them, sent to him promptly because he anticipated making extensive corrections and additions.[29] This practice, carried too far, was at least partly responsible for his break with Murray, but it did not cause him to mend his ways, so that he continued to demand of his publishers much more than any author nowadays would expect a publisher to tolerate.

Few of his corrected proof sheets survive – none for *Mahomet and His Successors;* but a dozen sheets of the 1848 edition of *Knickerbocker*, the first volume printed by Putnam in the new edition, afford an insight into Irving's method of revision at the time. For *Knickerbocker* he tore up and used two copies of the 1824 edition as printer's copy using the pages of the 1824 American edition for Volume I and of the 1824 French edition for Volume II. Many of these pages survive,

---

Jacob Blanck (BAL 10175) and because a detailed physical description will appear in the full-scale Irving bibliography to be published as the last volume of this edition by the University of Wisconsin Press. The Wisconsin edition is not specifically concerned with bibliographical details unless they bear on textual or editorial questions. Thus, while the full-scale collations undertaken list for record *all* textual variants noted, including damaged but still recognizable letters and punctuation marks, as well as missing characters, the former are not reported in this edition *unless* they could pass unnoticed or be misunderstood for intended revisions. Thus damaged semicolons appearing as commas or colons, exclamation points and question marks as periods, or commas as periods in the copy-text (or *h* appearing as *n* or *y* as *v*) are reported.

Completely missing end-of-line hyphenation in the copy-text which is the result of plate damage is normally emended but included in the List of Emendations only in the very few instances where in the Wisconsin edition the hyphens again fall at the end of the line; but for the record it is noted that such missing hyphens occur in the Putnam copy-text following "compan" (ARE I, 79.8; W 43.27), "pun" (ARE I, 96.3; W 52.32), "Ca" (ARE I, 332.26; W 195.17), and "inhabit" (ARE II, 465.25; W 489.38).

29. Irving to Murray, October 4, 22, 29, 1831 (McClary, *Irving and the House of Murray*, pp. 157–63).

along with twelve page-proof slips.[30] Author's alterations, short and long, in both indicate that Irving's correcting of proof, like Henry James's revision of text between printings, was literally a reseeing of the whole and involved completely rewriting lengthy passages. In seven instances marginal marks to indicate transpositions, insertions, cancellations, and substitutions were insufficient to indicate the changes Irving wanted made, so that he attached sheets of hand-written copy with notations such as "Correct p. 122 according to the following manuscript beginning at the end of the ninth line," followed in this particular case by 18 lines of rewritten material; another such interpolation runs to 26 lines. This was his procedure in 1848, while he was engaged on *Mahomet;* and he continued the process afterwards in *Washington*[31] in a less aggravated form presumably because for it, as for *Mahomet,* he presented recently hand-written copy rather than printed copy now a quarter century old. Accordingly his alterations for *Washington* are usually confined to a word or two, but he did not hesitate, when he thought it warranted, to write passages of 7, 19, 25, and 29 words into the margins, together with encirclements, arrows, and carets to show where they were to be inserted, in one instance pinning onto the proof sheet an odd-sized slip of paper containing 71 hand-written words to be inserted. Since these proof sheets were already paged, the havoc such last-minute revisions created among the workmen in the printshop can readily be imagined.

Again, Irving alone was not to blame. Considering the fact that the manuscript of *Mahomet* was written under extreme pressure from Putnam, who demanded copy for new books with which to vary the steady flow of Irving's old titles, the extant portions of MSb are surprisingly free of cancellations and insertions, though we may conjecture that the proof sheets were therefore all the more marked up with authorial revisions. For his part, Irving complained that because he had "knocked off" *Goldsmith* "in such an offhand manner," Putnam "thinks it is a very easy matter with me 'to blow up a dog' " overnight, as it were, and that *Goldsmith,* written at such a rate that he feared it smelled of the apoplexy, would simply have to "stay his [Putnam's] stomach a little longer." A manuscript for a book like *Mahomet and His Successors* required approximately 1,500 of his average-sized manuscript pages. Un-

30. These, along with the manuscript materials for *Knickerbocker,* are in the Henry E. Huntington Library, San Marino, California.

31. Eight author-corrected proof sheets for Volumes III and IV of *Washington* are preserved in the Arents Collection of the New York Public Library.

der the circumstances we can safely conclude that, as in the case of his earlier multivolume books, which Murray customarily began to set before all the manuscript was received, so early chapters of *Mahomet* were set in type while later chapters were not yet written, and successive chapters of *Mahomet's Successors* were similarly bolted through the press. The result would inevitably be a larger number of authorial corrections in the proofs than might normally be expected, the incidence of substantive corrections being especially high, partly because the accidentals went largely unnoticed.

Not having any author-corrected proof sheets for *Mahomet* by which to determine easily who was responsible for the variations that appear among texts, the editor falls back on what he can deduce from the data derived from multiple collations of the several editions and impressions, including of course the Murray edition which shows a considerable number of improvements, refinements, and corrections among substantives not found elsewhere – some of them acceptable, others questionable, most of them unacceptable for a variety of reasons.

The substantive differences that obtain between MSb and the corresponding portions of 50 are of three kinds: 5 additions, 15 substitutions, and 2 deletions. The editor's choices or decisions in most of them are complicated by the lack of corresponding proof sheets, which might provide positive evidence regarding whether the changes were made by Irving in the proofs or whether the compositor made them in the first place.

Among the additions made in 50 is "we implore" (155.19), which is prefixed to "his followers that they intercede with him in our favor" – a refinement that makes the construction parallel with the preceding clause and removes the possibility of misreading – one that the printer would not be likely to make, but that an author who read proofs in the way we know Irving did would be apt to make. Another addition is the insertion of "in addition to his African command" after "whether it were true that" and before "he was really appointed governor of Barca" (492.18–19). This, too, appears to be an alteration, added for emphasis, that only the author would be likely to make.[32] A clear-cut case is the insertion of "the slaughtered" in "the embalmed head of the slaugh-

---

32. A rule of thumb that is generally applicable in determining who is responsible for corrections in proof is that whereas a compositor or house editor may be expected to correct misspellings or errors of fact, because he is more cost-conscious than the author he is not as likely as the author to make stylistic changes that may involve costly resetting.

tered Cahina" (492.7). Others are recorded in the List of Emendations.

Substituted words occur more frequently. An interesting one is the change of the word "princes" to "provinces" in the synoptic head for Chapter XXXIII: "Subjugation of the neighboring provinces" (164.5). The text mentions two princes who are subjugated, rather than the provinces, which are not mentioned as such in this immediate context. A possibility is that Irving's formation of the word "princes," which is rather slurred, though perfectly legible to the careful eye, could have been misread by the compositor as "provinces," and so set, and that Irving, while reading proof, noticed that the over-all emphasis of the entire chapter is on the extension of Mahomet's power over territories or provinces of Syria, rather than on the subjugation of individual Syrian princes, and accordingly agreed that the substituted word was the better, and let it stand. In any case, the doubtful authority of MSb in other respects being what it is, we are justified in following the copy-text despite the fact that "provinces" was obviously not Irving's first choice; at all events, he sanctioned "provinces," and while sanctioning an alteration and himself making it are not the same thing, the odds appear to be in favor of the copy-text's authority.

A somewhat clearer case occurs in "Cahina" in the copy-text (491.32) – the form which Irving himself observed (490.29–30) is preferred to the alternate name "Dhabbá"; but in MSb (449.1) he originally wrote "Cahina," then cancelled it and substituted the less common form of "Dhabbá."[33] Whether Irving or the compositor (or possibly a Putnam reader) restored "Cahina" cannot be ascertained, although it would seem that Irving himself would have been the one to remember to make the change to the preferred form. A similar instance occurs in a case where we will never know for a surety whether the compositor misread a shakily written "wit" in "a war of wit" (MSb 304.21) and set it as "a war of ink," or whether Irving himself made the alteration in proof, or whether (if the printer made it) Irving decided to let it stand as preferable to what he had written in the manuscript, or whether he simply overlooked it in proof so that it came to stand in the copy-text by default, as it were. If we knew that Irving habitually and methodically compared his printer's copy with printer's proof, we might conclude that in allowing a printer's misreading to stand he did

33. The same alterations recur in MSb 449.9 (W 491.32) and MSb 450.7 (W 492.7–8).

so with knowing approval; but the little evidence we have that bears on the matter indicates that while his so-called correcting of proof involved making numerous changes, he did not do much checking of what the printer had set in type against what he had written in the first place. On receiving the first number of *The Sketch Book,* which Brevoort had seen through the press of Van Winkle, he wrote on July 28, 1819, expressing general satisfaction with what he called his "genteel appearance in print," yet voicing the opinion that it was "a little too *highly pointed,*" and that "High pointing is apt to injure the fluency of the style if the reader attends to all the stops." However he went on to admit that he did not in fact know whether this overpunctuation was the fault of his manuscript or the overzealousness of the printer.[34] Toward the end of the letter he specified three verbal changes he wanted made in the next printing, but said nothing about punctuation. Thus early there is evidence that he had already embarked on what later became his settled policy (in so far as it can be reconstructed from available evidence, including surviving author-corrected proof sheets and lists of corrigenda) of being meticulous about substantive matters (including spelling) but trusting the printer to supply whatever punctuation he neglected to incorporate in his manuscripts. Three decades later, on August 3, 1848, while asking Putnam to send him "proof of the introduction to the Sketch Book by mail," he added, "You need not send the copy with the proof." This would seem to imply that normally Putnam sent proof accompanied by copy, but there is nothing to suggest that Irving ever consistently read one against the other except perhaps to check cruxes as he came upon them. Instead, there is good reason for believing that during 1848–1849, with constant "fagging of the pen" and with the press "dogging at his heels," he did little more than read straight through the proofs without more than cursorily resorting to the printer's copy. This procedure would account not only for his inattention to the numerous printer's alterations of accidentals but also for his ready acceptance of the proofs so long as they satisfied him on the score of substantives. In short, in this area, which is from everlasting to everlasting debatable ground, the editor places his reliance on the reading of the copy-text when no clear authority can be attributed

34. On September 9 Brevoort replied that the overpunctuation was "not owing to the MS, but to the scrupulousness of Van Winkle," and added that in any reprinting of No. 1 "your corrections shall be carefully inserted, and the punctuation somewhat diminished."

to the manuscript, for whether Irving did indeed consider "ink" better than "wit" only Irving knew then, and nobody knows now.

A somewhat clearer case of an authorial alteration is the change from "Sending for Hassan therefore" (MSb 450.21–22) to "Sending for the latter" (492.16), as are the changes from "domination" (MSb 318.12) to "dominion" (165.35) and "drawn battle" (MSb 442.4) to "pitched battle" (486.14); and the moralizing sentence tagged on to the end of Chapter LIV, "His [Hassan's] cruel treatment of the heroic Cahina reconciles us to the injustice wreaked upon himself," is just such a bit of re-dressing as Irving was accustomed to make while reading proof.

Apart from the kind of alterations just observed between MSb and the copy-text, there are variants (1) within the copy-text itself, (2) between the copy-text and later impressions, (3) between the copy-text and the Murray edition, and (4) between the copy-text and the 237 reset pages of the 1857 impression.

The correct choices among variants that occur within the copy-text itself, or between the copy-text and later impressions (for some 840 pages of which there is no corresponding manuscript), are both easier and harder to make than those between the manuscript and the printer's version of it – easier because no manuscript exists to confuse the issues because of its inchoate state, and harder because the solutions have to be sought either in Irving's usage elsewhere in the copy-text or in other books of his that belong to the same general period. Once a complete list of suspect words in the copy-text (together with a record of their incidence) is in hand, and the evidence is sufficiently conclusive, the choice is usually relatively easy, but where the search extends to earlier or later books, it may become exhausting and frustrating, especially if, in the face of Irving's various shifts in usage, no viable pattern or answers emerge. If such cases involve inconsistencies, and no compelling reasons appear to the contrary, the editor has little choice but to let the copy-text govern and allow the inconsistency to stand – the assumption being that Irving did not seek consistency in this instance, or that usage varied at the time and that one form is as justifiable as the other.

By far the most significant variations that exist between the copy-text and later impressions are those made by Murray, the main one being Murray's revision and complete resetting of all the front matter of both Putnam volumes and then reversing the order of the Table of Contents and the Preface. A summation of variants that exist between the Murray and the first Putnam impression indicates 42 alterations – all of them efforts on the part of a Murray reader or shopman to repair or correct Irving's text as embodied in the plates supplied by Putnam. Of these 18 represent accidentals that were adopted for the Wisconsin edition. The remaining 14 are substantives, none of which are acceptable for emendation. They are dubious refinements, – chiefly British forms not in accord with Irving's practice at the time, many of them classifiable as either schoolmarmish or what Irving called officious; 3 of them are new errors.

Of 18 alterations made in the 237 reset pages for the 1857 impression that are recorded in the Lists of Emendations and of Rejected Substantives, no substantives (and only 11 of the accidentals) are acceptable for purposes of emendation; the other 7 are substantive alterations that are questionable "improvements" not in accord with Irving's known practice, or new errors. (For the great number of imperfections in the form of dropped or missing characters, as well as of accidentals not recorded in the Lists of Emendations and of Rejected Substantives, in the 1857 impression, see pages 592–593, above.)

Finally the degree to which critical decisions enter into the establishment of the Wisconsin text may be indicated by the fact that of 290 emendations made, 249 are made on the authority of this edition, that is to say, by editorial choice.

In all cases that are more than mere slips of the pen, by which for example Irving miswrites "Amir" for "Musa" (153.40) and Tokaia's husband Othman becomes her uncle (vii.18 and 45.4), or obvious printer's errors, such as "hy" for "by" (xii.11), adoptable variants by which copy-text is emended rest upon authority based on known or demonstrable authorial intent. For the sake of convenience and illustration, distinctions are made between the degrees of authority attaching to one text or another, but there is nothing intrinsic about the one that gives it more authority than the other except as it can be shown to be closer to the author's latest express wish or intention. The fact that a particular edition or impression employs a form which the editor chooses to adopt as an emendation is little more than a convenient or interesting illustration of the circumstance that he was not the first to do so. That is, a reading, from whatever source it derives (and this includes such emendations as the editor may choose to make solely on his own authority), is justified not by any authority that attaches to any of his sources (particularly because later impressions seldom involved authorial revisions), but only by the probability that it was Irving's intended reading. This probability approaches certainty the nearer it approximates what Irving demonstrably wrote; when what Irving actually wrote is not ascertainable, the editor reconstructs it as best he can on the basis of Irving's known practice as derived from all the relevant evidence. In all cases where the editor finds it necessary, on his own authority, to emend the copy-text, he does so only if (1) his emendation fits Irving's intended meaning in so far as it can be inferred from all the available evidence, and if (2) it improves the sense and context in which it is placed. If, in addition, it can be shown that the word under consideration as it stands in the copy-text could readily represent a misreading of the compositor's for the word intended, the justification for the emendation is strengthened all the more. Thus the editor has ample warrant for altering "who" to "whom" at 10.31, or for choosing "ink" over "wit" in the case already cited (see above, page 598), but he cannot proceed with the same assurance to change the awkward phrasing of Irving's "The hatred of Abu Jahl to the prophet" to the more idiomatic "Abu Jahl's hatred of the prophet" (50.9). These "improvements" that forever tempt the editor seeking to establish an eclectic, critical, but unmodernized text run all the way from printer's errors to dangling participial constructions in such a passage as the one in which Irving implies that God himself was an idolater: "Having fallen into blind idolatry, God sent a prophet of the name of Selah, to restore them [the children of Thamud] to the right way" (23.4–5). This kind of boner is not unique among instances crying for correction. None of them is intentional, but the editor has no justification for correcting unfortunate and obviously unintentional miscues of this kind – short of making the transition from editing to revising Irving's text.

A complicating factor stems from the inaccuracy with which Irving quotes from his sources – in which respect he was not better, and no worse, than his contemporaries. If it suited his purpose, he joined a portion of one sentence to a part of another without indicating the joinery, and he altered words or phrases at will. These liberties that Irving took with his authorities are often indicated, but no systematic effort is made to unscramble all such passages, which, as often as not, appear without quotation marks. Because the primary concern is to reproduce what Irving wrote, or intended to write, the editor has concentrated on what Irving's text shows and has noted or corrected Irving's alterations only when it can be shown that his modifications are erroneous or unintentional, or both. No emendations are made silently.

A further complication arises from the inability always to distinguish between substantive variants, such as changes of words that affect meaning, and accidental variants, such as spelling and hyphenation, which concern the forms of words. Generally useful as the distinction is, it is at best arbitrary and often too imprecise to mark the point where a change in an accidental becomes in effect a substantive change. The alteration of one character in a word may vitally change its meaning; synonyms or alternate proper names (totally different words) may not in fact change the meaning or texture of a passage, whereas the insertion of a hyphen between two words or the use of a comma to set off a relative clause may radically alter the meaning or a construction. Hence the list of substantive variants, which is designed to provide as much of historical collation as is practicable, includes some changes among accidentals that have a bearing on the direct as well as suggestive context.

TREATMENT OF ACCIDENTALS

In the handling of accidentals the editor walks a narrow path between the ever-threatening tyranny of the copy-text and the compelling temptation to impose consistency on Irving's text. Properly used, the copy-text is at once an index to what the editor may do and a guide to what he must not do, while the desire to impose consistency where it was not intended must be curbed by all ascertainable facts regarding what Irving actually wrote or probably intended. To do more, that is, to tamper with the accidentals of the copy-text except under unusually compelling circumstances would be to defeat the purpose of choosing a copy-text in the first place. On the whole, then, the temptation to impose consistency on the accidentals of the copy-text must be controlled (1) because many of the irregularities are characteristic of the author's manuscript itself, as the forty-three pages of existing printer's copy illustrate; (2) because they may constitute part of Irving's total suggestive expression, as in the case of his alternation between "spoil" and "spoils," "free-will" and "free will," or "cavalcade" and "cavalgada"; (3) because they may be part of an imperfectly realized effort on Irving's part to conform to a house style (see page 608, below, for his comment on Putnam's requirement of Webster's spellings); or (4) because whether they are intentional alternatives or unintentional oversights, authorial or compositorial, no amount of guesswork on the part of the editor will ever straighten out. These things being so, the editor must stick close to the forms of the copy-text, which, except for unauthorized printer's alterations or errors, are best treated as having had authorial approval.

However, not all inconsistencies are sanctioned because they exist in the copy-text. Certain irregularities of spelling, for example, may be attacked with confidence – especially those found among Irving's spelling of names. These he took some pains to get right and to spell consistently, and this care extended to oriental titles, such as Caliph, Fatimite, Sheikh, Emir, Satrap, and Najashee,[35] but he used "Kadhi" and "Cadi" interchangeably for "Judge." Acutely aware of the problem that the formidable array of oriental names presented, he sought a solution by rendering them (as he took care to say in the Preface) in "the old English nomenclature." But this procedure itself created difficulties because the Anglicization of Arabian names (based on an alphabet very different from the English) was far from uniform or consistent during the nineteenth century, so that in following one or another of his modern sources and authorities he had to be constantly alert to note and choose among various spellings – a procedure in which he failed repeatedly.[36] Thus he indiscriminately linked the region, the highlands,

---

35. The first three he capitalized consistently, but he wrote "Emir," "Satrap," and "Najashee" (Abbysinian for "king") upper and lower case depending on whether in the context he regarded the word as a proper noun (a specific title or part of a particular name) or a common, generic noun. Although in MSb "Emir" (occurring 12 times) is capitalized in whatever context it is used, it is clear that in proof he made a conscious effort to distinguish between "Emir" as used, for example, in the table of contents (xii. 19) as well as in the corresponding synoptic heading (Chapter XXXVI, 393.2), where he wrote "Moawyah, Emir of Syria," and later on the same page (393.10–11), "The late Caliph Omar . . . appointed him emir, or governor of Syria," where the noun is common or generic. Hence the copy-text forms are respected, the word being capitalized at xii. 19, 8.20, 393.2, and 423.28, and rendered lower case elsewhere unless the copy-text departs from Irving's self-imposed practice – in which case it is emended and recorded. "Caliphat," like "Caliph," is always capitalized.

36. Ordinarily, when quoting or adapting material from his authorities, Irving regularized proper names in accord with the forms he had already adopted; but sometimes he appears to have transcribed whatever form he found in his sources, and on some occasions he made simple errors of transcription, i.e., he garbled names as given in the sources he purports to be quoting. For examples, see the emendations at 17.37, 66.36, 66.37, 78.37, 99.40, 99.41, 130.38, and 130.39. These variations in his procedure introduce discrepancies that can be resolved only by individual editorial judgments as they are encountered.

and the city with variant spellings of "Hedjar," "Hedjas," "Hedjaz," and "Hegiaz," and "Hajar," depending presumably on which authority he was following at the moment: John P. Brown, Burckhardt, Conde, D'Herbelot, Gagnier, Gibbon, Green, Von Hammer-Purgstall, Marigny, Mills, Niebuhr, Ockley, Prideaux, Sale, Upham, Weil, or some other. Most of these contained variant spellings in themselves,[37] and Irving's

---

37. The problem is complicated by the fact that Arabic names originated in a wide variety of dialects and were further modified by the several avenues of transmission through which they came into English – Persian, Syriac, Turkish, Hebrew, Greek, and Latin among others. The lack of uniformity among Irving's sources was aggravated for him by the German and French spellings found, for example, in Von Hammer-Purgstall and in Gagnier, both of whom Irving relied on freely. Thus Von Hammer-Purgstall added "Bossra" and "Busrah" to Irving's spelling "Bosra" for the Syrian city, not to be confused with the Persian city whose name Irving spelled variously "Basra," "Basrah," and "Bassora." Von Hammer-Purgstall also added "Haffsa" to Irving's "Hafsa" and "Hafza," while Gagnier added "Ferrushzad" as an alternative to Irving's "Faruck-Zad," "Feruhk-Zad," and "Feruchsad," and compounded the confusion of Irving's "Hajar," "Hedjar," "Hedjaz," and "Hegiaz" by adding "Hegjaz" and "Heg'r." Ockley, Upham, and Prideaux, whom Irving also drew on extensively, added their mites – Ockley by spelling the word "Hejaz" and "Hadjr," Upham adding "Hagaz," and Prideaux, "Hagius"; while D'Herbelot's *Bibliothèque Orientale* used both "Higiaz" and "Hijaz" in addition to "Hegiaz." The last example is an extreme case, but instances of two and three variant spellings are not rare – some 120 examples having been observed. Of this number only a few can in good conscience be emended or normalized, either as authorial slips or compositorial errors not corrected in proof. The variations among diacritical marks used for the same as well as for different spellings of the same word (in both Irving and his sources) are so great that, except in a very few cases (as in "Merwân," where we know Irving intended to use the circumflex), finding the one "correct" form and regularizing the variants are simply impossible.

Irving himself often called attention to controversial spellings or to accepted variants among names, for example, "Kahtan"/"Joctan," "Omaya"/"Omeya"/ "Ommiah," "Mary"/"Mariyah"/"Miriam," "Khorassan"/"Korassan," "Khusestan"/ "Khurzestan," "Kadesia"/"Khadesiyah," "Rei"/"Rai"/"Rhages"/"Rhaga"/"Rhageia"/"Rages," "Hanef"/"Hanif," "Shiites"/"Shyites," and "Mosenna Ibn Haris"/ "Muthenna Ibn Hârith." He discussed in some detail the several derivatives of "Islam": "Moslem," "Moslems," "Muslim," "Musliman," "Muslimen," "Mussulman," "Musulman," "Musulmans," and "Musulmen," at the same time explaining his preference for "Moslem," "Musulman" and "Musulmen" (40.23–35); yet he slipped on four occasions and wrote "Mussulman" (147.37–38, 212.27, 340.6, and 409.38), and it is clear that he used "Beni"/"beni," "Omm"/"Um," "Ebn"/"Ibn," "Al"/"al," and similar forms indiscriminately. It is also clear that he preferred "Mahomet" over its many other forms, but it may be observed that in titles and quotations he was usually careful to follow the text before him.

It may be presumed that variants among proper names (and common-and-proper noun combinations) not included in the List of Emendations are to be regarded

adaptation of material from his sources often was so close that it included adopting their variant spellings. When among the authorities
Irving is known to have relied on, there is variation in spellings, and
Irving's several texts show no decided preference but follow first one
and then another form, the editor has no alternative to accepting the
different copy-text readings as permissible variants.[38] Variants remaining in the Wisconsin text are to be considered recognized and acceptable.

Of some help in this connection is a list that Irving prepared for his
own use or benefit (while checking the text of the first Putnam impression preparatory to a second printing) of 110 names, together with
brief remarks identifying many of them as to their familial relationships, their origins, their activities, or their importance. But this list
represents only a fraction of one per cent of the proper nouns he had to
deal with, and even for those he listed, he made numerous slips.[39] The

---

as acceptable or sufficiently common so as not to require alteration. That is, unless
there is evidence to show that Irving's variant is either erroneous or unprecedented
and unintentional, it is not emended.

38. Generally speaking, even a variant that occurs only once in one form, as
against another form that recurs several times, is allowed to stand if Irving's known
sources provide a precedent, unless the variant is obviously contrary to his intention
(as a typographical error would be that produced a markedly different word or as
a lone exception would be among many consistent spellings). Thus "Kaisan" and
"Keisan," each used once by Irving, are allowed to stand because Ockley, whom
Irving is following closely in the passage where the name occurs, used both forms
(as did others of Irving's authorities), and Irving simply adopted Ockley's variants.
"Hanef" and "Hanif" represent a similar case. "Ramadan," the form recognized by
the 1848 Webster and used by Ockley and Prideaux, and "Ramadhan," found in
Gagnier and D'Herbelot, are both retained; but his one use of "Rhamadan," which
does not occur in the sources he used, is emended as representing either an authorial
miscue or a misprint overlooked in proof.

39. The first four pages leave little doubt that among the 110 variants listed,
Irving preferred, at the time the list was prepared, "Azraïl" to "Asrael," "Jaafar"
to "Jaffar," "Maimuna" to "Maïmona," "Mosaab Ibn Omair to Musab Ibn Omeir,"
"Okaïder" to "Okaidor," "Rafe" to "Râfe," "Tabuc" to "Tabuk," "Tufiel" to
"Tafiel," and "Yathreb" to "Gothreb." Unfortunately the list falls short of being
a reliable index to Irving's preferences because beginning on page 5 he falters
when he spells the name of the Awsite prince "Saad Ibn Moad" (so identified at
118.19) "Saad Ibn Maadi" (168.21–22), and "Rustem Ibn Ferruchsad" on p. 5
of the list, on the next page becomes "Rustem Ibn Farruk-Zed or Feruchsad," thus
foreshadowing still more variant spellings of this name in Volume II ("Rustam
Ferukh-Zad (or Feruchsad)" at 347.29–30 and "Faruch-Zad" at 351.5, while
giving no hint for the reason why in Volume II the name is consistently spelled

conventional use of terms like "Abu," "Ibn," and "Omm" in Arabian nomenclature representing father, son, and mother relationships was
doubtless helpful, but for Greek, Jewish, Abyssinian, Egyptian, Persian, and other names he had no such built-in guides. There are occasionally mix-ups, as when the name of Hassan, the son of Ali and
grandson of Mahomet, is twice spelled "Hasan" (140.2 and 380.30). Similarly, misspellings of "Zobier" jostle the correct form, "Zobeir," on the
same page, once within two lines of each other (402-25–26). These are
not printer's errors, for misspellings of "Kaled" or "Caled" for "Khaled,"
"Mariyeh" for "Mariyah," "Ass" for "Aass," "Abdarahman" for "Abdal-
rahman," "Karegites" and "Karagites" for "Karigites," and scores of
others have a long history in MSa and MSb, as well as in copy-text and
later impressions. Here we are justified in regularizing Irving's unintentional variants, as we are in rectifying such occasional miscues as
"apostacy" for "apostasy," or changing "scimitar" to "scimetar," spelled
so in more than fifty other instances.

In this broader area of spelling in general we run into the uncertainties occasioned by our lack of information about which lexicographer,
if any, Irving chose to follow. During the period of his literary appren-
ticeship in New York he must have been fully conscious of the long-
regnant authority of Dr. Johnson, but he also became aware of native
forms as expressed in Webster's *American Spelling Book* while still a
schoolboy, and later as a budding young author he could not have remained entirely unaffected by Webster's controversy-provoking attempt in 1806 to crystalize these forms in his *Compendious Dictionary
of the English Language*. Granted that he acquired many American
spelling forms before his departure for England in 1815 (he was then
thirty-two), during the next seventeen years he tended toward a certain Anglicization of his style that every reader recognizes, and although he subsequently came under American influences and made con-

---

"Rustam," a consistency that casts doubt on the absolute authority of the list and
justifies accepting "Rustam" on its own face value in Volume II. Moreover, the
entries keyed to Volume I stop shortly after these confused spellings, and the 19
entries on the two pages that follow cover only the first 59 of the 500 pages that
comprise Volume II. Here the list ends abruptly, as if Irving had given up the
effort as thankless and impossible. It may be inferred that Irving found himself as
incapable of bringing regularity or uniformity into his spelling of proper names as
does the modern editor, and that in and of itself the list is not an infallible guide
to his final intention.

cessions to native customs (including American spellings, as these, in various degrees, were required first by Carey, Lea, and Blanchard, then by Harper & Brothers, and beginning in 1848, by G. P. Putnam), he never completely rid himself of all British forms, although *Webster's Unabridged* became the norm for the entire Author's Revised Edition.[40] For *Mahomet*, therefore, he followed, or tried to follow, the prescribed Webster spellings, though not without making some exceptions, and not without giving expression to his innate conservatism that balked at any radical departure from his accustomed ways of doing things. So he registered a characteristic gentle demurrer, not with Putnam, with whom it might have had some effect, but with a disinterested third party. Writing to M. D. Phillips on February 17, 1852, he intimated that Webster's prescriptions imposed limitations that he would disregard if he were a free agent: "I certainly do *not* make Webster's Dictionary my standard of orthography though I regret to say I often find myself inadvertently falling into some of the vitiations which the industrious circulation of his work has made so prevalent in our country. From the same cause also I find it almost impossible to have a work printed in this country free from some of his arbitrary modifications,

40. The problem of Irving's system (or lack of system) in spelling is complicated by our uncertainty regarding which authority he followed and when. Among a veritable store of reference works still preserved at Sunnyside, ranging from general compendia of knowledge, gazetteers, and encyclopedic volumes of various kinds, to books on rhetoric and syntax, as well as French-English, German-English, Dutch-English, Spanish-English, Portuguese-English, and Latin-English dictionaries, there are only three dictionaries devoted to his native language: (1) Samuel Johnson's *Dictionary of the English Language* . . . , by the Rev. Joseph Hamilton (London, 1807), (2) *Johnson's Dictionary* . . . (Philadelphia, 1813), and (3) *Webster's Dictionary, Unabridged* (Springfield, Mass., 1848) — a gift to Irving from G. and C. Merriam. The last obviously came too late to be of much use by way of influencing Irving's spellings during the period immediately following his return from Europe in 1832 except that inasmuch as it recorded or summarized current usage for a decade or more before its date of publication, it becomes an index to the kind of American forms that he was influenced by between 1832 and 1848, the year *Webster's Unabridged* appeared — which, be it observed, is also the year that Putnam (whose house style followed Webster) become his official publisher.

Meanwhile he could not have overlooked Webster's earlier epoch-making *American Dictionary of the English Language* of 1828, published so shortly before his return from his long years abroad, or, for that matter, the popular abridgment that followed, or the "Second Edition Corrected and Enlarged" of 1841, soon to become *Webster's Unabridged*.

which are pronounced provincialisms by all foreign scholars critical of the English language."[41]

Besides the equivocal influence of Johnson and Webster, there is the further possibility that Irving may have used John Walker's *A Critical Pronouncing Dictionary and Expositor of the English Language* (London, 1791), for he refers to Walker as early as 1803. Walker's lexicon reached its twenty-eighth "edition" in 1826, and circulated widely in America before the turn of the century, reaching a second American Edition by 1806.[42] What is noteworthy is that whereas Dr. Johnson and Noah Webster were not available in readily portable editions, Walker's dictionary appeared in a one-volume American Stereotype Edition of 576 pages in 1815, and in another one-volume New Stereotype Edition, enlarged to 609 pages plus 103 pages of appendix, in 1828, in relatively thin paper.[43] Several of the earlier editions were of a size that Irving might have found more manageable than the bulky Johnson and Webster multivolume tomes during his peripatetic years from 1815 to 1832. While nothing positive has appeared to prove that Irving did indeed carry Walker about in his peregrinations, or that he ever relied mainly or solely on Walker, the conclusion must be that unless for one reason or another consistency is demanded among Irving's spellings or uses of words, any variants among his forms that are confirmed by Johnson, Webster, Walker, or other contemporary sources should be respected as possibly representing Irving's choice.

As regards "-our" *versus* "-or", "-re" *versus* "-er", and "-ise" *versus* "-ize" spellings, Irving's practice, in so far as *Mahomet* provides an index, is not strictly consistent. In general, he appears to have adopted the "-or" form for words like "armor," "favor," "harbor," "labor," "savor," and "valor," but in MSb we find one instance, each, of "harbour" and "valour" – evidently lapses, which the printer regularized, and he was con-

41. Berg Collection, The New York Public Library, Astor, Lenox and Tilden Foundations.

Webster's placing Irving's name at the end of a list of distinguished American writers, beginning with Franklin and Washington, as among "the best models of composition" appears not to have had any mollifying effect.

42. Walker is said to have been used by Harvard students about 1800; among American authors, Emerson had a Walker on his shelves, and William Gilmore Simms relied on Walker's dictionary.

43. There were other American "editions" or printings between 1806 and 1828, and thereafter, until the vogue of *Webster's Unabridged* about the mid-century mark superseded both Walker and Johnson.

sistent throughout in his spelling of "saviour." Similarly, he appears to
have accepted "-er" endings, except for "centre," "lustre," "meagre,"
"sabre," "sceptre," "sepulchre," and "theatre," all of which he spells
consistently "-re."[44] But his "-ise" and "-ize" forms follow no discernible
pattern which could form the basis for emendation.[45]

Other individual variations, such as "salam" and "salaam" "indulgences" and "indulgencies," "cavalcade" and "cavalgada," and "spoil"
and "spoils" (of war) are examples of individual choice for which generalization is difficult and regularization hazardous. Some variations appear to be calculated, as in the spelling of "Khaibar"/"Kheibar" in "The
Jews inhabiting the tract of country called Khaibar are still known in
Arabia by the name of Beni Kheibar" (130.37–38). Here Irving is quoting his source, Niebuhr's *Travels*, II, 43, but manages to transcribe Niebuhr's "Khiebar" as "Kheibar." For others, however, it is difficult to ascertain whether varying authorities, deliberate choice, sheer whim, or
simple carelessness are accountable, especially when the examples are
few or when other books of the same general period contain no comparable examples.[46] Such a situation is presented by the words, "elegancies," "extravagancies," "incoherencies," "indulgences," and "indulgencies," each used only once or twice in *Mahomet*. Modernization of

44. "Reconnoitre," "reconnoitred," "reconnoitring," "reconnoiter," "reconnoitered," and "reconnoitering" are a special case about which he appears to have
been uncertain while writing *Mahomet*, in which he used the first, second, fourth,
and sixth forms (as listed); but his choice apparently became decisive by February
1, 1858, when Pierre M. Irving, doubtless at his uncle's behest, sent Putnam four
sheets of "Corrections Ordered" listing 87 changes he wished made in Volumes
I–III of *Washington*, then being corrected and reprinted. These include two changes
from "reconnoitered" to "reconnoitred" and six altering "reconnoitering" to "reconnoitring." In connection with one of the latter, he added (as if impatient with the
printer's obtuse persistence), "Omit the vicious e." This would seem to justify
adding "reconnoitre" to the list of words for which Irving preferred the "-re" form.

45. In MSb Irving wrote both "enterprise" and "enterprize," "stigmatise" and
"stigmatize," whereas in 50 the "-ise/-ize" words follow this pattern: "aggrandize,"
"apostatize," "authorize," "despise," "enterprise," "scandalized," "signalize," "solemnize," "stigmatize," "supervise," "surprise," "systematize," and "tranquilize,"
but he writes "apprise" four times and "apprized" once, so that there is no sound
basis for imposing consistency on his "-ise"/"-ize" spellings.

46. Even more confusing is the case where other books of the period, rather
than clarifying what Irving's intention was, introduce new inconsistencies. That
this lack of consistency holds for many words is shown when a full-scale tabulation is made of Irving's hyphenation and spelling practice in *A Tour on the
Prairies, Astoria, Goldsmith,* and *Mahomet* – books which ought to be very much
alike in these matters.

"-cies" to "-ces" forms had not yet crystallized in Irving's day, and both were used not only by Irving but other writers – Hawthorne, for example. In general, wherever variations of this order are tolerated or approved by usage in the mid-nineteenth century, regularization is not attempted except for good and stated reasons.

The same caution is exercised in treating Irving's hyphenation (his alternate "foot-soldiers" and "foot soldiers," for example), unless the evidence is clear that he preferred one form over another, as in the cases of "battering-rams," "bystander(s)," "fire-worshipper(s)," "palm-trees," "twoscore," "threescore," "fourscore."[47] But where it is found that the hyphenation of words varied (with no difference of meaning intended), and no preference can be detected in Irving's usage, *but* the 1848 Webster (which governed the Putnam house style that Irving presumably was obliged generally to follow) recognized only one of the forms, the editor cannot be very far wrong if he emends in favor of the accepted form. Thus "millstone"/"mill-stone" is an example in resolving which an editorial decision cannot be avoided. If, on the other hand a tabulation of Irving's forms shows a decided preference, this preference is respected, Webster notwithstanding. This procedure is applied with caution to spelling in general; but, as has been demonstrated, it cannot be extended with any assurance to cover oriental names because the wide variations among Irving's spellings and the even greater discrepancies among his sources, or authorities, make emendation doubly hazardous.

Changes in punctuation as found in the copy-text, too, are undertaken with caution. One very confusing aspect of Irving's punctuation is his tendency to omit commas between appositives and their antecedents in proportion as the relationship is close. Thus he omits the comma in "Khosru King of Persia" (132.33), "Khaled's friend Amru" (134.32), "his beautiful wife Zeinab" (136.21–22), "Fatima the wife of Ali" (193.26), "his wife Fatima" (225.25), and "his father Heraclius"

---

47. Irving's use of hyphens following "after," "all," "any," "ever," "re," and "well" in forming compounds or possible compounds follows no regular pattern or recognizable method on the basis of which regularization is justifiable; hence these variants in the copy-text are respected. However "co-," "fellow-," and "self-" regularly form hyphenated compounds, but "fore" (as in "forefathers") and "inter" as in "interwoven") do not, while "every" and "pseudo" are always written as separate words. Numerals ("twenty-four," "four-and-twenty," as well as "twenty-fourth") and fractions ("three-fourths") are consistently hyphenated compounds in the copy-text.

(388.4), but uses the comma in "the second Hegira, the flight of the Prophet himself from Mecca to Medina (49.5–7), "the Thamudites, one of the lost tribes of Arabia" (166.29–30), "Derar, the cherished champion in arms of Khaled" (249.32), and "many Copts, irreconcilable enemies of the Greeks" (388.13–14). However, his practice is so far from uniform that it is inapplicable as a basis for regularizing Irving's punctuation of appositional constructions; hence commas are added or deleted (and noted) only to correct obviously unintentional errors or to avoid misreading. This pocedure applies also to omitted commas normally used to indicate interjections or mild exclamations, as well as to missing marks of intended pairs, which he was usually careful to supply. Where superfluous marks became erroneous and are deleted, the deletions are recorded. No alterations in the copy-text are made silently.

An unusual use of the semicolon that carries over from MSa and MSb into the copy-text is that where terminal quotation marks are used in conjunction with the semicolon, the latter is usually placed before, rather than after, the quotation marks (for example, 40.3, 78.25, 79.17, 274.25, 378.16, 440.31, 448.3, 468.17, and 481.9). This practice appears to be habitual; hence the copy-text is not emended.

Another use of the semicolon that carries over from the manuscripts is one that today seems unnatural, especially when (as at 458.2 following "Yezid" and at 458.9 following "Ziyad" and "Bassora") the semicolon separates appositives from their immediately adjacent antecedents; but since they cannot be regarded as either unintentional or as obscuring the intended meaning, these copy-text forms, too, are respected.

An even more unorthodox practice of Irving's is his separation of the verb from its subject or its object (or complement) when either is complicated by internal comma division, or when it embraces either a clause or a phrase containing a verb form. This often produces the kind of over-pointing of which Irving himself once complained. It was fast disappearing about the middle of the nineteenth century; yet 179 instances of it have been observed in *Mahomet and His Successors*[48] –

48. Typical examples are "One of the first to avow himself a believer, was his servant Zeid . . ." (34.7), "Several of the prisoners who were poor, were liberated . . ." (95.23–24), "Women, children, monks, and the blind, were to be spared . . ." (136.33–34), ". . . the only reply was, to invoke the vengeance of heaven on his head (284.7–8), and "Khaled retorted, that it was all owing to his own obstinacy . . ." (300.33).

Although considered superfluous today, these commas in 122 of the 179 in-

enough to establish a pattern within the book and to demonstrate that deleting them would be in fact modernizing – one of the luxuries not allowed the twentieth-century editor of nineteenth-century texts.

In preparing the Wisconsin text, proof was read six times, and following the last revises a set of the unbound pages of the book was again scanned under the Hinman collating machine against a set of final revised page proof, in an effort to detect and correct any possible new errors resulting from last-minute resettings following damage or mishaps in the process of printing.

Although Irving's text is faithfully and critically rendered, no effort is made to reproduce exactly the so-called appurtenances of the text – that is, such typographical details as the precise arrangement of the title and half-title pages and other preliminary matter, pagination and lineation, the footnote symbols as they occur in the Putnam texts, the display capitals and the capitalized text letters following them, or the

---

stances noted had precedents in Irving's time, as typified by the examples just cited. Of the remaining 57, 32 may be explained as resulting from omitting one of intended pairs of commas or failing to set off appositives, parenthetical expressions, or other nonrestrictive modifiers (18.20, 18.23, 29.14, 30.20, 31.3, 34.21, 40.36, 92.37, 122.39, 148.26, 160.17, 279.11, 279.23, 317.21, 326.24, 330.12, 331.1, 343.5, 343.7, 362.37–38, 370.38, 372.6–7, 378.6, 398.30, 400.7, 404.2, 416.35, 432.4, 449.4, 459.1, 490.23, and 500.38), but Irving's practice is too erratic to provide a firm basis for emendation on that score alone – unless it be to guard against ambiguity or to facilitate reading (as at 160.17). In the other 25 cases (29.25, 33.12, 35.11, 40.36, 41.34, 57.24, 57.35, 125.24, 133.5, 136.33, 156.18, 297.4, 301.7, 320.18, 355.31, 362.35, 391.14, 396.6, 415.15, 430.2, 463.22, 473.4, 489.4, 493.5, and 504.31) the subject-predicate relationship is so direct and uncomplicated that the separating commas seem excrescences, but to delete them is to run the risk of altering a tone, nuance, pause, rhythm, or emphasis that Irving may have intended to convey. Hence these copy-text forms are not tampered with lest the alterations result in a text by just that much more removed from the missing manuscript.

After the anomalous use of commas just discussed, the next most idiosyncratic aspect of Irving's punctuation as exemplified in the ARE is his frequent use of semicolons for commas and of commas for semicolons, the most noticeable example of the latter being the commas between independent clauses not joined by simple conjunctions, although these never obscure the meaning and need no emending. Examples of the former are less striking, but they occur more frequently, as the following 11 examples on pp. 190–194 illustrate (190.32, 191.2, 192.14 (twice), 192.36, 192.38, 193.4, 194.15 (twice), 194.37, and 195.11). The incidence of these substitutions is so great that they must be considered intentional, and accordingly regularization is not justified, except for sufficient reasons duly recorded in the Discussions of Adopted Readings.

exact typography of the chapter titles, running heads, table of contents, synoptic chapter headings, and end-of-chapter notes. The last three, for example, employ the period in combination with the dash between items or entries. This is simplified here by using the dash only. Irving himself, while writing the table of contents and the synoptic chapter heads in MSb, used dashes only; Putnam was inconsistent, using the period-dash combination in most volumes (including *Mahomet*) and the dash only in four others (*Knickerbocker, Astoria, Bonneville,* and *Washington*). There being no uniformity among the Putnam volumes, the decision of the Press to drop the periods represents no radical innovation; but it is to be remembered that wherever in the Discussions of Adopted Readings or the Lists of Emendations and of Rejected Substantives, the period-dash form of punctuation in table of contents or synoptic chapter heads is cited, the period in the copy-text is consistently ignored, unless an abbreviation is involved.

Except for the details just enumerated, then, the Historical Note, the Textual Commentary, and the accompanying Discussions of Adopted Readings, together with the Lists of Emendations, of Rejected Substantives, and of End-of-Line Hyphenation, are designed to provide the reader with all the data needed to reconstruct the copy-text and to follow the steps by which the Wisconsin text of *Mahomet and His Successors* was established. Beyond this, the assembled evidence is designed not only to enable the reader so minded to examine and consider the bases on which all editorial decisions were made but to reconsider them, if he chooses, and in the process to see the relationships that exist among the several texts from the earliest draft of Irving's manuscript to a reasonably close approximation of the printed book the author intended it to be.

DISCUSSIONS OF ADOPTED READINGS

In these discussions of decisions to emend or not to emend, the symbols to designate texts used earlier (pages 583–584) are again employed:

MSa   Manuscript draft of *Mahomet* (1828–1832)

MSb   Manuscript fragment of printer's copy for 50

ARE   Author's Revised Edition (50 through 60 as listed below)

50, 51, . . . 60   Putnam's American impression (1850, 1851, . . . 1860), with earlier and later states of variant sheets within the 1850 Putnam impression indicated by 50a and 50b, respectively

E   Murray's English impression (1850)

W   Wisconsin edition

The page and line figures are keyed in each case to a word or words in the text to which the discussion or comment refers. A bracket separates the key word or words from the comment that follows.

ix.16   mountains] Whether the copy-text "Mountains" is an authorial or compositorial error, the adopted form both here (in the table of contents) and later in the synoptic chapter heading (151.2) requires lower-case for all common nouns except when they occur at the beginning of an item or entry. Accordingly "Mountains" is rendered lower case in both places.

ix.19   spoil] No clear pattern emerges from Irving's 18 uses of "spoil" and 30 of "spoils" that have been observed. The word is spelled both "spoil" and "spoils" in both MSa and MSb. Hence there is no basis for emending the copy-text except in one instance where in later impressions there appears to be an authorial change from "spoil" to "spoils" in 51 at 253.9.

ix.24   Tufiel] "Tafiel" here and at 158.6 is erroneously spelled. It is correctly "Tufiel" at 160.25. Irving included "Tufiel" in the list of names he intended to regularize, but apparently overlooked doing

so in these two instances. He also spelled the name "Tufiel" in MSb
at 302.7 and 308.2.

x.18   Successes] The addition in E of "Its" before "successes" represents a schoolmarmish refinement that cannot be regarded as in
accord with Irving's intention. It may be observed that the alteration was not made in the synoptic heading in E at 234.3.

x.20   for] The copy-text "to" in this connotation is not characteristic
of Irving's practice when he obviously meant "for." Hence "to" is
changed to "for" here, as well as in the synoptic chapter heading at
239.2. Irving was doubtless beguiled into using "to" by the elliptical
"succeed to." Whatever the cause, the passage as it turned out was
certainly not what Irving intended; hence the emendation appears
justified. Other unusual uses of "to" occur at 50.9, 192.37, and 470.10,
but none of these is as completely unprecedented in contemporary
usage as "Incompetency of Abu Obeidah to the general command of
Syria."

xii.4   subjugation] The copy-text reading "conquest" is changed to
"subjugation" because Irving uses the more idiomatic and accurate
"subjugation" in the same construction at xii.9, 285.34, and 372.2.
In conformity with the alteration made in the table of contents, the
word is also changed in the synoptic heading, 365.2.

xii.19   Emir] "Emir" capitalized here is acceptable as part of a title.

3.4   since] The E reading "ago" is a non-authorial "refinement" made
by Murray in accord with Dr. Johnson's distinction of using "since"
when reckoning time toward the present, as in "it is a year since it
happened," and "ago" when reckoning from the present, as in "it
happened a year ago." Webster is less specific, even listing the words
as synonyms – as, indeed, they were often used in Irving's time.
Irving uses "since" in the same sense at 417.3.

7.27   Arabia,] The omitted comma after "Arabia" in 57 is a mistaken
effort to "improve" Irving, who here accurately quotes from Ezekiel
27:21–23 (King James version).

9.15   herds,] Except for quoted passages in the copy-text where the
practice occurs (e.g., at 7.27–37, in a quotation from Ezekiel 27:23),
this is the first of one hundred seventy-nine instances observed where
commas separate the subject from the predicate, or the verb from its
object or the complement. Although outmoded today, commas in
these constructions being considered superfluous, their use was considered acceptable in Irving's time, and accordingly they are retained,

despite the manifest awkwardness created by their use in some instances – unless they result in ambiguity or misreading, in which case an alteration is made and recorded.

9.17 scimetar] The copy-text reading of "scimitar" is a misprint for a word consistently spelled "scimetar" throughout *Mahomet*.

10.30 most] Although Irving is normally careful to distinguish between the comparative and superlative degrees of adjectives and adverbs, his statement at 10.30 that as between Sabean and Magian faiths, the latter was the one to which the Arabs "most adhered" and the repetition of "most" in an almost identical construction at 13.13 are not merely coincidental errors, but explicable either as a conscious choice of "most" rather than "more" or as commonly accepted usage. The copy-text is therefore not emended in such instances. See also 449.2, where Irving uses "greatest" rather than "greater" for emphasis, and "longest" rather than "longer" at 50.7.

The misuse of "most" for "more" in the copy-text at 248.23 is not analogous, but represents an authorial slip; no overtone of meaning, or special emphasis, is intended; hence the copy-text is emended in this case.

12.13 fire-worshippers] The copy-text reading "fire worshippers" is changed to "fire-worshippers" in accord with Irving's consistent spelling of the word with a hyphen in every other instance in *Mahomet*.

12.29 ever] The effort in 57 to make "ever during" into a compound is not supported by Irving's practice in writing "ever living," "ever present," "ever increasing," and "ever ready" without hyphens; doubtless Irving intended "ever during" to be two words. It may be noted however, that he wrote "everlasting" as one word.

13.7 Wisdom] The context makes it clear that Irving intended to, and probably did, write "Wisdom of Solomon," the title of a book in the Apochrypha; but his capital "W" is often indistinguishable from his lower-case "w," and the printer could easily have misread the MS, so that "Wisdom" in the copy-text erroneously appears in lower case.

17.37 Kahtan] Quoting Burckhardt's *Notes on the Bedouins and Wahábys*, Vol. II, p. 47, Irving wrote "Katan" instead of Burckhardt's "Kahtan."

19.34 They] Although "They," used in close conjunction with "two individuals of the Amakelkites" and "Ishmael and his mother," may be mistaken as referring to the latter, a close reading of the text makes it clear that "They" refers to the Amakelkites. Hence no emendation is deemed necessary.

26.5　Zobeir] "Zobier" here is Irving's error; it is corrected also at 398.5, 398.11, 402.25, 405.33, and 412.30. There are several instances of "Zobier" in MSa, indicating that early and late the name gave him trouble. In 62 observed instances in *Mahomet* the name is spelled correctly "Zobeir."

36.24　brother,] The colon following "brother" in 50 is suspect because no other instance has been observed of Irving's employing it in an *a, b,* and *c* series. Moreover, in a nearly identical expression in the next paragraph (36.30) the comma is employed following "brother." The corresponding passage in MSa, too, uses a comma.

37.35　Antichrist] The copy-text reading of "anti-Christ" here is emended to the more conventional "Antichrist" preferred by Webster and also used at 207.30, as well as in MSa.

39.32　corner stone] There is no compelling reason for emending the copy-text "corner stone" to corner-stone," any more than there is to alter "foundation-stone" at 65.25 to "foundation stone."

41.21　fellow-man] The hyphenated form of "fellow-man" is adopted here, and at 82.31, because Irving wrote "fellow-man" at 125.16 and 307.18, and used "fellow-" in ten other combinations, such as "fellow-citizen," "fellow-laborers," and "fellow-sufferers."

46.30　me] In the confusion between indirect discourse in this passage and direct discourse in the sentence following, the mistaken use of "me" for "him" is understandable, if not excusable. It is emended as an error that Irving surely did not intend to make, and has not been observed to make elsewhere.

49.1　west] The copy-text reading by which "Jidda" (which the copy-text misprints as "Jodda") is placed "about two days' journey to the east of Mecca" is a slip of the pen for "west of Mecca."

50.9　to] The copy-text reading of "The hatred of Abu Jahl to the prophet" is retained as clear enough, although "of" or "for the prophet" (as at 105.13) might be preferred on stylistic grounds. But see x.20, 64.36, 65.6, 192.37, 410.26, 470.10, and the emendations at 239.2 and 425.7 for other instances of Irving's unconventional use of prepositions, including the use of "to" for "of" or "for."

52.31　Haschemites,] There is a blank space at the end of the line following "Haschemites" in 50 where the comma (apparently intended to add emphasis) was set but failed to print. The missing comma was not detected in the Putnam line until 57, when a hyphen was erroneously substituted; but it was clearly printed in E.

60.19 Al Lat] The copy-text "El Làt" is emended here and at 60.22 in accord with "Al Lat" readings at 159.34, 160.8, 160.16, MSa 411, and MSb 305[a].20, 306.21, and 307.10.

64.37 with] The copy-text reading "it was not with him to stay" (rather than the more idiomatic "it was not for him to stay") is retained because it is so written in MSa (161.8), and it is repeated a few lines later in the text, 65.5–6 (see MSa 162.2–3).

66.36 Bathra] In this passage derived from Humphrey Prideaux's life of Mahomet (p. 45) Irving misspells Prideaux's "Bathra" as "Bartha."

66.37 Ziz] The copy-text "Zig" is doubtless a printer's error for "Ziz," as the name is spelled in Prideaux (p. 45), whom Irving is quoting.

67.31 ¶Because] Another speaker (Musa) begins; hence the context requires a new paragraph. The corresponding passage in MSb is not extant, but in MSa (171.26), where the same passage occurs, the indentation, though not pronounced, is observed. If, as is likely, the indentation is MSb was equally light, the failure to observe it is best explained as a compositorial oversight.

73.22 Maadi] "Maads" in the copy-text is obviously a misprint for "Maadi" (see "Saad, the son of Maadi," 168.22). Elsewhere in the copy-text the name is consistently spelled "Saad Ibn Moad," for which there is ample authority in Irving's sources, whose spellings are predominantly "Moad," but occasionally "Moadh" and "Meadh," as well as "Maad."

75.15 ". . . to expel thee the city"] Although the expression seems unidiomatic, Irving quotes the passage accurately from the eighth chapter of Sale's Koran.

78.37 Salem] Here Irving erroneously writes Prideaux's "Salem" (p. 33) as "Salam."

80.32 burying-ground] Because Irving writes "burying-place," "burial-ground," and "burial-place," in addition to "burying-ground" elsewhere in *Mahomet* (and in *Goldsmith*), it may be presumed that this one departure from the norm in the copy-text was an oversight and was intended to be hyphenated.

82.31–32 say, 'What . . . him?'] The context indicates that the omitted single quotation marks in 50 are printer's errors. Both are properly supplied in a later parallel construction in the same paragraph.

84.13–14 new comers] Although the Putnam house style favored

"new-comers" (see *A Tour on the Prairies*, ARE 31.29, *Goldsmith*,
ARE 215.4, and the 1848 Webster dictionary), both the manuscript
and the first American edition of *A Tour on the Prairies* (36.21)
have "new comers." There would seem, then, to be no justification
for altering the copy-text's "new comers" in this context.

87.24   Medina, –] Irving's use in the copy-text of a semicolon after
"Medina" and after "desert" in the line following doubtless means
that he intended "fugitives" and "proselytes" to be regarded as in
apposition with the antecedent "converts," but no one reads this
involved sentence without wondering whether "converts," "fugitives,"
and "proselytes" are not to be interpreted as three coordinate mem-
bers of an *a, b, and c* series. Only as the sentence is re-read and
analyzed does Irving's true intent appear – all because the two semicolons used (in the hope that they would supply the accentuated
breaks that are required but that commas would not indicate clearly)
merely compound the unintentional ambiguity inherent in the structure of the sentence. Semicolons at these points in this complicated
sentence simply cannot accomplish what they are intended to, and
the only solution for resolving this anomalous situation (short of
completely rewriting the sentence) is to substitute dashes, preferably
commas and dashes, following "Medina" and "desert." The dash,
the main staple in Irving's early system of punctuation, is sparingly
used in his late writings. Instead of using it, especially in constructions where he considered the comma inadequate, he often employed
the semicolon. See the discussion for 234.14 days;]. This practice is
mainly responsible for the peculiarities that distinguish his punctuation from the forms in common use today.

89.1   enemies] Although a comma would normally be used to set off
the appositive, "the Koreishites," from its antecedent, "enemies," the
omission is not without precedent in Irving's practice; and since
misreading is not likely to follow, the copy-text reading is retained.

91.21   lay] Early and late, Irving confused forms of "lie" and "lay."
Here and at 385.23 he misused "laid" for "lay"; at 152.18 he did the
reverse. For early examples, see his journal for August 10, 1803, and
January 29, 1805; for later ones, see *A Tour on the Prairies* (1835),
97.24, 105.8, 263.5–6, and the MS designed for *Washington*, Vol. III,
Chap. 31, though not printed (preserved in the Seligman Collection
of the New York Public Library). See also the "Discussions of

Adopted Readings" for 173.38 ("lay"). At 262.39 and 263.1 "laid" is used conventionally, "lay" at 282.22 and 403.20, and "lain" at 18.3.

91.33 Burckhardt] Irving's misspellings of "Burckhardt (without the "c") at 9.26, 91.32, 91.38, and 99.41 in 50 were corrected in the Putnam plates before any sheets were printed from them or else the faulty sheets printed from the uncorrected plates were destroyed. It is to be noted that Irving also misspelled the name in MSb 307x.7.) The spelling of "Burckhardt" at 8.32, 17.39, 160.38, 191.23, 217.38, 218.32, and 218.36 appears to have been correct from the beginning. For further particulars, see pages 586–587, above.

99.40 *Thar*] In quoting Burckhardt's *Notes on the Bedouins and Wahábys,* Irving neglected to italicize "*Thar*" as he found it in his source at I, 314–15.

99.41 *Burckhardt's . . .* 314.] Because Irving's unusual ordering of the terms in his footnote, "*Burckhardt,* v. i. 314, Notes," erroneously suggests that his material is taken from the notes in Vol. I, p. 314, of Burckhardt's *Notes on the Bedouins and Wahábys,* the sequence is rearranged, and Irving's shortened title "Notes" is italicized – both in conformity with his habitual practice (e.g., at 95.40, 160.38, and 177.39–40) thus: "*Burckhardt's Notes,* v. i. 314." Actually, Irving's materials are drawn from both pp. 314 and 315.

105.18 Khaled] Both MSa and MSb demonstrate that Irving had trouble spelling "Khaled" consistently (using both "Caled" and "Kaled" besides "Khaled"); hence the error in the copy-text is doubtless Irving's rather than the compositor's.

107.5 Death !)] In constructions such as "Hamza set up the Moslem war-cry, Amit! Amit! (Death! Death!)" or "the shout of Allah Achbar! Allah Achbar! resounded through the Moslem host" (240.12–13) Irving often omitted the quotation marks around the battle cry. When, as at 146.9 quotation marks are used in the copy-text, they are reproduced as being so intended by the author.

112.19 this] The substitution of "his" for "this" in "Mahomet accepted . . . this pious sacrifice" is a questionable substantive 57 "improvement" in view of the next sentence, which begins "His nuptials with Zeinab . . . ." The use of "his" in the preceding sentence could easily cause confusion; hence the copy-text reading of "this" is retained.

125.12 courts,"] The copy-text's semicolon after "courts" is a printer's error, first corrected in 57.

128.24–25   their approach . . . their capital] Although the copy-text's
passage, "the Jews on their approach had laid waste the level country, and destroyed the palm-trees round their capital," *can* be misread, when read in its full context, it becomes clear that the first
"their" refers to the Arab's approach, and the second "their" refers
to the Jews' capital, Khaïbar; hence no emendation is made. The
corresponding passage in MSa (299–300) provides no basis for
emendation: "When the Jews knew of the advance of their [the
Arab] army they [the Jews] destroyed the palm trees round their
[the Jews'] capital and laid waste the level country."

130.38   Khiebar] Irving's source, Niebuhr's *Travels in Arabia* (II, 43),
has "Khiebar," not as Irving renders it, "Kheibar." Irving's own spelling of the word is customarily "Kaïbar."

130.39   Missead] Irving's source, Niebuhr's *Travels in Arabia* (II, 43)
has "Missead," not "Messiad."

141.26   spurned at] The phrase was considered idiomatic in Irving's
time. Dr. Johnson (1819) and Webster (1848) both cite Shake-
speare's "spurn at your most royal image." The phrase is repeated at
230.13 and 403.29.

146.12   female,] The omitted comma of an intended pair is added,
for MSa (376.4) employs the comma here; hence Irving's intention is
clear.

146.16   truth,] In quoting from Chapter LXI of Sale's Koran, Irving
correctly reproduces the comma after "truth" in the copy-text. The
omitted comma in E and 53–55 represents an error that was corrected
in 57.

147.17   proscribed] The copy-text's superfluous commas following
"proscribed" here and at 148.4 are deleted because the corresponding
passages in MSa (370 and 373) omit them. It may be observed that
among alterations made in 57, the superfluous comma was deleted
at 147.17, but overlooked at 148.4.

152.18   laid] See the discussion of 91.21 lay].

153.40   Musa] The copy-text "Amir" (for "Musa") is an authorial slip
by which Amir, who is slain in battle on p. 153, line 17, is permitted
to return in triumph to Medina in the last line on the same page.
The error was first corrected in 50b.

155.17   'we] The lower-case first word of a quotation not in direct discourse is common in Irving's practice and is not emended for the
reasons given in Discussions of Adopted Readings: 289.28 "for Allah

forbid,"]. Similar uses occur at 155.31, 159.19, 256.26, 305.2, 330.30, 446.11–12, 448.18, and 494.4.

155.19 we implore] The insertion of "we implore" following "and" of MSb is a stylistic improvement such as the author, not the printer, would make in the proofs.

155.23 Tamim] The confusion of "Tainem" in MSb (295.15) for "Tamim" as the word stands correctly in the copy-text is typical; the correction was doubtless made in proof by the author. At 295.6 of MSb Irving wrote "Tamim."

156.16 proportions,] The damaged comma following "proportions" appears as a period in all Putnam impressions.

159.7 ink] Apparently Irving accepted the printer's mistaken setting of "ink" as preferable to "wit," as the word stands in MSb 304.21.

160.17 blow,] The missing comma in the copy-text is one of an intended pair, and is added to facilitate reading.

160.29 poets] The superfluous comma following the subject "poets" is deleted because it does not appear in the corresponding passage of MSb (368.10). Presumably it is a printer's error.

160.37 defended] Irving's use of past tense "defended" in the same sentence immediately following the present tense "can raise" represents an awkward shift in tenses, but probably expresses what Irving intended to say.

163.7 Weil's Mohammed, p. 247] This reference to Weil, which is not present in MSb, appears to have been an authorial addition in proof.

164.5 provinces] MSb (314.6) has "princes," but the word is written in such a way and the context in which it occurs is such that the printer could easily have misread it as "provinces." In any case it is clear that "provinces" fits the context better than "princes," so that very probably Irving either approved the compositor's alteration or himself made the change in proof.

165.35 dominion] The 50 reading "dominion" appears to be either a compositorial misreading of "domination" (MSb 318.12) that Irving adopted or an authorial alteration made in proof as more accurate than "domination."

173.38 lay] The seeming unidiomatic "lay" occurs in the source that Irving is quoting and is therefore allowed to stand.

177.31 Lord,' in truth;] The semicolon following "Lord" and the comma after "truth" represent errors that Irving made in copying the passage from Lane's *Modern Egyptians,* II, 338. The emendations are made in accordance with Lane's text as necessary to clarify the intended meaning. A justifiable liberty that Irving took was to normalize Lane's spellings of proper names, in order to bring them in accord with spellings already generally adopted in his own text. For example, Lane has "Mooluck'ckin" for Irving's "Mulakken," "Ckoora'n" for "Koran," "Ka'abeh" for "Caaba," and "Ckib'leh" for "Kebla." Irvings choices are allowed to stand as representing his intentions.

191.17   Wahábys] The copy-text's "Wahabees" appears to be an error of transcription or an unauthorized compositorial alteration, for Irving's source, Burckhardt's *Notes on the Bedouins and Wahábys,* consistently spells the word "Wahábys." MSb (307x) has "Wahabys."

192.37   to] While "disregard for" or "disregard of distinction" would seem preferable to the copy-text "disregard to distinction," the idiom is not unusual in Irving's practice, and hence is accepted. See also Discussions of Adopted Readings, 50.9 to].

195.15   revelations] Apparently "relations" in the copy-text is a misprint for "revelations." It is only by a circuitous explanation that "revelations" mentioned earlier in the sentence can be construed as equivalent to "relations" – that is, revelations made in the form of "relations to himself [Mahomet]." The corresponding passage does not exist in MSa or MSb. Irving's habitually slurred handwriting provides a sufficient explanation of why "revelations" was mistakenly set as "relations."

197.20   finds] The awkward shift from past to present tense for the mid-section of the paragraph is a stylistic infelicity beyond the editor's jurisdiction to correct. See also 196.23–24 and 283.21.

204.21   inculcated] The sudden shift in a long passage from the past to the present tense is either an unintentional slip or an uncorrected printer's error; hence the copy-text "inculcates" is altered to "inclulcated" – in accord with the use of "inculcated" in parallel constructions at 203.4 and 203.15.

208.15   explanations] The passage, "Forty days, or, according to explanations, forty years of continued rain will fall," invites revision. The corresponding passage in MSa (498.11–12), "Forty days, or, according to other explanations, forty years . . . " does not get at the root of the problem. What Irving undoubtedly meant was "according to the varying explanations of the commentators," or, as he often put it with thinly-veiled irony when speaking of the Moslem historians and explicators, according to the several "learned" or "venerable

Doctors." But so extensive an alteration seems to represent an unwarranted tampering with the text, which, despite its vagueness, is
not likely seriously to mislead the reader. Hence the copy-text is not
emended.

210.25 camphire] Since the emphasis of the passage in which "camphire" occurs is on crystal streams, "running between green banks
enamelled with flowers, . . . flowing over beds of musk, perfumes,
and spices," the word "camphire" could be a misprint for "samphire,"
which, according to Webster, is a fleshy, tropical herb, with dense
heads of white flowers, common along beaches. In a passage (360.25),
where the emphasis is on "oriental perfumes, exquisite spices, odifer-
ous gums, and medicinal drugs," Irving mentions "camphor" among
the drugs, but uses the modern spelling rather than the obsolete
"camphire." In another passage (54.17), again in association with perfumes and musk, he mentions "camphor." But there is the Biblical
precedent: "My beloved is to me as a cluster of camphire in the vineyards of Engedi" (Song of Solomon 1:14). Moreover, "samphire" is
not a word that has been observed elsewhere in Irving's writings. It
is possible, of course, that Irving had in mind "henna," which Webster, 2d ed., gives as a second reading for "camphire," i.e., "an Old
World tropical shrub with small opposite leaves and axillary panicles
of fragrant white flowers, used by Buddhists and Mohammedans in
religious ceremonies." In any case, tempting though it be to alter
"camphire" to "samphire," the reasons for doing so are not sufficiently
compelling in the face of the copy-text's authority to justify the
emendation.

211.28 punishments; one] Although there are in the copy-text a number of instances in which Irving treats as separate elliptical sentences
certain phrases that explain the terms or amplify the meaning of the
preceding sentence, they are recognizable as such, and accordingly
are respected (e.g., 103.28–31, 231.36–37, 278.29, 323.19–23, 402.26.
See also 482.9.). However, Irving was not given to writing fragmentary sentences; hence in this particular instance, the unconventional period after "punishments" in the copy-text is altered to a semicolon, and the following capitalized "One" is rendered lower case,
in full accord with Irving's punctuation and capitalization in the
similarly constructed sentence of the next paragraph at 211.38–212.3.
See also 496.26.

219.9 votaries to] The substitution in E of "devotees at Mecca" is as unidiomatic as the copy-text's "votaries to Mecca." The context indicates that Irving meant to emphasize the discomfiture of the *pilgrims to* Mecca while wearing the scanty Ihram during a winter pilgrimage; but the use thrice within the same sentence of the word "pilgrim" doubtless caused him to make the unhappy choice of "votaries to Mecca" rather than the more idiomatic "pilgrims to Mecca." However, Irving's choice of phrase is clear enough and is not emended.

223.4   632] The erroneous "622" for "632" as the year of Mahomet's death was not corrected during Irving's lifetime in the Putnam line of impressions.

225.5   empire] Because there is evidence that Irving sometimes deliberately chose the accusative rather than the genetive form in subject-gerund constructions, it is very likely that his writing "there was danger of the newly formed empire falling into confusion" was a conscious choice and that he would have considered a substitution of "empire's" for "empire" an over-scrupulous refinement. Hence no emendation is made here, or in similar constructions at 379.32 and 478.36.

226.8   council] The copy-text's "counsel" is an error for "council." At 364.12 "councils" is misused for "counsels." In some 20 other instances Irving carefully distinguishes between "council" and "counsel."

226.23   in nominating] The E reading "to nominate" is rejected in favor of the copy-text reading as a kind of refinement that in another connection Irving called "officious."

234.14   days;] Among Irving's frequent substitutions of semicolons for commas are several instances in which, to set off appositives that are separated from their antecedents by intervening words, the copy-text employs semicolons to call attention to this delayed appositional relationship – cases in which dashes are commonly used today. Among the more striking examples are those at 87.24, 87.26, 234.14, and 346.21. In the first two instances emendations are made in conformity with modern practice in order to clarify the intended meaning, which the use of the semicolon obscures; but in the last two cases, while a dash (or comma and dash) would serve as readily as the semicolon, besides being less obtrusive, the semicolon does not obscure the meaning; and since it doubtless is in accord with the author's intention, the copy-text is not emended

236.7   cavalgada] The copy-text "cavalgada" appears to be an Irving coinage, based on the Spanish pronunciation of "cabalgada." Webster (1828, 1848) derives "cavalcade" from Spanish "cabalgada." Irving also has "cavalcade" at 102.13, but it is obvious that "cavalgada" is not a misprint for "cavalcade," since a misprint would not be likely to involve both an internal and an end letter.

238.36 joyed to see] The phrase "joyed to see" in 50 is an unusual but permissible idiom.

240.33 irruption] Irving is careful to distinguish between "irruption" (a breaking into) and "eruption" (a breaking forth). "Irruption" is used again at 373.31, 374.17, 374.20, and 375.6.

242.9 alarms] There is no recognizable difference between the unique copy-text reading "The bells rang alarums" at 242.9 and "the trumpets sounded alarms" at 264.14, or the use of "alarm" at 242.5, 264.39, 317.11, and 484.6. Hence the one use of "alarum" is emended to "alarm." Webster (1848) considered "alarum" a "corruption . . . not to be used."

243.1 wall,] The damaged comma in the last line on the page appears as a period in all Putnam impressions.

245.21 trotting] A "trotting brook" is an expression now rarely used, but not uncommon in Irving's time.

246.21 "fifteen] See Discussions of Adopted Readings, 381.4 "his].

247.11 foot soldiers] Although the 1828 Webster has "footsoldier," and the 1848 edition prefers "foot-soldier," and Irving used the hyphenated form once at 121.12, he evidently wrote "foot soldiers" here and at 261.14. Irving's preference being left in doubt, and neither form being given official preference, either by the lexicographers or common usage, Irving's variant spellings are respected.

247.11 soldiers,] There is a blank space at the end of the line in 50 following "soldiers" where a comma was apparently set but failed to print.

251.9 spoils] The substitution of "spoils" in 51 for copy-text "spoil" appears to be authorial, because no one at Putnam's would be likely to make the change.

272.30 was] In the face of Irving's habitual care to observe agreement between subject and predicate, it may be presumed that in writing "man and beast was ready to sink with fatigue," he considered the idiom "man and beast" to be singular in number, much as he might regard "bread and butter was his staple food" as preferable to "were his staple food." For an analogous, but converse instance, see Discussions of Adopted Readings, 363.14 were].

273.9 reconnoitred] Although Putnam house style apparently followed Webster's "-er" spelling, it is clear that Irving preferred "reconnoitred" (seee page 610, n. 44, above). Accordingly the copy-text
reading of "reconnoitered" is altered to "reconnoitred."

275.22 This] The copy-text "This" in "This it is to die a martyr" may
be a misprint for "Thus," but it may well be what Irving intended;
hence the copy-text is not emended.

281.24 from being] Awkward as the construction "from being" is in
50, it is clear enough and common in Irving's usage; hence it is not
altered.

289.28 "for Allah forbid,"] The unconventional lower-case beginning
of the quotation might be considered a printer's error by which
the initial quotation marks were placed before "for" instead of before "Allah"; but the copy-text rendition is neither ambiguous nor
conducive to misreading, and because constructions of this kind are
too numerous to be coincidental errors, "for Allah forbid" must be
presumed to represent what the author intended, and consequently
is not emended. Similar cases occur at 155.17, 155.31, 159.19, 256.26,
305.2, 330.30, 446.11–12, 448.18, and 494.4. It is to be observed that
in these passages Irving does not consistently employ a comma or
colon before the quotation.

291.27 him] "Him" used as a reflexive pronoun is uncommon but not
unprecedented in Irving's usage.

295.22 flight] The sequel makes clear that "flight" rather than "fight"
was intended, for the strategy of the Moslem army was to appear to
be in flight, rather than preparing to fight. The copy-text "fight" is
a printer's error overlooked in proof.

300.11 Abu Sofian] The Abu Sofian mentioned here, along with
Derar and Rafi, is of course the same as Yezed (i.e., Yezed Ibn Abu
Sofian) mentioned at 298.35 as one of the same triumvirate.

300.21 war-worn] The hyphen in "war-worn" appears as a faint dot in
all Putnam impressions, but clearly in E, and hence represents an im-
perfection in the Putnam plates.

305.23 Sophronius] The context requires "Sophronius" rather than the
copy-text reading of "Sempronius." See 305.9, 309.5, and 309.11.

308.17 ingress] The E reading of "egress" for copy-text "ingress" is an
erroneous "correction," for Irving meant "entrance to," no "going out
of" or "emergence from."

313.15 declined,] The Hinman collating machine shows an empty space following "declined" where in the Putnam impressions the comma was set but did not print. The Murray plates printed the comma.

319.12 Lucas,] The omitted comma after "Lucas" in 50 to set off the appositive is added in conformity with Irving's use of it in the identical construction at 319.32.

326.21 more brave] The fact that the word "more" is used with "brave" to form the comparative degree suggests that Irving intended "more brave" rather than "braver"; hence the copy-text reading is retained.

330.30–31 oath "by Christ !"] The expression "by Christ !" in the copy-text is not in this context properly a direct quotation or an appositive necessarily requiring a comma, so that neither a comma before "by" nor a capital "By" is necessary. For similar examples, see 381.4–8, 11–12.

332.1 between] See Discussions of Adopted Readings, 441.38 between].

331.39 deluges,] It is necessary to add a comma after "deluges" in the copy-text lest the interpretation be that "the deluges divided the earth into three parts," – clearly not Irving's intended meaning. Possibly the missing comma after "deluges" was mistakenly set after "parts," where it is unnecessary, though not entirely without precedent in Irving's method of punctuation.

336.2 with] In the copy-text "The people . . . capitulated with Amru," the word "capitulated" is not used in the sense of "surrendered to" but as "drawing up terms of a treaty or pact," in accord with Webster's first example: "thieves should offer to capitulate with him . . . ." Hence the "with," rather than "to," is acceptable.

339.10 This] Although "That of Misrah" would be preferable on stylistic grounds, it is obvious that the copy-text phraseology "This of Misrah" (meaning "This [siege] of Misrah") is what the author intended.

343.2 supplied] The copy-text, present tense "supply," instead of "supplied," is undoubtedly an unintentional authorial slip of the pen.

346.3 Arzemia –] The Murray addition after "Arzemia – " of "Her death – Elevation of Yezdegird to the throne – " in the synoptic chapter heading is an inappropriate interpolation not justified by the contents of the chapter. It is to be noted that the addition is omitted from the Murray table of contents (E II, xii.6).

346.21   father;] The reasons for allowing the semicolon following "father" to stand in the copy-text are the same as those given under Discussions of Adopted Readings, 234.14.

346.29   son,] Although Irving's use of commas with appositives is inconsistent (three other appositives appearing within this paragraph being separated by commas from their antecedents, while two are not), it is clear that in "His infant son Ardisheer, was placed on the throne" the comma omitted after "son" in the copy-text is one of an intended pair, and accordingly is added.

358.26   strongholds] The 50 reading of "strong-holds" is one of four instances in which Irving hyphenates the word, the others being at 376.33, 381.1, and 435.25. They apparently represent unconscious inconsistencies not in accord with Webster's preferance and the numerous instances in which Irving conforms to Webster, e.g., at 13.26, 52.12–13, 52.36, 60.18, 103.12–13, 159.33, 160–37, 342.9, 373.20, 496.27, and 508.4.

359.20   battering-rams] The copy-text reading of "battering rams" here is the only instance in which the word appears without a hyphen, and is therefore emended to "battering-rams."

362.5   Media] No attempt is made to regularize Irving's variant spellings of "Media," "Medea," and "Medean," all of which appear in his sources and apparently were tolerated.

363.14   were] Because Irving was careful about observing agreement between subject and predicate, presumably he regarded the copy-text reading "much" in "much of the stone, marble, and timber . . . were furnished" as having a collective meaning, much in the way that "part" in "part of the men, women, and children" may be regarded as a collective substantive. This may represent an unwarranted or too liberal interpretation on Irving's part, but unless it is regarded as an unintentional error or likely to cause misreading (neither of which is a tenable assumption), there is no justification for changing "were" to "was."

374.14   Sale] Copy-text "Lane" here is a slip of the pen for "Sale," as Irving's reference at the end of the paragraph and a check of Sale's text demonstrate.

376.10 conduct] Webster (1828, 1848) sanctions the use of "conduct" as an intransitive verb without using the reflexive pronoun "themselves" in such as construction as "men who conduct like you . . . ." Hence the copy-text is not emended.

376.26–27 'We . . . warfare.'"] "We are sons of Adam; but the angels of heaven are on our side and aid us in our warfare" is in direct reply to a direct question, but appears in the copy-text without single quotation marks. Since Irving was normally careful to use quotation marks in direct quotations, the missing marks are added, and the lower-case "we" is capitalized as an aid to the reader, and because the quotation is in direct discourse. If Irving had intended to indicate an indirect quotation, he would have written "we replied that we are the sons of Adam . . . ."

378.34 six] Here, at 381.13–16, and at 400.38, Irving follows his sources by calling Othman's electors "a council of six," though in reality, as Irving pointed out, there were seven, Othman himself being named by Omar to sit with Ali, Telha, Ibn Obeid'allah (Mahomet's son-in-law), Zobeir, Abda'lraman Ibn Awf, and Saad Ibn Abu Wakkâs.

379.32 Hamuzân] See the Discussions of Adopted Readings, 225.5 empire].

381.4 "his] The copy-text "his" is kept in lower case because here, as elsewhere, Irving does not capitalize the first word of a quotation that is not in direct discourse: "As has well been observed, 'his Caliphat . . . deserves . . . less than ten years.'" Another example occurs at 381.11–12: "Well may we say . . . , 'there were giants in those days.'" See also 246.21 and 330.30–31. But Irving was not consistent. See, for example, 382.4–5, where he uses the comma, the quotation mark, and the capital to designate the beginning of a quotation that is not in direct discourse; but see also 440.30–32: "The inscription of his signet was 'Every deed hath its meed;' or, according to others, 'All power rests with God.'"

390.30 pitched] The copy-text reading "drawn" (where "pitched" battle is clearly indicated) is Irving's oversight. He used "pitched" correctly at 119.10, 326.22, 460.7, 482.13, 485.33, and 490.17. Irving's erroneous "drawn" in MSb (442.4) was corrected to "pitched" in ARE II, 460.12, and appears so in W 486.14.

391.22 well contested] No clear pattern emerges as to Irving's hyphenation of words combined with "well"; hence the copy-text variants are respected as indicating individual authorial choices, especially when, as in this particular case, only one instance occurs.

393.2   Emir] The copy-text's capital "Emir" here is retained because the word is part of the title, "Emir of Syria." See also xii.19, 8.20, 393.2, and 423.28.

404.18   Syria;] The copy-text's erroneous comma between two independent clauses not joined by a conjunction is not without precedent in Irving's usage, but in this instance probably represents a compositorial error. A further consideration in favor of the emendation is the comfort of the reader.

410.36   commiserated] Webster (1848) cites examples of "commiserated" not followed by "with" from Denham and Locke; hence the copy-text "Ali commiserated the unfortunate man" is not emended.

412.6–13   His father, he said, had . . . manifested ?] It is to be noted that while the copy-text uses quotation marks before "His," after "father," and before "had," they are properly omitted after "manifested?" because the passage is in indirect discourse. (The direct quotation begins after "manifested?": "I . . . father," added Hassan, "those . . . me.") Apparently the compositor realized, when he came to the end of the passage, that he was setting indirect discourse, and accordingly omitted the terminal quotation mark after "manifested" but neglected to delete those already set.

414.14   hamstrung] The copy-text "hamstringed" is either a compositorial error or an unintentional authorial slip. The other two instances where the word occurs in *Mahomet* both have "hamstrung" (23.20 and 314.38), in conformity with the preferred listing of Dr. Johnson (1819), Walker (1828), and Webster (1828, 1848).

417.33–34   "What . . . God!] Although this sentence is phrased in the form of a question, no answer is expected, and the expression is properly regarded as exclamatory. Hence the copy-text's exclamation point following "God" is respected. A like example is found at 425.17.

418.39   sect] Elsewhere (e.g., at 396.19, 421.15, and 421.20) the Karigites are called "a sect," instead of "a set," of fanatics; the copy-text's "set" is a printer's error for "sect."

421.2   assassination] Lower-case "assassination" is required to be in accord with the table of contents, xii.29.

424.28–29   said, we want no fighting Caliphs.] The omission of internal
quotation marks in the passage "the people said, we want no fighting
Caliphs" is characteristic of Irving's practice in passages that express
a general feeling, sentiment, or slogan (in this case, of a people), instead of a direct quotation, i.e., the words actually expressed. Although this is one of the more awkward of such unorthodox omissions,
since misreading is not likely to follow, and no compelling reason
exists beyond the temptation to correct Irving's idiosyncrasies, no
emendation is made.

425.17   God!"] The quotation may be regarded as part of the governor's ejaculation rather than a separate question; accordingly the
copy-text's exclamation mark is not replaced by a question mark.

429.34   by-name] Since Irving writes "by-name" at 457.14 and 501.4,
and "by-road" and "by-stander(s)" in both *Mahomet* and *Goldsmith*, it may be presumed that the one use of "bye-name" represents
an oversight or unintentional inconsistency.

432.30   grandson] The copy-text "Constantine, a grandson of Heraclius" refers to Constantine IV – not to be confused with Constantine III, "the son of Heraclius" who is repeatedly mentioned by
Irving. Constantine III ruled only a few months following his father's
death in 1641. Constantine IV, actually the great-grandson of Heraclius, ruled from 668 to 685, and was in command of Constantinople
during 671–677 when the Greeks successfully withstood the Arabs'
siege. Irving apparently used the term "grandson" loosely (as was
not unusual) to include "great-grandson,"

434.33–34   none . . . seem] It may be observed that generally Irving
preferred, as in this instance, the plural form of a verb following
"none" as the subject.

435.32   nor] The double negative in "not a lion, tiger, leopard, nor
serpent" is a calculated use for emphasis, and is therefore not altered.

436.39   treatment?"] The question mark following ". . . I appeal to
your justice, whether I have merited such treatment?" in the copy-
text appears as a gratuitous addition, but it doubtless represents
Irving's intention, and hence it is not deleted.

437.36   which] The copy-text's superfluous comma after "which" is
unprecedented in Irving's usage and is deleted because it is either an
authorial slip or a printer's error.

439.28   Caliphat] This slip of the pen, "Caliph" for "Caliphat," in the

copy-text is emended as unintentional and to render the correct meaning. Irving consistently wrote "Caliphat," not "Caliphate."

440.31   was] In "The inscription of his signet was 'Every deed hath
its meed:' or, according to others, 'All power rests with God.'" the
comma after "was" is not in accord with Irving's practice of omitting
it except where the quotation is in direct discourse, and is doubtless
a printer's error overlooked in proof. The comma after "others" sets
off a parenthetical phrase – not the word of the inscription – and is
therefore retained.

441.38   between] Irving's use of "between" rather than "among" in
"to choose between the young Arab, the governor of Cufa, and himself" has ample justification in the 1828 and 1848 Webster, as well
as later editions, to indicate a choice between three or more things
severally or individually.

445.26   you;] The alteration of the copy-text's comma following "you"
to a semicolon is justified as representing Irving's practice and intent,
as well as necessary to clarify the meaning of the passage.

455.30   communicated] Whether Irving wrote "communicated" (as
the copy-text has it) or "was communicated" (which would be more
idiomatic) is a moot question. Because no real ambiguity is involved,
emendation is not justified.

457.2   abdication] The copy-text reading, "Abdication," is altered to
lower-case "abdication" in conformity with the table of contents at
xiii.7.

458.28   handsful] Usage varied from "handsful" to "hands full" and
"handfuls"; Irvings appears to have preferred "handsful."

470.10   to] The "to" in "many of the first people were disaffected to
him" seems unidiomatic, but it falls within the pattern of Irving's odd
but perfectly clear use of prepositions: "to" for "for" (450.22), "with"
for "for" (64.36), "to" for "at" (219.9), "through" for "from" (224.25),
in which questions of idiom, not of grammar or logic, are involved.
On the other hand, the misuses of "to" for "for" at x.20 and 239.2
result in nonsensical expressions and require mending.

472.32   "Fly,] The insertion of a comma following "Fly" in the copy-
text is in accord with Irving's customary practice and his specific use
of it in a similar construction at the beginning of the next paragraph.

476.27   catapults] It would seem odd that Irving, who had "small
Latin," and who rarely used classical terms, would choose to write
"catapultas" (Latin *catapulta,* plural *catapultae*), especially since he

had used "catapults" at 154.26, along with "battering-rams," precisely as in this instance.

481.2   emir] The copy-text "Emir" in this synoptic chapter heading is changed to lower case here because it is used as a common noun, in accord with the corresponding entry in the table of contents at xiii.21, as well as at xiii.24, 492.3, 492.24, and 493.2.

485.8   would] The change of MSb reading "should" to "would" in 50 is probably an authorial correction in proof.

485.15   farther] Webster (1828 and 1848), as well as general usage in Irving's day, allowed for Irving's indiscriminate use of "farther" and "further"; hence the copy-text "farther" is not emended.

486.14   pitched] The substitution in 50 of "pitched" for the MSb reading of "drawn" is probably Irving's correction in proof.

486.17   army] The substitution in 50 of "army" for "body" in MSb is probably an authorial correction made in proof.

487.21–22   "no . . . province"] Strictly construed, the passage in quotation marks is in indirect discourse so that the quotation marks are superfluous; but the meaning is clear enough, and may well be what the author intended. Hence the copy-text is not altered.

488.5   even] The unnecessary comma after "even" in 50 is a printer's error, probably intended to be placed instead after "fickle" (see the next note); it does not appear in MSb, and is excised in E.

488.5   fickle,] The missing comma following "fickle" in 50 (also missing in MSb, 462.2) appears to be Irving's error; Murray made the correction in E.

488.9   malady,] The omitted comma after "malady" in the copy-text is one of an intended pair, required to give the intended emphasis, and accordingly is added.

489.37   ladders,] The loss of the comma after "ladders" in 50 through plate damage was corrected in both E and 57.

491.15   fruit-trees] The hyphen is added here and at 491.22 in accord with Irving's "fruit-trees" (235.36), "fig-trees" (245.19), "date-trees" (8 times), "palm-trees" (11 times), and "palm-leaves" (6 times). Webster, it may be noted, prefers "fruit-trees."

491.27   Cahina] MSb (449.1 and 9) shows that Irving had trouble deciding which of the alternate names "Cahina" or "Dhabbá" to use; the substitution of the better-known form "Cahina" in 50 for "Dhabbá" in MSb was doubtless an authorial alteration made in proof. The alteration is made also at 491.32 and 492.7.

492.7   the slaughtered Cahina] The addition in 50 of "the slaughtered"
and the substitution of "Cahina" for "Dhabbá" of MSb (450.7) provide a typical example of Irving's "redressing" of the proof sheets.

492.16   the latter] The happy change for the MSb reading "Hassán
therefore" to "the latter" in proof is one that only the author would
be likely to make.

492.17–18   in . . . command] The insertion of "in . . . command" after
"that" in MSb is a typical authorial addition in proof.

492.31–32   His . . . himself] This is a typical Irvingesque comment,
which Irving doubtless added in 50 following "heart" while reading
proof.

496.26   country; some] The alteration of a period following "country"
in the copy-text to a semicolon and the change of capital "Some" to
lower case is required to maintain the parallel structure of the sentence. See also 211.28 punishments; one].

510.26   this;] The substituted "the" in E for "this" in 50 is a character-
istically misguided refinement attempted by someone in Murray's
establishment.

LIST OF EMENDATIONS

In this list of changes in the copy-text, the following symbols are used to designate the sources of the readings:

MSa	Manuscript draft of *Mahomet* (1828–1832)
MSb	Manuscript fragment of printer's copy for 50
50, 51, . . . 60	Putnam's American impression (1850, 1851, . . . 1860), with earlier and later states of variant sheets within the 1850 Putnam impression indicated by 50a and 50b, respectively
E	Murray's English impression (1850)
W	Wisconsin edition

These notes identify all emendations of the copy-text. The numbers before each note indicate the page and line. Chapter numbers, chapter or section titles, epigraphs, author's chapter or section summaries, texts, quotations, and footnotes are included in the line count. Only running heads and rules added by the printer to separate running heads from the text are omitted from the count.

The reading to the left of the bracket is the portion of the text under consideration or discussion and represents an accepted reading that differs from the copy-text. The source of the reading is identified by symbol after the bracket.

The reading after the semicolon is the rejected reading of the copy-text and any other text in which that reading occurs; if other alternatives are also available, they are recorded following that reading.

The swung (wavy) dash ~ represents the same word, words, or characters that appear before the bracket, and is used in recording punctuation variants; the caret ∧ indicates that a mark of punctuation is omitted. W signifies that a decision to emend or not to emend has been made on the authority of the editor of the Wisconsin edition. Some of these editorial decisions are explained among the Discussions of Adopted Readings, which include decisions to emend as well as some decisions not to emend. Discussion is identified by an asterisk *.

vii.18	husband] W; uncle 50
vii.21	Khattâb] W; Kattâb 50
viii.22	Kolthum] W; Kalthum 50
*ix.16	mountains] 57; Mountains 50
*ix.24	Tufiel] W; Tafiel 50
ix.29	Okaïder] W; Okaidor 50
*x.20	for] E; to 50
xi.31	III ∧] W; III. 50
*xii.4	subjugation] E; conquest 50
xii.11	by] E; hy 50
xii.32	I ∧] W; I. 50
3.10	Jesuits'] E; Jesuit's 50
3.12	out,] E; ~ ∧ 50
*9.17	scimetar] W; scimitar 50
9.42	ch.4] W; 4 50
10.31	whom] W; who 50
*12.13	fire-worshippers] W; ~ ∧ ~ 50
*13.7	Wisdom] W; wisdom 50
13.36	circumstances] W; ciscumstances 50
*17.37	Kahtan] W; Katan 50
19.6	Jidda] W; Joddah 50
19.9	Arafat] 50b, E; Ararat 50a
21.7	Kebla] W; kebla 50
21.21	expansive.] E, 57; ~ ∧ 50, 52–55
25.42	ii.] 57; ii, 50
*26.5	Zobeir] W; Zobier 50
27.26	Maïsara] W; Maīsara 50
27.28	Maïsara] W; Maìsara 50
36.21	Motâlleb] W; Motalleb 50
36.24	offer ?] W; offer. 50
*36.24	brother,] W; brother: 50
*37.35	Antichrist] W; anti-Christ 50
*41.31	fellow-man] W; ~ ∧ ~ 50
42.33	not.'] W; not." 50
45.4	husband] W; uncle 50
46.13	comparable?] W; comparable. 50
*46.30	him] W; me 50
49.1	Jidda] W; Jodda 50
*49.1	west] W; east 50

*52.31	Haschemites,] E, 57; ~ ∧ 50
53.12	adherents.] E; ~ ∧ 50
*60.19	Al Lat] W; El Làt 50
60.22	Al Lat] W; El Làt 50
63.24	sewn] W; sown 50
65.4	thee,] W; thee. 50
*66.36	Bathra] W; Bartha 50
*66.37	Ziz] W; Zig 50
*67.31	¶ "Because] W; no ¶ "Because 50
69.27	Horaira] W; Horeira 50
*73.22	Maadi] W; Maads 50
74.17	Eblis] W; Iblis 50
*78.37	Salem] W; Salam 50
79.17	calendar] W; Kalendar 50
*80.32	burying-ground] W; ~ ∧ ~ 50
82.25	fellow-man] W; ~ ∧ ~ 50
82.31	fellow-man] W; ~ ∧ ~ 50
*82.31–32	say, 'What . . . him?'] W; say What . . . him? 50
85.27	okks] W; okk 50
*87.24	Medina, –] W; Medina; 50
87.26	desert, –] W; desert; 50
*91.21	lay] W; laid 50
96.30	Dhu'l Fakâr] W; Dhul Fakar 50
99.7	Otha] W; Otho 50
*99.40	*Thar*] W; Thar 50
*99.41	*Burckhardt's Notes*, v. i. 314.] W; *Burckhardt*, v. i. 314, Notes. 50
100.34	Jaafar] 50b; Jaffar 50a, E
102.21	Merwân] W; Merwan 50
*105.18	Khaled] 50b; Kaled 50a, E
106.12	Solul] W; Solûl 50
106.18	Medina.] 52–53; ~ ∧ 50, E, 54–60
107.31	Wacksa] W; Waksa 50
109.14	handmill] W; hand-mill 50
110.35	millstone] W; mill-stone 50
111.24	Tabuc] W; Tabuk 50
112.2	Hareth] W; Horeth 50
121.4	Hoya] 50b; Hoyai 50a, E
*125.12	courts,"] 57; courts;" 50–55

127.18	Yathreb] W; Gothreb 50
128.32	Khattâb] W; Khattab 50
129.32	Rafe] W; Râfe 50
*130.38	Khiebar] W; Kheibar 50
*130.39	Missead] W; Messiad 50
131.5	Ahktab] W; Akhtab 50
131.9	eyes of] 50b; eyes 50a, E
132.12	was,] 57; ~ ∧ 50
134.18	Ihram] W; Iram 50
134.23	betrothed] W; bethrothed 50
135.5	Sarif] W; Serif 50
140.2	Hassan] W; Hasan 50
141.2	capture] W; Capture 50
*146.12	female,] W; ~ ∧ 50
*147.17	proscribed ∧] MSa (373.15); proscribed, 50
147.37–38	Musulman] W; Mussulman 50
148.4	proscribed ∧] MSa (370.8); proscribed, 50
151.2	mountains] 57; Mountains 50
152.15	Autas] W; Mutas 50
*152.18	laid] W; lay 50
*153.40	Musa] 50b; Amir 50a, E
155.20	favor.' "] W; ~ . ∧" 50
*156.16	proportions,] E, 57; proportions. 50, 52–55
157.19	imam] W; iman 50
158.6	Tufiel] W; Tafiel 50
160.16	stone.] E, 57; ~ ∧ 50, 52–55
160.17	blow,] W; ~ ∧ 50
*160.29	poets ∧] MSb; poets, 50
160.38	Wahábys] W; Wahabys 50
162.29	'I] W; ∧ ~ 50
162.30	own.'] W; ~ . ∧ 50
164.5	Okaïder] W; Okaidor 50
168.25	Tabuc] W, 57; Tabue 50
171.7	Safa] W; Sala 50
175.15	capital] W; capitol 50
*177.31	Lord,' in truth;] W; Lord,' in truth, 50
177.33	veracity;] W; veracity, 50
178.19	ejaculations.] 57; ~ ∧ 50–55
179.31	enemies."] W; ~ ∧" 50

180.1	Kaswa] W; Karwa 50
181.14	Weather-cock] E; $\sim_\wedge\sim$ 50–55; weathercock 57
185.5	he.] 57; $\sim_\wedge$ 50
185.17	Maimuna] W; Maïmona 50
186.22	Khattâb] W; Khattab 50
187.1	Mohadjerins] W; Mohejerins 50
188.23	approaching,] 57; $\sim_\wedge$ 50
189.18	Amram] W; Imram 50
189.35	apostasy] W; apostacy 50
*191.17	Wahábys] W; Wahabees 50
195.rh	IMPOSTURE] 50b; IMPORTANCE 50a, E
*195.15	revelations] W; relations 50
197.rh	IMPOSTURE] 50b; IMPORTANCE 50a, E
*204.21	inculcated] W; inculcates 50
206.18	sura] W; Sura 50
*211.28	punishments; one] W; punishments. One 50
212.27	Musulmen] W; Mussulmen 50
215.8	Ramadan] W; Rhamadan 50
*223.4	632] W; 622 50
223.9	Pharaohs;] E, 51; Pharaohs, 50
224.5	Bibliothèque] E; Bibliotheque 50
*226.8	council] W; counsel 50
231.22	apostasy] W; apostacy 50
239.2	for] W; to 50
*242.9	alarms] W; alarums 50
*243.1	wall,] E; wall. 50
243.5	signal shout] W; signal-shout 50
*247.11	soldiers,] W; $\sim_\wedge$ 50
248.23	more] W; most 50
*251.9	spoils] 51; spoil 50, E
256.6	Wakkâs] W; Wakkas 50
256.26	"for Christ] W; for "Christ 50
256.26	i'laha] W; I'laha 50
264.36	Jabiyah] W; Jabeyah 50
*273.9	reconnoitred] W; reconnoitered 50
276.31	man,] 57; man; 50
282.19	"and] W; $_\wedge\sim$ 50
286.8	Omeirah] W; Omeïrah 50
288.3	reproaching $_\wedge$] W; reproaching, 50

*295.22	flight] W; fight 50
297.15	Towaf] W; Towah 50
302.22	tent pole] W; tent-pole 50
*305.23	Sophronius] W; Sempronius 50
309.10	sheep-skin] W; sheepskin 50
311.3	Damâs] W; Damas 50
311.16	Abu] W; Abi 50
311.23	on] W; in 50
*313.15	declined,] W; ~ ∧ 50
314.37	sevenscore] W; seven score 50
*319.12	Lucas,] W; ~ ∧ 50
*331.39	deluges,] W; ~ ∧ 50
332.3	Kahtan] W; Kathan 50
334.26	seaport] W; sea-port 50
340.6	Musulman] W; Mussulman 50
*343.2	supplied] W; supply 50
*346.29	son,] W; ~ ∧ 50
347.9–10	vizier] W; vizir 50
350.3	III ∧] W; III. 50
353.10	Mukry] W; Muskry 50
353.19	hair-cloth] W; ~ ∧ ~ 50
353.33	hair-cloth] W; ~ ∧ ~ 50
*358.26	strongholds] W; strong-holds 50
*359.20	battering-rams] W; ~ ∧ ~ 50
360.6	Khosru !] W; Khosru, 50
360.7	another.] W; another ! 50
360.34	D'Herbelot] W; D'Herbolot 50
360.38	Nushirwan] W; Nashirwan 50
361.4	Mukry] W; Muskry 50
361.21	matter?] W; matter; 50
362.4	Wakkâs] W; Wakkas 50
364.12	counsels] W; councils 50
365.2	subjugation] W; conquest 50
365.26	headquarters] W; head-quarters 50
370.23	Hadîfeh] W; Hadîfah 50
372.3	Caucasian] W; Caucassian 50
*374.14	Sale] W; Lane 50
374.46	Ouseley] W; Ousley 50
375.23	Shahr-Zad] W; Shahr-zad 50

375.24	dominion] W; dominions 50
376.26–27	'We . . . warfare.' "] W; we . . . warfare." 50
376.33	stronghold] W; strong-hold 50
378.2	by] W; hy 50
380.30	Hassan] W; Hasan 50
381.1	strongholds] W; strong-holds 50
385.23	lay] W; laid 50
389.8	nomad] W; nomade 50
*390.30	pitched] W; drawn 50
391.29	Zobeir ∧] W; Zobeir, 50
395.24	dinars] W; dinârs 50
396.19	Karigites] W; Karegites 50
396.29	Merwân] W; Merwan 50
396.35	Merwân] W; Merwan 50
397.18	Merwân] W; Merwan 50
398.5	Zobeir] W; Zobier 50
398.11	Zobeir] W; Zobier 50
401.17	four-and-twenty] W; ~ ∧ ~ ∧ ~ 50
402.19	"However] W; ∧ ~ 50
402.25	Zobeir] W; Zobier 50
*404.18	Syria;] W; Syria, 50
405.33	Zobeir] W; Zobier 50
409.35	Alashari] W; Alashair 50
409.38	Musulman] W; Mussulman 50
410.24	Alashari] W; Alashair 50
*412.6–13	His father, he said, had . . . manifested ?] W; "His father," he said, "had . . . manifested ? 50
412.30	Zobeir] W; Zobier 50
413.7	Merwân] W; Merwan 50
*414.14	hamstrung] W; hamstringed 50
416.3	having been] W; having 50
416.33	five- and-forty] W; ~ ∧ ~ ∧ ~ 50
416.35	five-and-twenty] W; ~ ∧ ~ ∧ ~ 50
417.1	what] W; What 50
418.3	cousin-german] W; ~ ∧ ~ 50
*418.39	sect] W; set 50
*421.2	assassination] W; Assassination 50
422.9	Naharwan] W; Neharwân 50
425.7	for] W; to 50

427.2	I $_\wedge$] W; I. 50
427.3	Ziyad] W; Zeyad 50
*429.34	by-name] W; bye-name 50
430.3	Obeid'allah] W; Obeidallah 50
432.31	incapacity.] W; incapacity, 50
433.19	seigniors] W; seignors 50
435.25	stronghold] W; strong-hold 50
437.25	converting] W; convertimg 50
*437.36	which $_\wedge$] W; which, 50
439.24	Spain.] W; $\sim$ $_\wedge$ 50
*439.28	Caliphat] W; Caliph 50
*440.31	was $_\wedge$] W; was, 50
444.10	Nu'mân] W; Nu'màn 50
*445.26	you;] W; you, 50
445.30	test $_\wedge$] E; test, 50, 51–60
447.21	Zeinab] W; Zenaib 50
447.24	Zeinab] W; Zenaib 50
448.15	twoscore] W; two-score 50
*457.2	abdication] W; Abdication 50
457.12	for] W; to 50
459.9	Merwân] W; Merwan 50
462.2	the] W; thc 50
465.1	Tayef] W; Thayef 50
472.26	apparent.] W; $\sim$ $_\wedge$ 50
*472.32	"Fly,] W; $\sim$ $_\wedge$ 50
472.37	Mecca."] W; $\sim$ $_\wedge$ 50
474.18	Motazelites] W; Motalazites 50
474.39	Abd'alaziz] W; Abd $_\wedge$ alaziz 50
475.14–15	Azarakites] W; Azrakites 50
*476.27	catapults] W; catapultas 50
*481.2	emir] W; Emir 50
481.34	here?"] W; here, 50
481.34	Abd'almâlec.] W; Abd'almelec?" 50
482.19	Karigite] W; Karegite 50
482.37	doubtfully.] W; doubtfully, 50
484.29	Ahwâz] W; Awaz 50
487.11	sternly.] W; sternly." 50
487.12	"but] W; $_\wedge$ $\sim$ 50
*488.5	even $_\wedge$] W; even, 50

*488.5	fickle,] E; ~ ∧ 50
*488.9	malady,] W; ~ ∧ 50
*489.37	ladders,] E, 57; ~ ∧ 50–55
490.14	Caerwan] W; Caerwân 50
*491.15	fruit-trees] W; ~ ∧ ~ 50
491.22	fruit-trees] W; ~ ∧ ~ 50
491.23	Tangiers] W; Tangier 50
492.3	emir.] W; ~ ∧ 50
492.8	received] W; reeived 50
494.36	share.] E, 51; ~ ∧ 50, 52–60
496.18	Aulad-Arabi] W; Aulad-arabi 50
*496.26	country; some] W; country. Some 50
505.34	Gobi] W; Cobi 50
505.35	Tibet] W; Thibet 50
506.1	Khatiba] W; Katiba 50
506.12	Tayef] W; Thayef 50
509.13	reconnoitring] W; reconnoitering 50
509.33	Happy] W; happy 50
510.31	THE END.] E, 54–60; *omitted* 50–53

LIST OF REJECTED SUBSTANTIVES

In this list, which provides a historical record of substantive variants in the manuscripts and the authorized texts that appeared during Irving's lifetime, but that were not adopted for the Wisconsin text, the following symbols are used to designate the sources of the readings:

MSa	Manuscript draft of *Mahomet* (1828–1832)
MSb	Manuscript fragment of printer's copy for 50
50, 51, . . . 60	Putnam's American impression (1850, 1851, . . . 1860), with earlier and later states of variant sheets within the 1850 Putnam impression indicated by 50a and 50b, respectively
E	Murray's English impression (1850)
W	Wisconsin edition

*x.18	Successes] 50; Its successes E
xi.1	in] 50; in the E
xi.6	Siege] 50; The siege E
xi.12	Siege] 50; The siege E
xii.11	assassinated] 50; is assassinated E
xii.16	retaken] 50; taken again E
xii.36	Moslem conquests] 50; Conquests of the Moslems E
xiii.23	fate] 50; late 57
*3.4	since] 50; ago E
3.15	the] 50; that E
4.3	nor] 50; nor to E
92.28	inflicting a] 50, E, 57–60; inflicting 52–55
*112.19	this] 50; his 57
119.8	This] 50–55; The 57
123.6	Sword.] 50; *omitted* E
124.22	the] 50, E, 57; he 52–55
130.14	spat] 50, E. 57; pat 52–55
137.21	his] 50, E, 53–60; is 52

155.18	counsel] 50; council MSb
*155.19	we implore] 50; *omitted* MSb
*155.23	Tamin] 50; Tainem MSb
*159.7	ink] 50; wit MSb
162.18	counsel] 50; council MSb
*163.7	Weil's Mohammed, p. 247] 50; *omitted* MSb
*164.5	provinces] 50; princes MSb
*165.29	and their] 50; and their and their MSb
165.31	the] 50, 57; he 53–55
*165.35	dominion] 50; domination MSb
166.24	sit] 50; set MSb
167.12	an] 50; and 57
180.9	His] 50; He 57
180.10	He is] 50; His is 57
199.33	None-none-none!] 50; None-none! 57
218.5	to Mount Arafat] 50; to Arafat 57
219.4	at] 50; as 57
*219.9	votaries to] 50; Devotees at E
223.4–5	which did not occupy] 50; of less than E
223.5	and] 50; which E
223.30	merely intended] 50; intended merely E
224.13	through the pages of] 50; in the E
224.25	through] 50; from E
225.24	his wife Fatima] 50; Fatima his wife E
*226.22	in nominating] 50; to nominate E
*308.17	ingress] 50; egress E
316.7	men] 50, E, 51–52, 54–60; me 53
*346.3	Arzemia –] 50; Arzemia – Her death – Elevation of Yezdegird to the throne E
389.25	land] 50, E, 57; and 51–55
400.1	XXXVII] 50–52, 57; XXXVI E, 53–55
484.25	the] 50; the the MSb
*485.10	would] 50; should MSb
*486.14	pitched] 50; drawn MSb
*486.17	army] 50; body MSb
486.36	was] 50; as MSb
*491.27	Cahina] 50; Dhabbá MSb
*492.7–8	the slaughtered Cahina] 50; Dhabbá MSb
*492.16	the latter] 50; Hossán therefore MSb

*492.17–18   in addition to his African command] 50; *omitted* MSb
*492.31–32   His cruel treatment of the heroic Cahina reconciles us
                to the injustice wreaked upon himself.] 50; *omitted*
                MSb
509.3   a usurper] 50; an usurper E
510.26   this] 50; the E

LIST OF COMPOUND WORDS
HYPHENATED
AT END OF LINE

List I includes all compound and possible compound words that are hyphenated at the end of the line in the copy-text. In deciding whether to retain the hyphen or to print the word as a single-word compound (without the hyphen), the editor has made his decision first on the use of each compound word elsewhere in the copy-text; or second, when the word does not appear elsewhere in the copy-text, on Irving's practice in other writings of the period (chiefly *A Tour on the Prairies,* 1835, *Goldsmith,* 1949, and *Washington,* 1855–59); or finally, if the word does not appear in Irving's other writings of the period, on contemporary American usage, chiefly as reflected in Webster's dictionary of 1848. Each word is listed in its editorially accepted form after the page and line numbers of its appearance in the W text.

List II presents all compounds, or possible compounds, that are hyphenated or separated as two words at the end of the line in the W text. They are listed in the form in which they would have appeared in the W text had they come in mid-line.

LIST I

8.14	forefathers	91.10	sixty-one
9.30	wide-spreading	92.15	foot-print
9.34	saddlebags	134.11	warlike
9.40	short-hooked	160.1	stiff-necked
18.24	grandfather	168.38	overwhelming
37.35	Antichrist	176.19	overflow
37.39	forerun	178.15	insomuch
60.9	pomegranates	181.14	Weather-cock
60.18	strongholds	193.21	twenty-five
74.19	evesdropper	194.22	shoulder-blades
75.20	bloody-minded	199.15	insomuch

211.12	Seventy-two	427.13	great-grandfather
212.21	foresight	434.7	daylight
225.15	cousin-german	434.26	fifty-eighth
227.6	thoroughly-tried	434.27	forty-seven
243.5	signal shout	439.26	to-day
250.11	right-hand	446.6	forebodings
272.13	foot-prints	447.6	passports
277.21	wide-spreading	447.22	grandsire
282.30	horsemen	457.14	by-names
306.18	saddle-bags	481.9	densely-crowded
307.18	fellow-man	486.20	headlong
316.19	sunrise	487.26	horsemen
350.25	sunset	489.10	sixty-five
352.13	well-tried	489.12	sixty-five
359.16	panic-stricken	489.33	seaport
383.3	death-blow	502.34	gray-beard
402.6	bystander	504.6	well-stricken
411.35	non-resistance	508.1	far-famed
414.11	threescore		

LIST II

9.34	saddlebags	194.32	piecemeal
9.38	horsemen	208.32	mustard-seed
47.16	self-prescribed	219.10	half-naked
48.40	sea-coast	231.1	overran
53.5	stronghold	235.35	palm-tree
84.7	fifty-four	246.10	well garrisoned
84.13	new comers	247.8	horsemen
91.33	southeast	248.14	well armed
97.4	warfare	250.11	standard-bearer
103.12	stronghold	261.19	rear-guard
115.20	necklace	264.21	horsemen
153.2	well-known	271.12	downfall
165.14	lukewarm	277.6	ninety-seven
178.34	sixty-three	306.18	saddlebags
184.37	burying-place	317.13	draw-bridge
190.33	palm-leaves	350.25	sunset

353.23	husbandman	486.28	fifty-fourth
434.2	forty-seven	489.23	sea-coast
481.9	densely-crowded		

ERRATA

Page xii, line 33: *For* Ayesha *read* Amru
Page 387, line 19: *For* wordly *read* worldly (*twice*)
Page 400, line 17: *For* was the *read* was of the
Page 461, line 23: *For* verteran *read* veteran
Page 519, line 24: *For* eager *read* slow
Page 519, line 25: *For* slow *read* earlier
Page 540, line 26: *For* Five *read* Fire
Page 578, line 9: *For* remission *read* permission
Page 649, line 11: *For* 1949 *read* 1849